THE UNIVERSITY OF CHICAGO
STUDIES IN BALZAC

Edited by
E. PRESTON DARGAN

THE EVOLUTION OF BALZAC'S
Comédie humaine

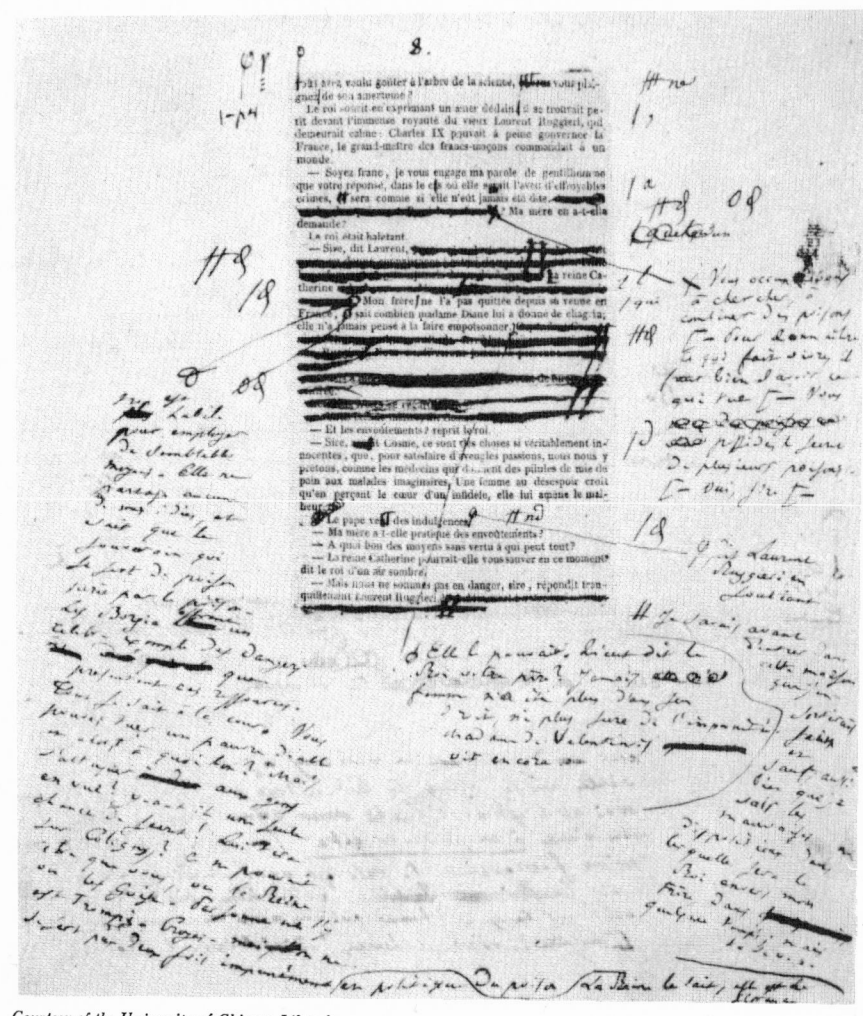

A PAGE FROM *LE SECRET DES RUGGIERI*

THE EVOLUTION OF BALZAC'S
Comédie humaine

Studies edited by

E. PRESTON DARGAN

AND

BERNARD WEINBERG

NEW YORK
COOPER SQUARE PUBLISHERS, INC.
1973

PRINTED IN THE UNITED STATES OF AMERICA
by SENTRY PRESS, NEW YORK, N. Y. 10013

PREFACE

THE present volume represents, in the opinion of its editors, the culmination of the "University of Chicago Studies in Balzac." Its redaction and publication have been delayed by unavoidable circumstances. Promised in the Preface to our Volume III (*Studies in Balzac's Realism*), it is complementary to that volume, because the master —we hope to show—whether in composing or revising his work, continued to lay emphasis on what are generally accepted as realistic features.

There have existed for some time at this University a Balzac project and a group of patient devotees who concern themselves mainly with the abundant textual variations in the *Comédie humaine*. The reason for this particular bent is not far to seek. In 1923 the acquisition by the University of Chicago Libraries of the notable Croué Collection furnished, as well as later editions, fifty-seven "firsts" of Balzac's novels. This gave the initial impulse. Since then, many more editions have been added, together with holograph manuscript proof and photostats of similar material. For example, the libraries possess the larger part of Balzac's own much corrected proof sheets of *Le Secret des Ruggieri;* and through the generosity of Mr. Stefan Zweig we have been allowed to photograph, to the extent of some seven hundred pages, the corrected proof of *Une Ténébreuse Affaire.*

Both of these treasures find their places in the following monographs, which offer also these contributions: A general editorial Introduction. A much needed and basic discussion, by Miss Brucia Dedinsky, of the George School, of how Balzac classified and reclassified his novels. This is preliminary to a series of studies (mainly portions of unpublished dissertations) on textual variations within particular stories. Miss Rachel Wilson, of Hollins College, has examined the variations in the masterpiece, *Le Curé de Tours.* Professor W. L. Crain, of the University of Kansas City, has contributed an "Introduction" to his still unpublished and remarkable critical edition of *Le Secret des Ruggieri.* A final chapter presents résumés of studies originally written by many hands.

The general intention of the volume is plain. We would uphold once more the great industry and growing artistry of Honoré de Balzac in his own realm, and we would demonstrate this with such abundant concrete evidence that these qualities can hardly again be called into question.

Chicago, Illinois
July 1940

E. P. D.
B. W.

Professor Dargan's untimely death in the fall of 1940 prevented him from seeing the publication of the final volume in the series that had occupied so many years of his life, the "University of Chicago Studies in Balzac." But during the spring and summer of that year he was able to direct and oversee the completion of the manuscript. Since that time every effort has been made to publish the work essentially as he had left it, with only such changes as were necessitated by editorial or legal exigencies. The title chosen is the one which he himself had suggested as early as the Preface to Volume I of the series, *A Balzac Bibliography;* the present volume represents a combination of Volumes IV and V of the series as originally planned.[1]

Had Professor Dargan lived, his keenest delight in the conclusion of this task would have been the pleasure of expressing his gratitude to those who contributed so much to its fulfilment: to his brother, Henry McCune Dargan, for editorial assistance over a period of many months; to W. Scott Hastings, for his expert advice, always so generously proffered; to William Hobart Royce, for the bibliographical information that all Balzacians have learned to seek from him; to William Albert Nitze and Dean Gordon J. Laing, for their constant encouragement and active help. To all these, all the contributors to the volume would join in expressing their sincere appreciation.

Finally, we would express our warm thanks to the American Council of Learned Societies, which has generously assumed a part of the financial burden of publication.

Chicago, Illinois
August 1941

B. W.

[1] Miss Brucia Dedinsky has graciously consented to the change of title of her chapter to "The Development of the Scheme of the *Comédie humaine*" from "The Evolution of the Scheme, etc.," in order to avoid confusion with the general title of the volume.

TABLE OF CONTENTS

LIST OF ABBREVIATIONS

Avant-propos.   In *Œuvres complètes,* éd. Conard, I, xxv–xxxviii.

*Béch.**   Editions published by Mme Charles-Béchet.

*Char.**   Editions published by Charpentier.

*Con.**   Editions published by Louis Conard.

Corr.   *Correspondance de H. de Balzac, 1819–1850 (Œuvres complètes,* éd. Calmann-Lévy, Vol. XXIV).

Corr. Carraud.   *Correspondance inédite avec Madame Zulma Carraud, 1829–1850,* éd. M. Bouteron (Paris: Armand Colin, 1935).

*Dum.**   Editions published by Dumont.

*Fur.**   Editions published by Furne, Dubochet et Hetzel.

*Gos.**   Editions published by C. Gosselin.

LEt.   *Lettres à l'Etrangère* (3 vols.; Paris: Calmann-Lévy, 1899, 1906, 1933).

LF.   *Letters to His Family,* ed. W. S. Hastings (Princeton: Princeton University Press, 1934).

Lov. Coll.   Lovenjoul Collection.

Lov., *Hist.*   Spoelberch de Lovenjoul, Charles de, *Histoire des œuvres de H. de Balzac* (3d ed.; Paris: Calmann-Lévy, 1888).

*Mame**   Editions published by Mame et Delaunay-Vallée.

MLN   *Modern Language Notes.*

MP   *Modern Philology.*

N.R.F.   *La Comédie humaine,* éditions de la Nouvelle Revue française (10 vols.; Paris, 1935–37).

OC.   *Œuvres complètes,* éd. Calmann-Lévy (24 vols.; Paris, 1869–76).

OD.   *Œuvres diverses,* Vols. XX–XXIII of *OC.*

PMLA   *Publications of the Modern Language Association of America.*

RDM   *Revue des deux mondes.*

RHL   *Revue d'histoire littéraire de la France.*

*Sou.**   Editions published by Hippolyte Souverain.

*Wer.**   Editions published by Werdet.

* This abbreviation may refer to any work of Balzac published by the publisher named; for its exact meaning at any given place the reader is referred to the individual chapters.

CHAPTER I

INTRODUCTION: BALZAC'S METHOD OF REVISION

By E. PRESTON DARGAN

I

THE object of this Introduction is to show, within a limited area of inquiry, how Balzac's abundant revisions follow the lines of his general method and of his realistic processes.[1] The material for such an investigation in any given case is almost overwhelming. Balzac's corrections and additions are likely to appear first on the manuscript of the story, then on the numerous proofs thereof, then in successive editions, up to and including the first collected edition of the *Comédie humaine*. A good part of the Lovenjoul Collection at Chantilly consists of bound volumes of Balzac's manuscripts and corrected proofs. The number of complete manuscripts found there is twenty-six; the number of novels at least partly represented in proof is approximately the same. From this material we select for present use portions of three novels: *Le Curé de Tours*, *La Rabouilleuse*, and *Histoire de la grandeur et de la décadence de César Birotteau*. The most important changes in these novels have been noted in the order just indicated: manuscripts, proofs, and various editions. For supplementary matter we utilize the results of an investigation made by Mario Roques on the manuscript and proofs of *Le Père Goriot*,[2] as well as the comparisons between the first and the final edition of *Les Chouans*, as treated in the monograph by Helen Barnes Wodrada.

Of the three novels chiefly studied, the following versions, mostly at Chantilly, have been in part collated.

A. The *Curé de Tours* has been used in these forms:

1. The manuscript of sixty-six pages,[3] of which page 1, one-half of page 51, and page 66 are available only in copies by Spoelberch de Lovenjoul. We shall refer to this manuscript as "*C.T. 1.*"

---

[1] Cf. chap. i of Dargan, Crain, and Others, *Studies in Balzac's Realism*.

[2] For this and other titles, see the Bibliography at the end of this Introduction.

[3] Lov. Coll., A 11.

2. Eighty-six pages of an early proof, of which pages 37, 38, 40, 42, 43, and 45 are missing (*C.T. 2a*). In the 1832 edition of the novel this proof covers page 309, line 18, through page 413; in the Conard edition, page 184, line 30, through page 248.[4] Also, a twelve-page proof (*C.T. 2b*—not final), which in the 1832 edition corresponds (not verbatim) to pages 281–95, line 21, and in the Conard edition to pages 169–77, line 13.[5]

3. Three successive editions of the *Curé de Tours* in 1832, 1834, and 1843, respectively.[6] This last-named is the first, or Furne, edition of the *Comédie humaine*, and a copy preserved at Chantilly contains for most of the novels marginal corrections in Balzac's hand.[7]

4. The Conard edition, IX, 167–248 (see Bibliography).

B. *La Rabouilleuse* is represented by these forms:

1. The original manuscript (*Rab.* 1).[8]

2. A *feuilleton* edition in *La Presse* of 1841–42 (*Rab.* 2).[9]

3. Five proofs, apparently set up for Souverain from the newspaper edition (*Rab. 3a, b, c, d, e*).[10] Of these *Rab. 3a* and *Rab. 3b* contain marginal corrections for Part I of *Les Deux Frères*, first edition in book form; the remainder are for Parts II and III of the novel. It should be said that portions of the last three sets ("épreuves en placard")[11] may have been run off from the manuscript, since Souverain probably did not await the end of the periodical publication. He wanted to strike while the iron was hot, probably to anticipate the publication of the novel in the *Comédie humaine* in the spring of 1843.[12]

4. The Souverain edition (*Sou.*), as *Les Deux Frères*, "1842" (really July, 1843). These two volumes include three parts, distributed thus: Part I (without title) in Volume I, pages 5–251; Part II, entitled "Un

---

[4] *Ibid.*, A 11.   [5] *Ibid.*, A 12.

[6] The novelette appears as *Les Célibataires* in Vol. III of *Scènes de la vie privée*, éd. Mame-Delaunay, 1832 (*Mame*); with the same title in Vol. II of *Scènes de la vie de province*, éd. Mme Charles-Béchet, 1834 (*Béch.*); as the *Curé de Tours* in Vol. VI of the *Œuvres complètes*), éd. Furne, Dubochet et Hetzel, 1843 (*Fur.*). See Miss Wilson's study, chap. iii, below.

[7] Lov. Coll., A 22.   [8] *Ibid.*, A 198.

[9] *Les Deux Frères*, February 24–March 4, 1841; *Un Ménage de garçon en province*, October 27–November 19, 1842.

[10] Lov. Coll., A 200.

[11] *Placard:* "épreuve d'imprimerie, en colonnes espacées, pour faciliter les corrections" (Larousse).

[12] Lov., *Hist.*, pp. 81–82; Hastings, *Balzac and Souverain*, p. 53.

Ménage de garçon en province," Volume I, pages 253–372, and Volume II, pages 5–222; Part III, entitled "A qui la succession?" Volume II, pages 223–380.

    5. Volume VI of the *Œuvres complètes* (Vol. II of *Scènes de la vie de province*) (Furne, Dubochet et Hetzel, 1843), pp. 63–317 (*Fur.*).

    6. The Conard edition, IX, 249–581 (see Bibliography).[13]

    C. For *César Birotteau*, the following material has been used:

    1. The original manuscript[14] (*C.B.* 1).

    2. Eight sets of proof[15] (*C.B.* 2*a*, *b*, *c*, *d*, *e*, *f*, *g*, *h*). *C.B.* 2*a* consists of nine *feuilles* (signatures) of impression intended for Volumes VI–X of the proposed Werdet edition of the *Etudes philosophiques*. The corrections probably date back as far as 1834–35.[16] *C.B.* 2*b* has much later corrections. It consists of two *feuilles* which represent pages 1–32 of the beginning, printed by Béthune et Plon, and intended for the *Figaro* edition, December, 1837 (dated 1838). *C.B.* 2*c* has slightly over six *feuilles* (pp. 1–101) of proof repeating and extending *C.B.* 2*b*. We find especially numerous corrections in this material designed for the first edition (*Fig.*). *C.B.* 2*d* has somewhat more than seven *feuilles* and runs to "peuple de douleurs" (*Fig.* I, 115, lines 14–15; *Con.*, p. 57, line 20). *C.B.* 2*e* goes as far as page 123 of *Fig.* I; *C.B.* 2*f* covers pages 65–126; *C.B.* 2*g* runs from page 65 to page 129 (eight *feuilles* in all); and *C.B.* 2*h* from page 65 to page 128, adding seven loose pages, which take the proof to *Fig.* I, 134, line 8, corresponding to *Con.*, page 66, line 14. The earlier proofs came from the office of Béthune et Plon.

    3. The first edition, in two octavo volumes, which the *Figaro* and the *Estafette* gave as a premium to their subscribers (*Fig.* I and *Fig.* II). This edition appeared in December, 1837, and was dated 1838.[17]

    4. The Furne edition of 1844 (*Fur.*).[18]

    5. The Conard edition, XIV, 1–341.

In the parenthetical references below the first printed text mentioned is the last one that is different from *Conard;* mention of manuscript or proof will indicate the place where the change was first made.

[13] The edition of Maurice Allem (Paris: Garnier Frères, 1932) has been found useful for the verification of variants and references.

[14] Lov. Coll., A 92.   [15] *Ibid.*, A 93–A 98.

[16] Spoelberch de Lovenjoul, "Les *Etudes philosophiques* de Honoré de Balzac," *RHL*, XIV, 411 and *passim*.

[17] Lov., *Hist.*, p. 112.

[18] *Scènes de la vie parisienne*, II (*Œuvres complètes*, Vol. X), 190–449.

The various forms of the *Curé de Tours* are easily handled and fairly typical. *La Rabouilleuse* offers some difficulties because of the interlocking and uncertain status of particular proofs. But by far the most complicated problem is offered by *César Birotteau,* which may be cited as a peculiar case. Altogether it takes seven quarto volumes, as compared with the usual one or two, to contain the manuscript and the multiple proofs of this work. As indicated above, eight partial proofs of the first sixty-six book pages (in the Conard ed.) of *César Birotteau* have been collated, and the entire first edition of 1838 has been compared with the definitive form.

But it is principally the proofs which are of interest in connection with this novel and many others. A word then as to Balzac's system of proof correction, concerning which a veritable legend has arisen. Frequently we have *placards* or galleys arranged in columns which were often printed at his own expense. These *placards* would be pasted on sheets of paper whose margin would receive the corrections. Later, *feuilles* of page proof (twelve or sixteen pages arranged end to end) would follow. Balzac would use either kind of proof, as we do typewritten material, for corrections and additions. This is especially true of the pages most recently written, set up in type, and returned. For example, we have page proof of *César Birotteau* which, while repeating the earlier material, adds successively one *feuille* of sixteen pages to each set. Thus Balzac would receive in one lot thirty-two, forty-eight, or sixty-four pages. For this sort of material we may use the term *cumulative* proof. The *interlocking* proof will repeat the stuff (eight or sixteen pages) where old is joined to new but will not repeat all the *feuilles* from the beginning. Now, the proof that has been examined has this special trait: it is usually the last *feuille* printed that is the most subject to revision. For instance, in the preparation of *César Birotteau* for the *Figaro* edition, pages 1–64 of the page proof were not retouched for proof *2f,* since they had undergone a quantity of corrections already; pages 65–101 were revised when first seen; next time it was the turn of pages 101–24, then of pages 124–29—always what was last set up or most recently delivered by the printer's devil. Thus Balzac's method is that of a snowplow plunging into a drift, boring a little farther each time and recoiling before each fresh effort. He drives ahead, first through the debris of his previous plunge and then into the untouched slowly yielding mass.

The manuscripts, written *currente calamo,* vary a great deal in legibility, but with regard to additions and corrections they usually offer much less material than the proof. The latter, furthermore, often adds whole paragraphs of manuscript. These may form pretty solid *dossiers*, lengthy expository insertions about an individual or an institution. Literally, as Champfleury says,[19] did Balzac follow Boileau's counsel: "Vingt fois sur le métier remettez votre ouvrage." It is on the proof that Balzac expended most of his second wind and his revising energy; it is on the proof that we find most of those *bouteilles*, as he called them, the pen circles inclosing hieroglyphic corrections. But first, in lighter vein, we shall quote from a journalist of the period a passage concerning the printer's difficulties with Balzac's proof revisions. "*Epreuves*, le mot peut s'entendre dans l'acceptation la plus pénible." So says Champfleury in his *plaquette* on *Balzac, sa méthode de travail*. He then quotes Ourliac, the journalist, to illustrate the procedure when, as so often, everybody was pressed for time:

L'imprimerie était prête et frappait du pied comme un coursier bouillant.

M. de Balzac envoie aussitôt deux cents feuillets crayonnés en cinq nuits de fièvre. On connaît sa manière. C'était une ébauche, un chaos, une apocalypse, un poème hindou.

L'imprimerie pâlit. Le délai est bref, l'écriture inouïe. On transforme le monstre, on le traduit à peu près en signes connus. Les plus habiles n'y comprennent rien de plus. On le porte à l'auteur.

L'auteur renvoie les deux premières épreuves collées sur d'énormes feuilles, des affiches, des paravents! C'est ici qu'il faut frémir et avoir pitié. L'apparence de ces feuilles est monstrueuse. De chaque signe, de chaque mot imprimé part un trait de plume qui rayonne et serpente comme une fusée à la congrève, et s'épanouit à l'extrémité en pluie lumineuse de phrases, d'épithètes et de substantifs soulignés, croisés, mêlés, raturés, superposés; c'est d'un aspect éblouissant.

Imaginez quatre ou cinq cents arabesques de ce genre, s'enlaçant, se nouant, grimpant et glissant d'une marge à l'autre, et du sud au septentrion. Imaginez douze cartes de géographie enchevêtrant à la fois villes, fleuves et montagnes. Un écheveau brouillé par un chat, tous les hiéroglyphes de la dynastie de Pharaon, ou les feux d'artifice de vingt réjouissances.

A cette vue, l'imprimerie se réjouit peu. Les compositeurs se frappent la poitrine, les presses gémissent, les protes s'arrachent les cheveux, les apprentis perdent la tête. Les plus intelligents abordent les épreuves et reconnaissent du persan, d'autres l'écriture madécasse, quelques-uns les caractères symboliques de Whisnou. On travaille à tout hasard et à la grâce de Dieu.

Le lendemain, M. de Balzac renvoie deux feuilles de pur chinois. Le délai n'est plus que de quinze jours. Un prote généreux offre de se brûler la cervelle.

[19] *Balzac, sa méthode de travail*, p. 18.

Deux nouvelles feuilles arrivent très-lisiblement écrites en siamois. Deux ouvriers y perdent la vue et le peu de langue qu'ils savaient.

Les épreuves sont ainsi renvoyées sept fois de suite. On commence à reconnaître quelques symptômes d'excellent français; on signale même quelques liaisons dans les phrases.[20]

With some caricature, this picture exhibits an outline of the truth. The same remark applies to Ourliac's statement[21] that *César Birotteau* was composed, written, and corrected some fifteen times by Balzac within twenty days, or that this novel "fut composé en vingt jours par M. de Balzac, malgré l'imprimerie, composé en vingt jours par l'imprimerie, malgré M. de Balzac."[22]

The facts in the case have, of course, been exaggerated. Balzac was not always illegible. Louis Loire, in his article entitled "A propos de la mauvaise copie de Balzac," discusses adversely what he calls "la légende Werdet" and its amplifications by Gautier and others. Yet we know that very often, in adding complications to his proofs, the author did his worst by the copyreader. And it was especially the sight of a proof, Champfleury maintains,[23] which acted as the *coup d'éperon* to Balzac's Pegasus.

II

Since the proof corrections are in the majority, the general reader may suppose that the changes now to be discussed are taken from one or another set of proofs, unless alterations from edition to edition are definitely indicated. At the same time, we have thought it well (for the benefit of those interested) to give proof references also, for the majority of the variations. These changes will fall into three divisions: (1) language and style; (2) realistic *procédés;* (3) general technique and devices solidifying the structure of the *Comédie humaine*.

Stylistic and linguistic considerations are prominent in the mind of Balzac and often affect as much as 90 per cent of the alterations. Such changes will be abundantly illustrated in the following chapters. For present purposes we shall not dwell too largely on variations of this type. They are, in our three novels, numerous enough; but only illustrative samples need be given. These represent, for the most part, fairly obvious, if distinct, improvements. They operate either for greater clearness or for

[20] *Ibid.*, pp. 9–12; the quotation is also found in the back of Vol. II of the 1st ed. of *César Birotteau.*

[21] Champfleury, *op. cit.*, p. 12.   [22] *Ibid.*, p. 13.   [23] *Ibid.*, p. 15.

concrete reference, exactness or concision. These qualities all really tend in the same direction, namely, the substitution of the *mot propre* for some vaguer term. Often, for example, a pronoun will be replaced by the definite noun, with or without modifiers. Among a dozen such cases we note that in *Les Chouans* "ce militaire" replaces "il";[24] in *César Birotteau* we find "la fatigue de l'apprenti" for "sa fatigue" (*Fig.* I, 56; *Con.* 26) and "fit trouver à César" for "lui fit trouver" (*Fur.* 207, *Con.* 26). The modifiers may add specific details; e.g., they frequently indicate the trade or profession of the person concerned: "La parfumeuse" for "elle" (*Fig.* I, 12; *Con.* 3); "cette prévoyante mère" for "Constance" (*Fur.* 370, *Con.* 238). This is very characteristic of Balzac, whose main intention is sociological and who views society as divided into species according to civil status or *métier*. Consequently, corrections of this sort are abundant, and often they add to our information. For instance, in the third edition of *La Rabouilleuse* we find "ce militaire réformé" as a substitute for "il" (*Sou.* I, 113; *Con.* 295), and earlier "cet ancien dragon" replaces the name Giroudeau (*Rab.* 2, *Con.* 296). After 1838 we find in *César Birotteau* "la notaresse" for "elle" (*Fig.* I, 336; *Con.* 170) and "l'amoureux" for "il" (*Fig.* I, 332; *Con.* 167). In the *Curé de Tours* there are many similar changes from the general to the specific—e.g., "égoïste" for "homme" (*Béch.* 44, *Con.* 175), and, of course, the frequent substitution of such a name as "Birotteau" for "il" or "lui." An example from *La Rabouilleuse* of multiple and complex word substitution may be cited. The passage concerns a loan of 1,200 francs which Agathe Bridau seeks through her godmother from J.-J. Rouget for the benefit of the rascally Philippe. The manuscript reads: "Elle écrivit à la vieille Madame Hochon de les demander à Jean-Jacques Rouget pour sauver son neveu. S'il refusait, elle *la* priait de les lui prêter." This confusion of pronouns is amended to read: "Elle écrivit à sa marraine, la vieille madame Hochon, de les demander à Jean-Jacques Rouget, pour sauver Philippe. Si Rouget refusait, elle pria *madame Hochon* de les lui prêter" (*Rab.* 1, *Con.* 352).[25]

Finally, substitution of the *mot propre* may be made for emphasis or fulness as well as for exactness: "Courez à Issoudun" instead of "Allez à Issoudun" (*Rab. 3c, Con.* 354); "Agathe Rouget se recommandait à l'admiration publique par une de ces figures..." for "Agathe Rouget *avait* une de ces figures..." (*Sou.* I, 23; *Con.* 257); and for "cette simplesse qui

---

[24] Wodrada, *Variations in Balzac's "Les Chouans,"* p. 24.

[25] Here, as in other quotations, italics are ours (to emphasize substitutions) unless otherwise indicated.

se trouve" we find "cette simplesse qui *surabonde* au début de la vie dans l'âme des artistes" (*Rab.* 2, *Con.* 283). Balzac also interpolates provincialisms, philological digressions, and the like—e.g., an addition with reference to the term "La Rabouilleuse" (*Rab. 3c, Con.* 390–91).

The purely stylistic alterations are not always so happy, particularly where some principle of harmony or elegance is at stake. On the one hand, Balzac is right in omitting certain absurd phrases from the *Curé de Tours,* and from *Les Chouans* sundry pedantic or purple passages that sound queer on the lips of Mlle de Verneuil. But frequently rhetorical questions seem to increase, and these often show a certain clumsiness. A typical example is the following: Before 1838 César said simply of Vauquelin's goodness: "elle est infinie." Now the passage reads: "n'est-elle pas infinie, dit-il d'un air fin" (*Fig.* I, 224, and Errata, p. 356; *Con.* 112). The change is hardly an improvement. Passive constructions are substituted needlessly; and vulgarities of expression are sometimes weeded out, sometimes left in. An example would be the famous "Hein" uttered by Mme de Beauséant in *Père Goriot* (*Con.* 293). With reference to this novel, Mario Roques[26] concludes that Balzac's chase after solecisms "est fort peu soigneuse, beaucoup échappent: par contre quelques constructions disparaissent, qui étaient fort bonnes." Mario Roques, however, seems too severe in his general conclusion that Balzac's corrections constitute a rapid and superficial labor and that *Père Goriot* has gained little or nothing in the process. A number of Balzac's revisions, here as elsewhere, seem very much to the point.

As a rule we have discussed additions and substitutions rather than omissions, which are decidedly in the minority, whether in regard to style or other matters. Balzac used his proofs less for purposes of subtraction than for piling Pelion upon Ossa. Some stylistic omissions may, however, be mentioned—e.g., in *César Birotteau* the suppression, after 1838, of the connective *car*, which had come to be a pet word and was too often misplaced. Balzac has a good deal of trouble with connectives, which, as a rule, he freely introduces; *alors* and *néanmoins* seem to have given him some difficulty. Mrs. Wodrada[27] mentions the numerous changes in *Les Chouans* affecting *alors* (it seems usually to be made postpositive), and Mario Roques[28] comments on the too frequent recurrence of *néanmoins.* "Balzac abuse des mots de liaison." Among others introduced, in the several novels considered, are *ainsi, donc, et, ici,* and *désormais.* Less ques-

[26] Art. cit., p. 42.   [27] *Op. cit.*, pp. 30–31.   [28] Art. cit., p. 41.

tionable is the introduction of speech-words (*dit-il*, etc.) and of time-notes, more of which might to advantage have been inserted, for the sake of "realism" if not of style.

Radical changes in dialogue are not very abundant, for a reason that will presently be mentioned. Yet some interesting cases occur. Witness the introduction of vivid dialogue on the lips of Philippe Bridau when he speaks of "La Rabouilleuse": "car elle," Philippe avers, "se tortillera comme un ver, elle jappera, elle fondra en larmes" (*Rab. 2, Con.* 517); or the horror of the Napoleonic officer who deplores a duel between brother-officers: "La Garde contre la Garde" is his reproachful expression, introduced as a repeated speech or "gag" (*Rab. 2, Con.* 519). Additional dialogue may also be used to amplify or stress a scene, as when Flore adduces more arguments for taking Max into the Rouget household (*Rab. 2, Con.* 414).

But the most interesting insertion of this kind concerns the verbal duel in the *Curé de Tours* between the Abbé Troubert and Mme de Listomère. Up to the second edition of 1834 these antagonists expressed themselves politely, with underlying veiled hostility. But from this edition on, the underlying hostility takes concrete form in a parenthetical accompaniment which gives what they really thought by the side of what they said. Every thrust and parry of the spoken dialogue is now accompanied by the written expression, italicized and in parentheses, of what the speaker really meant to convey, though he dared not say it. This most effective device is imitated, in fiction, by George Meredith and Joseph Conrad.[29]

III

The realistic qualities that are most conspicuous in these corrections are: (1) the emphasis on truth; (2) the addiction to materialism, visible in a certain *cynisme* of expression, as well as in the growing attention paid to objects and money; (3) a number of documents, *dossiers*, and partial *dossiers;* and (4) the sociological features.

A late insertion in the *Curé de Tours* declares that truth is essential "dans une histoire de mœurs" (*Béch.* 35, *Con.* 170), and we know that this was Balzac's belief in theory and practice. It often led him into painstaking researches, and he was not unaware of the difficulties in the path. Thus a long insertion in *La Rabouilleuse* illustrates how hard it is for provincials to get at the truth on account of local prejudice or gossip

---

[29] In *The Ordeal of Richard Feverel* and in *Chance*. For further discussion of this, see below, pp. 248–49.

(*Rab. 3e, Con.* 396). In the same novel a paragraph is inserted concerning the "horrible veracity" of Flore's subjugating old Rouget by her charms (*Rab. 3d, Con.* 428). Perhaps, says Balzac semiapologetically, you will blame the crudeness of this picture and you will think it the kind of verity that had better be left in darkness. But, he significantly adds, the scene is typically and extensively *true* and must therefore be recorded for its social value.

La *Rabouilleuse* has also several other insertions, emphasizing a certain naturalism, or *cynisme*, of observation and expression. "Philippe s'adressait à la Vénus des carrefours par une sorte de dédain brutal pour le sexe entier" (*Rab.* 2, *Con.* 314). This quality marks Philippe's maneuvers around "La Rabouilleuse," the manner in which he formidably threatens her, the account of how she feared him and came under his domination, finally how he allowed her to become degraded after their marriage. Other examples are not lacking; e.g., in *César Birotteau*, with regard to Roguin's repulsive physique and its effect upon his wife, Balzac adds (*C.B.* 2*f*, *Con.* 62): "Le mal physique, considéré dans ses ravages moraux … a peut-être été jusqu'ici négligé par les historiens des mœurs." Thus, anticipating the later Naturalists, he justifies his *cynisme* by considerations connected with sociohistorical veracity.

Still in the interests of accuracy, another group of examples likewise shows Balzac's concern with the military profession. In two novels, *Les Chouans* and *La Rabouilleuse*, we find a whole hierarchy of military titles set back into their proper epoch or changed into the suitable historical terms, Revolutionary or Napoleonic. In the former novel the titles are altered for the purpose of establishing the correct grades within the Republican Army: "sergent" for "caporal"; "adjutant" for "lieutenant."[30] In the latter story the titles concerning Philippe Bridau and his companions are changed (though not consistently) to the proper Napoleonic terms: "capitaine" for "commandant"; "escadron" for "compagnie"; "lieutenant-colonel" for "chef d'escadron" (*Rab.* 2, *Con.* 281–83).

Quite salient, in nearly every novel, is the number of corrections involving money and figures. In this respect Balzac's care for exactness is usually shown. For instance, when César Birotteau is bargaining with La Madou for her *noisettes*, one change in value (*Fig.* I, 198–99; *Con.* 99–100) necessitates a number of others, all correctly made. There are several alterations in the figures according to which César clears up his debts and

[30] Wodrada, *op. cit.*, p. 28.

re-establishes his credit. The figures here are increased, whereas in the
case of the *noisettes* they are diminished. We find provisionally a tendency
to further increases in large sums where it is a question of capital, income,
investments, and the like. "To him that hath shall be given." We may
remember the ease with which Balzac bestows millions on such characters
as Père Grandet. So in these corrections we find a lottery prize raised
from two to three millions (*Rab.* 2, *Con.* 333), and similar increases in
Philippe's pay (*Rab.* 2, *Con.* 282) and in the estimated fortune of Rouget
(*Rab. 3c, Con.* 494). In this last case the minor changes are due to the fact
that Rouget's savings had to be taken into consideration; various figures
and "deals" are again altered to correspond with the initial change. For
the sake of exactness, or *vraisemblance*, reduction in figures occurs in *La
Rabouilleuse* and notably in *Père Goriot*, with reference to the price of
board in the Maison Vauquer. This "abaissement progressif," according
to Mario Roques, is in order to harmonize with the "tendance à accentuer
la misère de la maison Vauquer."[31]

Substitutions in several business transactions have been noted; there
are also cases, whether in *La Rabouilleuse* or in *César Birotteau*, of additions further affecting such affairs. Notably Du Tillet's fortune is now
represented as made by speculating in accordance with the political barometer (*Rab. 3d, Con.* 579). Other mathematical changes concern dates,
ages, time-intervals, and the like. For the most part these alterations
seem plausible. For example, the action of *Père Goriot* is thrown back five
years, after the introduction of Rastignac, in order to agree with what
had been said before of this character in *La Peau de chagrin* and elsewhere.

It is known that Balzac, like other realists, was fond of inventing documents, of a semitechnical character, in his fiction. Several examples occur
of creating a document in the proof; notably the famous prospectus (*Con.*
38–40) concerning César Birotteau's toilet preparations, the "Double
Pâte des Sultanes," etc. This "pièce justificative" was not actually written[32] until the third proof and received many additions and retouches in
the fourth, fifth, and sixth proofs. Other documents which undergo
changes are the medals reproduced in *César Birotteau* (*Fig.* I, 295; *Con.*
149), the letter from Mme Hochon concluding the first part of *La Rabouil-*

---

[31] Art. cit., p. 40.

[32] Yet its genesis, as Dr. Fess maintains, may date back to 1830. See *MLN*,
XLIX, 516–19.

leuse (*Sou.* I, 244; *Con.* 352), and the insertion of a newspaper article in *César Birotteau* (*Con.* 134).

Documentation in another sense would apply to the introduction of that kind of biographical or social evidence that may be called *dossiers*.[33] Of all Balzac's variations, this is perhaps the most important kind: first, because of its frequency; then because of the amount of space which a fresh *dossier* will often cover; and finally because nothing is more revealing of Balzac's "encyclopedic zeal," his eager search for the truth, and the concrete and diversified way in which he presents his material. If, on the other hand, it be argued that some of these long digressions throw the narrative out of proportion artistically, the reason is partly in the fact that such a solid block is often added *après coup;* and, as a rule, there are still later additions and modifications, appearing in successive proofs. Of the many cases at hand, let us develop that of Du Tillet, the rascally clerk of César Birotteau. In the manuscript there is little about his life before or after his connection with Birotteau's business. But the third proof of this novel undergoes many changes, because, as we have mentioned, its date is two or three years later than the first proof, Balzac having changed his publisher in the meantime. So in this proof of 1837 we find a whole new *dossier* about Du Tillet (*C.B. 2c, Con.* 45 ff.). It begins with one of Balzac's familiar asides to the reader, concerning the necessity of saying more about this important personage. Then follows the biography of Du Tillet and an epitome of his character. A later proof (the fifth) adds details about his birth. Still later (sixth proof) we learn of Du Tillet's influence on Roguin's affairs, his dealings with Roguin's wife and mistress (*C.B. 2g, Con.* 65); the investments of this group are further complicated and extended. The range of Du Tillet in the world of the *Comédie humaine* is widened by other additions, and in various proofs there is much re-working of the latter part of the *dossier*, regarding the appearance and manners of this character. A passage stating that he is "encore garçon" was deleted (*Fig.* I, 39; *Con.* 48) to accord with his marriage in *Une Fille d'Ève.* Thus, through cumulative changes Du Tillet is planted very solidly on his feet, and his case is the best example of Balzac's snowplow process.

The same process, covering five proofs, is applied to Anselme Popinot, whose *dossier* amplifies the "good" apprentice as the foil to Du Tillet (*C.B. 2a, d, e, f, g; Con.* 57 ff.). This system of balance is paralleled in the *Curé de Tours,* where an account of Mlle Salomon, as the "good" *vieille*

---

[33] Cf. Dargan, Crain, and Others, *op. cit.*, p. 21.

fille, is added to set off Mlle Gamard (*C.T. 2a, Con.* 217 ff.). Other examples of lengthy *dossiers* inserted are: from the *Curé de Tours,* the type called "le vieux malin," or M. de Bourbonne (*C.T. 2a, Con.* 212 ff.); from *La Rabouilleuse,* the descriptions—historical, archeological, topographical—of Issoudun (*Rab. 3c* and *d, Con.* 356 ff.), together with several pages on the "histoire" and disintegrating vices of Jean-Jacques Rouget (*Rab. 3c, Con.* 401–5); also in this novel, the *dossier* on Max Gilet is extended by scattered additions concerning his paternity, character, and milieu, while Philippe's role as a spy is similarly built up.

One of the most far-reaching of Balzac's realistic qualities is his sociological intention—his purpose, already mentioned, to depict society according to groups and occupations, while accompanying the depiction with appropriate generalizations. Social *types* are stressed in one-third of the titles of the *Comédie humaine.* The various titles of the *Curé de Tours* indicate this preoccupation.[34] There are, for instance, many relics of Balzac's early intention to generalize about old maids.

While the final page of the *Curé de Tours*[35] offers us today reflections about the conflict between society and the individual, we have in *César Birotteau* fairly frequent touches that link up individual fortunes with the social or political environment: César, as a *parfumeur,* hates the Revolution because it suppressed the use of powdered wigs (*C.B. 2a, Con.* 28); he observes with complacency (*C.B. 2c, Con.* 22) that "since the peace [of 1819], the men are more assiduous around the ladies" and thus require more hair tonic. In *La Rabouilleuse,* too, the additions often emphasize the importance of groups, milieus, social pressure, or opinion. Thus, it is partly through group opinion that Flore is induced to marry Philippe (*Rab. 3c, Con.* 547–48). The phrase "socialement parlant" is inserted more than once by Balzac (e.g., *C.T., Con.* 189). Frequently he introduces generalizations about the middle class, about artists, soldiers, and the like. More is made generally of local *disettes,* or gossip. So in many ways the group idea is foremost, and through Balzac it controls the *roman social* in our own time.

IV

There are also alterations that affect general narrative technique. First, let us notice certain preliminary or external features that are changed in the various stories. The change in title of *La Vieille Fille* has

---

[34] For details, see below, pp. 192–94.

[35] The insertion was made in the 2d ed. (1834).

been mentioned. The final adoption of *La Rabouilleuse* as a title seems less satisfactory than *Les Deux Frères*;[36] "Un Ménage de garçon" had also been used as a title for the second part of the novel. This shifting indicated some uncertainty as to who is the principal character in the story. In most of the novels studied, chapter titles or divisions appeared in the manuscripts and the early editions. Had this system been maintained, it would have been a distinct advantage to the present-day reader, who wonders why the current text of the *Comédie humaine* is made even more heavy and compact by the omission of such divisions. The fault is usually not Balzac's but that of his publishers, who desired to economize space. The chapter titles originally chosen were often elucidative; they not only furnished a clue to the content of the chapter, but they were often indicative of social grouping: "Une Pension bourgeoise" as the first chapter title in *Père Goriot;* "La Famille Bridau" in *La Rabouilleuse;* "La Haute Banque" in *César Birotteau*. Other external changes concern fresh dedications or prefaces; and the business of shifting a story from one set of *Scènes* or *Etudes* to another—sometimes without an organic necessity for the shift.

In the suppressed Preface of 1838 to *César Birotteau*, we find Balzac speaking of "l'écrivain" as "ce grand rapporteur de procès." In examining his technique we should remember this emphasis on the *dossier* and the tendency to make the story at once a full biographical record and a social document. The strictly narrative value, as we know, is not usually the main thing in the mind of the author. Consequently, in the changes noted there is relatively little which concerns plot or intrigue, generally well mapped from the manuscripts down. But these fictional changes do concern character or type, exposition, description, detail, the development of milieu, and so on.

With regard to characters the first important point is the name of the personage. Balzac employed that system of *cognomologie*, according to which the name should suggest the individuality or the class of the character. He uses, for instance, names ending in *-ot* for the commercial bourgeoisie and names ending in *-ac* for his Méridionaux. These considerations are effective in the alterations. For example, Grindot is not a suitable name for a carpenter but is suitable for an architect; so Balzac makes this change in *César Birotteau (Fig.* II, 19; *Con.* 187). In *Père Goriot* Rastignac

---

[36] *La Rabouilleuse* was "indiqué postérieurement par Balzac" (M. Bouteron, in the notes to the Conard ed., p. 589).

was originally called Massiac, both names having the -*ac* termination.
Now for characterization. In the *Curé de Tours* the type of the *vieille fille* was the original preoccupation of Balzac.[37] In the manuscript there were more general observations on this type than now appear, and in the cases where these passages have been retained there has been more re-working of such general reflections. A few additions along this line have also been made, but not enough to make Mlle Gamard unduly prominent (*C.T.* 2*a*, *Con.* 200 ff.). This insertion concerning her is valuable as show-ing the nature of Balzac's transitional asides: "Pour bien peindre un être dont le caractère prête un intérêt immense aux petits événements de ce drame, et à la vie antérieure des personnages qui en sont les acteurs, peut-être faut-il résumer ici les idées dont l'expression se trouve chez la vieille fille" (*C.T.* 2*a*, *Con.* 199). On the other hand, to preserve the principle of contrast or balance (see above), we find today more about the "good" *vieille fille*, the "belle âme" of Mlle Salomon, and a sentence referring to several "belles âmes" for whom Abbé Birotteau served as confessor (*Béch.* 55, *Con.* 182). The latter's profession and type are well built up in the alterations. The abbé's brother, César Birotteau, shares in the family trait of social naïveté, and this is made to accord with his business shrewd-ness in a passage added in the third proof (*C.B.* 2*c*, *Con.* 53). To agree with the subsequent careers of characters, other passages are added or changed; e.g., those mentioned regarding Du Tillet, or those which fore-cast the career of Finot, who bought a journal which became the founda-tion of his fortunes (*Fig.* II, 74–75; *Con.* 212). To emphasize the devotion of the mother in *La Rabouilleuse*, a significant *finale* now concludes the first part of that novel. Joseph says: "O mère! tu es mère comme Raphaël était peintre! Et tu seras toujours une imbécile de mère!" (*Rab.* 2, *Con.* 355).

Thus maternity is the ruling passion of Agathe Bridau, as paternity is that of Père Goriot; and Balzac tends more and more to emphasize the determination of character by passion. Additions of this sort are found in the cases of Joseph Bridau, of the Curé de Tours and his "concupiscence mobilière" (*C.T.* 2*b*, *Con.* 173), and in a noteworthy conversation in *La Rabouilleuse*. Here Balzac introduces as *raisonneur* the clever Bixiou, who generalizes on the various passions which produce catastrophes in that story:

—Hélas! mes amis! dit Bixiou ... il suffit de livrer un homme à un vice pour se débarrasser de lui. ... Voilà! Ma grand'mère aimait la loterie et Philippe

[37] There are sixteen false starts using this title. See below, p. 192.

l'a tuée par la loterie! Le père Rouget aimait la gaudriole et Lolotte l'a tué! Madame Bridau, pauvre femme, aimait Philippe, elle a péri par lui! ... Le Vice! le Vice! mes amis! ... c'est le Bonneau de la mort.

—Tu mourras donc d'une plaisanterie! dit en souriant Desroches à Bixiou [*Rab. 3d, Con.* 574].

Balzac habitually took great pains with his exposition, which looms large as compared with the rest of the novel. The numerous changes so far discussed belong, for the most part, to the exposition of each of the novels treated. It may be noted that Balzac, as frequently, found some difficulty in getting started on *César Birotteau*. A dozen false beginnings are found in the manuscript. One fragment begins with a general reflection on fear, different from the text and called "Scène de nuit." "Avant-scène" was one title for chapter ii, in the first proof.[38] Again, the pages on César's ideas and education are transferred from the epoch of César's marriage to that of the girlhood of Césarine, a more logical position for them (*C.B. 2g, Con.* 42–44). Episodes are sometimes introduced, not always judiciously —e.g., inserting the story of a *cause célèbre* into *La Rabouilleuse* (*Rab. 3d, Con.* 361–62). Better placed is the account of Mme Hochon's visit to Philippe's home on the eve of his duel to pray for him and give him some relics as safeguards. This episodic scene makes an impression of profound verity in both the tone and the language. It is well chosen to indicate the character of each participant.

We also find examples of "decomposition" of action, that is, breaking up the action into separate fragments, for realistic or dramatic effect. The duel between Philippe and Max is made more detailed and dramatic partly by this means. Another case is the insertion of the passage where Agathe Bridau temporarily gives up Philippe after the lottery scandal: "Elle se jeta à genoux, pria Dieu de prendre cet enfant dénaturé sous sa protection, *et abdiqua sa pesante maternité*" (*Rab.* 2, *Con.* 338).

More fundamental are changes in the culminating scene, or what we call the "turn of the screw." Such, in *La Rabouilleuse*, is the death of Agathe Bridau, because of her wicked son's neglect. We wait until the edition of 1843 to get the actual death scene, fully and progressively described in about eight pages (*Rab.*, corrected *Fur.; Con.* 564 ff.), containing the agony of the mother, her *rapprochement* with her good son, Joseph, the ministrations of friends—with the callousness of Philippe preceding and accompanying this tragic event. The insertion is paralleled by a num-

---

[38] This is illustrative of our author's attachment to the word "scène" and to the idea of the "drame."

ber of death scenes regularly found in Balzac's novels of martyrdom or monomania.

Long descriptions are, of course, a *forte* with Balzac, and we should expect, in his revisions, numerous additions along this line. Some cases have already been considered as *dossiers*—e.g., the topographical account of Issoudun; this now includes a certain "tour de Richard Cœur-de-Lion" (*Rab. 3d, Con.* 381–82). The insertion is justified because the tower is made the scene of a prank played by the "Chevaliers de la Désœuvrance." We have also fresh additions about the appearance and costume of Philippe Bridau when he first visits his uncle. The description is keynoted around the "sinister physiognomy" of Bridau. Mario Roques remarks[39] that the touches added to the Maison Vauquer accentuate its keynote of *misère*—especially as regards the furniture of Goriot. Likewise, in the *Curé de Tours*, the furniture, typical of the priest's apartment, has now "une physionomie pleine de caractère" (*Mame* 289, *Con.* 174). Here, too, we find the introduction of the "salon jaune" as illustrative of the old maid's character (*C.T.* 2*a, Con.* 204). And there are more details, of an archeological sort, concerning the surroundings of the cathedral at Tours. Instances appear of the various kinds of Balzacian detail—especially the additional, the characteristic, and the cumulative. The phrase "sentant l'iris," stressing the perfume loved by the Curé de Tours, is an example (*Mame* 295, *Con.* 177).

A few scattered points in technique may be mentioned. Reference has been made to Balzac's way of considering the ideas of a given person—of the old maid, for instance, or of a Philistine (cf. Flaubert's M. Homais). A page full of César's bourgeois ideas and ideals is inserted in *César Birotteau* (*C.B.* 2*c, Con.* 43–44) within the lengthier passage ultimately shifted (*C.B.* 2*g;* cf. p. 16 above). Additions in the sixth proof develop the delight of this "paysan parvenu" in the number of his daughter's accomplishments (*C.B.* 2*f, Con.* 42). Again, many people have noticed the importance which Balzac attaches to local gossip, to what we have heard him call "les disettes." In *La Rabouilleuse* there are sundry passages reporting such *disettes;* there is the addition of *dictons*, or proverbs; there is an allusion in the *Curé de Tours* to the "médisances de la ville" (*C.T.* 2*c,*[40] *Con.* 190). At Issoudun particularly, the amount of gossip in circulation is almost incredible; the author inserts a whole page of local dialogue

---

[39] Art. cit., p. 40.

[40] This addition does not occur in 2*a*, which, however, modifies the same passage; it must have been made in the later proof, 2*c*, of which the pages extant do not include our passage.

about the duel (*Rab. 3c, Con.* 533), and on other occasions an effort is made to preserve the local point of view: "Aussi le peu que *la ville d'Issoudun* sut de la belle madame Rouget, ..." (*Sou.* I, 13; *Con.* 253).

A number of the changes already itemized tend toward the solidifying of that immense structure which is the *Comédie humaine.* The two main solidifying features still to be discussed are: (1) the use of generalizations as a sort of cohesive philosophy, and (2) the use of reappearing characters. With reference to *Père Goriot,* Mario Roques points out that Balzac adds psychological analyses and reflective moralizings about student life in Paris, about the *ménage à trois,* etc.,[41] and he quotes a typical phrase added by Balzac in the edition of 1835, concerning "les poésies de cette scène ... pleine d'observations et de couleurs locales ... ."[42] In three novels occur remarks about the dangers threatening unoccupied little minds. In the *Curé de Tours,* successive editions add observations tending to consolidate Balzac's philosophy of society—for example, he emphasizes the differences between the provincial priest and people of the world (*Mame* 302, *Con.* 181). He deduces conclusions about the monotony and lack of activity around Issoudun (*Rab. 3c, Con.* 359 ff.); he demonstrates a preference for Catholic, rather than lay, education (*Rab. 3c, Con.* 398); he shows his recurrent dislike for the bourgeois monarchy of Louis Philippe (*Rab. 3c, Con.* 370–72) and takes a fling at the "duplicity of the Liberals" (*Rab. 3d, Con.* 290–91). Other generalizations concern science, nature, art, and the supremacy of "l'intérêt, qui est le génie de l'argent" (*Rab. 3d, Con.* 549). As philosophy, this sounds like La Rochefoucauld brought up to date.

Balzac's explanatory asides often consist of apologies for cumbersome material. These asides are freely added. Thus, in the *Curé de Tours* he tells us that certain events "exigeaient cette longue introduction" (*Mame* 322, *Con.* 192) from an "exact historian" interested in minutiae. One insertion in *La Rabouilleuse* refers us to what comes later in the story (*Rab. 3d, Con.* 356), and another states that the "historian of manners" must clear up "archeological darkness" (*Rab. 3d, Con.* 357).

We now reach Balzac's frequent and familiar device of reappearing characters. As might be expected, there are a number of changes bearing upon this device. Sometimes the author alters the original name of a character and gives him the name of a personage who had appeared in other novels; or else he simply introduces characters from other novels, inserting

---

[41] Art. cit., p. 40.   [42] *Ibid.,* p. 72.

them bodily or by allusion into the fabric of the new story. This technique mortises together the different parts of the *Comédie humaine.* Let us consider first the revision of *César Birotteau.* Among the names substituted in the second edition are Camusot for Grasset, Granville for Marchangy (the character also changing in the latter case), Du Guénic for Bernier, etc. There are a dozen passages introduced to emphasize the Camusot-Cardot group of the *haute bourgeoisie.* Balzac is also fond of cataloguing the names of his reappearing characters, and such a list was inserted as early as the second proof of *César Birotteau (C.B. 2b, Con.* 18). It included "des Cochin, des Guillaume, des Roguin, des Saillard, des Popinot." Rather curiously, "des Goriot" was added in the following proof, although it was suppressed in the next but one (the fifth), since the unfortunate modern Lear hardly belonged to the class of successful merchants named. Other reappearing characters are mentioned in the exposition (later than the manuscript) of *César Birotteau.* In *Les Chouans*[43] there are fifteen changes affecting persons who recur in later novels; since this was the first published of the *Comédie humaine,* many alterations in names and characterizations were inevitable after Balzac had established this general scheme in 1833. In *Le Colonel Chabert,* according to Mario Roques,[44] there is an insertion of great interest which must have been made after 1834. The lawyer Derville is made to say: "J'ai vu mourir un père dans un grenier, sans sou ni maille, abandonné par deux filles auxquelles il avait donné 40000 livres de rente." Now this passage evidently refers to *Père Goriot* of 1834–35 and is not found in *Le Colonel Chabert* before that date. Of still greater interest is a change in the manuscript of *Père Goriot* itself (see Mario Roques, art. cit., pp. 38 and 179). In beginning this novel Balzac had no intention of using Eugène de Rastignac. His hero was called Eugène de Massiac through page 39 of the manuscript. A little later, page 43 (*Con.* 304), Rastignac boldly takes his place. This was evidently a swift decision to use a reappearing character, Rastignac having previously become known to the public in *La Peau de chagrin* and other stories.[45] But as Massiac, he seemed more sympathetic than under his new name—and Mario Roques gives examples of the coloring process by which Balzac gradually darkens this portrait.[46] E.g., Balzac deletes the phrase "ce joyeux garçon qui n'avait encore rien jugé"[47] and adds phrases emphasizing the *arriviste* character of the hero.

[43] Wodrada, *op. cit.,* p. 41.   [44] Art. cit., p. 34, n. 3.

[45] Cf. E. Preston, *Recherches sur la technique de Balzac,* pp. 132–39 and *passim.*

[46] Art. cit., pp. 38–39.   [47] *Ibid.,* p. 179.

In *La Rabouilleuse* we find casual introductions of Cardot, Sérizy, Léon de Lora (alias Mistigris), Schinner, César Birotteau "le célèbre parfumeur," le duc de Maufrigneuse, etc. Mention is also made of the beautiful Caroline (changed to Coralie in proof [*Rab. 3c, Con.* 552]), who later becomes the mistress of Lucien de Rubempré; and we hear a little of Florine and of old Lord Dudley, "le vrai père de de Marsay" (*Rab. 3d, Con.* 552). Certain reappearing characters are actually brought on in the flesh, especially in the extensive changes toward the end of the story. Among them are Bixiou, Bianchon, Loraux—all of whom appear during the final illness of Agathe Bridau. We also learn through successive insertions how Du Tillet and Nucingen beguile Philippe into various investments and finally ruin him (*Rab. 3d* and *Sou.* II, 377; *Con.* 579). Of all the kinds of insertions favored by Balzac, this introduction of reappearing characters seems one of the most common and perhaps the best worked out.

We have here attempted to show the principles which activated Balzac in making certain corrections, the results which he hoped to attain, and the methods which he used for this purpose. None of the novels discussed has been examined exhaustively. Our only aim has been to describe Balzac's general method. In the following chapters individual stories will be more particularly studied. But our first contributor is concerned rather with the development of the whole scheme and with Balzac's distribution, into divisions and subdivisions, of the numerous titles.

BIBLIOGRAPHY

BALZAC, H. DE. *Les Célibataires. Scènes de la vie privée*, III, 279–413. Paris: Mame-Delaunay, 1832.

———. *Les Célibataires. Scènes de la vie de province*, II, 31–164. Paris: Mme Charles-Béchet, 1834.

———. *Les Célibataires: Le Curé de Tours. La Comédie humaine* (éd. Furne, Dubochet et Hetzel), VI (1843), 1–62.

———. *Le Curé de Tours. Œuvres complètes* (éd. Conard), IX (1913), 167–248.

———. *Les Deux Frères*. Paris: Souverain, 1842. 2 vols.

———. *Un Ménage de garçon en province. La Presse*, October 27–November 19, 1842.

———. *Les Célibataires: Un Ménage de garçon. La Comédie humaine* (éd. Furne, Dubochet et Hetzel), VI (1843), 63–317.

———. *La Rabouilleuse. Œuvres complètes* (éd. Conard), IX (1913), 249–581.

———. *La Rabouilleuse* (éd. Maurice Allem). Paris: Garnier Frères, 1932.

———. *Histoire de la grandeur et de la décadence de César Birotteau*. Paris: Au Bureau du *Figaro*, 1838. 2 vols.

———. *Histoire de la grandeur et de la décadence de César Birotteau, etc. La Comédie humaine* (éd. Furne, Dubochet et Hetzel), X (1844), 190–449.

———. *César Birotteau. Œuvres complètes* (éd. Conard), XIV (1913), 1–341.

BARNES, HELEN ELCESSOR [Mrs. J. F. Wodrada]. *A Study of the Variations between the Original and the Standard Editions of Balzac's "Les Chouans."* Chicago, 1923.

CHAMPFLEURY. *Balzac, sa méthode de travail.* Paris: Patay, 1879.

DARGAN, E. PRESTON; CRAIN, W. L.; and OTHERS. *Studies in Balzac's Realism.* Chicago: University of Chicago Press, 1932.

FESS, G. M. "Balzac's First Thought of *César Birotteau*," *MLN*, XLIX (1934), 516–19.

HASTINGS, W. S. *Balzac and Souverain.* Garden City, New York: Doubleday, Page & Co., 1927.

LOIRE, LOUIS. "A propos de la mauvaise copie de Balzac," *L'Imprimerie*, July 15, 1888.

OURLIAC, ÉDOUARD. "Malheurs et aventures de César Birotteau avant sa naissance," *Figaro*, December 15, 1837.

PRESTON, E. *Recherches sur la technique de Balzac. Le Retour systématique des personnages dans la "Comédie humaine."* Paris: Presses françaises, 1926.

ROQUES, MARIO. "Manuscrits et éditions du *Père Goriot;* corrections et variantes," *Revue universitaire*, June 15, July 15, 1905, pp. 34–42, 71–76, 178–83.

SPOELBERCH DE LOVENJOUL, CHARLES Vᵀᴱ DE. *Histoire des œuvres de H. de Balzac.* 3d ed. Paris: Calmann-Lévy, 1888.

———. "Les *Etudes philosophiques* de Honoré de Balzac," *RHL*, XIV (July–September, 1907), 393–441.

CHAPTER II

DEVELOPMENT OF THE SCHEME OF THE *COMEDIE HUMAINE:* DISTRIBUTION OF THE STORIES

By BRUCIA L. DEDINSKY
George School, Pennsylvania

I. STATEMENT OF THE PROBLEM

IN THE following study the investigator is confronted with several fundamental questions: Do we know exactly what is the genesis of the *Comédie humaine?* Did the author from the start have a clear conception of his work? Or was this work a matter of the gradual accumulation of stories, written or projected, together with groupings of stories under collective titles,[1] which ultimately led Balzac to the idea of assembling all of his works into a unit and placing them under one all-inclusive title? In answer to these questions this investigation proposes to discover how Balzac planned and built up his "monument" and to define the organic structure of the whole *Comédie humaine.*

The earliest grouping of novels made by Balzac was published in 1830, in two volumes under the collective title *Scènes de la vie privée.* From 1833 to 1848 he continually rearranged the classification of his stories. Several novels appearing first in one group of *Scènes* or *Etudes* were moved, either temporarily or permanently, to another group. Our main problem, then, is to trace the history of Balzac's individual works from the earlier alignment of stories under collective titles and, as a corollary, to follow up the new classifications and additions of stories under the all-inclusive title *La Comédie humaine,* as the author left it in August, 1850.

The question of Balzac's classification and arrangement of his works has been touched upon by many admirers and critics. Le Breton considered it of little importance to know "sous quelle rubrique il [Balzac] a classé ses œuvres."[2] B. W. Wells[3] thought it time wasted to insist on a

[1] A "collective title" is a common title for volumes, published between 1830 and 1835, containing a group of stories similar in theme. Some of these titles are used, from 1834, to designate component parts of the *Etudes de mœurs,* and from 1842, parts of the *Comédie humaine;* therefore for the sake of clarity, as collective titles they will appear in italics, and as captions for divisions and subdivisions, in quotations.

[2] A. Le Breton, *Balzac, l'homme et l'œuvre,* p. 124.

[3] *A Century of French Fiction,* pp. 88–186.

classification that places a story in one series or another. On the other hand, Cabat emphasized the importance of knowing whether or not "la réunion de toutes les actions sous une même rubrique a sa raison d'être."[4] With Cabat we believe that the question of classification has a direct bearing on the development of the scheme of the *Comédie humaine*. Therefore the writer will endeavor to explain these changes in classification. Were they usually to satisfy the demands of publishers? Or had Balzac at times more urgent reasons—the reasons of a master-builder who must create his own plan? In the course of this study I have usually found in the stories themselves some element which could be interpreted as a basis for the author's varied classifications.

The opinions concerning the evolution of the scheme of the *Comédie humaine* are many and varied. It would seem that Sainte-Beuve, Taine, Baschet, Brunetière, and others tend to treat the *Comédie humaine* as one consistent body, conceived in its entirety. Brunetière states that about 1834 "l'œuvre *entière* de Balzac [est] *confusément contemporaine* dans sa tête."[5] But in 1834 Balzac had reached about the mid-stream of his career. What of the period before 1834? From what date did Balzac begin to carry the whole scheme in his mind? Brunetière is not sufficiently specific on this point; neither is Henry James,[6] who also maintains that Balzac early saw his work as a whole. This view is shared by Le Breton, who contends that at first Balzac wrote "à peu près au hasard et sans vue d'ensemble"[7] but that presently he had a sudden revelation of genius in which he saw "devant lui toute la *Comédie humaine*, comme une immense cité dont les toits et les clochers émergent soudain de la brume."[8] Of course, Le Breton evidently refers to the events of 1833, but again what about the years before 1833? Le Breton, in his discussion of the "Genèse et plan de la *Comédie humaine*,"[9] is cursory and general.

As early as 1864, however, Camille Chancel suggested that the *Comédie humaine* was a work of incubation and of slow development. The title of his article "La Genèse de la *Comédie humaine*"[10] is, nevertheless, misleading, since it gives merely a list of Balzac's compositions and indicates his new and original tendencies in depicting contemporary life. This article

[4] A. Cabat, *Etude sur l'œuvre d'Honoré de Balzac*, pp. 28–29.

[5] F. Brunetière, *Honoré de Balzac*, p. 87. Italics ours.

[6] *Notes on Novelists*, pp. 111 ff.; and *French Poets and Novelists*, pp. 77 ff.

[7] Le Breton, *op. cit.*, p. 112.

[8] *Ibid.*, p. 114.　　　　　[9] *Ibid.*, pp. 112–36.

[10] *Revue de Paris*, old ser., Vol. I (June, July, August, 1864).

fails entirely to show the "genesis." Paul Flat,[11] J. Merlant,[12] and Ernst Curtius[13] have treated the question of the genesis briefly and without specific details and have not materially advanced the knowledge of the problem. Other writers who knew Balzac personally—Félix Davin,[14] Gabriel Richard,[15] and Théophile Gautier[16]—seem to imply that the inception of the *Comédie humaine* was early and the growth slow. No one of these critics, however, has made a systematic and exhaustive study of the development of Balzac's scheme. The difficulty of the problem lies partly in the fact that the author published his work piecemeal and in a most bewildering variety of ways and partly in the lack of original documents recording his first steps. Only a chronological study of the novels and of the various classifications, therefore, can show the organic structure of the *Comédie humaine* and prove whether Balzac had from the beginning a clear conception of the whole scheme or whether he developed it by an evolutionary process.

The procedure in this investigation will be as follows: First, a chronological study (with a few inevitable exceptions) will be made of the volumes having collective titles, in the order of their publication up to 1833. After that date these volumes appeared in new alignments of stories, under collective titles—some new, some previously used—which now designate subdivisions; here again the treatment will be chronological. Then these stories, revised and enlarged, will be discussed as component parts of the *Comédie humaine*. Each story will be traced from its original place in those collective volumes to its final classification in the Conard edition of the *Comédie humaine*. Each classification or transference of a story from one grouping to another will be explained by textual analysis of the story under consideration. These shifts and final classifications will also be indicated by a table (p. 180).

The thirty-one years of Balzac's creative life are too many to be represented as on one plane of art and interest. His literary career, as a whole, falls into six definite stages, in spite of an inescapable overlapping of years. The first ten years comprise his apprenticeship; the last twenty must be divided into five periods, each distinguished by a paramount interest and marked by specific publications. Our study will be divided accordingly.

[11] *Essais sur Balzac*, I, 2–3.

[12] *Morceaux choisis de Honoré de Balzac*, pp. 36–39.

[13] *Balzac, sein Leben, sein Werk*, chap. xii.   [15] *Ibid.*, p. 482.

[14] Lov., *Hist.*, pp. 194–95.   [16] *Honoré de Balzac*, p. 42.

II. BALZAC'S YEARS OF APPRENTICESHIP: 1819-29

The works of Sir Walter Scott had doubtless a direct influence in suggesting the scheme of the *Comédie humaine*.[17] Balzac himself wrote that the lack of unity and co-ordination in the Waverley novels led him to seek a new technique and a new system for unifying scattered compositions and welding them into a correlated whole. Balzac's aim was to give a history of contemporary manners—what he called "un drame à trois ou quatre mille personnages que présente une société."[18] In order to make this "drama" interesting, he strongly felt the need of a system, for, he said, it is not enough to observe and to depict, it is necessary to depict and to observe with a definite aim in mind.[19] In March, 1830, while discussing a method of dealing with the numberless facts of history, Balzac states that they may be grouped under one general idea and then be classified and co-ordinated in order to show the "*enchaînement et la liaison qui en réunissent toutes les parties.*"[20] In 1835 Davin quoted Balzac as saying: "Le génie n'est complet que quand il joint, à la faculté de créer, *la puissance de coordonner ses créations.*"[21] Moreover, Davin, Balzac's mouthpiece, tells in no uncertain terms: "Nous devons l'unité de cette œuvre à une réflexion que M. de Balzac fit de *bonne heure* sur l'ensemble des œuvres de Walter Scott."[22] Finally, in 1842, Balzac becomes even more explicit on the matter of organization. In discussing Scott's lack of system, he says: "En apercevant ce défaut de liaison, qui d'ailleurs ne rend pas l'Écossais moins grand, je vis à la fois le système favorable à l'exécution de mon ouvrage et la possibilité de l'exécuter."[23] These statements plainly indicate the possible origin of Balzac's scheme.

Our next problem is to observe how Balzac achieved unity in his writings. First he conceived the happy idea of using the same characters in several novels. This device also might have been suggested by certain of the Waverley novels, in which Rob Roy, Claverhouse, and the Duke of

---

[17] For a full discussion of the influence of Sir Walter Scott on Balzac, see E. Preston Dargan, "Scott and the French Romantics," *PMLA*, XLIX (1934), 599–629. See also F. Baldensperger, *Orientations étrangères chez Honoré de Balzac*, chap. iv.

[18] *Avant-propos*, pp. xxviii ff.

[19] Quoted by Félix Davin, "Introduction aux *Etudes de mœurs au XIXe siècle*" (1835); reprinted in Lov., *Hist.*, pp. 46–64. References to this Introduction will be hereafter cited as "Lov., *Hist.*"

[20] *OD.*, III, 65. Italics ours.

[21] Lov., *Hist.*, p. 50. Italics ours.

[22] *Ibid.* Italics ours.

[23] *Avant-propos*, I, xxix.

Argyle reappear, and where still others, such as Henry Wynd and Flora MacDonald, are mentioned by name only.[24] It is barely possible that this *procédé* might have been suggested by Fenimore Cooper's Leather-Stocking series. As late as 1840 Balzac particularly admired, so he said, "la grandeur, l'originalité de Bas-de-Cuir, ce sublime personnage *qui lie entre eux les Pionniers, les Mohicans, le Lac Ontario, la Prairie.*"[25] However, the only novel of the Leather-Stocking series that Balzac could in all probability have known before he wrote *Annette et le criminel (Argow le pirate)* in 1824 was the *Pioneers*, which appeared in France on August 30, 1823.[26] Consequently, it is difficult to establish influence of Cooper at that early period.

Nevertheless, the first attempt to correlate novels by reappearing characters is made in *Le Vicaire des Ardennes*[27] and *Argow le pirate*[28] from the *Œuvres de jeunesse.*[29] In the Preface[30] to *Le Vicaire des Ardennes* Balzac states that the novel tends to become *en gros* a *cadre* into which the dramatized story is fitted. He hints at a plan for the co-ordination of a series of thirty projected novels in which characters will reappear.[31] At the end of *Le Vicaire des Ardennes* Balzac announced, in a "Note," a novel, *Le Criminel.* This was first published as *Annette et le criminel* but became, in 1836, *Argow le pirate.*[32] The connecting link between *Le Vicaire* and *Argow* is found in five reappearing characters.[33] Another linking device worthy of notice at that early period is a cross-reference by title to

[24] See Dargan, art. cit., *PMLA*, XLIX, 612–19.

[25] *La Revue parisienne*, July 25, 1840, pp. 69–70. Italics ours. See also Ethel Preston, *Recherches sur la technique de Balzac: Le Retour systématique des personnages dans la "Comédie humaine,"* p. 7. For a full discussion of Cooper's influence on Balzac, see E. Preston Dargan, "Studies in Balzac: I. Balzac and Cooper: *Les Chouans,*" *MP*, XIII (1915), 193–213. See also F. Baldensperger, *op. cit.*, pp. 68–73; and Margaret Gibb, *Le Roman de Bas-de-Cuir: Etude sur Fenimore Cooper et son influence en France*, pp. 149–75.

[26] *Bibliographie de la France*, 1823; the *Last of the Mohicans* appeared in 1826, the *Prairie* in 1827, and the *Pathfinder* in 1840.

[27] 4 vols.; Paris: Pollet, 1822.   [28] 4 vols.; Paris: E. Buissot, 1824.

[29] Cf. Wells, *op. cit.*, p. 93. See also Bellessort, *Balzac et son œuvre*, p. 45.

[30] *Le Vicaire des Ardennes*, I, iv.

[31] *Ibid.*, p. iv.   [32] Lov., *Hist.*, p. 256.

[33] They are: (1) Argow, or Maxendi, the leader of the rebels; (2) his accomplice, Vernyct; (3) M. de Saint-André, the admiral; (4) M. Badger, the banker; (5) Marguerite, the old priest's maid, who becomes the wife of the judge.

the *Vicaire des Ardennes*.[34] These two novels should therefore be considered as part of a correlated series, although the author had not as yet thought of a collective title. It is not unreasonable, then, to assume that in these novels originated, however vaguely, the method of relating stories through characters and cross-references.

During his later productive years Balzac borrowed some material from the *Œuvres de jeunesse;* for instance, *Eugénie Grandet, Melmoth réconcilié, Maître Cornélius*, and *Ursule Mirouët* all have their antecedents in the earlier novels.[35] According to his sister, Mme Surville,[36] young Balzac aspired to write a series of historical novels, each one characteristic of an epoch in the history of France. He definitely planned three; one, on a fifteenth-century theme, was to be entitled *Le Capitaine des Boutefeux*. This was never written, but the period chosen was later depicted in *Maître Cornélius*. The second projected novel, *Le Gars*, portraying the Chouannerie, actually appeared under the title *Les Chouans*. The publication of the third novel, *Les Trois Cardinaux, histoire du règne de Louis XIII*,[37] was announced for June 30, 1830.[38] Balzac wrote to his friend Mme Zulma Carraud,[39] on April 14, 1830, in terms which imply that he had begun the work; but in September, 1833, he tells her in another letter that the work is not finished. *Les Trois Cardinaux* never appeared, and no manuscript has been preserved. Of these three novels, therefore, probably only one, *Les Chouans*, was written. Nevertheless, this project is of great importance, because here Balzac first planned to cover a historical period in a series of novels with definite titles. This design is a positive step toward the formation of a plan for his writings after his somewhat vague announcement made in the Preface to the *Vicaire*.

---

[34] *Annette et le criminel*, III, 13.

[35] These borrowings will be indicated in the analyses of the novels.

[36] *Op. cit.*, p. 94.

[37] See Octave Uzanne, "A travers l'Œuvre de H. de Balzac, *"Les Zigzags d'un curieux* (1888), p. 161. He states that Balzac wanted to portray in this novel "le Père Joseph, dit l'Eminence Grise, Mazarin, et Richelieu." M. Bouteron, however, thinks that they were: "Mazarin, Dubois et le P. Joseph, l'Eminence grise de Richelieu"; cf. *Corr. Carraud*, p. 20.

[38] 2 vols., in octavo. See *Scènes de la vie privée* (1st ed., 1830), Vol. I. This announcement is printed at the end of the volume in the advertising pages. Cf. L.-J. Arrigon, *Les Débuts littéraires*, pp. 237, 268. See also Pierre Abraham, *Créatures chez Balzac*, pp. 68, 103.

[39] *Corr. Carraud*, p. 20.

In an unpublished manuscript, a fragment of a program,[40] now in the Lovenjoul Collection at Chantilly, Balzac planned new works: *La Physiologie du mariage*, *La Pathologie sociale*, and *La Monographie de la vertu*. These titles arrest our attention as being sociological rather than historical. He actually published between 1830 and 1831 a series of short "physiologies" or "pathologies." But the significant expression of this program, which must be considered as a basis and a background for the *Scènes de la vie privée* and later for the *Comédie humaine*, is *La Physiologie du mariage*.[41] After perusing the *Physiologie*, we find that the *Scènes de la vie privée*, as well as certain types in the *Comédie humaine*, proceed at least in part from this work. The characters of Augustine de Sommervieux, of Mme Firmiani, and of the daughters of Père Goriot originate there; certain ideas in *Gloire et malheur* (*La Maison du Chat-qui-pelote*), in *Une Double Famille*, and in *Mémoires de deux jeunes mariées* are already expressed in the *Physiologie*. These facts seem to prove that *La Physiologie* was a basis for the novels which Balzac later arranged under the general title, *Scènes de la vie privée*. *La Physiologie du mariage* is in three parts, each with divisions and with subdivisions. Within the work at least eight cross-references to the component parts of the book may be noted. And it should be recalled here that this method plays a vital part in the *Comédie humaine*. The diction in the *Physiologie* also occasionally forecasts that of the author's future work. At the outset Balzac says that as "l'humble *secrétaire* de deux dames, il a, tout en accordant leurs observations, accompli plus d'une tâche."[42] He also frequently refers to this work as an "Etude"; toward the end of the book we find a significant statement: "nous sommes parvenus au dernier cercle infernal de la divine comédie du mariage, nous sommes au fond de l'enfer."[43] It is noteworthy because it indicates at what an early date, 1824–29, Balzac had in mind the *Divine Comedy* of Dante.

A review of Balzac's apprenticeship (1819–29) reveals that these early writings profoundly influenced his later productions and supply a background for the *Scènes de la vie privée* and for the future *Comédie humaine*. The early signs of a plan or a system are found in the Preface to the

---

[40] Assigned by Lovenjoul to 1830. Lov. Coll., A 168, fols. 63–64. See below, p. 38.

[41] For a full account of the genesis of this work, see Prioult, *op. cit.*, pp. 213 ff. See also below, p. 166.

[42] *La Physiologie du mariage*, p. 13. Italics ours.

[43] *Ibid.*, p. 332. Cf. the opening pages of *La Fille aux yeux d'or*, where Balzac describes Paris.

Vicaire des Ardennes (1822), in the "Avertissement" to *Le Gars* (1827) and its marginal notes, and in the fragmentary program of 1830.

III. FIRST CONSTRUCTIVE PERIOD
APRIL, 1830—MARCH, 1833

Les Chouans opened for Balzac the road to fame. After this success, however, he turned from history and the past to the everyday life of the present—in the words of Mme Surville,[44] to "les mœurs de son époque." Contemporary life and manners became his field of observation, and so in the *Physiologie* he depicted the most intimate phases of private life. It is assumed, therefore, that about 1828 and 1829 the interest of Balzac was divided between the past and the life around him; or, as Helen Barnes (Wodrada) says, in a slightly different connection, "Balzac was pressing forward to the mark of socio-historical fiction."[45]

Balzac's reading at that period included *Proverbes romantiques* by A. Romieu (1827); *Scènes contemporaines*[46] by Romieu, Loève-Veimars, and Vanderburch (1828); and Henri Monnier's *Scènes populaires*,[47] which appeared in 1830. These works portray the customs and manners of the times, and they were evidently suggestive models for the *Scènes de la vie privée*. It is interesting to note that the term *Scène* was much in vogue; furthermore, the use of the term appealed to Balzac's interest in dramatic form. Paul Barrière emphasizes the fact that Balzac began his literary career with a drama—that he was haunted by the "enchaînement des scènes" and the logical development of action. By nature, Barrière avers, Balzac had "l'esprit de suite, d'organisation."[48]

By 1830 Balzac had written a great number of stories, some of which had appeared, often in a fragmentary form, in the leading periodicals. Out of these tales he selected six, two of which, *Gloire et malheur* and *La Paix du ménage*, had never appeared before, and published them in April, 1830, under the collective title *Scènes de la vie privée;*[49] the negotiations for the publication, however, started on October 22, 1829.[50] Here, for the

---

[44] *Op. cit.*, p. 95.

[45] *A Study of the Variations between the Original and the Standard Editions of Balzac's "Les Chouans,"* p. 6.

[46] Announced in the *Bibliographie de la France*, June 27, 1827. *Proverbes romantiques* and *Scènes contemporaines* were printed by Balzac in 1827 and 1828, respectively.

[47] L.-J. Arrigon, *Les Années romantiques de Balzac*, pp. 6, 66.

[48] *Honoré de Balzac et la tradition classique*, p. 198.

[49] 1st ed.; 2 vols.; Paris: Mame et Delaunay-Vallée.

[50] Lov. Coll., A 268, fols. 38–39.

first time, all the tales appeared in complete form. Each of these *Scènes* contains a character study of a young woman, while married life is the main theme; these stories continue the studies begun in the *Physiologie*. Balzac himself confirms this idea in a letter dated October 5, 1831, to his friend the Duchess of Castries:

Immédiatement après [*La Physiologie*], je fis, pour dévelloper [*sic*] mes pensées et les jetter [*sic*] dans les âmes jeunes par de frappans tableaux, *les Scènes de la Vie privée*. Dans cet ouvrage, tout de morale et de sages conseils, rien n'est détruit, rien n'est attaqué; je respecte les croyances auxquelles je n'ai pas foi. Je suis historien et jamais la vertu ne fut plus préconisée que dans ces *Scènes*.[51]

This passage shows Balzac's objective point of view and his aim at that time.

This is Balzac's first grouping of tales under a collective title, and it is of prime importance because it is the foundation for future enlargement and building up. Pierre Abraham aptly speaks of the title *Scènes de la vie privée* as "ce titre annonciateur de toute l'œuvre future,"[52] because a large number of stories and novels followed in the wake of the first edition of these *Scènes* and eventually were classed in subdivisions with similar general titles. The two volumes under consideration were given to the public April 13, 1830. The first volume contained a preface and three tales: *La Vendetta, Les Dangers de l'inconduite (Gobseck)*, and *Le Bal de Sceaux*. The three tales of the second volume are: *Gloire et malheur (La Maison du Chat-qui-pelote), La Femme vertueuse (Une Double Famille)*, and *La Paix du ménage*. The "Note" concluding the volume seems to be both a self-defense and an explanation of the author's technique. He states that invention is the distinctive feature of talent and that detail constitutes the merit of the novel.

The Preface to the first edition of these *Scènes* is important because in it Balzac gives his reasons for collecting, under a general title, stories with the same theme. Each of these six tales has been built around the fundamental principle that the romantic ideas and inexperience of young people bring disaster in their married lives. Young people, he says, are sincere and eager for happiness, but their obstinacy and lack of common sense result in misfortunes. His aim, he continues, is to depict faithfully the events which precede and follow marriage, inventing nothing, but only returning to the world what he had taken from it. These stories, he maintains, present true pictures of bourgeois home life, which are usually concealed from the casual observer. Balzac realized, as did no other writer

---

[51] *Correspondance de Balzac avec la duchesse de Castries*, pp. 3–4.

[52] *Balzac: Recherches sur la création intellectuelle*, p. 28.

of his day, the wealth of material offered by the French family circle and its customs. He drew into the limelight hidden thoughts, feelings, and interests of the family and of the individual. Concerned with manners and morals, he pleads for the education of women; he demands for them "une éducation solide sans nulle pédanterie,"[53] since, he believes, this will lead to a better understanding of matrimony and life in general and will better prepare for such experience the young women who will later appear "sur la scène sociale." These short narratives in which he pictures domesticity he appropriately compares to sketches of the Dutch school in their details regarding private and intimate life. With their common theme of the inner family sphere these stories are strung like beads on the same thread. Five of them are gloomy examples of unhappy marriages with tragic endings; *La Paix du ménage* is the only one with a happy conclusion.

The first story of this collection, *La Vendetta*,[54] is the tale of a blood-feud between two Corsican families. Baron Piombo learns that his daughter Ginevra loves Luigi, the scion of the Porta family. Neither of the young people has known of the feud. The strong wills of the father and the daughter now clash. The Baron, blinded by a passion equal in intensity to that of Goriot, but lacking in the self-sacrifice and utter devotion of the latter,[55] drives out Ginevra, who dies of privation. Since this is a study of affection and passion within the privacy of a family circle, the tale fittingly belongs in this grouping of the *Scènes de la vie privée*. When, in 1834, Balzac used this collective title to designate the first subdivision of the *Etudes de mœurs au XIXe siècle*, the story naturally remained in its original category.

Les Dangers de l'inconduite,[56] finally entitled *Gobseck*, is also a study of

[53] *Scènes de la vie privée* (1st ed.), I, 1.

[54] The first chapter of this story was published in *La Silhouette*, April 1, 1830; another fragment, according to Lov., *Hist.*, p. 11, appeared in *Le Courrier des électeurs*, May 9, 1830. However, a verification by N. E. Saxe shows that *Le Courrier des électeurs* was published only from January 9, 1829, to April, 1830 (courtesy N. E. Saxe). After its publication in the collection under consideration, *La Vendetta* reappeared in the successive editions of the *Scènes de la vie privée* (2d ed., 1832; 3d ed., 1835; 4th ed., 1839; 5th ed., 1842). It is now in *Con.*, Vol. III.

[55] Cf. Bellessort, *op. cit.*, p. 315.

[56] The first chapter, "L'Usurier," was published in *La Mode*, March 6, 1830 (error in Lov., *Hist.*, p. 26; courtesy N. E. Saxe). The complete tale appeared in the collection under consideration as well as in its 2d ed. In 1835 and 1839 it appeared in the "Scènes de la vie parisienne"; in 1842 it was again in the "Scènes de la vie privée." It is now in *Con.*, Vol. V.

an unhappy household. The original title indicates that the interest is centered on morals; it suggests the private life of the leading feminine character, the Comtesse de Restaud. The tale is, therefore, in keeping with the author's intentions as expressed in the Preface to this collection. In 1835 Balzac temporarily moved the narrative, with the new title, *Papa Gobseck*, to the third subdivision of the *Etudes de mœurs*, "Scènes de la vie parisienne." The new title shifts the interest to Gobseck, who, says Davin, personifies "l'avarice intelligente, puissante, haineuse."[57] It is possible that this temporary misplacement was due merely to the practical reason that Balzac did not have, at that time, enough stories with Parisian atmosphere to fill the four volumes of the additional subdivision. This view is supported by the fact that, in 1842, in the Furne edition, the story, now under the shortened title *Gobseck*, was permanently restored to its original group, "Scènes de la vie privée," where it naturally belongs. It is the story not only of the private life of the usurer Gobseck but also of the unhappy marriage of the countess and of the serious question of family inheritance.

Le Bal de Sceaux, ou Le Pair de France[58] is the study of a haughty heroine, Emilie de Fontaine, who scorns her lover, Maximilien Longueville, for his humble employment. He rises later in social standing and then, in turn, scorns her. Out of spite she marries her great-uncle, Count Kergarouët, who can give her the luxury and the social prestige which she is seeking. But Balzac says that her "luxe cachait imparfaitement le vide et le malheur de son âme souffrante," because, he explains: "Ce fut ainsi que l'influence exercée sur Emilie par une funeste éducation, tua deux fois son bonheur naissant et lui fit manquer toute son existence."[59] The sad tale of the unsuitable marriage and of the empty existence of the young woman forms an integral part of the *Scènes de la vie privée*, in which the author definitely placed it.

Gloire et malheur (La Maison du Chat-qui-pelote)[60] was written in Oc-

57 Lov., *Hist.*, p. 61.

58 A verification by W. S. Hastings indicates an error in Lov., *Hist.*, p. 144. The complete story, with the subtitle *Le Pair de France*, was published first in the *Scènes de la vie privée* (1st ed.) and later in the successive editions of these *Scènes*. It is now in *Con.*, Vol. I.

59 *Scènes de la vie privée* (1st ed., 1830), I, 392, 396.

60 A fragment of this story was published in *La Silhouette*, April 15, 1830. The complete story appeared in the collection now under discussion with the title *Gloire et malheur*—a title which it retained in the 2d, 3d, and 4th eds. of these *Scènes*. In the 5th ed. (Furne) it was published under its present title. The story is now in *Con.*, Vol. I.

tober, 1829, while Balzac was visiting at the Château de Mafliers, the home of Mme d'Abrantès. It is a study of quiet family life and of the marriage, beyond her station, of a merchant's daughter. Balzac contrasts the happiness of a young *bourgeoise* who has accepted "un mariage de raison" with the wretchedness of her sister, who married, against the wishes of her family, an artist, a man of a higher class and of a different outlook. The first title of the tale suggests the rise and fall in the life of Augustine; the second includes the home and the shop—in fact, a whole household consisting of the members of the family as well as the apprentices—and seems to indicate a sociological preoccupation on the part of the author. It is clear, therefore, that the story rightfully belongs to the *Scènes de la vie privée*, in which it was placed from the beginning.

La Femme vertueuse (*Une Double Famille*)[61] is built upon lines similar to those of the preceding story. The plot rises to the point of adultery and then gradually falls. Roger de Granville's marriage was a failure, partly because of his overvirtuous wife and partly because of his own intolerance. He disobeyed social laws and, consequently, suffered. The main theme of the story, frustrated happiness within the home, harmonizes perfectly with the basic idea of Balzac's grouping in the *Scènes de la vie privée*. In November, 1835, he moved the story temporarily to the third subdivision of the *Etudes de mœurs*, where it remained in the 1839 edition. An explanation for this shift may be found in the author's "Avis" to the first edition of this new subdivision. He states that the "calculs de l'auteur ont été dérangés par l'exécution de plusieurs scènes."[62] Balzac is not always clear in his explanations of shifts of stories. Here the term "exécution" probably means literally the execution or the process of writing rather than the completion of the tale. The author often planned the classification of projected, but as yet unwritten, works. *La Torpille*[63] is a case in point; it was assigned to the "Scènes de la vie parisienne" in 1835 but was not written at the time of their publication. Consequently, he filled the pages destined for *La Torpille* with the story *La Femme vertueuse;* ultimately, he restored *La Femme vertueuse* to the "Scènes de la vie privée" but gave it a new title, *Une Double Famille*, which is even more in harmony with the guiding thought of these Scenes.

[61] A fragment of this story, "La Grisette parvenue," appeared in *Le Voleur*, April 5 and 15, 1830. The complete story was published in the first two editions of the collection under consideration. In 1835 and 1839 it appeared in the "Scènes de la vie parisienne." In 1842 it was restored to its original category and is now in *Con.*, Vol. III.

[62] *OD.*, III, 392.   [63] Part I of *Splendeurs et misères des courtisanes.*

La Paix du ménage,[64] written at the home of Mme de Berny in 1829, is a domestic episode cleverly told. Arrigon[65] suggests that the subject was inspired by "L'Aventure du diamant," a tale from the collective volume, *Les Amusemens sérieux et comiques d'un Siamois*, by Charles Rivière du Fresny (1699). The scene of Balzac's story is a ball at which a young wife learns of her husband's fancy for a "femme légère" by recognizing her own gift to her husband, a diamond ring, on the finger of a stranger. In consequence her happy marriage is on the verge of dissolution when a friend, an older woman, brings about "la paix du ménage." This sketch remained in the "Scènes de la vie privée" for obvious reasons.

From the foregoing discussion we observe that, of the six stories assembled under the first collective title, four have permanently and two[66] have ultimately, after a temporary displacement, remained in the "Scènes de la vie privée"—the general title which was later given to the first subdivision of the *Etudes de mœurs au XIX*e *siècle*. The final classification of these stories as early as 1830 proves that the assembling of the tales was not done in a haphazard way but rather according to the pivotal theme which Balzac had established in his "Préface" to the first edition of the *Scènes de la vie privée*.

About a month after the appearance of these *Scènes*, on May 8, 1830, Balzac published in *La Mode* a short story, *Les Deux Rêves*, which is his first conception of the later *Sur Catherine de Médicis*, Part III. At the end of this story was a "Note," as follows:

> Ce morceau est l'un des plus importants que contiendra un livre auquel M. de Balzac travaille depuis longtemps et qui a pour titre: *Scènes de la Vie politique*. Cet ouvrage, digne de l'auteur des *Scènes de la Vie privée*, fait partie d'une collection remarquable publiée par la Maison Mame et Delaunay-Vallée. Nous avons déjà fait connaître à nos abonnés *el Verdugo*, extrait des *Scènes de la Vie militaire*.[67]

Since the *Scènes de la vie politique* and the *Scènes de la vie militaire* did not yet exist, we are reminded that one cannot always trust Balzac's enthusiastic announcements. We note, however, his claim that the story *Les Deux Rêves*[68] was an extract from a projected work, the *Scènes de la*

---

[64] This story first appeared in the *Scènes de la vie privée* (1st ed.); there it remained in all the subsequent editions. It is now in *Con.*, Vol. III.

[65] *Les Années romantiques de Balzac*, p. 12.

[66] See table (p. 180).   [67] Lov., *Hist.*, pp. 189–90.

[68] This story never entered the *Scènes de la vie politique* but was ultimately classified in the *Etudes philosophiques* as part of *Sur Catherine de Médicis*.

vie politique, parallel to the *Scènes de la vie privée*. From a third collective volume, the proposed *Scènes de la vie militaire*, one extract, *El Verdugo*, had previously been published in January, 1830. It appears, therefore, that during 1830 three groups of *Scènes*, not yet regarded as subdivisions, had been already tentatively projected and their titles chosen. Of these, only the *Scènes de la vie privée*, as has been shown, had actually seen the light of day. The choice of these three collective titles, as well as the stories in one case and the extracts in the other two cases, show that the idea of selective grouping was an early one, destined to a very gradual growth; it proves, furthermore, that the author at that time obviously intended to extend the range of his writings according to plans which had begun to take concrete forms. These facts warrant the dating of Balzac's tentative programs as of 1830, although their nebulous origin, as shown above, goes back to 1822.

The *Romans et contes philosophiques*[69] were the result of Balzac's keen interest in pseudo-scientific, fantastic,[70] mystical, and philosophical trends of thought. The origin of this interest may be traced to the readings of his youth. Mme Surville tells how he assimilated "tout ce qu'il y avait d'idées" in his mother's books on religion and mysticism—books by Saint-Martin, Swedenborg, Jacob Boehme, and Mme Guyon.[71] This bent toward the occult was encouraged by his mother, who knew "les magnéti-seurs et les somnambules célèbres de cette époque."[72] Félix Davin asserts that young Balzac toiled in his lonely garret from 1818 to 1820, "à com-parer, analyser, résumer les œuvres que les philosophes et les médecins de l'antiquité, du moyen âge et des deux siècles précédents, avaient laissé [*sic*] sur le cerveau de l'homme. Cette pente de son esprit est une pré-dilection."[73] At this time Balzac also read and re-read the works of Gall and Lavater,[74] who, from the twentieth-century point of view, are, per-

---

[69] Published by Charles Gosselin in 3 vols., September, 1831.

[70] For Balzac's great interest in the fantastic and in Ernst Theodore Hoffmann, see Baldensperger, *op. cit.*, pp. 104–11 *et passim*. Cf. Prioult, *op. cit.*, pp. xii, 300. Prioult emphasizes the influence of François-Benoît-Henri Hoffman, playwright.

[71] Balzac's indebtedness to several of these writers is worked out by P. Bernheim, *Balzac und Swedenborg, Einfluss der Mystik Swedenborgs und Saint-Martins auf die Romandichtung Balzacs*. See also Baldensperger, *op. cit.*, chap. ix.

[72] Surville, *op. cit.*, p. 106.

[73] Lov., *Hist.*, p. 196.

[74] F. J. Gall, *Anatomie et physiologie du système nerveux en général et du cerveau en par-ticulier* (4 vols., 1810–19). Also J. G. Lavater, *Physiognomonie* (4 vols., 1781–1803).

haps, only pseudo-scientists.[75] On August 20, 1822, Balzac informed his sister Laure that he had bought ten volumes of a "superbe Lavater."[76]

Although the fantastic and the supernatural early exercised a fascination for Balzac,[77] a lively interest in people and in the life around him, as well as his poverty, forced the young author to abandon these metaphysical meditations and turn to reality and the type of fiction demanded by the public. His varied interests—the pseudo-scientific, the mystical, and the social—seem to crowd each other in his teeming brain. Partly as a consequence of this, he seldom composed or published one single story at any given time. For example, in March, 1835, he wrote Mme de Castries: "J'ai une espèce de coquetterie littéraire qui me conseille de faire paraître à la fois, *Melmoth réconcilié, Séraphita, le Lys dans la vallée, la Fille aux yeux d'or, la Fleur-des-pois.*"[78] Thus he wrote as fancy led him, or else as the publisher required. Often, in the midst of a fantastic tale he would start a story dealing with private life, continue another depicting life in the provinces, and perhaps finish a fourth laid in the capital, writing and publishing, almost concurrently, historical, realistic, and philosophical fiction. This situation is evident from the coinciding dates of composition of the *Scènes de la vie privée* and of the *Romans et contes philosophiques.* He never lacked subjects, and he regretted not having a comrade who could develop, as he said, "les sujets que je conçois et qui reviennent trop en foule pour que je fasse tout."[79]

In Balzac's readings and interests mentioned above are the origins of his *Romans et contes philosophiques* and of the subsequent *Etudes philosophiques.* It would be well to establish from the start a clear understanding of what our author meant by "philosophique." A Balzacian philosophical story is frequently one which rests upon a mystical or supernatural idea; for example, the conception of human aspiration toward perfection in *Séraphita;* or in *La Peau de chagrin* the magic shrinking of the ass's skin upon every expressed desire of its owner. Such fantastic subjects, however, seemed to interest Balzac only so far as they revealed, or had a

[75] For a valuable discussion of the influence of these men on Balzac, see G. M. Fess, *The Correspondence of Physical and Material Factors with Character in Balzac.*

[76] *LF.,* p. 66.

[77] See *Œuvres de jeunesse: Le Centenaire, ou Les Deux Beringheld* (1822), and *La Dernière Fée* (1823).

[78] "Cahiers balzaciens," VI, 35.

[79] Letter to M. Victor Ratier, July, 1830. Quoted by Crépet, Preface to *Pensées, sujets, fragmens,* p. xviii.

bearing upon, human nature; for, above all else, he was an analytical observer of life.

La Peau de chagrin[80] is Balzac's first "roman philosophique." Soon after its publication he revealed the importance of this novel in a letter to the editor of L'Avenir, Comte Charles de Montalembert, August, 1831.

Elle [La Peau de chagrin] est donc le point de départ de mon ouvrage. Après viendront se grouper, de nuance en nuance, les individualités, les existences particulières, depuis la plus humble jusqu'à celle du Prêtre, derniers termes de notre société. Dans ces tableaux, je suivrai les effets de la pensée dans la vie ...[81]

There is a double significance in this statement. First, the author has sketched again the subjects of his future works for which La Peau de chagrin was to be the starting-point. This intention is reiterated in a letter to Mme de Castries of October 5, 1831: "... cet ouvrage [La Peau de chagrin] n'est pas destiné à rester seul; il est, pardonnez-moi cette scientifique expression, les premisses d'un ouvrage que je serai fier d'avoir tenté."[82] He emphasized the fact that the story was not an isolated piece of writing; his statements indicate that the novel was to serve as a nucleus for other romans philosophiques. Second, he has indicated to Comte de Montalembert "la pensée" as giving motive force for a group of stories, in supplying "le fil conducteur" for them. It is a specific form of "pensée," an exaggeration of any given thought; mania in scientific research; "desmesure" of pride in family name; excess of pleasure, of joy, sorrow, remorse, miserliness; extreme zeal in perfecting one's art. It is Balzac's firm conviction that thought which becomes an obsession ravages the mind. This is the basic idea in his philosophical tales and later in his Etudes philosophiques.

Balzac also left some information concerning La Peau de chagrin in his daily journal.[83] This was an oblong album, the size of a small notebook, in which Balzac jotted down fleeting thoughts, subjects for his work, fragments, names, etc. His explanation of the novel shows that, while he remained interested in actuality, his approach was to be philosophical and that he was endeavoring to work out a formula of human life. His definition is as follows: "La Peau de chagrin. L'Expression pure et simple de

---

[80] Published by Charles Gosselin and Urbain Canel in 2 vols., August, 1831.

[81] Revue bleue, 4th ser., XX (1903), 609. Italics ours.

[82] "Cahiers balzaciens," VI, 4.

[83] A copy of the journal is, at present, at Chantilly in the Lovenjoul Collection, A 181. It has been published, not always accurately, with a Preface and notes by Jacques Crépet (1910).

la vie humaine en tant que vie et que mécanisme. Formule exacte de la machine humaine. Enfin l'individu décrit et jugé [illegible] mais poètiquement."[84] Of this formula, Balzac had spoken earlier (1830) in connection with the projected treatise on social pathology,[85] from which the following passage summarizes with curious verbosity the ideas of the projected work:

Le 3ᵉ ouvrage est cette *Pathologie sociale ou méditations mathématiques et physiques et transcendantes* sur les manifestations de la pensée prise dans toutes les formes que lui donne l'Etat Social soit par le vivre et le couvert soit par la démarche et la parole et etc. ... Le titre bizarre en apparence est justifié par une observation qui m'est commune avec Brillat-Savarin.[86] L'Etat de Société a fait de nos besoins, de nos plaisirs, de nos nécessités autant de plaies de maladies par les excés auxquels nous nous portons poussés par nos goûts mais surtout par le dévellopement [*sic*] que leur donne la pensée. Il n'y a rien aujourd'hui où elle ne se trahisse. De là ce titre. En effet là où il n'y a pas maladie physique, il y a maladie morale. ... C'était donc un ouvrage de la plus haute importance que de rechercher les lois de cette existence extérieure et les ramener à une expression philosophique ...

He asserts that his intention is to examine how "l'homme social est fait."[87] This passage shows that Balzac endeavored to discover the laws of the outer existence and from them to deduce a philosophical axiom which became a basic conception. It is this: Ideas and passions by continual fermentation become the active dissolvents of the individual and, consequently, of society; or, in other words, thought can produce destructive effects in the lives of men.[88] This principle, says Davin,[89] is poetically formulated in *La Peau de chagrin*, a work in which the author considered man as an organism which may be destroyed by passion. Here the formula is: "La vie décroît en raison directe de la puissance des désirs ou de la dissipation des idées."[90] The life of Raphaël de Valentin, the hero of the novel, demonstrates this principle and serves as the starting-point for the tales in the collective volumes, *Romans et contes philosophiques*.

The history of the publication of *La Peau de chagrin* is given by H. H. Millott.[91] The novel deals with the field of moral philosophy and depicts,

[84] Lov. Coll., A 181, fol. 19. Crépet does not print the illegible words.

[85] See above, p. 28.   [86] Author of *La Physiologie du goût* (1826).

[87] Lov. Coll., A 168, fols. 63–64.

[88] Balzac's term, *la pensée*, is taken in a broad sense to include passion, as an obsession.

[89] Lov., *Hist.*, pp. 201, 203.   [90] *Ibid.*, p. 203.

[91] See Dargan, Crain, and Others, *op. cit.*, pp. 68–69.

interprets, and reduces human life to a formula conceived according to a philosophical principle. In Balzac's words to the Duchesse de Castries, the novel was also to "formuler le siècle actuel, notre vie, notre égoïsme."[92] The motivation of the story is egoism operating in a sensual and over-refined society. Uncontrolled desire, excess in passion, and self-centered thought lead Raphaël de Valentin to destruction. The talented student, not being able to attain the complete satisfaction of his intense soul and senses, is on the verge of suicide when he comes into possession of the small skin of a wild ass, which has the magic power of miraculously granting its owner's wishes—at the price of shortening his life. It shrinks with every expressed desire, thus symbolically representing Raphaël's ebbing life. In a last effort to prolong this life Raphaël attempts to exercise no will—an unnatural situation against which his physical nature revolts until death is the solution. It is easy to see, then, why Balzac designated *La Peau de chagrin* a *roman philosophique* in its first publication in book form and in 1835 placed it permanently in the *Etudes philosophiques*,[93] of which it is an integral part.

It is necessary to return to the letter addressed to the Comte de Montalembert in which, in addition to his comments on *La Peau de chagrin* and the *Romans et contes philosophiques*, Balzac discussed a proposed work, *Histoire de la succession du marquis de Carabas*. This project, although often mentioned by the author, was never carried out. The work, he says,

formulera la vie des nations, les phases de leurs gouvernements, et, sous une forme meilleure, démontrera évidemment que les politiques tournent dans le même cercle et sont évidemment stationnaires. ... Je vous expose succinctement *mon plan*, afin de faire excuser le retard que j'ai mis à vous offrir une œuvre incomplète encore.[94]

The question arises as to what Balzac meant by "mon plan"; certainly it was not yet *the* scheme which gradually evolved from these tentative beginnings into that explained in his "manifesto" of 1842. He must mean merely the scope and range of subjects he will treat in his books discussed in the letter to Montalembert. They will deal with contemporary life, representing almost every stratum of society, as well as with the whole nation in her political and governmental functions.

[92] "Cahiers balzaciens," VI, 4.

[93] *Wer.*, Vols. I–IV. In 1845 the novel entered the *Comédie humaine*, Vol. XIV, and is now in *Con.*, Vol. XXVII.

[94] *Revue bleue*, 4th ser., XX (1903), 609–10. Italics ours.

Meanwhile the collective volumes, *Romans et contes philosophiques*, were published in September, 1831. Balzac entreated Mme de Castries to read these tales and added: "Sous le titre de *Romans et contes philoso-phiques* j'ai un peu avancé dans mon plan."[95] By this he means that in these collective volumes he has carried out the intention, expressed earlier, to group *La Peau de chagrin* with tales of similar theme. The stories were headed by Philarète Chasles's Introduction,[96] to which Balzac alluded in the above-mentioned letter in these words: "Il [Chasles] a bien voulu sou-lever le voile de ma pensée intime et future." In this Introduction Chasles also speaks of a plan: "Ce vaste plan, caché sous ces fantaisies, a dû échapper à plusieurs yeux." He then enumerates the possible subjects in-cluded in Balzac's vast program. "Le paysan, le mendiant, le pâtre, le bourgeois, le ministre, ... le roi et le prêtre ... tous les degrés de l'échelle sociale,"[97] will be depicted, he continues, in situations showing the de-structive effects of egoism. This outline, like those given in the "Aver-tissement" and in the fragmentary program of 1830, as well as in the an-nouncement of the same year, was a fresh attempt to establish a guiding principle for Balzac's writings. To be sure, these earlier plans are tenta-tive and last only until a new one is drawn up. Nonetheless, the persistent and direct references to plans, together with the two published collective works, *Scènes de la vie privée* and *Romans et contes philosophiques*, and the projected titles *Scènes de la vie militaire* and *Scènes de la vie politique*, give evidence of Balzac's need of a system or scheme. Clearly, unity had to be created in the increasing number of his works. One conjectures that out of these tentative programs eventually was generated *the one scheme* carried through in the *Comédie humaine*.

It is pertinent now to analyze the contents of the *Romans et contes phi-losophiques* in order to see how they were connected with *La Peau de chagrin* and how many of them remained in the original grouping.

The success of *La Peau de chagrin* in August, 1831, was so great that Gosselin immediately proposed a new edition of the novel to be enlarged by twelve philosophical tales under the collective title *Romans et contes philosophiques*.[98] These additions were considered, says Balzac, "comme le complément nécessaire du système philosophique développé dans *la*

---

[95] "Cahiers balzaciens," VI, 4.

[96] Reprinted in Lov., *Hist.*, pp. 171–77. It is very probable that this Introduction was written under the influence of Balzac. See *LF.*, p. 111, n. 3.

[97] Lov., *Hist.*, p. 176.

[98] Published by Charles Gosselin in 3 vols., in octavo.

Peau de chagrin."[99] Chasles in his Introduction emphasized the fact, let us repeat, that, according to Balzac, a thought carried to the extreme is the cause of the disruption of man as an individual and as an "être social." This principle becomes the unifying "fil conducteur" in the twelve stories; these, with the exception of *Jésus-Christ en Flandre,* had appeared at intervals since 1830 in the leading periodicals.

The scene of *Sarrasine*[100] is laid in Italy. Wells[101] suggested that Balzac may have borrowed from the memoirs of Casanova. The study of Professor Henri David[102] establishes the indebtedness of Balzac to these memoirs in three specific respects: the name of the Théâtre d'Argentina where La Zambinella performed, the motif of a man singing the parts of a prima donna, and the idea of a man's almost womanly beauty. Professor David also formulates the theme of the story as "la puissance d'illusion qu'exerce la beauté." Charles de Bernard[103] justifies the temporary placing of the story in the collection under consideration by saying that "d'une idée il [Balzac] fait un drame," implying that an illusion which became an *idée fixe* was the cause of tragedy in the life of Ernest-Jean Sarrasine. The author's intention concerning this story was changing concurrently with his growing preoccupation with devising a scheme for the unity of his works. Thus, while at Aix, he wrote to his publisher, Mame,[104] in September, 1832, indicating the principle which he followed in grouping his stories under collective titles. He said that he would withdraw from the present collection certain stories, among which were *Sarrasine* and *Etude de femme,* because they were not sufficiently "philosophiques."[105] Curiously enough, on the same day, September, 1832, he wrote to Gosselin giving additional reasons for the removal of the story in question. He stated that he intended to "supprimer *Etude de femme* et *Sarrasine.* ... Les deux

---

[99] *OD.*, III, 405.

[100] This tale first appeared in *La Revue de Paris*, November 21 and 28, 1830. After its publication in the *Romans et contes philosophiques* and in the successive reprints, it was classified in 1835, in the "Scènes de la vie parisienne," Vol. IV. In 1844 it entered the *Comédie humaine,* éd. Furne, Vol. X. It is now in *Con.,* Vol. XVI.

[101] *Op. cit.,* pp. 100, 126.

[102] "Balzac italianisant: Autour de *Sarrasine,*" *Revue de littérature comparée,* XIII (1933), 457–68.

[103] See Lov., *Hist.,* p. 358.

[104] Balzac at that time was planning a "fourth" (in reality a third) edition of the *Romans et contes philosophiques* which appeared March, 1833, and was published by Charles Gosselin.

[105] Lov. Coll., A 250, fols. 1–2.

contes retranchés n'étaient ni assez philosophiques ni d'une donnée facile à découvrir, il faut ôter ce prétexte aux critiques."[106] His guiding thought, therefore, is that the stories here must be closely related in motives, situations, atmosphere, and theme in order to be assembled under a collective title.

The two stories withdrawn were to be replaced by new tales. Apparently those were not yet written; consequently, *Sarrasine* reappeared in the fourth edition of the collection (March, 1833), in spite of the instructions mentioned. Nevertheless, in May, 1835, the story was definitely placed in the "Scènes de la vie parisienne," the third subdivision of the *Etudes de mœurs*. The theme of the tale fits harmoniously in the *cadre* of the Scenes in which passions grow extreme. Balzac's mouthpiece, Félix Davin, asserts that without *Sarrasine* the large "vue de Paris n'eût pas été complète."[107]

La Comédie du diable,[108] a fantastic tale with many satiric allusions to contemporary events and personages, appeared in all the reprints of the *Romans et contes philosophiques* but was never published in the *Etudes philosophiques*.[109] Therefore, Davin's following statement contains a regrettable error, even though it reveals the important role this sketch played in Balzac's projects. Davin says:

> *La Comédie du diable*, si bouffonne en apparence, est devenue, dans cette édition, une âpre critique des gouvernements, une sorte de tohu-bohu des politiques, une sarcastique transition pour arriver à la conclusion de l'œuvre, à cette *Histoire de la succession du marquis de Carabas*, qui sera la formule allégorique de la vie collective des nations, comme *la Peau de chagrin* est la formule de la vie.[110]

Evidently the sketch was intended to serve as a prologue to a projected work which was never written. For this reason *La Comédie du diable* was classified neither in the *Etudes philosophiques* nor in the *Comédie humaine*. Davin's mention of the two story-titles may be explained, first, by the fact that Balzac announced, as late as September, 1836, *La Comédie du diable* on the cover pages of Volume XI of the *Etudes philosophiques;* sec-

---

[106] Lov. Coll., A 281, fol. 140.   [107] Lov., *Hist.*, p. 62.

[108] Part I appeared anonymously in *La Mode*, November 13, 1830; a fragment of Part II was published in *La Caricature*, November 18, 1830. The two parts were assembled in the collective volumes under consideration in 1831, as well as in the two reprints of 1832 and 1833. The narrative is now in *OD.*, Vol. I.

[109] The tale was, nevertheless, included in all the announcements of the projected volumes of the division.

[110] Lov., *Hist.*, p. 205.

ond, by his statement in Werdet's catalogue that the proposed "*l'Histoire de la Succession du Marquis de Carabas dans le fief de Coquatrix* [to which *La Comédie du diable* was to be the Prologue], qui doit terminer les *Etudes philosophiques*, est remise à l'année 1836."[111] Still later, in 1848, he announced *La Comédie du diable* in *L'Evénement*, published by Victor Hugo. Philarète Chasles, in his Introduction to these collective volumes, calls *La Comédie du diable* a "farce terrible" in which a bored "diable" offers a banquet to the dwellers of the Inferno.

Balzac wrote *El Verdugo* in 1829. Toward the close of the year Levavasseur introduced the young author to Armand Baschet,[112] who published the story[113] under the lengthy title *Souvenirs soldatesques. El Verdugo; guerre d'Espagne (1809)*. In the same periodical, May 8, 1830, *El Verdugo* was indicated as an extract from the projected collection, *Scènes de la vie militaire*.[114] The reason for temporarily assigning it to these *Scènes* is obvious, since it is a war story; yet it never appeared in this subdivision. In this hair-raising tale Balzac shows how a "chimère sociale," a magnified conception of one's title or dynasty, results in parricide and murder. "Aie du courage, lui dit son frère Philippe: autrement notre famille est éteinte."[115] In the Furne edition, 1845, Balzac made the following textual change: "... autrement notre *race presque royale* est éteinte."[116] By this variation he intensifies the idea of pride in a name. Whether it was saving a title, as Chasles[117] thinks, or a race, as Edmond Biré[118] asserts, matters little; the significant factor is the demonstration of excess of family

---

[111] See Spoelberch de Lovenjoul, "Les *Etudes philosophiques* de Honoré de Balzac (Edition Werdet)," *Revue d'histoire littéraire de la France* (July–September, 1907), XIV, 393–441.

[112] *Op. cit.*, p. 26.

[113] In *La Mode*, January 19, 1830. *El Verdugo* was published in the successive editions of the volumes now discussed. In 1835 it entered the *Etudes philosophiques*, Vol. V; and in 1846, the *Comédie humaine*, Vol. XV. Later a separate edition of *El Verdugo* appeared in 1847 with *Le Provincial à Paris (Les Comédiens sans le savoir)*. See *Causeries françaises* (Cercle de la librairie), No. 4 (February 16, 1923), p. 148, for the following item: "*Le Provincial à Paris*. Paris, Gabriel Roux, 2 vls. in-8° (1847)." It was announced in the *Bibliographie de la France*, June, 1848. We are indebted to Professor Hastings for the above information. Note also in Lov., *Hist.*, p. 133, an error in date which is corrected on p. 183. *El Verdugo* is now in *Con.*, Vol. XXVIII.

[114] See above, p. 35. [115] *Romans et contes philosophiques*, II, 78.

[116] *Comédie humaine*, éd. Furne, XV, 412. Italics ours.

[117] See Lov., *Hist.*, p. 172.

[118] Biré's edition of Balzac's *Scènes de la vie militaire*, Introduction by Biré to *El Verdugo*, p. 149. In this one-volume edition Biré collected all the war stories scattered throughout the *Comédie humaine*, including *El Verdugo*.

pride which causes an old marquis to force his heir to become a criminal. An entry in Balzac's notebook proves his psychological approach and emphasizes his interest in idea rather than in action: "Dans *El Verdugo*, un fils tua son père pour une idée."[119] This is precisely the reason for its grouping with *La Peau de chagrin*, and it explains its ultimate classification in the *Etudes philosophiques*.

Balzac began *L'Enfant maudit*[120] in 1831 and finished it in 1836. Part II of the story was preceded by a short Introduction (omitted in the subsequent editions) in which the author indicated the motivation of the action through the idea that "la maison d'Hérouville ne périrait point"[121]—a theme already treated in *El Verdugo*. In *L'Enfant maudit*, somewhat in the same manner as in *El Verdugo*, the egoism and the pride of the Duc d'Hérouville bring death to his wife and to his heir, Étienne, who are frail and delicate in physique but strong in faith. The old duke, possessed of family pride, forbids Etienne to marry Gabrielle, a social inferior whom he loves, and tries to force him to make a marriage of *convenance*. When Etienne resists, the duke draws his sword and so terrifies both Etienne and Gabrielle that they die of fear. Félix Davin calls *L'Enfant maudit* one of Balzac's "cinq grandes poésies," in which, he says (doubtless speaking for Honoré), Balzac "faisait courir un radieux rayon de foi, une mélodieuse métempsycose chrétienne qui commençait dans les douleurs terrestres et aboutissait au ciel."[122] Here are seen two aspects of Balzac's philosophical idea: maternal love of the countess and the attachment between Etienne and Gabrielle. This love, together with the exaggerated idea of the family name, brings the story in line with the motif of *La Peau de chagrin*. Thus the tale appropriately belongs in the philosophical category in which it remained.

L'Elixir de longue vie,[123] Balzac's first publication in *La Revue de Paris*,

---

[119] Lov. Coll., A 181, fol. 19.

[120] Part I of this story appeared in *La Revue des deux mondes*, January, 1831; it was published the same year in the collection under consideration and later in its subsequent editions. Part II, under the title *La Perle brisée*, was published in *La Chronique de Paris*, October 9, 1836. The two parts were assembled in 1837 as *L'Enfant maudit* and published by Werdet in the *Etudes philosophiques*, Vols. XV–XVI. In 1846 the story entered the *Comédie humaine*, Vol. XV, and is now in *Con.*, Vol. XXVIII.

[121] Lov., *Hist.*, p. 181.   [122] *Ibid.*, p. 206.

[123] The story first appeared in the collection under consideration and later in two reprints of 1832 and 1833. In 1835 it entered the *Etudes philosophiques*, éd. Werdet, Vol. V; in 1846 it entered the *Comédie humaine*, Vol. XI, and it is now in *Con.*, Vol. XXX.

appeared October 24, 1830. Although in the dedication to the reader Balzac admits that "cette fantaisie est due à Hoffmann de Berlin," he treats this agelong theme about the fountain of youth in his own way and makes the story a corollary to *La Peau de chagrin* and, consequently, a logical part of the *Etudes philosophiques*. Don Juan, the hero, impelled by egoism and by greed for his inheritance, does not revive his father with the potion, as he had been instructed to do. Balzac's Don Juan is a symbol of egoism and wickedness, as well as an allegorical figure of a social evil, greed.

Les Proscrits[124] appeared successively under three collective titles: *Romans et contes philosophiques*, *Le Livre mystique*, and *Le Livre des douleurs* —all anticipating the *Etudes philosophiques*, in which this tale was permanently classified. In this fantastic but moving legend Balzac gives a picture of Paris and the old Sorbonne of the thirteenth century, to which Dante and his young friend Godefroid have been exiled from Florence. Both men are symbolical figures. Dante personifies medieval philosophy and science, with a strong faith in the church; he also symbolizes patriotism in exile. He greatly desires to return to Florence in order to triumph over his enemies—a worldly ambition. His friend is a mystic whose contemplation of the beyond fosters disgust with this life. Both characters personify certain human sentiments or systems. This, then, is the reason for the story's being grouped with *La Peau de chagrin* and ultimately placed in the *Etudes philosophiques*.

When *Le Chef-d'œuvre inconnu*[125] was first published, it was accompanied by a subtitle, "Conte fantastique," which explains its affiliation with *La Peau de chagrin;* for, as Raphaël sought to capture the "Geheimnis des Lebens," so did old Frenhofer.[126] In 1837 Balzac definitely classified the story in the *Etudes philosophiques*. Nevertheless, for practical

---

[124] This story first appeared in *La Revue de Paris*, May, 1831. After its publication in the collection now analyzed and in the two reprints of 1832 and 1833, it appeared in *Le Livre mystique* in 1835 and again in 1836. In 1840 it entered the *Etudes philosophiques*, under the general title *Le Livre des douleurs;* in 1846 it was published in the *Comédie humaine*, Vol. XVI; and it is now in *Con.*, Vol. XXXI. Although the Souverain edition was published in 1840, the text is of 1836. See Spoelberch de Lovenjoul, art. cit., *RHL*, p. 436.

[125] This story first appeared in *L'Artiste*, July 31 and August 6, 1831. After its publication in the collection under consideration and in the two reprints of 1832 and 1833, it appeared in the *Etudes philosophiques*, Vol. XVII (1837). In 1845 it entered the *Comédie humaine*, Vol. XIV, and it is now in *Con.*, Vol. XXVIII.

[126] Curtius, *op. cit.*, p. 408.

reasons, to complete the required pages of the two volumes of *Le Provincial à Paris* (*Les Comédiens sans le savoir*), in 1847 Balzac temporarily
added *Le Chef-d'œuvre inconnu* under the title *Gillette* to these scenes of
Parisian life.[127]

The story, a study of art and artists, is laid in the seventeenth century.
Frenhofer, the painter, hides from his friend, Porbus, a masterpiece on
which he has been working for some time. Finally he unveils it before
Porbus and another artist, none other than Poussin. The two are astonished to see a confused mass of color without lines or attempt at composition, except a woman's foot admirably executed in the corner of the can-
vas. Old Frenhofer, says Merlant, has become a "victime de l'intensité
avec laquelle il se figure son idéal artistique; il y a chez lui rupture d'équi-
libre entre la vie intérieure et le sens commun."[128] Balzac maintained the
sane view that too much science or an overrefined conception of art renders the artist powerless to produce his masterpiece; the very intensity
of Frenhofer's conception of his ideal defeated him. Davin states that in
Le Chef-d'œuvre inconnu Balzac "nous montre l'art tuant l'œuvre."[129] The
painter, in his ardent desire to portray life, to get at its secret, has over-
done his retouching. In 1839, in the Preface to the *Fille d'Ève*, Balzac
himself throws light on the relation of this story to *La Peau de chagrin*.
He says that this is one of the works which "continuent pour ainsi dire
La Peau de chagrin, en montrant le désordre que la pensée arrivée à tout
son développement produit dans l'âme de l'artiste, en expliquant par
quelles lois arrive le suicide de l'art."[130] To realize the infinitely perfect
and beautiful is a human impossibility. Frenhofer became an "halluciné,"
a monomaniac, as detached from life and as absorbed in his art as was
Raphaël in himself and in his eager desires, or as was Balthazar Claës in
his arduous search for the composition of the atom. The painter dies of
despair because no one understands his aesthetic mysticism—a psychological and physiological phenomenon.

Le Réquisitionnaire[131] is a dramatic episode laid in Normandy during

---

[127] Cf. *Causeries françaises* (Cercle de la librairie), No. 4 (February 16, 1923), p. 148.
See also Lov., *Hist.*, pp. 133, 178, where there are errors in dates.

[128] Merlant, *op. cit.*, p. 347.

[129] Lov., *Hist.*, p. 204.   [130] *OD.*, III, 528.

[131] This story first appeared in *La Revue de Paris*, February 23, 1831. It was published later in the successive editions of the collection under consideration. In 1835 it
appeared in the *Etudes philosophiques*, Vol. XVII. In 1846 it entered the *Comédie humaine*, Vol. XIV; and it is now in *Con.*, Vol. XXIX.

the Reign of Terror. A mother, in agonizing suspense concerning her son's danger of death, thought that he had returned home safely. The next morning, however, she discovered that she had mistaken someone else for him. The intense shock brought on her death at the same moment that her son was shot by the Revolutionary troops. Davin summarizes the theme as "une mère tuée par la violence du sentiment maternel. Voilà donc la femme considérée ... comme mère, et devenant, ... victime de l'*idée*."[132] The tragic consequence of this story is due to a philosophical conception akin to that in *La Peau de chagrin:* excess of sentiment renders the nervous system so sensitive that a shock may result in death. Edmond Biré explains the grouping of the story among the philosophical tales in these words: "Le dénouement est dû moins à un fait qu'à une idée, et cette idée est celle-ci: l'amour maternel, porté au plus haut degré, peut devenir, en vertu de son excès même, un principe de mort."[133] Without doubt this was Balzac's reason for permanently placing *Le Réquisitionnaire* in the category of the *Etudes philosophiques,* with which it is closely linked.

Etude de femme[134] is a short study of a woman's passing fancy. Although originally grouped with *La Peau de chagrin,* it is out of keeping with the deeper themes of the philosophical tales, since it treats of ordinary private life. Because of such considerations the author made early plans, in 1832, as seen from letters to his publishers, Mame and Gosselin,[135] to remove it from this collection. He did not do so, however, until 1835, when, under the new temporary title *Profil de marquise,* the sketch was placed in the first edition of the "Scènes de la vie parisienne" in order to fulfil the required pages of these volumes. As the new title suggests, the interest of the story centers in the marquise. Mme de Listomère had, in Balzac's words, "une petite crise nerveuse" because she could not inspire such deep affection as did another woman, Mme de Nucingen. At first glance it would seem that the characters and events of the story harmonize with the trend of Parisian society life in which the sole occupation of women was to maintain their sovereignty in the *salons.* And yet it can be said

---

[132] Lov., *Hist.,* p. 203. Italics of Davin.

[133] Biré's ed. of Balzac's *Scènes de la vie militaire,* Introduction, p. 1.

[134] This tale first appeared in *La Mode,* March 12, 1830. It was published in all the editions of the volumes now discussed. In 1835 it was reprinted in the "Scènes de la vie parisienne"; it entered in 1842 the "Scènes de la vie privée" (*Comédie humaine,* Vol. I), and is now in *Con.,* Vol. III.

[135] Cited above, pp. 41–42.

that Balzac's acute sense of harmony and order ultimately induced him to place this sketch, under its original title, in the *Scènes de la vie privée*. *Etude de femme* belongs more appropriately in the *Scènes* in which are depicted "des émotions, des sensations irréfléchies."[136] Furthermore, the author himself stated in the Preface to *Une Fille d'Ève*[137] that the *Scènes de la vie privée* were to represent young people whose errors are due to inexperience of life. Certainly, this is the case in the sudden intrigue between the youthful Eugène de Rastignac and the sophisticated Mme de Listomère.

Balzac's interest in the period of religious wars dated from 1821. In a letter to Laure Surville, written November 23 of that year, he inquired whether he could obtain at Bayeux or at Caen books on the history of France. He informed his sister of his plans: "Le roman que j'irai faire [chez vous] sera, ou *la Démence de Charles VI*, ou *la Faction Armagnac et Bourguignonne*, ou *la Conspiration d'Amboise*, ou *la Saint-Barthélemy*."[138] The massacre of Saint-Bartholomew is touched upon in *Les Deux Rêves*, a story destined (in 1830) for a projected collective volume, *Scènes de la vie politique*,[139] but which never appeared there. After its first publication in *La Mode*, *Les Deux Rêves* came out again under a new title, *Le Petit Souper*,[140] with a subtitle, "Conte fantastique," which indicates its coloring. Omitting the subtitle and restoring the original title, as more specific, Balzac grouped the narrative with the twelve philosophical tales and subsequently classified it in the *Etudes philosophiques*.[141] In 1843 *Les Deux Rêves* became Part III of *Catherine de Médicis expliquée*[142] and served as a conclusion to the political principles expressed in Parts I and II of that novel.

Under either title this is the tale of two dreams told at a late dinner to a small group of guests. The first dream, related by a queer old lawyer,

[136] Lov., *Hist.*, p. 46.

[137] *OD.*, III, 519.   [138] *LF.*, p. 49.

[139] See above, p. 34. This title was used later, in 1846, as a general heading for the fourth subdivision of the *Etudes de mœurs*. See Lov., *Hist.*, pp. 145, 189.

[140] *La Revue des deux mondes*, December, 1830.

[141] *Wer.*, Vol. XII.

[142] Published by Souverain in 3 vols.; in 1846 *Les Deux Rêves*, still as Part III of *Sur Catherine de Médicis*, entered the second division of the *Comédie humaine*, Vol. XVI. It is now in *Con.*, Vol. XXX. This analysis will be completed in sec. vi, below, where the entire novel will be considered. For a full history of publication, see W. L. Crain, "A Critical Edition of Balzac's *Le Secret des Ruggieri*," chap. iv of this volume.

concerns Catherine de' Medici. She defends the Saint-Bartholomew massacre on the ground that for royal power "il fallait dans l'Etat un seul Dieu, une seule foi, un seul maître."[143] The second dream is told by a surgeon, who dreamed that during an operation he became aware of both a visible and an invisible universe, forming "une seule et même matière animée, depuis les marbres jusqu'à Dieu!"[144] These ideas presented allegorically in dreams align the story with *La Peau de chagrin* and therefore make it an integral part of the *Etudes philosophiques*.

Jésus-Christ en Flandre[145] is also an allegory with a mystical theme. Balzac gives a description of a catastrophe as told by the mariners of Ostend. In essence it is the legend of Christ walking upon the waves. The scene is a ferryboat, at one end of which are "les gens supérieurs," and at the other the "parias de la société."[146] Among the poor people is a stranger who comforts his fellow-men with mystic words; and during a storm they walk in faith with him safely ashore, while the haughty and the faithless perish. Davin describes the story in the following words: "*Jésus-Christ en Flandre* est la démonstration de la puissance de la foi, considérée aussi comme *idée*."[147] This circumstance explains why Balzac, from the start, grouped the story with the philosophical and mystical tales and ultimately classified it in the *Etudes philosophiques*. In 1845 *Jésus-Christ en Flandre* absorbed a short tale, *L'Eglise*, and, remaining in the same category, entered the *Comédie humaine* under the original title. It should be added that the fragment, *L'Eglise*, was originally a sketch, *Zéro*, with a subtitle "Conte fantastique,"[148] which may account for its inclusion with *Jésus-Christ en Flandre*. Furthermore, in analyzing this fragment, Davin

---

[143] *Romans et contes philosophiques*, III, 338.

[144] *Ibid.*, p. 348. On this idea of unity in the universe, cf. Diderot, *Le Rêve de D'Alembert* (*Œuvres complètes*, éd. Garnier), II, 138–39: "Tous les êtres circulent les uns dans les autres, par conséquent toutes les espèces ... tout est en flux perpétuel. ... Tout animal est plus ou moins plante; toute plante est plus ou moins animal. ... Il n'y a qu'un seul grand individu, c'est le tout." In this connection, on Balzac's great admiration for G. Saint-Hilaire, see Hélène d'Alsó, "Saint-Hilaire et M. de Balzac," *Revue d'histoire de la philosophie et d'histoire générale de la civilization* (Bruxelles), October 15, 1934, pp. 339–54.

[145] This tale first appeared in the collection under consideration and in its subsequent editions. In 1836 it was classified in the *Etudes philosophiques*, Vol. XIV; in 1845 it entered the *Comédie humaine*, Vol. XIV, and is now in *Con.*, Vol. XXVII.

[146] Chasles; see Lov., *Hist.*, p. 176.

[147] Lov., *Hist.*, p. 205. Italics ours.   [148] *Ibid.*, p. 465.

says: "Le rêve fantastique intitulé *l'Eglise* est une saisissante vision des idées religieuses se dévorant elles-mêmes, et croulant tour à tour les unes sur les autres, ruinées par l'incrédulité, qui est aussi une idée."[149] In *L'Eglise* the author tells of his dream in a cathedral. The church is represented as an old, degraded woman who suddenly is transformed into an angel of light. The last message of Balzac is that the church must be defended, because the great and magnificent things accomplished during the past ages surpass all the evil that may have been provoked.[150]

In direct opposition to *La Peau de chagrin*, which served as a starting-point for the collection, *Jésus-Christ en Flandre* stands as a concluding hopeful sign in Balzac's original analysis of the causes of suffering and evil. Whereas many of the preceding stories represent egoism, vice, pride, and skepticism, this legend portrays charity, humility, faith, and love.

It is interesting to note that out of these thirteen early stories, twelve are short, mostly *contes*, varying from 9 to 40 pages in length,[151] and only one, *La Peau de chagrin*, is really a novel, containing 290 pages. The binding threads are hardly visible to the superficial eye; nevertheless, they manifest a tendency toward unity and a purpose which will become stronger and more evident as the number of Balzac's works increases.

During the autumn of 1831 Paris was eagerly reading the *Romans et contes philosophiques*, while Balzac was writing and making plans for the publication of new works, either wholly his own or written in collaboration with other authors. In this manner, he published (February, 1832), anonymously, with Philarète Chasles and Charles Rabou, the *Contes bruns*,[152] a collection of gloomy stories in each of which was described some form of violent death. An anonymous critic—probably Honoré himself—explains the title in the following phrase: "... *bruns*, sans doute pour satisfaire aux lois de la couleur locale."[153] This *couleur locale* was aptly advertised on the title-page by a lithographed vignette. It served as a signature and represented a head turned upside down with hair on end, with wide-open, squinting eyes, and with thin lips drawn back showing large, strong teeth. The expression is cadaverous and terrified—therefore, in keeping with the tone of these exciting tales.

To the 398 pages which composed this volume Balzac contributed 122.

[149] *Ibid.*, p. 205.

[150] *Con.*, XXVII, 313-16.   [151] In the 1831 ed.

[152] Published by Urbain Canel and Adolphe Guyot.

[153] *La Caricature*, February 16, 1832. The article is reprinted in Lov., *Hist.*, p. 236.

Of these, 72 were later transposed to the *Comédie humaine*. It is necessary, therefore, to consider both this material and that which was discarded. Balzac's contribution consisted of twelve short stories under one common title, *Une Conversation entre onze heures et minuit*, and a separate story, *Le Grand d'Espagne*. Marcel Bouteron[154] has reprinted these tales with a Preface and notes and, for convenience, has given to ten episodes of the *Conversation* individual titles.[155] Balzac himself had already designated two of them as: "Histoire du chevalier de Beauvoir" and "La Maîtresse de notre colonel." The tales were told after dinner by the fireplace, around which are grouped a dozen people, men and women. Emile Henriot[156] states that Balzac insisted that such a gathering took place in the salon of Baron Gérard, which was frequented by Mérimée, Delacroix, and Stendhal. The last is referred to in the *Conversation* as "un homme gros et gras, homme de beaucoup d'esprit et qui devait partir pour l'Italie."[157] The women, guests of Baron Gérard, were Sophie and Delphine Gay and others. The opening pages of the first story, which M. Bouteron named "Un Salon parisien," serve as a framework for the twelve distinct episodes. Since each of these *récits* is a unit in itself, the author later transposed them, at will or at need, with changes and modifications to fit[158] them into various parts of the *Comédie humaine;* so *Autre Etude de femme*, for example, is shown by W. L. Crain[159] to be a mosaic partly made up of compositions taken from the *Conversation*.

It is possible that from their inception Balzac counted on transferring these *récits* from the *Contes bruns*. His changing plans are recorded in his correspondence. He had signed a contract with Mame on June 5, 1832,[160] for the publication of the *Conversation*, together with other works. He referred to the *Contes bruns* in a letter to his mother on June 10: "Comme ce que j'y ai fait sera réimprimé dans les *Causeries du soir*, tu dois peu

[154] H. de Balzac, *Contes bruns*, éd. M. Bouteron.

[155] These titles will be set within quotation marks.

[156] *Le Temps*, April 9, 1927.

[157] *Contes bruns*, éd. Bouteron, p. 71. Professor Robert Vigneron concurs in the probable presence of Stendhal at the meeting and adds that it must have taken place between September and November, 1830, the time at which Stendhal was appointed consul to Italy.

[158] The classifications and shifts of these stories will be discussed below.

[159] "The Reworking of Balzac's *Autre Etude de femme*" (unpublished Master's thesis, University of Chicago, 1925).

[160] *LF.*, p. 113, n. 1.

tenir à ceux [les contes] de Chasles et de Rabou."[161] The proposed volume of *Causeries du soir*, apparently a patchwork in the manner of *Une Conversation*, was never published.[162] Yet throughout July, August, and September, 1832, he frequently discussed the appearance of this work, even assuring his mother that it would be published by Mame the following February![163]

Balzac made another direct reference to the *Conversation* in *Les Marana*[164] of 1832; in the volume edition of this story (1834) he indicated (contrary to fact) that the *Conversation* had been classified in the "Scènes de la vie parisienne": "Ce divertissement de bivouac ["Histoire du capitaine Bianchi"] est raconté dans les *Conversations* par lesquelles cet ouvrage [*Scènes de la vie parisienne*] est terminé, ... [*Les Marana, Scènes de la vie parisienne* (1834), II, 5–6]." This passage remained the same in the Charpentier edition (II, 241–42), notwithstanding Davin's incorrect statement, in April, 1835, that the "*Conversations* ... ouvrent les *Scènes de la Vie politique*."[165] One cannot trust the statements of Balzac-Davin, for discrepancies in dates and facts obscure the true situation. For example, in the Preface to the "Scènes de la vie parisienne," August 30, 1835, our novelist stated that the "*Conversations* ... qui devaient terminer les *Scènes de la Vie parisienne* ... serviront d'introduction aux *Scènes de la Vie politique*."[166] This was not the case. And yet, in 1845, when the author shifted *Les Marana* to the "Etudes philosophiques," he perpetuated the error: "Ce divertissement de bivouac est raconté ailleurs (*Scènes de la Vie parisienne*)."[167] Curiously, this faulty cross-reference remained, even in the Conard edition,[168] despite the fact that neither the episode nor the *Conversation* was ever classified in the "Scènes de la vie parisienne" or "politique." Ultimately, however, some of the *récits* were classed in the two other subdivisions of the *Etudes de mœurs*, namely, the "Scènes de la vie privée" and the "Scènes de la vie de province."

It is interesting to follow each *récit* in its transpositions on the way to its final place in the *Comédie humaine*. "Un salon parisien"[169] was used

[161] *Ibid.*, p. 76.

[162] *Ibid.*, p. 76, n. 2; and p. 79, n. 1.   [163] *Ibid.*, p. 125.

[164] *La Revue de Paris*, December, 1832, pp. 235–36.

[165] Lov., *Hist.*, p. 49. These Scenes were published in 1846.

[166] *OD.*, III, 392.   [168] XXIX, 60–61.

[167] *Fur.*, XV, 221.   [169] *Contes bruns*, pp. 19–23.

for the description of Mme d'Esther's *salon* in *Le Conseil*.[170] Expanded, it served for the description of Mme d'Espard's *salon* in *Autre Etude de femme*.[171] To this story were also added the two long paragraphs in praise of Napoleon;[172] "La Maîtresse de notre colonel,"[173] now told by General Montriveau, while in the *Conversation* it was told by an artillery officer; and "La Femme du médecin,"[174] erroneously indicated by W. L. Crain as new material. "La Femme du médecin" in *Autre Etude de femme* becomes the death scene of Charlotte, Henri de Marsay's first love, which is told by Bianchon; in the *Conversation*, the dying woman was the wife of a German doctor, and the story was told by a young physician whose name was not given.

"Histoire du chevalier de Beauvoir" and *Le Grand d'Espagne*[175] joined *La Grande Bretèche*[176] under the title *La Grande Bretèche, ou Les Trois Vengeances*.[177] In journal publication the first two stories were permanently added to *Dinah Piédefer*,[178] and in lieu of *La Grande Bretèche* a paragraph summary was temporarily substituted. Next they reappeared, in volume publication, under the common title *La Muse du département*[179] (1843), but their individual titles were now omitted. When, in the same year, these old companions were republished in *Les Mystères de province*,[180] with the title *La Muse du département, ou Dinah*, Balzac restored the first title and made the following changes: "Histoire du chevalier de Beauvoir" was told by Lousteau; the title *Le Grand d'Espagne* was changed to "Histoire d'un croc où monsieur Gravier se pose crânement," and the story was told by Gravier; and *La Grande Bretèche* was told again in full by Bianchon. Finally, however, in 1845, this last story returned to its original classification in the "Scènes de la vie privée,"[181] as the concluding part

---

[170] *Scènes de la vie privée* (2d ed., 1832), Vol. III.

[171] *Ibid.* (5th ed., 1842), Vol. II.

[172] *Contes bruns*, pp. 31–33.   [174] *Ibid.*, pp. 95–97.

[173] *Ibid.*, pp. 58–70.   [175] *Ibid.*, pp. 35–46, 122–43.

[176] This story first appeared together with *Le Message* under the title *Le Conseil*, *Scènes de la vie privée* (2d ed., 1832), Vol. III. See below, p. 55.

[177] "Scènes de la vie de province" (1837), Vol. III; and Charpentier ed. (1839), Vol. I.

[178] This story first appeared in *Le Messager*, March 20–April 29, 1843.

[179] *Les Parisiens en province: II, La Muse du département* ("Scènes de la vie de province," *Comédie humaine*, Vol. VI).

[180] Published by Souverain in 4 vols., 1843–44.

[181] *Fur.*, Vol. IV.

of *Autre Etude de femme*. We see, therefore, that five borrowings from the *Conversation*, in addition to *Le Grand d'Espagne*, were used in the *Comédie humaine*. "Histoire du chevalier de Beauvoir" and *Le Grand d'Espagne* appeared five times each after they had left the *Contes bruns;* "La Maîtresse de notre colonel," "La Femme du médecin," and the paragraphs concerning Napoleon each appeared once; while the setting of the *salon* scenes, undergoing various changes, was used three times.

The remaining stories of the *Conversation* never entered the *Comédie humaine*. Part of the general *salon* setting; the "Histoire du capitaine Bianchi" with the enthusiastic praise of Napoleon, now reduced to a four-line paragraph; a discussion of contemporary civilization; "L'Avortement"; Stendhal's story of "Ecce homo"; "Le Tic du mort"; "Le Père du réfractaire"; "Le Gilet rouge"; "Le Président Vigneron"; "Le Bol de punch"; and "Le Général Ruska"—all these under a new common title, *Echantillons de causeries françaises*—were published *in toto* with the first edition of *Splendeurs et misères des courtisanes*.[182] Next, the *Echantillons*, with an additional paragraph from the introductory pages of the *Conversation*, was placed permanently in the *Œuvres diverses*, Volume I.[183]

The question now arises as to why Balzac utilized to such an extent his *Contes bruns*. The answer is, perhaps, seen in the dates of their peregrinations. Those begin in 1837 and go on steadily until 1845—a period during which the author was in full possession of his scheme. He was then enlarging his earlier subdivisions and adding new ones. In spite of certain adverse criticisms,[184] from the personal friends of Chasles and Rabou, Balzac fully realized the mechanical and artistic possibilities of these easily adaptable and movable *récits*. It is interesting to note that seven tales of the *Contes bruns* dealt with illicit love and its consequences, an aspect of life already touched upon in several stories of the first edition of the *Scènes de la vie privée*.

It will be recalled that the *Scènes de la vie privée* was Balzac's first collective title, used in 1830 for two volumes composed of six short tales, dealing with domestic life and morals. From the fact that our author used this collective title again for an enlarged grouping, and because there is a solidarity in the general trend of these stories, it is safe to assume that

[182] Published by De Potter in 3 vols., 1844.

[183] *OC.*, éd. Lévy, XX, 299–329.

[184] Cf. Anonymous, "Balzac et la tête à l'envers," *Chronique des lettres françaises*, XXVIII (1927), 518–19.

he now had a definite aim in view. These titles, moreover, throw light on his mode of thinking; he worked with related, and not with isolated, thoughts. Each of his *tableaux* or *scènes* (by which he meant tales) comprises an idea embodied in characters and in situations. Thus, a collective title represents a grouping of related thoughts under a general heading— a fact which becomes of prime importance in the author's scheme. The original and distinctive feature of the first period, let us repeat, is his persistence in using these collective titles.

On August 28, 1831, the novelist signed a contract with the publisher Mame for the reprinting of the first edition of the *Scènes de la vie privée* and for the publication of two additional volumes. The four volumes of the second edition[185] of the *Scènes* were on sale May 22, 1832. The contents of Volumes I and II corresponded to the same volumes of the first edition, both in titles and in text, although the pagination varied slightly. Volumes III and IV comprised nine new stories. In these fifteen stories Balzac deals with simple themes of bourgeois home life and morals. It is, indeed, a limited sphere of individual and family life, not as yet broadening to the sociohistorical preoccupations of his later years.

Le Conseil was a temporary caption for two distinct tales, *Le Message*[186] and *La Grande Bretèche;*[187] their individual titles were, however, omitted in the volumes now discussed. Both are stories told in the *salon* with similar themes of domesticity. The purpose of the *récits* was to warn— hence *Le Conseil*—the young hostess, Mme d'Esther, of the dangers of an illicit love affair with M. de La Plaine. As has been indicated above, Balzac had borrowed the description of her *salon* from the setting in the *Conversation*. The opening episode of *Le Conseil* is related by one of the guests, M. de Villaines, who had witnessed a fatal coach accident. His traveling companion, a dying man, intrusted to him the letters of his mistress. Burdened with the news of a lover's death, a lock of his hair, and the letters, M. de Villaines proceeded to find Juliette de Montpersan, a young married woman. The depth of her silent grief is briefly and simply presented. But the guests do not consider *Le Message* tragic enough, and the story-teller then offers a second *récit*, another warning to his hostess. *La Grande Bretèche* is a tale of jealousy and terrible vengeance. One night

---

[185] Published by Mame and Delaunay-Vallée. Announced in the *Bibliographie de la France*, May 26, 1832.

[186] First published in *La Revue des deux mondes*, February, 1832.

[187] This appeared first in the collection under consideration.

M. de Merret suspected that his wife was hiding her lover in a closet built in the wall of her room. She swore innocence upon her crucifix, but the husband's rage and suspicion wiped out all human feeling in him. In the dead of night he had a mason wall up the closet door. Then he remained in his wife's room for a fortnight, watching her agony while her lover died a lingering death.

Balzac's motive in placing *Le Conseil* in the *Scènes de la vie privée* is, we think, revealed in the concluding statement of the double story: "Il n'y a pas de bonheur assez grand pour faire affronter les secrètes tortures que les passions nous font subir."[188] Thus the author, by the principle of contrast, argues indirectly for quiet domestic happiness; this is his usual concern in the *Scènes de la vie privée*. Furthermore, in both episodes he depicts tragedy in private home life. This theme is in keeping with the general trend of these Scenes, to which the stories ultimately returned—the first tale with its restored individual title, *Le Message*,[189] in 1842, and the second in 1845.[190] Before reaching their final lodgment, however, the two stories underwent shiftings which throw more light on Balzac's growing scheme. While planning a third edition of these Scenes, he wrote to Mame on September 30, 1832, the following instructions:

> Je supprimerai *Le Conseil* [*Le Message* and *La Grande Bretèche*], puis *le Devoir d'une femme* dans le troisième volume, pour les remplacer par une nouvelle scène qui paraîtra dans la *Revue de Paris* et qui sera plus dans la nature et le genre des *Scènes de la vie privée* que les deux supprimés que je trouve un peu en dehors de la moralité du livre.[191]

The last part of this statement certainly applies to the second story, which, as will be shown presently, Balzac transposed finally to the *Etudes philosophiques*. The first story (*Le Message*, first episode of *Le Conseil*) he placed temporarily in the new subdivision, "Scènes de la vie de province."[192] In regard to this on November 1, 1833, he wrote to Mme Hanska: "... il faut, je crois, que je trouve quelque chose pour compléter mon second volume des *Scènes de la vie de province* ... il faudra une *scène* de

---

[188] *Scènes de la vie privée*, III (1832), 101.

[189] *Fur.*, Vol. II. The story is now in *Con.*, Vol. IV.

[190] See above, p. 53, and n. 181.

[191] Lov. Coll., A 250, fols. 1–2. *Le Devoir d'une femme* under the title *Adieu* entered in 1835 the *Etudes philosophiques*, Vol. IV. The "nouvelle scène" is *La Grenadière*, which appeared in *La Revue de Paris*, October, 1832.

[192] Vol. II. The volumes were on sale December, 1833, and the publisher was Mme Charles Béchet, not Mame, as the above-mentioned letter seems to imply.

quarante ou cinquante pages."[193] When a certain number of pages was needed for the completion of a volume, stories from the *Scènes de la vie privée* nearly always filled the gap. This temporary shift, then, of *Le Message* (later of *La Grande Bretèche*, as part of *Les Trois Vengeances*), notwithstanding the author's communication of September 30, 1832, was impelled by a practical reason with which he had continually to reckon as his scheme developed.

We may anticipate by saying that, besides *Le Message*, two other stories, *La Femme abandonnée* and *La Grenadière*, were used to meet the same need. These three, said Davin, Balzac's mouthpiece, formed "une trilogie des souffrances de la femme supérieure. ... Ces trois individualités ... font un type."[194] Therefore these tales were grouped (1835) together; and later, in 1842, when new stories, more in harmony with the principle of the "Scènes de la vie de province," were written, the trilogy was finally shifted to the "Scènes de la vie privée," where it properly belongs. *Le Message* was ultimately restored to the "Scènes de la vie privée," probably because, in the last analysis, Juliette de Montpersan was not too seriously compromised and was wise enough to return to conjugal life. The misfortune which followed clandestine love taught her, as it had taught some other women portrayed in this subdivision, the "douceurs d'un heureux ménage."[195]

La Grande Bretèche, separated after 1832 from its temporary mate, *Le Message*, suffered three shiftings before it was permanently restored in 1845 to its original subdivision, "Scènes de la vie privée." In 1837 it was coupled with two vengeance tales under the general title *La Grande Bretèche, ou Les Trois Vengeances*[196] and, like *Le Message*, was placed temporarily in the new subdivision, "Scènes de la vie de province." Here the three stories are told in a provincial *salon* by three guests to prove the innocence of their hostess, Mme de la Boudraye, and her supposed lover. M. Bouteron explains the combination of these three tales in this statement: "Il [Balzac] a besoin de copie pour corser la première nouvelle du volume: *La Grande Bretèche, ou Les Trois Vengeances*."[197] In addition to similarity of themes, the fact that the action is laid in the provinces may justify their temporary grouping. To harmonize these stories with the

---

[193] *LEt.*, I, 71. [194] Lov., *Hist.*, p. 60.

[195] Preface to *Une Fille d'Ève, OD.*, III, 519.

[196] An analysis of these stories is given below, pp. 100–101.

[197] *Contes bruns*, p. 10.

new subdivision, Balzac inserted an introductory paragraph depicting the dangers of illicit love in the provinces. It may be argued that the walling-up alive of a rival and the cutting-off of a wife's arm (which occurs in *Le Grand d'Espagne*) harmonize with the "sombres et douloureuses passions" of the "Scènes de la vie de province";[198] and, judging from a letter to Mme Hanska on February 10–12, 1837, one is led to believe that Balzac was satisfied with the transfer. He says that "*La Grande Bretèche* [est] rarrangée [*sic*], c'est-à-dire *encadrée mieux* qu'elle ne l'était primitivement et escortée de deux autres aventures."[199] Nevertheless, this classification was short-lived, for, as has been shown previously, in 1845, separated from these two stories and given a new framework, the tale becomes the "fin de *Autre Etude de femme*" and is permanently re-established in its more logical subdivision, the "Scènes de la vie privée."[200] Whether laid in the provinces or in the capital, it is essentially a tragedy of private life. Whereas these frequent shifts of stories (between 1833 and 1837) may be symptomatic of some uncertainty about the "plan" in Balzac's mind, they are definitely accounted for, in some cases, by precedence given to practical issues—the demands of the publishing firm.

We return to the second edition of the *Scènes de la vie privée*. *La Bourse*, a charming tale, is in harmony with the collective title under which it first appeared. The story represents Balzac's earlier conception of the narrow, but exquisite, setting of domesticity; in fact, the portrayal of the humble, and yet dignified, home of Mme de Rouville and her daughter, Adélaïde, has all the delicacy of an easel piece. Balzac must have thought of such a quiet home when he asserted in the Preface to the first edition of these *Scènes* that he painted therein "le tableau vrai de mœurs que les familles ensevelissent aujourd'hui dans l'ombre, et que l'observateur a quelquefois de la peine à deviner."[201] Hippolyte Schinner, the painter, is baffled by the mystery which surrounds the lives of these two women, although attracted by the sweetness of the young girl. He becomes a friend of the family and is commissioned to paint the father's portrait. One evening during a card game he misses his old, silk-embroidered purse. Unable to explain its disappearance, he withdraws. Later, however, he accepts an invitation from Mme de Rouville. After a while he notices before him a new purse, artistically embroidered. He then understands the gift as an

---

[198] "Scènes de la vie de province," préface de la première édition, *OD.*, III, 384.

[199] *LEt.*, I, 380. Italics ours.

[200] See above, p. 53.   [201] *OD.*, III, 379.

expression of gratitude for his work. Balzac skilfully depicts the awakening of love between the two young people and its fulfilment in a happy marriage—a contrast to the ending of many tales in these volumes. The events which take place in the life of Hippolyte and Adélaïde are in tune with the "Scènes de la vie privée," which, Davin says, reflect human life "dans son réveil matinal, et croissant pour fleurir."[202] *La Bourse* is closely integrated with this grouping and was classed therein permanently in 1842.[203] This classification came, however, only after a temporary placement in the first edition of the "Scènes de la vie parisienne,"[204] for which the author had not yet composed a sufficient number of stories. It is significant that he also placed temporarily in the "Scènes de la vie parisienne" two other tales of private life, *Une Double Famille* and *Gobseck.* Between these two stories, *La Bourse* "fait un contraste prodigieux," says Davin in his Introduction to the *Etudes de mœurs.* We surmise that again Davin is speaking for Balzac. Thus the emergency which necessitated the combining of stories for the completion of a volume apparently did not wholly destroy the novelist's feeling for artistic effects.

Le Devoir d'une femme had first been published as *Souvenirs soldatesques; Adieu,*[205] a title indicating its military coloring. It will be recalled that, at the time this tale appeared (1830, in journal publication), Balzac had announced two projected collective volumes, *Scènes de la vie politique* and *Scènes de la vie militaire.*[206] One will readily concur with Merlant[207] in his surprise that *Adieu* was not placed in "Scènes de la vie militaire." Possibly if Balzac had completed these Scenes, this story, with its famous description of the crossing of the Beresina, would have found its place in that subdivision. Since the story was classified in the *Scènes de la vie privée* under a new title, one may assume that the author deliberately emphasized not its military aspect but the character study of young Stéphanie, who, through duty, followed her husband on his long expedition—hence *Le Devoir d'une femme.* Here he anticipated the theme of the projected volumes, the *Etudes de femmes.* As this project was not realized, all these stories, special studies of women, were classified either temporarily or permanently in the "Scènes de la vie privée." Yet Balzac definitely

[202] Lov., *Hist.*, p. 197.

[203] *Fur.*, Vol. I. The story is now in *Con.*, Vol. I.

[204] 1835, in Vol. I; 2d ed., 1839, in Vol. I.   [206] See above, pp. 34–35.

[205] In *La Mode*, May 15–June 15, 1830.   [207] Merlant, *op. cit.*, p. 73.

stated[208] that *Le Devoir d'une femme* did not belong to these scenes because it is "en dehors de la moralité du livre." Davin, in an exceedingly illuminating passage, explains the temporary misplacement of *Adieu*. He approaches the problem of classification from the publisher's point of view, and his statement holds in regard to the other temporary classifications so far mentioned, as well as to those that will come hereafter. He argues:

> La mode, au-devant de laquelle courent les libraires, exigeait des livres à toute force; peu leur importait le sens des œuvres qu'ils publiaient. Ainsi, tel fragment n'avait rien de philosophique et convenait aux *Scènes de la Vie privée*, tandis que telle *scène* était une *Etude philosophique:* la fatalité du commerce, le besoin du moment les transposait. La première livraison des *Etudes philosophiques* en offre un exemple. *Adieu*, publié dans le troisième volume des *Scènes de la Vie privée*, et dont personne n'a compris la destination dans l'œuvre générale, est certes une des plus justes et des plus fermes déductions du thème inscrit sur *La Peau de chagrin*.[209]

Because the basic idea of *Adieu* is so closely related to that of *La Peau de chagrin*, Balzac in 1835 permanently classed the former story in the *Etudes philosophiques*. It is noteworthy that the author opened the story with an epigraph from *César Birotteau*[210] which clarifies his scientific idea: "Les plus hardis physiologistes sont effrayés par les résultats physiques de ce phénomène moral, qui n'est cependant qu'un foudroiement opéré à l'intérieur, et, comme tous les effets électriques, bizarre et capricieux dans ses modes."[211]

The fundamental idea of *Adieu* is similar to that of *Le Réquisitionnaire* and of *L'Enfant maudit*. The intensity of moral suffering or of great joy produces so strong a shock in the nervous system that death is the result. The young Comtesse de Vandières, wife of an old general who died in her presence at the crossing of the Beresina, loses her mind during that terrible retreat of the French army. A few years later in France, her lover, Colonel Philippe de Sucy, attempts to restore her mind by reproducing a close duplicate of the physical situation in which she became demented. This semiscientific device has been known, at times, to bring the desired results, and the method has an important place in the treatment of certain psychoses. The countess recognized her lover gradually, but the happi-

---

[208] See above, p. 56.   [209] Lov., *Hist.*, p. 195.

[210] This novel was, at that time, designed for the *Etudes philosophiques*.

[211] Lov., *Hist.*, p. 183.

ness was too great for her weakened mind and body, and she fell dead with a last "adieu." The distracted Philippe shot himself.

Les Célibataires[212] was the first study in which Balzac dealt with the attitude toward life and the habits of celibates. The original title of Le Curé de Tours was La Vieille Fille,[213] as is learned from the manuscript preserved at Chantilly. Apparently, Balzac first intended to show the two kinds of good and bad old maid, Mlle Salomon[214] and Mlle Gamard. The title, La Vieille Fille,[215] however, proved temporary, as Balzac realized that Birotteau had usurped the role of the principal character. The next title proposed was Le Prêtre catholique;[216] the present, Le Curé de Tours, appeared for the first time in 1843. These tentative captions are indicative of social classes; therefore, it is clear that by the early part of 1832 Balzac's interest in the limited sphere of individual and family life had broadened into a sociological preoccupation dealing with larger groups. The priest and, in fact, the whole ecclesiastical world were personified in the ambitious and powerful Troubert, who unfolded his wings outside of his domain.

The theme seems somewhat out of tune with the group of stories treating of love, marriage, and domestic problems; and Balzac may have placed it in the Scènes de la vie privée merely to produce, through contrast, an artistic effect. More probably he may have needed it to complete the volume. In 1833 he reclassified the story, putting it in the new subdivision, "Scènes de la vie de province," of which it is still a component part. Concurrently with this shift, Le Curé de Tours underwent a few changes,[217] in successive editions between 1833 and 1843, in order to harmonize it with the sociological trend of the Scènes to which the tale was permanently

---

[212] This story first appeared in the collection under consideration. In 1833 it was published in the "Scènes de la vie de province," Vol. II; in 1843 it entered the Comédie humaine, Vol. VI; and it is now in Con., Vol. IX. In regard to the title of this tale, Lovenjoul states: "Ce récit, ... dut un moment s'appeler L'Abbé Troubert" (Lov., Hist., p. 81).

[213] Lov. Coll., A 196, fols. 2–7.

[214] A reappearing character before 1833. Balzac gives a brief résumé of her antecedents and thus connects this story with Louis Lambert and Un Drame au bord de la mer.

[215] The title La Vieille Fille was used later for an entirely new story.

[216] Lov. Coll., A 196, fols. 27 and 16–23. It should be noted that the hero of this manuscript version (unpublished) was the Abbé de Vèze, and not Birotteau.

[217] Dr. Rachel Wilson's detailed study of the variations in the successive editions of Le Curé de Tours is now completed and published in this volume. A generalization concerning this aspect of the story will suffice here.

assigned. Balzac accentuated the narrow and set opinions of the old women; he placed greater stress on the contrast between the two priests; and he emphasized both the formidable character of Troubert and the *niaiseries* of the lamblike Birotteau. The latter is singled out, in the 1843 edition (*Con.*, IX, 169), as the "principal personnage de cette histoire." It could be argued that the author shifted the emphasis from the private life of priests to a more general field, the ecclesiastical group. This change was, after all, in keeping with the wider range of Balzac's developing plans for his works. In 1843 he permanently placed this story, together with his other studies of celibacy,[218] under a group title, *Les Célibataires*, already dealt with (in part), in the "Scènes de la vie de province." This final combination proves once more that the author had a systematic mind and a natural tendency to organize.

The childlike vicar, François Birotteau, the "sublime victime" of the scheming Troubert, owes all his misfortunes to a small vice—a taste for good living, which becomes so despotic as to ruin his whole life. Such is, in brief, the theme of the story; logically it belongs to the "Scènes de la vie de province," in which, says Davin, Balzac portrays

les tracasseries mesquines dont la périodicité concentre un intérêt poignant sur le moindre détail d'existence. Il [Balzac] nous initie au secret de ces petites rivalités, de ces jalousies de voisinage, de ces tracasseries de ménage dont la force, s'accroissant chaque jour, dégrade en peu de temps les hommes ...[219]

This is precisely the atmosphere in *Le Curé de Tours*, with its four characters whose celibacy the author condemns on the principle that the "état du célibataire est un état contraire à la société ... il y a des cas où les intérêts sociaux doivent l'emporter sur les intérêts particuliers."[220] This is, distinctly, one aspect of Balzac's sociological approach; another is the social role given to the church as an institution of both good and bad practices.

Volume IV, the last of the *Scènes de la vie privée* (1832), was composed of five fragments: *Le Rendez-vous, La Femme de trente ans, Le Doigt de Dieu, Les Deux Rencontres,* and *L'Expiation*. The volume opens with a "Note de l'Editeur," from Balzac's own pen. He asserts that the unity of these fragments rests in the life of one character, disguised under different names but caught at its beginning and followed to its end. Therefore,

---

[218] *Pierrette* and *Un Ménage de garçon en province* (later *La Rabouilleuse*).

[219] Lov., *Hist.*, p. 47.

[220] *Pierrette*, préface de la première édition (1840), *OD.*, III, 539–40.

the projected common title, *L'Esquisse de la vie d'une femme*, seems suited to these compositions.[221] It was, however, never used. In the second edition of the story[222] Balzac enlarged *Le Doigt de Dieu* by a new chapter, "La Vallée du torrent," and added a sixth episode, *Souffrances inconnues;* to these six *disjecta membra* the author now gave one caption, *Même Histoire.* The first mention of this collective title appears in his journal: "Un livre intitulé *Même Histoire*, composé de fragmens détachés sans queue ni tête en apparence, mais ayant un sens logique et secret."[223] He also wrote a preface (March, 1834), with the primary intention of pointing out the unifying thread in these fragments. The master said: "Le personnage qui traverse pour ainsi dire les six tableaux dont se compose *Même Histoire* n'est pas une figure; *c'est une pensée.*"[224] Since this *pensée* lacked continuity, the additional episode, *Souffrances inconnues*, was intended to fill the "trop forte lacune dans cette esquisse entre *le Rendez-vous* et *la Femme de trente ans.*"[225] The new chapter, "La Vallée du torrent," made the action of *Les Deux Rencontres* a logical outcome of the situation in which Hélène (the daughter of the woman of thirty) lived, as it motivated her elopement with the outlaw.[226] This otherwise irrational action is further clarified by the author in a "complément inédit," a later addition to the Preface of 1834. Explaining the girl's marriage, he said: "Chargée d'un fratricide, elle succombe sous les remords; elle ne se croit digne de personne; elle se voit en pensée la camarade des forçats. Son mariage avec un criminel est pour elle un ordre du ciel, une fatalité."[227] Besides these artistic and psychological justifications provided for the additions in *Même Histoire*, Balzac offered a more practical reason. In a letter of April, 1834, he wrote to Mme Charles Béchet: "Il faut, pour faire un volume de vingt-quatre feuilles avec l'ancien quatrième volume des *Scènes de la vie privée* [2d ed., 1832], ajouter quatre feuilles."[228] In this manner the new material met the need of the publishing firm. Moreover, the author did not fail to complain of the technical

[221] *OD.*, III, 382.

[222] "Scènes de la vie privée" (3d ed., 1834), Vol. IV.

[223] Lov. Coll., A 181, fol. 16.

[224] *OD.*, III, 383. Italics ours.   [225] *Ibid.*

[226] A theme that Balzac had already treated in *Argow le pirate* (1824).

[227] Lov., *Hist.*, pp. 415–16. So far as we know, critics have overlooked this additional information from Balzac's own pen.

[228] *Corr.*, p. 194.

difficulties in grafting the new episode and chapter to the old material. Nonetheless, these changes must have been motivated chiefly by his desire to achieve a certain artistic effect, for, in January, 1836, he wrote to Mme Hanska: "Nous réimprimons[229] en ce moment le quatrième volume des *Scènes de la Vie privée*, où j'ai fait de grands changements par rapport au sens général de *Même histoire*. Ainsi, la fuite d'Hélène avec le meurtrier est rendue presque vraisemblable; il a fallu longtemps pour trouver ces derniers nœuds."[230] In the Furne edition (1842) the story appeared as *La Femme de trente ans*, with six titled chapters, through all of which, for the first time, the characters bore the same names. But Balzac's logical mind was not yet satisfied with this second partial co-ordination. He was still tormented, while re-working the Furne edition,[231] by the lack of homogeneity and artistry in this novel. He shared these scruples with Mme Hanska in a letter of March 2, 1843. His intention had been, he said, to replace certain parts of the novel by something more suitable; but, he added: "... il fallait paraître, et je n'ai pas eu le temps de refaire ce mélodrame indigne de moi. Mon cœur d'honnête homme de lettres en saigne encore."[232] Thus, despite his several attempts, the novel remains an unfinished piece of work, with discrepancies in dates and flagrant offenses against psychology and artistic unity. The chief objection of most critics is based on the novelist's attempt to unify six distinct tales merely by ticketing different characters with the same names and endowing them with certain common characteristics. These defects have proved a reason for faultfinding by most of the critics since 1834.

Notwithstanding the difficulties of producing a unity of effect, Balzac had no hesitation about the classification of this novel. From the start it was essentially a portrait of the "jeune fille" and, later, of the "femme de trente ans"; therefore he rightfully placed it in the *Scènes de la vie privée*. Le Breton gave a somewhat terse characterization of the story, and unwittingly justified its classification, when he said: "... une forte étude de l'âme féminine, du mariage et de l'adultère."[233] The purpose of the novel (or mosaic) is given in the Preface of 1834. It is to "communi-

[229] This reprint of Vol. IV was issued by Werdet in 1837; it is not mentioned in Lov., *Hist.* See Canfield, art. cit., in *RHL*, XLI, 200. See also *MLN*, XLVIII (1933), 497.

[230] *LEt.*, I, 295.

[231] This volume with corrections made in Balzac's own hand may be consulted in the University of Chicago Libraries.

[232] *LEt.*, III, 118–19.   [233] Le Breton, *op. cit.*, p. 262.

quer à l'âme le vague d'une rêverie où les femmes puissent réveiller quelques-unes des vives impressions qu'elles ont conservées, de ranimer les
souvenirs épars dans la vie, pour en faire *surgir quelques enseignements.*"[234]
    La Femme de trente ans, as it stands today, is the story of Julie de Chat-
tillonest, who marries the dashing Victor d'Aiglemont against her father's
advice. The sensitive and imaginative Julie soon discovers the true character of her husband and silently suffers from abandonment and the
miseries of incompatibility. She meets a congenial friend in Lord Grenville but has learned to obey the social code; even at the cost of stifling
her hungry heart, she remains the mother of her small Hélène. When
Lord Grenville solves his problem by suicide, she retires to the country
in grief, with no compensating love for her child. Mme d'Aiglemont later
meets Charles de Vandenesse and loves again. The master-stroke of the
author in subjecting the heroine once more to the supreme test of honor
drew forth the following comment from Le Breton, usually a severe critic:
"Rien de plus vrai, rien de plus fort que les pages de *la Femme de trente
ans* où il [Balzac] met Mme d'Aiglemont en présence de Charles de Vandenesse ... de nouveau son [her] cœur va s'ouvrir, et c'est ce chaste, ce pur
amour d'autrefois qui aura préparé sa chute."[235] The eight-year-old Hélène
becomes her mother's silent judge. One wonders if Balzac had not had
occasion to observe the secret judgment of daughters upon their mothers
in the homes of Mme de Berny and of Mme d'Abrantès. No psychiatrist
of today could better analyze this child's actions than did Balzac in the
added chapter, "La Vallée du torrent"; thus he prepares for the grotesque
scene in the "Deux Rencontres." Mme d'Aiglemont's last ghastly punishment comes through her only remaining and favorite daughter Moïna,
who, ignorant of their relationship, falls in love with *her* half-brother, the
son of Charles de Vandenesse.
    In this psychological study of a woman's early struggle, for virtue's
sake, with her emotions, her aspirations toward an ideal love, and her
later transformation into a cruel mother, Balzac has penetrated into the
innermost soul of a woman. In spite of the piecemeal plot the heroine is
true to her nature and to her milieu. Her mode of living is the logical
product of her romantic imagination and of her ignorance of marriage,
just as variations in men are produced by occupations, and varieties in

---

[234] *OD.*, III, 383. Italics ours. Cf. Preface to the first edition of the *Scènes de la vie
privée, ibid.*, pp. 379-80.

[235] *Op. cit.*, p. 135.

animals by climate. Furthermore, Saint-Beuve asserts—and others have repeated the assertion—that Balzac is the inventor of the woman of thirty: "C'est là une de ses découvertes les plus réelles dans l'ordre du roman intime. La clef de son immense succès était tout entière dans ce premier petit chef-d'œuvre [*Même Histoire*]."[236] Even though he did not bring it to the artistic perfection which he sought, Balzac nevertheless achieved psychological consistency in the character of Mme d'Aiglemont. The author thought highly of this novel, and, in a letter to Mme Hanska, August 26, 1834, he said: "Mais c'est à faire frémir; tout cela est vrai. Jamais je n'ai été tant remué par une œuvre. C'est plus que *la Grenadière*, plus que *La Femme abandonnée*."[237]

This novel, with its careful analysis of domestic misery and its profound understanding of the motives of a woman's heart, naturally belongs to the *Scènes de la vie privée*.

Balzac had already, in the first edition of the *Scènes de la vie privée*, showed himself discerning in feminine psychology.[238] The study of women was one of his great preoccupations; hence they play an important role in the *Comédie humaine*. Our author owes his profound understanding of women to his intimate association with three devoted friends of this period, Mme de Berny, Mme Carraud, and Mme d'Abrantès. Doubtless the fickle Mme de Castries also contributed her share.[239] All these influenced his conception and portrayal of female character. Mme de Berny re-read and corrected his *Scènes de la vie privée;* Mme Carraud proved to be a most penetrating critic and a loyal friend, as is shown in her letters to the author; Mme d'Abrantès, during a long period of friendship (1825–38), revealed to him her innermost soul and that of her sex. Of Mme d'Abrantès, J. Turquan says: "Son influence dut donc être très grande et contribuer dans une large mesure à former la personnalité du jeune et déjà grand écrivain, surtout en l'éclairant sur les âmes des femmes, qu'elle ne lui peignait pas en beau."[240] It was she who helped Balzac to discover the woman of thirty. She was the prototype of the mature Mme d'Aigle-

---

[236] *Causeries du lundi*, II, 446. Sainte-Beuve prefers this novel in its early editions. Cf. Le Breton, *op. cit.*, p. 135; Wells, *op. cit.*, p. 112; Bellessort, *op. cit.*, p. 264.

[237] *LEt.*, I, 188. *La Grenadière* and *La Femme abandonnée*, also studies of conjugal unhappiness, were ultimately placed in the "Scènes de la vie privée."

[238] Bellessort concurs; *op. cit.*, p. 97.

[239] For a full treatment of the influence of women on Balzac, see Juanita H. Floyd, *Women in the Life of Balzac.*

[240] *La Générale Junot, duchesse d'Abrantès*, p. 371.

mont; and her daughter, Joséphine, was the model for Mme d'Aiglemont as "jeune fille." In 1831 Balzac wrote to Mme d'Abrantès asking that "Sœur Joséphine ne m'oublie pas en ses prières, moi qui me souviens d'elle en mes bouquins."[241] Balzac regarded some of these "bouquins" as character studies of women, to be used in a projected collective work, *Etudes de femmes*, to which he constantly referred in his notebook and in his letters. He hints in his *Avant-propos* at the difficulty of portraying women:

Quand Buffon peignit le lion, il achevait la lionne en quelques phrases; tandis que dans la Société la femme ne se trouve pas toujours être la femelle du mâle. Il peut y avoir deux êtres parfaitement dissemblables dans un mariage. ... L'Etat Social a des hasards que ne se permet pas la Nature, car il est la Nature plus la Société.[242]

The conception of the projected *Etudes de femmes* dates from the early spring of 1830. On April 16 of that year Balzac published in *La Mode* an article called "Visites: Un Pensionnat de jeunes demoiselles."[243] This is a sketch of a visit to a school where the author observed children at work and at play. The article was accompanied by a "Note" explaining the intentions of the author. "L'auteur se propose d'envisager, dans une série d'articles, la situation des femmes aux époques les plus intéressantes de leur vie. Il a dû commencer par l'enfance."[244]

The proposed *Etudes de femmes* was to consist of character studies, some of which were already written and published, either in the *Scènes de la vie privée*, in the *Romans et contes philosophiques*, or in the *Contes bruns*. There were to be others, not yet written, but already indicated by title. Balzac's plan for this work was so definite that he even asked Mme Émile de Girardin to write a preface for the volume. On July 29, 1832, he wrote to her, saying: "J'ai achevé un livre intitulé *Etudes de femmes;* il me faut une préface écrite par une femme. Voulez-vous me la faire?"[245] Balzac's term "achevé" is but an illusion—a perpetual illusion which makes him announce works as ready to appear which have not even been be-

[241] He spoke of her as "sœur" because she was for a while "sœur de charité" at Saint-Vincent-de-Paul; *ibid.*, p. 361.

[242] *Con.*, I, xxvii.

[243] Reprinted in *OD.*, II, 187. See also the "Catalogue des ouvrages" (*Con.*, I, xvi). It never entered the *Comédie humaine*.

[244] *Loc. cit.*

[245] See Spoelberch de Lovenjoul, *La Genèse d'un roman*, p. 113.

gun.[246] Still under the same self-delusion, he writes his mother on August 21, 1832: "J'ai fondu les *Etudes de femmes, les Conversations*, etc., dans une collection de trois ou quatre volumes originale [*sic*]."[247] He gives further details about the project to his publisher Mame in a letter from Aix, September 30, 1832:

> Vous aurez, vous, 3 volumes in-octavo prochainement: deux intitulés *Etudes de femmes* ... les *Etudes de femmes* se compléteraient de: *Etude de femme*, de *Sarrasine*, les deux histoires du *Conseil: Le Message* et *la Grande Bretèche*, de *Devoir d'une femme*, de la *Transaction*, bien refaite et corrigée, et bien d'autres choses. ... *La Femme abandonnée*, et d'autres que je garderai pour mettre de l'inédit ... [et] *Mme Firmiani*.[248]

One alignment of stories for this projected volume noted in Balzac's note-book includes, besides the above-mentioned titles, *Les Amours d'une laide* and *Une Fille d'Ève*.[249] A subsequent and enlarged grouping has these additional items: "*Dernières Etudes de femmes*, 8 vols. in-8°: *La Marana, La Succession, Les Orphelins (La Grenadière), Onda-Mulier, Saint-Jean, La Femme de trente ans*."[250] Further proof that *Etudes de femmes* was to be a collective title is found in an announcement, made early in 1833, of the ten volumes of the *Etudes de mœurs* divided into series. Among these are three volumes of *Etudes de femmes*.[251] This project was never realized; Balzac abandoned it after 1833, and the stories intended for the volumes were absorbed in the first three subdivisions of the *Etudes de mœurs*, with the exception of *Adieu*, which was placed in the *Etudes philosophiques*.

It would seem, then, that Balzac's announcement of a new plan made in the spring of 1833, at the home of Mme Surville, did away entirely with this project of a collection of women characters. It may be argued, also, that the collective title *Etudes de femmes* does not denote a setting, as

[246] E.g., *La Bataille, Les Trois Cardinaux*, and many other announced titles.

[247] *LF.*, p. 103. It is possible that Balzac meant "une collection originale de trois ... ."

[248] Lov. Coll., A 250, fols. 1–4. This letter is mutilated in the *Corr.*, p. 156. Of these tales, *Sarrasine* is now in the "Scènes de la vie parisienne"; *Le Devoir d'une femme (Adieu)* is in the "Etudes philosophiques"; all the others are in the "Scènes de la vie privée."

[249] Lov. Coll., A 181, fol. 18. The first tale never appeared; the second was placed in the "Scènes de la vie privée," *Fur.*, Vol. II.

[250] Lov. Coll., A 181, fol. 18. Item 1 is now in the "Etudes philosophiques"; 2, 4, and 5 never appeared; 3 and 6 are in the "Scènes de la vie privée."

[251] Lov., *Hist.*, p. 470.

does "Scènes de la vie privée" or "Scènes de la vie de province," since it is too general and vague. However, Balzac preserved the collective title in two stories, *Etude de femme* and *Autre Etude de femme;* the latter includes seven portraits of women. These might be divided into two groups: good women and "femmes légères." The four types defined in the first group are: (1) "la femme d'autrefois—la grande dame"; (2) "la femme moderne—la femme comme il faut[252] ou la femme élégante"; (3) "la femme bourgeoise"; (4) "la femme-auteur." The three types of the second group are concretely depicted in separate episodes narrating the punishments meted out to these "femmes légères." The first is Charlotte,[253] Henri de Marsay's first love; the tale is concluded by Bianchon, who says that her death "est une des plus belles que je connaisse." The second sketch is that of Rosina,[254] whose horrible punishment occurred during the French campaign in Russia. The last portrait of an adulteress is that of Mme de Merret, the heroine of *La Grande Bretèche.*

Balzac sought to portray women in most aspects of their social and private lives. His list of *femmes vertueuses* and *femmes criminelles*[255] proves that he ran almost the whole gamut of womankind—not, however, under the heading of *Etudes de femmes.* The projection of this work shows, nevertheless, that Balzac's evolving plan was a living, growing idea; that the shifting and adaptation of stories was a search for a harmonized and broader scheme. Although he did not completely carry out this project, he partly fulfilled it in a mosaic of stories included in the *Etudes de mœurs,* which is, of course, an enlargement of the narrow scope of the *Etudes de femmes.*

A few weeks after the *Scènes de la vie privée* had been given to the public, Balzac turned to the re-working of old and the writing of new tales of the philosophical type. To the twelve stories originally grouped with *La Peau de chagrin,* under the collective title *Romans et contes philosophiques,* Balzac now gave a briefer term, *Contes philosophiques,*[256] and, omitting the novel, reprinted them with the Introduction by Philarète

---

[252] Émile Blondet gives a detailed description of "la femme comme il faut." It originally appeared as an essay published by Balzac in the collective volumes, *Les Français peints par eux-mêmes* (1840).

[253] "La Femme du médecin," in *Contes bruns.*

[254] "La Maîtresse de notre colonel," *ibid.*   [255] *OD.,* III, 413.

[256] Published by Charles Gosselin in 2 vols., in octavo. Announced in the *Bibliographie de la France,* June 16, 1832.

Chasles in early June, 1832. The distribution of the stories in the two volumes differs from the 1831 edition, but there are no real changes in titles or in contents. This reprint was intended, says Balzac in the "Avis,"[257] to complete the set for those who bought the first edition of *La Peau de chagrin* in August, 1831.

In this same "Avis" Balzac announced a forthcoming volume, *Nouveaux Contes philosophiques*. Indeed, no sooner had he published the *Contes philosophiques* than he began on this new volume, to which he often referred as "le quatrième volume."[258] Since, in the 1831 edition of the *Romans et contes philosophiques* there were three volumes, this might be considered as the fourth volume of the whole collection. On the last cover page of the volume, among several announcements, is one which seems to confirm our view: "*Nouveaux Contes philosophiques*, formant le tome IV/ des *Romans et Contes*, troisième édition, ou le tome V de la première/édition de la *Peau de chagrin*. I vol. in-8, avec vignettes." This collective work was composed of four philosophical stories, two of which Balzac wrote in 1831, and two in 1832.

On June 10 the author wrote his mother to see Gosselin, the publisher, to whom he was promising "le manuscrit qui doit terminer le quatrième volume des *Contes* [*philosophiques*]."[259] Ultimately the volume ended with *Louis Lambert*, an autobiographical piece of fiction never previously published. In one of his self-deluding moods, Balzac informed Mme Carraud, on July 2, 1832, that he had but a few pages to add and that she should have the volume in a fortnight.[260] Yet it was far from being ready on July 20, for he then shared his fears and hopes about it with his sister: "... ce quatrième volume de *Contes philosophiques* doit être une dernière réponse à mes ennemis et doit faire pressentir une incontestable supériorité."[261] The volume was finally on sale in October[262] and contained: *Maître Cornélius, Madame Firmiani, L'Auberge rouge*, and *Louis Lambert*. This was the first volume-publication of the four stories; however, the first three had previously appeared in *La Revue de Paris*. As the collective title, *Nouveaux Contes philosophiques*, indicates, the tales were in a philosophical vein—hence in key with the central idea of *La Peau de*

---

[257] *OD.*, III, 405.

[258] *LF.*, pp. 77, 91.   [260] *Corr. Carraud*, p. 63.

[259] *Ibid.*, p. 77.   [261] *LF.*, p. 91.

[262] Published by Charles Gosselin, in 1 vol., in octavo. Announced in the *Bibliographie de la France*, October 20, 1832.

chagrin and the twelve old stories grouped with it. We now proceed to an examination of these narratives.

Baldensperger[263] thinks that Balzac was irritated by Sir Walter Scott's historical inaccuracy in *Quentin Durward*, and quotes Mme Surville as saying that Balzac "y riposte par *Maître Cornélius*." In the biography of her brother she adds: "... il trouvait que Walter Scott avait étrangement défiguré Louis XI, roi encore mal compris, selon lui. Cette colère lui fit composer *Maître Cornélius*, ouvrage où il met Louis XI en scène."[264] In view of the fact, however, that both portrayals of the king derive from the same sources, they are alike, maintains Professor Dargan[265] in his study. It is not unreasonable to suppose that Balzac was also annoyed by Scott's topographical errors, for he says: "Malgré la singulière fantaisie que l'auteur de *Quentin Durward* a eue de placer le château royal de Plessis-lez-Tours sur une hauteur, il faut se résoudre à le laisser où il était à cette époque, dans un fond, protegé de deux côtés par le Cher et la Loire."[266] But as to the location of the castle, Professor George D. Morris[267] says that "both Scott and Balzac are right." In all likelihood the castle was built on slightly rising ground in the middle of a large valley. Both L.-J. Arrigon and Pierre Abraham[268] assert that *Maître Cornélius* had its inception (between 1826 and 1828) in a projected historical novel, alluded to by Balzac as "un ouvrage consciencieux (*Le Capitaine des Boutefeux*), dont le sujet était pris dans les tems les plus orageux du 15e siècle."[269] This is precisely the period that Balzac depicted in *Maître Cornélius* (1831). Another interesting source is E. T. A. Hoffmann's *Fraülein von Scuderi*,[270] in which the obsession of a jeweler for his own work drives him to commit a series of murders. This general situation is paralleled in the case of the miser Cornélius. The vital interest, however, as pointed out by Professor Morris,[271] is centered in the figure of Cornélius, "the victim of his own avarice," and the devastating effects of the passion upon his personality.

---

[263] *Op. cit.*, pp. 67, 108. [264] Surville, *op. cit.*, p. 104.

[265] Art. cit. in *PMLA*, XLIX (1934), 616.

[266] *Nouveaux Contes philosophiques* (1832), p. 85.

[267] See *Three Stories by Balzac*, p. 183.

[268] *Les Débuts littéraires*, pp. 237–38; *Créatures chez Balzac*, p. 68.

[269] Cited by Pierre Abraham, *ibid.*, p. 103. Also see above, p. 27.

[270] Traduit de l'allemand par M. Loève-Veimars (Paris, 1830).

[271] *Op. cit.*, pp. xxvi–xxvii. Cf. also "Balzac's Treatment of History in *Maître Cornélius*," *Philological Quarterly*, X (1931), 356.

This continues Balzac's fundamental principle, as expressed in the *Peau de chagrin*, and for this reason the author from the start placed the narrative among the philosophical tales.

The first publication of the story was incomplete. This fact caused a growing coolness between Balzac and Amédée Pichot, the editor of the *Revue de Paris*, in which *Maître Cornélius* appeared in December, 1831. Spoelberch de Lovenjoul explains the misunderstanding: "*La Revue de Paris* inséra, sans que l'auteur fût mis à même d'en corriger les épreuves, l'une des plus intéressantes études philosophiques de Balzac: *Maître Cornélius*."[272] The publication of the curtailed and uncorrected manuscript sent Balzac into a fury. He declared everywhere, and wrote to Zulma Carraud on January 19, 1832, that his "*article Cornélius* [était] massacré par le directeur."[273] It appears, says M. Bouteron, that Pichot did not hesitate to cut out a few sentences here and there "pour bien tomber en pages."[274] Explanations and excuses by Pichot only aggravated the situation, and in March, 1833, Balzac broke his connection with the *Revue de Paris* entirely.

The character of Cornélius, the personification of avarice, parallels that of King Louis XI, whose banker and friend he was. The old Lombard, a somnambulist, hides his treasures in his sleep. On awakening, he does not remember and believes himself robbed. Two of his apprentices, accused of the theft, lose their lives unjustly; but the third brings about the downfall of the miser. This young man, Georges d'Estouteville, is of noble birth and the lover of the Comtesse Marie de Saint-Vallier, the favorite daughter of the king. In order to gain access to her apartment Georges disguises himself as an apprentice and so is admitted into the house of the miser, which adjoins that of the Comtesse de Saint-Vallier. His disguise is discovered, but with the help of the countess his innocence is proved. Who, then, is robbing the miser? The king shrewdly discovers the plight of the banker and thus brings his career to an end. The book form contains an inserted passage which clarifies the connection of *Maître Cornélius* with *La Peau de chagrin:*

> L'Idée la plus vivace et la mieux matérialisée de toutes les idées humaines, l'idée par laquelle l'homme se représente lui-même en créant en dehors de lui cet être tout fictif, nommé *la propriété*, ce démon moral lui enfonçait à chaque instant ses griffes acérées dans le cœur. ... Ses veilles durent être affreuses; il

---

[272] *Une Page perdue de H. de Balzac*, p. 42.

[273] *Corr. Carraud*, p. 47.   [274] *Ibid.*, n. 2.

[Cornélius] était seul aux prises avec la nuit, le silence, le remords, la peur, avec toutes les pensées que l'homme a le mieux personnifiées, instinctivement peut-être, ... cet homme si puissant, ... dut succomber aux horreurs du supplice qu'il s'était créé. Tué par quelques pensées plus aiguës que toutes celles auxquelles il avait résisté jusqu'alors, il se coupa la gorge avec un rasoir.[275]

Excessive miserliness destroys the miser himself. This philosophical study of the effects of a devouring passion forms an integral part not only of the collection under consideration but ultimately of the *Etudes philosophiques.*

Balzac placed *Madame Firmiani*[276] in the *Nouveaux Contes philosophiques;* but, since the tale did not depict the detrimental influence of exaggerated thought or passion, it did not belong there: he really intended to place the work in the projected volumes of the *Etudes de femmes,*[277] as he explained to Mame, who was to publish the *Nouveaux Contes philosophiques:* "Aussitôt que le IV⁶ volume de mes *Contes philosophiques* sera épuisé, j'en retirerai *Mme Firmiani* qui entrera dans les *Etudes de femmes.* Ce IV⁶ volume ayant 27 feuilles et *Mme Firmiani* trois feuilles, je n'aurai rien à y remplacer, 24 feuilles étant suffisantes."[278] It was Charles Gosselin, however, who actually published Volume IV of the collection in October, 1832, and to him Balzac gave similar instructions: "Dans le quatrième [volume] je retrancherai *Madame Firmiani.* Le volume a vingt-sept feuilles, elle n'en a que trois. Ainsi, le volume peut rester avec vingt-quatre sans danger, d'autant [plus] qu'il y aura une demi-feuille ajoutée dans [*Louis*] *Lambert.*"[279] As has been shown above, the projected *Etudes de femmes* had been abandoned; therefore, Balzac temporarily shifted *Madame Firmiani* to the first edition of the "Scènes de la vie parisienne,"[280] in order to supply the required number of pages for these volumes. Ultimately, in 1842, he placed the story in the "Scènes de la vie privée,"[281] where it rightfully belongs, for it is in this subdivision that he gives a series of portraits of women who are, says Davin, "marquées du même sceau, celui du sentiment égarant un moment la vertu. ... la femme n'est jamais fautive que par passion."[282] Balzac's first conception of Mme Firmiani, as it stands in his notebook, suggests that the heroine might not

[275] *Nouveaux Contes philosophiques* (1832), pp. 129–30.

[276] This story first appeared in *La Revue de Paris*, February, 1832.

[277] See above, pp. 67–69.

[278] Lov. Coll., A 250, fols. 1–4.

[279] Lov. Coll., A 281, fol. 140.

[280] Mme Béchet, 1835; Vol. IV.

[281] *Fur.*, Vol. I. It is now in *Con.*, Vol. III.

[282] Lov., *Hist.*, p. 54.

have been qualified for his list of "femmes vertueuses,"[283] but he ultimately portrayed, under the name of Mme Firmiani, a superior type of woman. Like *La Bourse* (also finally classified in the "Scènes de la vie privée"), *Madame Firmiani* is an optimistic work. The heroine, serious, intelligent, and noble, is the talk of the town. She is devoted to Octave de Camps, who, so runs the rumor, has lost his fortune because of her. After the death of her husband she marries Octave secretly at Gretna Green and makes him pay his father's debts. When his name is thus cleared, she announces their marriage. Octave's old uncle, M. de Bourbonne, touched by Mme Firmiani's actions and words, says to her: "Ma nièce, ... autrefois nous faisions l'amour, aujourd'hui vous aimez."[284] Thus he emphasizes the contrast between women of the old regime and those of modern times.

Balzac told Charles Rabou, in a letter dated May 18, 1831, that he wrote *L'Auberge rouge*[285] as a relief from his labors on *La Peau de chagrin*. He took this "distraction" somewhat strenuously, since in the same letter he continues: "Je suis en ce moment à cheval sur un crime, et je mange, je me couche dans *l'Auberge rouge*, de manière à donner, mardi matin ... un joli petit manuscrit ... une copie sans ratures, léchée, pourléchée, coquettement corrigée."[286] In order to provide a setting for his story he asks Rabou for exact details concerning the Republican Army in Germany. Here Balzac's theory of the ravaging influence of thought upon personality is realistically portrayed. According to Davin, it is in this tale that "les plus sévères déductions du thème général"[287] of the *Etudes philosophiques* converge in the secret remorse which causes the disintegration of Mauricey's personality. His overwrought nerves, under the continual remembrance of the crime, effect the complete disorganization of his system and his eventual death. This outcome naturally brings the story in line with *La Peau de chagrin*. In *L'Auberge rouge*, the plan of the murder is conceived by one man and involuntarily transmitted to the mind of another, who carries it out. The transference of thought is a psychic phenomenon now acknowledged by many psychologists. Balzac's imagination creates a situation, as in *Le Réquisitionnaire*, in which an idea

---

[283] Lov. Coll., A 181, fol. 44.

[284] *Nouveaux Contes philosophiques*, p. 177.

[285] This story first appeared in *La Revue de Paris*, August 10–27, 1831. See Ruth B. Dunn, "Variations in the First and Second Editions of Balzac's *L'Auberge rouge*" (unpublished Master's thesis, University of Chicago, 1924).

[286] *Corr.*, pp. 85–86.   [287] Lov., *Hist.*, p. 204.

leads to definite action. The author makes a distinction between fact and the idea which begets it; he contrasts divine and human justice; he proves that man's own conscience can be far more terrible in its devastating effects than the death, even of an innocent man, administered by law.

In the 1837 edition of *L'Auberge rouge*,[288] on the back of the title-page, Balzac gave a quotation omitted in the subsequent editions of the story: "Une idée causer des souffrances physiques, hein! qu'en dis-tu? *Etudes philosophiques*, t. XXII, *Histoire intellectuelle de L. Lambert*, 3ᵉ éd." The later omission of this quotation is regrettable, for it makes clear his purpose and the relation of the story to the basic principle of the philosophical tales. That Mauricey suffered morally and physically amid his blood-stained wealth, that he was pursued by remorse for his crime, is reason enough for Balzac's grouping *L'Auberge rouge* with the philosophical tales and later keeping it consistently in the *Etudes philosophiques*.

The *Notice biographique sur Louis Lambert* concludes the collective volume of the *Nouveaux Contes philosophiques*. It deals with Balzac's own "état d'âme," his theories, his treatise on the will—in fact, it contains more concerning the author's childhood, youth, and beliefs than any of his semi-autobiographical works, such as *La Peau de chagrin*, *Albert Savarus*, *César Birotteau*, or Part II of *Illusions perdues*. On this point Champfleury, Bettelheim, and Curtius[289] agree, despite Mme Surville's assertion that only the first part of *Louis Lambert* portrays her brother.[290]

The first conception of *Louis Lambert*, although under a different title, dates back to 1827 or 1828. In the "Avertissement"[291] to *Le Gars* (*Les Chouans*), Balzac gives a fictitious biography of the author, "Victor Morillon," one of his own pen-names. This life, maintains Pierre Abraham,[292] anticipates in many points the biography of *Louis Lambert*. Balzac actually began the novel in June, 1832, and finished it in July of the same year. Greatly preoccupied with *Louis Lambert*, he spoke of it at length in letters written in 1832 and the early part of 1833. His ambition in this work was to emulate Goethe and Byron.[293] His hopes for a good sale and popularity ran high.[294] On November 26, 1832, he wrote from Nemours to

---

[288] *Etudes philosophiques*, Vol. XVII (Delloye et Lecou).

[289] *Balzac au collège*, p. 32; *Balzac*, pp. 125–26; *Balzac, sein Leben, sein Werk*, p. 315 and *passim*.

[290] Surville, *op. cit.*, p. 20. See also Gautier, *op. cit.*, p. 14.

[291] Lov. Coll., A 13, fols. 1–6. See above, pp. 27, 29.

[292] *Créatures chez Balzac*, pp. 79–88.

[293] *LF.*, p. 91.   [294] *Ibid.*, p. 99.

76   EVOLUTION OF BALZAC'S "COMEDIE HUMAINE"

Charles Gosselin: "*Louis Lambert*, œuvre de mélancolie ne nuira pas plus à la vente des *Romans et Contes* [*philosophiques*] que *Atala* n'a nui au *Génie du christianisme*. Il popularisera cette longue entreprise."[295] While supposedly resting at Aix in September, 1832, Balzac wrote to Zulma Carraud of laborious emendations and additions: "J'ai comme une ourse léché mon petit. ... En somme, je suis satisfait, c'est bien; c'est une œuvre de profonde mélancolie et de science."[296] George Sand approved of the novel, which she called "votre beau et bon livre,"[297] while Paul Bourget said that *Louis Lambert* was the "monographie de sa [Balzac's] propre intelligence."[298]

The center of interest in *Louis Lambert* is not the plot, which is very slight, but the psychology of Balzac.[299] This work particularly reflects the author's readings on mysticism and his study of Swedenborg's writings. *Louis Lambert* showed progress in the development of the theory that a ruling passion or obsessive interest in any one thing destroys personality. Thought introverted, so to speak, prodding into the innermost parts of the soul, or, in the words of Bellessort, into "les mystères du moi, dans les abîmes de la personnalité humaine,"[300] leads to the insanity and ultimately to the death of Lambert. Balzac himself often conceived of thought as a physical entity. His *alter ego*, Louis Lambert, says: "Aussi, la Pensée m'apparaissait-elle comme une puissance toute physique, accompagnée de ses innombrables générations. Elle était une nouvelle humanité sous une autre forme."[301] An idea, Balzac said in *L'Auberge rouge*, can cause physical suffering; and to prove his theory he describes thought thus: "Si, par exemple, je pense vivement à l'effet que produirait la lame de mon canif en entrant dans mon doigt, j'y ressens tout à coup une douleur aiguë comme si je m'étais réellement coupé: il n'y a de moins que le sang."[302] This aspect of the reality of thought is succinctly expressed by Félix Davin: "*La lame use le fourreau*, dit le peuple. M. de Balzac, lui, écrit *Louis Lambert* ... Pour Louis Lambert, y dit-il, *la Volonté, la Pensée*

[295] Lov. Coll., A 287, fols. 103–24.

[296] *Corr. Carraud*, p. 71.

[297] Art. cit., *Nouvelles littéraires*, July 26, 1930.

[298] Introduction to the *Répertoire de la Comédie humaine de H. de Balzac*, by A. Cerfberr and J. Christophe, p. ix.

[299] See Chancel, *op. cit.*, p. 459.   [301] *Nouveaux Contes philosophiques*, p. 343.

[300] Bellessort, *op. cit.*, p. 96.   [302] *Ibid.*, p. 319.

étaient des forces vives."[303] He considers this novel the most penetrating expression of the fundamental principle of the *Etudes philosophiques*, "la pensée tuant le penseur." It is evident why Balzac grouped *Louis Lambert* with the philosophical tales and placed it permanently in *Etudes philosophiques*, of which it is as truly a part as is *La Peau de chagrin*. In the Preface to the *Livre mystique* (1835), in which the novel was included, Balzac explains his work: "*Louis Lambert* est le mysticisme pris sur le fait, le voyant marchant à sa vision, conduit au ciel par les faits, par ses idées, par son tempérament; là est l'histoire des voyants."[304]

Louis Lambert, Séraphita, Les Proscrits, and *Jésus-Christ en Flandre,* all in the same category, deal with the same theory, which includes elements of mysticism, Swedenborgianism, and pseudo-science. Balzac's idealistic theory of thought and of the will or soul is considered by Taine, in his classical essay[305] on Balzac, as romance in the field of psychology and metaphysics. In this novel Balzac once more applies the principle of *La Peau de chagrin* and, generally, of the *Romans et contes philosophiques.* Thought can be the cause either of good or of evil; an idea can find expression in a devouring desire or ambition, as in *La Peau de chagrin;* in remorse, as in *L'Auberge rouge* or *Melmoth réconcilié;* or in maternal and paternal love, as in *Le Réquisitionnaire* and *Un Drame au bord de la mer.* In all these philosophical tales thought is transformed into sentiment and then into action, good or bad—usually bad.

Louis Lambert is the story of the school days of a sensitive and intelligent youth to whom the rigid discipline of the college brings great suffering of mind and body. The second phase of his short life begins in Paris with his struggles as a student in the clutches of poverty. Ill-health brings him back to provincial life, where he meets Pauline de Villenoix, the only one who understands his philosophical ravings. He falls in love and is to marry her; but the absorption of his mind in metaphysics completely detaches him from daily life, and he becomes insane. His fiancée alone understands his folly and devotes herself to him until his death. Balzac's

---

[303] Lov., *Hist.*, p. 202. In this connection, M. B. Ferguson in a recent study states: "La Volonté apparaît surtout chez Balzac comme une force agissante dont le moteur prédominant est la passion. ... La Volonté ... régit la conduite extérieure." The superior form of this "Volonté" is "la pensée" (*La Volonté dans la "Comédie humaine" de Balzac*, pp. 92–94).

[304] *OD.*, III, 424.

[305] *Nouveaux Essais de critique et d'histoire*, "Balzac," pp. 63–70.

doctrine as held by Lambert, coupled with his passionate temperament, results in a disordered mind and an untimely end.

Of the four stories just discussed, three[306] were permanently classed in the *Etudes philosophiques* for very good reasons. Yet Balzac did not include them in the third (marked fourth[307]) edition (March, 1833), of the *Romans et contes philosophiques*[308]—a collective title then appearing for the last time before it gave way to the more comprehensive *Etudes philosophiques*. When Charles Gosselin brought out the first edition of *La Peau de chagrin*, little did he imagine that from August, 1831, to March, 1833, the publication of Balzac's philosophical stories would be one of his chief occupations. In a letter to Mame of September 30, 1832,[309] Balzac indicated that he was already planning a fourth (really a third) edition of the *Romans et contes philosophiques*. He confirmed this plan in a letter to his mother in October: "J'ai aussi un remaniement des *Contes philosophiques* pour la quatrième édition, qui se fera aux environs d'avril."[310] This edition entailed a good deal of labor, in revisions and additions, although no new stories were added. Toward the end of January, 1833, he tells Mme Hanska: "Je travaille dix-huit heures par jour. Je me suis aperçu des défauts de style qui déparent *la Peau de chagrin;* je la corrige pour la rendre irréprochable; mais après deux mois de travail, ... je découvre encore une centaine de fautes. Ce sont des chagr:ns de poète."[311] Early in March, 1833, Gosselin put the four volumes on sale. The first two contained *La Peau de chagrin*, omitted from the *Contes philosophiques*, and the last two were identical in distribution of stories with the two volumes of the June, 1832, edition. From a letter to Gosselin dated November 13, 1833, we learn that Balzac was not satisfied with this edition; he considered it "mal conçue et mal fabriquée."[312] Be that as it may, the note-

[306] All except *Madame Firmiani*.

[307] See *OD.*, III, 406–7. Balzac explains the confusion in numbering these editions thus: The first edition was published in August, 1831; the second was published in 3 vols., September, 1831, and was designated as the third on account of its two printings (which should have been marked as the second and the third). The fourth edition (or the third, should the two printings be considered as one edition) was published in 4 vols., March, 1833.

[308] Published by Charles Gosselin in 4 vols.

[309] Lov. Coll., A 250, fols. 1–4.

[310] *LF.*, p. 128.   [311] *LEt.*, I, 7.

[312] Lov. Coll., A 287, fols. 103–24. See also *Revue bleue*, XX (1903), 644.

worthy fact about all these philosophical tales is that they form the nucleus of the *Etudes philosophiques*, the second great division of the *Comédie humaine*, just as the 1830 edition of the *Scènes de la vie privée* is the basis of the *Etudes de mœurs*, the first great division of Balzac's final structure.

With this third edition of the *Romans et contes philosophiques* ends the first period of Balzac's literary career.[313] It is pertinent, therefore, to review briefly his achievements and the progress of his changing plans up to 1833.

By this time he had issued six publications under four collective titles and had announced two projected collective titles: the *Scènes de la vie politique* and the *Scènes de la vie militaire*. Of these, only extracts had as yet appeared. Three of the six publications were enlargements of previous editions. Under the first collective title, the *Scènes de la vie privée*, the author grouped together fifteen domestic stories similar in theme and atmosphere; under the *Romans et contes philosophiques* and the *Nouveaux Contes philosophiques* he assembled seventeen stories developing the same basic idea, to wit, that exaggerated thought and passion may disorganize personality.

No shifting of stories occurs within this period, but after 1833 ten[314] out of those thirty-two tales were moved temporarily or permanently to other subdivisions. One, *La Comédie du diable*, was never admitted to the *Comédie humaine*. Of the six tales in the first edition of the *Scènes de la vie privée*, two were later moved temporarily to the "Scènes de la vie parisienne" but were ultimately restored to their original classification. Of the fifteen titles in the second edition of the *Scènes de la vie privée*, nine were new. Five of these were shifted: three temporarily, one to the "Scènes de la vie parisienne" and two to the "Scènes de la vie de province"; and two permanently, one to the "Scènes de la vie de province" and the other to the "Etudes philosophiques."

From the *Romans et contes philosophiques*, as has just been said, one tale was discarded; two were moved to the "Scènes de la vie parisienne"—one permanently, the other temporarily; this latter was ultimately classified in the "Scènes de la vie privée." To this group was also added permanently one tale from the *Nouveaux Contes philosophiques*.

These temporary misplacements were due, in some instances, to the exigency of filling a definite number of pages in the new volumes. In

313 See above, p. 79.
314 All these shiftings are indicated in the table (p. 180).

1840 Balzac, commenting upon the arrangement of his earlier volumes, stated that he was aware of certain defects which had arisen from the "nécessité où se trouve l'auteur de publier séparément les différentes parties d'un grand tout."[315] However, when the number of novels for the new subdivisions had increased, the author rearranged his classifications logically and restored some of the misplaced stories to their original rubrics. It is remarkable that, even in the first period of Balzac's literary career, there is a rather high percentage of stories—twenty-six out of thirty-two—that were, at the very beginning, placed in the groups to which they were ultimately assigned. Such a high percentage of correct classification from the start points to Balzac's conscious primary urge toward order and unity in his writings; this order becomes characteristic of his way of thinking and is also disciplinary in its effects. His grouping already represents two major types of fiction—contemporary manners and philosophical tales—which anticipated the two grand divisions of the second period, the *Etudes de mœurs au XIXᵉ siècle* and the *Etudes philosophiques*.

Meanwhile, in the *avis*, prefaces, introductions, and in the letters of this period, Balzac alludes to and discusses his various plans aligning the fields and the scope of his writings. Out of these tentative programs gradually developed the one plan toward which he had been feeling his way in these six publications.

IV. SECOND PERIOD IN BALZAC'S LITERARY CAREER: 1833–37

Before we enter upon a discussion of the second period of Balzac's career certain literary devices which had intruded into his work should be recognized and dealt with as an influence in the ripening of his scheme. In the autumn of 1832 he had been making plans to publish, toward the middle of 1833, a complete edition[316] of his works to date. In the ensuing revision of previously published novels he must have become aware of the possibilities for expansion, as well as of certain methods unconsciously used.

We shall note three factors or devices which led to Balzac's announcement in the home of Mme Surville and to future developments. First, he recognized that certain passages held germs of plots for future novels. For

[315] Preface to the first edition of *Pierrette*, *OD.*, III, 544.

[316] This later became the *Etudes de mœurs*, published between 1833 and 1837.

example, in *Les Dangers de l'inconduite (Gobseck)*,[317] a lawyer, Derville, retells in the *salon* of Mme de Grandlieu the professional experiences related to him by Gobseck: "Hier une tragédie: un père s'asphyxie parce qu'il ne peut plus nourrir ses enfants ... un vieux négociant sur le penchant d'une faillite, une mère qui veut cacher la faute de son fils."[318] This passage remained unchanged in the edition of 1832; but Balzac, in 1834, added the following plot: "Un grand sur le déclin de la faveur, et qui, faute d'argent, va perdre le fruit de ses efforts."[319] The first quotation suggests the theme of *Père Goriot* (1834), even though Goriot died a natural death. The "négociant" could easily be identified with César Birotteau, who died at the age of fifty-one. To Balzac still in his thirties, the time at which he began the novel at Frapesle[320] in April, 1834, fifty-one might have seemed "vieux," or in writing he may have changed his idea of the character's age. "Une mère qui veut cacher la faute de son fils" is probably Agathe Rouget in *La Rabouilleuse (Les Deux Frères)*.[321] Philippe Bridau had stolen his aunt's savings; everyone knew his guilt, but his mother, to protect her favorite son, pretended that she took the money. "Je l'ai prise [la somme] pour Philippe, j'ai cru pouvoir la remettre avant que vous ne vous en aperçussiez."[322] On looking for her silver, to pawn it and replace the stolen sum, she found only a receipt from the broker's shop. "Un grand sur le déclin ..." is perhaps an allusion to Rabourdin in *Les Employés*, an honest and superior man, who after six years of work on an administrative plan failed because of bureaucratic corruption. His opponent, M. Baudoyer, bought the support of the influential men at first in favor of Rabourdin.[323]

A passage of similar prophetic nature in *La Peau de chagrin* has remained essentially the same in subsequent editions. Émile, the journalist and drinking companion of Raphaël, addresses Aquilina, "une femme légère": "As-tu donc, comme ta patronne, un noble et terrible *conspira-*

[317] Cf. Preston, *op. cit.*, p. 20. Miss Preston does not show the evolution of the passage.

[318] *Scènes de la vie privée* (1830), I, 194–95.

[319] "Scènes de la vie parisienne" (1834), I, 258. In all subsequent editions the passage remained the same.

[320] *LEt.*, I, 149. See also *Corr. Carraud*, pp. 210, 276.

[321] These later titles reach beyond the period now considered.

[322] *Les Deux Frères*, éd. Souverain (1842), I, 193.

[323] *La Femme supérieure*, éd. Werdet (1838), II, 148, 177.

teur qui t'aime et sache mourir pour toi? ... dit vivement Émile réveillé par cette apparence de poésie. —Je l'ai eu! ... répondit-elle; mais la guillotine était ma rivale."[324] This information concerning Aquilina's executed lover leads to the subplot in *Melmoth réconcilié* (1835).[325] Castanier, having sold his soul to Melmoth, had acquired the latter's power, through which he learned that Aquilina had deceived him and had hidden in her closet his rival, a young officer. When Castanier forced him to come out, the officer challenged him to a duel. Castanier answered: "Pourquoi vous tuerais-je? Vous avez sur le cou une ligne rouge que je vois. La *guillotine* vous attend. Oui, vous mourrez en place de grève. ... Vous *conspirez* contre le gouvernement."[326]

Second, during this re-working Balzac saw that a few characters reappeared in his pages: Pauline de Villenoix, Captain Bianchi, and Mme de Beauséant.[327] Not only had the author made some use of reappearing characters at this early period (December, 1832), but he definitely documented them as they appeared in the earlier story—for instance, in the case of Captain Bianchi. This method was frequently employed after 1835. In the first edition of *Les Marana*, a reference to the captain led Balzac to give the gist of the story in which he had appeared previously:

> Au siège de Tarragone, les Italiens perdirent leur célèbre capitaine Bianchi, le même qui, pendant la campagne, avait parié manger le cœur d'une sentinelle espagnole, et le mangea. Ce divertissement de bivouac a été raconté récemment dans un livre[328] où se trouvent, sur le 6ᵉ de ligne, des détails qu'il est inutile de répéter ici.

Balzac continues with an account of Bianchi's military bravery and his death, concluding with an apology: "Cette digression était nécessaire pour expliquer comment le 6ᵉ de ligne entra le premier dans Tarragone, et pourquoi le désordre dégénéra si promptement en un léger pillage."[329] By such means the novelist established points of connection between individual stories, but the arresting fact is that reappearing characters existed in 1832, notwithstanding M. Bouteron's statement that one would

[324] *La Peau de chagrin* (1st ed.), I, 194. Italics ours.

[325] See below, p. 114.

[326] *Etudes philosophiques*, éd. Werdet, XXII, 130–34. Italics ours.

[327] Appearing respectively in *Le Curé de Tours*, *Les Marana*, and *La Duchesse de Langeais*.

[328] *Contes bruns*, "Une Conversation entre onze heures et minuit."

[329] "Les Marana," *La Revue de Paris*, December, 1832, pp. 235–36.

seek "vainement la trace de ce procédé dans les premiers romans de Balzac publiés de 1829 à 1832, sa découverte ne semble pas antérieure à 1833."[330] The artistic possibilities of reappearing characters as an effective device for unification in a growing plan must have struck Balzac with illuminating force.

Third, by 1832 the author conceived the idea of social classification, thereby introducing the sociological interests of his novels. Mme Carraud, in reading Part II of *Les Marana* (1832), saw this implication and criticized it as unsound: "... vous érigez en principe la nécessité des classifications sociales, et voulez parquer l'espèce humaine d'après le hasard de la naissance."[331] Balzac firmly answered that the principle of social classification is for him "indiscutable, ... c'est un point arrêté."[332] He held that a man is inevitably conditioned by his inheritance and environment,[333] and in *Les Marana* he emphasized the fact that Juana and Diard belong to different "social species." From the data of Juana's inheritance and environment Balzac determines her behavior in certain circumstances and conditions. In like manner he characterizes her husband, Diard, by his habits of the "mauvais ton de l'armée, des mœurs de sa province et d'une incomplète éducation," and represents him as entirely "incapable de monter les hauts échelons de l'ordre social."[334] This deterministic theory, based on observation of society,[335] doubtless lay back of Balzac's idea of classifying mankind into groups, not only according to milieu but according to trades and professions as well.[336] In 1839 he said: "Il n'y a plus d'originalité que dans les professions, de comique que dans les habitudes."[337] Anticipating this theory, he had already adopted, in 1832, the approach and method of the biologist in arranging and classifying his material as if according to the established scientific laws. He recognized,

[330] Introduction to Balzac's *Comédie humaine*, Editions de la Nouvelle Revue française (1935), I, xx. All subsequent references to this volume will be "*N.R.F.*, I."

[331] *Corr. Carraud*, pp. 131–32.

[332] *Ibid.*, p. 137.

[333] Cf. theories of G. Saint-Hilaire. See below, sec. v.

[334] *Con.*, XXIX, 107.

[335] It is pertinent to add that 1832 was the year of Balzac's infatuation with the Marquise de Castries; he keenly felt the social barrier between them. This experience must have sharpened his growing conviction of the influence of environment and of social distinctions.

[336] Cf. Merlant, *op. cit.*, p. 374; Preston, *op. cit.*, chap. iv.

[337] Preface to *Une Fille d'Ève, OD.*, III, 521.

nevertheless, that social differences do not have the complete fixity of natural laws.[338] For artistic purposes, however, this method of grouping was precisely that needed later to present systematically the great wealth of material which French society offered.

To Balzac, working as critic and artist in the revision and arrangement of his works during the winter of 1832 and 1833, the three factors just discussed afforded a prospect, hitherto unperceived in its fulness, of expanding and unifying his novels into a complete whole in which all the component parts would be logically connected.

The crystallization of this conception can be traced in his correspondence. On September 22, 1832, he wrote to his mother of his plans for a complete edition (the later *Etudes de mœurs*): "J'offrirai ainsi un bel ensemble d'œuvres";[339] in January, 1833, he informed Mme Hanska that he wished to "construire un monument, durable plus par la masse et par l'amas des matériaux que par la beauté de l'édifice";[340] and by March, 1833, he seemed to feel certain of success, even if he had, as he says, "à travailler pendant trois ans," for, he adds, "il faut refaire, recorriger, mettre tout à l'état monumental."[341] These successive statements indicate a preoccupation with the scope and number of novels, with totality and massiveness rather than with artistry.

The strain of Balzac's work at that time was tremendous. He wrote to Mme Carraud that he lived in an atmosphere of ideas, plans, and conceptions "qui se croisent, bouillent, pétillent dans ma tête à me rendre fou."[342] By April, 1833, he was forced to seek rest at La Poudrerie. A month later he returned to Paris, where, according to M. Bouteron, he resumed "comme par magie, son grand travail, ses seize heures par jour et la plus grande somme de courage et d'inspiration."[343] There, in white heat, Balzac hammered into shape an idea latent in his brain which was eventually to insure that unity and solidity which he sought for his work. This conception had behind it years of thinking and preparation and culminated in the joyous cry "Eureka!" uttered before his sister. The date of this announcement is open to dispute. Unfortunately, Mme Surville did not record this occurrence until 1856, twenty-three years later. It remains a question, therefore, whether she used her brother's exact words or wrote in the light of what he had accomplished since 1833. She states:

338 *Avant-propos*, pp. xxvi–xxvii.

339 *LF.*, p. 120.

340 *LEt.*, I, 4.

341 *Corr. Carraud*, p. 137.

342 *Ibid.*, p. 129. Letter dated February, 1833.

343 *Ibid.*, pp. 144, 147.

Ce ne fut que vers 1833, lors de la publication de son *Médecin de campagne,* qu'il pensa *à relier tous ses personnages pour en former une société complète.* Le jour où il fut illuminé de cette idée fut un beau jour pour lui! ... Saluez-moi, nous dit-il joyeusement, car je suis tout bonnement en train de devenir un génie! ... Il nous déroule alors son plan qui l'effrayait bien un peu; quelque vaste que fût son cerveau, il fallait du temps pour y emménager ce plan-là.[344]

Mme Surville here dates her brother's declaration as contemporary with the publication of *Le Médecin de campagne,* known to be in September, 1833. However, he had employed prior to that date, as shown above, a method of unity usually assumed as motivating his famous announcement, that of reappearing characters. Another tenet of unity, also prior to September, 1833, is evinced in his extended grouping of stories in the "Scènes de la vie parisienne" (second subdivision of the *Etudes de mœurs*). The negotiations for their publication were already in process between May 29 and June 1, 1833. It is precisely in *Les Marana* and *La Duchesse de Langeais,* included in this grouping, that there are found earlier examples of reappearing characters. It seems impossible that he should not announce until September what he embodied in works prior to May. These facts lead me to believe that Balzac made his declaration in May, 1833, during the arrangements for the publication of the "Scènes de la vie parisienne," rather than in September. Mme Surville continues her report as if in the words of Balzac: "Comme je me laisserai tranquillement traiter de *faiseur de nouvelles* à présent, tout en taillant mes pierres! Je me réjouis d'avance de l'étonnement des myopes quand ils verront le grand édifice qu'elles formeront." She tells of her brother's musing over his characters as if they were real people: "Je n'invente pas la nature humaine, je l'observe dans le passé et le présent, et je tâche de la peindre telle qu'elle est."[345]

The three outstanding points, we repeat, in Mme Surville's account are: (1) the correlation of characters; (2) the purpose to create a complete, representative society; (3) the vastness of the author's plan for coordination. The *plan* as here used by Balzac had undergone a modification. This word no longer connotes merely subjects and scope of his works; but now in 1833, according to the author's sister, it implies methods, guiding principles, the underlying theory of his writings, and their correspondences—in short, the *plan* has become a matter of procedure as well as of material and scope; it has developed into a whole scheme, for, as he says

---

[344] Surville, *op. cit.,* pp. 95–97. Italics ours.
[345] *Ibid.*

of himself, it is not enough to be "un homme, il faut être un système."[346]

To perfect the scheme further steps were needed; some of these are recorded in Balzac's correspondence. As stated previously, on May 29—June 1, 1833, he informed Mme Hanska of his contract for the publication of the "Scènes de la vie parisienne";[347] on August 19, 1833, he announced *Eugénie Grandet* as a story of the "Scènes de la vie de province."[348] In the same month he wrote Gosselin, who was then expected to publish the whole work, that it would contain four series;[349] and by the end of August he spoke to Mme Carraud of the "achèvement des *Etudes de mœurs*,[350] which, however, were still unfinished on October 24.[351] These statements indicate that by August, 1833, Balzac was in the process of co-ordinating the first three parts of the *Etudes de mœurs* and that his intentions for the *Etudes* were more comprehensive than those for the *Scènes de la vie privée* of 1830, or for the *Romans et contes philosophiques* of 1831.

While the publication of the *Etudes de mœurs* was going on, the novelist formulated plans for a parallel publication of the *Etudes philosophiques*,[352] the contract for which was signed with Werdet on July 19, 1834.[353] Soon after this date he printed two prospectuses,[354] which reiterated, in the main, his general statements of 1830 and 1831[355]—with, however, a new vision of the "petits faits" of everyday life: he will record all phases of individual and social activity, all classes of people whose actions, habits, and gestures he scrutinizes. He proposes to give minute descriptions of interiors, because, he says: "... de leur minutieuse description, s'exhale une révélation lumineuse du caractère de ceux qui les habitent, des passions et des intérêts qui les préoccupent, de toute leur vie en un mot."[356]

---

[346] Quoted by Félix Davin, Lov., *Hist.*, p. 50. In this connection it is interesting to note the report of another contemporary of Balzac, Théophile Gautier. He emphasizes the immensity of the plan (*op. cit.*, pp. 70–71). Still another, Edmond Werdet, at one time friend and publisher of Balzac, speaks of the plan as "une idée littéraire des plus heureuses ... de réunir en faisceau tous les personnages de ses [Balzac's] romans ... ." This idea he calls "idée-type, idée-mère" from which derived first the *Etudes de mœurs* and later the *Comédie humaine* (*Portrait intime de Balzac*, p. 81).

[347] *LEt.*, I, 27.   [350] *Corr. Carraud*, p. 157.

[348] *Ibid.*, p. 33.   [351] *LEt.*, I, 62.

[349] *Corr.*, p. 181.   [352] *Ibid.*, I, 168, 170.

[353] Spoelberch de Lovenjoul, art. cit., *RHL*, 1907, p. 398.

[354] Reprinted in *ibid.*, pp. 403–4.   [355] See above, pp. 30, 38, 40.

[356] Spoelberch de Lovenjoul, art. cit., *RHL*, 1907, p. 404.

There had been, as yet, no sign of definite co-ordination of parts; but on October 18–19, 1834, he gave for the first time an inclusive title for the "grande édition générale de l'œuvre qui, sous le titre d'*Etudes sociales*, comprendra tous ces fragments, ces fûts, ces chapiteaux, ces colonnes, bas-reliefs, murs, coupoles, enfin le monument qui sera laid ou beau, qui me vaudra le *plaudite cives* ou les gémonies."[357] That the scheme was being gradually worked out is again confirmed by Balzac in a letter of October 26, when he writes to Mme Hanska concerning these *Etudes sociales*, which will be a "monument dans notre beau langage. Je crois qu'en 1838 les trois parties[358] de cette œuvre gigantesque seront, sinon parachevées, du moins superposées, et qu'on pourra juger de la masse."[359] The whole work, he continues, will describe, judge, and analyze man, society, and humanity. Then he gives a brief exposition of the scheme in its main parts. Balzac uses architectural terms: the *Etudes de mœurs au XIX*e siè-cle is the foundation upon which the other two divisions will be built. In this division he intends to present social history in all aspects; to trace the history of the human heart, phase by phase, and to depict the three stages of life from childhood to old age; and to treat of politics, justice, and war. He will portray every type of man, every situation and manner of living in every social stratum; his *Etudes* will thus represent all social phases of French life. The *Etudes de mœurs*, in twenty-four volumes, will comprise the whole stage of human action.[360]

In the *Etudes philosophiques*, the second division of the projected *Etudes sociales*,[361] Balzac proposes to give the motivating causes and mechanism of action presented in the first division. This section is the *coulisse* which holds all the machinery controlling the action on the stage. The *Etudes philosophiques* will be more compact, and therefore contained in fifteen volumes.

In the third division, the *Etudes analytiques*, the author will analyze the underlying principles, primary motives of both causes and effects, and in this manner will establish interdependence among the three main parts. Part III, still more condensed, will be comprised of nine volumes only; the tripartite division of the whole work is here closely and definitely interrelated and unified.

---

[357] *LEt.*, I, 196.

[358] Meaning the *Etudes de mœurs, Etudes philosophiques, Etudes analytiques*.

[359] *LEt.*, I, 205.   [360] *Ibid.*, p. 206.

[361] This title, although suggested in a letter to Mme Hanska, was not used for the publication discussed.

Balzac had discussed this scheme with his friend and critic, Félix Davin, who at the instigation of the author wrote two introductions, one to the *Etudes philosophiques*,[362] dated December 6, 1834; the other to the *Etudes de mœurs*,[363] dated April 27, 1835. The novelist[364] actually made contributions to both and frankly acknowledged his pen in the first; while later, publisher Hetzel[365] disclosed the fact that Balzac had a hand in the second also. Both introductions amplify and develop the scheme succinctly given by the author to Mme Hanska. These documents are long winded and contain some irrelevant matter and many repetitions. Yet the Davin-Balzac discussion of the three main parts and of the six subdivisions of the *Etudes de mœurs* constitutes an important contribution to the subject.

This discussion adds that the systematic reappearances of characters link the novels one with another and give a unified and complete picture of life and movement; it emphasizes the evolutionary development of the scheme; it recognizes the function of Balzac as the historian[366] of French society[367] and the originator of what is now called the *roman social;* furthermore, it points to his untiring search for truth, because of which he cannot

faire choix entre le beau et le laid, le moral et le vicieux. ... Il doit, sous peine d'inexactitude et de mensonge, dire tout ce qui est, montrer tout ce qu'il voit. ... Enfin, n'a-t-il pas fallu tout savoir du monde, des arts et des sciences, pour

[362] Appeared first in the *Etudes philosophiques*, éd. Werdet, Vol. I; reprinted in Lov., *Hist.*, pp. 194–207.

[363] Appeared first in the "Scènes de la vie privée" (3d ed.), Vol. I; see above, p. 25, n. 19.

[364] *LEt.*, I, 222. See below, p. 111.

[365] Spoelberch de Lovenjoul, *Autour de Honoré de Balzac*, p. 239. See below, p. 132.

[366] In an article dated October, 1833, Balzac states: "Il y a dans tous les temps un homme de génie qui se fait le secrétaire de son époque. Homère, Aristote, Tacite, Shakespeare, L'Arétin, Machiavel, Rabelais, Bacon, Molière, Voltaire, ont tenu la plume sous la dictée de leurs siècles" (*Théorie de la démarche, OD.*, I, 584). Balzac hesitated as to whether he was the "historien" or the "secrétaire" of society, and used the two terms almost synonymously. In one instance only (so far as we know) has he made a clear distinction between the function of the historian and that of the secretary. In his *Avant-propos* Balzac stated: "La Société française allait être l'historien, je ne devais être que le secrétaire." That is, Society—the historian—dictated, and Balzac—the secretary—wrote down and kept the records.

[367] In 1839 Balzac gave his reasons for choosing French society as the subject of his writings: "Les mœurs françaises sont, littérairement parlant, au-dessus de celles des autres pays comme variété de types, comme drame, comme esprit, comme mouvement; tout s'y dit, tout s'y pense, tout s'y fait" (Preface to *Une Fille d'Ève, OD.*, III, 521).

avoir entrepris de configurer la société avec ses principes organiques et dissol-
vants, ses puissances et ses misères, ses différentes morales et ses infamies? ... Il
voulait peindre les maisons et les intérieurs, les portraits et le costume, les replis
du cœur et les aberrations de l'esprit, la science et le mysticisme, l'homme dans
ses rapports avec les choses et avec la nature.[368]

The last portion of this statement shows Balzac chiefly interested in man
as a social being. In that connection we note that his character sketches
written between 1830 and 1831 had attested his interest in the individual,
whom he saw as conditioned by a diversified and complex system of modern society outside of which he cannot exist. The titles of these sketches—
L'Epicier, Le Ministre, Le Banquier, Un Commis voyageur[369]—are self-
explanatory. He treated these individuals as representatives both of
their trades or professions and of their social milieus. His preoccupation
with social categories was again manifest in some of his early stories: in
La Maison du Chat-qui-pelote (1829) Balzac had portrayed an apprentice
group; in *Le Curé de Tours* (1832) he had depicted the ecclesiastical group,
on the one hand, and the celibate, on the other; in *L'Illustre Gaudissart*
(1833) he had devoted six pages to a disquisition on the traveling agent as
an "espèce sociale"; again in *Histoire des Treize*, of the same year, he
had given a cross-section of contemporary society comprising the nobility, the middle class, and the populace. It would seem that by 1833 his
interest in the individual has broadened out; he is interested in him not
only per se but as a member of a social group. For Balzac, "l'homme
n'était que le détail [et] le moyen" to a study of society—his goal. The
unity of the whole work has become for him completely vested in society.

From 1832 one can trace a sustained effort toward the *roman social*.
Balzac found fiction restricted almost to one passion—love—and that
usually idealized. He widened the scope of the novel, which with him became the *roman réaliste*—a social document, a comprehensive record of all
human activities and the experiences of all milieus. He justly said of his
works: "Ce sera ce qui se passe partout ... les choses sociales comme elles
sont."[370] Within this vast sociological synthesis the *roman social* was
born. The trend may be readily recognized in the general title *Etudes de
mœurs au XIXe siècle* and in its six subdivisions, all indicative of the sociological range of the growing scheme.

In 1837, at the end of our present period, the Preface to *Illusions per-*

[368] Lov., *Hist.*, pp. 54–57.

[369] Reprinted in *OD.*, Vol. II.   [370] Preface to *Le Livre mystique* (1835).

dues elucidated further Balzac's guiding principle: "L'état social adapte tellement les hommes à ses besoins et les déforme si bien, que nulle part les hommes n'y sont semblables à eux-mêmes, et qu'elle [la société] a créé autant d'*espèces* que de *professions;* qu'enfin l'humanité sociale présente autant de variétés que la zoölogie."[371] This statement proves that Balzac had sensed the significance of scientific theory and sought to approximate its method by applying the laws of classification to society. Concurrently with this trend of thought grew up his plan of divisions and subdivisions in which he grouped his novels according to his own analyses of organized society, and in harmony with his intentions for each category, so that in the end each story has its particular niche in the complete whole.

The period from 1833 to 1837 is essentially that of the *Etudes de mœurs*. The author's notebook shows several proposed alignments of subdivisions, one of which suggests the final form adopted. The notation is:

Scènes de la vie privée,   introduction par George Sand
Scènes de la vie du monde, préface par Mme Belloc
Scènes du salon,   préface par Mme D'Abrantès
Scènes du village[372]

The first subdivision remained unchanged; the second and the third clearly suggest the later "Scènes de la vie parisienne"; and the fourth obviously anticipates the "Scènes de la vie de campagne." Of the ultimate six subdivisions, only half (the "Scènes de la vie privée," the "Scènes de la vie de province," and the "Scènes de la vie parisienne") were published between 1834 and 1837; the other half (the "Scènes de la vie politique," the "Scènes de la vie militaire," and the "Scènes de la vie de campagne") were merely announced in 1835 to appear soon.

Balzac called each subdivision a "cadre,"[373] by which he meant a setting for stories alike both in coloring and in atmosphere. The *cadre* first adopted was that of domestic life portrayed in the collective volumes of the *Scènes de la vie privée*, but in his second literary period the expanding conception of the *cadres* included the wider space of the provinces and the capital. The novelist creates in a medium of both space and time— i.e., he depicts youth in the first and old age in the last subdivision; furthermore, the looseness with which he interprets his term may connote not only place and age but also social level or profession. The term

[371] *OD.,* III, 389. Balzac's italics. Cf. *Avant-propos*, p. xxvi.

[372] *Pensées, sujets, fragmens*, éd. Crépet, p. 99.

[373] *OD.,* III, 388.

"cadre," therefore, is not specific; this lack of definiteness constitutes a weakness and points to a genuine deficiency in his system of classification; it gave ground for an attack from a now long-forgotten critic, Chaudes-Aigues,[374] who objected to the reclassifications of stories. Apparently, it did not spoil the effectiveness of the *Comédie humaine;* nor did it lessen Balzac's talent. Nevertheless, it should be borne in mind that the six sets of Scenes are not a fully organized analysis of society and are neither exhaustive nor mutually exclusive. It is obvious, as Jared Wenger[375] says, that the provincial background, for example, is not entirely restricted to the stories grouped in the "Scènes de la vie de province." On the other hand, had the author been able to carry out his analysis of society on the model of a strictly scientific classification, his distribution of novels might have been static, but there would have still remained the query as to whether it was truly artistic. Admitting that his distinctions between the *scènes* are not clear cut, each scene has, nevertheless, its *raison d'être* in that it clarifies Balzac's world and correlates his characters as they come and go from one setting to another.

Because of the mass of material required in portraying all aspects of life and because of the multiplicity of facts and the impetuosity of movement, the history of the "mœurs modernes mise en action" must, of necessity, be presented in order and unity. These effects Balzac achieves by closely interrelated divisions and subdivisions. Just as one character may evoke another, so one *cadre*, or subdivision, may lead to the next; for instance, the "Scènes de la vie de province" is a pendant to the "Scènes de la vie privée," and in turn is a contrast to the "Scènes de la vie parisienne," to which the "Scènes de la vie politique" and the "Scènes de la vie militaire" serve as a complement; with all of these are contrasted, in a general way, the "Scènes de la vie de campagne."

This consecutive progression from the first to the last category is attained by the final story, designed in each subdivision to serve as a transition to the next. For example, *La Femme de trente ans*,[376] the closing story of the "Scènes de la vie privée," links with the "Scènes de la vie de province," in which *Illusions perdues* leads up to the "Scènes de la vie parisienne," which in turn is tied with the "Scènes de la vie politique" by

---

[374] "Ecrivains contemporains: III, M. de Balzac, *Une Fille d'Ève*," *Revue de Paris*, new ser., XI (1839), 20–38.

[375] *The Province and the Provinces in the Work of Honoré de Balzac.*

[376] *OD.*, III, 384, 568.

L'Envers de l'histoire contemporaine. Balzac has made his world the more real to his reader by the continuity of his characters now playing major roles in one subdivision, then reappearing in another in minor parts. Recognition is noted by Aristotle as one of the deeply seated, almost instinctive pleasures of man. In the world of Balzac it exercises this function and produces an illusion of reality. These particular figures are always vigorously active, always striving to reach higher levels of society, as in the case of Rubempré or Rastignac.

Despite the close weaving of the subdivisions, each has its intrinsic theme, variously presented in different novels. Throughout the six subdivisions the complex and diversified "machine sociale" of French society of the nineteenth century is dominant. Obviously, the names of some of these subdivisions have had their origin in titles previously used by Balzac for collective volumes, as in the case of the *Scènes de la vie privée,* which had two editions, or in the *Scènes de la vie politique* and in the *Scènes de la vie militaire*—which, however, were at first announced only as titles to be used for volumes. The importance of the early collective volumes and the projected titles is great, since upon these bases the author has gradually built up the *Etudes de mœurs.*[377] The growth of single parts and their later fusion into one corpus, the *Comédie humaine,* proves the evolutionary nature of the total scheme.

Although the *Etudes de mœurs au XIXᵉ siècle,*[378] bought by Mme Veuve Charles-Béchet between October 9 and 13, 1833, were built essentially upon previously published works, we still have to deal with two kinds of material: on the one hand, old stories revised, enlarged, and linked both by reappearing characters, some of whom are now renamed, and by cross-references which had the ostensible purpose of fitting the novels into the growing plan; on the other hand, new novels composed for the scheme and designed to suit a definite category. The two types of material, old and new, are harmoniously integrated and established in the appropriate *Etude, Scène,* and group, such as *Les Célibataires, Les Parisiens en province,* and *Les Rivalités.* This expansion of the scheme is evinced by the variations in texts between the first and the final form of many novels.[379] Our

---

[377] A similar situation, except for the absence of subdivisions, exists in the case of the *Etudes philosophiques.*

[378] In 12 vols. (3d ed. of the "Scènes de la vie privée," 4 vols.; 1st ed. of the "Scènes de la vie de province," 4 vols.; 1st ed. of the "Scènes de la vie parisienne," 4 vols.), published by Mme Charles-Béchet and later by Werdet, 1834–37.

[379] This type of revision is established by several variation studies done in connection with the Balzac Project.

next necessary step is to examine the first subdivision of the *Etudes de mœurs*, the "Scènes de la vie privée," third edition.

In the Preface to the first edition of the *Scènes de la vie privée*, Balzac had stated, as noted in Section III, the general theme of those collective volumes. But when, in 1833, he transferred the volume title to designate the first subdivision of the *Etudes de mœurs*, he widened the scope of his program. This extension was explained in the Davin-Balzac introductions, and later, in 1839, by the author himself in his Preface to *Une Fille d'Ève*. The "Scènes de la vie privée" portray "une face de la vie individuelle"—the periods of childhood and of adolescence, when sentiments are unselfish and generous, when hopes are naïve and run high. No violence is permitted here; only noble sentiments are depicted. Davin-Balzac explains: "Cette première vue de la destinée humaine était sans encadrement possible. Aussi l'auteur s'est-il complaisamment promené partout: ici, dans le fond d'une campagne; là, en province; plus loin, dans Paris." Here is obviously stressed the concept of time—youth; for this reason a story in this subdivision may have the setting either in the capital or in the provinces—which proves that the subdivisions are not watertight compartments.

The contents of the third edition of the "Scènes de la vie privée," now to be discussed, differ somewhat from those of the first and second editions. In the way of new[380] material we note (1) two additional episodes· "Souffrances inconnues" and "La Vallée du torrent" in *Même Histoire;* and (2) two fresh stories: *La Fleur-des-pois* (*Le Contrat de mariage*) and *La Recherche de l'absolu*.

Balzac finished *La Fleur-des-pois*[381] at the home of Mme de Berny in October, 1835.[382] The tale was written for the "Scènes de la vie privée," in which it has remained permanently since it forms an integral part of the subdivision. In his correspondence he spoke of the story as "une grande *Scène de la vie privée*."[383]

Paul de Manerville, nicknamed "La Fleur-des-pois"—young, naïve, kind—was in love with Natalie Evangélista, the daughter of an ambitious and spendthrift mother, who arranged Natalie's marriage with Paul.

---

[380] See Sec. III for analyses of the first two editions of the *Scènes de la vie privée*. New stories only will be discussed in this section.

[381] This story first appeared in the subdivision under consideration. In 1839, it was published in the Charpentier ed. of these Scenes; in 1842 it entered *Fur.*, Vol. III; it is now in *Con.*, Vol. VII.

[382] *LF.*, p. 151.   [383] *Ibid.*, p. 157.

Later she succeeded in spending Paul's fortune, and finally ruined his good name by spreading rumors of disgraceful action on his part. Trustful and ignorant alike of her intrigues and of his wife's infidelity, Paul went to India to seek another fortune. A letter from his friend, Henri de Marsay, disclosed the facts concerning Paul's wife and her scheming, unscrupulous mother. In this tale Balzac did more than simply portray domestic infelicity. He wrote a *roman social*, in which he emphasized the great importance of the marriage contract in regard to property; he stressed also the professional type, the "espèce sociale," of the notary. He characterized sympathetically the old family lawyer, Mathias, in contest with the young and tricky solicitor, Solonet, each representing one of the contracting parties. Balzac says: "Ces *Condottieri* matrimoniaux, qui s'allaient battre pour leurs clients, et dont les forces personnelles devenaient si décisives en cette solennelle rencontre, les deux notaires représentaient les anciennes et les nouvelles mœurs, l'ancien et le nouveau notariat."[384] The scene between the two lawyers just before signing the marriage contract is subtly contrasted with that between the people most vitally concerned in the matter. Balzac is direct, simple, powerful: "Il se passa donc une double scène. Au coin de la cheminée du grand salon, une scène d'amour où la vie apparaissait riante et joyeuse. Dans l'autre pièce, une scène grave et sombre où l'intérêt mis à nu, jouait par avance le rôle qu'il joue sous les apparences fleuries de la vie."[385] This is the pivotal scene in the story, the "bataille d'hommes d'affaires." That the social significance of the "convenances pécuniaires" becomes uppermost in the author's mind is manifested by his change of title, in 1842, to *Le Contrat de mariage*. Paul's aunt voices the universal French idea concerning marriage: "Le contrat, mon enfant, le contrat est le plus saint des devoirs!" The struggle of interests and the emphasis on the marriage document would seem to group the novel among the "Scènes de la vie parisienne." Nevertheless, Balzac placed *Le Contrat de mariage* (with other legal stories which will be discussed later) in the "Scènes de la vie privée"; probably the family considerations, the heritage of the young people, were foremost in the author's mind. This is a story not only of French marriage customs and laws but also of conjugal unhappiness. The novelist's comment within the narrative brings *Le Contrat de mariage* in line with other tales classified in the same division. He says: "Les événemens et les idées qui ame-

---

[384] "Scènes de la vie privée" (3d ed., 1835), II, 81.

[385] *Ibid.*, p. 87.

nèrent le mariage de Paul avec mademoiselle Evangélista sont la préface de l'œuvre, uniquement destiné à retracer la grande comédie qui précède toute la vie conjugale."[386]

The inception of *La Recherche de l'absolu*[387] can be traced to June 10, 1832,[388] when Balzac became interested in the life and work of Bernard Palissy, whom he thought to be an alchemist and whom he intended to make the hero of a projected novel, *Les Souffrances de l'inventeur*.[389] This title appears also in the author's notebook,[390] with a name—M. Claës—which indicates that Bernard Palissy was the prototype of Balthazar Claës, the hero of our novel.[391] J. Merlant[392] suggests that the theme of *Les Amours d'une laide*, a story projected but never finished,[393] was also incorporated in *La Recherche de l'absolu*.

A recent work[394] attributes the temporary placement of *La Recherche* entirely to Mme Béchet's urgent demand for an additional novel to complete the third edition of the "Scènes de la vie privée." This tentative classification shows, however, that at first Balzac did not stress Balthazar's gradual detachment from life and his increasing absorption in science, but rather his devotion to his wife and family. One could argue that the story is a study of a Flemish home and of conjugal happiness; this view is supported by the original chapter headings, now omitted. Chap-

---

[386] *Ibid.*, p. 60.

[387] This novel first appeared in the subdivision under consideration; next it was published by Charpentier in the 4th ed. of the same *Scènes*, Vol. I (1839). In 1845 it appeared in the *Etudes philosophiques*, éd. Furne, Vol. XIV. Georges Vicaire lists a Figaro ed. (1838) of the novel (see *Manuel de l'amateur de livres du XIXᵉ siècle, 1801–1893*, Vol. I, col. 197). This edition is not mentioned in Lov., *Hist*.

[388] *LF.*, p. 75.

[389] *LEt.*, I, 52. The story was never written, but the title was used for Part III of *Illusions perdues* (1843).

[390] Ed. Crépet, p. 132.

[391] See M. Georges Thouvenin, "La Genèse d'un roman de Balzac, *La Recherche de l'absolu*," *RHL*, XVIII (1911), 865–84. He maintains that M. Hoëne de Wronski, a Pole, was an influence in Balzac's conception of Claës. Cf. *LEt.*, I, 168–69. Wronski created, in 1819, a stir with his search for the Absolute and exercised a great influence on the minds of his students. However, Balzac's interest in alchemy is shown in *La Confidence des Ruggieri* (1836) rather than in *La Recherche de l'absolu*.

[392] *Op. cit.*, p. 168.   [393] *LF.*, p. 109.

[394] A. J. Williamson, "*La Recherche de l'absolu*. The Determination of Balzac's Method of Composition and Revision" (unpublished Ph.D. dissertation, Princeton University, 1938).

ter i, "La Maison Claës," with emphasis on "maison," is, in a way, a symbol of the family traditions; in fact, the presentation of the house of Claës has a sociohistorical value in depicting several generations of a whole clan.[395] Chapter ii, "Histoire d'un ménage flamand," enhances the "vie domestique" of the young couple, with a gradual building-up of the husband's interest in and passion for Lavoisier's discoveries. Finally, says Balzac, this interest became "une maladie morale"; and Mme Claës, realizing that she had a rival in science, felt that she and the children were victims of Balthazar's monomania. Chapters iii–vii are a study of Balthazar as the martyr of his *idée fixe*, of his mental and physical degradation and its effects upon his family. The fact that in 1845 the author withdrew the novel from the "Scènes de la vie privée" and placed it permanently in the *Etudes philosophiques* shows that he considered the development essentially psychological. In reality it is less a "tableau de mœurs" than a study of exaggerated thought,[396] which becomes a blind passion and ravages the mind of Claës to the extent of making him a maniac. On October 11, 1846, Balzac justifies to Hippolyte Castille his final classification: "... le héros de *la Recherche de l'absolu* représente les efforts de la chimie moderne, ... et tout personnage typique devient colossal par ce seul fait. C'est, d'ailleurs, une œuvre *placée à son lieu* dans les *Etudes philosophiques*, où il n'y a que des *symboles*."[397] One of those symbols is certainly the smoke rising from the chimney of the laboratory, watched with despair by the dying wife. Balzac says: "Elle voyait s'enfuir en fumée la fortune de ses enfants; mais elle sauvait la vie de leur père."[398] The central idea of the *Etudes philosophiques*, said Davin, is "la Pensée tue"; that is, when one thought possesses a man to the exclusion of all others, he becomes the martyr of his own ideal, and death is the only solution. The same intensity of conception is portrayed in *La Recherche de l'absolu* as in *La Peau de chagrin* and *Le Chef-d'œuvre inconnu;* logically, therefore, the novel under consideration should be included in the same division. That the story was closely connected in Balzac's mind with *Le Chef-d'œuvre inconnu* is indicated by his notations in the corrected Furne edition of the *Comédie humaine:* "La Recherche de l'absolu doit être placée immédiatement après *Melmoth réconcilié* et le *Chef-d'œuvre in-*

---

[395] Dargan, "Studies in Balzac, II," *MP*, XVI (1918), 366.

[396] See above, pp. 38, 41.

[397] *OD.*, III, 365. Italics ours.

[398] *La Recherche de l'absolu* ("Scènes de la vie privée" [1834]), III, 165.

connu aller après *la Recherche de l'absolu.*"[399] These lines are crossed out and on the back of the flyleaf of the same volume is written, "Retrancher de ce volume *La Recherche de l'absolu*," meaning simply that it was to be placed just before *Le Chef-d'œuvre inconnu* in another volume of the *Etudes philosophiques*, as it eventually was.

This closes our discussion of the new material in the first subdivision of the *Etudes de mœurs*.

The first edition of the second subdivision, the "Scènes de la vie de province," made its initial appearance in 1833. In the Davin-Balzac introductions were given the author's intentions for the subdivision. They were (1) to depict the mature period of life, as contrasted with that of youth; (2) to paint love motivated by self-interest and material advantage; (3) to portray selfish calculations and egotistical passions set against the narrow background of provincial life, in which setting he aimed to disclose "les tracasseries mesquines dont la périodicité concentre un intérêt poignant sur le moindre détail d'existence."

Balzac chose the provinces as a setting, Davin continues, because it is the most harmonious and the richest in effects of chiaroscuro; Balzac himself gave further reasons for his portrayal of provincial life as a whole in the Preface to *Eugénie Grandet*, where he added that there is still poetry in the provincial atmosphere, still interest in thought rather than in action, still original characters to be found, and that life, although monotonous, is rich in detail.

These were ostensibly Balzac's reasons and intentions, artistic and psychological, for the stories to be grouped in the "Scènes de la vie de province"; but both reasons and intentions reveal an ultimate aim, and here we concur with Jared Wenger,[400] to contrast life in the provinces generally with that of the capital and to make the provinces subservient to Paris.

It should be noted that the "Scènes de la vie de province" was never used as a collective title—that is, on the same basis as the *Scènes de la vie privée*. The name was first mentioned to Mme Hanska in a letter dated August 19, 1833. From that time Balzac continuously discussed the stories which he classified in this subdivision.[401] This first edition was

[399] Lov. Coll., A 30. See also *Etudes philosophiques* (*Comédie humaine*, éd. Furne), XIV, 283.

[400] *Op. cit.*

[401] Vols. I and II were published by Mme Béchet, December, 1833 (dated 1834). Vols. III and IV were published by Werdet, February, 1837.

composed of nine stories, of which three—*Le Message, Le Curé de Tours,* and *La Grande Bretèche* (the last episode of *Les Trois Vengeances*)—had been previously published in the *Scènes de la vie privée*[402] and six tales (plus the first two episodes of *Les Trois Vengeances* dealt with in part) were new material, which will be the subject of discussion.

Eugénie Grandet,[403] announced to Mme Hanska on August 19, 1833, as "une *Scène de la Vie de province,* dans le genre des *Célibataires,*"[404] was from the beginning placed in this subdivision; for here the author portrays life where, in the words of Davin, "les intérêts positifs contrecarrent à tout moment les passions violentes aussi bien que les espérances les plus naïves."[405] This statement aptly characterizes the plot of the novel; on the one hand is Eugénie, naïve and trusting; on the other are her father, with his passion for gold, and the contesting parties of the Cruchotins and the Grassinistes. The novel is essentially a *roman social.* Its sociological aspect is revealed in Balzac's minute study of Grandet's occupation and fortune, his social status in the town and in the set in which he moves. The chapter titles of the story, later discarded, clarified its sociological nature—for instance, chapter i, "Physionomies bourgeoises." Both Bellessort[406] and Maurice Serval[407] suggest that the original conception of the character of Eugénie is to be found in Annette Gérard, the heroine of *Argow le pirate.*[408] Eugénie gives money, as does Annette, but under different circumstances. The mainspring of the action is Félix Grandet's domineering, avaricious character, which blighted the destinies of both his wife and daughter. Since the initial pages of this novel convey so admirably the atmosphere of provincial life, it is well that *Eugénie Grandet* should open the "Scènes de la vie de province." Sainte-Beuve[409] has commended Balzac's instinctive choice of locality for his stories. And it is with just pride that the novelist tells Mme Carraud that *"Eugénie Grandet ... peint si bien la vie de province."*[410] From the first pages the keynoting

---

[402] See above, pp. 55 ff.

[403] The first chapter was published in *L'Europe littéraire,* September 19, 1833; the complete story appeared in Vol. I of the *Scènes de la vie de province;* in 1839 it appeared independently in 1 vol. in the Charpentier ed.; in 1843 it entered the Furne ed., *Comédie humaine,* Vol. I; and is now in *Con.,* Vol. VIII.

[404] *LEt.,* I, 33.

[405] Lov., *Hist.,* p. 47.

[406] *Op. cit.,* pp. 45–46.

[407] *Autour d'Eugénie Grandet,* pp. 32–33.

[408] See above, pp. 26–27.

[409] *Portraits contemporains,* II, 340.

[410] *Corr. Carraud,* p. 197.

and harmonizing, along lines of melancholy, are done with the utmost care in order to fit the tale of small-town life into the category. The street, the house, and the costume of the Saumur miser are in keeping with the narrow circle of his friends, the Des Grassins and the Cruchots; their tittle-tattle, scheming and greed for Eugénie's dowry, the intrigues and cupidities, especially evident in provincial life with its narrow horizons, are all depicted with a masterly hand.

La Femme abandonnée,[411] after its temporary classification in the "Scènes de la vie de province," was permanently placed in 1842 in the "Scènes de la vie privée," of which it is an organic part. Although the setting is provincial life, the story is essentially that of a young man and of his sincere love for a woman, Mme de Beauséant, abandoned by her first lover, Ajudo-Pinto. In this tale Balzac demonstrates the havoc played by illicit love in the life of Gaston de Nueil and his consequent incapacity for the joys and duties of home life. After nine years of happiness with Mme de Beauséant, Gaston was overruled by his mother and tricked into a marriage of expediency. The author's interest is sharply focused upon the relation of Gaston and "la femme abandonnée." He has presented the soul analysis of one man and one woman, with the inevitable debacle of the man's marriage and his ensuing suicide.[412]

La Grenadière[413] was originally called *Les Orphelins*. The latter title, frequently mentioned by Balzac in his correspondence, is not unsuited to the story, which deals with a mother and two fatherless boys. Here we have a really charming picture of child life in Touraine. However, this was not the motive for Balzac's brief artistic narrative. Its theme is indicated in his notebook: "Une mère mourante soignée par deux fils, elle n'est pas mariée. Son enterrement."[414] This is the gist of *La Grenadière*, except for the fact that Lady Brandon, the heroine, was married. It is essentially an account of a woman whose life was ruined by passion; remorseful for the errors of her past and unpardoned by her husband, she

[411] This story first appeared September 16, 1832, in the *Revue de Paris*. In 1834 it was published in the "Scènes de la vie de province," Vol. II; and in 1839 in the 2d ed. of this collection by Charpentier, Vol. I. In 1842 it entered Vol. II of the *Comédie humaine*, "Scènes de la vie privée." It is now in *Con.*, Vol. IV.

[412] It is interesting to note the two allusions to this "femme abandonnée" of 1832 in *La Duchesse de Langeais*, written in 1833.

[413] This story was first published in the *Revue de Paris*, October, 1832; after its appearance in the 1st and 2d eds. of the "Scènes de la vie de province," it entered in 1842 the "Scènes de la vie privée," éd. Furne, Vol. II. It is now in *Con.*, Vol. IV.

[414] Lov. Coll., A 181, fol. 18.

retired to Touraine with her children. Weakened by sorrow and anxiety, she soon died. This melancholy tale of private life blighted by illicit love was also temporarily placed in the subdivision under consideration, where it served as a "filler" to supply the required volume pages. In 1842 the story was permanently classed, together with *La Femme abandonnée*, in the "Scènes de la vie privée," to which they both rightfully belong.

L'Illustre Gaudissart[415] is a short story written in the broadly jesting spirit which Balzac could adopt upon occasion. It is an amusing episode, almost a caricature, of Gaudissart, nicknamed "L'Illustre," a loquacious, self-confident traveling agent, who is outwitted by a Tourangeau innkeeper. Gaudissart, unabashed by his failure, returns to Paris to relate the incident to his own advantage. The satire of this sketch is pointed by the author's statement to Mme Hanska in a letter of July 15, 1834, that the publisher, the "illustre Werdet," resembles a little the "illustre Gaudissart."[416]

The commercial traveler, says Davin, is essentially a creation of modern society. Since Balzac purposed to present all types and all professions, Gaudissart has his place in the picture, per se; he also serves as a link between the capital and the provinces. This doubtless was the novelist's idea when, in 1843, he coupled this sketch with *La Muse du département* under a general title, *Les Parisiens en province*, to establish a dual connection between the two subdivisions and to show the continual trekking of people from the provinces to the capital and thence to the provinces again.

Balzac's lengthy Preface to the tale is a disquisition on high-powered salesmanship as developed in Paris and practiced on the provincials. With his increasing sociological interest he discussed the commercial agent as "une espèce"; the scene of Gaudissart's activities as he reappears is varied; in this sketch he is limited to the sphere of the small town, a circumstance which decides its permanent classification in the "Scènes de la vie de province."

Volume III of the "Scènes de la vie de province," Werdet edition, contained *Les Trois Vengeances* (*La Grande Bretèche*)[417] and *La Vieille Fille*.

[415] After this sketch appeared in the 1st ed. of the "Scènes de la vie de province," it was published in the 2d ed. by Charpentier in 1839. It entered in 1843 the *Comédie humaine*, Vol. VI, and is now in *Con.*, Vol. X.

[416] *LEt.*, I, 173.

[417] This story (the third episode of revenge) has been partly dealt with above, pp. 53, 55–58.

The former consists of three tales of revenge. The gist of the first, "Histoire du chevalier de Beauvoir," told by M. Gravier, a guest of Mme d'Espard, is as follows: When Napoleon was first consul, the Chevalier, a political prisoner, had the imprudence to fall in love with the wife of the commandant of the garrison; immediately he was locked in a dungeon. The husband contrived a scheme for vengeance which would inevitably result in the prisoner's death by his falling into an abyss. The Chevalier, however, discovered the precipice in time, succeeded in killing his jailer, and safely made his escape.

The second vengeance episode, "Le Grand d'Espagne," laid in the Restoration period, is far more tragic. It is told by Lousteau, who, on his way to Spain in 1823–24, attended a ball in Tours, where he joined a group of story-tellers. Among these was an old man who related a tale supposedly heard in Madrid. It was an account of unfaithfulness, jealousy, and bloody revenge told with the usual Balzacian verve and emphasized by the presence in the *salon* of the characters involved. These episodes with their typically provincial setting of the *salon* remained in the "Scènes de la vie de province," but only as fitting parts of *La Muse du département.*[418]

In *La Vieille Fille*,[419] Rose Cormon, the wealthy heiress of Alençon, is the very symbol of provincial life; says Balzac: "... elle concordait à l'esprit général et aux mœurs des habitants qui l'aimaient comme le plus pur symbole de leur vie, car elle s'était encroûtée dans les habitudes de la province, elle n'en était jamais sortie, elle en avait les préjugés, elle en épousait les intérêts, elle l'adorait."[420] She is the heroine of this patently provincial story, which the author classified from the start in the "Scènes de la vie de province." In this story, as in *Eugénie Grandet*, of the same subdivision, the plot hinges on the marriage of an heiress whose fortune was frankly coveted by the Chevalier de Valois, the gallant royalist and Voltairian, and by the energetic bourgeois Du Bousquier, a liberal and republican. The third pretender, Athanase Granson, nineteen years her junior, a talented and bashful youth, really loved Mlle Cormon without mercenary aim. "La province," says Balzac, "calcule et arrange le mariage," while Eugénie Grandet, or Rose Cormon, or Athanase—each a sin-

---

[418] See below, p. 143.

[419] This novelette first appeared in *La Presse*, October 23–November 4, 1836. In 1837 it was published in the subdivision under consideration; and in 1839 in the Charpentier ed. of the same scenes; in 1844 it entered the *Comédie humaine*, Vol. VII. It is now in *Con.*, Vol. X.

[420] *La Vieille Fille*, "Scènes de la vie de province," III (1837), 211.

cere, idealistic soul—became the victim of such egotistical matrimonial calculations. Around the old maid the author arranged a tableau of provincial society. Her *salon* is the link between the two factions of the town: the old, impoverished aristocracy, of which the Chevalier is the symbol, and the rising antireligious bourgeoisie, with the ambitious Du Bousquier as its representative. Balzac shows himself a true historian of a passing aristocratic society and of a coming new type, somewhat commercial and vulgar.

In 1844, under a general but pertinent title, *Les Rivalités*, the author grouped *La Vieille Fille* with *Le Cabinet des antiques*, in which the conflict of old and new social ideas in the sphere of marriage widened into the political domain. Anticipating a second edition of the *Comédie humaine*, Balzac made important revisions in Volume VII[421] of the first Furne edition. *La Vieille Fille*—still under the general title, *Les Rivalités*—was to be grouped with two projected stories, *L'Original* and *Les Héritiers Boirouge*; but inasmuch as these were never written and the second edition of the *Comédie humaine* was not published until after the death of its author, *La Vieille Fille* remained as the single story of the *Rivalités*,[422] since it had been separated from its sequel. A study of the variations of the novel[423] shows that Balzac's prime interest in rehandling the story was of a sociological nature, as the general title indicates.

Balzac designed (1837) the last novel of the "Scènes de la vie de province," *Les Deux Poètes* (Part I of *Illusions perdues*),[424] to serve as a transi-

---

[421] Lov. Coll., A 23.

[422] For *Le Cabinet des antiques*, see below, p. 144.

[423] Rachel Wilson, "A Study of the Variations between the First and the Definitive Editions of Balzac's *La Vieille Fille*" (unpublished Master's thesis, University of Chicago, 1925).

[424] This novel comprises three parts: Part I, "Les Deux Poètes," first appeared in the subdivision under discussion. Part II, "Un Grand Homme de province à Paris," was first published by Souverain in 1839, in 2 vols. Two chapters of this part, "Comment se font les petits journaux" and "Le Souper," appeared on June 8, 1839, in *L'Estafette*. Part III, "Les Souffrances de l'inventeur," first appeared June 9–19, 1843, in *L'Etat;* it was also published, under the title "David Séchard, ou Les Souffrances de l'inventeur," in *Le Parisien d'Etat*, July 27–August 14, 1843. The same year these three parts, under the general title *Illusions perdues*, entered the *Comédie humaine*, éd. Furne, Vol. VIII; Parts I and II kept their individual titles, whereas Part III was given a new one, "Ève et David," which had also a separate publication in 1844, under the title "David Séchard," in 2 vols. *Illusions perdues* is now in *Con.*, Vols. XI–XII. Although Parts II and III belong to a later period, it is expedient here to discuss the classification of the

tion to the third subdivision of the *Etudes de mœurs*, the "Scènes de la vie parisienne." With this end in view he refers clearly in Parts I and III to the journeys of the hero to Paris, and at the end of Part II he anticipates the return to the province. It is here that Bérénice gives her ill-gotten money to Lucien that he may leave Paris. Balzac says: "... cet argent lui brûlait la main et il [Lucien] voulait le rendre; mais il fut forcé de le garder comme un dernier stigmate de la vie parisienne."[425] Part III closes with another forward look to Paris: "Quant à Lucien, son retour à Paris est du domaine des *Scènes de la vie parisienne.*" It is in *Splendeurs et misères des courtisanes* that Balzac concludes the career of his hero, Lucien, who weeps in his prison cell over his lost illusions.

In Parts I and III the novelist portrays life in the province and relates the touching story of David Séchard and his wife, Eva, the sister of Lucien. They accept the quiet, uneventful life of Angoulême, which the author contrasts with the feverish life of the capital—in fact, he claims that the general sense of *Illusions perdues* is "un plaidoyer pour la famille." The young printer, Séchard, and his wife stand out among the most sympathetic types that Balzac has created; their sacrifice and courage contrast impressively with the selfishness and moral weakness of Lucien. The author's personal recollections of the vicissitudes of a printer and a journalist have made his description of the French literary youth around 1822 keenly significant and, as he claimed, "d'une réalité désespérante."

For each part of this trilogy Balzac wrote a preface in which he clarifies his intentions regarding the ensuing novel and its classification. In the Preface to Part I, *Les Deux Poètes*, the author says: "Il ne s'agissait d'abord que d'une comparaison entre les mœurs de la province et les mœurs de la vie parisienne; ... mais, en peignant avec complaisance l'intérieur d'un ménage et les révolutions d'une pauvre imprimerie de province ... le champ [the scope] s'est agrandi malgré l'auteur."[426] In portraying Lucien, the personification of ambition, the author thought of the "grande plaie de ce siècle, au journalisme, qui dévore tant d'existences, tant de belles pensées, et qui produit d'épouvantables réactions dans les modestes régions de la vie de province."[427] Thus the tableau of individual

---

complete novel. For a full treatment of the novel, see Margaret Anderson, "The Background of Balzac's *Illusions perdues* and Variations in the Principal Editions" (unpublished Ph.D. dissertation, University of Chicago, 1930).

[425] *Con.*, XII, 361.

[426] *OD.*, III, 390. [427] *Ibid.*

life is extended to include a whole section of contemporary society—literary men, journalists, and their "mœurs intimes."

Most changes and variations[428] in this novel are of a sociological nature, centered in the social groups of literary men, journalists, printers, as well as of usurers, inventors, and provincials in Paris—men with whom Balzac was himself associated. Moreover, the changes demonstrate his determination to solidify and unify the novel within its *cadre* and within the whole *Comédie humaine*. The theme of the novel and its treatment make it, as a whole, a part of the "Scènes de la vie de province," in which it was classified from the beginning. On the basis of Part II, *Un Grand Homme de province à Paris*, the story might have been in keeping with the "Scènes de la vie parisienne"; however, since the hero of the trilogy is a provincial and Parts I and III are laid in Angoulême, the whole is more appropriately placed at the close of the "Scènes de la vie de province," where it leads directly to the next subdivision and our present topic.

The first edition of the third subdivision of the *Etudes de mœurs* was designated "Scènes de la vie parisienne,"[429] a general title not used before. Balzac first mentioned it in a letter to Mme Hanska dated May 29–June 1, 1833, when he told her of the contract signed for the publication of these Scenes. On August 19 he informed her that they would appear during the winter. They were published between March, 1834, and November, 1835.

With the publication of the Parisian series Balzac had reached, with an ever widening scope, the mid-point of his total scheme. Of the nine stories included in the first edition of the "Scènes de la vie parisienne," six[430] had appeared in earlier collections. The author temporarily[431] transferred this old material to the new subdivision in order to fill the number of pages required in these volumes. In the following passage, a typical one, he accounts for the misplacement of some novels prior to their final classification:

> Les fragments de l'œuvre entreprise par l'auteur subissent ... les lois capricieuses du goût et de la convenance des marchands. Tel journal a demandé un morceau qui ne soit trop long, ni trop court, qui puisse entrer dans tant de colonnes et de tel prix. ... On les [stories] expose dans les deux premiers volumes

---

[428] See Anderson, *op. cit.*

[429] In 4 vols., published by Mme Béchet; Vol. I appeared in November, 1835; Vols. II and III, March 15, 1834; Vol. IV, May, 1835.

[430] Discussed above, pp. 31, 33, 41, 47, 58, 73.

[431] Except for one story, *Sarrasine*, which remained permanently in this subdivision.

venus. Il faut subir les exigences de la librairie ... elle veut deux volumes ni plus ni moins, ou un bout de conte pour mettre à ceci plus d'ampleur. Elle a ses habitudes de format, elle tient à ses marges.[432]

In the second edition[433] of this series the distribution of stories per volume was different from the first; and one tale, *L'Interdiction*, was added. Otherwise, there were no changes.

In his Preface[434] to the first edition Balzac harks back to *Illusions perdues*, as the link connecting the two subdivisions and showing "la province venant chercher Paris par un calcul d'amour-propre et de vanité." The intermingling of provincial and Parisian life is continuous, he asserts; the portrayal in the Parisian series is on a broader scope and done, he claims, with a more "sober and somber brush." Here the stories depict the *arriviste* on a wider and more metropolitan scale, more advanced and yet more materialistic and pessimistic, with emphasis on the "machine sociale." According to the author, Paris is the only possible setting for the portrayal of the clash of selfish interests, of the life in which passion, vices, abuses, and all extremes dissolve social principles. It is in Paris, Davin-Balzac had earlier said, that "tout se subtilise, s'analyse, se vend et s'achète," that "l'humanité n'a plus que deux formes, le trompeur et le trompé ... tout s'exploite, se débite."[435] The stories of this subdivision will presently be analyzed in the light of these intentions.

The third subdivision of the *Etudes de mœurs* contained only three new titles: *Les Marana, Histoire des Treize,* and *La Comtesse à deux maris.* Balzac stated the theme of *Les Marana:*[436] "Une femme tuant son mari qui a fait un crime ignoble et qui, en mourant sur l'échafaud, déshonorerait ses enfants."[437] In this statement he strikes the keynote, family honor. This and two other stories, *El Verdugo* and *L'Enfant maudit,* also

[432] Preface to *La Femme supérieure, La Maison Nucingen,* and *La Torpille, OD.,* III, 507–8.

[433] In 2 vols., published by Charpentier, 1839.

[434] *OD.,* III, 391.   [435] Lov., *Hist.,* p. 47.

[436] This novel first appeared in the *Revue de Paris,* December 15, 1832—January 15, 1833. After its first appearance in the 1st ed. of the subdivision under consideration it was published, together with *Ferragus,* by the Bureau du *Figaro,* in 1838; this edition is not listed in Lov., *Hist.* See A. G. Canfield, *MLN,* XLVIII (1933), 497–501. In 1846 the story appeared in the *Etudes philosophiques, Comédie humaine,* Vol. XV. It is now in *Con.,* Vol. XXIX.

[437] Lov. Coll., A 181, fol. 18.

embodying the presentation of an abstract idea, were ultimately and logically classified in the *Etudes philosophiques*.

Juana de Mancini, the heroine of the story, motivated by a high sense of honor, killed her husband rather than suffer the shame of his execution to fall upon her children. This dramatic tale, written with great economy in characters and exposition, places its emphasis on the conception and development of two characters only. One, Diard, a hero on the battlefield, was really a moral coward incapable of self-sacrifice. Balzac, believing in social castes, carefully prepared the denouement by keynoting Diard's character along lines of a certain weakness leading to infamy. His courage failed when his wife expected him to be a man of moral stamina. Diard was the victim of an inferiority complex which he could not overcome and was therefore incapable of facing "le monde" on equal terms. He gradually slipped back into his former "vie infernale" and eventually wrought his own destruction. In the author's intentions Diard belongs, along with Montefiore, whom he stabbed and robbed, to those "grands hommes manqués, que la société marque d'avance au fer chaud, en les appelant des *mauvais sujets*."[438] As a contrast, Balzac explains Juana, the second character, in a careful *dossier*.[439] Her inherited pride, sense of honor, and social background justify her action. It is clear that *Les Marana* is not primarily an *étude de mœurs*, since it derives rather from a contemplation of ideas of honor and moral courage, of infamy and cowardice. Because of these features, the tale forms an integral part of the *Etudes philosophiques*, in which it remained after 1846.

Balzac gave the general title *Histoire des Treize*[440] to three stories concerning a secret gang known as the "Thirteen," adventurers and "grands seigneurs," who for their own benefit and pleasure had sworn mutual protection. Ferragus, a convict and leader of the band, was the loving father,

---

[438] *Les Marana, Con.*, XXIX, 60.   [439] *Ibid.*, p. 97.

[440] Part I, "Férragus chef des dévorants," first appeared in the *Revue de Paris*, March and April, 1833. In 1838 it was published, together with *Les Marana*, in 1 vol. in octavo. See above, n. 436. Of Part II, "La Duchesse de Langeais," chap. i appeared in *L'Echo de la jeune France*, March, 1833. Of Part III, "La Fille aux yeux d'or," one fragment, "Le Petit Mercier," appeared in *La Caricature*, December 16, 1830; another, "Les Jeunes Gens de Paris," was published in Vol. IV of the *Nouveau Tableau de Paris au XIXe siècle* (a collective work) (1834–35). These three parts, under the general title *Histoire des Treize*, first appeared together in the subdivision under consideration; in 1839 under the same general title the first two parts only were published by Charpentier in 1 vol. In 1843 the novel entered the *Comédie humaine*, Vol. IX. It is now in *Con.*, Vol. XIII.

almost *à la* Goriot, of Marie, happily married to a respectable bourgeois, M. Jules Desmarets, who was ignorant of his wife's antecedents. Auguste de Maulincour, a sentimental and bored aristocrat, infatuated with Marie, unjustly told Desmarets that she was unfaithful. By this act Auguste brought death upon himself at the hands of the powerful Ferragus and, indirectly, caused that of the innocent young wife.

The secret power of the "Thirteen" is again presented in a second tale, which recalls Balzac's own experiences as a rejected lover. Of this tale Bellessort says: "... on y trouve l'analyse la plus dramatique de la coquetterie féminine dans tout ce qu'elle a d'instinctif et de calculé, d'intelligent et de félin."[441] Briefly, it is the story of Armand de Montriveau, one of the "Thirteen," passionately in love with the Duchesse de Langeais, a modern Célimène. With the help of his associates Armand kidnapped her; then, with a violent revulsion of feeling, threatened to brand her; and finally with scorn freed her. Later she entered a convent off the Spanish coast as a nun. Here, after five years of search, the repentant and still devoted Armand found her. Again with the aid of the "Thirteen," he succeeded in penetrating the convent, but only to carry off the body of the duchess—death had defeated the powerful band.

In the last story Balzac relates the third failure of the secret gang, confronted now with perverted passion and ultimate death. Since his plan obliged him to be universal, he maintained that his picture of modern Sodom would be incomplete without this episode, of which he spoke to Mme Hanska as "cette bêtise de *la Fille aux Yeux d'or.*"[442]

These three plots are melodramatic; but the long disquisitions of the *Histoire des Treize* on life in the aristocratic *faubourg* of Saint-Germain under the Restoration, and the great variety of social types, such as the magistrate, the speculator, the banker, the lawyer, the petty merchant, the workingman—all seeking, says Balzac, money and pleasure—make this novel the broadest social picture which the author had yet written about Paris. It is a study par excellence of Parisian life and forms an integral part of the "Scènes de la vie parisienne," in which it was permanently classified and appropriately placed as the opening scene of the subdivision in the first Furne edition of the *Comédie humaine.*

Le Colonel Chabert[443] is the pathetic tale of an officer of the *Légion d'hon-*

---

[441] Bellessort, *op. cit.*, p. 252.   [442] *LEt.*, I, 240.

[443] This story first appeared in serial form in *L'Artiste*, February–March, 1832; and the same year in Vol. I of the *Salmigondis*, under the title *Le Comte Chabert;* in 1835 it

neur, wounded at Eylau and reported dead. Reviving, he crawled out from under the heap of bodies. After a miserable life in Germany he returned to France, wishing to reinstate himself in his former social position. His wife, married again and enjoying her first husband's fortune, refused to recognize him. In his desperate struggle the poverty-stricken soldier interested the honest lawyer, Derville, who attempted to rehabilitate him. The revelation of his wife's wickedness was so revolting to the upright, stoic nature of Chabert that he gave up the fight when Derville had almost won his case for him. The hero of Napoleon's army later sank to the lowest depth of poverty in a public institution.

The shift in titles indicates Balzac's change in interest. At first it centered in the complicated legal procedure which led to a compromise; hence the original title, *La Transaction*. In the second title, *Le Comte Chabert*, the author turned the spotlight on the rehabilitation of the hero's social and military status. Next, he shifted the emphasis to the psychology of the main characters, especially to that of the wife, whose problem is indicated in the third title, *La Comtesse à deux maris*. Later, however, since the stoic colonel was, after all, the chief character, Balzac finally adopted the present title, *Le Colonel Chabert*. He wrote to Mme Hanska in regard to this story: "J'ai trouvé cela détestable, manquant de goût, de vérité."[444] Hence the changes and corrections. Apparently, he was at last satisfied, for Davin-Balzac says: "Maintenant, grâce aux changements heureux que l'auteur vient de faire subir à *la Comtesse à deux maris* ... cette étude est une histoire irréprochable."[445]

The changes in title, as well as the textual insertions concerning the types of the law offices, indicate, first, Balzac's sociological preoccupation and, second, his desire to fit the story into the general scheme of the *Comédie humaine*. In the 1835 edition of the novel he added the Derville tirade, in which he summarized, along with other stories, *Le Père Goriot*. Furthermore, he developed the reappearing characters, whose relationships were further clarified in the next edition of 1844. On the flyleaf of the corrected Furne edition[446] Balzac indicated *Le Colonel Chabert* as being a part of the "Scènes de la vie privée," to which the tale was conse-

---

was published in Vol. IV of the "Scènes de la vie parisienne"; it reappeared in the 2d ed. of the same series in 1839; it entered the *Comédie humaine*, Vol. X, in 1844. It is now in *Con.*, Vol. VII.

[444] *LEt.*, I, 243. Letter dated March, 1835.

[445] Lov., *Hist.*, p. 63.   [446] Lov. Coll., A 17 and A 25.

quently shifted. This novel, together with a group of other legal stories, such as *Le Contrat de mariage*, *L'Interdiction*, and *Un Début dans la vie*, forms an essential part of the first subdivision of the "Etudes de mœurs." It is evident, nevertheless, that there was a doubt in Balzac's own mind as to the exact classification of these Scenes laid in Paris; each narrative deals with an individual private life; probably this consideration induced the author to place this group of stories in the "Scènes de la vie privée."

Since *L'Interdiction* is the only new story in the second edition of this category,[447] it seems expedient to discuss it at this point. *L'Interdiction*,[448] according to Balzac's notations on the corrected Furne edition of the *Comédie humaine*, is now classified in the "Scènes de la vie privée," to which it logically belongs. It had originally, in 1836, been placed inappropriately in the *Etudes philosophiques*, Werdet edition. In 1839 and again in 1844 it filled the required pages in the subdivision now under consideration. The final classification of *L'Interdiction* is explained by two parallel scenes: Judge Popinot's interviews, first, with the Marquise d'Espard, and then with her husband. In these scenes the author reveals and contrasts two lives. In the first, the marquise employs her coquetry and craftiness to seduce the honest and kindhearted Popinot in order to obtain from him a decree of restraint for her husband and thus secure control of the latter's fortune. In the second scene the judge visits the marquis and his sons. Here Balzac presents a quiet, peaceful home life devoted to the rearing of two boys and to assiduous work. During this visit the judge is convinced of Mme d'Espard's true motives in seeking to place a legal injunction upon her husband. The following words make the reader feel that Balzac primarily intended to portray private life: "Le marquis tendit sa main à Popinot, et Popinot y frappa doucement de la sienne en jetant à *ce grand homme de la vie privée* un regard plein d'harmonies pénétrantes."[449] The outstanding figure in the story is Popinot, the philanthropist and honest man-of-law. This story completes the series

---

[447] Ed. Charpentier, 2 vols., 1839.

[448] This tale first appeared in the *Chronique de Paris*, January–February, 1836; the same year it was published in the Werdet ed. of the *Etudes philosophiques*, Vols. XXIV–XXV. After its appearance in the Charpentier ed. of the "Scènes de la vie parisienne" it was placed in the Furne ed. of the *Comédie humaine*, Vol. X (1844). It is now in the "Scènes de la vie privée," *Comédie humaine*, éd. Conard, Vol. VII.

[449] *Con.*, VII, 194. Italics ours. It is interesting to note that the above statement should appear in the original manuscript and remain unchanged subsequently. See photostat of the manuscript in the University of Chicago Libraries.

now included in the *Etudes de mœurs*. However, the publication of the *Etudes philosophiques*, later to become the second main division, had already been begun.

It has been shown that from the beginning of his constructive period there were in Balzac's mind parallel drives toward the *Etudes de mœurs* and the *Etudes philosophiques*. From 1833 to 1837 he was engaged in the publication of the first three subdivisions of the former and did but little on the latter. However, his plan to utilize earlier collections of the philosophical tales for the second main division of the future *Comédie humaine* is hinted in his "Note" (1835) to the fourth edition of *La Peau de chagrin*. He says: "Aujourd'hui l'œuvre entière prend le seul titre (*Etudes philosophiques*) que l'auteur avait voulu lui imposer dès l'origine."[450] Balzac had expressed a similar intention in a letter to his publisher, dated November 13, 1833. For several years he had been promising Gosselin a novel, *Le Privilège*, never written. In this letter he offered him two new volumes of the *Contes philosophiques* in place of *Le Privilège*, but the publisher was unwilling to accept the substitute. Somewhat angered, the novelist wrote in reply: "Je crois, Monsieur, que vous ne compreniez pas toute l'importance de cet ouvrage [*Contes philosophiques*], comme publication. ... Si vous continuez à rejeter ce que je vous propose dans notre intérêt commun, je vois que l'entreprise des *R. et c.* [*phil.*], sera soumise au même dédain que les *Etudes de mœurs*."[451]

The altercation seems to have been a bad omen for the future *Etudes philosophiques*, eventually published by Edmond Werdet. This publication—in four series, or *livraisons*, of five volumes each—appeared between 1835 and 1840; the first series was on sale in January, 1835; the second in September, 1836; of these Werdet was the sole publisher. In October, 1836, however, he claimed bankruptcy;[452] consequently, the third series was published conjointly by Delloye and Lecou. Although this series was registered in the *Bibliographie de la France* on July 8, 1837, it did not appear until August 17.[453] The fourth and last series, published by Hippolyte Souverain, appeared on June 4, 1840. This protracted publication, by three different firms as well as by different printers, is partly responsible for the very complicated numbering of those volumes which actually ap-

[450] *OD.*, III, 407.

[451] Lov. Coll., A 287, fol. 103. This letter has been published in the *Revue bleue*, 4th ser., XX (1903), 644.

[452] Spoelberch de Lovenjoul, art. cit., *RHL*, 1907, pp. 393 ff.

[453] *Ibid.*, p. 395.

peared. Balzac repeatedly announced that the complete series would contain twenty-five or thirty volumes. The numeration and contents of volumes varied in each announcement in the Werdet catalogues, as well as on the cover pages of the *Etudes de mœurs*, then in course of publication. In the summer of 1834 Balzac printed two prospectuses, of which the *en-têtes* were identical; but again the contents of these volumes were shifted.[454] Of the projected volumes of the *Etudes philosophiques*, only twenty appeared. The numbers of these were later arbitrarily changed to give the impression of a continuous series of twenty volumes.

In this second main division of Balzac's future *Comédie humaine* the questions of *mœurs* and *roman social* are not paramount; for up to 1833 at least half of his work belonged to the "philosophical" type of fiction in which he deals with mental and moral deviation and in which passions are treated as the driving forces of human life. Balzac's plans for the *Etudes philosophiques* are set forth in his correspondence, in his prefaces, and in the Davin-Balzac Introduction of 1834. Of this last the novelist wrote frankly to Mme Hanska in a letter dated December 22, 1834—January, 1835: "Vous devinerez facilement que l'*Introduction* m'a autant coûté qu'à ce M. Davin, car il a fallu le *serinetter* et le recorriger jusqu'à ce qu'il eût exprimé convenablement ma pensée."[455] In the *Etudes philosophiques* the author sought to explain the hidden mechanism of human life. The characters are individualized types, yet symbols of abstract ideas—for example, Maître Cornélius, a symbol of avarice. The basic idea, says Davin-Balzac, is that "la pensée, augmentée de la force passagère que lui prête la passion, et telle que la société la fait, devient nécessairement pour l'homme un poison, un poignard."[456] The novelist reiterates in 1839 ideas already expressed in 1831 concerning this group of tales which were to continue *La Peau de chagrin* by showing "le désordre que la pensée arrivée à tout son développement produit dans l'âme ... [and that] la fantaisie y [*Etudes philosophiques*] dominera d'une manière sensible."[457] This type of fiction, then, springs from the treatment of abstract ideas and symbols.

It would seem that Balzac attempted to devise subdivisions for the *Etudes philosophiques*, as he had done for the *Etudes de mœurs*. A memorandum in his notebook listed titles of stories, now included in the *Etudes*

454 *Ibid.*, p. 403.

455 *LEt.*, I, 222. For Balzac's participation in the "Introduction" to the *Etudes de mœurs*, see below, p. 132.

456 Lov., *Hist.*, p. 201.   457 Preface to *Une Fille d'Ève, OD.*, III, 528–29.

philosophiques, under the following proposed subdivisions: "la vie d'action," "la vie du cœur," and "la vie du cerveau"; these groupings, however, were never used. As in the case of the *Etudes de mœurs* series, the *Etudes philosophiques* were largely an extension of previously published collective volumes.[458] Balzac was, in reality, doing double work: revising, enlarging, and fitting into his scheme previously written stories and at the same time creating new ones for the second division of the future *Comédie humaine*. Therefore, here also we deal with two kinds of material, old and new. Of the twenty-five stories in the twenty volumes, first issued under the general title *Etudes philosophiques*, eleven were new in the division; of these, two—*Adieu* and *L'Interdiction*—have been analyzed in other categories. Consequently, we shall discuss only nine new stories,[459] in the chronological order of their appearance in the *livraisons*.

Although the order adopted in this study is chronological, it becomes, upon occasion, advisable to give precedence to logical sequence. Hence we shall now analyze a collective volume, *Le Livre mystique*,[460] not originally published in the series under discussion; but since the title and contents of *Le Livre mystique* are suggestive of this category, it may be considered as one of its subdivisions. The three stories (*Louis Lambert, Séraphita, Les Proscrits*) in this volume are obviously mystical and philosophical and were ultimately classed in the proper division. In the Preface to the first edition of *Le Livre mystique* (1835) Balzac himself brings out the relation of this collective volume to the *Etudes philosophiques*, while defending the mystical and the idealistic views expressed in the stories. He says: " ... ce livre est destiné à offrir l'expression nette de la penseé religieuse, jetée comme une âme en ce long ouvrage."[461] He continues his explanation by asserting that, since Louis Lambert and Séraphita are mystics, they must speak and act in character; they symbolize both human sentiment and systems: "Séraphita, blanche et pure expression du mysticisme ... connaît l'infini, les mesures du fini doivent alors lui paraître mesquines."[462]

Séraphita,[463] the only new title in the *Livre mystique*, was, then, per-

---

[458] See above, pp. 40, 70.

[459] Of which four—*Séraphita, Melmoth réconcilié, Gambara*, and *Massimilla Doni*—had been published earlier in individual volumes but not yet in divisions.

[460] 1st ed. (December, 1835); 2d ed. (February, 1836), in 2 vols., published by Werdet.

[461] *OD.*, III, 418.   [462] *Ibid.*, pp. 418–27.

[463] The beginning of this story was published in the *Revue de Paris*, June–July, 1834. The complete tale appeared in the two editions of *Le Livre mystique* (1835 and 1836) and

manently classed in the *Etudes philosophiques* (1840 and subsequently) because of its purely mystical philosophy. For Balzac the character of Séraphita was the symbol of celestial perfection, and the novel was intended as a fitting conclusion for the category of the *Etudes philosophiques*. He wrote the story under the influence of the work of Swedenborg, whose mystical raptures are voiced by Séraphita-Séraphitüs, a creation of mixed nature—half-human, half-angelic. Taine states that in Séraphita "la destinée humaine est présentée comme une suite de vies ascendantes où l'âme, guidée d'abord par l'amour de soi, puis par l'amour des êtres et enfin par l'amour du ciel, traverse tour à tour le monde naturel, le monde spirituel et le monde divin."[464] Wilfrid personified self-love: Minna, womanly love; and Séraphita, love of God. Both Wilfrid and Minna symbolize the purification of human passion through divine aspiration and their desire to unite themselves with the Infinite. It is appropriate that the story should be aligned with *Louis Lambert*, also inspired by the Swedenborgian doctrine of faith. In *Séraphita*, in *Les Proscrits*, in *L'Enfant maudit*, and in *Jésus-Christ en Flandre* Balzac emphasized faith as a comforting factor in life and as a purifying element of the human spirit in its ascent toward the mystery of eternity. Having established the logical connection between *Le Livre mystique* and the *Etudes philosophiques*, we shall now continue our discussion of the first *livraison* of the latter.

Only one new story was added to the first *livraison*, *Un Drame au bord de la mer*.[465] It continues the study of remorse which Balzac made earlier in *L'Auberge rouge*. In the *Drame au bord de la mer*, as in *El Verdugo* and in *Les Marana*, an exaggerated idea of family honor leads to murder. Logically, then, this story is classified with the other three in the *Etudes philosophiques* and later in the division of the same title. We have here a dramatic account of how a father, a Breton fisherman, preferred to see his dissipated son dead rather than imprisoned and publicly executed. He

---

was reprinted in 1840 by Souverain, under a new collective title, *Le Livre des douleurs*, in Vols. XXVIII and XXIX of the *Etudes philosophiques*. In 1842 it appeared, together with *Louis Lambert*, in 1 vol., published by Charpentier; in 1844 it entered the *Comédie humaine*, Vol. XVI, and is now in *Con.*, Vol. XXXI.

[464] *Nouveaux Essais de critique et d'histoire*, p. 92.

[465] This story, with a new title, *La Justice paternelle*, reappeared in 1843, together with *La Muse du département*, *Rosalie* (*Albert Savarus*), and *Le Père Canet* (*Facino Cane*), under the general title *Les Mystères de province*, published by Souverain in 4 vols. Under its present title it entered the *Comédie humaine*, Etudes philosophiques, Vol. XV (1846). The story is now in *Con.*, Vol. XXIX.

says: "Je ne veux pas qu'un Cambremer soit fait mourir sur la place du Croisic."[466] He threw his son from a cliff into the ocean; then, tortured by remorse, he became a hermit, lived on bread and water, and dwelt in the shadow of a cross on the scene of his crime.[467]

In the second *livraison* (September, 1836) we note only two new stories, *L'Interdiction*[468] (already dealt with) and *Melmoth réconcilié*.[469] The latter had its origin in *Le Centenaire* (*Le Sorcier* or *Les Deux Beringheld*) of 1822 but was more directly inspired, as Balzac stated in his "Note" to the first edition,[470] by the *Melmoth* of the Rev. Charles R. Maturin.[471] In 1828 Balzac bought from the publisher, Hubert, a translation of the English story, by M. Jean Cohen.[472] The subject must have haunted the novelist's mind, for there is an allusion to it in the first edition of *La Peau de chagrin* (1831). In *Melmoth réconcilié* the author used the Faust theme. His Melmoth possessed magic powers but could neither overcome remorse nor satisfy his desire—to save his soul—unless he passed on his demoniac passion to another human being. The victim chosen was Castanier, a dishonest clerk in a banking-house, who, to escape the consequences of a theft, exchanged his soul for the fatal powers of Melmoth. After satisfying his passions, Castanier reached satiety, where his almost unlimited power became the source of his greatest wretchedness—he had sold his soul "au prix de son éternité bienheureuse."[473] Driven by remorse and fear, he sought in turn to save his soul from the demon. He found a suitable subject, Claparon, at the Exchange, where, says Balzac, since 1815 the principle of honor had been replaced by that of greed. From Claparon this diabolical power passed in turn through many hands until it perished with a miserable clerk, who died without remorse and without repentance.

[466] *Con.*, XXIX, 193.

[467] It is noteworthy that this story, written in November, 1834, should contain two reappearing characters, Louis Lambert and Pauline de Villenoix.

[468] See above, p. 109.

[469] This story first appeared in Vol. VI of the *Livre des conteurs*, a collective work compiled by several authors and published by Lequien, June, 1835. The same year it was published in the *Etudes philosophiques*, Vol. XXII (changed to Vol. XIV in 1840), and not in Vol. V, as indicated in Lov., *Hist.*, p. 178. The error was not repeated, however, on p. 163. The story entered the *Comédie humaine*, Vol. XIV (1845), and is now in *Con.*, Vol. XXVII.

[470] *OD.*, III, 417–18.   [471] Translated into French in 1821.

[472] For this information we are indebted to M. Marcel Bouteron.

[473] *Con.*, XXVII, 355.

Balzac's purpose in this is precisely that developed elsewhere in the *Etudes philosophiques*—to show the destructive effect of an intensified *idée fixe* which, when it becomes passion, exalts and then annihilates man. It is self-evident that *Melmoth réconcilié* continues the idea of *La Peau de chagrin* and is a component part of the *Etudes philosophiques*, in which it was permanently classified—whether as a "set" or as a main division of the *Comédie humaine*.

Between March, 1835, and September, 1836, Balzac made four different announcements regarding the third *livraison*, but no others appeared until August 17, 1837, when *La Presse* advertised the sale of the volumes. Spoelberch de Lovenjoul[474] explains this long silence by Werdet's pseudo-bankruptcy, of October, 1836. The volumes of this series had been handled by several firms; new publishers continued the publication, as indicated by their names on the inside title-pages of Volumes XII, XV, XVI, and XVII of this third *livraison*. These shifts reveal the harassing conditions under which the *Etudes philosophiques* were published and give evidence of a situation which partly explains the flagrant errors in content and pagination of these volumes.

The third *livraison* contained most of the new material in the series. There were nine stories, of which five were new; of these, *La Messe de l'athée*[475] was at first placed temporarily in the division under consideration; then, in 1844, in the "Scènes de la vie parisienne." In both cases the misplacement was due to the exigency of completing the *feuilles*, a matter always irritating to Balzac. But, on planning a second edition of the *Comédie humaine*, he indicated, in his own hand, on a leaf pasted in Volume I[476] of the first Furne edition, that *La Messe de l'athée*, together with other stories[477] of the "Scènes de la vie parisienne," was to be permanently classified in the "Scènes de la vie privée." Consequently, in the prospectus of 1846, to which the Conard edition conforms, these stories are listed in the designated subdivision. *La Messe de l'athée* is the story of Dr. Desplein, the inner meaning of whose life was inadvertently discovered by his disciple and friend, Bianchon. In a touching manner Balzac

---

[474] See art. cit., in *RHL*, 1907, pp. 394–95, 426.

[475] This story first appeared in *La Chronique de Paris*, January 3, 1836. After its publication in the *Etudes philosophiques* it entered, in 1844, the *Comédie humaine*, Vol. X ("Scènes de la vie parisienne," Vol. II). It is now in *Con.*, Vol. VII ("Scènes de la vie privée").

[476] Lov. Coll., A 17.

[477] *Le Père Goriot, Le Colonel Chabert, Pierre Grassou*, and *L'Interdiction*.

tells how the profound gratitude of the scientific and skeptical Desplein disrupted his own principles. For twenty years he had been paying for annual Masses which he attended in respectful memory of the simple faith of a water-carrier, a humble Auvergnat, who had sacrificed his life-savings and ambition to aid the youth in attaining his own aim to become a famous physician. It is a charming tale of brotherly love, which, according to Balzac, belongs and was finally classified in the "Scènes de la vie privée."

The next new story in Volume XII of the third *livraison* is *Facino Cane*.[478] Although essentially an *étude de mœurs*, it served first as a "filler" for this volume. For the same purpose, but under the title *Le Père Canet*, Balzac later grouped it with other stories under the collective title *Les Mystères de province*. Ultimately, in 1844, he classified this short sketch in the "Scènes de la vie parisienne," in which the typical Parisian setting, the intensity of passions, and the resultant murder, as in the case of *Sarrasine* and of *La Fille aux yeux d'or*, definitely belong. In these stories the author ferrets out the hidden secrets of human lives which have been distorted by some abnormal bent of mind or by an unfavorable milieu. *Facino Cane* is the story of a blind musician, a former Venetian prince, who possessed the magic power of seeing hidden gold through walls. After a series of murders and escapades, and blind and impoverished, he descended to the deepest degradation. This story is also one of the semi-reminiscent tales of a period of Balzac's youth spent in the Rue Lesdiguières. In an interesting passage he explains his intuitive power of penetrating another person's mind and soul and of projecting his own personality into his characters and living, so to speak, their lives.[479]

The last story in Volume XII is *Les Martyrs ignorés* (*Fragment du Phédon d'aujourd'hui*),[480] written in dialogue. A few writers and scholars are accustomed to gather in the evenings around the "Table des Philosophes" at the Café Voltaire. The action takes place in December, 1827,

---

[478] This tale first appeared in *La Chronique de Paris*, March 17, 1836. After publication in the category under consideration it was published with a new title, *Le Père Canet*. See above, n. 465. In 1844, but under its first title, the story entered the *Comédie humaine*, Vol. X ("Scènes de la vie parisienne"), and is now in *Con.*, Vol. XVI.

[479] See Paul Bourget, *Essais de psychologie contemporaine*, II, 87 ff.

[480] After this tale appeared in the division under consideration it was, together with *La Dernière Incarnation de Vautrin* and *Une Rue de Paris et son habitant*, published by Chlendowski in 3 vols., in 1848. It is now in the *OD.*, I, 351–88.

a time when Balzac actually lived in the neighborhood of the café.[481] Each of the group tells a story which illustrates the ravaging effects of exaggerated thought upon men, "les martyrs ignorés." This feature aligns the story with *La Peau de chagrin, Louis Lambert, Melmoth réconcilié*, and others in the *Etudes philosophiques*, where the author originally placed it. One of the speakers gives the main idea: "La pensée est plus puissante que ne l'est le corps, elle le mange, l'absorbe et le détruit; la pensée est le plus violent de tous les agents de destruction, elle est le véritable ange exterminateur de l'humanité qu'elle tue et vivifie, car elle vivifie et tue."[482] Next, the interlocutor varies his thought but slightly: "Savez-vous ce que j'entends par penser? Les passions, les vices, les occupations extrêmes, les douleurs, les plaisirs sont des torrens de pensées. Réunissez sur un point donnée quelques idées violentes, un homme est tué par elles comme s'il recevait un coup de poignard."[483] In spite of these definitions, obviously classifying *Les Martyrs ignorés* as belonging to the philosophical series, the story never entered the *Comédie humaine*. One is tempted to conjecture that, had Balzac lived to complete his work, this tale would have remained among the *Etudes philosophiques* and later been included in the second division of the *Comédie humaine*.

Volume XIII, also of the third *livraison*, contained but one story, *Le Secret des Ruggieri*.[484] Here Balzac takes up the events after the massacre of Saint Bartholomew, when the king, Charles IX, became aware of his mother's insatiable ambition, her passion for power to which all other sentiments were sacrificed. He himself consulted Laurent and Cosme as to the future and thus learned the extent of their influence on his mother's policy.[485] This tale, under a less appropriate title, *La Confidence des Ruggieri*, now forms Part II of *Sur Catherine de Médicis*. The reason for this

[481] Baldensperger, *op. cit.*, p. 103.

[482] *Martyrs ignorés, Etudes philosophiques*, éd. Werdet, XII, 251–52.

[483] *Ibid.*, pp. 252–53.

[484] This story first appeared in *La Chronique de Paris*, December, 1836. With an "Introduction," it was published by Souverain in 1842, in 3 vols., together with *Le Martyr calviniste*, under the general title *Catherine de Médicis expliquée;* under the same title the story was published by Chlendowski in 1845, in 3 vols. In 1846, under the new title *La Confidence des Ruggieri*, it was placed as Part II of *Sur Catherine de Médicis* in the *Etudes philosophiques, Comédie humaine*, Vol. XVI; it is now in *Con.*, Vol. XXX. See W. L. Crain's unpublished Ph.D. dissertation, "A Critical Edition of *Le Secret des Ruggieri*" (University of Chicago, 1937), and chap. iv of this volume.

[485] *Sur Catherine de Médicis* was not finished until 1842. The complete novel will be discussed in the section on the Furne ed. of the *Comédie humaine*.

change in title is obscure. *Le Secret des Ruggieri* refers definitely to the information withheld by the Ruggieri from Charles IX, who sought to learn whether the queen, his mother, had attempted to poison him. This title, therefore, seems more closely related to the action of the story than the rather vague *La Confidence*. Since *Les Deux Rêves*, now Part III of the same novel, was published in 1831 under the collective title *Romans et contes philosophiques*, it is logical that *Le Secret des Ruggieri* should be likewise classified in the same series. In this story Balzac presents the cabalistic doctrine of the brothers Ruggieri, whom he calls "les deux personnages philosophiques."[486] These counselors to Catherine, whom she trusted implicitly, were seeking by means of their astrological formulas the mystery of life. The following characterization of Catherine also has a bearing on the classification of the story:

Deux mots expliquent cette femme si curieuse à étudier. ... Ces deux mots sont Domination et Astrologie. Exclusivement ambitieuse, Catherine de Médicis n'eut d'autre passion que celle du pouvoir. Superstitieuse et fataliste comme le furent tant d'hommes supérieurs, elle n'eut de croyances sincères que les Sciences Occultes.[487]

Volume XVI, the last of the third *livraison* to be discussed, contained only one new story, *Une Passion dans le désert*,[488] an episode from a projected novel, *Les Français en Egypte*. Obviously from its title, this novel was intended for the proposed *Scènes de la vie militaire* but was left unfinished. In order to fill two *feuilles*[489] for the completion of this volume, Balzac put the story temporarily in the *Etudes philosophiques*. In 1846, however, this tale, the experience of a soldier during the French campaign in Egypt, rightfully took its place in the limited group of military stories. There is some controversy as to its origin. Mme Surville[490] maintains that it was suggested by Martin, the famous trainer of animals; on the other hand, Ratier,[491] the editor of *La Silhouette*, claims the honor for himself. It is more than probable that both sources were involved. This tale concludes our discussion of the third *livraison*.

[486] *Con.*, XXX, 268.   [487] *Ibid.*

[488] This story first appeared in *La Revue de Paris*, December, 1830. After its publication in the *Etudes philosophiques*, it was published, together with *Modeste Mignon* and *Un Episode sous la Terreur*, by G. Roux and Cassanet in 4 vols. In 1846 it entered the "Scènes de la vie militaire" (*Comédie humaine*, Vol. XIII), and is now in *Con.*, Vol. XXII.

[489] *Pensées, sujets, fragmens*, éd. Crépet, p. 103.

[490] *Op. cit.*, p. 105.   [491] See Lov., *Hist.*, p. 403.

Chronologically speaking, *Le Livre des douleurs*, published[492] in 1840, does not belong to the second period of Balzac's literary career. Since, however, it forms the fourth *livraison* of the *Etudes philosophiques*, it should be considered under the present caption. When, in 1835, the author planned this *livraison*, he designated for it a particular story,[493] *Le Livre des douleurs* and indicated its main idea and coloring in his notebook:

Le Livre des douleurs est une étude destinée à prouver qu'il existe un point d'appui matériel dans la pensée pour supporter les plus effroyables douleurs et que ce n'est pas un secours venu d'en haut. En ôtant l'idée religieuse chrétienne et prenant trois exemples authentiques: Béatrice de Cenci.—Le tailleur de Henri II ou tout autre martyr protestant et un régicide Chatel ou Damiens.[494]

No single story of like title was ever written; but the subject was developed in *Les Martyrs ignorés*,[495] particularly in the tale of the unbroken spirit of Robert-François Damiens, who had been first tortured, then quartered, for having struck Louis XV with a penknife.[496] When, finally, the fourth *livraison* went on sale, June 4, 1840, it bore the title *Le Livre des douleurs*, which may be, like *Le Livre mystique* (1835 and 1836), properly considered a subdivision of the later *Etudes philosophiques*.

Le Livre des douleurs, the only *livraison* bearing a general title, included four stories. Of these, *Les Proscrits* and *Séraphita* had been previously published, together with other philosophical tales, under collective titles, while *Gambara* and *Massimilla Doni* had been temporarily grouped with still other novels in individual volumes.

Gambara[497] is, above all, a study of a master-passion, an ideal in art, the pursuit of which, as in *Le Chef-d'œuvre inconnu*, led to a human tragedy. Paolo Gambara—"ce Louis Lambert," as Balzac designates him in a letter—is only a theorist: his great desire to regenerate music and his passion to attain the ideal in sound, as Frenhofer sought to do in painting, key him up to an "extase musicale" but paralyze all creative ability with-

---

[492] By Souverain, in 5 vols.

[493] Spoelberch de Lovenjoul, art. cit., *RHL*, 1907, pp. 436, 441.

[494] Lov. Coll., A 181, fol. 99.

[495] See above, p. 116. [496] *Larousse du XXᵉ siècle.*

[497] This story first appeared in *La Revue et gazette musicale de Paris*, July–August, 1837. In 1839 it was published, together with *Le Cabinet des antiques*, by Souverain in 2 vols. It entered the category under consideration in 1840, and in 1846 the *Comédie humaine*, Vol. XV. It is now in *Con.*, Vol. XXVIII.

in him. When he attempts to interpret his ideas in composition and in execution, he is no longer understood except by his wife, Marianna.[498] This great artist, the inventor of the panharmonicon, an instrument designed to replace a whole orchestra, is finally reduced to singing duos with his wife on street corners. Gambara becomes the mouthpiece of his creator, whose theory he analyzes lucidly:

> ... nous sommes victimes de notre propre supériorité ... quand la musique passe de la sensation à l'idée, elle ne peut avoir que des gens de génie pour auditeurs, car eux seuls ont la puissance de la développer. Mon malheur vient d'avoir écouté les concerts des anges et d'avoir cru que les hommes pouvaient les comprendre. ... Ah! Monsieur, dit-il d'une voix sourde, au moins fallait-il me laisser ma folie.[499]

The temporary coupling, in 1839, of *Gambara* and a story of life in the provinces, *Le Cabinet des antiques*, was merely a question of expediency. In two letters dated December, 1839, Balzac comments on this exigency to his publisher, Souverain. He states that *Gambara* will supply the lacking twelve *feuilles* for the completion of the volume.[500] Moreover, in one of his typical prefaces he confirms the fact: "... *Gambara* [est] une *Etude philosophique* ajoutée à une *Etude de mœurs* pour arriver au nombre de feuilles exigé par la jurisprudence bibliographique."[501] Balzac announced the central purpose of the story in a letter of May 29, 1837, to Maurice Schlesinger, editor of *La Gazette musicale*. It was, the author said, to "exprimer mes idées en musique, si toutefois je puis réduire mes sensations à l'état d'idées, et en tirer quelque chose qui ait l'air d'un système philosophique."[502] Again, in a letter to Mme Hanska, he justifies his classification of *Gambara* and *Le Chef-d'œuvre inconnu* in this *livraison*.

> *Massimilla Doni* et *Gambara* sont, dans les *Etudes philosophiques*, l'apparition de la musique, sous la double forme d'*exécution* et de *composition*, soumise à la même épreuve que la pensée dans *Louis Lambert*, c'est-à-dire l'œuvre et l'exécution tuées par la trop grande abondance du principe créateur, ce qui m'a dicté le *Chef-d'œuvre inconnu* pour la peinture. ...[503]

---

[498] In her love for Gambara there is something of the devotion and understanding which Pauline de Villenoix has for Louis Lambert; in both cases the women seem to be in love with genius.

[499] *Con.*, XXVIII, 106, 101. Cf. the situation of Frenhofer, the painter, in *Le Chef-d'œuvre inconnu*.

[500] W. S. Hastings, *Balzac and Souverain*, pp. 19–20.

[501] Preface to *Une Fille d'Ève* and *Massimilla Doni*, OD., III, 528.

[502] *Ibid.*, p. 495.   [503] *LEt.*, I, 398–99. Letter dated May 24, 1837.

This statement is important, since it embodies Balzac's own alignment of the major illustrations of his theory as demonstrated in the *Etudes philosophiques*.

The small number of variations[504] between the first edition (1837) and the Conard proves that Balzac had well in mind, from the beginning, the specific niche into which the novel was to be fitted. In 1846 he inserted a brief comment to link *Gambara* more intimately with the *Etudes philosophiques* and placed it finally in the *Comédie humaine*.

Closely related in thought and method to the preceding story is *Massimilla Doni*;[505] in fact, Taine considers the two tales as a "petit roman en deux parties."[506] In *Massimilla Doni* Balzac continues his exposition of the ideal of art in general and of music in particular, as presented in *Gambara* and in *Le Chef-d'œuvre inconnu*. The story, in which he deals with thought and passion as destructive of creative ability and of human life, becomes, therefore, an integral part of the *Etudes philosophiques*. In explaining Genovese's failure to sing the aria, Balzac makes the following claim:

> Quand un artiste a le malheur d'être plein de la passion qu'il veut exprimer, il ne saurait la peindre, car il est la chose même au lieu d'en être l'image. L'art procède du cerveau et non du cœur. Quand votre sujet vous domine, vous en êtes l'esclave et non le maître. Vous êtes comme un roi assiégé par son peuple. Sentir trop vivement au moment où il s'agit d'exécuter, c'est l'insurrection des sens contre la faculté![507]

One is inclined to believe that the author here interprets his own experience. Apparently, he was satisfied with *Massimilla Doni*, for on May 24, 1837, he wrote to Mme Hanska that he had just finished the story, and added: "Si je puis réaliser toutes mes idées comme elles se sont présentées dans ma tête, ce sera, certes, un livre aussi étourdissant que la *Peau de chagrin*, mieux écrit, plus poétique peut-être."[508] In his long disquisitions on music and in his careful analysis of Rossini's opera *Mosé*, Balzac de-

---

[504] See H. S. Graybill, "Variations and Realism in Balzac's *Gambara*" (unpublished Master's thesis, University of Chicago, 1927).

[505] This story was first published, together with *Une Fille d'Ève*, by Souverain in 2 vols. A fragment, "Une Représentation du *Mosé* de Rossini à Venise," appeared in *La France musicale*, August 25, 1839. After its appearance in *Le Livre des douleurs* (1840), the story entered the *Etudes philosophiques*, *Comédie humaine*, Vol. XV (1846), and is now in *Con.*, Vol. XXVII.

[506] Taine, *op. cit.*, p. 73.

[507] *Con.*, XXVII, 462.   [508] *LEt.*, I, 398.

velops an interesting thesis of mysticism in music; he says that the emotion aroused by music detaches the listener from reality and lifts him into the metaphysical spheres and into the infinite.[509] Man can attain similar mystical voluptuousness, he continues, through platonic love, as did Emilio de Varese,[510] or through opium, as did Vendramin.

The story is almost plotless. Interest is centered in the development of artistic theories rather than in action or in characters. The latter exist merely to demonstrate the author's thesis. The love between Emilio and Massimilla, the loss of Genovese's voice, the disintegration of Vendramin's personality, merely supply loose connecting threads of narrative. Contrary to the other philosophical tales, this one ends well, through the intervention of the materialistic and wise French physician, who brings about the happiness of the lovers and restores to Genovese his beautiful voice; for Vendramin, the opium addict, the physician can do nothing. Balzac, soon after his return from Italy in 1837, announced this story as a philosophical study. Its first title, Les Deux Amours, later kept as a chapter caption, was changed to the more specific Massimilla Doni. This story concludes our analyses of the Etudes philosophiques, Werdet edition, and closes Balzac's second period.

The significant features of the second period in Balzac's literary career are: (1) the development and the crystallization of his scheme, in structure and scope; (2) its unification through the introduction of reappearing characters (May, 1833); (3) his decision to become the social historian of French society of the nineteenth century; and (4) his creation of the roman social as a medium suitable for carrying out his intentions. At the basis of his scheme lies a deterministic, scientific view founded on his theory that environment, trades, and professions divide men, so to speak, into social species comparable to the classifications of the zoölogical world. This theory, discernible in 1830, was fully adopted as a basic working principle by 1837.

In the process of development, as he observed and analyzed society, Balzac reached the conclusion that only a few fundamental principles actuate numerous causes, which in turn bring about numberless effects or actions occurring in everyday life. The three motivating factors in human society—principles, causes, and effects—underlie the three main divisions of the plan which form different levels in the structure of the future Comédie humaine.

[509] Con., XXVII, 425. [510] Ibid., pp. 425, 427.

By 1837 Balzac's plan had taken concrete form in the publication of fifty classified stories, of which twenty-two were new, while twenty-eight consisted of old material, revised, enlarged, and fitted to the growing system. The scheme now comprised two main divisions: the *Etudes de mœurs* and the *Etudes philosophiques*. The first edition of the former series contained twenty-five stories, of which eleven were new (plus the two last episodes of *Les Trois Vengeances*). These, distributed among the three subdivisions, were ultimately retained as such in the *Comédie humaine*. Within the second period the third edition of the "Scènes de la vie privée" was made to include two of the new titles; the first edition of the "Scènes de la vie de province" was assigned six; the "Scènes de la vie parisienne," three, since the *Histoire des Treize* is regarded as one novel. Of these eleven new stories in the first edition of the *Etudes de mœurs*, five were later transposed: one each from the "Scènes de la vie privée" and the "Scènes de la vie parisienne" were permanently placed in the *Etudes philosophiques;* one from the "Scènes de la vie parisienne" and two from the "Scènes de la vie de province" were ultimately shifted to the "Scènes de la vie privée."

The almost equal number of new stories in each main division seems to indicate an interest evenly divided among the groups. Such is not the case; there was an overlapping. Although the new stories of the *Etudes de mœurs* were published strictly within the second period (1833–37), the publication of the eleven new stories of the *Etudes philosophiques* was extended into the third (1833–40). Of these stories, four were presently reclassified: one was permanently assigned to the "Scènes de la vie parisienne"; two others were temporarily placed in the same subdivision and finally put in the "Scènes de la vie privée"; one was directly transferred to the "Scènes de la vie militaire."

During the second period Balzac's novels exhibit the growth of a sociological interest which leads to a still greater broadening of the scheme toward the all-inclusive scope of the third period. This will be the matter for analysis in our next section.

V. THIRD PERIOD: 1837–41

Our discussion of the third period in Balzac's literary career (1837–41) is necessarily short, since there were no new serial publications except the reprint of the *Etudes de mœurs*. The period embraces, however, an important phase in the development of the novelist's general plans.

In the preceding section we discussed the formulation and the establishment of Balzac's scheme; we analyzed the classification of stories in the first edition of the *Etudes de mœurs* and the *Etudes philosophiques*. However, his classification at that time was not final, since it did not yet include all works produced during the second period (1833–37). Three important social studies—*Le Médecin de campagne, Le Père Goriot,* and *Le Lys dans la vallée*[511]—were published independently of subdivisions between 1833 and 1836 and were not included in the second edition of the *Etudes de mœurs* (1839). Balzac also published, in separate volumes, between 1837 and 1839, seven other unclassified novels:[512] *Histoire de la grandeur et de la décadence de César Birotteau, La Maison Nucingen, Illusions perdues* (Part II, *Un Grand Homme de province à Paris*), *La Torpille* (Part I of *Splendeurs et misères des courtisanes*), *La Femme supérieure* (*Les Employés*), *Le Cabinet des antiques,* and *Une Fille d'Ève.*

These titles arrest our attention; each demonstrates a sociological interest either in groups or in institutions and indicates Balzac's more intensive study of types and groups. Such a view is strengthened by his insertions,[513] which usually took the form of more extensive *dossiers* concerning sociohistorical institutions and events. The ten novels cited are of importance in a study of the development[514] in Balzac's plans; the stages are shown not only in the novels but also in the prefaces written for them.

It is well now to check the aspects of the unfolding scheme apparent especially in the last seven novels. In *Histoire de la grandeur et de la décadence de César Birotteau* and in *La Maison Nucingen* Balzac portrays private business and banking on a large scale and thus affords a view of various milieus. This is done, in the first novel, Part I, by giving a detailed account of a busy day in the life of César and by presenting his grand ball. One hundred and four reappearing characters figure in the first novel, and fifty in the second. *Illusions perdues,*[515] Balzac's largest tableau of life, including the work of literary men, journalists, printers, lawyers, and usurers, contains one hundred and sixteen reappearing characters. In *Splendeurs et misères des courtisanes* he gives a new aspect of

[511] See below, pp. 145, 147, 163.

[512] For the analyses and classification of these novels, see below, pp. 148, 150, 146, 152, 151, 144, 136.

[513] See studies in variations in other chapters of this volume.

[514] In Sec. III, in the analyses of certain stories, we were forced to anticipate, to some degree, the present discussion.

[515] Part I, *Les Deux Poètes;* see above, p. 102.

French society, the Bohemian life of actresses and courtesans, with the highest number of reappearing characters—one hundred and fifty-five. These last two compositions present "le monde exceptionnel."[516] Indeed, the first novel may be called "epic" in structure and spirit. It portrays the life and work of Lucien de Rubempré, whose "illusions," nurtured in Angoulême, are lost in Paris, the all-devouring monster. In *Les Employés*, the novelist depicted a large bureaucratic group—the clerks of the government. In this novel Mary Scott has reported ninety-six recurring characters.[517] In *Le Cabinet des antiques*, in which Ethel Preston[518] counted fifty-six reappearing characters, Balzac pictured a very large circle of aristocrats and politicians both in the provinces and in the capital. In *Une Fille d'Ève* he returned to the depiction of domesticity disturbed by the Bohemian type of journalist; this story contains forty-two reappearing characters. We see, therefore, that in these novels (written between 1836 and 1839) he reached his widest scope in presentation of French society, including the financial, the political, the literary, and the theatrical world. Moreover, in this depiction, as Brunetière has justly said, our novelist achieved "l'incomparable solidité."[519]

This solidity and massive effect Balzac largely attained by bringing into relation character with character, story with story, thereby closely integrating the component parts of his literary monument. These recurring characters, like threads on the weaver's loom, cross and recross each other and give verisimilitude to an interdependent society. In this manner all the material, moral, and spiritual factors of group life are artistically correlated. The number of reappearing characters, greater than those introduced prior to 1836,[520] is conclusive evidence of the development of his plan.

This growth is manifest not only in the larger number of reappearing characters, in insertions, and in revisions of sociological import but also in Balzac's concurrently written prefaces. Of special interest are the prefaces[521] to *Illusions perdues* (1837 and 1839); to *Les Employés*, *La Maison*

[516] See above, p. 102, n. 423.

[517] "Variations between the First and Second Edition of Balzac's *Les Employés*," *MP*, XXIII, 331.

[518] *Op. cit.*, Appen. VI.   [519] *Op. cit.*, p. 157.

[520] Cf. Canfield, art. cit., *RHL*, XLI, 15.

[521] Partly discussed from a different point of view; see above, p. 105.

Nucingen, and *La Torpille* (1838); and to *Le Cabinet des antiques* and *Une Fille d'Ève* (1838).

The significance of the Preface[522] to *Illusions perdues*, Part I (1837), lies in the fact that here, for the first time since Davin's introductions, Balzac gave the range and the scope of his categories and explained the basic principle, a view of contemporary society, as an organization based on the analogy of zoölogy.[523] The Preface to Part II (1839), in which he restated with greater emphasis the sociological aspect of his work, takes the form of an indignant outburst against the wiles of journalism and is also a plea for the independence of writers. In the Preface to *Le Cabinet des antiques* (1839) and in that to Part III of *Illusions perdues* (1844)—it is necessary to anticipate, since the latter to a degree reiterates the former— Balzac stressed the closer interlocking of all the component parts of the scheme, thus securing, as he stated, a more harmonious and integrated whole. Furthermore, he introduced a new aspect of his theory: the notable opposition between the provinces and the capital by statement of parallels and differences. Also, he indicated the links which connect the provinces with Paris; the unifying force is embodied in the young men Lucien de Rubempré and the Count of Esgrignon, who, said the author, "vont et viennent de la province à Paris, ayant quelques-unes des conditions du talent sans avoir celles du succès."[524] In *Le Cabinet des antiques* an impoverished provincial aristocracy seeks means and ways in Paris to re-establish its lost fortune; in *Illusions perdues* an ambitious poet welds provincial and metropolitan life in his quest for fame; in *Les Mitouflet*,[525] a projected work, Balzac intended, so he said, to portray a wealthy manufacturer seeking honors in the capital. Nobility, genius, wealth—in representative characters—became, then, the nexus between the provinces and Paris in the second and third subdivisions of the *Etudes de mœurs*.

One further point must be made in regard to this integration of categories in the *Etudes de mœurs*. Balzac felt in 1839 that even with *Illusions perdues* and *Le Cabinet des antiques* his picture of provincial life was not yet complete. He said: "*Les Scènes de la vie de province* n'auraient-elles pas été incomplètes, si, après avoir accusé le mouvement ascensionnel de la province vers Paris, l'auteur n'indiquait pas le mouvement opposé?"[526] This project was carried out in 1843 through *Les Parisiens en province:*

[522] See preceding note.

[523] Cf. Sec. IV, p. 90; Sec. VI, pp. 133–35. [525] This work was never published.

[524] *OD.*, III, 514. [526] *OD.*, III, 515.

Part I, *L'Illustre Gaudissart*, a reprint of 1833; Part II, *La Muse du département*. He said further that after the composition of the projected *Les Héritiers Boirouge*[527] there would still remain to be done "la peinture de la garnison des villes de province et celle de quelques figures assez originales aperçues après coup, pour que cette partie de l'œuvre soit achevée."[528] This plan was never fulfilled.

In the Preface to *La Femme supérieure*, *La Maison Nucingen*, and *La Torpille* (1838), Balzac speaks less of the co-ordination of his scheme and more of his own function as a historian.[529] He gives in his novels, he says, "l'esprit des événements ... il les synthétise." In the Preface to *Une Fille d'Ève* (1839) he recapitulates briefly the main ideas of the *Etudes de mœurs* with greater emphasis on the device of reappearing characters which tie up the divisions of the plan. For example, in the persons of the actress Florine and Rastignac, the novelist connects the first three subdivisions of the *Etudes de mœurs*.[530] These instances illustrate the proportions of the scheme. Its further development, given in his prefaces written in 1842 and later, is, of course, evinced in the Furne edition of the *Comédie humaine*.

At once the question rises whether this growth of purpose caused Balzac to reclassify the novels and tales reprinted during this brief period. The second edition of the *Etudes de mœurs*, published by Charpentier in 1839, points to a negative answer. It contained the fourth edition of the "Scènes de la vie privée," the second of the "Scènes de la vie de province," and the second of the "Scènes de la vie parisienne." Each of the three groups appeared in two volumes; they did not, however, include all the stories of the Béchet-Werdet edition. The long stories, such as *La Recherche de l'absolu*, *Eugénie Grandet*, and *Histoire des Treize* (the first two episodes), were each published (1839) in separate volumes; consequently, the twenty-six tales of the first edition of the *Etudes de mœurs* are all reprinted in the second edition. There were no new tales except *L'Interdiction*,[531] temporarily placed in the "Scènes de la vie parisienne." It is clear, therefore, that the order but not the classification of the stories in each volume differed from that of the first edition of the *Etudes de mœurs*.

---

[527] *Fragments d'histoire générale. Scène de la vie de province* (fragment publié par le vicomte de Spoelberch de Lovenjoul, *RDM*, XLII [1917], 881–84). Chap. ii, "Ursule Mirouët," contains two lines only. See below, p. 141.

[528] *OD.*, III, 515.

[529] See above, p. 88, n. 366.

[530] *OD.*, III, 522–23.

[531] See above, p. 109.

It is impossible to trust Balzac's frequent statements concerning his revisions and corrections. The Charpentier edition is a case in point. One would expect considerable variations between the first and the second edition of the *Etudes de mœurs*. But the second, practically a reprint of the first, contains no textual changes except those of punctuation: a greater number of commas is introduced, making for greater clarity. Therefore, the period between 1837 and 1839 was an interregnum in which no new serial publications were added. In spite of the fact that Balzac was revising, inserting, and re-writing his works during the third period, the most sweeping changes[532] in text and classification of stories occur in the later Furne edition of the fourth period.

Here another question arises, that of the expansion of Balzac's purview upon his choice of a general title. With the drift toward the integration of more and more novels into a co-ordinated whole the idea of an all-inclusive title must have been coexistent in his mind. At least, such is the impression made by his letters of this period. It has been pointed out in Section III that, concurrently with the publication of the first edition of the *Etudes de mœurs*, Balzac had proposed a general title for all his works to date, namely, *Les Etudes sociales*.[533] On March 30, 1835, he wrote to Mme Hanska concerning a second edition of the *Etudes de mœurs;* in May of the same year he definitely stated, although contrary to fact, that "dans l'année 1837 ... mes œuvres deviendront les *Etudes sociales*."[534] By this title the author draws attention to the developing sociological aspect of his work. This proposed general title was to include the three main divisions: "Etudes de mœurs," "Etudes philosophiques," and "Etudes analytiques." The work was to be published "par mode de tontine,"[535] a system devised by Lorenzo Tonti (*ca.* 1653) in which subscribers become shareholders in the publication. For this project three thousand subscribers were needed, and the plan failed. The proposed edition was to have been illustrated and is referred to by the novelist as *Balzac illustré*. This scheme was partly realized in the publication of one volume, *La Peau de chagrin*,[536] which appeared under the general title *Balzac illustré* and

---

[532] See studies in variations in other chapters of this volume.

[533] See above, p. 87.   [534] *LEt.*, I, 242, 247.

[535] *Ibid.*, pp. 409, 413. For the interest which the Balzac family had in the *tontine* Lafarge, see *Con.*, XXI, 439. Cf. *LF.*, p. 30, n. 4, and p. 199.

[536] *Bibliographie de la France* (1838). See Dargan, Crain, and Others, *op. cit.*, pp. 68–72.

under the subtitle *Etudes sociales*. According to the author's letter of February, 1838,[537] the sale of this volume was good; nevertheless, after that date there is no further mention of *Balzac illustré* or of the *Etudes sociales*. Apparently, this general title did not completely express the author's idea, and the search for a more comprehensive title continued.

How and when Balzac decided upon the title *La Comédie humaine* has long been a point of interest among his various critics. Baldensperger[538] seems to credit the claim of Henry Reeve that the latter had suggested the title in a conversation with Balzac. In a letter to his friend E. H. Handley, Reeve, apparently relaying his conversation with the Frenchman, wrote: "If Balzac wants a title . . . . I shall beg to suggest the parody of Dante's 'Divina Commedia'—for this modern 'Commedia' is *tutta diabolica*."[539] This communication does not necessarily assert that Reeve actually made the suggestion to Balzac. Moreover, there is no evidence for Reeve's advice in Balzac's letters. Lovenjoul[540] believed the title had its origin in the enthusiasm of the novelist's friend, the Marquis de Belloy, for Dante's epic; Le Breton[541] likewise accepted this theory. Curtius,[542] however, concurs with Julien Lemer[543] in holding that, since the author named his subdivisions *scènes*, the whole work should logically take the name "drama," and *comédie* was a simple, fitting term. Curtius elaborates the point and discovers analogies from Plato down to Diderot's *Le Neveu de Rameau;* he asserts that the expression *comédie* was applied to prose fiction during the first half of the nineteenth century by Gautier, Musset, and others. Marie-Jeanne Durry finds a *rapprochement* between the title and a statement made by Stendhal in 1836, which she quotes: "Depuis que la démocratie a peuplé le théâtre de gens grossiers incapables de comprendre les choses fines, *je regarde le Roman comme la Comédie du XIXe siècle*."[544] Her contention is that the two great contemporaries independently of each other had a similar conception of the function of the novel.

[537] *LEt.*, I, 460.

[538] "Une Suggestion anglaise pour le titre de *la Comédie humaine*," *Revue de littérature comparée*, I (1921), 638–39.

[539] Sir John K. Laughton, *Memoirs of the Life and Correspondence of Henry Reeve*, I, 39–40.

[540] Lov., *Hist.*, p. 414.   [542] *Balzac*, pp. 333–35.

[541] *Op. cit.*, p. 115.   [543] *Balzac. Sa vie, son œuvre*, p. 148.

[544] "A propos de *la Comédie humaine*," *RHL*, January–March, 1936, p. 98.

Whatever relationship may be suggested in the term *comédie*, Balzac's early (1829) and frequent allusions[545] to Dante's *Divine Comedy* show the association as present in his mind. In his letters to Mme Hanska from November, 1833, to September, 1841, I have found nine allusions—three to Beatrice, five to the "Inferno," and one to the "Paradiso." In seven instances he compares his love for Mme Hanska to that of Dante for Beatrice; in two, he likens Paris, which he wishes to forget, to the Inferno.

References to Dante increase steadily in Balzac's work between 1829 and 1841. Their nature is varied. During that period I have noted fifty-one[546] direct and several miscellaneous and incidental allusions. These are significant and, I believe, led to the use of the title *Comédie humaine*.

Among the more important of these instances is that in *La Physiologie du mariage;*[547] that in *Les Chouans* (1829);[548] several in *Les Proscrits* (1831), where Dante is presented as a leading character; one in *Un Lendemain,*[549] in which the author alludes to the Francesca da Rimini episode, repeated in the *Illusions perdues* (1834) and in *Le Lys dans la vallée* (1836). Further, in *La Fille aux yeux d'or* (1834) he refers to Paris as an Inferno which would someday have its Dante. This prophetic allusion implies a definite relation to his adoption of the title. In *L'Expiation (La Femme de trente ans* [1832])[550] he draws analogies between the denizens of the Inferno and those of his own created world. In speaking of the structure of the *Divine Comedy* Balzac calls it a "gigantic labyrinth";[551] frequently he mentions Dante's vision in *Le Livre mystique* (1835–36) and especially in *Séraphita* and *Louis Lambert*. Dante's treatment of adultery finds an echo in Balzac's *La Muse du département* (1837),[552] and in *La Torpille*[553] he claims that certain torments are not included in the Inferno. Aside from its significant title, the novel *Béatrix* (1839) contains many allusions, even though his conception of this character is entirely different from that of Dante. Finally, there are miscellaneous and incidental references to the poet ad libitum throughout Balzac's works. In view of both character and number of the instances cited above, it is the definite conclusion of the present writer that our novelist's early and increasing interest in the

---

[545] See above, p. 28.

[546] For some of these I am indebted to Professor Furman A. Bridgers.

[547] Noted above, p. 28.   [549] *OD.*, I, 264.

[548] III, 147.   [550] IV, 351.

[551] *L'Enfant maudit (Romans et contes philosophiques* [1836]), IV, 132.

[552] III, 16.   [553] Ed. Werdet, 1838, p. 180.

Divine Comedy had a direct bearing on his creation of the synthetic title, *La Comédie humaine*, so admirably adapted to his works.

The next question that confronts us is whether Balzac used the title, as is commonly asserted, in 1841 or earlier. J. F. Jackson[554] has based his argument for 1838 on a letter from our novelist to Mme Hanska dated January 20 of that year. This letter is to be found in Balzac's *Correspondance*,[555] a volume which is now generally known to be wholly unreliable. If we concede that the dating of the letter may be correct, there is still serious doubt as to the authenticity of its contents. A comparison of the document in question with its counterpart printed in the *Lettres à l'Etrangère*[556] (whose text is usually more reliable than the *Correspondance*) makes us critical of Jackson's suggestion, since the particular passage cited by him is omitted. Therefore, for want of more accurate proof, it is safe to assume that, so far as present evidence shows, Balzac mentioned the title for the first time on June 1, 1841.[557]

At this point in our study certain steps bring us to obvious conclusions: (1) an expansion of sociological import is evinced in the lengthy novels not classified until 1842; (2) the increasing frequency and the nature of references to the *Divine Comedy* ultimately led Balzac to the adaptation of the title for his own works; and (3), so far as I am now able to ascertain, his first mention of *La Comédie humaine* to Mme Hanska was in a letter dated June 1, 1841.

Having reached these conclusions, we must now turn to the paramount objective of this study, the classification of the novels under the general title *La Comédie humaine* (Furne ed.).

VI. FOURTH PERIOD: 1842-48

Under this comprehensive title, *Comédie humaine*, Balzac now includes the tripartite division of his works:[558] "Etudes de mœurs" (3d ed.), "Etudes philosophiques" (5th ed.), and "Etudes analytiques" (1st ed.). An agreement for publication was signed on October 2, 1841,[559] with Furne, Dubochet, Hetzel, and Paulin. Soon after, April 10, 1842,[560] our

---

[554] "Dating Balzac's Adoption of the Title *La Comédie humaine*," *MLN*, XLII (December, 1927), 525-26.

[555] *OC.*, XXIV, 276.   [556] *LEt.*, I, 451-56.

[557] *Ibid.*, p. 557. This date is confirmed by M. Bouteron. It is regrettable that the writer has had no access to the original letter of 1838, the very existence of which is questionable.

[558] Anticipated in a letter to Mme Hanska, October 26, 1834. See above, p. 87.

[559] *LEt.*, II, 30.   [560] See *N.R.F.*, I, xvi.

writer announced in a prospectus the *Comédie humaine* in sixteen volumes, stated very briefly the plan and the main ideas of the work, and gave what he then called the "definitive order" of the stories. Moreover, concerning the general title, now used for the first time, he informed his readers that *"La Comédie humaine* ... résume la pensée de l'écrivain et ... éclaire l'ensemble aussi bien que chaque détail"[561] of his work.

In 1846,[562] even before all the volumes of the first edition were published, Balzac, in another prospectus, announced a forthcoming edition of the *Comédie humaine* in seventeen volumes. Volume XVII,[563] according to M. Bouteron, was the first supplement to the original sixteen and the last to appear during the life of the novelist. After his death three more supplementary volumes (XVIII, XIX, XX) were published between 1853 and 1855 by Mme Houssiaux; of these three, Volume XVIII[564] alone was included in the *Comédie humaine*. Volume XVII was composed of two long novels of Parisian life, written after 1845; these appeared under the collective title: *Les Parents pauvres:*[565] Part I, *La Cousine Bette;* Part II, *Le Cousin Pons*.

The first *livraison* of the *Comédie humaine* in sixteen volumes was announced on April 23, 1842.[566] Balzac prefaced this edition with his famous manifesto, our next topic of discussion.

In the Preface to *Le Cabinet des antiques* (1839) Balzac perhaps anticipated the *Avant-propos* when he said: "Ces avertissements et ces préfaces doivent disparaître tout à fait lorsque l'ouvrage sera terminé et qu'il paraîtra dans sa véritable forme et complet."[567] While the first edition of the *Comédie humaine* was in process of being printed, Hetzel, the publisher, wrote to Balzac in June, 1842: "Il est impossible de reproduire ces préfaces signées Félix Davin. Elles ont le tort d'avoir l'air écrites en grande partie par vous[568] et d'être signées d'un autre nom ... leur effet, à la tête d'une chose capitale comme notre édition complète, serait détestable."[569] Hetzel explained further that he wanted "un résumé, une brève

561 *Ibid.*, p. xviii. 562 *Ibid.*, p. xix.

563 Published by Furne alone on November 18, 1848. See *ibid.* Cf. *LF.*, p. 304, n. 1, which contains an error.

564 See below, p. 152, n. 679; p. 159, n. 714. Vol. XIX contained *Le Théâtre;* and Vol. XX, *Les Contes drolatiques*.

565 See below, p. 218. 567 *OD.*, III, 518.

566 *Bibliographie de la France* (1842). 568 See above, pp. 88, 111.

569 Spoelberch de Lovenjoul, *Autour de Honoré de Balzac*, p. 239.

explication de la chose écrite, signée par vous, ce qui implique une grande sobriété, une mesure très grande. ... Parlez comme un de vos héros, et vous ferez une chose utile, *indispensable.*"[570] One cannot forego citing this letter, because it definitely establishes the fact of Balzac's personal participation in Davin's Introduction (discussed earlier in this study); and it seems to warrant our assumption that at least in part the *Avant-propos* is the condensed and harmonized form in which are merged statements found previously in prefaces, prospectuses, and introductions. It is an artistic synthesis of the ideas elaborated in the *Comédie humaine* and is generally accepted as one of the most important literary manifestoes of the nineteenth century. Balzac fully realized its significance, for on July 13, 1842, he wrote: "Ces vingt-six pages m'ont donné plus de mal qu'un ouvrage, car elles prennent, par la circonstance, un caractère de solennité qui effraie celui qui prononce ces quelques paroles en tête d'une collection si volumineuse."[571]

The *Avant-propos*, not corrected in Balzac's annotated volume of the *Comédie humaine*, Furne edition,[572] was published with variations on October 25, 1846 (in *La Presse*). However, the text in Conard (I, xxv–xxxviii) differs from the two just cited, notwithstanding Bouteron's[573] statement that he utilized the variations of the 1846 printing. The Conard does contain some of the variations of 1846, yet remains closer to the edition of 1842. The irrelevant nature of the passages omitted and the elaboration of the additions in *La Presse* indicate that Balzac strove for a concentrated and clear statement of the basic philosophy in his *Comédie humaine*.

It has been stated above that the *Avant-propos* is in part a synthesis of Balzac's previously published prefaces. There still remains to be seen, however, what new vision the novelist expressed in his manifesto. Its importance consists in the light it throws on the total scheme now erected.

First, Balzac definitely indicates the time of his conception of the *Comédie humaine* as being "depuis bientôt treize ans," that is, from 1829, the year of *Les Chouans*. Next, he makes a final statement concerning his "biological" distinction among social species, which originated, he de-

---

[570] *Ibid.*, p. 240.   [571] *LEt.*, II, 56.

[572] I, 7–32. The text reprinted in *N.R.F.*, I, 3–16, is identical with the uncorrected Furne ed., 1842.

[573] *Con.*, I, 429.

clares, in his sustained comparison "entre l'Humanité et l'Animalité." Of this approach he had already spoken in 1837.[574] His point of departure here was contemporary scientific thought as concerning unity in the composition of life. He says: "Il n'y a qu'un animal. ... [Il] est un principe qui prend sa forme extérieure, ou, pour parler plus exactement, les différences de sa forme, dans les milieux où il est appelé à se développer."[575] It is precisely in these differences, Balzac maintains, that the variety of zoölogical species originates; and, he continues, mankind resembles animals in that the human being is a result of his environment. He seeks to integrate man in nature and to find in natural laws a justification of social laws. He asserts, therefore: "Il existera de tout temps des Espèces Sociales comme il y a des Espèces Zoologiques, *en dépit de notre théorie sur l'égalité*."[576] However, he adds: "Dans l'humanité par un immense courant de vie, *nous voyons s'accomplir sous nos yeux la transfusion des espèces inférieures dans la haute sphère.*" This assertion implies, according to the novelist, that a grocer may rise to the rank of a peer, that a peer may degenerate into the lowest strata of society; and that the wife of the former may be worthy of a prince, whereas that of the latter may not be worthy even of a merchant. In other words, chance, "le hasard," is admissible in society, although impossible in nature because of the immutability of its laws.

For this universal law, unity of composition, Balzac gratefully acknowledged his indebtedness by an enthusiastic dedication of *Le Père Goriot* to the "grand et illustre Geoffroy Saint-Hilaire comme témoignage d'admiration de ses travaux et de son génie." From the first page of the *Avant-propos* he glorified the scientist whose eternal honor it is, he says, to have proclaimed the system of unity in nature. Imbued with this idea—a digression at this point is not out of place—Balzac gives a scientific (physiological) description of social species throughout his *Comédie humaine* and especially voices his admiration in *Séraphita*[577] and in *Ursule Mirouët*.[578] His analogical conception has a vital place in the plan of his works, as vital as the hub around which a wheel revolves; although his method of classification is not exactly based on social species, it is, nonetheless, the symbol of unity[579] in the *Comédie humaine*. It derives (see

[574] *OD.*, III, 389; see above, pp. 90, 126.   [575] *Con.*, I, xxvi.

[576] The italics indicate additions in the text printed in *La Presse*, October 25, 1846.

[577] *Con.*, XXXI, 198.   [578] *Ibid.*, VIII, 68.

[579] Notwithstanding the objection raised by Chaudes-Aigues (see *La Revue de Paris*, new ser., XI [1839], 20–38).

Sec. IV) from Saint-Hilaire's ideas of (1) one principle, i.e., unity of composition in nature, and of (2) cause and effect; upon this theory Balzac sought to build his three main divisions. Furthermore, the scientist's law of environment gave rise to Balzac's conception of both milieu and period of human life reflected in the six subdivisions: the family is usually the setting or the theme for the *Scènes de la vie privée;* the capital of the *Vie parisienne;* the province for the most part of the *Vie de province;* the rural districts of the *Vie de campagne;* and then, without any restricted habitat but with definite themes and characters, come the military and political spheres. These subdivisions are not absolutely fixed and must be considered as shifting planes, but in each of them Balzac shows himself the physiologist and the painter of "mœurs transformistes,"[580] the disciple of Saint-Hilaire. The remaining topics of the manifesto—Balzac's function as a historian and his analysis of the novel as a genre—have been treated in Section IV. With this analysis of the *Avant-propos* I shall now return to the discussion of the stories in which are illustrated its principles.

It is well to keep in mind that the first edition of the *Comédie humaine* contained three main divisions: "Etudes de mœurs," "Etudes philosophiques," and "Etudes analytiques"; and that the first division exhibits great expansion. For the first time it is made up of the six subdivisions indicated in 1834–35: "Scènes de la vie privée" (5th ed.); "Scènes de la vie de province" and "Scènes de la vie parisienne" (both 3d eds.); "Scènes de la vie politique," "Scènes de la vie militaire," and "Scènes de la vie de campagne" (all 1st eds.). Since Balzac's intentions for the first subdivision have been stated in connection with earlier editions, we shall proceed directly to the consideration of the fifth edition (1842–45) of the "Scènes de la vie privée." It contained, in all, twenty-three stories;[581] of these, fourteen had appeared in previous publications, but nine were new and will now be discussed.

La Fausse Maîtresse[582] is the story of Thaddée Paz and of his unselfish devotion to the wife of a lifelong friend, Adam Laginski. This theme and

---

[580] Hélène d'Alsó, art. cit., *Revue d'histoire de la philosophie et d'histoire générale de la civilisation,* p. 354.

[581] *La Grande Bretèche* is not counted separately because it is indicated in the Furne ed. as the "fin" of *Autre Etude de femme.*

[582] This tale first appeared in *Le Siècle,* December, 1841. Next it was published in the subdivision under consideration; in order to make up the necessary forty-four *feuillets* of Vol. II, published by Dumont in 1844, our tale was temporarily coupled with *Un Début dans la vie.* It is now in *Con.,* Vol. IV.

its treatment fully harmonize with the atmosphere of the "Scènes de la vie privée," where it was placed from the start and to which it rightfully belongs.

Albert Savarus,[583] an autobiographical story, deals with the love between Albert and the Duchesse d'Argaiolo and ends tragically because of the interference of an ignorant girl, Rosalie. In her *dossier* the novelist harks back to ideas expressed in his Preface to the first edition of the *Scènes de la vie privée;* he deplores Rosalie's lack of proper education and her insincerity because they poison her home life; "ce combat secret avait lieu dans l'enceinte la plus secrète de la vie domestique à huis clos."[584] Rosalie's reading of other people's letters is the worst, continues Balzac, of all hidden crimes "dans les mystères de la vie privée." Such passages fit the setting of the "Scènes de la vie privée" and help to justify the classification of the tale there.

Mémoires de deux jeunes mariées,[585] an epistolary novel, is the story of two young women, "amies de couvent." The romanesque Louise de Chaulieu marries for passion; the more prudent Renée de Maucombe, for expediency. Renée's letters depict charming scenes of private family life; the letters of Louise, showing excess of passion, form an effective contrast. The author's emphasis on the happiness of Renée, who conquers life by a will to do her duty, makes clear his reason for placing the novel from the start and permanently in the "Scènes de la vie privée," in which it holds an important position.

The opening pages of *Une Fille d'Ève*[586] are taken up with a discussion on the education of the two sisters, Marie-Angélique and Marie-Eugénie de Granville. Again Balzac is preoccupied with "la vie de famille," or, as he calls it, "la zone domestique," in which grows up Marie-Angélique de Vandenesse, the heroine of *Une Fille d'Ève*. Young, with a romanesque

---

[583] The story, first published in *Le Siècle*, May–June, 1842, entered the subdivision under discussion in the same year. It appeared as a complement to *La Muse du département*, together with *Un Drame au bord de la mer* and *Père Canet* in 1843, in 2 vols. It is now in *Con.*, Vol. III.

[584] *Fur.*, I, 417.

[585] This novel was first published in *La Presse*, November, 1841—January, 1842. The same year it appeared in 2 vols., published by Souverain. Next it entered the "Scènes de la vie privée" (*Comédie humaine*, éd. Furne), Vol. XI; it is now in *Con.*, Vol. I.

[586] This tale first appeared in *Le Siècle*, December, 1838—January, 1839; next it was published by Souverain, together with *Massimilla Doni*, in 2 vols., in 1839; in 1842 it entered the "Scènes de la vie privée" (*Comédie humaine*), Vol. II. It is now in *Con.*, Vol. IV.

imagination, without experience, she is completely ignorant of the world about her. The novelist gives the minutiae of her narrow education, watched over by a devout and despotic mother, and shows how inadequate it is to meet the problems of social life. Married to a man of the world much older than herself, and somewhat neglected by him, she becomes attracted to a Bohemian type of journalist, Raoul Nathan, a man of vulgar taste, whom she innocently believes to be a genius. Her husband, however, realizing the situation, saves her from a foolish passion by skilfully presenting the false lover in his true light. This, as a narrative of youthful folly, fits logically into the grouping of the "Scènes de la vie privée," for which it was intended from its conception. Although the tale was not written until 1838, Balzac wrote to Mme Hanska in 1833 that *"Une Fille d'Ève ...* sera le type de la *Femme abandonnée* prise entre quinze et vingt ans";[587] and in 1834 he indicated its place in the first subdivision of the "Etudes de mœurs";[588] finally in 1839 he asserted: *"Les Scènes de la vie privée* eussent été moins complètes sans l'ouvrage principal de la présente publication, *Une Fille d'Ève."*[589]

It has been shown previously that *Autre Etude de femme*[590] was made up of six separate episodes; they are unified by the idea of infidelity in love or in marriage. This theme is in harmony with those in the first subdivision of the "Etudes de mœurs." It is true, however, that only a few of these episodes have been consistently placed in the subdivision; others underwent shiftings to the "Scènes de la vie de province" but, ultimately assembled under the title *Autre Etude de femme*, were permanently classified in the subdivision under consideration. Although the setting in all the component parts is not clear cut, the fact remains that all deal with family life and problems; therefore, Balzac rightfully placed his composite story in the "Scènes de la vie privée."

The novelist frankly stated in a letter to Mme Hanska[591] that, although the subject had really been suggested by George Sand, nevertheless in *Béatrix*[592] he had portrayed some of his own friends. The novel, laid in

---

[587] *LEt.*, I, 6.

[588] Lov., *Hist.*, p. 197.   [589] *OD.*, III, 518.

[590] This novel was partly dealt with above, pp. 51, 53–56, 58; see also Canfield, art. cit., XLVIII, 498.

[591] *LEt.*, I, 464, 527.

[592] Parts I and II of the novel first appeared in *Le Siècle*, April–May, 1839; in January, 1840, the novel was announced in the *Bibliographie de la France* and was published

Brittany, is to a great degree the story of Calyste du Guénic, without whom, Balzac said, "*Les Scènes de la vie privée* auraient manqué un type essentiel, celui du jeune homme dans toute sa gloire, offrant à la fois beauté, noblesse et sentiments purs."[593] He is the central character, presented as a youth, lover, husband, father, and finally as the lover of Béatrix. In three young men—Calyste, Albert Savarus, and Thaddée Paz (in *La Fausse Maîtresse*)—Balzac described the experiences of first love, a theme which he assigned from the start to the *Scènes de la vie privée*. Consequently, the three novels in which these characters figure form an integral part of that subdivision. Another aspect which calls for this classification is the author's claim that "sans Béatrix, l'auteur aurait oublié de peindre les sentiments qui retiennent encore les femmes, après une chute."[594] Furthermore, in 1839 he stated that the two novels, *Béatrix* and *Une Fille d'Ève*, would, for good reason, greatly advance *Les Scènes de la vie privée*.[595]

Since *Béatrix* appeared as a separate publication in close conjunction with the Furne edition, it was, from the beginning, intended as a *scène* in the *Comédie humaine*, and so included the necessary links in continuity and solidity.[596] Another point is the change in chapter titles to demonstrate exact sociological intent.

The theme of *Modeste Mignon*[597] was suggested by Mme Hanska.[598] Soon after its publication Balzac wrote: "Il y a des gens qui commencent à dire que M[odeste] Mi[gnon] est un chef-d'œuvre."[599] It is one of his few novels which end happily, and is a charming scene of private life where common sense and peace prevail. The theme, one of Balzac's favorites, is that the best security in married happiness is a "mariage de raison." The plot recalls that of Cyrano and Roxane, with the difference that Modeste, guided by her father and a devoted friend, Butscha, recognizes

---

by Souverain in 2 vols. In 1842 the two parts entered the "Scènes de la vie privée," Vol. III. Part III first appeared in *Le Messager*, December, 1844—January, 1845; in 1845 it was published by Chlendowski in 2 vols.; the same year Part III entered the "Scènes de la vie privée," Vol. IV. The complete novel is now in *Con.*, Vol. V.

[593] *OD.*, III, 536, Preface to *Béatrix*.   [595] *Ibid.*, p. 524.

[594] *Ibid.*   [596] See above, p. 125.

[597] This novel first appeared in *Le Journal des débats*, April, May, July, 1844; the same year it was published, together with *Un Épisode sous la Terreur* and *Une Passion dans le désert*, by Roux and Cassanet in 4 vols. In 1845 the story entered the subdivision in question, and it is now in *Con.*, Vol. IV.

[598] *LEt.*, II, 321, 325, 331.   [599] *Ibid.*, p. 404.

in time her true lover, Ernest de la Brière, a man of integrity and positive virtues.

Balzac's letters show that he meditated for a long time on the classification of this novel. On March 17, 1844, he wrote: "[*Modeste Mignon*] sera la dernière *Scène de la Vie privée*, dans l'ordre et le classement définitif des idées que chacune présente. C'est la lutte entre la poésie et le fait, entre l'illusion et la société; c'est le dernier enseignement avant de passer aux scènes de l'âge mûr."[600] Aside from this clear statement, there are several unmistakable indications that *Modeste Mignon* is a "drame" and a "scène domestique," in which the minutiae of private life hold the interest. Balzac keenly analyzes Modeste's "amour platonique si rare, si peu compris, la première illusion des jeunes filles, le plus délicat de tous les sentiments."[601] Again, the following passage illustrates his method of harmonizing the tales with the main ideas formulated in the Preface to the first edition of the "Scènes de la vie privée." Ernest de la Brière, writing to Modeste, pleads for common sense: "Destinée à la vie bourgeoise, obéissez à la loi de fer qui maintient la société ... Croyez-moi, pour une fille, comme pour une femme, la gloire sera toujours d'enfermer dans la sphère des convenances les plus serrées, ses ardents caprices."[602] Further methods of interlocking his works at that time are Balzac's allusions by content and title to *Le Lys dans la vallée*, to *L'Interdiction*, and to *L'Enfant maudit*.[603]

In *Honorine*[604] the novelist again says, in answer to the problem of passion in marriage, that "le mariage exclut la passion." Octave de Bauvan, because of the infidelity of his romantic wife, seeks consolation in excessive work. Later, after Honorine's sincere repentance and expiation, he forgives her, but she cannot forget her sin; it is, as Balzac says, "un cas de conscience conjugale" which gradually undermines her health and brings death. Incidentally, the author pleads for the rehabilitation of the penitent woman.

There was no hesitation in the classification of this tale. On January 17 Balzac wrote: "*Honorine* est supérieure au *Message*, à *la Femme abandonnée*, et à tout ce que j'ai taillé sur ce patron."[605] The last two narra-

---

[600] *Ibid.*, p. 331.

[601] *Fur.*, IV, 152.

[602] *Ibid.*, p. 175.

[603] *Ibid.*, pp. 253–54.

[604] The novel first appeared in *La Presse*, March, 1843; in 1844 it was published, together with *Un Prince de la Bohème*, by De Potter in 2 vols.; finally, in 1845, it entered the category under consideration. It is now in *Con.*, Vol. IV.

[605] *LEt.*, II, 100.

tives were classified in the "Scènes de la vie privée"; it is fitting, therefore, that *Honorine* should be permanently placed in the same category.

Concerning *Un Début dans la vie*,[606] the author wrote on April 17, 1843, to Mme Hanska: "Il y a bientôt un an que *Mistigris* est fait. ... Cela se trouvera dans le quatrième volume des *Scènes de la vie privée* ... sous le titre de: *un Début dans la vie*."[607] The original title, *Mistigris*, meaning a "dabbler in colors,"a nickname imposed upon Léon de Lora by the studio of Schinner,[608] was not in harmony with the general theme of the "Scènes de la vie privée." The subject was suggested by Laure Surville under still another title, *Les Jeunes Gens*. The present title, however, is better suited to the category and the theme, which is the beginning of Oscar Husson's career, and, moreover, points to the sociological importance of the story.[609] The interesting description of the picturesque "coucou," Pierrotin's stage-coach, shows a part of the life of that period, 1822; the evolution in the social scale is demonstrated by the rapid rise of the bailiff Moreau, who becomes a deputy; and the law offices, clerks, and Oscar's private life in his poverty-stricken but decent home all form parts of the environment now paramount in the novelist's mind. The principal theme concerns the errors of the youthful Oscar Husson, who insists on leading a romantic life and who commits a series of foolish mistakes; the secondary theme is the family tragedy of De Sérisy. These two aspects definitely align the tale with the "Scènes de la vie privée," where it was permanently classified. With this tale we conclude our discussion of the nine new stories in the fifth edition of the "Scènes de la vie privée" and proceed to the analysis of the second subdivision of the *Etudes de mœurs*.

The "Scènes de la vie de province," third edition (1843–44), had thirteen titles (the three parts of *Illusions perdues* are counted separately). Of these, five had been published previously and eight (counting separately Parts II and III of *Illusions perdues*) were new. Brunetière[610] maintains that no artist has depicted life in the provinces of France, between 1830 and 1850, with a more universal quality than Balzac. The novelist

---

[606] This fiction first appeared in *La Législature*, July–September, 1842, under the title *Le Danger des mystifications;* in 1844, under the present title, it was published, together with *La Fausse Maîtresse*, by Dumont in 2 vols. In 1845 it entered the subdivision under discussion, and it is now in *Con.*, Vol. II.

[607] *LEt.*, II, 138, letter dated April 7, 1843, continued on successive days.

[608] *Con.*, II, 344.

[609] Cf. another story of the same category, where a nickname used as a title, *La Fleur-des-pois*, is changed to one having a social bearing, *Le Contrat de mariage*.

[610] *Balzac*, p. 101; cf. also Wenger, *op. cit.*

felt, however, in 1844 that even with these eight new novels his portrayal
of the provinces still lacked a "tableau d'une ville de garnison frontière,
celui d'un port de mer, celui d'une ville où le théâtre est une cause de désordre, et où les comédiens et les comédiennes de Paris viennent faire leur
récolte."[611] This new project was an enlargement of that of 1839,[612] but
neither plan was ever carried out. As in the case of the "Scènes de la vie
privée," Balzac's objectives in the "Scènes de la vie de province" have already been discussed.[613] It suffices now to recall briefly the main intentions to portray: (1) mature people; (2) their material outlook on life;
(3) the limited sphere of intrigue in the provinces, as contrasted with the
metropolis. In this light we proceed to analyze the themes and the classifications of the new stories.

In *Ursule Mirouët*,[614] as in *La Rabouilleuse*, of the same category, Balzac is interested in the question of inheritance. This interest is to be found
in one of his *Œuvres de jeunesse*, *L'Héritière de Birague* (1822), and possibly
originated in some experience during his apprenticeship in a lawyer's
office. In a fragmentary manuscript at Chantilly, *Les Héritiers Boirouge,
ou Fragments d'histoire générale*,[615] a projected chapter bears the title
"Ursule Mirouët." *Les Héritiers Boirouge*, although listed in the catalogue of 1845 as Part II of *Les Rivalités*, was never completed. Its theme
of inheritance, however, was utilized in the novel *Ursule Mirouët*.

The author calls Ursule a "sœur heureuse"[616] of Eugénie Grandet, since,
like Eugénie, she is wooed by several suitors for her fortune; but, unlike
Eugénie, she is finally happily married. The fact that a swarm of greedy
cousins quarrel over her inheritance and plot against the young girl
stamps the main theme as a "lutte des intérêts matériels," which is set
against the background of the monotony of provincial life. It is appropriate, therefore, that *Ursule Mirouët* be classified, together with *Eugénie
Grandet*, in the "Scènes de la vie de province."

In *Pierrette*,[617] with its martyrdom plot, Balzac continues the study of

[611] *OD.*, III, 569.

[612] Cf. above, pp. 126–27.   [613] See above, pp. 90, 97.

[614] This novel first appeared in *Le Messager*, August–September, 1841; in 1842 it
was published by Souverain in 2 vols.; in 1843 it entered the subdivision now discussed. It is now in *Con.*, Vol. VIII.

[615] Lov. Coll., A 167, fols. 214–48. See above, p. 127.   [616] *LEt.*, II, 67.

[617] This story first appeared in *Le Siècle*, January, 1840; the same year it was published, together with *Pierre Grassou*, by Souverain in 2 vols.; in 1843 the tale became
Part I of *Les Célibataires* and entered the subdivision under consideration; the novel is
now in *Con.*, Vol. IX.

celibacy begun in *Le Curé de Tours* (1832). Sylvie Rogron, an abnormally jealous and cruel spinster, tracks to death her victim, Pierrette, as Troubert did François Birotteau. Here, again, Balzac gives voice to his somewhat persistent hatred of "tout être improductif," such as he created in Silvie Rogron, whose only motive in life is the persecution of the pretty, melancholic orphan. Since the provincial intrigues and rivalries in this novel equal those of *Eugénie Grandet* and of *Ursule Mirouët*, it is logically classified with them in the "Scènes de la vie de province."

Les Célibataires forms the collective title for three separate stories: Part I, *Pierrette*, just analyzed; Part II, *Le Curé de Tours;*[618] Part III, *La Rabouilleuse*. Of the last, Balzac wrote, October 29, 1842: "C'est la troisième histoire de[s] *Célibataires* et avec *L'Abbé Troubert*[619] et *Pierrette*, cela complète ce que je voulais écrire sur le célibat."[620] Balzac changed the title of this novel twice before he decided on *La Rabouilleuse*. Such shifting of titles betrays a doubt in the author's mind as to which was the leading character.

Part I of *La Rabouilleuse*, *Les Deux Frères*,[621] deals with the brothers Philippe and Joseph Bridau. Part II, *Un Ménage de garçon en province*,[622] seems to stress the celibacy of Philippe. The two parts under the title of Part I came out in book form in 1843, published by Souverain in two volumes. The same year, but under the title of Part II, *Un Ménage de garçon*, and designated as the third series of the *Célibataires*, the novel was classified in the "Scènes de la vie de province."[623] Balzac indicated the present title, *La Rabouilleuse*, in his plans[624] for the second edition of the *Comédie humaine*. Nevertheless, during the same period he announced the novel under a fourth title, *Le Bonhomme Rouget*. Each of these titles points to a separate theme in the story: the first and second have been explained; in *La Rabouilleuse* the interest is shifted from the two brothers to Flore Brazier. The term "rabouilleuse" designates a person who stands over a stream and frightens the fish in order to catch them more easily. Flore was seen doing that. In *Le Bonhomme Rouget* the spotlight is focused on

[618] See above, pp. 61 ff.

[619] One of the projected titles of *Le Curé de Tours*.

[620] *LEt.*, II, 73.

[621] This part first appeared in *La Presse*, February–March, 1841.

[622] *Ibid.*, October–November, 1842.

[623] *Fur.*, Vol. VI; it is now in *Con.*, Vol. IX.

[624] Lov. Coll., A 297, fol. 56; A 159, fols. 14–15.

the imbecile Rouget, whose wealth is coveted by the unscrupulous Philippe and by the tyrannical Flore and her criminal lover, Maxence Gilet. All these characters are celibates, at least during a good part of the action.

Balzac indicated the classification of the novel in a preface of 1840, in which he wrote: *"Le Bonhomme Rouget (un Ménage de garçon en province)* sera la troisième *Scène de la vie de province* où il [Balzac] essayera de peindre les malheurs qui attendent les célibataires pendant leur vieillesse."[625] The setting and atmosphere of the small town made the tale distinctly one of provincial existence. Furthermore, in later editions the author inserted passages, mostly generalizations of a sociological nature, concerned with the lives and manners of provincials.

The other collective title in the third edition of the "Scènes de la vie de province" is *Les Parisiens en province;* this contained two stories: *L'Illustre Gaudissart*[626] and *La Muse du département (Dinah Piédefer).*[627] The latter is Balzac's second composite story (cf. *Autre Etude de femme*); here, besides the salon setting and the three episodes of vengeance—*Histoire du Chevalier de Beauvoir*, a summary[628] of *La Grande Bretèche*, and *Le Grand d'Espagne*, discussed previously—are also passages from *La Femme de province*[629] and from *Olympia, ou Les Vengeances romaines.*[630] For practical reasons the first and third episodes had temporarily been utilized in the "Scènes de la vie privée"; but, since the setting and characters in both stories are essentially provincial, they now were permanently placed in the "Scènes de la vie de province" as parts of *La Muse du département*, in which they furnish the background for the life of Mme de la Baudraye.

Her life is the unifying thread in this composite tale; Mme de la Baudraye is the Balzacian Mme Bovary who, after a sincere repentance, is rehabilitated and returns to her provincial home and family. Although she lives for a while in Paris with the unworthy Lousteau, her life is closely

[625] *OD.*, III, 546.   [626] See above, pp. 100–101.

[627] Partly discussed; see above, pp. 53, 101.

[628] But *La Grande Bretèche* was given in full in the Souverain ed. of *La Muse du département* (1843). It could not be given in full in the subdivision under consideration because the whole episode became the conclusion in *Autre Etude de femme*, "Scènes de la vie privée" (1845), of the *Comédie humaine*.

[629] This narrative first appeared in *La Province des français peints par eux-mêmes*, Vol. I (1840).

[630] This story appeared under the title "Fragments d'un roman publié sous l'Empire par un auteur inconnu" in *Les Causeries du monde*, September, 1833.

bound to the provinces, where she was the "muse" of provincial talent. A passage in a letter to Mme Hanska throws light on the composition and placement of the novel. On March 2, 1843, the novelist wrote: "... le sixième volume de *la Comédie humaine*, *le Curé de Tours*, et *un Ménage de garçon* font, avec *l'Illustre Gaudissart*, vingt-deux feuilles, et comme il en faut trente, il s'ensuit qu'il faut un roman de la dimension d'*Une Fille d'Ève*[631] [a scene in the series of private life]." This statement recalls the earlier practical reasons given whenever the author was in want of material; but *La Muse du département*, with its provincial pattern despite "the Parisian influence,"[632] is truly the appropriate space-filler in the second category.

Le Cabinet des antiques[633] appeared with *La Vieille Fille* under a collective title, *Les Rivalités*. On February 12, 1837, Balzac wrote that *"Le Cabinet des antiques* servira de clôture à *la Vieille Fille."*[634] In his plans for a second edition of the *Comédie humaine* Balzac indicated that *Le Cabinet des antiques* was to be severed from its companion story and was to appear with a projected novel, *Jacques de Metz* (never written), under another collective title, *Les Provinciaux à Paris;* this caption points to a province-Paris axis as his objective. *La Vieille Fille*, however, was to remain with two projected novels, *L'Original* and *Les Héritiers Boirouge*, under *Les Rivalités*. Despite the fact that the proposed novels were never written, *Le Cabinet des antiques*, with its Parisian-provincial theme, is now *Les Provinciaux à Paris*, Part I. Both this collective title and the earlier *Les Rivalités* are adapted to our story, with its bitter rivalries between degenerating provincial aristocracy and the rising energetic bourgeoisie, together with the experiences of provincials in Paris.[635] The title *Le Cabinet des antiques* also suggests ruined nobility, "les antiques," who rallied around the venerable Comte d'Esgrignon. Whether it be considered as a portrayal of provincial intrigues and quarrels or of provincials in the metropolis, it remains a typical tale of the "Scènes de la vie de province," in which it holds its legitimate position.

---

[631] *LEt.*, II, 120.   [632] Wenger, *op. cit.*, p. 26.

[633] Part I of this novel, under the present title, appeared in *La Chronique de Paris*, March, 1836. Part II, *Les Rivalités en province*, was published in *Le Constitutionnel*, September–October, 1838; in 1839 both parts joined under the first title, together with *Gambara* (as a "filler"), were published by Souverain in 2 vols. In 1844 our novel was placed in the category under discussion; it is now in *Con.*, Vol. XI. *Le Cabinet des antiques* was partly dealt with in connection with *La Vieille Fille;* see above, p. 102.

[634] *LEt.*, I, 380.   [635] See above, pp. 126 ff.

It is generally accepted that Mme de Mortsauf, the heroine of *Le Lys dans la vallée*,[636] is modeled upon Mme de Berny and that Félix de Vandenesse represents, to some degree, the author himself. The novel, laid in the countryside near Tours, is a melancholy tale of struggle between passion and duty, and duty triumphs at the cost of the heroine's life.

Balzac's letters show that from the first he designed this novel for the last (rather than the second) subdivision of the *Etudes de mœurs*. On March 11, 1835, he wrote to Mme de Castries: "(*Le Lys dans la vallée*) ... sera la dernière scène des *Etudes de mœurs* comme *Séraphita* est la dernière *Etude philosophique*. Au bout de chaque œuvre se dressera la statue d'une image de la perfection sur la terre, d'abord, puis dans le ciel, n'est-ce pas une grande idée."[637] Consequently, the Introduction of April, 1835, gives the classification of the novel in the "Scènes de la vie de campagne." Davin-Balzac states that in *"Le Lys dans la vallée* se retrouvent, à un degré peut-être supérieur, les qualités du *Médecin de campagne*,"[638] which belonged to the same series; Balzac himself confirmed that classification in 1839.[639] In spite of these definite assertions, the author was forced, for practical reasons,[640] to place the novel temporarily in the "Scènes de la vie de province." On November 14, 1843, he complained to Mme Hanska that Volume VII (now under consideration) of the *Comédie humaine* lacked "quinze feuilles";[641] on February 28, 1844, he continued: "Je me décide à finir le tome VII de *la Comédie humaine* avec *Le Lys dans la Vallée* qui, certes, peut passer pour une *Scène de la Vie de Province*."[642] Seemingly he is not convinced that the novel is a provincial scene, but uses it to complete the volume. Later, however, on the flyleaf of his own copy of the corrected Furne edition, Balzac stated: *"Le Lys dans la vallée* sera rapporté aux *Scènes de la vie de campagne*."[643] There is little justification for placing the novel in the provincial scenes.[644] On the other hand, the

[636] The first instalment of this novel was published in *La Revue de Paris*, November–December, 1835. The complete novel was published by Werdet in 1836, 2 vols.; in 1839 it was published by Charpentier in 1 vol. In 1844 *Le Lys dans la vallée* appeared in the subdivision under discussion; it is now in *Con.*, Vol. XXVI.

[637] "Cahiers balzaciens," VI, 34. Cf. *LEt.*, I, 237.

[638] Lov., *Hist.*, p. 49.   [639] *OD.*, III, 522.

[640] Cf. Marc Blanchard, *La Campagne et ses habitants dans l'œuvre de Honoré de Balzac*, p. 33.

[641] *LEt.*, II, 225.   [643] Lov. Coll., A 21.

[642] *Ibid.*, p. 317.   [644] Cf. Wenger, *op. cit.*, p. 19.

typically rural episodes of vintage and harvest carry out the author's intentions to depict rustic occupations in the fields.[645] Moreover, the heroine, in whom he claimed to have attained "terrestrial perfection,"[646] definitely belongs among those "plus purs caractères"[647] destined for the last category. For these reasons the novel is better adapted to the themes of the "Scènes de la vie de campagne" than to those of the "Scènes de la vie de province."

Un Grand Homme de province à Paris and *Ève et David*, respectively Parts II and III of *Illusions perdues*, although new in this edition of the subdivision, have been dealt with earlier in this study,[648] in connection with Part I of the trilogy. In Part II, Balzac deals with literary movements in Paris; hence its title, *Un Grand Homme de province à Paris*— that is, Lucien, the poet, and his relations with men of letters and with journalists. In the Preface to Part II the novelist says: "... le talent de province a contre lui la vie de province, dont la monotonie fait aspirer tout homme d'imagination aux dangers de la vie parisienne."[649] *Illusions perdues*, as a whole, fittingly concludes the "Scènes de la vie de province" and logically leads to the third subdivision of the "Etudes de mœurs," the "Scènes de la vie parisienne."

Balzac's intentions for the "Scènes de la vie parisienne," given in his introductions and prefaces (ending with 1839), have already been dealt with in this study.[650] For the sake of clarity we recapitulate. The main points are: (1) the approach of old age; (2) the type of the social climber; (3) the passions, vices, and abuses as dissolving social principles; and (4) Parisian life versus the provincial. It is pertinent now to see what new theories, if any, have been developed by the novelist since 1839 concerning the third subdivision of the "Etudes de mœurs."

In the *Avant-propos* Balzac recast his earlier statements in regard to this category, in which he now asserted "se rencontrent à la fois l'extrême bien et l'extrême mal."[651] By 1844 he had enlarged his picture of Parisian life by adding *Splendeurs et misères des courtisanes*. He maintained, nevertheless, at that time that his portrayal of Paris was not yet complete; in order to achieve his task, he asserted in this Preface that the descriptions of "*le palais de justice, le monde du théâtre, et le monde des*

---

[645] Lov., *Hist.*, p. 48.   [646] *LEt.*, I, 237.

[647] *Avant-propos*, p. xxxvii. Cf. *OD.*, III, 549. The conception of character had a bearing on the classification of the novel.

[648] See above, p. 102.   [650] See above, p. 105.

[649] *OD.*, III, 534.   [651] *Con.*, I, xxxvi.

savants"[652] should be added. Of these projects, the second, "le monde du théâtre," was actually realized in *Splendeurs et misères*. The first and third remained unfinished. Guided by these objectives, we shall now analyze the new stories in the "Scènes de la vie parisienne," third edition (1843–46).

It contained seventeen titles, of which six (*Histoire des Treize, Le Colonel Chabert, Facino Cane, La Messe de l'athée, Sarrasine,* and *L'Interdiction*) had previously appeared and eleven (counting the three episodes of the *Splendeurs et misères des courtisanes* as one novel) were new.

A statement in Balzac's notebook indicates the subject of *Le Père Goriot:*[653] "Un brave homme—pension bourgeoise—600 fr. de rente—s'étant dépouillé pour ses filles qui toutes deux ont 50.000 fr. de rente, mourant comme un chien."[654] This is the gist of the poignant tale of Goriot, the French King Lear, in which, the author said in 1835, he intended to "saisir la paternité dans tous les plis de son cœur, de la peindre tout entière."[655] And in *Le Père Goriot,* so Balzac wrote to Mme Hanska, he presented a man "qui est *père* comme *un saint, un martyr est chrétien.*"[656] Balzac punished this excess of paternal love, carried to a degrading idolatry, by making his hero a monomaniac abandoned by his children, dying wretchedly and alone.

There was some doubt in the author's mind concerning the classification of the novel which, although published in book form in 1835, was not, until 1843, placed in the "Scènes de la vie parisienne" in which Le Breton says it was "si bien à sa place."[657] The entire action, laid in Paris, the truly Parisian characters, the age and tragedy of Goriot—all tenets of Balzac's theory for the category—justify the classification of the novel in the third subdivision. However, in accordance with his directions for a definitive edition of the *Comédie humaine,* the story was later and permanently classified with the other tales (*La Vendetta, Le Bal de Sceaux, Une Double Famille*) of paternal love in the "Scènes de la vie privée." Balzac's

---

[652] *OD.,* III, 575. Italics Balzac's. Cf. *LEt.,* II, 301.

[653] The novel first appeared in *La Revue de Paris,* December, 1834—January–February, 1835; the same year two editions were published by Werdet and Spachman, as well as a reprint by Werdet in 4 vols.; in 1839 *Le Père Goriot* was published by Charpentier in 1 vol.; in 1843 it entered the subdivision under discussion; it is now in *Con.,* Vol. VI.

[654] *Pensées, sujets, fragmens,* éd. Crépet, p. 114.

[655] *OD.,* III, 417.

[656] *LEt.,* I, 195. Italics Balzac's.   [657] *Op. cit.,* p. 124.

reasons for reclassification of *Le Père Goriot* may be explained by similarity of theme rather than by background and characters. This shift, it may also be argued, emphasizes the private lives of the leading characters. As in *Le Lys dans la vallée*, so in *Le Père Goriot*, the pattern is not clearly exclusive but might fit in either category. The pro and con are a matter of individual emphasis.

The origins of the *Histoire de la grandeur et de la décadence de César Birotteau*[658] may be found in a letter from Dr. Nacquart, dated November 23, 1830. He answers a query of Balzac concerning the care of the skin and ends his letter by saying, "... j'ai voulu vous donner des matériaux,"[659] a combination of medical and cosmetic information that Balzac used later in this novel.

The first mention of the title and brief allusions to the book occur in the author's correspondence[660] with Mme Carraud in the letters of September 17 and October 5, 1833. He began *César Birotteau* (as he stated later[661]) in April, 1834, at Frapesle; from there he wrote to Mme Hanska: "... je fais une œuvre capitale, *César Birotteau*, le frère de celui que vous connaissez, victime comme son frère, mais victime de la civilisation parisienne, tandis que son frère n'est victime que d'un seul homme. Ce sera plus grand, plus vaste que ce que j'ai fait jusqu'alors."[662] Like his brother, François, César is naïve in all social matters except business; he was temporarily successful in his "petit commerce parisien" but could not cope with the intrigues and the dishonesty of the "fauves" and the "reptiles" of the great business world of Paris; he fell prey to the metropolitan jungle. Concerning the character of César, Balzac wrote much later, in 1846, to Hippolyte Castille:

J'ai conservé *César Birotteau* pendant six ans à l'état d'ébauche, en désespérant de pouvoir jamais intéresser qui que ce soit à la figure d'un boutiquier assez bête, assez médiocre, dont les infortunes sont vulgaires et symbolisent ce dont nous nous moquons beaucoup, le petit commerce parisien. Eh bien, monsieur, dans un jour de bonheur, je me suis dit: "Il faut le transfigurer, en en faisant l'image de la *probité*."[663]

[658] This novel was first published by the Bureau du Figaro, December, 1837, in 2 vols.; in 1839 it was reprinted by Charpentier, and in 1844 it entered the subdivision under consideration; it is now in *Con.*, Vol. XIV.

[659] "Cahiers balzaciens," VIII, 2–5.

[660] *Corr. Carraud*, pp. 168, 176.

[661] *Ibid.*, p. 276, letter dated January, 1837.

[662] *LEt.*, I, 149, letter dated from Frapesle, April 10, 1834.

[663] *OD.*, III, 365. Italics Balzac's. Letter dated October 11, 1846.

César, who showed much fortitude in all his misfortunes, the "type parfait du négociant probe ... ne soutient pas la joie et la vie."[664] His sudden emotion upon regaining his honest name kills him; and Balzac concludes the novel: "Voilà la mort du juste!"

According to Balzac's announcement (September, 1834) on the verso cover page of the *Etudes de mœurs*, Volume III, and an earlier agreement with Werdet (July 16-19, 1834), this novel was to come out in the *Etudes philosophiques* (January, 1835). It was stated in the Werdet document:

M. de Balzac aurait ainsi l'obligation de compléter le nombre de vingt volumes, dont rigoureusement doivent se composer les *Etudes Philosophiques*, par cinq volumes d'œuvres inédites, sous le titre de l'*Histoire de la grandeur et de la décadence de César Birotteau, marchand parfumeur, adjoint au maire du deuxième arrondissement de la ville de Paris*. Ces cinq volumes formeront la quatrième livraison de l'œuvre.[665]

This publication was postponed first to March, 1835, then to 1836, and finally to 1837, to appear in the fifth *livraison* (Vols. VI–X[666]), with an addition in the title "chevalier de la Légion d'honneur"—perhaps to emphasize the hero's rising grandeur. The printing of the work really began in 1834–35 but was left unfinished. Subsequently a few of the proof sheets, set up for the *Etudes philosophiques*, were found and used later for the publication of the novel by *Le Figaro* in two volumes, in December, 1837 (dated 1838). In this, however, the story was designated as a "nouvelle scène de la vie parisienne." The new classification is by far more justifiable, since the composition carries out Balzac's expressed intentions for the category in which, Davin said, "les calculs s'y font au grand jour et sans pudeur, l'humanité n'a plus que deux formes, le trompeur et le trompé, ... l'honnête homme est un niais ... tout s'exploite, tout se débite."[667]

César Birotteau is par excellence the social document among Balzac's novels; here the group idea is foremost: the business world, the financiers, Birotteau's relatives and friends—many interlocking social classes—all characteristic of Parisian life. Most of the variations occur in the exposition and in the *dossiers* of the characters; a number of them (as seen above) offer generalizations about social categories, types, bourgeois,

---

[664] Lov., *Hist.*, p. 204.

[665] Spoelberch de Lovenjoul, art. cit., *RHL*, 1907, p. 400.

[666] *Ibid.*, pp. 410–11, 424, 434. These delays were caused by the liquidation of Werdet's business.

[667] Lov., *Hist.*, p. 47.

artists, etc.; the author's emphasis, therefore, is consistently on the *étude de mœurs*, as illustrated in the capital.

La Maison Nucingen[668] had been first announced as *La Haute Banque*, a title which, although not unsuitable, was never used. It was possibly too general, whereas the present title is more specific. Nucingen, whom Balzac likens to a "loup-cervier," is a motor-force in the Parisian financial world, of whom P. Barrière aptly said: "... l'habileté criminelle ... jointe au sens pratique réussit, et donne à un malhonnête homme l'apparence de l'honneur tandis que Birotteau a l'apparence du déshonneur."[669] Balzac refers to Nucingen and his henchmen as "ces spirituels *condottieri* de l'industrie moderne"[670] whose obscure speculations bring them millions and peerages but inflict ruin on the public. This dishonest situation falls in line with the author's objective for the category, to portray the "deceiver and the deceived." In both novels he shows a profound knowledge of bankruptcy and speaks of *César Birotteau* and *La Maison Nucingen* as "born twins."[671] Since these novels represent two sides of Parisian life in which the integrity of César is contrasted with the craftiness of the "fauve" Nucingen, they are rightfully given an important position in the "Scènes de la vie parisienne."

Pierre Grassou[672] is a short composition in which Balzac depicts the life and work of a mediocre painter who caters to the public taste; his persistence and hard work bring him financial success but not the satisfaction of a true artist. Guided merely by common sense and not by the passionate genius of Gambara or of Frenhofer, Pierre does not belong to the same category of philosophic artists; and therefore the narrative, of which the setting and spirit are of the French capital, is appropriately classified in the "Scènes de la vie parisienne" rather than in the "Etudes philosophiques." Balzac showed, however, some hesitancy in the classification of the tale, for in the catalogue (1845) he listed it temporarily in the "Scènes de la vie privée."[673] A reason for the projected shift may be

---

[668] This novel, together with *La Femme supérieure* and *La Torpille*, was published by Werdet in 1838, in 2 vols.; in 1844 it entered the subdivision under consideration. It is now in *Con.*, Vol. XIV.

[669] *Op. cit.*, pp. 109–10.   [670] *Fur.*, XI, 2.   [671] *OD.*, III, 496.

[672] This tale first appeared in *Babel*, a collection by several authors published in 1840, in 4 vols. The same year it appeared, together with *Pierrette*, in 2 vols., published by Souverain. In 1844 the sketch entered the subdivision under discussion; it is now in *Con.*, Vol. XVI.

[673] See also Lov. Coll., A 27.

seen in the youth and occupation of Grassou, which recall Mistigris in
Un Début dans la vie of the first subdivision. Far more significant, however, is the presentation of the typical Parisian atelier, of expositions, of
the shrewd art-dealers, together with the episode of the *crise ministérielle*,
May, 1839—these motifs, essentially those of the capital, recommend the
story for a permanent position in the "Scènes de la vie parisienne."

Les *Secrets de la princesse de Cadignan*[674] is an "étude de femme" and
recalls *La Duchesse de Langeais*, except that the princess is, as Balzac
calls her, a "Célimène amoureuse."[675] Her lover, the poet Daniel d'Arthez,
is, to a large degree, Balzac himself. The first rather general title, *La
Princesse parisienne*, was changed in 1844 to *La Princesse de Cadignan*,
which is more specific. The background of this character sketch—the
Faubourg Saint-Germain after the July Revolution, the social set of the
Parisian salon and its intrigues; the crafty, worldly heroine, a typical
Parisian coquette who personifies, as the author says, "le dernier degré de
la dépravation dans les sentiments"[676]—these aspects harmonize with the
standard pattern of the "Scènes de la vie parisienne," in which the tale
was permanently grouped.

In *Les Employés, ou La Femme supérieure*[677] Balzac is preoccupied with
administrative reforms; he endeavors to discover the cause and the effect
of bureaucratic procedure, proposes to simplify the governmental machine, and seeks to improve the position of the employees. In this idealistic program the honest M. Rabourdin failed; a man of integrity like César
(the hero of another Parisian scene), he also plays into the hands of his
unscrupulous rivals, Baudoyer and Des Lupeaulx. Miss Scott[678] clearly
shows how the author's lengthy additions and insertions, borrowed from
La Physiologie de l'employé (1841) and *Les Petits Bourgeois* (still unpublished in 1844), had shifted the interest from the official's capable wife to
that of the bureaucratic group. Consequently, the *feuilleton* title, *La*

---

[674] This story first appeared in *La Presse*, August, 1839, under the title *La Princesse
parisienne;* retaining the same title, it was included in *Le Foyer de l'opéra*, a collective
work by several authors published by Souverain in 1840. In 1844, under the present
title, it entered the category under consideration; it is now in *Con.*, Vol. XVI.

[675] *LEt.*, I, 519.   [676] *Ibid.*

[677] This novel first appeared as *La Femme supérieure* in *La Presse*, July, 1837. In
1838 it was published by Werdet, together with *La Maison Nucingen* and *La Torpille*,
in 2 vols. In 1844, under the present title, it entered the third category; it is now in
Con., Vol. XIX.

[678] Art. cit., *MP*, XXIII (1926), 315–36.

Femme supérieure (Mme Rabourdin) was no longer suitable for the Furne edition of the story, and the more precise *Les Employés* was adopted. Since in this novel Balzac has realistically depicted political, administrative, and financial Paris, it remains an indispensable part in the 'Scènes de la vie parisienne."

Splendeurs et misères des courtisanes[679] is composed of four parts, of which only three appeared in the Furne edition of the *Comédie humaine.* It is logical, however, that the last part, although not included in the novel until 1855, should be considered under the present caption, since it was listed as Part IV of the novel in the catalogue of 1845. In this immense "fresco" Balzac assembled his created world of men of letters and of law, of financiers, politicians, and magistrates. In addition to these are here revealed, so he said in the Preface, "les existences, dans toute leur vérité, des espions, des filles entretenues et des gens en guerre avec la société qui grouillent dans Paris."[680] When the novelist was reproached for introducing such types, he stated in self-defense, "mais il faut faire Paris vrai,"[681] and claimed that the novel was composed of "détails profondément vrais, pour ainsi dire historiques."[682] For the sake of truth, he continued, he had undertaken "l'analyse et la critique de la Société dans toutes ses parties"; consequently, he was obliged to portray "ces figures si curieuses, de la courtisane, du criminel, et de leurs entourages."[683]

The idea of rise and fall suggested in the title *Splendeurs et misères*

---

[679] Of Part I, *Comment Aiment les Filles,* a fragment, *La Torpille,* was published by Werdet, together with *La Femme supérieure* and *La Maison Nucingen,* in 1838, in 2 vols. The remainder of *La Torpille,* with a large section of Part II, *A combien l'Amour revient aux vieillards,* appeared in *Le Parisien,* May–July, 1843, under the title *Esther, ou Les Amours d'un vieux banquier;* it was composed of three sections, to which Balzac soon added a fourth. De Potter published the whole under the present title in 1844, in 3 vols. The same year the novel entered the third category, under the present title: Part I, *Esther heureuse;* Part II, retaining its first title; Part III, *Où Mènent les Mauvais Chemins;* this part was first published in *L'Epoque,* July, 1846, as *Une Instruction criminelle.* In 1847 it was published by Souverain under the title *Un Drame dans les prisons,* together with *Esquisse d'homme d'affaires (Les Roueries d'un créancier).* Part IV, *La Dernière Incarnation de Vautrin,* first appeared in *La Presse,* April–May, 1847, and the following year was published, by Chlendowski, with *Les Martyrs ignorés* and *Une Rue de Paris et son habitant,* in 3 vols. In 1855 Part IV entered the *Comédie humaine,* Vol. XVIII, a supplementary volume published by Houssiaux (see above, p. 132). The four parts are now united under the collective title *Splendeurs et misères des courtisanes, Con.,* Vols. XV–XVI.

[680] *OD.,* III, 575.

[681] *LEt.,* I, 175.

[682] *OD.,* III, 576.

[683] *Ibid.,* pp. 576–77.

(cf. *Histoire de la grandeur et de la décadence de César Birotteau* of the same category) is itself a key to the classification of the novel, with its interwoven plots and intrigues all typical of the capital. Moreover, in the character of Vautrin is presented the archcriminal of the underworld in his true environment of rascals and courtesans. The death scene of Esther savors the degradation to which life may sink in the great metropolis. Marcel Barrière[684] maintains that the *Splendeurs et misères* is the outstanding work of the "Scènes de la vie parisienne." It forcibly illustrates the "extrêmes de Paris qui dissolvent incessamment les principes sociaux,"[685] and fulfils the author's expressed intention for the third subdivision.

The three compositions to be considered next are short sketches each affording a glimpse of the *mœurs parisiennes* through the characterization of a definite type. The first of these, *Un Prince de la Bohème*,[686] recalls Balzac's early salon stories, except that here the tale is read instead of being told. Its original title, *Les Fantaisies de Claudine*, was too narrow, for it stressed only the whims of Claudine; the new caption, *Un Prince de la Bohème*, is far better suited to its contents and the social category portrayed. Through the idle, adventurous life of La Palferine, one of the "jeunes gens" of the *Comédie humaine*, Balzac acquaints the reader with the social set in the cafés on the Boulevard des Italiens. The Parisian *boulevardiers*, with their meaningless existence *à la bohème*, properly belong to the "Scènes de la vie parisienne," in which our sketch was classified from the start.

Esquisse d'homme d'affaires d'après nature,[687] like the preceding tale, characterizes another member of the "jeunes gens," Maxime de Trailles. It is a clever sketch, depicting the trickery of Maxime's creditor, Cérizet, which explains the first title, *Les Roueries d'un créancier*. When finally,

[684] *L'Œuvre de Honoré de Balzac*, p. 157.

[685] *OD.*, III, 392.

[686] This short story, under the title *Les Fantaisies de Claudine*, first appeared in *La Revue parisienne*, August 25, 1840; in 1844, under its present title, it was published, together with *Honorine*, by De Potter, in 2 vols. In 1846 it entered the category under consideration; it is now in *Con.*, Vol. XVIII.

[687] This tale was first published in *Le Siècle*, September, 1845, under the title *Les Roueries d'un créancier*, as chap. iii of a series, *Etudes de mœurs*. In 1846, entitled *Esquisse d'homme d'affaires d'après nature*, it entered the category under discussion. In 1847, retaining the same title, it completed Vol. II of *Un Drame dans des prisons* (Part III of *Splendeurs et misères des courtisanes*), published by Souverain. The tale under a new title, *Un Homme d'affaires*, is now in *Con.*, Vol. XVIII.

in 1846, the tale was classified in the third subdivision, Balzac bestowed on it the second title, which involves a larger sociological group and is more in keeping with the author's growing scheme. The sketch, however, is not listed in the catalogue of 1845, for the simple reason that it had not yet been written. In 1846 the novelist, while revising Volume XI[688] of the Comédie humaine, wrote on the back of the inside cover of the book a third caption, Un Homme d'affaires. In this he gained brevity but still retained the connotation of the title in the first edition. The character of Maxime de Trailles, the Parisian dandy, and of his crafty creditor, together with the atmosphere of the demi-mondains, is a true "étude de mœurs" in the capital and plays an important part in the "Scènes de la vie parisienne," in which it was ultimately classified.

Gaudissart II,[689] the last sketch, presents the type of the perfect sales-man; in him Balzac personified "la passion des vendeurs." It is a comic skit of a few pages in which is shown how Gaudissart II is more successful in a Parisian shop than was L'Illustre Gaudissart in Touraine. Although the sketch was not included in the catalogue of 1845, it remains in the corrected Furne edition[690] as part of the "Scènes de la vie parisienne," where it was logically and permanently classified.

The last story in Volume IV of the "Scènes de la vie parisienne," Les Comédiens sans le savoir (Le Provincial à Paris),[691] portrays an additional scene in the life of provincials in Paris.[692] It is comic in nature and offers an effective contrast to the tragedy of Un Grand Homme de province à Paris, Lucien de Rubempré of Illusions perdues. Gazonal, the country-

[688] Lov. Coll., A 28.

[689] First appeared in La Presse, October 12, 1844, under the title Un Gaudissart de la rue Richelieu; les Comédies qu'on peut voir gratis. It also appeared in Le Diable à Paris, a collective work by several authors published by Hetzel in 1844–46, in 2 vols. In 1846, under its present title, it entered the subdivision under discussion; it is now in Con., Vol. XIX.

[690] Lov. Coll., A 25 and A 28.

[691] This story first appeared in Le Courrier français, April, 1846; the same year it entered the third category. In 1848 it was reprinted under the title Le Provincial à Paris, together with Gillette (Le Chef-d'œuvre inconnu), Le Rentier, and El Verdugo. Three episodes of the story appeared separately: Un Espion à Paris: Le Petit Père Fromenteau, bras droit des gardes du commerce and Une Marchande à la toilette, ou Madame Ressource in Le Diable à Paris, published by Hetzel in 2 vols., in 1845–46, in the series Les Comé-dies qu'on peut voir gratis à Paris; Etude de mœurs: II, Le Luther des chapeaux, in Le Siècle, August, 1845.

[692] Cf. Les Provinciaux à Paris: Le Cabinet des antiques.

man, comes to the capital to settle a lawsuit. There his cousin, Léon de Lora, a painter, and Bixiou act as *ciceroni*. With Gazonal the reader is taken on a tour into the "infernal regions" of Paris; here Balzac presents a gallery of metropolitan portraits, the "Comédiens sans le savoir": the barber, the haberdasher, the hatter, the usurer, the fortune-teller, the concierge, the police spy, the politician—they all mystify and amuse our provincial, who, after winning his case, returns to his province more informed and completely convinced of the superiority of the metropolis.

A proposed title, *Les Comiques sérieux* (listed in the catalogue of 1845), and the one used in 1848, *Le Provincial à Paris*, as well as the present and final title, are all appropriate, for each points to a specific aspect of the narrative. These secondary Parisian types and the true Parisian milieu demand the classification of *Les Comédiens sans le savoir* in the "Scènes de la vie parisienne," in which the story retained its position permanently.

With this story ends our discussion of the original four volumes of the "Scènes de la vie parisienne" (Furne ed.). In 1848, however, Balzac published a supplementary,[693] a fifth, volume of the series, which should logically, despite chronology, be considered under the same caption as the first four.

This supplementary Volume XVII of the *Comédie humaine* contained the twin novels *La Cousine Bette* and *Le Cousin Pons*, under the collective title *Les Parents pauvres*.[694] This work, written in June, 1846, and published in October, 1847, belongs to the last creative period of our novelist, during which he portrayed his characters with extreme realism, bordering on naturalism, monomania, and even pathology in the case of Bette. The first, a novel of several themes, centers around a poor relative, Bette, who endeavors to bring about the ruin of her cousin, Adaline, despite the fact that she has been kindly treated by the family. Her motivation is vengeance born of unrestrained envy and pettiness. *Le Cousin Pons*, the second novel, is a complement and contrast to the first. Pons, too, is a poor relation, but one who is humiliated and despised by his wealthy kin. A simple soul, like François Birotteau (of the same category), Pons is beset

---

[693] See above, p. 132.

[694] The original title of the diptych was *Histoire des parents pauvres;* it appeared in the *Constitutionnel: La Cousine Bette,* October–December, 1846, and *Le Cousin Pons* (the projected title was *Les Deux Musiciens*), March–May, 1847. The two novels were joined in book form and published by Chlendowski and Pétion in 1847–48, in 12 vols. In 1848 they entered, with their present titles, the subdivision under consideration. The two stories are now in *Con.*, Vols. XVII, XVIII.

by "les petits vices," especially by *gourmandise;* to satisfy this weakness he gradually becomes a parasite in the homes of his well-to-do relatives. He has, however, a master-passion which, noble in itself, has effected his complete ruin—namely, his love of art and the uncontrollable mania of a collector. His collection is the true heroine of the story and the love of his heart. During his illness his persecuting family learns the value of the art museum, joins the cohorts of rival art-dealers and shysters, and abets the rapacious concierge, La Cibot. Piece by piece, they despoil him of his treasures.

Balzac proposed to change not only the original collective title, *Histoire des parents pauvres,* but also the subtitle of the second novel. First it was *Le Bonhomme Pons;*[695] next it became *Le Vieux Musicien,* who is, Balzac says, "le parent pauvre accablé d'injures, plein de cœur." *Le Cousin Pons, La Cousine Bette,* and *Pierrette,* continues Balzac, "constitueront *L'Histoire des parents pauvres.*"[696] Still another proposed title, *Les Deux Musiciens,* was on June 28, 1846, replaced by *Le Parasite* and designated as "le titre définitif."[697] When this, however, was not approved by Mme Hanska, the author decided on the present title, *Le Cousin Pons,* which implies a clearer connection with its companion, *La Cousine Bette.* Each of the rejected titles reveals his indecision as to which aspect of Pons's character most completely harmonizes with the theory in the third category. *Le Cousin Pons* suggests kinship and the greedy expectation of inheritance,[698] a feature of Parisian life, which Balzac intended to portray in the "Scènes de la vie parisienne."

The title of *Les Parents pauvres* indicates, furthermore, a social category within which Balzac opposes contrasting characters: Pons and his faithful friend Schmucke, innocent martyrs, symbolize the "extrême bien"; the Marville family—La Cibot, Rémonencq, and Bette—personify the "extrême mal," another objective in the author's general design for the "Scènes de la vie parisienne." The facts that the theme of young love holds a very minor role (Hortense and Wenceslas in *La Cousine Bette*) and that the work is essentially a study of vicious and cruel Parisian life in all social levels align the novels logically in the third subdivision of the *Etudes de mœurs.*

[695] *LEt.,* III, 254.

[696] *Ibid.,* p. 256. See above, p. 142, on *Les Célibataires: Pierrette.*

[697] *LEt.,* III, 281.   [698] Cf. Lov., *Hist.,* p. 47.

The last three categories[699] of the "Etudes de mœurs": "Scènes de la vie politique," 1846, "Scènes de la vie militaire," 1845, and "Scènes de la vie de campagne," 1845, had had no previous publications; therefore the titles were not used as subdivisions until 1845, although much earlier Balzac indicated the "Scènes de la vie politique" and the "Scènes de la vie militaire" as collective titles (May 8, 1830).[700] Of the six categories, these remained the least developed, even though their pattern was distinctly outlined by the author. For our purposes it seems advisable (1) to consider them as a group, (2) to discover Balzac's intentions for each, (3) to follow up his realization in individual stories, and (4) on such bases to discuss the pro and con of the classifications.

It should be recalled that all three categories were announced as a group in the Davin-Balzac introductions, 1834 and 1835, respectively, at which time they were designed in general to depict "les spectacles atroces mais pompeux des masses sociales luttant entre elles ... la vie et les intérêts incarnés dans quelques hommes chargés d'en prévoir les nécessités et de mettre aux prises les individus entre eux. Ce seront les *Scènes de la vie politique* et les *Scènes de la vie militaire*."[701] The last category, Davin-Balzac continued, was to portray the haven for the "débris des hommes brisés par la politique, par la guerre et par les orages de la vie." These statements show that the author was no longer particularly interested in individuals but in personalities representative of the masses and nations. His general objective in the last three categories was a study of antagonism between large groups of people. Apparently the author planned a greater number of novels for these subdivisions than he actually completed. On May 10, 1840, he wrote to Mme Hanska that he had yet to compose "*les Scènes de la vie politique* et *les Scènes de la vie militaire*, deux portions bien longues et bien difficiles. Il me faudra pas moins de six années de travaux pour en venir au bout."[702] The work advanced slowly, for in September, 1841, he reported: "Quant aux *Scènes de la Vie politique, militaire et de campagne*, il en manque les deux tiers, et je dois tout avoir fini en sept ans, sous peine de ne jamais faire la *Comédie humaine*."[703]

Balzac's specific intentions[704] for the "Scènes de la vie politique" were (1) to consider political issues and dictatorial power after the Revolution;

---

[699] Partly dealt with; see above, pp. 91 ff.

[700] See above, p. 34.   [702] *LEt.*, I, 537.

[701] Lov., *Hist.*, p. 198.   [703] *Ibid.*, p. 565.

[704] Lov., *Hist.*, pp. 48–49; *Avant-propos*, p. xxxviii.

(2) to portray the will of the majority symbolized by the elected; (3) to depict organized power, the administration versus individual liberty. We shall now see to what degree he realized these purposes in the stories eventually placed in the category.

Besides the four actually published, other compositions were planned for the first edition of the "Scènes de la vie politique." To repeat, *Les Conversations*[705] were intended to open the category because, the author explained, "elles forment une transition naturelle entre la peinture des extrêmes de Paris ... et ... des *Scènes de la vie politique*, où l'homme se met au-dessus des lois communes, au nom des intérêts nationaux."[706] This project, as stated above, was not carried out, and *Les Conversations* did not enter the category.

Un Épisode sous la Terreur[707] became ultimately the opening scene of the subdivision. This is a short narrative, written in 1830, to which Balzac gave a historical background. Here the monarchy is represented by the priest and two nuns, while the Revolution and the action of the masses are personified by the executioner of Louis XVI; the executioner seeks comfort and forgiveness in a Mass held secretly in an attic by the priest in hiding. The idea of one man as expressing the voice of a people harmonizes with the author's design for the "Scènes de la vie politique"; therefore the tale holds rightfully a significant place in the category.

Bellessort[708] maintains that in *Une Ténébreuse Affaire* Balzac utilized the secrets of the imperial police communicated to him by his friend, Mme d'Abrantès. This view is confirmed by the author's statement that the story "est une œuvre ... vraie comme événement, et vraie comme détail."[709] The action is based upon a historical fact, the kidnapping of Senator Clément de Ris, in September, 1800, although Balzac has changed the time and place of the event. This incident has been discussed by G. Lenôtre in *Histoires de police et d'aventures*,[710] where it is shown that

---

[705] See above, p. 52.   [706] *OD.*, III, 392, Preface, 1835.

[707] The *Épisode* first appeared anonymously as an introduction to the *Mémoires de Sanson sur la Révolution française*, published by Mame et Delaunay in 2 vols., 1829. The tale had also appeared in *Le Cabinet de lecture*, January–February, 1830. In 1842, in a somewhat modified form, the story was published in the *Royal Keepsake* under the title *Une Messe en 1793;* in 1844–45 it completed Vol. IV of *Modeste Mignon*, published by Roux et Cassanet. In 1846 the story entered the *Comédie humaine*, Vol. XII; it is now in *Con.*, Vol. XXI.

[708] *Op. cit.*, p. 108.   [709] *LEt.*, II, 132. See also *OD.*, III, 559.

[710] Published by Flammarion in 1936. Cf. G. Mongrédien, *"Une Ténébreuse Affaire,"* *Les Nouvelles littéraires*, December 26, 1936.

Malin de Gondreville, in Balzac's story, was modeled upon Clément de Ris. The title of the novel was appropriate, for the real kidnapping remained for a long time a "ténébreuse affaire." Corentin and Peyrade, who personify the imperial police, claim to avenge society, while in reality they avenge their personal pride. Malin de Gondreville stands for the opportunist politician who, like a chameleon, changes with every regime. Une Ténébreuse Affaire is an important political and social document in its disclosure of the corrupt relations between the police and high government officials of France from 1803 to 1806, and so was correctly classified as an essential part of the "Scènes de la vie politique."

The origin of Z. Marcas[711] may be found in a jotting of Balzac's notebook: "Pour les Scènes de la vie politique. Un homme d'Etat agissant pour le pays et pour lui. Un pauvre diable pour sa famille, les mêmes scènes en bas et en haut. Le ministre a une statue, l'artisan est au bagne. Intituler. Les Deux Extrêmes."[712] This specific work was never published, but the subject was treated in our story, where Marcas, an ambitious young man, a born statesman, is exploited by a mediocre but successful minister. Of the hero the author observes: "Il avait cru voir la trahison au cœur du pouvoir, non pas une trahison palpable, saisissable, résultant de faits; mais une trahison produite par un système, par une sujétion des intérêts nationaux à un égoïsme."[713] Despite his high ideals, Marcas falls a victim to corrupt politics; and in his person the novelist criticizes the French government, before the revolution of 1848, for not utilizing the young and talented generation of that period. From its first conception Balzac designed this tale for the "Scènes de la vie politique," because in every detail are illustrated his declared objectives for the category.

The last story of this series, L'Envers de l'histoire contemporaine,[714] con-

---

[711] This sketch was published in the first number of the Revue parisienne, August 25, 1840; in 1841, under a new title, La Mort d'un ambitieux, it appeared in Le Fruit défendu, a collection by several authors; in 1846 the tale entered the Comédie humaine, Vol. XII; it is now in Con., Vol. XXI.

[712] Pensées, sujets, fragmens, éd. Crépet, p. 115.

[713] Fur., XII, 432.

[714] Two episodes of Part I of this novel appeared in September, 1842, and September, 1843, in Le Musée des familles; the first episode was entitled Les Méchancetés d'un saint, and the second, Madame de la Chanterie; under the same title a third episode was published in October and November, 1844, in the same journal. These three fragments, united under a common title, L'Envers de l'histoire contemporaine (premier épisode), entered in 1846 the Comédie humaine, Vol. XII. This part, under a new title, La Femme de soixante ans, together with L'Enfant maudit, L'Epicier, Le Notaire, and La Femme de

sists of two episodes: I, *La Femme de soixante ans* (*Madame de la Chan-terie*), and II, *L'Initié;* although the latter was not added until 1855, it should logically be dealt with in the present period. A. Prioult[715] states that the source of Part I of our novel is to be found in *Sophie, ou L'Enfant volé*, published by L. Legay, 1822. Balzac's hero, Godefroid, seems to be modeled upon De Meran, the hero in *Sophie.* Godefroid, who lacked a motive in life, under the inspiration of practical evangelism became active in good works and was finally initiated into the secret band dedicated to a service of kindly deeds. The fundamental theme of the whole novel is charity combating misery and transforming the lives of men.

But there is a broader aspect from which the work may be considered. In 1844 Balzac explained that he was preparing

comme contre-poids et comme opposition, un ouvrage où se verra l'action de la vertu, de la religion et de la bienfaisance au cœur de cette corruption des capi-tales, et c'est une œuvre à la fois si longue et si difficile, qu'il y a bientôt trois ans qu'il y travaille sans pouvoir la terminer. *Les Méchancetés d'un saint* et *la Baronne de la Chanterie* sont deux fragments extraits de cet ouvrage (*l'Envers de l'histoire contemporaine*), formidable de vertus et où chacun pourra compter les misères affreuses sur lesquelles repose la civilisation parisienne.

En commençant les *Scènes de la vie parisienne* par *les Treize*, l'auteur se pro-mettait bien de les terminer par la même idée, celle de l'association faite au pro-fit de la charité, comme l'autre au profit du plaisir.[716]

It is, then, designed as a contemporary novel depicting a humanitarian phase of Parisian life, and as such the story is now classified in the "Scènes de la vie parisienne." In harmony with this final arrangement and remaining in the same category, it is so listed in the catalogue of 1845. Nevertheless, in 1846 Part I was temporarily used as the conclud-ing story of the "Scènes de la vie politique." On the basis of certain ideas and episodes the novel could pass for a political scene. In it Balzac con-demns the Civil Code; the police episodes recall the Chouannerie;[717] M.

province, was published by Roux et Cassanet in November, 1847, in 3 vols. In 1854, retaining the same title, the story was published by De Potter in 1 vol. Part II, al-though announced as *Les Frères de la consolation*, appeared as *L'Initié* in the *Spectateur républicain*, in August–September, 1848. Together with *El Verdugo*, it was published by De Potter in 2 vols., 1854. In 1855, *L'Initié*, as Part II of our story, entered the *Comédie humaine*, Vol. XVIII, published by Mme Houssiaux. The whole novel is now in *Con.*, Vol. XX.

[715] *Op. cit.*, p. 141.

[716] *OD.*, III, 575–76, Preface to *Splendeurs et misères*.

[717] The novel is linked with *Les Chouans* through the brother of Alphonse de Montau-ran, M. Nicolas, one of the "Frères de la consolation."

de Bourlac's death sentence and Mme de la Chanterie's speech of forgive-ness are both, in essence, political episodes. Although these elements commend the story as a logical transition to the political scenes, far more significant are the truly Parisian setting and characters. The picture of the capital would have been neither true nor complete without the charity work which was then (after the Romantic period) taking root. The hu-manitarian aspect is, in fact, a feature of contemporary Parisian life. With this novel we conclude our discussion of the fourth category and shall now turn to the fifth of the "Etudes de mœurs."

Despite the fact that the "Scènes de la vie militaire" continuously oc-cupied the mind of Balzac from 1829 or even earlier, they remain the least developed of the "Etudes de mœurs." The general design was given in the Davin-Balzac Introduction[718] already dealt with. The author in-tended to portray the masses led "en marche pour se combattre"; and consequently, as he said, he had to describe "les mœurs d'une armée, ... d'un champ de bataille, ... le choc de la France et de l'Europe, ... le trône des Bourbons, que veulent relever dans la Vendée quelques hommes généreux, ... l'émigration aux prises avec la République dans la Bretagne, ... la nation tantôt triomphante et tantôt vaincue."[719] In 1839[720] Balzac accentuated his purpose—the details of military life will be personified, he said, in historical men, "dont l'histoire ne tiendra jamais compte." And in the Avant-propos he explained that society will be shown "dans son état le plus violent"; nevertheless, he regretted, at that time, that the series was still the least complete portion of his work. In his dedication of Les Deux Frères Balzac disclosed further features designed for the sub-division. He wrote "Assez de beaux caractères, assez de grands et nobles dévouements brilleront dans les Scènes de la vie militaire."[721] Again in his letters he alluded to the projected series which would entail a journey to the battlefields of Germany and of Austria.[722] An analysis of the military tales will presently show which of these objectives were ultimately carried out.

The title of the fifth subdivision of the "Etudes de mœurs," like the fourth and the sixth, had had no publication previous to this issue except for the fact that the phrase had been used as a collective volume title for a

[718] See above, pp. 91, 157.   [719] Lov., Hist., p. 48.

[720] OD., III, 525, Preface to Une Fille d'Ève.

[721] Les Deux Frères, éd. Souverain (1842), I, iii.

[722] LEt., I, 537, 544, 569, and passim; II, 288, 340, and passim; III, 26.

projected work of which only one extract, *El Verdugo*,[723] had been published in 1830.

Of the two stories actually published in the series under consideration, *Une Passion dans le désert*[724] has been dealt with earlier in our study. We now pass directly to the discussion of the second, *Les Chouans, ou La Bretagne en 1799*.[725] There are two themes in this historical novel: the royalist insurrection in Brittany of 1799 and the love of Marie de Verneuil for "le Gars," the Marquis Alphonse de Montauran. Together with his followers, chiefly Breton peasants, Montauran represents the royalist front as opposing the republican. Through a police intrigue he loses both his cause and his life. In the background of the actual revolt, as well as in the historical incident and characters,[726] Balzac definitely realized some of his intentions. As a tableau of the civil war in the nineteenth century the novel is in keeping with Balzac's design for the series in which it was legitimately classified in 1845; together with *Une Passion dans le désert* it forms an integral part of the unfinished "Scènes de la vie militaire."

Although the title of the sixth and last subdivision of the "Etudes de mœurs," the "Scènes de la vie de campagne," was mentioned by Balzac as early as November, 1833,[727] it had previously been used neither as a volume title nor as a subdivision. To the author's plans in regard to this series, discussed earlier in this study, should now be added a more specific statement of design. He purposed to portray: "... les hommes froissés par le monde, par les révolutions, à moitié brisés par les fatigues de la guerre, dégoûtés de la politique. Là donc le repos après le mouvement, les paysages après les intérieurs, les douces et uniformes occupations de la vie des champs après le tracas de Paris ... les idées religieuses, la vraie philanthropie, la vertu sans emphase."[728] In the *Avant-propos* Balzac again extended his objective to include, he said, "les plus purs caractères

---

[723] See above, pp. 34, 43–44.

[724] The shifting of this story from the "Etudes philosophiques" to the "Scènes de la vie militaire" has been discussed and justified above, p. 118.

[725] Partly dealt with; see above, p. 27. This novel was published in 1829, under the title *Le Dernier Chouan, ou La Bretagne en 1800*, by Urbain Canel, in 4 vols.; in 1834 it was published, under its present title, by Vimont in 2 vols.; in 1836, by Werdet. In 1845 the story entered the *Comédie humaine*, Vol. XIII; it is now in *Con.*, Vol. XXII. For a complete history of publication and variations, see Barnes, *op. cit.*; and Dargan, Crain, and Others, *op. cit.*, pp. 33–65.

[726] Dargan, Crain, and Others, *op. cit.*, pp. 41 ff.

[727] *LEt.*, I, 91.   [728] Lov., *Hist.*, p. 48.

et l'application des grands principes d'ordre, de politique, de moralité."
By this he meant that in the last category he would declare his faith in a
social order, in politics and ethics. All these tenets are to be symbolized
by characters, setting, and action. A discussion of the novels placed in
the category at that time will reveal the concrete expression of the author's ideas and so warrant the classification.

The first edition of the series contained *Le Médecin de campagne* and
Le Curé de village.

Le Médecin de campagne,[729] together with *Les Chouans*, is among Balzac's notable productions; the latter opened the way to fame, and during
the composition of the former he conceived the idea of reappearing characters. He spoke of *Le Médecin de campagne* as his "œuvre de prédilection"[730] and hoped it would win him "le prix Montyon."[731] The political, economic, social, and religious ideas in this novel are, in large part,
expressed by the author's spokesman, Benassis, the country doctor,
mayor, and benefactor of the community, through whose life and work
Balzac shows the efficacy of philanthropy and demonstrates that in order
to improve men one must better their milieu. The novel is essentially a
sociological study but contains some military episodes, the most important of which is the "Napoléon du peuple." Upon the basis of such passages, it may be argued, *Le Médecin de campagne* might be classified in the
"Scènes de la vie militaire"; and had this subdivision been completed,
probably these episodes, as well as others, dispersed in various novels,
would have been parts of the military series. But in our novel the military passages are incidental to the narrative, which is essentially concerned with the social reforms brought about by the country doctor. In
1840[732] Balzac indicated the story as a scene in the last subdivision of the
"Etudes de mœurs" in which it was classified in 1846 and of which it
forms a component part. For in this novel, as well as in the next, the
author developed certain ideas on religion and social reforms designed, as
stated above, particularly for the "Scènes de la vie de campagne."

[729] This novel first appeared in September, 1833, in 2 vols., published by Mame-
Delaunay; the 2d and 3d eds. were published by Werdet in 1834 and 1836, respectively;
in 1839 Charpentier reprinted it in 1 vol. In 1846 the novel entered the *Comédie humaine*, Vol. XIII; it is now in *Con.*, Vol. XXIV.

[730] *LEt.*, I, 24.

[731] *Corr. Carraud*, p. 82. Cf. Surville, *op. cit.*, p. 201. See also Bouteron, "Balzac et
le prix Montyon," *RDM*, XVIII (December 15, 1933), 927.

[732] *LEt.*, I, 536.

In the Preface to the first edition of *Le Curé de village*[733] Balzac stated that this novel, a "pendant" to the one just discussed, contained "l'application du repentir catholique."[734] Here we find the practical idealist, Abbé Bonnet, aided by Véronique Graslin and others, undertaking and achieving the material and moral regeneration of the inhabitants of the wretched village, Montégnac. Bonnet suggests to the unhappy Mme Graslin that she use her wealth for the irrigation of the countryside of Montégnac in order to fertilize the plateau and to transform for the better the lives and the morale of the villagers. Véronique Graslin, therefore, in seeking expiation of her own sin, becomes the benefactress of the people.

There was no doubt in Balzac's mind concerning the classification of this novel; from the start it was destined for the "Scènes de la vie de campagne." On June 2, 1839, he wrote that the work "sera beaucoup plus élevé, plus grand, plus fort que *Le Lys dans la vallée* et que le *Médecin de campagne*,"[735] both classified in this subdivision.[736] The country setting, a few rural characters and their occupations, together with the religious and philanthropic ideas in *Le Curé de village*, fully justify its inclusion in the category. With this novel we conclude our discussion of the "Etudes de mœurs au XIXe siècle," first division of the *Comédie humaine* (Furne ed.), and shall now pass to the second main division, the "Etudes philosophiques."

In comparison with the "Etudes de mœurs," just discussed, there was very little development or new material in the "Etudes philosophiques"; of the twenty-two titles comprised in the division, only one was new, *Le Martyr calviniste*.[737] Although the last to be written, this work became Part I of *Sur Catherine de Médicis*. The earlier title of this episode, for which three *feuilles* were actually set up by Charles Plon, was *Un Martyr*.[738] It was, however, successively announced as *Le Pelletier de la reine*, *Le Fils du pelletier*, *Les Lecamus, ou Catherine de Médicis prise au piège*,[739] but finally published as *Les Lecamus*. Even this was ultimately changed

---

[733] This story first appeared in *La Presse*, January 1–7, June 30–July 13, and July 30–August 1, 1839. It was published in book form, May, 1841, by Souverain in 2 vols.; in 1845 the novel entered the *Comédie humaine*, Vol. XIII; it is now in *Con.*, Vol. XXV.

[734] *OD.*, III, 547.   [735] *LEt.*, I, 513, 536.

[736] *Le Lys dans la vallée* was added later.

[737] This episode first appeared as *Les Lecamus* in *Le Siècle*, March 23–April 4, 1841.

[738] Lov. Coll., A 281, fols. 300, 305.

[739] Lov., *Hist.*, p. 186. See also *Con.*, XXX, 398; Crain, *op. cit.*, pp. xix–xxvi.

to *Le Martyr calviniste* in the Souverain edition of the complete novel. Each of these titles has a direct bearing on the contents, which deal with the conspiracy of Amboise, with the part played in it by Catherine, and with the life of the young Calvinist, Christophe Lecamus, the son of the queen's furrier.

In 1843, when the three parts of the novel were assembled under the general title *Sur Catherine de Médicis*, Balzac added an "Introduction," in which he pointed out Catherine as the unifying *fil*, and thereby justified the title of the book. Here, also, as well as in a letter to Mme Hanska, he stated the purpose of the work. He wrote: "Je viens d'achever une petite étude, intitulée *Le Martyr*, qui avec *Le Secret des Ruggieri* et *Les Deux Rêves*, me complète l'étude du caractère de Catherine de Médicis."[740] Balzac's interest in Catherine's complex nature is obvious in the "Introduction"; the whole novel is, indeed, an explanation and a defense of the queen and her policy of absolute monarchy. Although the classification of this novel has been previously discussed on the basis of *Les Deux Rêves* and *Le Secret des Ruggieri*, it is well to add the following passage from the author's notebook:[741]

19 X^bre 1836. Résolu d'introduire dans les *Etudes philosophiques*, autant de scènes historiques qu'il y a de siècles depuis l'invasion des Francs jusqu'en 1800, pour montrer le ravage des hautes idées de la politique, ce qui a fait l'esprit des siècles, l'antagonisme, et cela dans les proportions du *Secret des Ruggieri*. Environ 15 scènes. *Les Ruggieri* seront complétés par *Les deux Rêves*, dans l'édition future.

This jotting and a letter to Mme Hanska[742] give the reasons for placing a historical work in the "Etudes philosophiques." Moreover, the "Introduction" contains a further reason for the classification; Balzac says: "Si ce travail se trouve parmi les *Etudes philosophiques*, c'est qu'il montre l'esprit d'un temps et qu'on y voit clairement l'influence de la pensée."[743] Catherine's *idée-fixe*—the absolute power of royalty, with its Machiavellian politics; the egoism of power, the prime motive of all her life and actions—is the underlying philosophical principle in the novel. This is a good reason and justifies the inclusion of *Sur Catherine de Médicis* in the second main division, where the story rightfully holds a significant place.

Balzac conceived and announced in 1834, as stated above, the idea of

740 *LEt.*, I, 399, letter dated May 28, 1837.

741 Ed. Crépet, p. 138.

742 *LEt.*, II, 134.   743 *Fur.*, XV, 478.

grouping all his novels under three captions; the realization, necessarily slow, was carried out between 1842 and 1848. Consequently, the third and concluding section of the *Comédie humaine*, the "Etudes analytiques," the least developed and articulated of the three, was here added. Its general line of thought had been indicated, as for the first two main divisions, in the Davin-Balzac Introduction;[744] and no new purpose was enunciated in the *Avant-propos*. Nonetheless, this part was not written without a somewhat elaborate earlier preparation.

The analytical essays[745] concurrent with the publication of the *Physiologie du mariage* show a definite kinship with this work and with the author's intentions for the division. Here, through their exterior manifestations, as Davin-Balzac stated, were sought the hidden principles of human nature. Hence, a significant title was projected, *Le Traité de la vie extérieure*, of which, according to Balzac, fragments had already been published. The other title projected for the division, at that time (1834), was *La Monographie de la vertu*.[746] From these announced works and from a number of short compositions published between 1830 and 1831[747] we conjecture that Balzac planned a series of "physiologies" and "pathologies." Although this assumption seems fully warranted, the present writer has nowhere found a specific statement by Balzac in regard to such a series. These short essays, sometimes alluded to as "traités," or "codes," were to fill the "Etudes analytiques," for which the author was ostensibly now apprenticing himself. They indicate a search for the human nature hidden by outward appearances, and a consequent interest in physiognomy, gait, and manners, in so far as these reveal to Balzac the inner life of man.

Planned only on these broad lines, the division contained at the time of the author's death but one work,[748] *Physiologie du mariage*,[749] published anonymously in 1829. Curiously enough, there exists a preoriginal of this work, bearing no title. It is bound in a volume with *Histoire de la*

---

[744] See above, p. 88.   [745] See above, p. 28.

[746] Lov., *Hist.*, p. 206. Neither of these works was published.

[747] See above, p. 28.

[748] The second composition added to this division later is analyzed in Sec. VII.

[749] Partly discussed above, pp. 28–29. This work was first published anonymously in December, 1829, by Levavasseur and Canel. In 1834, signed by the author, it was published by Ollivier in 2 vols.; and in 1838 by Charpentier in 1 vol.; in 1846 it entered the *Comédie humaine*, Vol. XVI; and it is now in *Con.*, Vol. XXXII.

rage, written by B.-F. Balzac, father of the novelist, and printed in 1826–27.[750] The *Physiologie* is not a novel; instead it is a satire on marriage and a sociological analysis of passion in its diverse manifestations. In keeping with his objective for the division, the author seeks to establish the principle that legal equality between husband and wife should be the basis of the family. The various reasons for this principle were shown in the "Etudes philosophiques," and the effects were illustrated in the "Etudes de mœurs." It should now be obvious, if not before, that the *Physiologie* logically belongs to the "Etudes analytiques," in which it was ultimately classified. With this division we close the fourth period of Balzac's literary career and complete our discussion of the first edition of the *Comédie humaine*.

It is now pertinent to summarize the chief points of advance in the fourth period: (1) in this serial publication, *La Comédie humaine*, the one inclusive general title, is used for the first time; (2) "Etudes analytiques," the third main division, is added to the original "Etudes de mœurs" and "Etudes philosophiques"; (3) new works are included and new dispositions of novels are also made. The "Etudes de mœurs" in the Furne had sixty-one titles, of which thirty-five were new:[751] nine in the first category, eight in the second, eleven in the third, four in the fourth, one in the fifth, and two in the sixth. An explanation of the counting is necessary: the three parts of *Illusions perdues* are counted separately, but those of *Histoire des Treize* and *Splendeurs et misères* are considered as one novel.

The "Etudes philosophiques" comprised in the original *Comédie humaine* twenty-two titles, of which only one was new; the three episodes of *Sur Catherine de Médicis* are counted separately.

The "Etudes analytiques," as has just been shown, contained only one title; therefore the grand total of novels in the sixteen volumes of the first edition of the *Comédie humaine* was eighty-four, of which thirty-seven were new. Among these we note the following shifts. To the "Scènes de la vie privée" were restored: (1) *La Bourse, Une Double Famille*, and *Gobseck*, after a temporary placement in the "Scènes de la vie parisienne," from which also came *Madame Firmiani* and *Etude de femme*, both originally of the philosophical tales; (2) *Le Message* and parts of *Autre Etude de femme*, after a temporary classification in the "Scènes de la vie de province," from which were also added *La Grenadière* and *La Femme*

[750] Prioult, *op. cit.*, pp. 213–22.

[751] That is, they had not been previously classified in the subdivisions.

abandonnée. To the "Scènes de la vie parisienne" were shifted *Facino Cane* and *La Messe de l'Athée,* both from the "Etudes philosophiques," Werdet edition. From the same division was moved *Une Passion dans le désert* to the "Scènes de la vie militaire." Therefore, during the fourth period there resulted, in all, twelve shifts; of these, five[752] were restored to the first category; seven were reclassified—six[753] permanently and only one[754] temporarily. This proportion is significantly small in comparison with the reclassifications that took place in the second period. This fact is a most convincing proof of his increasing control over the scheme. The publication of the first edition of the *Comédie humaine* is followed by the fifth and last period of Balzac's literary career.

VII. THE FIFTH AND FINAL PERIOD: 1845-50

In formulating final statements as to the novels included and their placement in Balzac's last arrangement of his *Comédie humaine,* it will be of value to recapitulate briefly the main points of the two preceding sections. Of these, Section V dealt with that period of expansion in Balzac's scheme which paved the way for the first edition of the *Comédie humaine.* This was the only complete edition published during the author's life and was discussed in Section VI. His creative vein continued, although with slower tempo, into his last years, so that later (1848-70) there were added eight compositions which will be noted or discussed in the first part of the present section. The second part will consider those projects of which only fragments or titles now remain, together with the final disposition of the novels.

Three of the eight novels in question were left unfinished[755] and were published posthumously, but we shall discuss only those portions really written by Balzac. Although, for convenience, the chronological order of stories has usually been adopted in this study, nevertheless, logical order is given precedence wherever good sense dictates; consequently, four novels—*La Cousine Bette, Le Cousin Pons, L'Initié* (Part II of *L'Envers*

---

[752] *La Bourse, Une Double Famille, Gobseck, Le Message,* and *La Grande Bretèche* of *Autre Etude de femme.*

[753] *Madame Firmiani, Etude de femme, La Grenadière,* and *La Femme abandonnée* in the "Scènes de la vie privée"; *Facino Cane* was moved to the "Scènes de la vie parisienne"; and *Une Passion dans le désert,* to the "Scènes de la vie militaire."

[754] *La Messe de l'athée.*

[755] *Les Paysans,* later completed by Mme Ève de Balzac; *Les Petits Bourgeois* and *Le Député d'Arcis,* completed by Charles Rabou. See below, pp. 169, 170, 171.

de l'histoire contemporaine), and *La Dernière Incarnation de Vautrin*[756] (tail end of *Splendeurs et misères des courtisanes*)—have already been discussed under their appropriate classifications; therefore, there now remain only four stories to be analyzed.

Les Paysans,[757] the first of the unfinished novels, was conceived, Balzac said,[758] in 1837. In 1838 he composed[759] Part I, *Qui terre a, guerre a,* and four chapters[760] of Part II but published only Part I. Recognizing the completion of the work as a great task, he wrote: "Je ne me pardonnerai jamais de ma vie de m'être fourré dans *Les Paysans.*"[761] According to Spoelberch de Lovenjoul[762] and M. Bouteron,[763] it was his widow who completed the novel. The story is one of the obstinate attachment of the French peasants to the soil. A group of them, aided by the local small bourgeoisie, forced the landowner, M. Moncornet, to sell his large property by lots; here Balzac depicts the struggle between classes. The setting and the episodes of the narrative are definitely *campagnards;* the characters and their *mœurs* are predominantly rural, and on such a basis the story naturally belongs to the "Scènes de la vie de campagne," in which it was later classified as the author had directed.[764] Marc Blanchard[765] claims for Balzac the honor of having introduced into French literature "la campagne et ses habitants."

According to Balzac's letters,[766] *Les Petits Bourgeois,*[767] planned in 1839,

[756] See above, pp. 155, 160, 152 ff. Since these novels were published in the supplementary Vols. XVII and XVIII, they are not counted in the above-given total of eighty-four novels but will be added later. See below, p. 172.

[757] Part I (thirteen chapters) appeared in *La Presse,* December 3-12, 1844; Part II (first four chapters), in *La Revue de Paris,* April–June, 1855; the same year the two parts were published by De Potter in 5 vols. (*Bibliographie de la France,* 1855). Again, in 1855, the complete novel was published by Mme Houssiaux, in the supplementary Vol. XVIII (*Bibliographie de la France,* 1856). Next it appeared in *OC.,* Vol. XIV. It is now in *Con.,* Vol. XXIII.

[758] *LEt.,* II, 434, 453.   [760] Lov. Coll., A 175.

[759] *Ibid.,* I, 488.   [761] *LEt.,* II, 471.

[762] *La Genèse d'un roman de Balzac: "Les Paysans."*

[763] *Con.,* XXIII, 393 ff.   [765] *Op. cit.,* p. 317.

[764] Lov. Coll., A 17.   [766] *LEt.,* II, 268.

[767] This novel first appeared in serial form in *Le Pays,* July–October, 1854; next it was published by De Potter in 8 vols., 1856–57—the first four under the title *Les Petits Bourgeois,* and the last four called *Les Parvenus.* In 1870 the complete novel entered the *Comédie humaine,* éd. Michel Lévy, Vol. XI; it is now in *Con.,* Vol. XX, and contains only the portions written by Balzac and left unfinished.

was not begun before 1843. For this work, as for many of his others, he considered successive titles: *Gendres et belles-mères, Un Grand Artiste, Les Petits Bourgeois de Paris,* and finally the present title. Each is definitely related to a theme in the novel: the first tentative title emphasizes the marriage motif; the second reveals the character of Théodose de la Peyrade, of whom the author speaks as the "cousin germain de Tartuffe";[768] the third was suggested by the publisher Hetzel in the hope that the title would give "une immense valeur de vente à l'œuvre."[769] This last Balzac ultimately shortened to *Les Petits Bourgeois;* the composition is a satirical epic[770] concerning the fairly well-to-do element of the lower Parisian bourgeoisie. It tells of Louis-Jérôme Thuillier and his sister, children of the concierge at the Ministry of Finance, both motivated by political and social ambitions. Céleste, the daughter of Louis-Jérôme, and her dowry are sought by Théodose de la Peyrade, called by the author "avocat des pauvres"[771] and "artiste en hypocrisie," who tries to win the good graces of the family by promising political advances to the father.[772]

Through the portrayal of social and political climbers and their dishonest intrigues and abuses—all staged against the background of the Latin quarter in old Paris—Balzac gave in this novel, as he said, "une scène de la vie parisienne."[773] Although unfinished, *Les Petits Bourgeois* was, according to his instructions,[774] ultimately classified in the Parisian series, where it obviously belongs, together with *Les Employés,* presenting the government group; *La Maison Nucingen,* the world of high finance; and *César Birotteau,* both big and small business.

Les Petites Misères de la vie conjugale,[775] which the novelist wrote at different periods in his career, is a patchwork of short psychological analyses of human nature in general and married life in particular. Balzac

[768] *Con.,* XX, 91.   [770] *Ibid.,* p. 337.

[769] *LEt.,* II, 263.   [771] *Con.,* XX, 55.

[772] *Ibid.,* pp. 464 ff. At this point ends Balzac's manuscript as verified by M. Bouteron according to the material in the Lovenjoul Collection at Chantilly. The rest of the novel was written at the request of Mme Ève de Balzac by Charles Rabou, who, however, did not acknowledge his completion of the story. Rabou had collaborated with Balzac in the *Contes bruns.*

[773] *LEt.,* II, 264.   [774] Lov. Coll., A 17.

[775] This work was first published by Chlendowski in 1 vol., in 1845; partial reprintings were made in 1846; the same year Roux and Cassanet published the whole composition in 3 vols. In 1855 it was classified and appeared in Vol. XVIII, éd. Houssiaux. It is now in *Con.,* Vol. XXXIII.

maintains that in married life, as in the life of society, the greatest evil comes from falsehood and unfaithfulness and that legal equality should be the basis of the association and foundation of the family. Marriage is considered as a social bond which places definite obligations upon both husband and wife. The author illustrates somewhat satirically the "miseries" a wife may inflict upon the husband and the cruelties he, in return, may impose. *Les Petites Misères*, like its companion work, *La Physiologie du mariage*, can hardly be called a "novel," since there is no plot, intrigue, or close delineation of character. The fragmentary form of the composition recalls the "monographs" and "codes" noted above and discussed in connection with *La Physiologie*. In compliance with the author's wishes *Les Petites Misères* was added posthumously (1855) to the "Etudes analytiques." The analytical nature of the two works—the search for principles underlying human behavior—amply fulfils Balzac's objectives for this division.

Balzac wrote only Part I of *Le Député d'Arcis*.[776] Again at the request of Mme Ève de Balzac, Rabou completed the unfinished novel, and this time acknowledged his work. Our study, however, is concerned only with the part written by the novelist himself and now published in the Conard edition of the *Comédie humaine*, Volume XXI. This text also has been verified by M. Bouteron according to the manuscripts in the Lovenjoul Collection.

In *Le Député d'Arcis* the author depicted the political elections in the provinces and characterized the ambitious politicians who, like the provincial poet and nobleman, gravitated toward the capital. In this connection he stated in 1844: "Quant au mouvement politique, à l'ambition du député, c'est une Scène qui appartient aux *Scènes de la Vie politique*, ... elle est intitulée *le Député à Paris (le Député d'Arcis)*."[777] The setting and the characters are intrinsically provincial; the emphasis is placed, as the novelist ironically said, upon "les splendeurs de la vie politique"[778] and

---

[776] Part I, "L'Election," was published in *L'Union monarchique*, April 7–May 3, 1847; Rabou inaccurately reprinted this in *Le Constitutionnel*, September–October, 1853; the same journal published Rabou's completion of the novel, October, 1853—January, 1854. The whole novel appeared in 13 vols., published by De Potter in 1854–55. In 1865 it was reprinted and added to Vol. XII of the *Comédie humaine* (1st ed.) by Mme Houssiaux. Next the story entered the Michel Lévy ed., Vol. XIII. Only Part I of the novel is now in *Con.*, Vol. XXI.

[777] *OD.*, III, 568. Cf. *LEt.*, II, 93, 125. See also Lov. Coll., A 17.

[778] *Con.*, XXI, 286.

the procedure in the election of a deputy—in short, upon departmental politics and their effect on the community. Balzac was a severe critic of representative government and was opposed to the July Monarchy.[779] He declared sarcastically "cette Scène est écrite pour l'enseignement des pays assez malheureux pour ne pas connaître les bienfaits d'une représentation nationale, et qui, par conséquent, ignorent par quelles guerres intestines, aux prix de quels sacrifices à la Brutus, une petite ville enfante un député!"[780] This statement reflects Balzac's unfortunate personal experience in taking an active part in politics and himself aspiring to the office of deputy; his defeat embittered him and fostered an ironic attitude toward the conduct of contemporary politics. On the basis of ideas and situations in Part I alone, *Le Député d'Arcis* is unquestionably a typical political scene and was rightfully assigned from the start to the category of the "Scènes de la vie politique."

With these analyses we conclude our discussion of the additional eight compositions, even though three were left unfinished by the author. The grand total of stories in the *Comédie humaine*, therefore, has now risen from eighty-four to ninety-two.[781]

Balzac's literary career falls, as a whole, into definite periods, according to his partial or successive publications of the "Scènes" and the "Etudes"; there are, nevertheless, certain inevitable overlappings among these; this is particularly true in the case of his final period, which we date from 1845, when his classification was nearly complete. Our division has occasionally necessitated an anticipation of events. The close of the discussion now demands a review of those projects made concurrently with, and partly carried out in, the original Furne edition and its successors.

Although between 1843 and 1848 the novelist frequently referred in his letters[782] to a forthcoming second edition of his *Comédie humaine*, there was, in reality, no second edition prior to his death. But since throughout this period he was adding new novels and slightly modifying the distribution in tentative lists, there grew up later a sort of extension of the Furne, Dubochet, and Hetzel edition; this extension began in 1855 with the pub-

[779] For a full discussion of Balzac's political views, see Bernard Guyon, *Un Inédit de Balzac: "Le Catéchisme social" précédé de l'article "Du Gouvernement moderne."*

[780] *Con.,* XXI, 289.

[781] The *Echantillons de causeries françaises* has not been included because it is not a part of the *Comédie humaine.* Cf. *N.R.F.,* I, xiv.

[782] *LEt.,* II, 143; III, 42.

lication of Volume XVIII[783] and was issued by Mme Houssiaux,[784] who had bought out the firm noted above. The volume contained: *L'Initié* (*L'Envers de l'histoire contemporaine*), *Dernière Incarnation de Vautrin* (*Splendeurs et misères*), *Les Paysans*, and *Les Petites Misères de la vie conjugale*. This expansion, however, is not to be regarded in any way as a second edition.

During the same years (1843–48) Balzac indicated in successive lists of his works an increase in the number of volumes from the original sixteen (to which he had added a supplement, Vol. XVII) to the final twenty-six in the "Catalogue des ouvrages que contiendra *La Comédie humaine.*"[785] This "Catalogue" was first published by Amédée Achard in *L'Epoque*, May 22, 1845, and was again printed in *L'Assemblée nationale*,[786] August 25, 1850, shortly after Balzac's death. The "Catalogue," drawn up in 1845, comprised, in all, the titles of one hundred and thirty-eight novels (in reality one hundred and thirty-seven, since there is an error in including *La Femme supérieure* twice), of which fifty-one were never finished. This study would be incomplete without a final consideration of these projects which, even though unfinished, were distributed among the divisions of the *Comédie humaine:* forty-two were designated for the "Etudes de mœurs"; five for the "Etudes philosophiques"; and four for the "Etudes analytiques." Within the "Etudes de mœurs" the distribution of projected stories in the first category was: *Les Enfants, Un Pensionnat de demoiselles, Intérieur de collège*, and *Gendres et belles-mères;*[787] in the second: *Les Gens ridés, Une Actrice en voyage, L'Original, Les Héritiers Boirouge,*[788]

[783] *Bibliographie de la France* (1856).

[784] She also published, between 1853 and 1855, a reprint of the 17 vols. of the original Furne ed., together with three supplementary volumes: XVIII, XIX, XX. See above, p. 132, n. 564.

[785] *Con.*, I, xiv–xvi.

[786] Here should be noted a few errors, doubtless misprints, in these publications. In *L'Epoque*, No. 7, read *La Danse* instead of *La Bourse;* No. 22, *Léonine*, should be *Honorine*. In *L'Assemblée nationale*, No. 19, *Le Ménage*, was a mistake for *Le Message*, and No. 24, *Gabrielle*, should be *Gobseck*. Both journals indicate a projected work, *Les Grands, l'hôpital et le peuple*, as actually published; under this title only a fragment appeared in 1846. The preceding errors are corrected in the *Histoire des œuvres* and in Vol. I, Conard ed., of the *Comédie humaine;* in the latter, nevertheless, we must note the date of Achard's reprinted article erroneously given as 1860 instead of 1850 (see *Con.*, I, xvi, n. 1).

[787] This was a tentative title for *Les Petits Bourgeois;* see above, p. 169.

[788] See above, pp. 127, 141.

and *Jacques de Metz;* in the third: *Les Grands, l'hôpital et le peuple,*[789] *Une Vue du palais, Entre Savants,*[790] and *Le Théâtre comme il est;*[791] in the fourth: *L'Histoire et le roman, Les Deux Ambitieux, L'Attaché d'ambassade,* and *Comment on fait un ministère;* the fifth category will be considered below; in the sixth are included only *Le Juge de paix* and *Les Environs de Paris.*

It is already obvious that, of the forty-two projected compositions for the "Etudes de mœurs," nineteen were planned for first, second, third, fourth, and sixth subdivisions, beginning with the "Scènes de la vie privée"; whereas the remaining twenty-three were all assigned to the fifth category, "Scènes de la vie militaire." Such apparent disproportion demands a more detailed treatment.

It has been shown, in Section III, that the inception of these never completed scenes dates from Balzac's historical projects of 1827. Early in his literary career he gathered material for the "Scènes de la vie militaire";[792] and in January, 1830, he even made an agreement with Mame for the publication of a projected novel, *La Bataille de Wagram,* which held a prominent place in his plans up to his last years but was never written. Le Breton believes, perhaps justly, that several of the projected stories for the series must have been sketched but were lost after the author's death by "la très négligente Madame Hanska."[793] In confirmation of the critic's view there exist several brief jottings in Balzac's notebook concerning this project—titles, names of characters, and situations.

The contemplated extent of the series may be judged from the "Catalogue" noted above, in which are listed proposed titles for the "Scènes de

---

[789] A fragment of this project was published in *Le Diable à Paris* (1846).

[790] The beginning of this work was printed as "Une Rue de Paris et son habitant," in *Le Siècle,* July 28, 1845. It was reprinted by Chlendowski in 1848, together with *La Dernière Incarnation de Vautrin,* in 3 vols. The unfinished *Entre Savants* was published by Spoelberch de Lovenjoul in the *Annales politiques et littéraires,* May–June, 1901. See *La Comédie humaine,* éd. *N.R.F.,* X, 1053.

[791] No. 68 in the catalogue of 1845, listed among the "Scènes de la vie parisienne." See *La Comédie humaine,* éd. *N.R.F.,* X, 1055, where the title is erroneously indicated as a "Scène de la vie de province."

[792] M. Bouteron, "Un Conseiller de Balzac, le l^t colonel Périolas," *RDM,* January 15, 1922, pp. 422–27. See also Arrigon, *Les Années romantiques,* pp. 206–8. Cf. *Corr. Carraud,* p. 298.

[793] *Op. cit.,* p. 129, n. 1.

la vie militaire," from No. 82 to No. 106, inclusive. Of these, only two were written: *Les Chouans* and *Une Passion dans le désert*.[794]

Although the list of the projected military stories is lengthy, it is worth indicating here because it reveals the author's intended scope for the series, which was to cover the whole of Europe and Egypt as well: (1) *Les Soldats de la République*,[795] (2) *L'Entrée en campagne*, (3) *Les Vendéens*;[796] (4) *Le Prophète* and (5) *Le Pacha* under the general title *Les Français en Egypte;* (6) *L'Armée roulante*, (7) *La Garde consulaire;* under the general title *Sous Vienne:* (8) *Un Combat*, (9) *L'Armée assiégée*, and (10) *La Plaine de Wagram;* (11) *L'Aubergiste*, (12) *Les Anglais en Espagne*, (13) *Moscou*, (14) *La Bataille de Dresde*, (15) *Les Traînards*, (16) *Les Partisans*, (17) *Une Croisière*, (18) *Les Pontons*, (19) *La Campagne de France*, (20) *Le Dernier Champ de bataille*, (21) *L'Emir*, (22) *La Pénissière*, (23) *Le Corsaire algérien*. Some of these titles are strongly suggestive of certain stories within the *Comédie humaine;* for example, *Moscou* recalls *L'Adieu*, now among the philosophical tales; *La Bataille de Dresde* evokes *Le Colonel Chabert* of the private scenes. These projects show, in part, Balzac's desire to round out neglected categories. Had all these novels been written, their numbers would have more equally balanced those of the first three categories. Moreover, by completing the projected "Scènes de la vie militaire," the author would have developed the main interest and ideal of his life—Napoleon and his era.

Of the five proposed titles for the "Etudes philosophiques," two were partly carried out: *Le Phédon d'aujourd'hui*, now called *Martyrs ignorés*, *fragment du Phédon d'aujourd'hui*,[797] and *La Vie et les aventures d'une idée*, known as *Aventures administratives d'une idée heureuse*.[798] The remaining three—*Le Président Fritot*, *Le Philanthrope*, and *Le Nouvel Abeilard*— were never written.

The titles of the four projected compositions for the "Etudes analytiques"—*Anatomie des corps enseignants*, *Pathologie de la vie sociale*, *Monographie de la vertu*, and *Dialogue philosophique et politique sur la perfection du XIX⁰ siècle*—show a similarity to the short studies (noted

---

[794] See above, pp. 162 ff.   [795] Planned in three parts.

[796] In regard to this work, on the flyleaf of Vol. I of the corrected Furne ed., Balzac made this notation: "*Les Vendéens* feront un Vol. 14 avec *Les Chouans*" (Lov. Coll., A 17).

[797] *OD.*, I, 351. See also *Etudes philosophiques*, éd. Werdet, Vol. XII (1837).

[798] *OD.*, I, 339. A fragment was published in *Les Causeries du monde* (1837).

above), the "monographs," "pathologies," and "codes." Apparently they, too, were intended to illustrate the basic social principles—Balzac's objective for the third main division of the *Comédie humaine*—and with them closes our discussion of Balzac's unfinished works. It should be added that this "Catalogue," naturally, did not include the novels composed between 1845 and 1848.

It now behooves the writer to recapitulate the changes[799] made during the final period in the distribution of novels really written and published. The changes between the Furne first edition and the "Catalogue" were the following: (1) *Le Père Goriot, Le Colonel Chabert, La Messe de l'athée, L'Interdiction,* and *Pierre Grassou*—all "Scènes de la vie parisienne"— were to become "Scènes de la vie privée"; (2) *L'Envers de l'histoire contemporaine* was to be shifted from the "Scènes de la vie politique" to the "Scènes de la vie parisienne"; *Le Cabinet des antiques,* originally grouped with *La Vieille Fille* under the common title *Les Rivalités,* was now to appear under a new designation, *Les Provinciaux à Paris.*

In 1846 Balzac drew up a new prospectus[800] which was practically a reprint of 1845 but to which he added what proved to be his final directions, to the following effect: *Pierre Grassou*—after a tentative inclusion in the "Scènes de la vie privée," in which it was, in fact, never published—was to remain in the "Scènes de la vie parisienne"; *Le Lys dans la vallée* was to be shifted from the "Scènes de la vie de province" to the "Scènes de la vie de campagne"; *Un Ménage de garçon en province* was to become *La Rabouilleuse; Les Frères de la consolation* should bear the title *L'Envers de l'histoire contemporaine.*

The Michel Lévy edition[801] of the *Comédie humaine,* said to be definitive, claimed to be based on the corrected Furne; but in reality the distribution of novels follows in part that of the uncorrected Furne, in part that of the "Catalogue" (1845), and in part the prospectus (1846). According to the line-up in the "Catalogue," *Le Lys* still remained, in the Lévy edition, in the "Scènes de la vie de province"; *Le Cabinet des antiques* was placed under the common title *Les Provinciaux à Paris;* and the recommended shiftings of *Le Père Goriot, L'Interdiction, Le Colonel Chabert,* and *La Messe de l'athée* were also carried out. On the other hand, the classification of *L'Envers de l'histoire contemporaine* in the "Scènes de la

---

[799] The reasons for these changes were given above in the analyses of the novels in question.

[800] *N.R.F.*, I, xix.   [801] *OC.*, Vols. I–XVII (1869–76).

vie politique" follows the uncorrected Furne edition rather than Balzac's later directions; whereas *Pierre Grassou* remained in the "Scènes de la vie parisienne" according to the prospectus of 1846 and the corrected Furne. These circumstances confirm our view that the publishers, Michel and Calmann-Lévy, did not utilize in full the corrected Furne, as is generally believed.

The Conard edition of the *Comédie humaine*,[802] which contains, in all, ninety-two stories, is regarded as both critical and definitive, since the text and the classification of novels have been revised on the basis of the corrected Furne and in keeping with Balzac's final directions. *Le Lys dans la vallée* is placed in the "Scènes de la vie de campagne," *L'Envers de l'histoire contemporaine* in the "Scènes de la vie parisienne," and *Le Cabinet des antiques* appears again under the original common title, *Les Rivalités*.

A brief summary of this section will emphasize several definite points: (1) Eight compositions were added[803] to the *Comédie humaine*, of which three, although left unfinished, contained, nonetheless, certain features which determined the placement of the stories; (2) fifty-one works projected for the three main divisions show the wider scope contemplated by the author for certain categories within his *Comédie humaine;* (3) the problem of classification was in Balzac's mind to the last; (4) six novels underwent reclassification during the final period.

VIII. GENERAL CONCLUSIONS

The main problem of this investigation has been to trace systematically the history of the publication of Balzac's novels in order to discover whether or not the scheme of his *Comédie humaine* was the result of an evolutionary development. As a corollary, it has been necessary to follow up his method of distribution of stories and to seek within the texts reasons for classification and later reclassification of certain novels.

In considering the above problem it was shown that (1) suggestions of Balzac's general plan are found as early as 1822 in the Preface to *Le Vicaire des Ardennes*, and again in 1827 in the "Avertissement" to *Le Gars;* that (2) the novelist's intentions have become clearer by 1829, when, in his "Avis" to *Les Chouans*, he designated this novel as a cornerstone for

---

[802] Vols. I–XXXIII (1912–28).

[803] In 1848, *La Cousine Bette, Le Cousin Pons;* in 1855, *L'Initié, La Dernière Incarnation de Vautrin, Les Paysans,* and *Les Petites Misères de la vie conjugale;* in 1865, *Le Député d'Arcis;* in 1870, *Les Petits Bourgeois.*

future construction; that (3) definite stages of progress are reached in 1830, with the *Scènes de la vie privée*, from which later grew the "Etudes de mœurs" (1833–37), and again in 1831 with the *Romans et contes philosophiques*, from which later arose the "Etudes philosophiques" (1836–40); that (4) these developments became the original two main sections of the all-inclusive *Comédie humaine* (1842–48), with its final threefold division embracing ninety-two stories. The instances cited establish concrete forms in the inception of the plan and indicate gradual growth in these successive publications.

The scientific basis which underlies Balzac's work consists of two major principles—unity in fundamental nature and environment as a determining factor in the development of species. This theory inspired Balzac to place man in the scale of biological development as a zoölogical and sociological being subject to social laws and dependent upon them as is an animal upon laws of nature; and, consequently, to explain social laws through analogy with the biological. As a scientist observes effects, finds causes, and deduces principles, so Balzac sought to discern those three factors in society; these served as the bases for his three main divisions: "Etudes de mœurs," "Etudes philosophiques," "Etudes analytiques." His scientific beliefs, corroborated by his observations of society, took concrete form in novels arranged in still smaller groupings. Throughout the "Etudes de mœurs," conceived in terms of space—province, Paris, country—and in social circumstances of private, political, and military life, prevails the idea that trades, professions, and environment mold man into species. Here the author approximates deterministic philosophy. The "Etudes philosophiques" and the "Etudes analytiques" had no formal subdivisions. Yet, in the material included, the general drive tended, in the second category, toward considering exaggeration of thought and sentiment as a cause for mental disorder, and, in the third category, toward deducing principles which govern human behavior. The last category suffered comparative neglect. Between 1830 and 1833 two groupings comprise thirty-two stories and represent two major types of fiction: contemporary mores and philosophical tales; from 1833 to 1840 was noted a wider scope in the increased number of stories—fifty in all; the period between 1842 and 1848 marks the peak in the development of the scheme of grouping and is manifest in eighty-four works, and finally in ninety-two.

It has also been shown that the idea of grouping the stories was conceived early, and with it arose the problem of classification which dominated the mind of the author from 1833 to his last year. A careful perusal of his letters, prefaces, and introductions and a thorough analysis of each grouping and of the texts of stories have revealed two chief reasons as governing classification: one, of practical necessity, when Balzac yielded to the exigencies of publishing firms which required a definite number of pages for separate volumes; and the other, logical, artistic, or sociophilosophical, in which preference was given to similarity of themes, ideas, characters, episodes, and setting. Furthermore, it became evident in the course of this study that the original paucity and subsequent increase in the quantity of novels occasioned a good deal of reclassification. Of the ninety-two stories included in the first edition of the *Comédie humaine*, twenty-two[804] underwent a change in position: thirteen[805] were reclassified once and nine twice before final appropriate placement. The latter group includes: *Madame Firmiani, Etude de femme, La Messe de l'athée, L'Interdiction, Gobseck, La Grande Bretèche (Autre Etude de femme), Le Message, Une Double Famille,* and *La Bourse.* The last five were ultimately restored to their first setting, "Scènes de la vie privée," after having been used as "fillers" in the "Scènes de la vie parisienne" and in the "Scènes de la vie de province." The remaining seventeen of the twenty-two stories were permanently removed from their original classifications. The time element of these peregrinations is self-explanatory, for it was during the publication of the two major series, both marking steps in the progress of the author's plan, that they occurred—namely, from 1833 to 1840 and from 1842 to 1848.

Moreover, it has been shown in the course of this investigation that the temporary classification of eleven stories (*Une Double Famille, Etude de femme, Le Message, Adieu, Madame Firmiani, La Femme abandonnée, La Grenadière, L'Interdiction, La Messe de l'athée, Une Passion dans le désert,* and *Le Lys dans la vallée*) was explained by practical reasons, and the reasons were couched in typical statements which have been cited from Balzac's letters.[806] Later, when the exigencies no longer existed, these eleven, together with other tales, were permanently classified (as were the seventy that never changed their original positions) in the light of common elements and in harmony with the intentions expressed for

---

[804] On the diagram (p. 180) are listed the twenty-two stories with their successive shifts.

[805] *La Grenadière, La Femme abandonnée, Le Père Goriot, Le Colonel Chabert, Le Curé de Tours, Facino Cane, Sarrasine, Une Passion dans le désert, L'Envers de l'histoire contemporaine, La Recherche de l'absolu, Les Marana, Adieu, Le Lys dans la vallée.*

[806] See above, pp. 56, 104.

CLASSIFICATION AND SUCCESSIVE SHIFTS OF TWENTY-TWO STORIES

Name of Story	Scènes de la vie privée, 1830–32	Romans et contes philosophiques; Nouveaux contes, 1831–33	Etudes de mœurs, 1833–37	Etudes philosophiques, 1836	Charpentier, 1839	Comédie humaine, 1842–48	Catalogue, 1845	Prospectus, 1846; Corrected Furne	Lévy	Conard
La Bourse	Privée		"Paris"			"Privée"	"Privée"	"Privée"	"Privée"	"Privée"
Une Double Famille	Privée		"Paris"			"Privée"	"Privée"	"Privée"	"Privée"	"Privée"
Madame Firmiani		Nouveaux contes	"Paris"			"Privée"	"Privée"	"Privée"	"Privée"	"Privée"
Etude de femme		Romans et contes	"Paris"			"Privée"	"Privée"	"Privée"	"Privée"	"Privée"
Le Message	Privée		"Province"		"Province"	"Privée"	"Privée"	"Privée"	"Privée"	"Privée"
La Grenadière			"Province"		"Province"	"Privée"	"Privée"	"Privée"	"Privée"	"Privée"
La Femme abandonnée	Privée		"Province"		"Province"	"Privée"	"Privée"	"Privée"	"Privée"	"Privée"
Gobseck			"Paris"		"Paris"	"Privée"	"Privée"	"Privée"	"Privée"	"Privée"
Le Père Goriot						"Paris"	"Privée"	"Privée"	"Privée"	"Privée"
Le Colonel Chabert			"Paris"		"Paris"	"Paris"	"Privée"	"Privée"	"Privée"	"Privée"
La Messe de l'athée				Etudes philosophiques		"Paris"	"Privée"	"Privée"	"Privée"	"Privée"
L'Interdiction				Etudes philosophiques	"Paris"	"Paris"	"Privée"	"Privée"	"Privée"	"Privée"
La Grande Bretèche	Privée		"Province"		"Province"	"Privée"	"Privée"	"Privée"	"Privée"	"Privée"
Le Curé de Tours	Privée		"Province"		"Province"	"Province"	"Province"	"Province"	"Province"	"Province"
Facino Cane				Etudes philosophiques		"Paris"	"Paris"	"Paris"	"Paris"	"Paris"
Sarrasine		Romans et contes	"Paris"		"Paris"	"Paris"	"Paris"	"Paris"	"Paris"	"Militaire"
Une Passion dans le désert				Etudes philosophiques		"Militaire"	"Militaire"	"Militaire"	"Militaire"	"Militaire"
L'Envers de l'histoire contemporaine						"Politique"	"Paris"	"Paris"	"Politique"	"Paris"
La Recherche de l'absolu			"Privée"		"Privée"	"Etudes philosophiques"	"Etudes philosophiques"	"Etudes philosophiques"	"Etudes philosophiques"	"Etudes philosophiques"
Les Marana			"Paris"		"Paris"	"Etudes philosophiques"	"Etudes philosophiques"	"Etudes philosophiques"	"Etudes philosophiques"	"Etudes philosophiques"
Adieu	Privée			Etudes philosophiques		"Etudes philosophiques"	"Etudes philosophiques"	"Etudes philosophiques"	"Etudes philosophiques"	"Etudes philosophiques"
Le Lys dans la vallée						"Province"	"Province"	"Province"	"Province"	"Campagne"
Pierre Grassou*						"Paris"	("Privée")	"Paris"	"Paris"	"Paris"

* Although indicated in this table, *Pierre Grassou* is not included in the twenty-two stories because it was never in reality published in the "Scènes de la vie privée." See above, p. 176.

each special category. An exact weighing of factors in the final classification of these twenty-two novels warrants the ultimate disposition of all but three: *Le Colonel Chabert* and *Le Père Goriot* in the "Scènes de la vie privée," and *Le Lys dans la vallée* in the "Scènes de la vie de campagne." The placement of these must be left an open question, since it depended on the author's subjective choice in which at one time certain features of the story, more than others, exercised a stronger appeal.

As an outcome of this systematic and chronological study of Balzac's works, the writer is led to believe that the scheme of the *Comédie humaine* is the result of a slow and evolutionary development. An exhaustive examination of the texts of novels usually in their first editions has revealed that Balzac's guiding principles for classification were, primarily and in the last analysis, artistic, logical, or sociophilosophical. Three stories alone militate against this conclusion—cases which must remain debatable, since factors determining the varied classification of these stories are in no instance mutually exclusive.

BIBLIOGRAPHY

Balzac, H. de. *Béatrix, ou Les Amours forcés. Scène de la vie privée.* 1st ed.; Paris: H. Souverain, 1840. 2 vols.

———. *Le Cabinet des antiques. Scène de la vie de province.* 1st ed.; Paris: H. Souverain, 1839. 2 vols.

———. *Contes bruns* (éd. Marcel Bouteron). Paris: Delpeuch, 1927.

———. *Contes philosophiques.* Paris: Gosselin, 1832. 2 vols.

———. "Correspondance inédite de Honoré de Balzac," *Revue bleue*, 4th ser., XX (1903), 609–12.

———. *Correspondance inédite de Honoré de Balzac avec le lieutenant-colonel L.-N. Périolas (1832–1845)* (éd. Marcel Bouteron, "Cahiers balzaciens," No. 1). Paris: Castellan, 1923.

———. *Correspondance inédite de Honoré de Balzac avec la duchesse de Castries (1831–1848)* (éd. Marcel Bouteron, "Cahiers balzaciens," No. 6). Paris: Lapina, 1928.

———. *Correspondance inédite de Honoré de Balzac avec le docteur Nacquart (1823–1850)* (éd. Marcel Bouteron, "Cahiers balzaciens," No. 8). Paris: Lapina, 1928.

———. *Correspondance inédite avec Zulma Carraud (1829–1850)* (éd. Marcel Bouteron). Paris: Armand Colin, 1935.

———. *Le Curé de village. Scène de la vie de campagne.* 1st ed.; Paris: H. Souverain, 1841. 2 vols.

———. *Les Deux Frères.* 1st ed.; Paris: H. Souverain, 1842. 2 vols.

BALZAC, H. DE—*continued.* *Etudes philosophiques.* Paris: Werdet, 1835–40. 20 vols.

———. *La Femme supérieure, La Maison Nucingen, La Torpille.* 1st ed.; Paris: Werdet, 1838. 2 vols.

———. *La Femme de trente ans,* pp. 1–4, 177–356, 356–60. Page proof with author's corrections in manuscript. Paris, 1842. Rare Book Room, Harper Library, University of Chicago.

———. "Les Héritiers Boirouge. Fragments d'histoire générale. Scène de la vie de province," *Revue des deux mondes,* 6th ser., XLII (1917), 871–84.

———. *Histoire de la grandeur et de la décadence de César Birotteau. Nouvelle Scène de la vie parisienne.* 1st ed.; Paris: Bureau du Figaro, 1838. 2 vols.

———. *Lettres à l'Etrangère.* Vol. I, *1833–42.* Paris: Calmann-Lévy, 1899. Vol. II, *1842–44.* Paris: Calmann-Lévy, 1906. Vol. III, *1845–46.* Paris: Calmann-Lévy, 1933.

———. *Letters to His Family, 1809–1850* (edited with Introduction and notes by W. S. Hastings). Princeton: Princeton University Press, 1934.

———. *Le Livre des douleurs.* Paris: H. Souverain, 1840. 2 vols.

———. *Le Livre mystique.* Paris: Werdet, 1835. 2 vols.

———. *Le Lys dans la vallée.* 1st ed.; Paris: Werdet, 1836. 2 vols.

———. *Le Médecin de campagne.* Paris: Mame-Delaunay, 1833. 2 vols.

———. *Le Médecin de campagne* (introduction et notes par Maurice Allem). Paris: Garnier frères, 1931.

———. *Morceaux choisis* (éd. J. Merlant). Paris: Didier, 1912.

———. *La Muse du département, ou Dinah et Rosalie.* 1st ed.; Paris: H. Souverain, 1843. 4 vols.

———. *Nouveaux Contes philosophiques.* 1st ed.; Paris: Gosselin, 1832.

———. *Œuvres complètes.* Paris: Furne, Dubochet et Hetzel, 1842–48. 17 vols. 3 suppl. vols., éd. Houssiaux, 1853–55.

———. *Ibid.* Paris: Michel Lévy, 1869–76. 24 vols.

———. *Ibid.* Paris: Conard, 1912–38. 39 vols.

———. *Ibid. La Comédie humaine.* Paris: Nouvelle Revue française, 1935–37. 10 vols.

———. *Œuvres de jeunesse.* 1. *Le Vicaire des Ardennes,* par M. Horace de Saint-Aubin (pseud.). Paris: Collet, 1822. 4 vols. 2. *Annette et le criminel,* par Horace de Saint-Aubin (pseud.). Paris: E. Buissot, 1824. 4 vols. 3. *Le Centenaire, ou Les Deux Beringheld,* par Horace de Saint-Aubin (pseud.). Paris: Pollet, 1822. 4 vols. 4. *La Dernière Fée, ou La Nouvelle Lampe merveilleuse,* par Horace de Saint-Aubin (pseud.). Paris: J. N. Barba, 1823. 2 vols.

———. *La Peau de chagrin, roman philosophique.* 1st ed.; Paris: Canel et Gosselin, 1831. 2 vols.

———. *Pensées, sujets, fragmens* (éd. Jacques Crépet). Paris: A. Blaizot, 1910.

——. *Romans et contes philosophiques.* 2d ed.; Paris: Gosselin, 1831. 3 vols. 3d ed.; Paris: Gosselin, 1833. 4 vols.

——. *Scènes de la vie parisienne.* 1st ed.; Paris: Mme Béchet, 1834–35. 4 vols. 2d ed.; Paris: Charpentier, 1839. 2 vols.

——. *Scènes de la vie privée.* 1st ed.; Paris: Mame et Delaunay-Vallée, 1830. 2 vols. 2d ed.; Paris: Mame-Delaunay, 1832. 4 vols. 3d ed.; Paris: Mme Béchet, 1835–37. 4 vols. 5th ed.; Paris: Charpentier, 1839. 2 vols.

——. *Scènes de la vie de province.* 1st ed.; Paris: Mme Béchet, 1834–37. 4 vols. 2d ed.; Paris: Charpentier, 1839. 2 vols.

——. *Splendeurs et misères des courtisanes.* Paris: L. de Potter, 1845. 3 vols.

——. *Ursule Mirouët.* 1st ed.; Paris: H. Souverain, 1842. 2 vols.

ABRAHAM, PIERRE. *Balzac. Recherches sur la création intellectuelle.* Paris: Rieder, 1929.

——. *Créatures chez Balzac.* Paris: Gallimard, 1931.

ALSÓ, HÉLÈNE D'. "Balzac, Cuvier et Geoffroy Saint-Hilaire (1831–1843)," *Revue d'histoire de la philosophie et d'histoire générale de la civilisation,* new ser., fasc. 8 (October 15, 1934), pp. 334–54.

ALTSZYLER, HÉLÈNE. *La Genèse et le plan des caractères dans l'œuvre de Balzac.* Paris: Alcan, 1928.

ANDERSON, MARGARET. "Background of *Illusions perdues* and Variations in the Principal Editions." Unpublished Ph.D. dissertation, University of Chicago, 1932.

ANONYMOUS. "Balzac et la tête à l'envers," *Chronique des lettres françaises,* XXVIII (1927), 518–19.

ARRIGON, L.-J. *Les Années romantiques.* Paris: Perrin, 1927.

——. *Les Débuts littéraires d'Honoré de Balzac.* Paris: Perrin, 1924.

BALDENSPERGER, FERNAND. *Orientations étrangères chez Honoré de Balzac.* Paris: Champion, 1927.

——. "Une Suggestion anglaise pour le titre de la *Comédie humaine,*" *Revue de littérature comparée,* I (1921), 638–39.

BARNES, HELEN E. [Mrs. J. F. Wodrada]. *A Study of the Variations between the Original and the Standard Editions of Balzac's "Les Chouans."* Chicago: University of Chicago Press, 1923.

BARRIÈRE, MARCEL. *L'Œuvre de H. de Balzac.* Paris: Calmann-Lévy, 1890.

BARRIÈRE, PAUL. *Honoré de Balzac et la tradition littéraire classique.* Paris: Hachette, 1928.

——. *Honoré de Balzac. Les Romans de jeunesse.* Paris: Hachette, 1928.

BASCHET, A. *Honoré de Balzac. Essai sur l'homme et sur l'œuvre.* Paris: D. Giraud et J. Dagneau, 1852.

BELLESSORT, ANDRÉ. *Balzac et son œuvre.* Paris: Perrin, 1924.

BERNARD, CLAUDE. *An Introduction to the Study of Experimental Medicine* (trans. Henry Copley Greene). New York: Macmillan, 1927.

BERNHEIM, P. *Balzac und Swedenborg; Einfluss der Mystik Swedenborgs und Saint-Martins auf die Romandichtung Balzacs.* Berlin: Ebering, 1914.

BETTELHEIM, ANTON. *Balzac: Eine Biographie.* München: Beck, 1926.

BIRÉ, EDMOND. Edition with "Introduction, notes et appendices" of *Scènes de la vie militaire* (anthology). Paris: Lamarre, 1908.

BLANCHARD, MARC. *La Campagne et ses habitants dans l'œuvre d'Honoré de Balzac.* Paris: Champion, 1931.

BOURGET, PAUL. *Essais de psychologie contemporaine.* Paris: Plon-Nourrit, 1899. 2 vols.

BOUTERON, MARCEL. "Balzac et le prix Montyon," *Revue des deux mondes,* XVIII (December 15, 1933), 926–34.

BRUNETIÈRE, FERDINAND. *Honoré de Balzac.* Paris: Calmann-Lévy, 1906.

CABAT, AUGUSTIN. *Etude sur l'œuvre d'Honoré de Balzac.* Paris: Perrin, 1889.

CANFIELD, A. G. "Notes on Lovenjoul's *Histoire des œuvres de Honoré de Balzac,*" *Modern Language Notes,* XLVIII (1933), 497–501.

———. "Les Personnages reparaissants dans *La Comédie humaine,*" *Revue d'histoire littéraire de la France,* XLI (1934), 15–34, 198–214.

CERFBERR, ANATOLE, et CHRISTOPHE, J. *Répertoire de la "Comédie humaine" de H. de Balzac avec une introduction de Paul Bourget.* Paris: Calmann-Lévy, 1887.

CHAMPFLEURY [Jules Fleury]. *Balzac. Sa Méthode de travail.* Paris: Patay, 1879.

———. *Balzac au collège.* Paris: Patay, 1878.

CHANCEL, CAMILLE. "La Genèse de *la Comédie humaine,*" *Revue de Paris,* old ser., I (June, July, August, 1864), 81–98, 241–58, 455–69.

CHAUDES-AIGUES, J. "Ecrivains contemporains. III. M. de Balzac: *Une Fille d'Ève,*" *Revue de Paris,* new ser., XI (November, 1839), 20–38.

CRAIN, W. L. "A Critical Edition of Balzac's *Le Secret des Ruggieri.*" Unpublished Ph.D. dissertation, University of Chicago, 1937. The "Introduction" is printed as chapter iv of the present volume.

———. "The Reworking of Balzac's *Autre Etude de femme.*" Unpublished Master's thesis, University of Chicago, 1925.

CURTIUS, E. R. *Balzac, sein Leben, sein Werk.* Bonn: Friedrich Cohen, 1923.

DARGAN, E. PRESTON. "Scott and the French Romantics," *Publications of the Modern Language Association,* XLIX (1934), 599–629.

———. "Studies in Balzac: I. Balzac and Cooper: *Les Chouans,*" *Modern Philology,* XIII (1915), 193–213.

DARGAN, E. P., CRAIN, W. L., and OTHERS. *Studies in Balzac's Realism.* Chicago: University of Chicago Press, 1932.

DAVID, HENRI. "Balzac italianisant: Autour de *Sarrasine,*" *Revue de littérature comparée,* XIII (1933), 457–68.

DIDEROT, DENIS. *Le Rêve de d'Alembert. Œuvres complètes*, II, 138–39. Paris: Assézat et Tourneux, [1875–79].

DURRY, M. J. "A propos de la *Comédie humaine*," *Revue d'histoire littéraire de la France*, XLII (January–March, 1936), 96–98.

FERGUSON, MURIEL B. *La Volonté dans la "Comédie humaine" de Balzac*. Paris: Courville, 1935.

FESS, G. M. *The Correspondence of Physical and Material Factors with Character in Balzac*. Menasha: Banta, 1924. (University of Pennsylvania Ph.D. dissertation.)

FLAT, P. *Essais sur Balzac*. Paris: Plon-Nourrit, 1893–94. 2 vols.

FLOYD, JUANITA H. *Women in the Life of Balzac*. New York: Holt, 1921.

GALL, F. J. *Anatomie et physiologie du système nerveux en général et du cerveau en particulier*. Paris: Schoell, 1810–19. 4 vols.

GAUTIER, T. *Honoré de Balzac*. Paris: Poulet-Malassis et De Broise, 1859.

GIBB, MARGARET M. *Le Roman de Bas-de-Cuir. Etude sur Fenimore Cooper et son influence en France*. Paris: Champion, 1927.

GRAYBILL, H. S. "Variations and Realism in Balzac's *Gambara*." Unpublished Master's thesis, University of Chicago, 1927.

GUYON, BERNARD. *Un Inédit de Balzac: "Le Catéchisme social" précédé de l'article "Du Gouvernement moderne*." Paris: La Renaissance du Livre, 1933.

HANOTAUX, G., and VICAIRE, G. *La Jeunesse de Balzac. Balzac imprimeur* (new edition adding correspondence of Balzac with Mme de Berny). Paris: Ferroud, 1921.

HASTINGS, W. S. *Balzac and Souverain*. New York: Doubleday, Page, 1927.

HOFFMANN, E. T. A. *Contes fantastiques* (trans. M. Loève-Veimars). Paris: Eugène Renduel, 1830.

JACKSON, J. F. "Dating Balzac's Adoption of the Title *La Comédie humaine*," *Modern Language Notes*, XLII (December, 1927), 525–26.

JAMES, HENRY. *French Poets and Novelists*. New York: Macmillan, 1893.

———. *Notes on Novelists*. New York: Charles Scribner's Sons, 1914.

LAUGHTON, SIR JOHN KNOX. *Memoirs of the Life and Correspondence of Henry Reeve*. London and New York: Longmans, Green, 1898.

LAVATER, J. G. *Essai sur la physiognomonie*. La Haye: (no publisher given), 1781–1803. 4 vols.

LE BRETON, ANDRÉ. *Balzac, l'homme et l'œuvre*. Paris: Colin, 1905.

LOÈVE-VEIMARS, VANDERBURCH, et ROMIEU. *Scènes contemporaines, laissées par feue madame la vicomtesse de Chamilly*. 2d ed.; Paris: Urbain Canel, 1828.

MILLE, PIERRE. "Balzac," *A travers la Librairie*. Paris: Cercle de la Librairie, 1923.

MORRIS, G. D. "Balzac's Treatment of History in *Maître Cornélius*," *Philological Quarterly*, X (1931), 356–68.

———. Preface to *Three Stories by Balzac*. Boston: Ginn, 1932.

PRESTON, ETHEL. *Recherches sur la technique de Balzac. Le Retour systématique des personnages dans "la Comédie humaine."* Paris: Les Presses Universitaires, 1921.

PRIOULT, A. *Balzac avant "La Comédie humaine"* (*1818–1829*). Paris: Courville, 1936.

ROMIEU, A. *Proverbes romantiques.* Paris: Ladvocat, 1827.

ROYCE, WILLIAM HOBART. *A Balzac Bibliography. Writings Relative to the Life and Works of Honoré de Balzac.* Chicago: University of Chicago Press, 1929.

———. *Indexes to A Balzac Bibliography.* Chicago: University of Chicago Press, 1930.

SAINTE-BEUVE, CHARLES-AUGUSTIN. *Causeries du lundi,* Vol. II. Paris: Garnier, 1850.

———. *Portraits contemporains,* Vol. II. Paris: Didier, 1889.

SAND, GEORGE. "Une Correspondance inédite de George Sand avec Balzac," *Les Nouvelles littéraires,* July 19, 1930.

SCOTT, MARY. "Variations between the First and the Final Edition of Balzac's *Les Employés," Modern Philology,* XXIII (1926), 315–36.

SEILLIÈRE, ERNEST. *Balzac et la morale romantique.* Paris: Alcan, 1922.

SERVAL, MAURICE. *Autour d'"Eugénie Grandet."* Paris: Champion, 1924.

SPOELBERCH DE LOVENJOUL, CHARLES DE. *Autour de Honoré de Balzac.* Paris: Calmann-Lévy, 1897.

———. "Correspondance inédite de H. de Balzac," *Revue bleue,* 4th ser., XX (1903), 609–12, 641–45, 673–77, 705–8.

——— "Les *Etudes philosophiques* de Honoré de Balzac (Edition Werdet)," *Revue d'histoire littéraire de la France,* 14th year (July–September, 1907), 393–441.

———. *La Genèse d'un roman de Balzac: "Les Paysans."* Paris: Société d'éditions littéraires et artistiques, 1901.

———. *Histoire des œuvres de H. de Balzac.* 3d ed.; Paris, 1888.

———. *Une Page perdue de Balzac.* Paris: Ollendorff, 1903.

SURVILLE, MME L. *Balzac, sa vie et ses œuvres, d'après sa correspondance.* Paris: Jaccottet, Bourdilliat, 1858.

TAINE, H. *Nouveaux Essais de critique et d'histoire.* 3d ed.; Paris: Calmann-Lévy, 1880.

THIEME, HUGO P. *Bibliographie de la littérature française, 1800 à 1930.* 3 vols.; Paris: Droz, 1933.

THOUVENIN, GEORGES. "La Genèse d'un roman de Balzac, *La Recherche de l'absolu," Revue d'histoire littéraire de la France,* XI (1911), 864–84.

TURQUAN, JOSEPH. *La Générale Junot, duchesse d'Abrantès, 1784–1838.* Paris: Montgrédien, 1901.

UZANNE, OCTAVE. *A travers l'Œuvre de H. de Balzac. Les Zigzags d'un curieux.* Paris: Quantin, 1888.

VICAIRE, GEORGES. *Manuel de l'amateur de livres du XIXe siècle, 1801–1893.* Paris, 1894–1910. 7 vols.

WELLS, B. W. *A Century of French Fiction.* New York: Dodd, Mead, 1903.

WENGER, JARED E. *The Province and the Provinces in the Work of Honoré de Balzac.* Menasha: Banta, 1937. (Princeton Ph.D. dissertation.)

WERDET, E. *Portrait intime de Balzac: Sa Vie, son humeur et son caractère.* Paris: Dentu, 1859.

———. *Souvenirs de la vie littéraire.* Paris: Dentu, 1879.

WILLIAMSON, A. J. *"La Recherche de l'absolu.* The Determination of Balzac's Method of Composition and Revision, Based on a Study of the Manuscript and Successive Editions of the Novel." Unpublished Ph.D. dissertation, Princeton University, 1938.

WILSON, RACHEL. "A Study of the Variations between the First and the Definitive Editions of Balzac's *La Vieille Fille.*" Unpublished Master's thesis, University of Chicago, 1925.

CHAPTER III

VARIATIONS IN *LE CURE DE TOURS*

By RACHEL WILSON
Hollins College

I. INTRODUCTION

A. The Scope of This Study

THIS study will analyze the variants in the *Curê de Tours* from manuscript[1] to definitive edition. With these two forms of the novel I have compared such proofs as are found at Chantilly in the Lovenjoul Collection[2] and the texts of the first, second, third, and fourth editions.

The *Curê de Tours*, which is dated "Saint-Firmin, avril 1832," appeared for the first time in May, 1832, under the title of *Les Célibataires*. It was published by Mame-Delaunay and formed a part of the *Scènes de la vie privée*, second edition, Volume III.[3] The second edition of the story was brought out by Mme Veuve Charles Béchet in December, 1833 (dated 1834). The title is unchanged, but Balzac has shifted this study of manners once for all to Volume II of the *Scènes de la vie de province*, of which this is the first edition.[4] In 1839 Charpentier issued the second edition of the *Scènes de la vie de province*, the first volume of which contains our novel under the original title. In 1843, with the addition of the date and its present dedication to "David, statuaire," the story appeared as Vol-

---

[1] Lov. Coll., A 11.

[2] *Ibid.*, A 11–A 12. For the manuscript and proofs I have used photostatic copies. These materials, with the exception of one twelve-page proof in photostat which Professor Dargan kindly lent me, are the property of the University of Chicago Libraries. They are catalogued here as *"Les Célibataires (Le Curê de Tours) 1832*, Manuscrit et épreuves corrigées (Paris, 1929)," of which there are two copies, and *"Supplement to Les Célibataires (Le Curê de Tours) 1832*, Manuscrit et épreuves corrigées (Paris, 1929)." I have used copy 1 of the manuscript and author's proofs and copy 2 in case of doubt. Through the courtesy of Professor Walter Scott Hastings, of Princeton University, I have been able to check the *cotes* of these and other materials in his transcript of the catalogue of the Lovenjoul Collection.

[3] Lov., *Hist.*, pp. 5, 81.   [4] *Ibid.*, pp. 65, 81.

ume II of the third edition of the same *Scènes*, occupying pages 1–62 of Volume VI of the first edition of the *Comédie humaine*. It was here that the *deuxième histoire* of *Les Célibataires* became one of three and received its present title, *Le Curé de Tours*. The publishers were Furne, Dubochet et Hetzel. The definitive edition of *Le Curé de Tours* is found in Volume IX of the Conard edition, *Œuvres complètes*, edited by Bouteron and Longnon. Our volume appeared in 1913. In this edition *Le Curé de Tours* is, as in the Furne, the second of three stories comprising a group entitled *Les Célibataires*.[5]

The manuscript and the proofs, taken together, furnish a solid basis for a study of the evolution of the story before publication; but they must be used to supplement each other, as no one item is extant in its entirety. The manuscript, to which we shall refer as "*C.T.* 1," contains sixty-six pages; but pages 1, one-half of 51, and 66 are copies made by Lovenjoul. The duplicate of page 1 has been made from proof *2b;* pages 51 and 66 have been copied from proof *2a*. These restorations do not, of course, have the authenticity of the original holograph pages. Page 39 of the manuscript is missing entirely in the photostatic copy. Our earliest proof, *2a*, is also incomplete. Although the pages of this version are numbered from 1 to 86, they do not include the first part (about one-fifth) of the story. Moreover, six of the eighty-six numbered pages are missing. These are pages 37, 38, 40, 42, 43, and 45. This proof has been cut and pasted on sheets of white paper, the margins of which are used for corrections. The third available early form is a twelve-page proof (*C.T.* 2b). And, lastly, we have two fragments, one of eleven and one of sixteen pages, of page proof (*C.T.* 2c) for the *princeps*.[6]

---

[5] The story occupies the following pages in the editions mentioned: Mame-Delaunay, pp. 279–413; Béchet, pp. 31–164; Charpentier, pp. 1–105; Furne, pp. 1–62; Conard, pp. 167–248.

[6] There are no pages of *C.T.* 2a which correspond either to *C.T.* 2b or to the first fragment of *C.T.* 2c. *C.T.* 2b, p. 1—p. 9, line 9, corresponds to the first fragment of *C.T.* 2c, pp. 279–88. *C.T.* 2a, p. 101, l. 3 (autograph correction)—p. 118, l. 21, corresponds to the second fragment of *C.T.* 2c, pp. 337–52.

C.T. 2a corresponds to—
Mame, p. 309, l. 17—p. 352, l. 6; p. 355, l. 10—p. 356, l. 10; p. 357, l. 23—p. 360, l. 6; p. 362, l. 12—p. 363, l. 12; p. 365, l. 8—p. 413.
Con., p. 184, l. 29—p. 208, l. 30; p. 210, l. 21—p. 211, l. 3; p. 211, l. 32—p. 213, l. 8; p. 214, ll. 14–31; p. 215, l. 28—p. 247, l. 2.
C.T. 2b corresponds to—
Mame, pp. 281–95, l. 21.
Con., pp. 169–77, l. 13.

[Footnote 6 continued on following page]

Le Curé de Tours, short though it is, is one of Balzac's best stories and an excellent example of his genius.[7] Balzac himself compares the story to *Le Cousin Pons* and calls it "great" and "heartbreaking."[8] His good friend and critic, Mme Zulma Carraud, wrote him in 1833 that *Birotteau*, as she called *Le Curé de Tours*, was her "œuvre de prédilection"; and she summed up the story as "ce chef-d'œuvre d'une intelligence investigatrice, qui avait trouvé le mystère du prêtre et de la vieille fille."[9] Stendhal admired the portrayal of provincial life in the novel. In 1838 he wrote in recounting his travels: "J'ai trouvé dans ma chambre un volume de M. de Balzac, c'est l'*Abbé Birotteau*, de Tours. Que j'admire cet auteur! qu'il a bien su énumérer les malheurs et petitesses de la province!"[10] In her study of *Le Curé de Tours* Miss Marhofer has cited the opinions of a number of other writers regarding the novel.[11] Recent criticism has not neglected this small Balzacian volume. M. Ferdinand Duviard, in concluding his monograph on Balzac and *Le Curé de Tours*, says:

Ce *Curé de Tours*, mérite en somme, par son contenu une place éminente dans la *Comédie Humaine*. Il en offre les défauts énormes, et les beautés fulgurantes.

On y trouve, condensé en moins de cent pages, si j'osais dire, "catalytiques," le modèle du réalisme tel que Balzac l'a compris, tel qu'il l'a *créé* ...[12]

Another contemporary critic, Alain, has praised Balzac's skill in composing the story:

... le commencement de cette nouvelle est admirable par une description de choses petites et sottes (Serai-je chanoine? Me suis-je enrhumé? Pourquoi mon bougeoir ici et non là?). ... Toute la fin de ce court récit consiste en délibérations de province, où les choses et les gens sont réellement pesés à leur poids.[13]

C.T. 2c corresponds to—
Mame, pp. 281–91, l. 15; 337–52, l. 17.
Con., pp. 169–75, l. 9; p. 199, l. 24—p. 209, l. 2.

[7] For a detailed analysis of *Le Curé de Tours* as representative of Balzac's realism, see Miss Marhofer's study in Dargan, Crain, and Others, *Studies in Balzac's Realism*, pp. 91–120.

[8] *LEt.*, III, 281.   [9] *Corr. Carraud*, p. 168.

[10] Stendhal, *Mémoires d'un Touriste*, p. 72.

[11] Dargan, Crain, and Others, *op. cit.*, pp. 94, 98, 99, 100, 104, 105, 113, 114, 116, 119.

[12] *Un Prédécesseur de Ferdinand Fabre, Balzac romancier clérical dans Le Curé de Tours*, p. 49.

[13] Alain (pseud. of Émile Chartier), *Avec Balzac*, pp. 73–74.

While the critics have perhaps most often commented on the excellent provincial picture drawn in *Le Curé de Tours*, they have also brought out other characteristic Balzacian features in the story, among them the monomaniacs and the conspiracy plot involving the cruel martyrdom of a weak individual by two strong and sinister characters.

Arguing from the principle of zoölogical species, Balzac tells us in the *Avant-propos* of the *Comédie humaine* that society, too, has its species, distinguishable according to *condition*, profession or trade, and habitat.[14] Characteristically we find in *Le Curé de Tours* two types of *célibataires:* priests and old maids. These are further differentiated, the good but weak of each "species" succumbing to the powerful and vindictive. Colors, too, have a symbolic value for Balzac. Thus Mlle Gamard's parlor is keynoted in yellow. Her careless habits of dress and her dull costumes are indicative to Balzac of her warped femininity. His belief in cognomology runs through the story from the first edition to its final form. Mme de Listomère's name is suggestive of her character.

The fact that the action of the novel is laid in Tours, where Balzac was born and where his family lived until 1814, adds color and accent to this provincial scene. How well he knew Saint-Gatien his sister Laure has told us.[15] The shadow of the cathedral is no darker than the lives of Balzac's four celibates who dwelt almost under its great buttresses! The picture of provincial society is not much less somber. Town and cloth are equally implicated in an intrigue in which the law is deviously used. The passages in *Le Curé de Tours* dealing with lawyers are not numerous; but they have been carefully re-worked, and they remind us that Balzac studied law and spent three unhappy years in the offices of a lawyer and a notary.[16] His own lawsuits, too, may have added bitterness to his pen.

The novel is then related in several ways to Balzac's own experience. It illustrates a number of favorite Balzacian theories and devices. It can be studied in a number of forms from manuscript to final edition. These facts make it an interesting subject for a variations study. Let us turn now to an analysis of the numerous changes which Balzac introduced in his story from stage to stage of its evolution.

[14] *Avant-propos*, I, xxvi.   [15] *Corr.*, p. xiii.

[16] L.-J. Arrigon, *Les Débuts littéraires d'Honoré de Balzac*, pp. 2, 3, 9–10, 17; G. Hanotaux et G. Vicaire, *La Jeunesse de Balzac: Balzac imprimeur; Balzac et Madame de Berny*, p. 22.

B. The *Brouillons* and the Search for a Title

The title of the story has undergone a series of changes. As we know, the story was first called *Les Célibataires;* but Balzac had once thought of naming it *La Vieille Fille,* or perhaps, *Le Prêtre catholique.* Of these two titles, he first chose the former. Moreover, in 1843, when he finally found his definitive title, *Le Curé de Tours,* although he added the explanation at the beginning of the story that the Abbé Birotteau is "le principal personnage de cette histoire" (*Fur.* 1), he did not diminish the role of the old maids. The final title is interesting because it adds to the connotation implied in "curé" the suggestion of the milieu in which this social species will be depicted.

The idea of centering the story around an old maid was strong in Balzac's mind when he began this novel, for there are sixteen false starts bearing the title *La Vieille Fille.*[17] (This title was later used by Balzac, but the story has no connection with *Le Curé de Tours.*[18]) Balzac was groping for his opening sentences. Of the sixteen discarded beginnings, nine[19] suggest the opening of the story as we know it today; five[20] are variations in shorter form of the passage which now begins: "Jadis, il existait dans le Cloître ... ."[21] One is the brief passage:

Si tout doit avoir une fin dans la société comme dans le monde, il y a certes quelques existences dont il est impossible de deviner le but ou l'utilité. La morale et l'économie politique réprouvent également certains êtres qui consomment sans produire, ou tiennent ici-bas une place sans repandre autour d'eux ni bien ni mal [*MS* 11].

These two sentences, with slight variations, have endured. Today they are imbedded in an analysis of the *vieille fille* found on page 199 of Conard. The last *brouillon* has only the words: "Pourquoi ne soup [*sic*] ... ."

The only extant early text of the actual beginning of the story is the proof 2*b*, from which Lovenjoul copied one page of the manuscript.[22]

---

[17] In the photostatic versions which I have used, ten of these are bound with the manuscript and six are bound in the *Supplement.* Reference to the pages in the *Supplement* will be marked "*S.*" Those from the manuscript will be marked "*MS.*"

[18] M. Bouteron suggests in the third issue of "Les Cahiers balzaciens," *Lettres de femmes adressées à Honoré de Balzac, Première Série (1832–1836),* that *La Vieille Fille* of 1836 may be Balzac's answer to a criticism of *Les Célibataires* made to him by Mlle Adèle, *une vieille fille.* M. Bouteron adds that Mlle Cormon would hardly have satisfied the critic. Letter viii of this "Cahier" (pp. 23–27), from Mme L. St-H, takes issue also with Balzac for his analysis of *la vieille fille* (in *Le Curé de Tours*).

[19] *S.* 24, 26, 28, 30, 34; *MS* 15, 17, 19, 21.

[20] *S.* 32; *MS* 23, 25, 27, 29.   [21] *Con.* 170–71.

[22] *S.* 2. Note in Lovenjoul's handwriting, signed "S. L." (Lov. Coll., A 12).

This version bears the title *La Vieille Fille* and proves Balzac's first intention.

However, the idea of the provincial priest was also in his mind from the first. There are three *brouillons* called today *Le Prêtre catholique*, of which two, according to Lovenjoul, are false starts for *Le Curé de Tours*.[23] In one of these, which we shall call *P.C.* 1,[24] a house in the shadow of Saint-Gatien is owned by a widow, Mme Berger, who has lived in it some twelve years with her daughter Mlle Sophie Berger. The mother and daughter have a lodger, a canon of the cathedral, on whom they bestow every attention.[25] In this fragment Balzac has applied to the life of the two women the often quoted phrase "l'occupation dans le vide et le vide dans l'occupation" (*S.* 31), which he used subsequently, with slight variations, to describe the Abbé Birotteau's existence (*2a*/ms, 116;[26] *Con.* 207). We find also in this early version the substance of page 171 of Conard. Even very characteristic phrases of the definitive text occur in the *brouillon*. The expression in *P.C.* 1, *un lieu plein de physionomie* (*S.* 25), becomes in Conard, *une solitude pleine de physionomie* (*Con.* 171); *une solitude de pierres* (*S.* 25) becomes the *désert de pierres* (*Con.* 171). This fragment is obviously, then, a beginning of our story.

Although *P.C.* 1 is nearer the actual story than any of the *brouillons* under the caption of *La Vieille Fille*, Balzac was still clinging to the second title. Each of the six pages of *P.C.* 1 has on the verso a false start under the title *La Vieille Fille*.[27]

There is a second version of *Le Prêtre catholique*, which we shall call *P.C.* 2 and which, with its setting in Tours, seems to be yet another start for our novel. In this fragment Balzac introduces a young priest who has many of the Abbé Troubert's traits: among others, his paleness, his mystery, his calm, his lowered eyes, his ill-health, his apparent ambition.[28]

[23] *S.* 22. Note in Lovenjoul's handwriting (Lov. Coll., A 196).

[24] *S.* 23, 25, 27, 29, 31, 33.   [25] *Ibid.*, 27, 29, 33.

[26] The addition of "ms" to a version indicates an autograph correction on a proof. After quotations the manuscript and three proofs will be abbreviated as "1," "2a," "2b," and "2c," respectively. The references to "1" and "2a" relate to the page on which the quotation is found in the bound photostatic copy of *MS*. Although 2b, which is unbound, is printed in the format of pages, no numbers are found, so that it has been necessary to make up a pagination. The separate pages have been numbered consecutively from 1 through 12, and references to this proof are to these numbers. References to 2c relate to the printed number which each page bears.

[27] *Ibid.*, 24, 26, 28, 30, 32, 34.

[28] *Ibid.*, 36, 37. According to Lovenjoul, both *P.C.* 1 and *P.C.* 2 were written in 1831 or 1832 (*S.* 21, 22, 35). The first page of both fragments is missing. Lovenjoul

The third fragment entitled *Le Prêtre catholique* is dated by Lovenjoul as of 1834.[29] This version is quite different from the two preceding, for, although the mysterious and pale young *abbé* reappears with his lowered eyes, the scene has been moved to Angoulême. But *Le Prêtre catholique* was never finished. However, if Lovenjoul's date for *P.C.* 3 is correct, this fragment should probably be connected with the projected novel of that title which Balzac mentions in letters to his sister and to his publisher in October and November, 1833.[30]

One other title for *Le Curé de Tours* was considered by Balzac. Lovenjoul tells us that Balzac thought for a moment of calling this novel *L'Abbé Troubert*.[31] This statement is borne out in a letter to Mme Hanska dated October 29 [1842]: "J'avais terminé *les Deux Frères* pendant la nuit de ce jour-là. Ces *Deux Frères* prendront dans *la Comédie Humaine*, le titre de: *un Ménage de Garçon*. C'est la troisième histoire de[s] *Célibataires* et, avec *L'Abbé Troubert* et *Pierrette*, cela complète ce que je voulais écrire sur le célibat."[32]

The definitive title was chosen before February 1, 1843. Balzac writes to Mme Hanska on March 2, 1843: "Voici, le 1er février, que dans le sixième volume de *la Comédie Humaine*, le *Curé de Tours* et *un Ménage de Garçon* font, avec *l'Illustre Gaudissart*, vingt-deux feuilles ... ."[33]

The differences of title are obviously connected with Balzac's conception of his story. Certain other changes that have been mentioned should be recalled.

As we have seen, the story was lifted bodily from the *Scènes de la vie privée* and reset in the *Scènes de la vie de province* in the 1834 edition. This resetting did not necessitate any fundamental re-writing of the story. It was already an account of small or mean lives in a provincial city. A second new feature was the addition for the *Comédie humaine* of the dedication mentioned above. It was also for the Furne edition that Balzac added for the first time the date and place of composition of the novel.

C. The General Evolution of the Story

A number of *brouillons* are not our only evidence that Balzac had difficulty in starting this story. He writes to his mother on July 15, 1832:

thinks Balzac had called these versions *La Vieille Fille* and that he destroyed these first pages to avoid confusion in his manuscripts. He thinks also that the false start entitled *La Vieille Fille* (*S.* 32), which is written on the back of fol. 6 (*S.* 31) of *P.C.* 1, is a version of one of the destroyed first pages (*S.* 21, 22. Notes in Lovenjoul's handwriting [Lov. Coll., A 196]).

[29] *S.* 42. Note in Lovenjoul's handwriting (Lov. Coll., A 196).
[30] *LF.*, p. 133; *Corr.*, p. 189.   [32] *LEt.*, II, 73.
[31] Lov., *Hist.*, p. 81.   [33] *Ibid.*, p. 120.

"Madame de B[erny] a bien vu à Saint-Firmin, ce que c'était que le travail de tête. Il m'a fallu dix jours avant d'inventer et de penser *Les Célibataires*."[34] The plot, however, is fixed in the main lines in the manuscript. Balzac may fumble for a title, thus shifting the sociological accent; but the characteristic central theme, that of the martyr done to death, will not change.

However, probably no better example could be found to show how Balzac poured his energy out in the correction of detail. Swamped, as he always was, with proof and copy, he was nonetheless tormented by his desire to express himself well and circumstantially.[35] One would naturally expect the greatest number of variations in the early versions of the story and in the editions which appeared when Balzac was reorganizing his scheme. Our study of the variants confirms this supposition. Moreover, Balzac's letters to Mme Hanska at the time he was getting ready the first edition of the *Scènes de la vie de province* and that of the *Comédie humaine* bear witness to the careful rehandling he gave the story for these editions.[36]

There are in all the texts examined a total of approximately five thousand variants.[37] Of these the greatest number, about 63 per cent, occur between the manuscript and the *princeps*.[38] Between Mame and Béchet there is not only the usual revision of detail, but there are important additions. Between Béchet and Charpentier the only changes are a few corrections of obvious errors. Between Charpentier and Furne there is, as elsewhere in the first edition of the *Comédie humaine*, a definite effort to compress the story typographically. There is a general tendency to take out titles—to change, for example, *monsieur l'abbé* to *l'abbé*—and to cut out paragraph divisions wherever possible. There are, of course, other types of changes. Between Furne and Conard paragraphs are still further reduced in number, since Balzac strikes out nineteen paragraph divisions on his Furne copy of *Le Curé de Tours*. He indicates also a few mechanical variations, such as capital letters for small. The changes in the text are, at this stage, so slight that these variations may be said statistically to have no importance. Table 1 shows the number of changes made as the story took

[34] *LF.*, p. 87.

[35] See his letter of 1839 to Louis Desnoyers, *Corr.*, p. 332.

[36] *LEt.*, I, 64, letter of October 26, 1833; I, 74, November 6, 1833; I, 87, November 20, 1833; II, 73, October 29, 1842; II, 120, March 2, 1843.

[37] The figures here and elsewhere in this study are approximate, since it is impossible to control this kind of material with absolute accuracy.

[38] This term will be used for brevity instead of the more usual *édition originale*.

its definitive form. Of the approximately one thousand sentences which compose the Conard edition, there are only twenty-nine that do not represent a revision at some stage of the story.

Stylistically, one characteristic stands out as true for all versions. There is a steady tendency to break up sentences. The sentences are frequently long and involved in the manuscript, sometimes incorrect. These are naturally shortened, but the process continues from edition to edition.

TABLE 1

APPROXIMATE NUMBER OF CHANGES IN TEXT

Changes	Manuscript (C.T. 1) to Early Proofs	Proofs to Princeps	Mame to Conard
Stylistic (including sentence divisions)..	525	2,750	1,730
Realistic....................	15	82	128

About 33⅓ per cent of the sentences have been broken up. The opposite change, of combining sentences, occurs about one-third as often.

II. VARIATIONS

Let us turn now to a detailed study of the variations themselves. These will be considered first stylistically and then with regard to Balzac's general realistic method and technique, following the outline as suggested by Professor Dargan in his study of Balzac's realism.[39]

The variations will be arranged in three groups: first, those changes that Balzac introduced between his manuscript and the incomplete proofs; second, the changes between the proofs and the *princeps;* third, the changes that were introduced after the first edition, whether in Béchet, Furne, or Conard. This arrangement involves a certain inevitable monotony but has been adopted to show not only what corrections Balzac tended to make in general in his revisions but also that particular changes are characteristic of certain periods of the story's evolution.

The stylistic variations have been studied from the standpoint of sentence structure, rhetorical devices, and parts of speech. They convince the student that Balzac was working toward greater accuracy, concision, and clearness. They are not, of course, invariably happy. They far outnumber, as is usually true of Balzac's corrections, the realistic variations, constituting about 95 per cent of the changes.

[39] Dargan, Crain, and Others, *op. cit.*, pp. 1–32.

A. Changes from *Manuscript (C.T.* 1) to Early Proofs (*2a, 2b, 2c*)

I. STYLISTIC VARIATIONS

a) According to sentence structure.—Balzac's changes in sentence structure are frequent. Sometimes they may leave one in doubt as to his purpose, as they do when he shifts back and forth between two constructions seemingly without reason. One example of this practice will suffice to illustrate the point.

In the manuscript Balzac wrote of the Abbé Birotteau: "... il ne tira pas sa montre sans effroi en voyant quatre heures et quelques minutes. *Or, connaissant* la ponctualité de Mademoiselle Gamard, il se hâta de se rendre au logis ..." (1, 50).[40] When he corrected *2a*, he joined these two sentences by substituting "car il connaissait" for "Or, connaissant" (*2a*/ms, 112). The dependent construction was, however, promptly struck out when it appeared in the text of *2c*. The new sentence was again broken into two, the second beginning: "Connaissant" (*2c*/ms, 346). This form is found in Mame (346), but in Béchet (93) Balzac returned to the finite form and began his sentence: "Il connaissait." This construction he did not change in subsequent editions.

Whatever stylistic sense urged Balzac to alternate finite and participial constructions, the change is a frequent one in all versions of the text. Substitutions of one of these forms for the other occur fourteen times between the manuscript and proofs and often involve the breaking-up of sentences. Sometimes the change has no great effect and yet adds smoothness to the style, as in the example cited below. Here the substitution of the participial phrase, which makes possible also the omission of the conjunction *et*, breaks up a long succession of clauses:

... quelques vestiges de l'arcade gothique qui *s'harmoniait* sans doute avec l'ensemble du monument *et* formait jadis le portail ... [*2b*, 3]	... quelques vestiges de l'arcade gothique qui, *s'harmoniant* avec l'ensemble du monument, formait jadis le portail ... [*2c*, 282; *Mame* 284][41]

[40] Unless otherwise noted, italics are used to indicate variations between texts.

[41] When a given change persists essentially down through Conard, a plus sign (+) is attached to the last reference cited. When, however, the text is altered, a second reference is given to show the last version in which the variation occurred. In both cases, other changes may, of course, occur in the passage. When the texts which are being compared do not follow each other chronologically, there is no extant intervening version of the passage quoted. All quotations are given as in the original texts, including idiosyncrasies of spelling and punctuation.

Sometimes Balzac makes the opposite change:

... les meubles d'acajou, et le tapis d'Aubusson *décorant* cette vaste pièce peinte à neuf ... [2*b*, 9]	... les meubles d'acajou, et le tapis d'Aubusson *qui ornaient* cette vaste pièce peinte à neuf ... [2*c*, 288+]

The reason here is obvious. In the preceding sentence Balzac has replaced the phrase of *C.T.* 1, 8, "en arrangeant le salon" by "en décorant le salon" (2*b*/ms, 8+). The change of "décorant" in the above sentence to "qui ornaient" may be taken as typical of the great number of variations of this sort which Balzac introduced in the course of his revisions.

The following example illustrates the change from finite verb to participial construction and shows Balzac working toward a smoother style:

Néanmoins, *comme* le pavé du cloître *est* toujours sec, et *que* l'abbé Biroteau *venait de gagner* trois livres dix sous ... [2*b*, 2]	Néanmoins, le pavé du cloître *étant* toujours sec, et l'abbé Birotteau *ayant gagné* trois livres dix sous ... [2*c*, 280; *Char.* 2]

Changes of this sort seem to occur more frequently in dependent, than in independent, clauses. The proportion is about eight to one. The reason may be the large number of sentences that are broken up into shorter sentences where the finite verb is needed.

However, independent clauses are frequently reduced to dependent constructions by this type of alteration, as is seen in the examples below:

Or, feu l'abbé Chaploud chanoine de Saint-Gatien *était* l'ami intime, de l'abbé Biroteau ... [2*b*, 5]	Or, feu l'abbé Chapeloud, chanoine de Saint-Gatien, *ayant été* l'ami intime de l'abbé Birotteau ... [2*c*, 284; *Mame* 286]

Independent clauses are also replaced by relative clauses. This change produces a more compact style. In speaking of Birotteau's faithfulness to Chapeloud, Balzac originally used an independent co-ordinate clause, "et son amitié resta la même" (1, 9). This becomes, with some re-writing, "dont l'amitié resta toujours la même" (2*b*/ms, 10+). This form evidently satisfied Balzac, because he does not touch it again.

Another means by which Balzac works for an easier and more closely woven style is by substituting for either independent or dependent clauses a past participle. The following case is characteristic:

Cette maison étant au nord de Saint-Gatien se trouve toujours dans l'ombre *que projette* cette grande cathédrale ... [2*b*, 3-4]	Cette maison, étant au nord de Saint-Gatien, se trouve continuellement dans les ombres *projettées* par cette grande cathédrale ... [2*c*, 282+]

The total number of variations for sentence structure between the manuscript and proofs is forty-five. Of these the greatest number are in dependent clauses. This fact is largely explained, as has been said, by the tendency throughout the versions to break the many long sentences of the manuscript into shorter ones, in which participial constructions and clauses cannot replace the finite verb.

b) According to rhetorical devices.—An amplification is defined as the elaboration of an expression. In the manuscript and proof corrections of his story Balzac uses this process seven times. His purpose may be, at times, to replace a colorless expression, as in the following illustration, in which the keen social observation in the revision heightens the reader's sense of the *abbé*'s persecution by the mean old maid:

Ces contrariétés devinrent constantes ... [*2a*, 115]	*Les mille et une contrariétés qu'une servante peut faire subir à son maître, ou une femme à un mari dans les habitudes privées de la vie,* furent devinées par Mademoiselle Gamard ... [*2c*, 348+]

Or Balzac may elaborate an expression simply to clarify his idea, as he does in the following example:

... [les vieilles filles] sont jalouses à vide, et ne connaissent que les malheurs de la seule passion *qui se pardonne.* [*2a*, 102]	... elles sont jalouses à vide, et ne connaissent que les plus affreux malheurs de la seule passion *que les hommes pardonnent parce qu'elle les flatte.* [*2c*, 339+]

Additions are used in much the same way as are amplifications. Balzac introduces them to heighten an effect, to complete an expression, to clarify, or simply to define. In the following example Balzac has made many changes, but it is the addition of the final prepositional phrase that sharpens our impression of the unequal struggle we are witnessing:

La vieille fille, heureuse de vivre par un sentiment aussi plein que celui de la vengeance, se plaisait à planer sur Birotteau, comme un oiseau de proie sur un mulot, à lui peser ... [*2a*, 116]	Heureuse de vivre par un sentiment aussi fertile en émotions que l'est celui de la vengeance, la vieille fille se plaisait à planer sur le vicaire, comme un oiseau de proie sur un mulot *avant de le dévorer* ... [*2c*, 349+]

An addition may quite simply clarify:

Le hazard voulut qu'il trouvât heureusement pour lui beaucoup d'occupation à Saint-Gatien, où il fit plusieurs enterremens, un mariage et deux baptêmes ... [*2a*, 112]	Il trouva par hasard et heureusement pour lui beaucoup d'occupation à Saint-Gatien, où il se fit plusieurs enterremens, un mariage et deux baptêmes; *alors il put oublier ses chagrins.* [*2c*, 346+]

The total number of additions from the manuscript through 2c is exactly half a hundred.

Balzac thickened his texts more often than he thinned them. This tendency is well illustrated in the early versions of this story. Nevertheless, he had to correct and prune the hastily written manuscript. In correcting his proofs Balzac seems to have concentrated on getting rid of *remplissages*. There are fifteen omissions and eighteen compressions at this stage of the novel.

In the example below he has improved a wordy and really bad clause. The first revision is not the best that Balzac can do, but it is a smoother and more compact expression than the original. It is not, however, until the Mame edition that the expression is effectively shortened:

... si la conscience *que nous avons de l'utilité dont nous sommes aux autres nous* donne un sentiment de satisfaction ...   [2a, 101]

... si la conscience *de notre utilité pour les autres* donne *à l'être agissant* un sentiment de satisfaction ...   [2c, 337]

... si la conscience de *son* utilité donne à l'être agissant un sentiment de satisfaction ...   [*Mame* 337][42]

How slowly the passage evolved, but how revealing it is of the effort Balzac made to write concisely! Surely the man who had the patience to go over and over his material in this minute fashion had a sense of the inadequacies of his style!

In studying the corresponding pages of the early versions of the story from the manuscript through 2c, we find that Balzac has omitted five sentences and an occasional clause and phrase. The sentences went because they repeated what had already been said. In one case, omitting the clause resulted in a rhythmical and closely knit phrase, whereas the original expression was jerky and cumbersome at the same time:

... la nature des persécutions *qu'il éprouvait,* interdisait à Birotteau ...   [2b, 116]

... la nature de ses chagrins interdisait à Birotteau ...   [2c, 349+]

Balzac corrected his texts frequently by transposing sentences or parts of sentences. A comparison of the passages of which there is more than one proof shows that there are thirty-one transpositions within sentences.

---

[42] In *Fur.* 25+, "travail" replaces "utilité."

These are frequently made to bring together the verb and its subject or its object (*2a*, 116; *2c*, 349+, and *2a*, 117; *2c*, 350+). In the following instance the rearrangement gives to the sentence a climactic ending in keeping with the tragedy that we are witnessing:

... la vieille fille lui dit d'un son de voix où *la joie de le trouver en faute et le reproche se peignaient également* ... [*2a*, 112]

... la vieille fille lui dit d'un son de voix où *se peignaient également le reproche et la joie de la trouver en faute* ... [*2c*, 347+]

In the example below, the words "clochers" and "cloches" follow each other too closely in the original text; and, furthermore, the short final phrase gives an unfinished and jarring effect. Balzac avoids these errors in his revision by placing the phrase before the two longer expressions:

... interrompu seulement *par le chant des offices* qui bourdonne au dehors de l'église, ou bien par les cris des choucas logés dans le sommet des clochers, *ou par le bruit des cloches.* [*2b*, 4]

... interrompu seulement par *le bruit des cloches, par le chant des offices,* qui franchit les murs de l'église, ou par les cris des choucas logés dans le sommet des clochers. [*2c*, 282+]

The above examples suffice to show the importance of transpositions in Balzac's corrections.

Variations involving figures of speech are rare between the manuscript and the proofs. One familiar metaphor Balzac does retouch, though none too successfully:

... Birotteau ne pouvant plus douter qu'il vivait *sous l'œil de la haine* la plus active, *sous un œil* qui ne sommeillait jamais ... [*2a*, 116]

... Birotteau ne pouvait plus douter qu'il vécût sous *le sceptre d'une haine dont l'œil* était toujours ouvert sur lui. [*2c*, 348]

Balzac himself was not satisfied with this figure. In Béchet 95+ he replaced "sceptre" by "empire," but the metaphor is still badly mixed.

In the next case we have an example of Balzac's use of figures of speech which are applicable to the calling of his characters. The substituted figure is not only more unusual but, with the addition, serves to explain more clearly why the gouty *abbé* does not mind getting caught in a sudden downpour:

Puis, *il avait les pieds chaussés d'un canonicat,* caressait sa chimère, un désir déjà vieux de vingt ans, son désir de tous les soirs, sur le point de s'accomplir ... [*2b*, 2]

Puis, en ce moment il caressait sa chimère, un désir déjà vieux de douze ans, son désir de tous les soirs qui était sur le point de s'accomplir, et *il s'enveloppait trop bien dans l'aumusse d'n canonicat pour sentir l'intempérie*[43] *de l'air.* [*2c*, 280+]

[43] *2b*/ms reads here " les intempéries," and Balzac corrects *2c* to read thus also.

This concludes our analysis of the early changes involving rhetorical devices. Amplifications and additions are characteristically more numerous in the proofs than are compressions and omissions. However, whether Balzac elaborates his text or condenses it, his first aim is clearness and exactness. Other stylistic effects, such as vividness, movement, and smoothness are his second goal. Transpositions are frequently made in an effort to bring together the logically related elements in a sentence. Changes in word order are also effected for the sake of emphasis and occasionally for that of sound. The figures of speech introduced between the manuscript and proofs are few in number, but they are none the less typical. Balzac's rhetorical figures do not always escape banality; but when he invents a figure, it is usually arresting because it expresses so aptly the *condition* of a character or harmonizes so exactly with a description.

In the small number of pages for which there exists more than one proof, there are one hundred and twenty-five changes involving rhetorical devices. As there are, in all, some five hundred variations in these pages, we may, perhaps, conclude that rhetorical devices would account for about one-quarter of the stylistic changes which Balzac made in correcting the proofs of this story.

c) According to parts of speech.—Balzac's verbal corrections are, of course, important and numerous. Between the manuscript and the proofs there are some three hundred and thirty-five changes which affect words. Throughout all the versions of the story these small corrections tend to make his style more accurate, more exact, and often more colorful. We shall, for purposes of convenience, classify these variations according to the parts of speech, which will be further subdivided into substitutions, additions, and omissions. Between the manuscript and proofs the parts of speech most frequently affected are verbs, nouns, adjectives, adverbs, and conjunctions.

There are eighty changes involving verbs. Omissions are rare, and even additions are infrequent. Substitutions, on the other hand, are very common. In the following example both omission and addition are effected by a simple transposition. Mlle Gamard's remark on the vicar's tardiness at dinner becomes blunter in the process:

... vous *devez savoir* que *nous ne nous*   Vous *savez* que nous *ne devons pas nous*
attendons jamais!   [2a, 115]   attendre!   [2c, 347+]

In the instance below, the omission of the auxiliary gives a more conversational tone to the Abbé Chapeloud's remarks to his friend Birotteau. The canon is lauding Mlle Gamard's housekeeping. This speech becomes even more natural in the first edition, where Balzac shortens and, so to speak, harmonizes the last clause by further omissions:

Je trouve toujours chaque chose en
place ... mes meubles *sont* frottés, et
tout est si bien essuyé que ...   [1, 10]

> Je trouve toujours chaque chose en
> place ... mes meubles frottés, et *tout est*
> *si bien essuyé* que ...   [2b, 12]

>> Je trouve toujours chaque chose en
>> place ... mes meubles frottés, et *tou-*
>> *jours si bien essuyés* que ...
>>   [*Mame* 295+]

In one case involving both addition and substitution Balzac has not only achieved grace but has enhanced the imagery of a sentence that was originally both heavy and unevocative because of a colorless verb and the stark enumeration with which it ended. This happy effect was not, however, completely attained until the *princeps*. Balzac, in describing Mlle Gamard's house, tells us that it lies continually in the shadow of Saint-Gatien:

... cette grande cathédrale sur laquelle
le tems a jetté son manteau noir, et
mis ses rides, ses mousses, ses herbes,
son froid humide.   [2b, 4][44]

> ... cette grande cathédrale, sur laquelle
> le temps a jeté son manteau noir, *im-*
> *primé et semé* ses rides, son froid hu-
> mide, ses mousses, ses hautes herbes.
>   [2c, 282]

>> ... cette grande cathédrale, sur laquelle
>> le temps a jeté son manteau noir, *im-*
>> *primé* ses rides, *et semé* son froid hu-
>> mide, ses mousses, ses hautes herbes.
>>   [*Mame* 284+]

Cases of substitution occur fifty-three times. Many of these changes

[44] 2b/ms reads: "... noir, *imprimé* ses rides, son froid humide, *et semé* ses mousses, ses hautes herbes."

are made to avoid repetitions. There is a tendency to replace the verb *être* by other, more specific verbs, such as, for example, *devenir* (*2a*, 115–16; *2c*, 348; *Char.* 49) and *paraître* (*2a*, 116; *2c*, 349+). The substituted verb may suggest a much more concrete image, as in the following case:

| ... et malgré les chaussons de flanelle dont il *enveloppait* en tout temps ses pieds ... [*2b*, 2] | ... et malgré les chaussons de flanelle dont il *s'empaquetait* les pieds en tout temps ... [*2c*, 280+] |

The substitution in the next example was made for the sake of accuracy:

| ... les personnes habituellement réunies chez madame de Listomère lui *avaient assuré* que la place de chanoine, vacante au chapitre ... lui serait donné ... [*2b*, 2] | ... les personnes habituellement réunies chez madame de Listomère lui *avaient presque garanti* sa nomination à une place de chanoine, alors vacante au chapitre ... [*2c*, 280–81+] |

It may be that the substitution of another word in a phrase led Balzac to change his verb, as when he replaced "accomplir ce vœu" (*2b*, 5) by "satisfaire cette cupidité" (*2c*, 285+).

Balzac's tendency to replace a single verb by two should be mentioned. Sometimes he merely incumbers his style, as when he changes "avait pris" (*2b*, 5) to "s'était chargée d'entretenir" (*2c*, 284+).

There are fifty variations involving nouns. Twelve of these changes are omissions, eight are additions, and thirty are substitutions. In general, superfluous nouns are omitted. In the following example the omission of the noun avoids redundancy in the revised text. The Tourangeaux do not criticize Mlle Gamard for owning a "bien national" under the Restoration:

| ... soit que les gens religieux lui supposassent l'intention de le léguer au chapitre *par son testament* ... [*2b*, 4] | ... soit que les gens religieux lui supposassent l'intention de le léguer au chapitre ... [*2c*, 283+] |

Nouns are usually added for the sake of emphasis. For example, when the vicar asked Troubert to intercede with Mlle Gamard in his behalf, the canon

| fit une de ces réponses qu'il fallait étudier longtemps avant d'en bien comprendre toute la portée ... [*2a*, 118] | fit une de ces réponses dont il fallait étudier longtemps *toutes les paroles* avant d'en bien comprendre la portée ... [*2c*, 352] |

This passage is almost entirely re-written for the Furne edition where the meaning is made even more specific: "... le chanoine fit une de ces réponses dont toutes les paroles devaient être long-temps étudiées pour que leur portée *fût entièrement mesurée*" (*Fur.* 31+).

Substitutions are frequently made to avoid repetitions. A favorite device is to exchange proper and common nouns. Having introduced the word "ami" just above the phrase "l'appartement de son ami" (2b, 9), Balzac naturally changes this expression to "l'appartement de Chapeloud" (2c, 288+). In re-writing the following clause Balzac was led by his sense of the *mot propre* to substitute a word connoting greater cruelty, a more exact noun:

Tant que *l'inimitié* de la vieille fille avait été sourde ... [2a, 116]	Tant que la vieille fille avait sourdement exercé sa *vengeance* ... [2c, 348+]

Again, the substituted noun may be a more evocative term, as it is in the case cited below. Balzac has told us that Chapeloud and Birotteau were sons of peasants. In revising his text he consequently seeks to suggest their poverty more strongly. The added adjective emphasizes still further their slender means:

... ils avaient épuisé toutes leurs *ressources* à passer le temps malheureux de la révolution. [2b, 6]	... ils avaient épuisé leurs minces *économies* à passer le temps malheureux de la révolution. [2c, 285+]

Another substitution should be mentioned. To call Troubert Birotteau's "collègue" (2a, 118) may be exact, but it tells the reader nothing. To call him "ce prêtre mystérieux" (2c, 351+) is equally exact, and at the same time it sums up dramatically what Balzac has been saying about the canon in the immediately preceding sentences.

Variations involving verbs and nouns are much more frequent than those for the other parts of speech. However, adjectives, adverbs, and conjunctions are concerned in the variants almost as often as are nouns and verbs. The other parts of speech are more rarely varied.

Changes affecting pronouns do not occur often in the early versions of *Le Curé de Tours*. There are only seventeen such variations. Balzac had the habit, which became even more pronounced later, of replacing pronouns by nouns. The next example illustrates this tendency. In describing Chapeloud's bookcase Balzac writes:

C'était un très beau morceau ... [2b, 7]	*Cette bibliothèque* était un très beau morceau ... [2c, 286]

Later, in *Fur.* 5+, Balzac omits the clause entirely, as it is redundant. The next case is even more typical of this kind of variation than is the example just quoted. Balzac is analyzing the unhappiness of old maids, of whom he says:

... *elles* éprouvent toujours une gêne intérieure ... [2a, 103]	... *les vieilles filles* éprouvent toujours une gêne intérieure ... [2c, 340+]

Adjectives and adjectival phrases are varied some forty-seven times between the manuscript and proofs. Substitutions are more frequent than are omissions and additions. We have seen in the discussion of nouns how an added adjective was used for stylistic effect by Balzac. The cases of omission are rare and unimportant. Substitutions occur twenty-six times. The changes are, characteristically, often made for the sake of definiteness. The substituted phrase may be more evocative, as well as more exact. The cruel Mlle Gamard takes delight in yielding to

un sentiment aussi *plein* que celui de la vengeance ... [2a, 116]	un sentiment aussi *fertile en émotions* que l'est celui de la vengeance ... [2c, 349+]

One substitution is particularly interesting because it shows us that Balzac sought new and unusual adjectives. However, in this instance he quite correctly abandoned his scientific term. In describing Mlle Gamard's stiff, queer gestures he says:

Ses mouvements avaient une soudaineté *télégraphique* ... [2a, 105]	Ses mouvements avaient une soudaineté *bizarre* ... [2c, 342+]

Variations involving adverbs and adverbial phrases occur forty-one times. There are seven omissions, five substitutions, and twenty-nine additions. The omitted adverbs are frequently introductory phrases, such as *en effet* (1, 9; 2b/ms, 11+) or *du reste* (2a, 105; 2c, 341+). Sometimes Balzac is uncertain whether to omit an adverb or not. Mlle Gamard's false hair gives both the author and the wearer some difficulty! Her *tour* is said to be "*assez souvent* mal bouclé" (2a, 104), "mal bouclé" (2c, 341), "*presque toujours* mal bouclé" (*Mame* 341), and, finally, "*assez* mal bouclé" (*Béch.* 89+). The definitive version suggests, as did 2c, that Mlle Gamard is invariably untidy. A telling substitution has to do with an expression of time. The intensity of the amended phrase brings out more clearly the progression of the Abbé Birotteau's tragic suffering:

... *chaque jour* la terreur que lui causait la perspective d'une explication avec Mademoiselle Gamard s'étant accrue ... [2a, 117]	... la terreur que lui causait la perspective d'une explication avec mademoiselle Gamard s'étant accrue *de jour en jour* ... [2c, 350+]

Adverbs are added usually for the sake of clearness or emphasis—for clearness in the following instance:

... tout le mobilier que le pauvre chanoine put y mettre consistait en un lit, une table ... [2b, 7]	... tout le mobilier que le pauvre chanoine put *d'abord* y mettre, consistait en un lit, une table ... [2c, 286+]

The adverb has been inserted for emphasis in the example quoted below. The Abbé Chapeloud delighted in his spotless apartment:

| Avez-vous vu un grain de poussière chez moi? [1, 10] | Avez-vous vu un grain de poussière chez moi? *Jamais!* [2*b*/ms, 12+] |

While these variations are small, they add vividness and life to the style. Their very number makes them significant.

Variations affecting conjunctions are also notable for their frequency. They occur forty-nine times. There are fifteen cases of substitution, twelve of addition, and twenty-two of omission. The conjunction *et* is more frequently affected than any other. It is omitted thirteen times, added five, and replaced by different conjunctions seven times. The omissions are usually due to the breaking-up of the long and often badly organized original sentences. In the re-writing, one sentence becomes two or more, and the superfluous conjunctions are dropped, as, for example, in the instance following:

| Alors, Chaploud se mit chez mademoiselle Gamard, *et* lorsque Birotteau ... [2*b*, 6] | Ce fut alors que Chapeloud se mit chez mademoiselle Gamard. Lorsque Birotteau ... [2*c*, 285+] |

Other examples show how the addition of the conjunction *et* was used to effect a more evenly flowing style (2*a*, 104; 2*c*, 340+) or to achieve variety (2*a*, 101; 2*c*, 337+).

As regards the other conjunctions, variations affecting *car* are the most numerous, and these occur only five times. This conjunction, so frequently omitted in the Béchet text, as we shall see, was struck out only twice in the proofs (2*b*, 8; 2*c*, 287+). It was added twice (1, 9-10; 2*b*/ms, 11; *Mame* 294, and 2*a*, 112; 2*c*, 346+), and it was replaced by *et* once (2*b*, 6; 2*c*, 285).

Variations involving other parts of speech are infrequent and unimportant. Articles are concerned in nine of the changes; prepositions in eight. In no case is the style appreciably affected.

The total number of verbal corrections of all sorts is impressive when compared to the other kinds of variations. It is evident that Balzac spent much time in his effort to discover the exact word, whether it was an essential verb or a small conjunction. That he so often did find the expression he sought is witnessed by the fact that the *mot propre* is considered a salient trait of his style.

To conclude our study of the stylistic variations in the manuscript and proof versions of *Le Curê de Tours* we note first the slowness with which the text evolved. The manuscript is frequently incorrect: words are misspelled; sentences and paragraphs are run together regardless of topic; ideas are repeated, or they are suggested but not developed. In short, Balzac did not stop for correctness in the heat of composition. As each proof was returned to him, he patiently weeded out the errors, but not always all of them each time. Sometimes his manuscript changes on the proofs were themselves incorrect! However, from proof to proof the paragraphs are reorganized, the sentences are shortened, the style is usually improved ultimately. There is an obvious effort to avoid repetitions, padding, and obscurity. Balzac's ideal of truth led him to make the minute verbal corrections which we have discussed. These small variations involving the parts of speech are significant not only because of their frequency but because they often contribute color and movement to the style.

Balzac will introduce many stylistic variations in his text as the editions succeed each other. The general trend of these changes will not, however, be greatly different from that of the proof corrections. His main stylistic objectives will always be clearness and exactness.

2. REALISTIC VARIATIONS (BETWEEN MANUSCRIPT AND PROOFS)

The realistic variations are always far less numerous than those which Balzac introduced for the sake of style. They are, on the other hand, always interesting, whereas the stylistic and linguistic changes are often routine corrections. The realistic variations may involve Balzac's general realistic qualities, or they may be due to his narrative technique.[45] Let us consider, then, under these two headings the realistic changes found in the corresponding pages of the manuscript and proofs.

a) General realistic qualities.—We may quickly enumerate the few changes of a general realistic nature. In the *Avant-propos* Balzac tells us that the novel must be "vrai dans les détails."[46] Hence we find him, in the following example, bringing his story closer to actuality—that is, to truth—by adding a detail which is essential to an accurate depicting of the situation:

... l'abbé Birotteau s'imagina qu'il empêchait mademoiselle Gamard et le chanoine de se promener, et *cette idée grossie par sa bonté* lui fit abandonner la place. [2a, 112]	... l'abbé Birotteau s'imagina qu'il empêchait mademoiselle Gamard et le chanoine de se promener. *Cette idée inspirée tout à la fois par la crainte et par la bonté*, prit un tel accroissement qu'elle lui fit abandonner la place ... [2c, 346+]

45 Dargan, Crain, and Others, *op. cit.*, pp. 15–31.
46 *Con.* I, xxiii.

The materialistic viewpoint—the emphasis on things—is illustrated in two cases. Balzac often raises sums of money from one version to another, and we find him here changing the legacy inherited by Chapeloud from "mille francs" (2b, 7) to "deux mille francs" (2c, 286+). He adds to the furnishings of Mlle Gamard's dining-room a barometer[47] and eliminates the enumeration of the obvious articles:

... dans laquelle [la salle à manger] il n'y avait que deux consoles, un buffet, des chaises, et une table ... [2a, 106]	... dans laquelle il n'y avait que deux consoles pour tout ornement et un baromètre ... [2c, 343+]

One interesting sociological phrase which emphasizes succinctly both the species and the milieu is substituted for a longer expression; Balzac is speaking of Mlle Gamard's rooms:

Enfin les deux pièces situées au rez de chaussée, sous son appartement, et où elle recevait ses deux pensionnaires étaient en rapport avec sa physionomie et ses idées. Un papier verni représentant des paysages turcs ornait les murs de la salle à manger ... [2a, 106]	Cette figure typique du genre vieille fille[48] était très bien encadrée par les grotesques inventions d'un papier verni représentant des paysages turcs ... [2c, 343+]

Other general realistic changes occur, as we shall see, at different stages of the revision of the novel.

b) Technical elements.—At only one time in correcting this story did Balzac shift his material in blocks. These transpositions were made when he revised 2a for the printer.

Let us first examine the whole passage that was rearranged, as it appears in the manuscript. Balzac has just finished his exposition, and the morning of the second day of Mlle Gamard's open persecution of Birotteau has dawned. The vicar, the canon, and their hostess are seated at breakfast. Birotteau expects Mlle Gamard to apologize, at least, for his having been locked out the night before, and he is appalled to have her tell him that his coming in late has disturbed her rest. In the manuscript the narrative is here interrupted by the reference to Mlle Gamard as an excellent illustration of the "nature élégiaque et désolée de la vieille fille" (1, 41). Sitting there opposite Birotteau, Balzac interpolates, she looks so sulky and catlike that the poor priest, seeing her for the first time with open eyes, wonders why he never noticed before the lack of goodness in

[47] Cf. Jared Wenger, *The Province and the Provinces in the Work of Honoré de Balzac*, p. 38, for the "fanatical deference" which Balzac's provincials felt for a barometer.

[48] Balzac italicized "vieille fille."

her face. This observation serves as a transition to Mlle Gamard's appearance. Balzac tells us that she is rather tall, that she is "d'une seule pièce," and that she walks like the Commander! Her face, he continues, is in accord with her attitude, because life makes the soul and "l'âme fait la physionomie" (1, 41). Here Balzac introduces an analysis of the old maid as a social species. He then loops back to the physical portrait of Mlle Gamard; next he proceeds to the description of her dining-room and salon, and, to complete our impression of the old maid's personality, he brings her pet, a fat old pug dog, into the picture. Such was the person, he adds, in whom Birotteau had awakened the only passion of which she was capable—hate. At this point in the manuscript Balzac returns to the breakfast scene. He tells us where the two *abbés* and their hostess are seated at table and discloses Birotteau's consternation at Mlle Gamard's rigid silence, for she has said nothing since her spiteful complaint about being kept awake. The vicar is suffering acutely because he believes that talking at meals is good for the health. Mlle Gamard agrees with this theory, as heretofore she has responded willingly to the Abbé Birotteau's platitudes. Here Balzac recounts at length what these two provincials discussed every morning. This particular morning, however, Mlle Gamard is so angry that Birotteau's tongue is frozen. Nevertheless, unable to bear the silence, he hazards the remark that the coffee is excellent. He receives no answer. He tries again; commanding all his self-respect and courage, he observes: "Il fera plus beau aujourd'hui qu'hier ... ." No reply! Mademoiselle glances graciously at Troubert, then glares at Birotteau, who fortunately has looked away. Finally Troubert, who seems to come out of his reverie for the sake of politeness, answers: "Oui, il fera beau."

It is obvious that in this first version the several themes are woven into a somewhat irregular pattern. In the revision in *2a* the outline is more symmetrical. Balzac first combines all the scattered material relating to the breakfast scene which he is depicting. Isolated bits—for example, the seating arrangements in the dining-room and the description of the spoiled old dog—are brought together and completely re-written to form a logical sequence. Three entire pages are moved forward from the end of the passage and placed here in the dining-room setting. These are the paragraphs dealing with Birotteau's loquacity at meals, the unvarying topics that he and Mlle Gamard discuss daily, and his ill-received remarks about the coffee and the weather. Thus Balzac points up dramatically, with setting, dialogue, and characters, the breakfast scene before he introduces his generalizations on the *genre vieille fille* and his observations on Mlle Gamard in particular.

A second transposition in 2*a* was made to unite in one place the two parts of Mlle Gamard's portrait. In the manuscript, as we have seen, Balzac's remarks about her tall form and her manner of walking precede his analysis of old maids. In the rearranged text these detached details have been placed so that they conclude Mlle Gamard's portrait, of which the keynote is rigidity. Thus the gaunt figure and the walk, which was stiff as a statue's, form an effective climax in the revision.

One other short transposition was made, this time within the disquisition on old maids. The passage, which deals with the vengeance unhappy creatures take on those around them, came originally after the observation that society's reprobation of old maids is reflected in their dour faces. In the corrected version it is placed between the remark that their lack of happiness makes old maids austere and morose and a generalization on their want of grace. The exact location of the transferred blocks is indicated in Table 2.

Following the discourse on old maids the paragraphs succeed each other in the same order in the revised text of 2*a* as in the original. The whole passage now ends with the paragraph explaining Mlle Gamard's hatred of Birotteau. Here Balzac picks up Troubert's tardy reply to the vicar: "Oui, il fera beau." Thus the author has brought us back to the breakfast table, and from here he plunges again into his narrative. The order of ideas thus established in correcting 2*a* must have satisfied Balzac, for he did not again change it after this proof.

These transpositions were not, however, effected without some other readjustments. Moreover, in reorganizing this material Balzac re-wrote much of it, notably the parts having to do with the breakfast scene and with the old maid as a social type. The variations within these transferred passages have been discussed elsewhere. Let us consider here, however, those changes which Balzac made in order to fit the transpositions into their new setting.

The first adjustment entailed by the reblocking process was the substitution of an aside to the reader for the particularized passage on Mlle Gamard's formidable ill-humor and its effect on Birotteau (1, 41; 2*a*, 99). Balzac was fond of thus addressing his reader, and in this case he has used the aside as a transition to the long digression on old maids: "... mais pour bien peindre un être dont le caractère prête un intérêt immense aux petits événemens de ce drame et à la vie antérieure des personnages qui en sont les acteurs, peut-être faut-il résumer ici les idées dont une vieille fille est l'expression" (2a/ms, 99).[49]

A second variation due to the transpositions is the omission of a sentence to the effect that Mlle Gamard's face harmonized with her attitude

TABLE 2

TRANSFERRED PASSAGES

Order of Subjects after Revision (Cf. *Con.* 196–202)	Location in Manuscript	Original Location in 2a	Location in 2a after Revision
Birotteau's astonishment at Mlle Gamard's asperity	41	99	98/ms
The description of the three persons at table	47	107–8	98/ms
The pet dog	46	106	98/ms
Birotteau's loquacity Mlle Gamard's talkativeness	47–48	108–9	Inserted between 98 and 99
Topics discussed by these provincials	48	109–10	Inserted between 98 and 99
Birotteau's uneasiness and humble remarks Mlle Gamard's disdainful silence	48–49	110–11	Inserted between 98 and 99
Mlle Gamard exemplifies the elegiac nature of her kind	41	99	99, following inserted pages
Disquisition on old maids The vengeance sought by unhappy creatures	42–44 42–43	100–104 101	100–104 102
Physical portrait of Mlle Gamard Her figure and her walk	44–46 41–42	104–5 100	104–5 105

(1, 42; 2a/ms, 100). This sentence originally followed the description of her walk and became superfluous when that passage was moved elsewhere.

Transplanting the passage about Mlle Gamard's dog also involved additional minor readjustments. In the manuscript the description of the old maid's pet came after the *dossier* on her apartments. Here we learn that her dining-room walls were hung with a paper grotesquely ornamented with Turkish landscapes. A few lines beyond Balzac tells us that

[49] In Furne, however, the final clause reads: "... dont l'expression se trouve chez la vieille fille" (25+).

the Abbé Birotteau is so abashed by Mlle Gamard's manner that he doesn't dare speak to her or even look at her. Consequently, "[il] avait pour toute perspective la figure muette et aride de l'abbé Troubert, *ou les horribles paysages turcs dont il connaissait tous les détails*" (1, 47). But, as we have seen, the breakfast tableau was shifted in the revision far ahead of the description of Mlle Gamard's rooms. Balzac has therefore substituted in the corrected proof the fat old dog for the "horribles paysages turcs." The passage reads here: "... n'osant regarder ni la figure aride de Troubert ni le visage menaçant de la vieille fille, [Birotteau] *se tourna, par contenance, vers un gros carlin chargé d'embonpoint*" (2a/ms, 98+). The transplanted description of the dog is given at this point, but it is interruped by an addition, a bit of dialogue. This line of inserted speech serves two purposes: stylistically, it breaks up a long passage; technically, it reveals character directly rather than by description. Birotteau remarks timidly to the unresponsive old animal: "Hé bien mon mignon! tu attends ton café!" (2a/ms, 98+). This humble effort of the *abbé* to ingratiate himself with his hostess by noticing her pet is a pathetic unmasking of his soul.

This concludes the variations due to the transpositions. One other change of a technical nature is found, however, between the manuscript and the proofs of our story. It was in correcting the proofs that Balzac began to emphasize the color of Mlle Gamard's salon. Yellow becomes clearly in 2c the symbolic keynote of the room in which the old maid spends most of her time:

Le salon était parqueté, garni d'un meuble en velours d'Utrecht jaune, les flambeaux et la pendule en cristal.

[2a, 106]

Le salon commun dans lequel elle passait la majeure partie de la journée, sera tôt connu, en faisant observer qu'il se nommait *le salon jaune* et qu'il y avait sur la cheminée des flambeaux et une pendule en cristal ...

[2c, 343+]

Later, in Béchet, we shall find this keynote perhaps overemphasized.

It is not surprising to find so small a group of realistic variations in our few extant pages of proof. Balzac's main intention was always, of course, to transfer to his pages the world he observed around him. Consequently, even in its earliest form *Le Curé de Tours* has its broad realistic traits. Since the purpose of the story is to depict milieu and *conditions*, the sociological features are especially well developed in the manuscript. Notable among these sociological elements are: the provincial setting; the small-town intrigues with counterplots in Paris, involving church and even state; the selfish priests, who are either dangerous or useless to mankind; and the bitter old maid who takes her revenge for social ostracism. As regards the corrections, there are only four which derive from Balzac's general realistic qualities. His sociological interests are illustrated in one of these early changes. A second variation was made for the sake of truth. The two others exemplify Balzac's belief in the importance of "things."

The variations introduced for technical reasons are also infrequent. The most important of these is a series of transpositions. Balzac transplanted a number of paragraphs in order to build up dramatically his first scene between Mlle Gamard and her victim, the *débonnaire* Birotteau. Two additional transpositions were made in order to bring together related material. The only other change involving technique has to do with a familiar Balzacian device—the keynoting of descriptions. Our attention is focused on the color of Mlle Gamard's salon. However, the dominant color tone is less strongly emphasized here than it will be in the same passage of the 1834 text.

What is the significance of these small changes? Or, one may ask, what realistic traits of our author are so important that they are found in even a scant number of his pages? The technical variations illustrate two deep-rooted Balzacian tendencies: his inclination to dramatize a scene, and his habit of keynoting a description. As regards his more general realistic qualities, the changes involve truth, sociology, and things—the very bases on which he founded the realistic novel.

B. Changes between the Proofs and the First Edition

Since none of the three proofs for Le Curé de Tours is extant in its entirety, the variations for this stage of our story involve sometimes one set of proofs, sometimes another. In every case, of course, the *princeps* has been compared with the latest extant preceding version.

It should be noted, moreover, that 2c, our last proof, is not final for the Mame edition. In the two fragments of this page proof there are some eighty-eight sentences, fifty-three of which are different from the corresponding sentences in the first edition. Many of the marginal corrections of 2c/ms do not appear in the Mame edition. One such case has been cited below (see p. 221). Sometimes the differences between the two texts affect only a word or two, as, for example:

... lorsque Birotteau vint *le visiter* ...   ... lorsque Birotteau vint visiter *le*
                [2c/ms, 285]   *chanoine* ...   [*Mame* 287]

Again, the two texts may be quite divergent, as in the next instance:

Conservant le teint de brunes, ses che-veux *étaient* noirs; *mais d'affreuses mi-graines, les avaient blanchis ce* qui la contraignait à porter un tour *qu'elle ne savait point* mettre de manière à en dissimuler la naissance ... [2c/ms, 341]

Brune, ses cheveux, *jadis* noirs, *avaient été blanchis par d'affreuses migraines, accident* qui la contraignait à porter un tour; *mais ne sachant pas* le mettre de manière à en dissimuler la naissance ... [*Mame* 341+]

These examples, chosen from both fragments of 2c, suffice to show that for these pages, at least, Balzac must have had certainly one more proof before he was ready to publish his story.

I. STYLISTIC VARIATIONS

Let us now consider the general stylistic variations which occur between the proofs and the *princeps*. As is usual in Balzac's corrections, these variants are more than abundant. We can give examples of the most frequent and most important types of changes only. These will again be considered from the point of view of sentence structure, rhetorical devices, and parts of speech.

a) According to sentence structure.—A careful examination seems to indicate that the majority of Balzac's changes in sentence structure are made to vary the turn of his phrases. A change from the participial to the finite form in one sentence, for example, will lead to the opposite change in a closely following sentence. As has been noted above (see p. 196), there is a definite effort to break up sentences. There is also, of course, the drive toward clearness and toward concision.

One of the most frequent changes under sentence structure is the reduction of independent clauses to dependent constructions. This change occurs thirty times and is usually made in the interest of smoothness. The favorite method of correction is to substitute a participial phrase for a finite clause:

Mademoiselle Gamard *prit* avec plaisir le vicaire en pension, *et* il participa dès-lors à toutes les félicités de la vie ma-térielle que lui vantait le défunt cha-noine.   [2b, 11]

Mademoiselle Gamard *ayant pris* le vicaire en pension, il participa dès lors à toutes les félicités de la vie matérielle que lui vantait le défunt chanoine.   [*Mame* 294+]

To get a true picture of Balzac's stylistic variations, however, one must remember that he frequently makes a correction in one text only to take it out again in the following edition. In many instances he returns to his original phraseology. These restorations are particularly characteristic of the variations involving finite and participial constructions. They are, moreover, usually fully justified stylistically. In the following example the original correction was perhaps made in the interest of smoothness; but when Balzac corrected his text, he saw that an even style was not suited to the passage. He has therefore deliberately returned to the staccato tempo of the finite construction in order to sustain the impression of surprise he had created. He has also broken his sentences differently in each text. In summing up the events which followed Birotteau's disgrace Balzac writes:

Trois mois après, M. le vicaire-général
fut nommé évêque, et madame de Listomère était morte. *Elle laissait* quinze
cents francs de rente par testament à
M. l'abbé Biroteaux.   [*2a*, 163]

       Cinq mois après, M. le vicaire-général
       fut nommé évêque, et madame de Lis-
       tomère était morte, *laissant* quinze
       cents francs de rente par testament à
       M. l'abbé Birotteau.   [*Mame* 410]

              Cinq mois après, M. le vicaire-général
              fut nommé évêque. Madame de Lis-
              tomère était morte, et *laissait* quinze
              cents francs de rente par testament à
              M. l'abbé Birotteau.   [*Béch.* 159+]

    Between the proofs and the first edition, dependent clauses are reduced to shorter elements thirty-eight times and in a variety of ways. Sometimes a more closely knit sentence is achieved by the substitution of a past participle for the clause:

D'où venait cette susceptibilité *qu'elle*   D'où procédait cette susceptibilité stu-
portait en tout ... ?   [*2a*, 86]   pidement *portée* en toute chose ... ?
                                                      [*Mame* 318+]

Greater concision results in five cases from the substitution of a noun for a dependent clause. For example, Mlle Gamard used to say:

... qu'elle s'était heureusement aper-   ... qu'elle s'était heureusement aper-
çue à temps de la mauvaise foi *de celui*   çue à temps de la mauvaise foi *de son*
qui prétendait l'aimer ...   [*2c*, 343]   *amant* ...   [*Mame* 342+]

In the interest of a more compact style Balzac often substitutes an adjective for a dependent clause. In the first instance cited below, he has also avoided cacophony:

... le vent poussait par momens sur lui   ... le vent poussa par momens sur lui
des bouffées de pluie *comme si c'eus-*   certaines bouffées de pluie *semblables à*
sent été des douches.   [1, 12]   *des douches.*   [*Mame* 297+]

Thus, in the very next sentence "le tems qu'il fallait" (1, 12) becomes "le
tems nécessaire" (*Mame* 297+). For the sake of concision, a dependent
clause may be reduced by the substitution of a phrase:

Quand elle était de bonne humeur ...   *Dans ses momens* de bonne humeur ...
          [2c, 105]   [*Mame* 342+]

Dependent clauses are changed to independent constructions in eleven
cases. The following example is characteristic of Balzac's effort to simplify his style:

Ce fut ainsi que l'avoué des libéraux   L'avoué des libéraux entama donc
entama l'affaire ...   [2a, 146]   l'affaire ...   [*Mame* 392+]

There are, in all, ninety-three changes in sentence structure between
the proofs and the first edition of this short novel. The reader of Balzac
often has the impression that his sentences bristle with clauses. These
variations suggest that Balzac himself had the same impression, for they
all tend in one direction—toward a less involved style. He shortens his
sentences and reduces his clauses constantly in his effort to achieve simplicity.

b) According to rhetorical devices.—Elaboration of expression may be
made for emphasis, as when Balzac expands the idea contained in the adjective "bon" in the example below:

Oui, mais vous logerez bientôt à l'ar-   Oui, mais vous logerez bientôt à l'ar-
chevêché! dit le *bon* Birotteau ...   chevêché! ... dit le vicaire, *voulant que*
          [2a, 95]   *tout le monde fût heureux ...*
                                                   [*Mame* 329+]

An amplification may be used merely to define. One wonders if the expanded form is superior to the original in the following example:

Ainsi, le premier jour où il vint dîner et   Ainsi, le premier jour où il vint dîner
coucher chez la vieille fille, il fut retenu   et coucher chez la vieille fille, il fut
dans son salon *par une fausse politesse,*   retenu dans son salon par le désir de
et aussi par son désir de faire connais-   faire connaissance avec elle, *aussi bien*
sance avec elle.   [2a, 82]   *que par cet inexplicable embarras qui*
                                       gêne souvent les gens timides, ou leur
                                       fait craindre d'être impolis en interrom-
                                       pant une conversation pour sortir ...
                                                   [*Mame* 312+]

Additions serve also to clarify. In the example below, the insertion is made for the sake of clearness. M. de Bourbonne is explaining to Birotteau why he should not sue Mlle Gamard:

Mais, tous vos amis, quoique pleins de bonnes intentions vous mettent dans un mauvais chemin. [2a, 136]	Mais, tous vos amis, quoique pleins de bonnes intentions, vous mettent dans un mauvais chemin, *d'où vous ne pourrez vous tirer* ... [*Mame* 380+]

In the following example the added clause makes for exactness:

... toute espèce de choix implique d'ailleur un mépris. [2a/ms, 87]	... toute espèce de choix implique un mépris *pour ce que l'on refuse.* [*Mame* 319; *Béch.* 69; *Char.* 29]

Again, an addition may be used for the sake of balance. It may, at the same time, give us needed information, as when we learn that the Baron de Listomère's ambition is achieved:

Le legs de madame de Listomère à Birotteau fut attaqué par M. le baron de Listomère sous prétexte de captation. [2a, 164]	Le legs de madame de Listomère à Birotteau fut attaqué par M. le baron de Listomère sous prétexte de captation; *mais le baron fut nommé capitaine!* [*Mame* 411+]

There are one hundred and sixty-one variations in this category. There are more than three times as many additions as there are amplifications. The latter occur only thirty-eight times, whereas the former reach a total of one hundred and twenty-three.

Compressions naturally tend toward a more concise style. They frequently result in greater smoothness. In the following example the emended form is not only smoother but clearer than the original one:

... car les vieilles filles ont toutes un certain talent pour accentuer *leurs petites traîtrises qui imprime un caractère particulier aux actions et aux mots que la haine leur suggère.* [1, 18]	... car les vieilles filles ont toutes un certain talent pour accentuer *les actions et les mots que la haine leur suggère.* [*Mame* 302+]

Concision and clearness are also achieved by the omission of clauses, phrases, and even sentences. Sentences are usually omitted because they repeat an idea that has been used elsewhere. Phrases and clauses are taken out in order to simplify the style. One example employing both condensation and omission will serve to illustrate Balzac's efforts to write more clearly and more simply:

Birotteau, pour son malheur, avait développé chez elle les seuls sentimens qu'il fût possible à cette femme d'éprouver, ceux de la haine, qui jusqu'alors *étaient restés* latens, par suite du calme *où elle avait vécu, et du peu d'événemens accomplis dans le cercle resserré tracé par la vie de province,* dont l'horizon s'était encore rétréci pour elle ...   [2c, 344]

Birotteau, pour son malheur, avait développé chez elle les seuls sentimens qu'il fût possible à cette femme d'éprouver, ceux de la haine, qui, latens jusqu'alors, par suite du calme *et de la monotonie d'une vie provinciale* dont l'horizon s'était encore rétréci pour elle ...   [*Mame* 344+]

Balzac's royalist sympathies may explain one omission. Through 2a the Abbé Birotteau and his hostess recount tales of "conspirations tous les quinze jours" (2a, 109). This phrase does not occur in the *princeps* (*Mame* 334).

In summing up the changes in this class we find that there are forty-three compressions and seventy-four omissions. The total figure of one hundred and seventeen is not small and convinces us that, despite his natural exuberance of expression, Balzac could, and did, delete with a will.

Transpositions are less frequent between the proofs and the first edition than are the other changes involving rhetorical devices which we have studied. Even so, their number is not insignificant, as Balzac made at least ninety-one such transfers within sentences. Sometimes these changes are made for logical reasons, as in the example cited below. The young nephew of Mme de Listomère has heard that he is about to be retired from the Royal Navy and has gone up to Paris in great haste to seek the help of his uncle, the deputy:

Aussi le jeune homme attendit, avec la plus vive anxiété, *la fin de la séance dans la voiture de son oncle.*   [2a, 148]

Aussi attendit-il avec la plus vive anxiété, *dans la voiture de son oncle,* la fin de la séance.   [*Mame* 393-94+]

In the following instance the sentence is made smoother by bringing together the widely separated subject and verb:

... *l'abbé* tout en cherchant lui-même ses pantoufles qu'il ne trouvait pas au milieu du tapis de son lit comme elles étaient jadis *fit* sur la manière dont Marianne était habillée certaines observations ...   [1, 14-16]

Tout en cherchant lui-même ses pantoufles qu'il ne trouvait pas au milieu de son tapis de lit, comme elles y étaient jadis, *l'abbé fit* sur la manière dont Marianne était habillée certaines observations ...   [*Mame* 300+]

Again, it may be the verb and its object which are joined (2a, 153-54; *Mame* 400+).

One example will serve to illustrate the transpositions of single words and of short phrases. In the example quoted, the change seems to have been made principally for the sake of rhythm. Mlle Gamard, seen from a distance, had seemed to the Abbé Birotteau

le type de la femme de l'évangile, la femme sage, décorée de toutes les vertus humbles et modeste qui répandent *un parfum céleste sur la vie.*
[2a, 81]

le type de la femme de l'évangile, la femme sage, décorée de ces vertus humbles et modestes qui répandent *sur la vie un parfum céleste.*
[*Mame* 311]

In the Béchet edition "céleste" is placed before its noun, the transposition serving to stress the adjective (*Béch.* 61+).

There are no important changes in dialogue at this stage of *Le Curé de Tours*, but in several cases narration is broken up by the introduction of direct speech. Thus, in the example below the heavy effect of a series of clauses is lightened. Balzac tells us that each day the Abbé Chapeloud recounts to Birotteau how excellent Mlle Gamard's dinner has been:

... et il était bien rare que, pendant les sept promenades de la semaine, il ne lui arrivât pas de dire *que cette excellente fille avait eu pour vocation le service ecclésiastique.*
[2b, 12]

... et il était bien rare que, pendant les sept promenades de la semaine, il ne lui arrivât pas de dire ou moins quatorze fois: —*Cette excellente fille a, certes, pour vocation le service ecclésiastique.*
[*Mame* 295+]

Direct speech for narration adds life and swiftness to the style in the scene in which Mme de Listomère and her friends advise Birotteau that the way to secure his canonship is to leave Mlle Gamard's house. One dissenting opinion is expressed, that of "le vieux malin" (2a/ms, 122; *Mame* 362+). Speech-words indicating the speaker are frequently added, with or without modifiers (2a, 148; *Mame* 394+). A parenthetical phrase to indicate the person addressed is often introduced for clearness. It may, at the same time, add naturalness to the scene:

—Si ce n'est que cela! ... donnez! ... dit dit Madame de Listomère.
[1, 56]

—N'est-ce que cela? ... Signez! ... dit madame de Listomère *en regardant Birotteau* ...
[*Mame* 363+]

Variations involving figures of speech occur eight times between the proofs and the first edition. Of these, three are metaphors and five are similes. The most interesting of these figures are the similes. Two of these concern the Abbé Chapeloud's apartment, which is in each case compared to a woman. The canon's rooms were at first only poorly furnished. In correcting 2c, Balzac adds: "... l'appartement était donc comme une belle femme en haillons" (2c/ms, 286; Mame 288+). But with the years the apartment became more and more elegant. Balzac adds at one point the following simile: "Semblable à une jolie femme qui, passe par degrés de la misère à la pauvreté, l'appartement s'était vêtu de soie, et couvert de joyaux étincelans" (2c/ms, 288). This comparison, which occurs fairly near the one just cited, is not found in the princeps (Mame 291), for the probable reason that it seems to repeat too closely the idea of the first simile.

No doubt Balzac felt it was inappropriate to liken the Abbé Birotteau to a tun of wine rolling down the nave of Saint-Gatien. He therefore substituted for that picturesque figure a description of the vicar's manner of walking:

... le bon Birotteau trottinait en pa-   ... le bon vicaire y circulait sans gra-
raissant rouler comme une tonne de vin.   vité, trottait, piétinait, en paraissant
                             [2a, 93]   rouler sur lui-même.   [Mame 326+]

The metaphors are not unusual in their nature. To leave Tours would be a kind of death for Birotteau (2a, 137; Mame 381+). The jealous struggle of Mlle Gamard against the aristocrats of Tours is characterized in the first edition as "le combat du peuple et du sénat dans une taupi-nière" (Mame 385).[50] But through 2a (140) the phrase read "dans un trou."

We find, in looking back on the variations involving rhetorical devices, that they constitute about four hundred of the stylistic changes introduced between the proofs and the first edition. Amplifications and additions outnumber compressions and omissions, which, in turn, are more frequent than transpositions. Changes which concern dialogue, speech-words, and figures of speech comprise less than one-tenth of the total number of variations due to rhetorical devices.

The general trend of the elaborations and additions is toward exactness and clarity, as we have seen. Insertions were also made for emphasis and for symmetry. A surprisingly large number of omissions and contractions indicates that Balzac sought, in correcting his proofs, to achieve concision and compactness—qualities which were suited to the brevity of his novel. Omissions were also made for accuracy, for smoothness, and for reasons of logic. Transpositions serve both to bring together related ideas and to give a more even and rhythmical movement to the original sentences.

[50] Béch. 129+ reads "du sénat romain" for "du sénat."

Of the less frequent changes studied, speech-words are the most numerous. They are added more than twenty times and contribute not only clearness but a certain dramatic quality and vigor to the style. Vividness was attained by the judicious adding of two bits of dialogue which break up long stretches of narration. On the other hand, the figures of speech are familiar and less evocative than those which Balzac creates when he bases his analogies on the vocations of his characters.

c) According to parts of speech.—Changes of a purely verbal character are numerous. Substitutions are more prominent than additions and omissions. The purpose behind all these changes is, in general, the search for the *mot propre.*

Variations involving verbs occur two hundred and sixty-eight times and are more frequent than those affecting any other part of speech. Omissions are extremely rare, occurring only six times. Verbs are added twenty-four times. In the following example the insertion in the revised text was made both for balance and for emphasis; but the word chosen did not please Balzac, for he changed it in the Furne edition. The original sentence became two in Béchet (120). The Curé de Tours has just learned of the defeat of all his hopes:

L'abbé Poirel était chanoine, et lui,
Birotteau, sans asile, sans fortune et
sans mobilier.   [2a, 132]

       L'abbé Poirel était chanoine, et lui,
       Birotteau, *restait* sans asile, sans for-
       tune et sans mobilier!   [*Mame* 375]

              L'abbé Poirel était chanoine! Lui, Bi-
              rotteau, *se voyait* sans asile, sans for-
              tune et sans mobilier!   [*Fur.* 41+]

We can illustrate only a few of the one hundred and seventy-two cases of substitution. Balzac frequently replaces the verb *avoir* by a more pointed word. In the following instance the substitution suggests the profession of the speaker, the young naval officer:

... si [l'abbé Birotteau] a du cœur et   Si le vicaire a du cœur et veut suivre
veut suivre mes avis, il *aura* sa tran-   mes avis, il *aura* bientôt *conquis* sa
quillité.   [2a, 120]   tranquillité.   [*Mame* 358+]

The substitution of a picturesque verb for a less evocative one is a happy change in the next example, in which Balzac describes the rigid Mlle Gamard's manner of walking:

... elle était, pour ainsi dire, d'une seule pièce, et *marchait* comme la statue du commandeur. [2c, 342]	... elle était, pour ainsi dire, d'une seule pièce, et *semblait surgir, à chaque pas,* comme la statue du Commandeur. [*Mame* 342+]

Again, Mlle Salomon's devotion to her insane lover is more vividly suggested by the following substitution:

... elle s'était, avec le courage de l'amour, consacrée au bonheur mécanique de ce malheureux, dont elle avait aussi *étudié* la folie pour ne plus y croire. [2a/ms, 127]	... elle s'était, avec le courage de l'amour, consacrée au bonheur mécanique de ce malheureux, dont elle avait assez *épousé* la folie pour ne plus y croire. [*Mame* 369+]

As regards verbs, Balzac has a tendency to add modal auxiliaries. These changes may make for accuracy of meaning, as in the following example, which shows him struggling toward this goal through three texts. The Abbé Birotteau has returned to his apartment to find Troubert ensconced in it. After a long gaze into Troubert's motionless eyes, the *abbé* says: "... si mademoiselle Gamard *est* impatiente de vous mieux loger, elle *est* cependant assez juste pour me laisser le tems d'enlever mes livres et mes meubles" (2a, 129). The italicized verbs are first changed to read respectively: "a pu se montrer" and "doit être" (2a/ms, 129). However, in the first edition they have become "a pu être" and "doit se montrer" (*Mame* 372+). The substitutions may, on the other hand, merely serve to emphasize, as when, in the famous breakfast conversations between Birotteau and Mlle Gamard, Balzac makes the following elaboration:

... elle disait qu'un homme nourri d'un œuf chaque matins, mourrait à la fin de l'année ... [2a, 110]	... elle disait qu'un homme nourri d'un œuf chaque matin, *devait infailliblement mourir* à la fin de l'année ... [*Mame* 334+]

As for nouns, the changes are again abundant, totaling one hundred and eighty-two. Additions and omissions occur in almost equal ratio, but their numbers are not large. Simplicity and directness are achieved by striking out mere verbiage in several instances. For example, the Abbé Birotteau analyzed Mlle Gamard's hostility to him:

Avec cette *espèce de* sagacité questionneuse que contractent les prêtres habitués à diriger la conscience des vieilles filles ... [1, 18]	... avec cette sagacité questionneuse que contractent les prêtres habitués à diriger la conscience des vieilles femmes ... [*Mame* 302+]

Again, Mlle Gamard resents Mme de Listomère's defense of the vicar:

Avec *toute* la *science de* vanité qui dis- Avec la *vanité subtile* qui distingue les
tingue les vieilles filles ... [2a, 137] vieilles filles ... [*Mame* 382+]

Probably the desire for emphasis led Balzac to add the noun and adjective in the following case, though these are not the only important changes which he made in the passage:

L'air ambitieux de Troubert avait con- ... l'air ambitieux de Troubert, en don-
tribué à le faire redouter et à le laisser nant lieu de le redouter, avait contri-
simple chanoine ... [2a, 93] bué peut-être à le faire condamner *au*
 rôle insignifiant de simple chanoine ...
 [*Mame* 326+]

Substitutions occur many times. These are especially interesting when the *mot propre* replaces a vaguer word. In the example below, Balzac's tendency to use exact, technical terms is illustrated. The Abbé Birotteau, who has had more than one attack of gout, is unhappily forced to stand in the rain while a servant unlocks his door:

Mais les peines du *goutteux* ne finis ant ... mais les peines du *podagre* ne fi-
pas aussitôt qu'il le croyait ... [1, 12] nirent pas aussitôt qu'il le croyait ...
 [*Mame* 298+]

The celebrated phrase "concupiscence mobilière," used to describe Birotteau's longing for his friend's apartment, occurs for the first time at this stage of the story:

... le début de sa *convoitise* mobilière ... le début de sa *concupiscence* mobi-
fut semblable à celui d'une passion lière fut semblable à celui d'une pas-
vraie ... [2c/ms, 285] sion vraie ... [*Mame* 287+]

"Concupiscence," a word which a priest might well have used in the above connection, is an interesting example of Balzac's ability to find expressions suggestive of the calling of his characters. Similarly, in the illustration below, the substituted phrase is suited to the occasion and suggests what the Abbé Birotteau himself might have said. At Mlle Gamard's funeral:

... une seule personne ... pleura; ce fut Une seule personne ... pleura; ce fut
Birotteau, qui ... pria sincèrement Birotteau, qui ... pria sincèrement
pour la *vieille fille* ... [2a, 160] pour l'*âme de la défunte* ...
 [*Mame* 406–7+]

Variations involving pronouns are found one hundred and seventeen times. Common and proper nouns replace pronouns frequently. These changes make for definiteness, but they are often routine corrections introduced to avoid repetitions. In the following case, for example, the substitution avoids a succession of clauses beginning with *il*. Birotteau has just realized Mlle Gamard's ill-will toward him:

... *il* semblait accablé ...   [1, 16]   *Le bon homme* semblait accablé ...
                                                             [*Mame* 301+]

On the other hand, in the following case the change is due to Balzac's effort to be exact and specific. When M. de Bourbonne asks to see the contract between Mlle Gamard and Birotteau, the vicar replies, "*Il* est ..." (2*a*, 123), then "*Cela* est ..." (2*a*/ms, 123), and finally, "*L'acte* est chez moi" (*Mame* 365+). Pronouns are added some thirty times. Sometimes the pronoun is introduced because of a change in sentence structure. Frequently it is inserted for the sake of exactness (1, 24; *Mame* 307; *Béch.* 57+). Omissions, strange to say, are found almost as often as additions. Of the twenty-seven pronouns which Balzac struck out, many were deleted in order to avoid redundancy. Some pronouns were omitted because they were inexact (2*c*, 338; *Mame* 338+); others for the sake of smoothness (2*a*, 147–48; *Mame* 393; *Char.* 82).

Many changes involve adjectives. Eliminations occur only fifteen times and are made, in general, to avoid repetitions. For example, since everything Balzac has told us about Mlle Gamard has emphasized her aridity and thinness, he omits, in the following instance, a further reference to these characteristics:

Mademoiselle Sophie Gamard était   D'une taille assez élevée, elle se tenait
d'une taille assez élevée, *maigre et*   très droite ...   [*Mame* 342+]
sèche. Elle se tenait droite ... [2*c*, 342]

Additions involving adjectives number about thirty-five. The insertion may be made in the interest of accuracy:

Le titre de chanoine était pour [Birot-   Le titre de chanoine était devenu pour
teau], comme la pairie pour un mi-   lui ce que doit être la pairie pour un
nistre ...   [1, 12]   ministre *plébéien*.   [*Mame* 296+]

In many cases the qualifying word is introduced for the sake of emphasis. When Mlle Salomon learns that the Abbé Birotteau has been transferred to Saint-Symphorien, she expresses her indignation thus:

Quelle combinaison!   [2*a*, 162]   Quelle *atroce* combinaison!
                                                             [*Mame* 410+]

There are more than three times as many adjectival substitutions as there are additions. Usually Balzac is seeking the exact word in making these changes. Occasionally the variation is made to avoid monotony in form and similarity in sound (2a, 134; *Mame* 378+). A number of cases illustrate Balzac's search for the *mot propre;* for example:

| ... Mademoiselle Gamard fit de l'abbé Birotteau un portrait *un peu sombre* ... [2a, 88] | Mademoiselle Gamard fit de l'abbé Birotteau un portrait *si peu flatteur* que ... [*Mame* 320+] |

Troubert's face is described as "cambrée" (*Mame* 326+) rather than "creuse" (2a, 93). When Mlle Gamard refuses to talk to Birotteau at breakfast, the vicar finds this silence "effrayant" (2a, 100). In the Mame edition the silence has become "dangereux pour son estomac" (335+).

Two examples show Balzac striving for stylistic effects. In both cases the changes were made for the sake of antithesis. In the first illustration the clause has been re-written to stress the contrast. In Troubert's oration at Mlle Gamard's funeral:

| ... le tableau de la vie de la vieille fille fut tracé avec le style de Bossuet ... [2a, 160] | ... le tableau de la vie *étroite* menée par la testatrice prit des proportions *monumentales.* [*Mame* 407+][51] |

As Troubert's sermon is later called a "pompeux discours" by M. de Bourbonne, the antithesis in the revision is acceptable. The contrast in the emended clause is in keeping with Troubert's peroration; at the same time it suggests Bossuet's style, which was evidently still the model for provincial funeral orations, and yet it does not discredit the great orator as the direct allusion of the original sentence had done. In the second example, however, the contrasts are too exaggerated, too many adjectives are piled up, and the striving for effect is too obvious. Balzac is speaking of the gossips of Tours:

| ... cette congrégation de langues possédait une influence qui devenait terrible quand un intérêt majeur la dirigeait. [2a, 140] | Cette congrégation *oisive et agissante, invisible et voyant tout, muette et parlant sans cesse,* possédait alors une influence que sa nullité rendait en apparence peu nuisible, mais qui cependant devenait terrible quand elle était animée par un intérêt majeur. [*Mame* 384–85+] |

Adjectives are replaced by other qualifying phrases fifty-five times. The total number of variations in which adjectives are concerned reaches the figure of one hundred and eight.

Adverbs are even more frequently involved than adjectives in the vari-

[51] 2a/ms reads "proportions immenses."

ations now under consideration. As opposed to the other parts of speech, however, adverbs are added much more often than they are omitted or substituted. Additions occur one hundred and ten times; omissions, eighteen; and substitutions, twenty-six.

As usual, we find Balzac striving for exactness. This tendency leads him to strike out several adverbial expressions. The following example is a case in point. Mlle Salomon is speaking of the Abbé Birotteau, who has been exiled, really, to the parish on the other side of the Loire from Tours:

Lui qui, depuis ses malheurs, peut à peine marcher, serait obligé de faire une lieue *tous les jours* pour nous voir.
[*2a*, 162]

Lui qui, depuis ses malheurs, peut à peine marcher, serait obligé de faire une lieue pour nous voir.
[*Mame* 410+]

Omissions are sometimes made to avoid repetitions, as when "sans doute," occurring twice in the same sentence, is deleted the second time in the revision (*2a*, 162; *Mame* 408–9+). Repetitions are also avoided by means of substitutions. Thus, in order not to repeat *ici* too often, Balzac uses the phrase "dans ce logement" (*2a*, 129; *Mame* 373+). Vivid phrases replace monotonous terms (*2a*, 129; *Mame* 372+). Other substitutions may be accounted for on the grounds of accuracy (*2a*, 139; *Mame* 384+).

Conjunctions figure prominently in the variations we are now considering. Seventy-three omissions are made, fifty-seven substitutions, and fifty-one additions. The connective most frequently involved is *et*, which is omitted forty-four times and added seventeen. The conjunction *car*, which Balzac struck out many times between the first and second editions of his story, is omitted only five times between the proofs and the Mame edition. It is added five times also at this same stage of the corrections. Both *et* and *car* are usually dropped because Balzac has broken a sentence into shorter components. For example, in the first edition the following sentence becomes two by the omission of *et:* "Le vieux propriétaire voulut voir cette espèce d'acte de renonciation, *et* monsieur Caron le lui apporta" (*2a*, 123; *Mame* 365; *Char.* 62). In the illustration below, the omission of the conjunction *que* gives greater smoothness to the style of the corrected text. Old maids, according to Balzac, are bitter:

... parce qu'un être qui a manqué sa vocation est malheureux; *qu'*il souffre, et *que* la souffrance engendre la méchanceté ...
[*2c*, 339]

... parce qu'un être qui a manqué sa vocation est malheureux; il souffre, et la souffrance engendre la méchanceté.
[*Mame* 338–39+]

The addition of *et* sometimes results in a more rhythmical sentence (*2a*, 126; *Mame* 368; *Béch.* 113). *Car* is inserted more than once to permit

Balzac to fuse transitional remarks into his sentences (2b, 11–12; *Mame* 294; *Béch.* 45). As regards the substitutions, there is a tendency to interchange *et* and *or*. The following case is characteristic. The Abbé Chapeloud used to pay a short visit to Mlle Gamard every evening before dinner:

... *et*, pendant cette espèce de visite polie il lui avait fait durant les douze ans qu'il passa sous son toit les mêmes questions ... [1, 24]	*Or*, durant cette espèce de visite polie, il lui avait fait, pendant les douze années qu'il passa sous son toit, les mêmes questions ...

[Mame 307; Char. 20]

Variations according to other parts of speech are less numerous by far than those which we have been analyzing. They are also less interesting and do not noticeably affect Balzac's style. Of these changes, thirty-nine affect articles; thirty-three, prepositions; and twelve, negatives.

The total number of verbal changes is about eleven hundred and bears witness once again to Balzac's infinite care for detail. Verbs are affected more frequently than any other part of speech. Nouns and conjunctions are varied more often than are the remaining elements. The high ratio of conjunctions is explained by the fact that Balzac made many changes in sentence structure; thus connectives were dropped or added. Adverbs are involved in this group of variations almost as frequently as nouns and conjunctions, while pronouns and adjectives are changed slightly less often. These numerous minute changes are made principally for definiteness and emphasis and contribute as much as any other changes Balzac made to the vividness and exactness of his style in *Le Curé de Tours*.

2. REALISTIC VARIATIONS (BETWEEN THE PROOFS AND THE FIRST EDITION)

a) General realistic qualities.—One way in which Balzac seeks to create the impression of truth is by accuracy of statement. We therefore find him changing a phrase about the Abbé Troubert's "absence totale d'esprit" (2a, 94) to "l'apparence d'un manque total d'esprit" (*Mame* 326; *Char.* 34). "La commisération" (2a, 154) expressed for Mlle Gamard when she falls ill becomes "une feinte commisération" (*Mame* 400). For reasons of truth Balzac sometimes omits an exaggerated statement. For example, the generalization that old maids are "malheureuses dans toutes les affections de leur sexe " (2c, 339–40) does not appear in the *princeps* (339). The phrase "son seul bien" used to describe the Abbé Birotteau's health in 2c (350) is omitted in the first edition (349), obviously because it is not true.

Balzac may harmonize discrepancies in the interest of truth. Mme de Listomère and her friends are the aristocrats of Tours and do not mingle with Mlle Gamard, the daughter of an "espèce de paysan parvenu," and her bourgeois set. Consequently, in revising the following example, Balzac struck out the phrase "et la petite bourgeoisie." He is speaking of the salons of Mme de Listomère, Mlle Merlin de la Blottière, and "autres dévotes en possession de recevoir la société pieuse *et la petite bourgeoisie* de Tours" (*2a*, 84; *Mame* 315). In another example the word "honteuse" is certainly more *vraisemblable* in the mouth of Mme de Listomère than is "sale":

Nous consulterons, nous plaiderons s'il faut plaider, et comme cette affaire est assez *sale* pour mademoiselle Gamard, et peut nuire à l'abbé Troubert, il y aura une transaction. [*2a*, 135]	Nous consulterons des avocats, reprit madame de Listomère, nous plaiderons s'il faut plaider; mais comme cette affaire est assez *honteuse* pour mademoiselle Gamard, et peut nuire à l'abbé Troubert, nous obtiendrons sans doute quelque transaction. [*Mame* 379+]

Balzac makes an effort to weed out discrepancies of time, but he does not always succeed. For example, in the manuscript (p. 4) the Abbé Birotteau has longed for twenty years to become a canon. The twenty years became twelve in a correction on *2b* (p. 2), but a few sentences later we find, even in the *princeps*, that the apartment which Birotteau occupied had been "comme l'était alors le canonicat, l'objet de son envie et son *hoc erat in votis*[52] pendant une *dizaine* d'années" (*Mame* 285–86). It is not until the Béchet edition that Balzac makes this statement accurate by substituting "douzaine" for "dizaine" (*Béch.* 37–38+).

Another tangle involving time is never straightened out. We are never quite sure just when Mlle Gamard first manifested her ill-will toward the Abbé Birotteau or at what time he began to be unhappy under her tyranny. When the story opens, the *abbé* is returning to Mlle Gamard's house, in which, we are told, he has been living for two years. Arriving at his door, he finds himself locked out; but this circumstance is less upsetting than the discovery that there is no fire in his room and that his candlestick and slippers are not in their accustomed places. He realizes, apparently for the first time, that something is wrong. At this point Balzac writes: "Alors il se souvint que depuis environ quinze jours, il était sevré de tous ces petits soins qui lui avaient rendu la vie si douce pendant dix-

___
[52] Italics by Balzac.

huit mois ..." (1, 16; *Mame* 300+).[53] The simple priest, Balzac continues, "venait de reconnaître, un peu tard à la vérité, les signes d'une persécution sourde exercée sur lui depuis environ trois mois par mademoiselle Gamard ..." (1, 18; *Mame* 302+). A little later, however, we learn that "dix-huit mois après l'avoir pris en pension" she hates him and that he has become for her "l'objet d'une persécution sourde et d'une vengeance froidement calculée" (2a, 89;[54] *Mame* 321+). Yet, Balzac, with his love for exact figures, has carefully inserted a little earlier in the first edition a still further conflicting period of time:

Il se coucha dans l'espoir d'éclaircir le lendemain matin la cause de la haine qui devait détruire à jamais le bonheur dont il jouissait après l'avoir si longtems désiré. [1, 20]	Il se coucha dans l'espoir d'éclaircir le lendemain matin la cause de la haine qui devait détruire à jamais ce bonheur dont il avait joui *pendant une douzaine de mois* après l'avoir si longtemps désiré. [*Mame* 304]

This last inconsistency Balzac corrects in the Furne edition, where he changes "une douzaine de mois" to "deux ans" (*Fur.* 11+), a period which conforms with the reader's first impression that Birotteau's unhappiness dates from the very night the novel opens.

However, the author allows still another discrepancy to stand. Toward the end of the story, when the poor vicar is trying to comprehend his fate, we are told that "il se demandait mille fois pourquoi la première année passée chez mademoiselle Gamard ayant été si douce, la seconde était si cruelle" (1, 57;[55] *Mame* 367–68+). These exact references to time are less definite than they seem. Balzac makes no attempt to adjust the conflicting remarks that Mlle Gamard began her persecutions of Birotteau three months, and six months, before the story opens; and he makes only one effort to harmonize the statements that the *abbé* was gay and contented at the beginning of the novel, that his first year only had been happy at Mlle Gamard's, and that his life there had been "douce" for eighteen months. Of course, what Balzac is primarily interested in is not the time, but the effect, of the old maid's persecution of the vicar. He has used exact figures because it is his habit to be specific, not because he was trying to place his psychological problem in an absolutely accurate time-setting.

On the other hand, it was no doubt for the sake of greater probability

[53] There are slight stylistic variations between these two texts.

[54] The prepositional phrases are transposed in 2a.

[55] Variants in the manuscript: "il se demandait *toujours*." The sentence structure is also different.

that Balzac lengthened the time of the denouement. Birotteau is sent to Saint-Symphorien, and *"Cinq* mois après, M. le vicaire-général fut nommé évêque, et madame de Listomère était morte ..." (*Mame* 410+). The original period was "trois mois" (*2a*, 163). At the end of the story, we find in *2a:* "Ce n'était plus que le squelette du Birotteau qui roulait, *six mois auparavant,* si vide, mais si content, à travers le cloître" (*2a*, 164). In the *princeps* Balzac stretches the time to "dix mois" (*Mame* 412; *Char.* 103).

Changes involving sums of money and figures in general are characteristic of Balzac. Between the proofs and the first edition of *Le Curé de Tours,* contrary to his more usual custom of increasing sums of money, he has reduced or omitted several amounts. The first of these changes has to do with Mme de Listomère's wealth: "Tout le monde sut bientôt, dans la ville de Tours, que madame la baronne de Listomère, veuve d'un lieutenant général, *et riche de vingt-quatre mille livres de rente,* recueillait M. l'abbé Birotteau, vicaire de Saint-Gatien" (*2a*, 137). The parenthetical phrase about the income of the baroness is, quite uncharacteristically, simply dropped in the first edition (*Mame* 382+).

Balzac's more general tendency to increase monetary values is illustrated in a difference he makes in the Abbé Birotteau's fortune. In the same passage, contrary to his familiar full inventorial method, he condenses the enumeration of the vicar's possessions. In order to help the vicar in his suit against Mlle Gamard, the nephew of Mme de Listomère has had the *abbé*'s belongings evaluated by a connoisseur:

L'ancien expert du Musée avait estimé la Vierge de Valentin *sept mille francs,* c'était en effet un morceau capital, et le Christ de Lebrun *quatre mille francs;* quant à la bibliothèque et les meubles gothiques, le goût dominant qui s'accroissait de jour en jour à Paris pour ces sortes de choses, leur donnaient une valeur fictive de douze mille francs; mais *l'expert déclara que leur valeur réelle était de six mille francs; et il y avait, en outre selon l'opinion d'un commissaire priseur, pour huit mille francs de livres en égard aux reliures, et pour deux mille francs de meubles.* [2a, 146]	L'ancien expert du Musée avait estimé *onze mille francs* la Vierge du Valentin et le Christ de Lebrun, morceaux d'un beauté capitale; quant à la bibliothèque et aux meubles gothiques, le goût dominant qui s'accroissait de jour en jour à Paris pour ces sortes de choses, leur donnaient une valeur fictive de douze mille francs; mais *enfin l'expert, vérification faite, évalua le mobilier entier à trente mille francs.* [*Mame* 391–92][56]

---

[56] *Béch.* 134–35+ reads "dix mille écus" instead of "trente mille francs."

Changing the value of the *abbé*'s property necessitated another variation a little later. The total having been raised, as we have seen, from 27,000 to 30,000 francs, Balzac omits in the following example the original amount, which has now become inexact:

Or, il était évident que M. Birotteau, n'ayant pas entendu donner à mademoiselle Gamard, *la somme énorme de vingt-sept mille francs*, il y avait judiciairement parlant, lieu à réformer leurs conventions ... [2a, 146]	Or, il était évident que M. Birotteau, n'ayant pas entendu donner à mademoiselle Gamard *cette somme énorme*, il y avait, judiciairement parlant, lieu à réformer leurs conventions ... [*Mame* 392+]

The number of valuable pictures which the vicar inherited is reduced from three to two (2a, 145; *Mame* 390). Balzac's preoccupation with mere numbers is shown in an addition which is too mathematical, although it introduces a good balance: "... il était bien rare que, pendant les sept promenades de la semaine, il ne lui arrivât pas de dire *au moins quatorze fois:* ... (2b, 12; *Mame* 295).

By far the most important variations introduced for the first edition are three *dossiers*. For the first of these we have no proofs; for the other two we have the autograph corrections on 2a.

The first *dossier* is the shortest, but it has the added interest of conveying a clear statement of Balzac's belief in *cognomologie*. It contains also a characteristic reference to the novelist as a historian:

Ici, l'historien serait en droit de crayonner le portrait de cette dame; mais il a pensé que ceux même auxquels la cognomologie de Sterne est inconnue ne pourraient pas prononcer ces trois mots: MADAME DE LISTOMÈRE! ... *sans le la peindre noble, digne, tempérant les rigueurs de la piété par la vieille élégance des dorures monarchiques et classiques, par des manières polies; se permettant la Nouvelle Héloïse, la comédie, et se coiffant encore avec ses cheveux.*

[1, 53; *Mame* 357;[57] *Béch.* 104+]

In the second *dossier* inserted in 2a, Balzac sets before us a well-developed provincial type, M. de Bourbonne, whom he has merely sketched in the manuscript as "un vieux propriétaire qui connaissait le pays" (1, 54). This *dossier* is an excellent example of Balzac's eager effort to give us the biographical and social background of his characters. It is also interesting for its specific references to Tours and the Tourangeaux:

[57] Here and hereafter, italics *throughout* a quotation mean that the whole passage is lacking from the first text noted and is an addition *en bloc* in the second text; the first reference (of two or more references in one parenthesis) applies merely to *locus*, or context, and is given to permit verification.

In the present case Balzac italicized *cognomologie* and *Nouvelle Héloïse*.

Ce vieux propriétaire, nommé M. de Bourbonne, résumait toutes les idées de la province aussi complètement que Voltaire a résumé l'esprit de son époque. C'était un homme sec et maigre, professant en matière d'habillement toute l'indifférence d'un propriétaire [1] dont la valeur territoriale est cotée dans son [2] département. Sa physionomie, tannée par le soleil de laTouraine, était moins spirituelle que fine. Habitué à peser ses paroles, à combiner ses actions, il cachait sa profonde circonspection sous une simplicité trompeuse. Aussi fallait-il une légère observation [3] pour s'apercevoir que, semblable à un paysan de Normandie, il avait toujours l'avantage dans toutes les affaires. Il était très supérieur en œnologie, la science favorite des Tourangeaux; et, comme il avait su arrondir les prairies de sa terre aux dépens des laisses de la Loire en évitant tout procès avec le domaine de l'Etat, il passait pour un homme de talent [4]. Si, charmé par la conversation de M. de Bourbonne [5], vous eussiez demandé ce qu'il était à quelque Tourangeau:

—Oh! *c'est un vieux malin!* ...

Etait la réponse proverbiale faite par tous ses jaloux [6], car, en Touraine, la jalousie forme, comme dans la plupart des provinces, le fonds de la langue [7].

[*Mame* 359–60][58]

The third *dossier* is interesting from several points of view. It is that of a "good" *vieille fille*. Mlle Salomon, the friend of Birotteau, offsets Mlle Gamard, his vindictive enemy. If we examine this long addition, we find that it parallels the disquisition on unloving and unloved old maids and the *dossier* on Mlle Gamard—passages which Balzac carefully re-wrote for 2a, as we have seen. Generalizations on the "good" type contrast with those on the "mean" species. Then we are told that Mlle Salomon is an illustration of the noble old maid, as we have been told that Mlle Gamard's eyes betray her distorted nature. Next come details on each old maid and, last, the attitude of each toward Birotteau.

The most striking part of this *dossier*, however, is the allusion to the unfortunate Louis Lambert, whom Mlle Salomon was to have married. Although the suitor's name is not given, his identity is unmistakable. He became insane, we are told, and his fiancée consecrated herself to his care until the day of his death. Mlle Salomon de Villenoix is, then, one of Balzac's first reappearing characters, although at this stage of the story Balzac has not worked out the time interval between *Louis Lambert* and

[58] Variations in 2a/ms, 120–21: (1) "la profonde indifférence du propriétaire"; (2) "le"; (3) "de l'observation"; (4) "il paraissait un homme de génie"; (5) "charmé de sa conversation"; (6) "de ses jaloux," *faite* does not occur; (7) "provinces, une maladie permanente." The sentence structure is also different. The italics are found in the text. Such differences as occur in the succeeding editions have been discussed under their proper categories.

Le Curé de Tours, and he makes Mlle Salomon too old.[59] This *dossier* is so important that it must be given here, as it first appeared:

Dans la *citta dolente* des vieilles filles, il s'en rencontre beaucoup, surtout en France, dont la vie est un sacrifice noblement offert tous les jours à de nobles sentimens. Les unes restent fièrement [1] fidèles à un cœur que la mort leur a trop promptement ravi; et [2] martyres de l'amour, trouvent le secret d'être femmes par l'âme. Les autres, obéissant à un orgueil de famille, qui, chaque

[59] Cf. A. Canfield, "Les Personnages reparaissants dans la *Comédie humaine*," *Revue d'histoire littéraire*, XLI (1934), 17. Mr. Canfield says: "[Balzac] semble ne s'être souvenu que vaguement de Pauline [de Villenoix] en décrivant la 'vieille fille' du *Curé de Tours*." And he adds later: "Il est évident que Mademoiselle de Villenoix, en reparaissant dans le *Curé de Tours*, ne joue nullement le rôle des personnages reparaissants qui rappellent un groupe de personnages connus et représentent un milieu social. D'ailleurs, les deux romans en question sont tous deux de 1832, et personne n'a songé à faire remonter l'origine de ce procédé au delà de 1833." One cannot deny, however, that Mlle Salomon contributes to that impression of solidity which Balzac sought to give his social order, nor can one be too sure that Balzac remembered her only vaguely when he put her in *Le Curé de Tours*. Had she really been thought out as a character of *Louis Lambert* when Balzac was correcting *C.T.* 2a? In our manuscript the connection with Louis Lambert does not, of course, exist. In 2a, however, he has added the details to which Mr. Canfield objects but which are, with one exception, explained by the fact that Balzac thought of her at this time as a much older woman than she is in *Louis Lambert*. He writes: "... pendant vingt années, elle s'était avec le courage de l'amour, consacrée au bonheur mécanique de ce malheureux" (2a, 127). Since *Le Curé de Tours* is dated April, 1832, and appeared in May of that year, and since *Louis Lambert* is dated June–July, 1832, and appeared in October, 1832 (Lov., *Hist.*, p. 190), it may well be that Balzac had not yet thoroughly conceived *Louis Lambert* when he was correcting 2a. He therefore makes Mlle Salomon too old for her role in *Louis Lambert*. He also makes her a member of the aristocratic set of Tours, whereas, as Mr. Canfield points out, in *Louis Lambert* provincial prejudice excludes her from noble society. In the first edition of *Louis Lambert* Balzac writes: "Mais l'origine de mademoiselle de Villenoix et les préjugés que l'on conserve en province contre les Juifs, ne lui permettaient pas, malgré sa fortune et celle de son tuteur, d'être reçu dans cette société toute exclusive qui s'appelle, à tort ou à raison, la Noblesse" (*Notice biographique sur Louis Lambert, Nouveaux Contes philosophiques* [1832], p. 363). But in the manuscript of our story Mlle Salomon is, at first, just *une autre vieille fille* who comes to see Mlle Gamard. It is in the corrections in 2a (see p. 239) that her visits are paid to the *abbé*, who is an old friend, and that she is said to belong to the aristocratic group. One would have to compare the manuscripts of the two novels in order to work out the genesis of Mlle Salomon's role, but it looks as though Balzac introduced a rather shadowy Mlle Salomon in *Le Curé de Tours* (1), and then set her solidly on her feet in 2a both as a friend of Birotteau and as the woman beloved of Louis Lambert. When he later thought out her role more completely for *Louis Lambert* she was too integral a part of the plot of *Le Curé de Tours* to be greatly changed there; so he merely made her younger in his effort to harmonize the two stories more accurately.

jour, déchoit à notre honte, se dévouent à la fortune d'un frère, ou à des neveux orphelins; celles-là se font mères en restant vierges. Mais en consacrant les sentimens de la femme au culte du malheur, ces vieilles filles atteignent à tout l'héroïsme de leur sexe, et en idéalisant, pour ainsi dire, la destination, en renonçant aux récompenses et n'en acceptant que les peines. Elles vivent alors entourées de la splendeur de leur dévouement, et les hommes inclinent respectueusement la tête devant leurs traits flétris. Mademoiselle de Sombreuil n'a été ni femme, ni fille; elle fut et sera la poésie vivante.

Or, mademoiselle Salomon appartenait à ces créatures [3] héroïques, et son dévouement était religieusement sublime, en ce qu'il devait être sans gloire, après avoir été une souffrance de tous les jours. Belle, jeune, elle fut aimée, elle aima. Le jeune homme dont elle devait être la femme perdit la raison. Pendant vingt années, elle s'était, avec le courage de l'amour, consacrée au bonheur mécanique de ce malheureux, dont elle avait assez épousé la folie pour ne plus y croire.

C'était, du reste, une personne simple de manières, franche de langage, et dont le visage pâle ne manquait pas de physionomie, malgré l'irrégularité de ses traits. Elle ne parlait jamais des événemens de sa vie; mais, parfois, les tressaillemens soudains qui lui échappaient en entendant le récit d'une aventure ou affreuse ou triste, révélaient en elle les belles qualités que développent les grandes douleurs. Elle était venue habiter Tours, après avoir perdu son compagnon; et, ne pouvant y être appréciée à sa juste valeur, elle passait pour une *bonne personne*. Elle faisait beaucoup de bien; et s'attachant, par goût, aux êtres faibles, le pauvre vicaire lui avait inspiré naturellement un profond intérêt.

[*Mame* 368–70][60]

Balzac, as we know, liked to cite documents. Thus he has, in *Le Curé de Tours*, quoted the full text of a legal agreement between Mlle Gamard and the Abbé Birotteau. This document is made more specific and more binding by three additions inserted in *2a*. The first of these limits the time during which the Abbé Birotteau may pay less than Mlle Gamard usually receives from her lodgers: "... attendu qu'il reconnaît être hors d'état de donner *pendant plusieurs années* le prix payé par les pensionnaires de la demoiselle Gamard ..." (*2a*, 133; *Mame* 377+). The second addition is a part of the clause on which Birotteau's lawyer will later accuse Mlle Gamard of intention to defraud his client:

60 Variants in *2a*/ms, 126–27: (1) "fièrement" does not occur; (2) "et" does not occur; (3) "était une de ces créatures." The sentences are longer also. The italics are found in the text.

Variants in the editions: This passage is considerably changed stylistically in Béchet. Additional stylistic variations are made for the Furne. One realistic variation is made in Béchet, where "vingt ans" becomes "cinq ans" (114).

... ledit Birotteau s'engage à laisser à mademoiselle Gamard à titre d'indemnité, le mobilier dont il se trouvera possesseur ... [2a, 133]

... et eu égard à diverses avances faites par ladite soussignée, ledit Birotteau s'engage à lui laisser à titre d'indemnité le mobilier dont il se trouvera possesseur ... [Mame 377+]

The third insertion, involving time again, gives Mlle Gamard more strength with which to strike her enemy, a power which we understand later in the story: "... lorsque, par telle cause que ce soit, il viendrait à quitter volontairement, *et à telle époque que ce puisse être,*[61] les lieux à lui présentement loués ..." (2a, 134; Mame 377–78).

Balzac's sociological intention is one of his salient realistic qualities. In an aside inserted in 2a, 90+ of our story, he calls himself an "historien exact," and in the *Avant-propos* he speaks of himself as "copiant toute la Société."[62] One of his fundamental ideas is, as we have seen, that of the *espèces sociales*. And one of his most characteristic traits is his habit of generalizing about these same groups or about the larger social order of which they are a part.

In *Le Curé de Tours* the first emphasis is, of course, on *les célibataires*. We have seen that Balzac, in inserting Mlle Salomon's *dossier* in 2a, added generalizations about the "good" *vieille fille* (2a/ms, 126–27+). In reworking the passage about the old maids of Mlle Gamard's type he omitted one such general remark: "La femme qui n'a pas été instruite par l'amour dans le grand art de plaire, n'en connaît l'usage, ni les ressources" (2a, 102–3). We learn that to forgive a passion must be "moins facile à un prêtre" (Mame 292+) than merely to divine it (2b, 10). Apropos of the Abbé Birotteau's innocence of the world and its *mœurs*, we are told, in an addition in Mame, why he would never understand the secret motives of Mlle Gamard's hatred of him: "*Il n'y a qu'un homme de génie ou un intrigant qui se disent:—J'ai eu tort! ... parce que l'intérêt et le talent sont les seuls conseillers consciencieux et lucides*" (1, 20; Mame 304+).

The second sociological purpose of the novel is to depict the provincial scene. This particular scene Balzac knew very well, and he added at this stage of his story a number of thrusts at the Tourangeaux as typical provincials.

We have seen (p. 233) that in the *dossier* of M. de Bourbonne "le vieux malin" is characterized as a man who "résumait toutes les idées de la province" and who "semblable à un paysan de Normandie avait toujours

[61] 2a/ms reads here "que ce soit"; Béch. 122+ reads "que ce soit."
[62] Con. I, xxxii.

l'avantage dans toutes les affaires" (*2a*, 120). The daily conversations of Mlle Gamard and of Birotteau offer "une peinture achevée de la vie toute béotienne des provinciaux" (*Mame* 333+) rather than merely a picture of "la vie des niais" (*2a*, 109). "La monotonie d'une vie provinciale" is stressed between *2c* (344) and Mame (344+). The conspiracy against the Abbé Birotteau becomes in Mame "cette intrigue si bien en harmonie avec la vie de province" (1, 53; *Mame* 357+). At first Balzac writes that Mme de Listomère's friends "commençaient à s'amuser de cette intrigue jetée dans le vide de leur vie provinciale" (*2a*, 122), but later he emphasizes the empty boredom of their life in the provinces by substituting for "s'amuser" the stronger expression, "se passionner" (*Mame* 362+). The shrewd presentiment which tells these aristocrats that they must fight Troubert as well as Mlle Gamard is characterized in an addition in the *princeps* as "un instinct provincial" (*2a*, 136; *Mame* 380+). The self-interest of this same provincial group is brought out in a substitution which accentuates social, rather than personal, implications. When the Abbé Birotteau's aristocratic friends are urging him to sue Mlle Gamard and are promising him their support, the "vieux malin" takes him aside and says to him:

Des quatorze personnes qui sont ici, vous n'en aurez pas une pour vous, dans quinze jours, et si vous avez besoin de quelqu'un, vous ne trouverez guère que moi *qui puisse vous rendre service, parce que je n'ai jamais laissé à personne de prise sur moi, et que je défierais même Troubert de me causer la moindre peine.* [*2a*, 136]	Des quatorze personnes qui sont ici ... il n'y en aura pas une pour vous dans quinze jours! Alors, si vous avez besoin d'appeler quelqu'un à votre secours, vous ne trouverez peut-être que moi *d'assez hardi pour prendre votre défense, parceque je connais la province, les hommes, les choses, et mieux que cela encore, les intérêts.* [*Mame* 380+]

Provincial jealousy is stressed, as we have seen, in the *dossier* on M. de Bourbonne. It is "tous ses jaloux" who call him "le vieux malin," jealousy being in Touraine, as in most of the provinces, "le fonds de la langue." The phrase "tous ses jaloux" is further emphasized in Béchet by the addition of "et il en avait beaucoup" (*Béch.* 106+).

The gossip of Tours is scored in several variations. In Mame the Abbé Troubert speaks of "les médisances de la ville" (*Mame* 319+).[63] Mlle Salomon is worried by "les suppositions et les calomnies" (*Mame* 361+) that are repeated against Birotteau in Mlle de La Blottière's salon. The passage recounting the ramified activities of the gossips who supply the

[63] This addition does not occur in *2a*, our only proof for this passage.

silent Troubert with the information he wants for the Congrégation is fully re-written (2a, 138-41; Mame 382-86).

Other additions tell us that Touraine is "un pays où personne ne veut se déranger, même pour aller chercher un plaisir" (1, 52; Mame 354+); that the "science favorite des Tourangeaux" is "œnologie" (2a/ms, 121; Mame 359+); and that the heroic Mlle Salomon cannot be appreciated "à sa juste valeur" (2a/ms, 127; Mame 370+) in Tours.

This concludes our study of Balzac's general realistic traits, as they are exemplified in the variations between the proofs and the first edition. Although the total number (forty-nine) is not large, these changes contribute important features to our story.

Eleven variants illustrate Balzac's ideal of truth. Exaggerated statements are toned down, and discrepancies are harmonized. Conflicting periods of time are made to conform when they are essential to the impression of truth.

Although his bent toward materialism led Balzac to increase one sum of money between the proofs and Mame, we find that he has also omitted two amounts and shortened an enumeration of personal property. There is, then, no exaggeration in these variants.

Variations involving dossiers and documents are significant. The most important changes introduced for the first edition were the dossiers. Two of these are masterly examples of Balzac's skill in presenting his characters and their background en bloc. Pertinent additions to a contract attest to Balzac's accurate knowledge of the law and to his care in the use of legal terminology.

The sociological changes, totaling twenty-six, are the most numerous of these realistic alterations. Generalizations concerning priests and old maids as types are introduced. Variations stressing the dulness and smallness of provincial life add more than one darkening touch to the story. The importance of gossip in small communities is emphasized in several changes, while others score the laziness of the Tourangeaux. In short, the picture of life in Tours, that is, in the provinces, becomes less flattering with each change. Finally, among the sociological changes are several comparisons of Balzacian characters to historical personages. Thus Balzac links effectively his world to society in its full scope.

b) Technical elements.—We know that Balzac had some difficulty in getting this story under way; witness the *brouillons* discussed above (pp. 192 ff.). He seems, too, to have been somewhat uncertain at first as to the role of Mlle Salomon—a role of considerable importance to the exposition and the plot. Through the first proof the Abbé Birotteau makes her acquaintance in Mlle Gamard's salon, where she is a frequent guest; yet she is spoken of as a member of the exclusive noble set of Tours (*2a*, 82, 87). When, however, Balzac corrected *2a*, he had Mlle Salomon, as we know her, clearly in mind. We know that he inserted her *dossier* at this time. By means of this *dossier* Balzac created, as we have observed, a certain balance in the particular social scene he was depicting.

The author also introduced a few variations in the exposition of his story which change the relationship of Mlle Salomon to Mlle Gamard and the vicar. She now comes to the former's home because of her friendship for Birotteau:

Une autre vieille fille *étant venue voir Mademoiselle Gamard ...* [2*a*, 82]	Une autre vieille fille, *amie de Birotteau, nommée mademoiselle Salomon de Villenoix, étant venue le voir ...* [*Mame* 312+]

Her aristocratic connections are stressed and explain Mlle Gamard's great pride in her visits:

Ses paroles furent d'autant plus humblement altières et abondamment doucereuses, que mademoiselle Salomon de Villenoix appartenant [1] à la société la plus aristocratique de Tours, elle [Mlle Gamard] triomphait de l'avoir chez elle, [2] quoique mademoiselle Salomon y vînt uniquement [3] par amitié pour le vicaire.   [*Mame* 314+][64]

Balzac made, in all, four changes dealing with Mlle Salomon in his exposition. They seem to bring out more clearly the gulf between the aristocratic and the bourgeois circles of the two old maids, and they add to the reader's understanding of Mlle Gamard's bitter revenge. The greater her success has been, the deeper is her disappointment at the failure of her salon.

The exposition as a whole is long, as Balzac's introductions tend to be. To explain this length he added, in correcting *2a*, an aside in which he reiterates the necessity for exactness on the part of the novelist:

... les événemens qui constituent en quelque sorte l'avant-scène de ce drame de bas étage, mais où les sentimens dont la vie humaine est agitée, se retrouvent tout aussi violens que s'ils étaient excités par de grands intérêts, *ont exigé cette espèce d'introduction, dont il était difficile à un historien exact de resserrer les développemens nécessaires.*   [*Mame* 322]

[64] Variants in *2a*/ms: (1) "appartenait"; (2) this clause does not occur; (3) "et consentait à venir chez elle" instead of "quoique ... uniquement."

The explanation replaced a simple prepositional phrase, "sur un théâtre élevé," in 2a, 90. Two interesting variations are introduced in this passage in later editions. In Béchet, Balzac lays further stress on the importance of detail in the novel by substituting for "les développemens nécessaires" the phrase "les minutieux développements" (*Béch.* 72+). In Furne "ce drame de bas étage" becomes "ce drame bourgeois" (*Fur.* 19+), a change which suggests perhaps the significance which Balzac attached to *conditions*.

With regard to characterization we have already seen that Balzac introduced three important *dossiers* at this stage of *Le Curé de Tours* (cf. above, pp. 232–35). The importance which he attached to the name of a character is brought out in the first of these, that of Mme de Listomère. Those of M. de Bourbonne and of Mlle Salomon are excellent examples of Balzac's method of giving his reader, in a block, both the biographical and the sociological background of his characters.

The *dossier* is not, however, Balzac's only method for standing his characters on their feet. One effective device which he uses is that of scattered detail. This detail he frequently accumulates and harmonizes around a keynote, or, as we say in the case of his monomaniacs, around a ruling passion. A number of variations between the proofs and the first edition are due to scattered changes in detail which build up the characters both physically and psychologically.

Mlle Gamard's driving passion is her ambition. We therefore find Balzac substituting for "la vieille fille" (2a, 84) the specific "l'ambitieuse Gamard" (*Mame* 315+). The deep-rooted sense of inferiority which torments this woman is well brought out in the following change:

... elle dit à ses bonnes amies en sortant de Saint-Gatien que les personnes qui désiraient la voir pouvaient bien venir, le soir chez elle ... [2a, 84–85]	... un soir, en sortant de Saint-Gatien, elle dit aux bonnes amies, *dont elle se considérait comme l'esclave jusqu'alors,* que les personnes qui désiraient la voir, pouvaient bien venir une fois par semaine chez elle ... [*Mame* 314+]

Her egotism is illustrated by an addition in the Mame edition, where we are told that the Abbé Chapeloud was always, every day, "sûr de caresser toutes les vanités de la vieille fille" (1, 24–26; *Mame* 308+).

Balzac emphasizes the Abbé Birotteau's passion for Chapeloud's possessions by changing it from a mere "convoitise" (2c, 285) to a "concupiscence mobilière" (*Mame* 287+). The simple goodness of the vicar is stressed in an early addition: "Mais le bon vicaire n'ayant pas en lui des qualités qui pussent contraster avec les défauts de son hôtesse, fut obligé, pour les reconnaître et pour en être choqué, de subir la douleur, ce cruel avertissement donné par la nature à toutes ses créations" (*2a*/ms, 86;[65] *Mame* 317). This same trait of the vicar is further stressed in a revision in which, "voulant que tout le monde fût heureux" (*2a*, 95; *Mame* 329+), Birotteau tells Troubert that the latter will soon be living in the archbishop's palace. Birotteau's love of comfort is brought out by the addition of a prepositional phrase in the *princeps*: "Puis, il resta, *selon son habitude*, plongé dans les rêvasseries somnolescentes pendant lesquelles Marianne avait coutume de lui allumer du feu" (*2a*, 91; *Mame* 323+). Another variation emphasizes the same desire for creature comforts:

Mademoiselle Gamard vue de loin et à travers le prisme du *bonheur idéal* qu'il avait rêvé près d'elle lui semblait une créature parfaite ... [*2a*, 181]	Mademoiselle Gamard, vue de loin, et à travers le prisme des *félicités matérielles* qu'il avait rêvé de goûter près d'elle, lui semblait une créature parfaite ... [*Mame* 311+]

Love of ease was also a dominant trait of the clever Abbé Chapeloud. Balzac's use of concrete detail to bring out a psychological trait is well illustrated in the following addition, which appears *en bloc* in Mame. Chapeloud is speaking:

Voilà vivre! ... N'avoir rien à chercher, pas même ses pantoufles! ... Trouver toujours bon feu, bonne table ... Enfin, mon soufflet m'impatientait, parce qu'il avait de larynx embarrassé ... Je ne m'en suis pas plaint deux fois ... le lendemain, elle m'a donné un très joli soufflet, et cette paire de badines avec lesquelles vous me voyez tisonner! ...   [*Mame* 295–96+][66]

The adjective "adroit" is added in Mame to the description of Chapeloud as an "égoiste spirituel" (1, 22; *Mame* 306+). The wily canon avoids taking his suppers at Mlle Gamard's (1, 24). An added detail in Mame gives us his reason for doing so and emphasizes his adroit selfishness:

... il avait évité *le souper* en prenant tous les soirs du thé dans les maisons où il allait passer ses soirées ... [1, 24]	... il avait évité *les ennuis du souper* en prenant tous les soirs du thé dans les maisons où il allait passer ses soirées ... [*Mame* 307+]

A few touches are added to Troubert's character. His persistence is suggested in an addition in Mame where he is called "fidèle et patient"

---

[65] The manuscript correction reads "l'avertissement" and "une douleur." The whole addition forms a lengthy clause in *2a*/ms.

[66] We have no proof for this addition. *2b*, the only extant proof for this part of the story, stops just before Chapeloud's speech.

(*2a*, 83; *Mame* 314+). When the dispossessed Birotteau enters his former apartment, Troubert's "air sardonique" reveals to him at long last the full measure of Troubert's perseverance and hatred. The adjective is an insertion in the first edition (*2a*, 128; *Mame* 371+). Troubert's love of power and his egotism are made more prominent in the following thoroughgoing revision, which concerns Mme de Listomère's call on the man she must conciliate:

[Troubert] *ne fut pas insensible peut-être au plaisir de la recevoir* dans la bibliothèque *de Troubert*[67] et au coin de cette cheminée ornée des deux fameux tableaux. *Elle dut sans doute à ce sentiment, le succès de sa demande.* [*2a*, 154]	*Flatté peut-être de voir* dans la bibliothèque *de Chapeloud*, et au coin de cette cheminée ornée des deux fameux tableaux, *une femme qui l'avait méconnu, Troubert fit attendre la baronne un moment, puis consentit à la recevoir.* [*Mame* 401][68]

Voice and gesture are often indicative of character with Balzac. One addition illustrates the use of voice in this way. When Mlle Gamard disdainfully remarks that the Abbé Birotteau rarely reads his "gros livres," the vicar answers by inquiring about her health "d'une voix flûtée" (*2a*, 97; *Mame* 330+). Nothing could be more indicative of the *abbé*'s timidity than the added detail about his voice.

Gesture is used to stress the character of M. de Bourbonne. His decisive manner of closing his snuffbox or of putting it down is a *tic* that harmonizes with his quick mind and wary nature. It is a language that even the naïve Birotteau understands. Mme de Listomère has just remarked that, since the vicar proposes to leave Mlle Gamard's apartment, there is no inconvenience in signing a legal statement to that effect:

—Cela est juste! ... dit le propriétaire en fermant sa tabatière; mais il est toujours dangereux d'écrire ... [1, 56]	—Cela est juste! ... dit M. de Bourbonne en fermant sa tabatière *par un geste sec dont il est impossible de rendre le langage télégraphique.* Mais il est toujours dangereux d'écrire, *ajouta-t-il en posant sa tabatière sur la cheminée, d'un air à effrayer le vicaire.* [*Mame* 364; *Char.* 61]

We have seen how voice and gesture are used by Balzac to stress character. Detail regarding costume may also be used to keynote a personality. Mlle Gamard's drab appearance is indicative of her uninteresting

---

[67] Balzac corrects this slip on *2a*.

[68] The last phrase is changed in *Béch.* 147, as we shall see.

nature. In the following variation the substituted adjective suggests not only the color but the uniformity of a nun's habit, and the reader's sense of the monotony of Mlle Gamard's dress is at once heightened:

Sa robe, *de couleur puce*, et de taffetas en été, de mérinos en hiver ... [*2c*, 341]

Sa robe, de taffetas en été, de mérinos en hiver, *mais toujours couleur carmélite* ... [*Mame* 334+]

Details of physical appearance may be used in the harmonizing of a personality. In the following example the added information concerning Mlle Gamard's thinness is a case in point:

[Sa robe] ... lui serrait sa taille et les bras. [*2c*, 341][69]

... serrait sa taille *disgracieuse* et ses bras *maigres*. [*Mame* 341]

Having added these details to the physical portrait of Mlle Gamard, Balzac took out two others: "Elle avait le pied gros et la main desséchée" (*2c*, 341; *Mame* 341). Omission of detail is so unusual that it is always striking. However, the graceless figure and thin arms are more evocative than a dried-up hand and would justify the omission of the latter detail. Perhaps, too, Balzac thought that the old maid's large feet could be surmised from her peasant origin.

One other similar addition is interesting because it shows us Balzac's desire to explain a physical characteristic by a psychological cause and also because it increases our impression of Mlle Gamard's tonelessness: "A dix-huit ans, elle avait pu être fraîche et grasse, mais il ne lui restait aucune trace ni de la blancheur ni des couleurs qu'elle se vantait d'avoir eues; *et les tons de sa chair avaient contracté une teinte blafarde assez commune chez les dévotes*" (*2c*, 342;[70] *Mame* 341+).

Usually descriptions of the milieu are varied from the proofs to the first edition by means of added details. There are many examples, of which we can mention only a few. We are not told at first, for example, that the chairs which Chapeloud buys are carved: "Puis, le chanoine eut assez de goût pour chercher et trouver de vieux fauteuils en bois de noyer *sculpté* ..." (*2c*, 287; *Mame* 289+). *Le petit pavé* (1, 12) on which the wooden shoes of Mlle Gamard's servant clack is called "caillouteux" in Mame (298+). The noise of the shoes seems at once louder to the reader!

[69] Balzac's autograph corrections here read "*une* taille disgracieuse" and "*des* bras maigres."

[70] The text of *2c* reads: "... elle avait dû être ... mais il ne restait ... ." "Pu" and "lui" are marginal corrections. The added autograph clause reads "*car* les tons" and "*avaient cette* teinte ..." (*2c*/ms).

Mlle Gamard's house bore a close architectural resemblance to Saint-Gatien. We learn, moreover, in the *princeps* that "[cette maison] avait toujours été occupée par des abbés ..." (*2c*, 283; *Mame* 285+). This added clause is characteristic of Balzac's tendency to tell us all he knew about a person or thing, to clutter his descriptions with information. However, by means of this insertion the house takes on a certain realistic solidity, a character which tells us as much about it as do the architectural details and which harmonizes with the events in the story. It is perhaps less important that the supplementary feature seems to be based on actual fact[71] than that it creates an impression of reality.

Another variant between the proofs and the *princeps* illustrates the use of an added detail for both realistic and psychological effect. In the passage describing Mlle Gamard's *salon jaune*, Balzac inserts between *2c* and the first edition the remark that the room was "digne d'elle" (*2c*, 343; *Mame* 343+). The addition is important, since it stresses the *coquille* idea—the room and the hostess explain each other.

In correcting this novel for the first edition Balzac made no large changes for technical reasons. The only alteration affecting the plot was the easily accomplished change in the role of Mlle Salomon. Accentuating her friendship for the Abbé Birotteau set in higher relief Mlle Gamard's hatred of him and of his aristocratic friends. Variations affecting the characters occur twenty-two times. In each case additional detail is introduced to make the characterization more explicit. Descriptions are enriched by this same method. Thus the milieu becomes more exact, and "things" are more and more concretely visualized. The salient feature of the technical corrections between the proofs and Mame is, then, the use of supplementary detail. This device accounts for all but five of the variations which derive from Balzac's technique.

C. CHANGES BETWEEN THE SEVERAL EDITIONS
I. STYLISTIC VARIATIONS

Balzac's constant effort to improve his style is amply illustrated in the changes he introduced in the text of *Le Curé de Tours* from edition to edition. These variations are of the same character as those which we have studied for the other stages of the novel; consequently, we shall mention in our present discussion only the most striking and the most frequently occurring changes.[72]

[71] See Miss Marhofer's study in Dargan, Crain, and Others, *op. cit.*, p. 98.

[72] This study has been made independently of Maurice Allem's edition of *Le Curé de Tours* (Paris: Garnier Frères, 1937), which lists the variants between Mame and

a) According to sentence structure.—Although for the Furne edition Balzac several times combines two sentences into one, his more pronounced tendency to break up sentences continues from text to text. There are one hundred and forty-five cases of shortened sentences in the Béchet text alone. In one instance a single overcrowded sentence of the manuscript has become seven separate elements in the 1834 edition.[73] The original sentence comprised the whole of Troubert's cold reply to the Abbé Birotteau when the vicar returned to his former apartment to claim his furniture.

The most frequent changes in sentence structure occur in dependent clauses. We find a number of examples of the characteristic reduction of a clause to a participial phrase:

Madame de Listomère retourna chez elle, espérant que l'archevêque achèverait l'ouvrage *qu'elle avait* si heureusement *commencé* ...	Madame de Listomère retourna chez elle, espérant que l'archevêque consommerait une œuvre de paix si heureusement *commencée.*
[*Mame* 405]	[*Béch.* 155+]

The opposite change, however, from participial phrase to clause, also occurs (*Char.* 1; *Fur.* 1+). Relative clauses introduced by *dont* are changed to *qui* or *que* constructions in several instances in the 1843 edition. The change does not seem especially significant, except for the fact that Balzac was always self-conscious about his *donts:*

... écoutant et cherchant à comprendre le sens des rapides paroles *dont tout le monde était prodigue.* [*Char.* 61]	... écoutant et cherchant à comprendre le sens des rapides paroles *que tout le monde prodiguait.* [*Fur.* 37+]

These examples will suffice to illustrate the most typical changes which Balzac made in sentence structure for the various editions of our novel. The total number of changes involving sentence structure is one hundred and forty-five.

b) According to rhetorical devices.—The most obvious case of amplification is the long passage (see below, p. 267) added by Balzac after the *princeps* to the end of the story. This passage expands and elaborates the

---

Conard. The present analysis is, by its very nature, much more detailed. I find, too, that sometimes M. Allem does not include all the variants. For example, he does not note on his p. 3, l. 18, "la" (*Béch.; Char.*) for "cette"; p. 7, l. 24, "l'humble ami" (*Mame; Béch.; Char.*) for "le camarade"; p. 9, l. 4, "lui" (*Mame; Béch.; Char.*) for "à Birotteau"; p. 9, l. 22, "il" (*Mame; Béch; Char.*) for "celui-ci"; p. 25, ll. 31–32, "un homme difficultueux" (*Mame*), etc.

[73] These sentences may be located in *Con.*, IX, 220, ll. 9–22.

idea of the final sentence: "Or, nous vivons à une époque où le défaut des gouvernemens est d'avoir fait la société moins pour l'homme, que l'homme pour la société" (*Mame* 413+). From the point of view of style the passage is badly written. Moreover, it makes the ending of the book cumbersome and uninteresting. Amplifications of the more usual sort may be illustrated in the following elaboration, which emphasizes the naïveté of the Abbé Birotteau, who was "toute expansion":

... s'amusant *de tout avec simplicité.*	... et s'amusait *d'une bagatelle avec la*
[*Mame* 325]	*simplicité d'un homme sans fiel, ni malice.* [*Bêch.* 74-75+]

Additions are especially important between the *princeps* and the Béchet edition. Two long passages, fifty-five sentences, and forty-two shorter additions were inserted in the 1834 volume. One of the passages is the long conclusion we have just mentioned. The other is largely dialogue and will be considered under that heading. Seventeen of the sentences are the parenthetical thoughts introduced in the conversation between Mme de Listomère and Troubert (see below, p. 268). The rest are scattered throughout the story and deal primarily with the Abbé Birotteau's naïveté, M. de Bourbonne's astute worldly wisdom, the self-interest of the Listomères, and Troubert's relentless hatred of Birotteau (*Bêch.* 97, 100–101, 105, 143, 145, 146, 148, 160). Generalizations account for two sentences: one on the church, another on the price man pays for his ambitions; philology is the subject of still a third addition (*Bêch.* 129-30, 144, 162). Stylistically, the longer additions are used as transitions, for emphasis, or to round off and complete a paragraph. For example, Balzac introduced the following transitional sentences in order to explain the intercalated thoughts in the interview between Mme de Listomère and Troubert:

Quelques dessinateurs se sont amusés à représenter en caricature le contraste fréquent qui existe entre *ce que l'on dit* et *ce que l'on pense.*[74] Ici, pour bien saisir l'intérêt du duel de paroles qui eut lieu entre le prêtre et la grande dame, il est nécessaire de dévoiler les pensées qu'ils cachèrent mutuellement sous des phrases en apparence insignifiantes.   [*Bêch.* 148+]

Repetitions are extremely rare in this novel, but we find Balzac inserting one in Béchet in order to stress a situation. When Mme de Listomère explains to the Abbé Birotteau the measures which must be taken to combat Troubert's power, the vicar, in his consternation, repeats one of her

[74] The italics are found in the text.

remarks to himself: *"Et, peut-être avec le secours de Monseigneur l'archevêque pourra-t-on en finir!"*[75] (*Béch.* 145+). In the following example the original sentence was an interpolation which interrupted the narration of Birotteau's awakening sense of doom. The addition not only continues the figure of speech fittingly, but it also concludes the paragraph logically. Balzac, in speaking of Mlle Gamard's cruelty to Birotteau, says of old maids of her type:

Elles égratignent à la manière des chats; et non seulement elles blessent, mais elles éprouvent du plaisir à blesser, et à faire voir à leur victime qu'elles l'ont blessée. [*Mame* 302]	Elles égratignent à la manière des chats. Puis, non-seulement elles blessent, mais elles éprouvent du plaisir à blesser, et à faire voir à leur victime qu'elles l'ont blessée. *Un homme du monde ne se serait pas laissé griffer deux fois; mais le bon Birotteau avait besoin de plusieurs coups de patte dans la figure, avant de croire à une intention méchante.* [*Béch.* 53+]

Shorter additions occur frequently. They serve, as usual, to explain and clarify (*Mame* 375–76; *Béch.* 120; *Fur.* 41). Balzac may use these short insertions for technical emphasis. In the following example the italicized phrase is an addition in Béchet. Mme de Listomère's nephew is forced by Troubert to sue Birotteau, and we are told: *"Quelques jours après l'exploit introductif d'instance*, le baron fut nommé capitaine de vaisseau" (*Mame* 411; *Béch.* 161+). Again, Mme de Listomère stresses Birotteau's rights, which, she says in an addition in Béchet, are "reconnus par des avocats distingués" (*Mame* 404; *Béch.* 153+).

Compressions are, as usual, less frequent than additions and elaborations. However, it must not be supposed that Balzac did not strive constantly to make his style more concise and exact. Among a number of examples, let us quote two typical changes. In speaking of Mlle Salomon, Balzac writes:

Le jeune homme dont elle devait être la femme perdit la raison. [*Mame* 369]	*Son prétendu* perdit la raison. [*Béch.* 114+]

Similarly the clause "les sentimens dont le cœur humain est agité" (*Char.* 31) is condensed to "les passions" (*Fur.* 19+).

The number of omissions occurring between the published texts is, as usual with Balzac, not large. If, however, one counts here the suppression of almost all titles, such as *monsieur* and *l'abbé*, for the Furne edition (see

---

[75] The italics are Balzac's.

above, p. 195), the total is considerably increased. The most striking type of omission, that of conjunctions, will be discussed later. In one case Balzac has happily lightened his style by the omission of a clause containing a pedantic phrase:

> En effet, ayant agi jadis très logiquement en obéissant aux lois naturelles de son égoïsme, il lui était impossible de deviner ses torts envers son hôtesse; *car l'intus-susception des âmes et le pouvoir du "connais-toi toi-même!*[76] *..." composent une science inconnue aux gens médiocres.*   [*Mame* 322]

The italicized clause does not occur in Béchet (71). The total number of contractions and omissions is sixty-eight. Compressions are effected fourteen times. Six sentences are struck out to avoid repetitions. There are nineteen cases of omission, exclusive of titles. In the latter category there are twenty-nine changes in the Furne edition.

Direct speech is introduced four times in the Béchet edition. Of these, two are important changes. A long scene between Mme de Listomère, her nephew, and *le vieux malin* is inserted in this 1834 text (see below, p. 268). This material is intercalated between a conversation occurring in Paris and one taking place in Tours. It serves as a transition and at the same time is a very excellent example of Balzac's ability to write dialogue. No important changes have been made in this scene since it first appeared. The dialogue is natural, moves quickly, and serves considerably to lighten the style at this point in the story. The most interesting insertion of dialogue, however, is that in the *duel de paroles* (see below, p. 268). Mme de Listomère and Troubert are fencing verbally. To stress the real animosity which exists between the two adversaries, Balzac adds in the Béchet edition a series of italicized sentences which represent the hostile thoughts of each speaker. This clever device adds much piquancy to the dialogue. We cannot quote the entire conversation, but two small sections will serve to illustrate the stylistic effectiveness of the added "thoughts." Mme de Listomère begins by saying how much she regrets the Abbé Birotteau's suit against Mlle Gamard. Then she adds that she would like to see the affair settled to the satisfaction of both parties. Troubert answers piously, all the while impiously thinking:

> —Le mal est fait, madame, dit l'abbé d'une voix grave, la vertueuse mademoiselle Gamard se meurt.
> —*Je ne m'intéresse pas plus à cette sotte fille qu'au Prêtre-Jean*, pensait-il; *mais*

---

[76] This phrase is italicized in the text.

je voudrais bien vous mettre sa mort sur le dos, et vous en inquiéter la conscience, si vous êtes assez niais pour en prendre du souci.[77]   [*Mame* 401; *Béch.* 149+]

The canon, who could easily have Mme de Listomère's nephew retired, asks with polite malice whether the young officer has not been to Paris. His crafty thought is: *"Vous avez eu là de mes nouvelles ... Je puis vous écraser, vous qui m'avez méprisé. Vous venez capituler"* (*Mame* 402; *Béch.* 150+). But Mme de Listomère is as skilful as her antagonist. She answers in the affirmative, thanking Troubert for his interest in the baron, and adds aloud: *"Il y retourne ce soir, il est mandé par le ministre, qui est parfait pour nous, et voudrait ne pas lui voir quitter le service"* (*Mame* 402; *Béch.* 151+). This "sweet" speech, the whole of which is an addition in Béchet, is accompanied by the acid thought: *"Jésuite, tu ne nous écraseras pas ... et ta plaisanterie est comprise"* (*Mame* 402; *Béch.* 151+).

Speech-words are introduced in dialogue ten times in the Béchet edition and occasionally in the Furne. Their general purpose is to clarify. For example, Troubert attempts to intimidate Mme de Listomère with a glance from his sinister orange-colored eyes. Their dialogue having been interrupted, Balzac adds, when the baroness resumes the conversation: *"... dit-elle en continuant"* (*Char.* 96; *Fur.* 57).

Some mention should be made of Balzac's tendency to use rhetorical questions. The number introduced between the editions of *Le Curé de Tours* is, however, not large. These are inserted in the Béchet edition. When they do not occur too close together, they add variety and lightness to the style. They are usually substituted for a dependent clause, as in the example below:

C'était pour lui une sorte de mort, car *c'était* briser toutes les racines par lesquelles il s'était planté dans le monde. [*Mame* 381]	C'était pour lui une sorte de mort. N'était-ce pas briser toutes les racines par lesquelles il s'était planté dans le monde. [*Béch.* 125+]

Of the seven figures of speech involved in the variations between the published texts, four are metaphors and three are similes. Six of the changes occur in Béchet. Two of the metaphors are illustrative of Balzac's use of figures of speech which are in keeping with the profession of his characters. When the Marquis de Listomère tells his nephew, the naval officer, that to be promoted to a captaincy he must propitiate Troubert, the nephew makes his decision quickly. The entire sentence below is an

[77] The italics here, and in the other "thoughts" quoted, are in the text. The parentheses which today inclose the italicized sentences were not added until the Furne edition.

addition in Béchet: "*—Je ne veux pas, dit-il à son oncle, recevoir une seconde bordée ecclésiastique dans mes œuvres-vives!*" (*Mame* 395; *Béch.* 138–39+). And when M. de Bourbonne is counseling caution in dealing with Troubert, he says to the young officer: "*D'ailleurs, marchez la sonde en main, M. le marin*" (*Mame* 395; *Béch.* 141+). One of the metaphors is less happy and seems to have displeased Balzac, since this is the third time he has retouched it (see above, p. 201). In the final metaphor of the four, M. Caron, the lawyer of Mlle Gamard, is called "le ronge-papiers" (*Mame* 356; *Béch.* 103+).

The similes are more usual. The victimized Abbé Birotteau "devait succomber comme un agneau sous le coup du boucher" (*Mame* 354; *Béch.* 101+). Mlle Gamard's voice is like a trumpet in his ears (*Mame* 374; *Béch.* 119+). And, lastly, the poor Abbé is "doué d'une loquacité vide et sonore comme l'est un ballon" (*Mame* 333; *Béch.* 81+).

To sum up our analysis of the variants due to rhetorical devices, we find that between the editions Balzac made two hundred and eighty changes of this nature. Amplifications and additions, occurring one hundred and twenty-seven times, are the most frequent of these changes. Of these, the most salient are the ninety-nine insertions which were introduced for the 1834 volume. These intercalations are especially important for the dialogue in the story, notably in the *duel de paroles*. Compressions and omissions are effected about one-third as often as the additions and are found almost evenly distributed between the Béchet and the Furne texts. A number of transpositions, which have not been illustrated, were made for clarity or smoothness and occur three times more often in Béchet than in Furne. Rhetorical questions are seldom run in, despite Balzac's liking for them. One single repetition was added for the sake of emphasis. A few speech-words were inserted for the same reason. Six new figures of speech were introduced in the 1834 edition. Of the total number of changes involving rhetorical devices, the ratio between the Béchet and the Furne texts is fairly even. The most significant variations were, however, introduced in the earlier volume.

c) According to parts of speech.—When we consider the verbal changes, we find again that, except in the cases of adverbs and conjunctions, substitutions occur more frequently than either additions or omissions. These changes are also, as usual, nearly all due to Balzac's effort to find the exact word.

Verbs are affected in two hundred and five of the variations between the editions. One hundred and one of these changes are substitutions. A few examples will illustrate Balzac's practice. In the citation below, the substituted verb is perhaps not more exact than the original term, but it contrasts more logically with the verb of the principal clause. When the Abbé Birotteau accepts the reassurances of his aristocratic friends that a visit to Troubert will insure his nomination to the longed-for canonship, Balzac says of the vicar:

Les gens faibles se rassurent aussi facilement qu'ils *se désolent.*
[*Mame* 367]

Les gens faibles se rassurent aussi facilement qu'ils *s'effrayent.*
[*Béch.* 112+]

In the next illustration the substitution has been made in the first instance to avoid a repetition, but the particular verb "séduire" has no doubt been used with stylistic intent. A little earlier in the text Balzac has compared Chapeloud's apartment to a woman and has said that Birotteau's "concupiscence mobilière" began like the "passion vraie" of a young man for the woman he will always love:

Enfin, trois ans avant sa mort, l'abbé Chapeloud avait complété le confortable de son appartement en décorant le salon, dont le meuble, quoique simplement garni de velours d'Utrecht rouge, *avait ébloui les yeux de* Birotteau.
[*Char.* 8]

Enfin, trois ans avant sa mort, l'abbé Chapeloud avait complété le confortable de son appartement en décorant le salon. Quoique simplement garni de velours d'Utrecht rouge, le meuble *avait séduit* Birotteau.   [*Fur.* 6+]

In nine cases Balzac replaces a single verb by a verb plus an infinitive, as, for example, "jugea" by "sut juger" (*Mame* 306; *Béch.* 57+). His aim is no doubt exactness, but the compound form does not always achieve greater definiteness. A number of variations result from the substitution of a more exact verb for *avoir* and *être*. In the following example greater precision results from the changed form. Mlle Gamard was persecuting the poor vicar daily, but

Birotteau s'efforça de ne pas *être* sensible.
[*Mame* 319]

Birotteau s'efforça de ne pas *se montrer* sensible.   [*Béch.* 68+]

Vividness, as well as accuracy, is attained in the majority of the substitutions. Two examples involving past participles illustrate Balzac's effort to find the evocative word. In the first case, Balzac is speaking of the silence around Saint-Gatien, which is, he says, sometimes broken

par les cris des choucas *logés* dans le sommet des clochers. [*Mame* 284-85]

par les cris des choucas *nichés* dans le sommet des clochers.   [*Béch.* 37+]

In the second instance, the thorough demolitions of the rapacious *Bande*

Noire are more graphically called to mind in the revision. Balzac is speaking of the Abbé Chapeloud:

... il employa cette somme à l'emplète d'une bibliothèque en chêne, provenant de la démolition d'un château *acheté* par la bande noire. [*Mame* 289]

Il employa cette somme à l'emplète d'une bibliothèque en chêne, provenant de la démolition d'un château *dépecé* par la bande noire. [*Béch.* 40+]

Exactness accounts for the addition of eleven verbs: seven in the Béchet edition, four in the Furne. For example, Mlle Gamard and her prying friends

employaient toute leur journée à tamiser les pas, les démarches de leurs voisins ...   [*Mame* 383]

employaient toute leur journée à tamiser les paroles, *à scruter* les démarches de leurs voisins ... [*Béch.* 127+]

In the Furne edition "employaient" is replaced by "passaient" (*Fur.* 45+).

Seven omissions are made for the sake of concision and simplicity. For example, when Chapeloud moved into his apartment, Balzac tells us:

... tout le mobilier que le pauvre chanoine *put* d'abord y *mettre, consistait* en un lit, une table ...   [*Mame* 288]

Pour tout mobilier, le pauvre chanoine y mit d'abord un lit, une table ... [*Béch.* 40+]

Nouns are affected in one hundred and twenty-one of the variations now under consideration. The majority of these changes, seventy-six in number, occur in Furne. Forty-two nouns are involved in the Béchet corrections, but only three in the Conard text. Substitutions, the most frequent type of change, occur eighty-seven times in the three editions. Many of these are made to avoid repetitions; others are made in the effort to find the exact word. An imaginative expression may replace a general term, as when Mme de Listomère says to the Abbé Birotteau:

Cédez, comme je le fais à *ces circonstances* ...   [*Mame* 397]

Cédez, comme je le fais, à *cet orage* ... [*Béch.* 143+]

Again a concrete and evocative noun takes the place of a vague one. Mlle Salomon says that in the cold, damp rectory of Saint-Symphorien, Birotteau

va se trouver enterré dans un *fond* ... [*Mame* 410]

va donc se trouver dans un *véritable sépulcre.* [*Béch.* 159+]

Emphasis results from a number of the substitutions, such as "minuties" (Béch. 51+) for "petites choses" (*Mame* 300). Again, the substitution may be made for affective reasons, as in the following example, where added details help to awaken our pity for the stricken Birotteau. The citation illustrates how small verbal alterations play their part in the evolution of Balzac's style:

Il était pâle et maigre.   [*Char.* 103]

> *Ce curé frappé par l'archevêque* était
> pâle et maigre.   [*Fur.* 61]

> > *Ce pauvre prêtre frappé par son* Arche-
> > vêque était pâle et maigre. [*Con.* 246]

Fully half the substitutions, however, are due to Balzac's desire for accuracy. For example, in the following phrase the italicized word replaces an original "richesse" (*Char.* 68): "combien la haine sut mettre de *nuances* dans l'accentuation de chaque mot" (*Fur.* 41+).

Other changes involving nouns are infrequent. Nouns are omitted ten times because they are not needed. They are added eighteen times in the interest of clear or precise expression.

Pronouns are involved in eighty-seven of the variations which Balzac introduced in the published texts. The most interesting changes are fifty cases of the substitution of nouns, both proper and common, for pronouns. Seven-tenths of these substituted nouns are found in the Furne edition, a factor which explains, in part, why the style in this edition tends to be more definite and concrete than that of the preceding volumes. A few examples chosen from the several texts follow.

One effective substitution is made in the funeral oration which Troubert delivered for Mlle Gamard. The style of such a sermon is cleverly suggested by the change from a pronoun to the Christian name of the old maid:

Heureux ceux qui peuvent reposer, ici-bas, en paix avec eux-mêmes, comme *elle* repose maintenant au séjour des bienheureux dans sa robe d'innocence! [*Char.* 99]	Heureux ceux qui peuvent reposer ici-bas, en paix avec eux-mêmes, comme *Sophie* repose maintenant au séjour des bienheureux dans sa robe d'innocence! [*Fur.* 59+]

Another change affects Troubert, who, en route to his diocese, passed along the quay of Saint-Symphorien. There he saw resting in the sun an old and ill man, Birotteau:

L'évêque *lui* lança un regard de mépris et de pitié ... [*Fur.* 61]	L'Evêque lança *sur sa victime* un regard de mépris et de pitié ... [*Con.* 246]

One further example will conclude our illustrations of this very frequent type of variation. In the case below, the substitution was no doubt made for the sake of emphasis. Mademoiselle is dying because of Birotteau's lawsuit, according to the gossips of Tours:

"Birotteau *la* tuait ..."   [*Char.* 91]   "Birotteau tuait *sa bienfaitrice* ..."
[*Fur.* 54+]

Adjectives are added twenty-five times between the editions, while they are struck out eighteen times. There are thirty-eight cases of substitution. The changes are rather evenly distributed between the 1834 and 1843 texts. Twenty-one insertions add vividness or psychological intensity to the style. In the following example, familiar though the simile be, Birotteau's utter helplessness becomes more poignant in the revision because of the added adjective. In the struggle with Mlle Gamard:

... il devait succomber comme un agneau sous le coup du boucher.   ... il devait succomber comme un a-gneau, sous le *premier* coup du boucher.
[*Char.* 54]   [*Fur.* 32+]

Similarly, "un grain de poussière" becomes "un *seul* grain de poussière" (*Mame* 295; *Béch.* 46+). Omissions are made when the adjectives contribute nothing to the style (*Mame* 293; *Béch.* 44) or when they detract from the forcefulness of expression (*Mame* 336; *Béch.* 84). The substitutions are not especially significant. For example, "des choses du monde" becomes "mondaine" (*Char.* 23; *Fur.* 14+).

Adverbs are freely added from edition to edition. These small insertions add color and variety to the style. They may be run in with much effectiveness in surprising places, as, for example, in the contract between Mlle Gamard and Birotteau, where Balzac intercalates that the *abbé* was "surabondamment" unable to pay the usual price of the pension (*Mame* 377; *Béch.* 122). Omissions occur twenty-nine times. Unnecessary adverbs are struck out (*Mame* 286; *Béch.* 39+). There is, moreover, a tendency to omit *en effet* and *alors*. One-fourth of the omissions under discussion concern these two expressions and are typical of the uncertainty Balzac seems to have felt about connectives. In the next example the introductory phrase is struck out in Béchet: "*En effet*, la distribution intérieure et la contenance de sa maison n'avaient pas permis à mademoiselle Gamard d'avoir plus de deux pensionnaires ..." (*Mame* 286; *Béch.* 38+). In the same way the transitional "alors" is omitted in the following instance: "*alors*, il ne laissa s'établir ..." (*Mame* 307; *Béch.* 57+).

Substitutions involving adverbs are made twenty-seven times. About a quarter of these again concern *alors*. In one instance we find Balzac hesitating about this troublesome little word from the manuscript through the Furne edition (1, 22; *Char.* 19; *Fur.* 12+). Another fourth of the substitutions were made for the sake of emphasis. For example, manifestations of Mlle Gamard's tyranny are said to occur not "souvent" (*Mame* 318) but "presque tous les soirs" (*Béch.* 67–68+). The substitution of adverbial phrases for adverbs is not, however, a frequent change between the editions. One case should be mentioned, since it shows Balzac wisely restoring the original phrase of the manuscript (1, 5). He is speaking of Mlle Gamard's house:

Quoique ce bien eût été acquis *natio-*   Quoique ce bien eût été acquis *de la*
nalement, pendant la terreur, par le   *nation*, pendant la Terreur, par le père
père de mademoiselle Gamard ...   de mademoiselle Gamard ... [*Fur.* 3+]
[*Char.* 4]

Between the editions of *Le Curé de Tours* Balzac made, in all, one hundred and fifteen changes involving adverbs. Additions are twice as frequent as substitutions or omissions. All types of changes, however, occur in almost equal proportions in the Béchet and the Furne texts.

Conjunctions figure more prominently than any other part of speech in the verbal corrections now under consideration. There are two hundred and fifty-four variants in this category. Conjunctions are added fifty-four times for smoothness or where structural changes demand them. The majority of the twenty-four cases of substitution are made to avoid repetitions. The omissions are due primarily to the shortening of sentences. We have seen that one hundred and forty-five sentences are reduced in length in the Béchet text alone. In ninety-nine of these cases conjunctions are eliminated. Some twenty to thirty further omissions are made in this text in the interest of concision. Except for the breaking-up of sentences, the omissions of conjunctions is, then, the most frequent correction made for the Béchet edition. The conjunction most often affected is *et*, which is eliminated fifty-four times. *Car* is dropped thirty-four times. Conjunctions are struck out in the Furne edition some thirty times. *Et* is omitted eight times; *car* three. Only one conjunction is deleted for the Conard edition. The total number of conjunctions omitted in all the editions is about one hundred and seventy-six.

Variations according to other parts of speech may be briefly recorded, since they do not affect the style perceptibly. Articles are involved in forty-three of these changes, negatives in six, and prepositions in twenty-one.

To summarize the analysis of the variations according to parts of speech, we find that Balzac made nine hundred and sixty-two verbal changes between the editions. Conjunctions are varied more often than any other part of speech. The omission of these connectives is, as we have seen, a feature of the Béchet corrections. After conjunctions the most frequent changes affect verbs. These variations, usually made in the interest of definiteness, are rather evenly distributed between the Béchet and Furne texts, in both of which substitutions predominate. However, nouns, the next largest category, are more often changed in the Furne text than in the earlier volume. The same is true for pronouns. Substitutions involving both nouns and pronouns are salient in the Furne corrections. Since the majority of these variants tend in the direction of the *mot propre* and of greater concreteness, the style of the 1843 volume is more exact than that of the preceding editions. Greater vividness and color are at times achieved by the variations in which adjectives and adverbs are concerned. The changes are fairly evenly distributed between the Béchet and the Furne texts. While adjectives are usually substituted, adverbs are more frequently inserted. We have already noted, both in the corrections for the proofs and in the *princeps*, this tendency on Balzac's part to run in adverbs.

Just as verbal changes predominate in the earlier corrections, so they outnumber all other changes between the editions. The importance of these small variants is not, however, their number but their effectiveness. Although Balzac has left a number of pedantic words in the final text of *Le Curé de Tours*, his corrections have eliminated others, notably "intussusception"! His effort, from edition to edition, to find the exact word culminated in the concrete phraseology of the Furne, a style which must have pleased him, since he made so few changes in it for his proposed next edition. If Balzac's style in this little story has a certain vigor and strength, we may attribute much of this effect to the many careful verbal changes he made between the editions.

2. REALISTIC VARIATIONS (BETWEEN THE SEVERAL EDITIONS)

Let us now consider the realistic variations which Balzac introduced in his novel after the *princeps*. The most important editions for these changes are, of course, the Béchet, when the story was set in the *Scènes de la vie de province*, and the Furne, or first edition of the *Comédie humaine*. The Charpentier edition of 1839 was practically untouched, as we have said; and there are no realistic changes in the Conard. In studying these editions the changes deriving from Balzac's general realistic qualities will be analyzed first; then those variations which are due to his fictional technique.

   a) General realistic qualities.—We know that the first article in Balzac's credo as a novelist was the necessity for truth. This belief he reaffirms in a variation introduced in the Furne edition:

... *la vérité historique* oblige-t-elle à dire ... [*Char.* 2]	... *la vérité, si essentielle dans une histoire de mœurs* oblige à dire ... [*Fur.* 2+]

Later in the Furne text he adds further: "... cette histoire est de tous les temps" (*Char.* 24; *Fur.* 15+). Many variations are due to his painstaking efforts to realize this ideal of universal truth.

   One way in which Balzac creates his impression of reality is by accuracy of statement. Thus he changes a reference to Saint-Gatien as "cette église" (*Mame* 287) to "la cathédrale" (*Béch.* 39+). Birotteau's "instant de désespoir" (*Mame* 376) when he learns that his rival has been chosen for the long-coveted canonship is more truthfully characterized in Béchet as a "commencement d'aliénation mentale" (*Béch.* 120+). Truth also obliges Balzac to add that it was not entirely a sense of the justice of the Abbé Birotteau's cause which led the vicar's friends to move unhurriedly in his defense:

Les amis du vicaire, animés par le sentiment que donne la justice d'une bonne cause, ayant remis le commencement de l'instance au jour où ils reviendraient à Tours, avaient laissé prendre les devans aux amis de mademoiselle Gamard ... [*Mame* 387]	Les amis du vicaire, animés par le sentiment que donne la justice d'une bonne cause, *ou paresseux pour un procès qui ne leur était pas personnel,* avaient remis le commencement de l'instance au jour où ils reviendraient à Tours. Les amis de mademoiselle Gamard purent donc prendre les devans ... [*Béch.* 130–31+]

It is for actuality's sake, no doubt, that Balzac changes the rank aspired to by "le lieutenant de vaisseau" from "capitaine de frégate" (*Char.* 82) to "capitaine de corvette" (*Fur.* 49+), since the former was the higher command.[78]

   We have seen above (pp. 229–31) that the time-intervals in the story are not entirely accurate and that Balzac made a few changes which tend to harmonize them. We have referred to the substitution in Furne of "deux ans" for "douze mois" to straighten out the length of time that the Abbé

[78] *Grande Encyclopédie* (Paris, *s.d.*), XII, 1122.

Birotteau has occupied Chapeloud's apartment. With a two-year period in mind, Balzac alters a passage (*Char.* 49) describing the *abbé*'s relations with Mlle Gamard to include the phrase "une trame ourdie depuis six mois" (*Fur.* 30+). The allusion to a plot laid six months earlier is consistent with the assertion that Mlle Gamard's persecution of Birotteau began eighteen months after his coming to lodge with her, but is at variance with the statement that her ill-treatment of him has been going on "depuis environ trois mois" (*Con.* 180) when the story opens.

For the sake of probability Balzac continues to make corrections which lengthen the time of the denouement of the story. Consequently, we find the following change:

Ce n'était plus que le squelette du Birotteau qui roulait, *dix mois* auparavant, si vide, mais si content, à travers le cloître.   [*Char.* 103]

Ce n'était plus que le squelette du Birotteau qui roulait, *un an* auparavant, si vide mais si content, à travers le Cloître.   [*Fur.* 61+]

Likewise Mlle Gamard's death is postponed a few hours longer after Mme de Listomère's call:

Madame de Listomère apprit *dans la soirée* la mort de mademoiselle Gamard.   [*Char.* 98]

Madame de Listomère apprit *le lendemain* la mort de mademoiselle Gamard.   [*Fur.* 58+]

One allusion to time in the story is never very clear; and when, in Béchet, Balzac changes the date of the opening of the novel from 1824 to 1826 (see below, p. 261), the reference becomes even more obscure. Throughout all versions of our text Chapeloud occupies his apartment for twelve years, and Birotteau is in his second year of residence in the same rooms (1, 5+). However, the following statements, with slight variations, run through the story from the manuscript to the definitive edition: "Quand Napoléon rétablit le culte catholique, l'abbé Chaploud fut nommé chanoine de St-Gatien et Biroteau, devint vicaire de l'Eglise. Alors, Chaploud se mit chez Mademoiselle Gamard ..." (1, 6+).[79] If Balzac refers to the Concordat of 1801, that year should be the date of Chapeloud's coming to Mlle Gamard's—not 1810, as in the first, or 1812, as in the later, editions of the story. There may be an explanation, however, for this discrepancy, because in nine of the *brouillons*[80] the story begins in 1816. In the early pages of his manuscript Balzac may have had this date

[79] See *Con.* 173 for the definitive text.

[80] *S.* 26, 28, 30, 34, and *MS* 15, 17, 19, 21—all false starts entitled *La Vieille Fille; S.* 27, *Le Prêtre catholique*, p. 1.

in mind when he traced the fourteen-year background of the Abbé Birotteau's "concupiscence mobilière," and he may have thought of Chapeloud as coming to lodge with Mlle Gamard in 1802. Farther along in the manuscript, however, Balzac placed the action of the story in 1824 (1, 48). Perhaps, at the time, he had forgotten his earlier reference to the reopening of the churches and so did not change it, a slip which he never later corrected.

Balzac's propensity to increase fortunes is illustrated in one change between the editions. In this case he suggests greater wealth for M. de Bourbonne:

Il avait su arrondir les prairies *de sa terre* aux dépens des laisses de la Loire en évitant tout procès avec le domaine de l'Etat.   [*Char.* 58]

Il avait su arrondir les prairies *d'un de ses domaines* aux dépens des lais de la Loire en évitant tout procès avec l'Etat.   [*Fur.* 34+]

In one instance a sum of money is omitted. Originally (1, 77), Troubert, having inherited Mlle Gamard's fortune, "donna la bibliothèque et les livres de Chapeloud au petit seminaire, en y joignant un capital de cent mille francs" (*Char.* 102). In the Furne edition the newly elected bishop gives only the bookcase and the books (*Fur.* 60+), probably because, as the "vieux malin" suspects, he is ambitious of being sent to the *Chambre haute* and so keeps the money in order to maintain his rank fittingly in Paris some day.[81] There is only one other variation which concerns money, and that is an addition in the Furne text which tells us that the legacies left to Chapeloud by his "pieuses pénitentes" were not large (*Char.* 7; *Fur.* 5+).

There are two instances of increased figures. The number of victims who died by the guillotine during the Revolution is at first thought by Mlle Gamard and the vicar to have been "trois cent mille" (*Mame* 334). Later their number is "treize cent mille" (*Béch.* 82+). The length of the bridge that connects Tours and Saint-Symphorien is changed from "dixsept cents pieds" (*Char.* 100) to "dix-neuf cents pieds" (*Fur.* 59+). Neither figure is exact, as the bridge is said to be 434 meters long.[82]

In two cases numbers are omitted. In the first instance, however, Balzac suggests a larger, rather than a smaller, figure by the omission. He is speaking of the Abbé Birotteau:

... il était le *confesseur de deux pensionnats de jeunes filles* ...   [*Mame* 305]

... en sa qualité de *confesseur des pensionnats de la ville* ...   [*Béch.* 55+]

---

[81] For Troubert's motives, see pp. 270–71.

[82] *Grande Encyclopédie*, XXXI, 251.

In the second example Balzac has wisely struck out in the revision the precise number. Its very exactness seemed unnatural in the context. Having given up his apartment, the bewildered Birotteau exclaims:

—Où vais-je mettre tous mes meubles? ... et mes livres, ma belle bibliothèque, mes *deux* beaux tableaux, mon salon rouge, enfin tout mon mobilier? [*Char.* 62–63]

—Où vais-je mettre tous mes meubles? ... et mes livres, ma belle bibliothèque, mes beaux tableaux, mon salon rouge, enfin tout mon mobilier! [*Fur.* 37+]

Balzac's "encyclopedic zeal" often led him to introduce digressions of a technical or semitechnical nature. Sometimes the inserted material is merely cumulative information. The example below shows how the author amplifies a simple statement of fact with additional lore:

Il existe dans le cloître *un passage qui aboutit à la grande rue.* [*Mame* 283]

Jadis, existait dans le cloître, *du côté de la Grande-Rue, plusieurs maisons réunies par une clôture, appartenant à la Cathédrale et où logeaient quelques dignitaires du chapitre. Depuis l'aliénation des biens du clergé, la ville a fait du passage qui séparait ces maisons une rue, nommée rue de la Psalette, par laquelle on va du cloître dans la Grande-Rue. Ce nom indique suffisamment que là demeurait autrefois le grand Chantre, ses écoles et ceux qui vivaient sous sa dépendance.* [*Béch.* 35–36+]

Of a semitechnical nature is a semantic digression introduced to explain a dialectical word. The persecuted Abbé Birotteau speaks of himself as a "bourrier de la rue." "Ce mot Tourangeau," adds Balzac, "n'a point d'équivalent, et ne peut être traduit que par le mot *brin de paille*"[83] (*Mame* 398+). In Béchet, Balzac adds: "Mais il y a de jolis petits brins de paille, jaunes, polis, rayonnans, qui font le bonheur des enfans: tandis que le bourrier est le brin de paille décoloré, boueux, roulé dans les ruisseaux, chassé par la tempête, tordu par les pieds du passant'" (*Béch.* 144+). The use of this word peculiar to the milieu is characteristic of Balzac and may be cited as an example of one way in which he sought to introduce local color in his stories.

The skill with which Balzac fitted the many parts of the *Comédie humaine* together is well known. Five variations illustrating this solidifying

---

[83] The italics are in the text.

technique occur between the editions of our novel. Three concern time. The two others introduce a reappearing character.

We have seen (cf. above, p. 258) that Balzac changed the time of the action of the novel from 1824 to 1826 (*Mame* 334; *Béch.* 82+). In the Furne edition he emphasizes the latter date by inserting it in the first line of the story (*Fur.* 1+). This time-change he probably made in order to interlock *Louis Lambert* and *Le Curé de Tours* more carefully than he had done in the 1832 versions of the novels. A later substitution concerning time seems to justify this conclusion. The action of *Louis Lambert* takes place from 1812 to 1824. In the first edition[84] Balzac establishes the date 1820 as the time when Louis Lambert first met Mlle Salomon, and then continues: "Mademoiselle de Villenoix avait alors vingt ans, et sa beauté remarquable, les grâces de son esprit, étaient pour sa félicité des garanties moins équivoques que toutes celles que donne la fortune."[85] The author tells us later that "Lambert mourut à l'âge de vingt-huit ans, le 25 septembre, 1824."[86] Now, originally in our novel Mlle Salomon was in 1824, as we learned from her *dossier*, a much older woman than she is in *Louis Lambert*. In the first edition of our story she is said to have consecrated twenty years of her life to the "bonheur mécanique" of Louis Lambert (*Mame* 369). As has been suggested above (see p. 233; also n. 59, p. 234), when our novel appeared in May, 1832, Balzac probably had not completely thought out Mlle Salomon's role in *Louis Lambert*, which appeared, dated "June–July 1832," in October of that year.[87] After the first edition of *Louis Lambert* he made what changes he could in *Le Curé de Tours* to make Pauline de Villenoix consistent in the two stories. In the Béchet edition he therefore makes the following substitution concerning the length of time she devoted herself to her ill-fated lover: "Pendant *cinq* années, elle s'était, avec le courage de l'amour, consacrée au bonheur mécanique de ce malheureux, dont elle avait si bien épousé la

---

[84] According to Lov., *Hist.*, p. 190, the novel was first published in October, 1832, by Charles Gosselin in *Nouveaux Contes philosophiques* under the title: *Notice biographique sur Louis Lambert*.

[85] *Notice biographique sur Louis Lambert*, p. 365; for the other details concerning the meeting of Louis Lambert and Mlle Salomon, cf. *ibid.*, pp. 359, 361, 362.

[86] *Ibid.*, p. 425. The statements from *Louis Lambert* are found in all the editions of that novel which cover the period of publication for *Le Curé de Tours*, through the Furne. Lovenjoul (*Histoire des œuvres*, p. 190) lists these editions after the first as follows: Gosselin, 1833; Werdet, 1835; Charpentier, 1842.

[87] Lov., *Hist.*, p. 190.

folie qu'elle ne le croyait point fou" (*Béch.* 114+). This change makes her age tally in the two novels. The earlier change of setting the action of our novel forward two years makes more plausible Mlle Salomon's well-established position in Tours, since it is stated that she came to that city "après avoir perdu le compagnon de sa vie" (*Béch.* 115+). By means of these time-changes Balzac has thus harmonized more accurately the part played by Mlle Salomon in the two novels and has once more added to that impression of substantial reality which the *Comédie humaine* creates.

If Mlle Salomon's role as a reappearing character evolves slowly, that of Troubert seems to have been the invention of a moment. Up to the publication of the *Comédie humaine* Troubert's see is not given; he is spoken of merely as "Monseigneur Hyacinthe évêque de ..." (*Char.* 101, 102–3). In the Furne edition he becomes the "évêque de Troyes" (*Fur.* 60+, 61+). In a later novel, *Le Député d'Arcis*, Troubert reappears as the Bishop of Troyes. The interesting thing about this fact is that at the very time Balzac was getting Volume VI of the *Comédie humaine* ready for publication he was also working on *Le Député d'Arcis*. He writes Mme Hanska under the date of March 2, 1843: "Après m'être élancé à corps perdu dans *le Député d'Arcis*, voici le libraire qui ne veut pas de politique."[88] He then mentions almost immediately *Le Curé de Tours* as part of the sixth volume of the *Comédie humaine* (see above, p. 194). However, since Balzac wrote only the first seventeen chapters of *Le Député d'Arcis*,[89] one might question whether he or Charles Rabou, who finished the story for book form,[90] introduced Troubert in the novel. Conclusive proof that Balzac did so is found in the Conard edition, which publishes only Balzac's part of the story. The text of *Le Député d'Arcis* in this edition is based on that of the *Union monarchique*, in which Balzac's seventeen chapters first appeared from April 7 to May 3, 1847,[91] and on the manuscript in the Lovenjoul Collection.[92] In the Conard, Troubert appears as "Monseigneur Hyacinthe, évêque de Troyes."[93] All the evidence seems to justify our conclusion, then, that Troubert's role as a reappearing character is due to the fact that Balzac was working on the two stories at about the same time and swiftly interlocked them by means of the wily Congréganiste.

---

[88] *LEt.*, II, 119–20.   [89] Lov., *Hist.*, p. 155.

[90] *Ibid*. The volume was published in 1854 by L. de Potter.

[91] *Ibid*.

[92] *Con.* XXI, 445; Lov. Coll., A 55.   [93] *Con.* XXI, 367.

There are between the various editions of *Le Curé de Tours* thirty-two variations which illustrate Balzac's sociological bent. The definitive title with its emphasis on type and milieu was chosen, we know, for the *Comédie humaine* edition. Having changed his title, Balzac inserts in Furne the phrase that the Abbé Birotteau is "le principal personnage de cette histoire" (*Fur.* 1+), though he in no way at this time decreases the importance of the other *célibataires* in the story. He does, however, increase the references to the smallness and meanness of life in a provincial city, thus further justifying his inclusion of the name of Tours in the new title.

The small-town intrigue which we are witnessing becomes even more nefarious in the variations. For example, when the Liberal lawyer undertook Birotteau's case, the writ which he drew up against Mlle Gamard condemned her so clearly that

trente ou quarante copies en furent *faites, et coururent* par toute la ville.	trente ou quarante copies en furent *méchamment distribuées* dans la ville.
[*Mame* 392]	[*Béch.* 135+]

Between the first and second editions Balzac emphasizes the jealousy of Mlle Gamard's set who, he adds in Béchet, regards "comme ennemis" the salons frequented by the aristocrats (*Béch.* 129+). We already know that Mlle Gamard's friends are less important socially than Birotteau's; hence the insistence on their hostility as a group to the aristocrats darkens the picture Balzac is painting. The ease with which the rest of the town picked up the gossip and animosity of the bourgeois circle is stressed. Mlle Gamard's friends say Birotteau is killing her. The town "obligingly" repeats the news (*Mame* 400; Béch. 147+). The jealousy of the Tourangeaux receives an added touch, as we have seen. An insertion in Béchet stresses the large number of M. de Bourbonne's fellow-townsmen who are envious of him (*Mame* 359–60; *Béch.* 106+).

The generalizations introduced by Balzac in the later versions of *Le Curé de Tours* are of a broad scope and tend to sum up his social philosophy on the types and the scene he is depicting. For example, several insertions emphasize the difference between the provincial priest and people of the world. A man of social experience would never have been "clawed" twice in Mlle Gamard's catlike maneuvers (*Mame* 302; *Béch.* 53+). Balzac adds later in Béchet: "... *les yeux du bon vicaire n'étaient jamais à ce point d'optique qui permet aux gens du monde de voir et d'éviter si promptement les aspérités du voisin ...*" (*Mame* 317; *Béch.* 67+). The increased dangers of celibacy in contemporary society are stressed by an addition:

Mais le célibat a, pour les célibataires et pour la société, ce vice capital que, concentrant les qualités de l'homme sur une seule passion, l'égoïsme, elle les rend ou nuisibles ou inutiles.	*Mais aujourd'hui que l'Eglise n'est plus une puissance politique, et n'absorbe plus les forces des gens solitaires,* le célibat a, pour la société, ce vice capital que, faisant converger les qualités de l'homme sur une seule passion, l'égo-
[*Mame* 412–13]	ïsme, il rend les célibataires ou nuisi-
	bles ou inutiles. [*Béch.* 162+]

Le Curé de Tours ends today with a long passage on the struggle between man and society.[94] This sociophilosophic disquisition was added to the novel for the first time in the Béchet edition (pp. 162–64+); that is, well after Balzac had finished his story. The passage is both obscure and tedious, but as an example of Balzac's tendency to sum up and to generalize on his particular types and scenes it is an interesting variation. This use of generalizations as a sort of "cohesive philosophy" to bind together his social order is one of the author's most characteristic solidifying devices.

A group of variations concerning the Congrégation illustrates Balzac's close linking of the real world and his own. The Congrégation's power under Charles X, who was himself a member of the organization, was great.[95] Thus, in our story Troubert turns out to be "l'homme le plus important de la province" because he is the representative of this politico-religious society in this region. Troubert's authority is increased in the variations; this is in accordance with Balzac's tendency to expand the scope and power of certain of his characters. The secret agent's prestige is well defined in the following addition, which was inserted as a whole in Béchet:

> La position du chanoine au milieu du sénat femelle qui faisait si subtilement la police,[96] de la province, et sa capacité personnelle l'avaient fait choisir par la congrégation, entre tous les ecclésiastiques de la ville, pour être le proconsul inconnu de la Touraine: l'archevêque, le général, le préfet, grands et petits, étaient sous son occulte domination. [*Mame* 395; *Béch.* 138+]

Another addition stresses the fact that "les plus chères espérances de la famille de Listomère" (*Mame* 395; *Béch.* 139+) are dependent on the Congrégation, because if Troubert is not appeased the marquis will not be made a peer, nor will the nephew become a captain. But the family bows, recognizing—another insertion tells us—"le pouvoir occulte de la

---

[94] *Ibid.*, IX, 247, l. 2, to end of story, p. 248.

[95] *Ibid.*, p. 585 (notes).   [96] The comma here is obviously an error.

Congrégation" (*Mame* 400; *Béch.* 146+). The social reaction to the society's hidden power is emphasized in an addition in which "le vieux malin" counsels Mme de Listomère to guard well Troubert's secret:

—*Madame, ... oubliez que j'ai deviné l'invisible influence de ce prêtre, et j'oublierai que vous la connaissez également. Si nous ne nous gardions pas le secret, nous passerions pour ses complices; nous serions redoutés et haïs. Imitez-moi: feignez d'être dupe; mais sachez bien où vous mettez les pieds.*

[*Mame* 395; *Béch.* 140+]

Fear of the Congrégation dominates all circles. Justice itself is endangered, as M. de Bourbonne well knows when he urges Birotteau, in another passage, not to sue Troubert's friend: "—Excepté l'avoué des Libéraux, je ne connais, à Tours, aucun homme de chicane qui voulût[97] se charger de ce procès *sans avoir l'intention de vous le faire perdre,* ... et je ne vous conseille pas de vous y embarquer" (*Char.* 79; *Fur.* 47+). The italicized phrase is an insertion in the Furne text.

There are, in all, eight changes—mostly additions—in this group. In every case the variants stress the power of the Congrégation, either linking it more clearly with the fate of individuals or emphasizing its broader social implications, its church and state ramifications, and its psychological and moral effect upon the society of the day.

In one other instance, however, the Congrégation is replaced by an important office of the king's household. The Marquis of Listomère inquires of the Minister of the Marine why his young nephew is to be retired. In reporting this conversation to his nephew the uncle says that the minister has accused the young man of being at the head of the Liberals of Tours and of not following the line of the government. He continues:

Son Excellence a fini par m'avouer que tu étais mal avec *la Congrégation.* [*Char.* 83]	Son Excellence a fini par m'avouer que tu étais mal avec *la Grande-Aumônerie.* [*Fur.* 49+]

Since the marquis goes on immediately to say, "Bref, en demandant quelques renseignements à mes collègues, j'ai su que tu parlais fort légèrement d'un certain abbé Troubert ..." (*Fur.* 49+), and since he commands his nephew to make his peace with Troubert at once, it may be that the substitution was made to extend the range of Troubert's influence to the court itself. Certainly the allusion to the office of the *grand aumônier* adds to the impression of actuality in the young baron's situation, since the incumbent in 1826 is known to have been particularly zealous.[98]

---

[97] The Charpentier edition reads "veuille."

[98] E. Lavisse, *Histoire de France* (Paris: Hachette, 1921), IV, 245.

One single variation of a purely political nature occurs: this is an allusion to "l'Opposition," which is added in Furne (48+).

Just as men in the real world are compared to historical figures, so in Balzac the social types are epitomized in such comparisons. Up to the Furne edition Troubert is likened to "Philippe II ou Richelieu" (*Char.* 103); in the 1843 edition Balzac says of him: "Nul doute que Troubert n'eût été en d'autres temps *Hildebrandt ou Alexandre VI*" (*Fur.* 61+). The new comparisons keep Troubert more within his own domain, of course, and perhaps symbolize his strength and pitilessness. One wonders, however, if, by substituting the two popes for the fanatically religious Philip and the powerful prime minister, Balzac was answering Sainte-Beuve's criticism of the projection of Troubert to the stature of a Richelieu. In November, 1834, Sainte-Beuve had written: "Son chanoine Troubert se grossit et s'exagère vers la fin au point de nous être donné comme un petit Richelieu."[99] Whatever Balzac's reason for this change, it is interesting to observe that it is the only one of its kind which he makes for the Furne edition. Equally exaggerated comparisons in the very last sentence of the story, a sentence added in Béchet, are not touched: "L'histoire des Innocent III, des Pierre-le-Grand, et de tous les meneurs de siècles prouverait au besoin, dans un ordre très élevé, cette immense pensée que Troubert représentait petitement au fond du cloître Saint-Gatien" (*Béch.* 164+).

The most important realistic variations which Balzac made in revising *Le Curé de Tours* are the sociological changes. Allusions to contemporary organizations are multiplied. In the Béchet edition particularly, the variants set in relief the popular conception of the Congrégation, which was currently credited with great political influence and even a "pouvoir mystérieux" under the government of Charles X. In the Furne a reference to another contemporary institution, the *grande aumônerie*, brings out further the prestige of the "parti-prêtre" under Charles and thus strengthens the impression of actuality in the story. In the Béchet text a number of changes emphasize the pettiness and mediocrity of life in the provinces, a favorite Balzacian subject. Larger generalizations in the same edition develop the theme of the celibate in contemporary society and that of man in the modern world.

Next in importance are those changes which fit *Le Curé de Tours* into the Balzacian world. There are only five such variations, two of which occur in Béchet, and three in Furne. Although the changes in themselves

---

[99] Sainte-Beuve, *Portraits contemporains*, II, 343.

are small, they link effectively both characters and action into Balzac's interlocking scheme and thus contribute to the solidity of the *Comédie humaine*.

As regards truth, thirteen variations illustrate Balzac's effort to bring his story closer to the real world. About half of these alterations are made to secure greater accuracy of expression; two concern truth as an ideal in the novel, and the rest have to do with the actual time of the story. The principal change involving time, that of shifting the action of the story from 1824 to 1826, occurs in Béchet. The other variations made in the interest of truth are slight and are three times as frequent in the Furne text as in the Béchet.

Balzac's penchant for materialism is illustrated in about a dozen changes, but there is no tendency to increase greatly either figures or sums of money. The only exaggeration, that of the number of persons who were guillotined during the Revolution, is justified by the context, since it is the Abbé Birotteau and Mlle Gamard who raise the total figure in their own imaginations. This particular change is found in the Béchet text, but most of the other variants in this category were made for the Furne.

Finally, two short documentary digressions were inserted, illustrating another of Balzac's most prominent realistic traits. Both additions were made in the Béchet text.

This analysis shows that the most important changes took place, then, when our story was set in the framework of the provincial scenes (1834). As we should expect, the sociological variations are outstanding in this edition. Variations concerning truth and solidity are more numerous in the Furne. As regards solidity, however, the changes in Béchet are more significant. On the other hand, Balzac's tendency toward materialism is more manifest in Furne.

b) Technical elements.—No important change in plot is made in *Le Curé de Tours* in its published versions, but the composition is slightly affected by additions which are inserted in the Béchet text. Some of these are used for purposes of anticipation; others explain and sum up action. Interpolations of a different kind which date from the 1834 edition are found in the celebrated duel of words. Here italicized remarks in parentheses show us what the characters are really thinking while they are saying something quite different (see above, p. 246). Let us now consider these changes from the point of view of composition.

Two solid blocks of material are inserted. One of these is the passage on the individual and society which was added at the end of the story

(*Béch.* 162–63+). From the point of view of composition the passage detracts from, rather than adds to, the novel. Balzac may have thought that his story ended abruptly. It now ends tediously and no more logically. The other passage (*Béch.* 138–42+)[100] is a combination of narration and dialogue which is used to point up the scene in Paris between the Baron de Listomère and his uncle and to anticipate the maneuvers which the Listomères make in Tours to outwit Troubert. This insertion marks an improvement in the composition, since it suggests a necessary passage of time and forms a logically built-up transition between episodes widely separated in time and place. In the *princeps* these episodes had been set apart merely by a short clause.

At times, additions may be used to sum up the action: "Ainsi les instructions de M. de Bourbonne étaient sagement exécutées" (*Mame* 400; *Béch.* 146+). Other insertions exemplifying this use are found on pages 100–101+, 145–46+, and 161+ of the Béchet text.

The most important addition is that of the series of unspoken thoughts inserted in the *duel de paroles*. From the point of view of composition, this masked dialogue enables Balzac to give us in quick and dramatic fashion, and without further comment, the psychological accompaniment of the battle of wits that is taking place. He also uses the device once for action: Troubert's decision to accept the overtures of the Listomères. In this instance the author omits a longer explanation of that same decision:

... il est probable que des raisons péremptoires le décidèrent, pendant le débat, à se faire de la famille de Listomère plutôt une alliée qu'une ennemie.
[*Mame* 405]

—*La vieille fille va crever, j'entamerai les Listomère, et les servirai, s'ils me servent!* pensait-il. *Il vaut mieux les avoir pour amis que pour ennemis.*[101]
[*Béch.* 155+]

The quick, concise "thought" is better composition than the slow-moving explanation, and would be so even if stylistically the explanation were less involved, because the thought gives the terms on which Troubert accepted a peace pact with the Listomères. These terms we recall at the turn of the screw, when Troubert a second time threatened the career of the young Baron de Listomère. At this point Balzac inserts the following explanation: "*L'ambitieux marin vint le voir, et le prêtre implacable lui dicta sans doute de dures conditions; car la conduite du baron attesta le plus entier dévoument aux volontés du terrible congréganiste*" (*Mame* 410; *Béch.* 180+). After the interview with the new Bishop of Troyes the lieutenant

---

[100] *Con.*, p. 232, l. 14 to p. 235, l. 4.   [101] The italics are in the text.

contested his aunt's legacy to Birotteau, and "*Quelques jours après l'exploit introductif d'instance*, le baron fut nommé capitaine de vaisseau" (*Béch.* 161+). The italicized phrase replaced the conjunction "mais" (*Mame* 410).

From the point of view of plot and composition, these changes are not of great importance. They are, however, interesting examples of Balzac's method of correction.

From edition to edition of our story Balzac makes many small changes which tend to touch up his characters. There are no new *dossiers*, but details and incidents are added which emphasize the *faculté maîtresse* of the individuals. Generalizations may be introduced which serve to stress the type and profession of the character. For example, after telling us that the two great concerns of Birotteau's life are his desire to be made a canon and his yearning to live in Mlle Gamard's comfortable boarding-house, Balzac adds in Béchet:

... *et peut-être résument-elles* [ces deux grandes affaires] *exactement l'ambition d'un prêtre, qui, se considérant comme en voyage vers l'éternité, ne peut souhaiter en ce monde qu'un bon gîte, une bonne table, des vêtemens propres, des souliers à agrafes d'argent pour satisfaire les besoins de la bête, et un canonicat pour calmer les impatiences de l'amour-propre.*   [*Mame* 286; *Béch.* 38+]

The self-indulgence of both Birotteau and Chapeloud is further stressed. More is made of Birotteau's pleasure in lying in bed while his room grows warm in the mornings (*Mame* 323; *Béch.* 72+), for the vicar was not a man to rise without a fire. Chapeloud, who takes his breakfast coffee in bed, likes it *à la crème*, we are told in Furne (12+).

Emphasis is laid on Chapeloud's ingratiating personality. He is called instead of merely "l'abbé" (*Char.* 8), "cet homme aimable" (*Fur.* 5+). On the other hand, his egotism is stressed:

L'abbé Chapeloud, *homme franc*, aimable et indulgent ... [*Char.* 9]	L'abbé Chapeloud, *égoïste* aimable et indulgent ... [*Fur.* 6+]

Chapeloud's adroitness in handling Mlle Gamard is played up. For his own comfort he accords her only certain courtesies, but in these he knows he must be "plus infaillible que n'est le pape" (*Char.* 20; *Fur.* 12+). This phrase, added in 1843, is an interesting example of Balzac's effort to make his characters speak and think according to their profession.

If Chapeloud's wiles are emphasized, it is Birotteau's family trait of naïveté and even his *niaiserie* which are stressed. His face expresses a "bonhomie sans idées" (*Mame* 325; *Béch.* 74+). He remarks *niaisement* of Troubert: "Je ne sais pas à quoi lui sert de passer les nuits!" (*Mame* 395; *Béch.* 138+). "Un homme du monde" would have known at once that Mlle Gamard was persecuting him with sadistic pleasure. Not so the "bon Birotteau," who had to be hurt by a series of successive scratches in the face "avant de croire à une intention méchante" (*Mame* 302; *Béch.* 53+). In one instance Balzac omits a reference to the vicar's naïveté and simplicity, probably because it is a repetition of the idea contained in the addition to Béchet last mentioned. The following statement does not occur after the *princeps:* "Or, comme le pauvre prêtre avait un grand fonds d'indulgence, les piqûres d'épingle par lesquelles mademoiselle Gamard commença l'attaque ne l'atteignirent pas tout d'abord ..." (*Mame* 321). His innocence and simple goodness are brought out in the scene in which Mme de Listomère reveals to him Troubert's malevolence and power. Balzac inserts after her explanation: *"L'innocent Birotteau joignit ses mains comme pour prier, et pleura de chagrin à l'aspect d'horreurs humaines que son âme pure n'avait jamais soupçonnées"* (*Mame* 396; *Béch.* 143+). A number of variations bring out his weakness. After the first edition Mme de Listomère is made to say to Troubert: "Birotteau, *dont vous devez connaître le caractère faible* ..." (*Mame* 404; *Béch.* 153+). He is spoken of as "la plus faible de toutes les victimes" (*Mame* 411; *Béch.* 161+).

We learn more of Troubert's power, of his varity, and of his vengeful spirit. He is spoken of as "le terrible congréganiste" (*Mame* 410; *Béch.* 160+). M. de Bourbonne advises the Listomères to withdraw their support of Birotteau's lawsuit; if the vicar should win, it would be too late to make peace with Troubert: "Il peut encore vous pardonner d'avoir entamé le combat; mais, après une défaite, il serait implacable" (*Char.* 87; *Fur.* 51+).[102] In another addition Troubert is called "le prêtre implacable" (*Mame* 410; *Béch.* 160+), and Balzac inserts a passage to stress the furious hatred and vindictiveness of this strong-willed churchman:

> *Furieux d'avoir été joué par une femme à laquelle il avait donné la main tandis qu'elle tendait secrètement la sienne à un homme qu'il regardait comme son ennemi, Troubert menaça de nouveau l'avenir du baron et la pairie du marquis de Listomère. Il dit en plein assemblée, dans le salon de l'archevêque, un de ces mots ecclésiastiques, gros de vengeance et pleins de mielleuse mansuétude.* [*Mame* 410; *Béch.* 160+]

Troubert gives to Saint-Gatien the property he has inherited from Mlle Gamard, but not for reasons of piety. Birotteau is placed under an interdict, and Balzac explains in an addition: *"Si Monseigneur Troubert*

[102] The sentence, as a whole, is an addition in Béchet. "Vous" and "d'avoir entamé le combat" were added in Furne.

avait conservé la succession de la vieille fille, il lui eût été difficile de faire censurer Birotteau" (*Mame* 412; *Béch.* 161+).

M. de Bourbonne suspects, an addition tells us, that Troubert's vanity may be even greater than his hatred: "*Pliez devant Troubert: si sa haine est moins forte que sa vanité, vous vous en ferez un allié; mais si vous pliez trop, il vous marchera sur le ventre*" (*Mame* 395; *Béch.* 140–41+). A number of additions in Béchet develop the vanity of Troubert. One amusing phrase suggests his colossal self-esteem. When Mme de Listomère comes to call, he makes the baroness wait, and then: "... il consentit à lui donner audience" (*Mame* 401; *Béch.* 147+). He makes Mme de Listomère tell him why she has come to him with Birotteau's nonsuit, not because he does not know, but because, an insertion tells us, the vengeful priest is "*excité par un sentiment analogue à celui qui pousse une femme à se faire répéter des complimens*" (*Mame* 404; *Béch.* 153+). We even learn in these additions that Troubert has a characteristic gesture. M. de Bourbonne tells Mme de Listomère: "*S'il se caresse le menton, vous l'aurez séduit*" (*Mame* 401; *Béch.* 148+). When the baroness invites the canon to her salon, Balzac inserts: "Troubert se caressa le menton. —*Il est pris! Bourbonne avait raison*, pensait-elle, *il a sa dose de vanité!*"[103] (*Mame* 405; *Béch.* 154+). And Balzac adds: "—*En effet, le grand-vicaire éprouvait en ce moment la sensation délicieuse contre laquelle Mirabeau ne savait pas se défendre, quand, aux jours de sa puissance, il voyait ouvrir devant sa voiture la porte cochère d'un hôtel autrefois fermé pour lui*" (*Mame* 405; *Béch.* 155+).

A few touches are added to the portrait of Mme de Listomère. Balzac inserts in her *dossier* that she is "*bonne, mais un peu raide; légèrement nasillarde ...*" (*Mame* 357; *Béch.* 104+). In her verbal duel with Troubert, one of her "thoughts" tells us what she thinks of herself. When she remarks that she takes little interest now in Birotteau, Troubert interrupts by reminding her that the vicar is, after all, her *pensionnaire*. She replies: "—Non, monsieur, il n'est plus chez moi. —*La pairie de mon beau-frère et le grade de mon neveu, me font faire bien des lâchetés*, pensait-elle" (*Mame* 403; *Béch.* 152+). But family solidarity is a characteristic of the Listomères, and Mme de Listomère's remark emphasizes her adherence to the family code.

M. de Bourbonne's quick insight is again stressed by means of his *tic*. Having shown the Listomères how to placate Troubert, he adds: " '*J'ai dit.*' Et il fait claquer sa tabatière" (*Mame* 395; *Béch.* 142+). The wiliness

---

[103] These italics are in the text.

of the old gentleman is brought out when we are told in Béchet that, wishing to know what the Baron de Listomère had learned in Paris, "*Le vieux malin n'avait prématurément cherché sa canne et son chapeau que pour se faire dire à l'oreille: —Restez, nous avons à causer*" (*Mame* 395; *Béch.* 139+).

Descriptions both of people and of the milieu are built up by means of added detail as our story progresses from edition to edition. Mlle Gamard's lean rigidity is emphasized by the fact that her dress is too tight (*Char.* 44; *Fur.* 27+). Just as her nose reveals the despotism of her ideas, Balzac adds in Béchet that the flatness of her forehead betrays their narrowness: "... la forme *plate* de son front en trahissait l'étroitesse" (*Mame* 342; *Béch.* 89+). The adjective is an addition in Béchet.

The *salon jaune*, which is so expressive of the vindictive old maid's personality, is retouched. The furnishings are now listed in a typical Balzacian enumeration. Each new article suggests the keynote of the room:

Le salon commun où elle recevait était digne d'elle; il sera bientôt connu, en faisant observer qu'il se nommait le salon jaune, et *qu'il y avait sur la cheminée des flambeaux et une pendule en cristal.* [*Mame* 343]	Le salon commun où elle recevait, était digne d'elle. Il sera bientôt connu en faisant observer qu'il se nommait le salon jaune; *que les draperies en étaient jaunes, le meuble et la tenture jaunes; que sur la cheminée garnie d'une glace à cadre doré, des flambeaux et une pendule en cristal jetaient un éclat dur à l'œil.* [*Béch.* 91+]

The kinds of detail used by Balzac in his descriptions may differ greatly. A detail may be simply cumulative, as when Mlle Gamard's "chaise" (*Mame* 332) becomes a "chaise à patin" (*Béch.* 80+). Again, we are told that the jambs and lintel of Chapeloud's fireplace were made of badly carved stone. Balzac changes this description in Furne to read: "Les chambranles des cheminées en pierre mal sculptée *n'avaient jamais été peints*" (*Char.* 6; *Fur.* 5+). The detail may be merely additional. Balzac adds to the information concerning the length of the bridge of Tours a detail to suggest its beauty: "Ce pont, *un des plus beaux monumens de l'architecture française*, a dix-sept cents pieds de long ..." (*Mame* 409; *Béch.* 158+).

The causal detail is illustrated by one variation, an addition in Béchet. Tormented and harassed by Mlle Gamard, the Abbé Birotteau is so unhappy that his health is affected. It is not, however, until he realizes one morning that his legs have grown much thinner that he decides to take some measures against her persecutions:

Un matin, en mettant ses bas bleus chinés, il reconnut une perte de huit lignes dans la circonférence de son mollet; stupéfait de ce diagnostic si cruellement irrécusable, il résolut de faire une tentative auprès de l'abbé Troubert, pour le prier d'intervenir officieusement entre mademoiselle Gamard et lui.

[*Mame* 349; *Béch.* 97+]

A variation illustrating Balzac's use of exact detail has been quoted above (p. 260) as an example of documentary digression. In this description Balzac accumulates historical and architectural details concerning the surroundings of Saint-Gatien.

To summarize the variations deriving from Balzac's narrative technique, now fully matured, we find that, numerically, those concerning characterization are the most important. Changes in description and detail are next in order of frequency, while alterations which pertain to composition are the least common.

As regards the composition, we have seen that it was not materially affected by the variations. It should be noted, though, that such changes as there are, were all made for the Béchet edition.

Eleven changes enrich descriptions both of the personages and of the milieu. In every case the method of revision is that of added detail. Again, it is the second edition of the story which is most affected by these variants, since nine of the changes are found in Béchet.

Balzac's preoccupation with characterization is evidenced by twenty-eight variants which he introduced in revising the editions of our story. Behind all these changes is the author's principle of harmonizing or keynoting a character. The variations are usually small inserted details which emphasize the dominant trait of the individual, though an occasional generalization may stress his type. Of these emendations, twenty-three were made in the Béchet edition, the rest in the Furne.

Our summary of the technical emendations shows us, first, that the variations in this category are, for the most part, short. The fact, however, that the changes are small is in itself significant, since it proves once more Balzac's infinite care in detail in every feature of his writing. We learn, in the second place, that, just as the majority of the changes deriving from his general realistic qualities were more significant in the Béchet volume, in like manner the variants considered specifically under his technique are more important in this same text. Thus, of all the editions of *Le Curé de Tours*, the second is the most fruitful in examples of Balzac's realistic method as illustrated in his corrections.

III. CONCLUSION

The several texts of our story have yielded a host of variants. Although not all these changes are felicitous, the majority of them seem warranted. The style of the definitive edition of *Le Curé de Tours* is more correct, vigorous, and exact than that of the manuscript. Moreover, in accord with Balzac's realistic method, a number of variations introduced between the first and final versions have heightened the realism of the novel.

The variants are not difficult, except for the fact that there is such a plethora of them. Undue importance must not, of course, be attached to the mere number of changes, since in any given category the variations are never of equal importance. The numbers do, however, indicate the predominant trends in Balzac's corrections. Our problem has been to find what kinds of variations the author introduced most often in his revisions and to try to determine how effective these changes were. Let us now examine our results and endeavor to see with what concepts of his art Balzac was most concerned in his corrections.

The numerous stylistic variations attest to his desire to perfect his prose. From the manuscript to the definitive edition we have seen Balzac striving for greater simplicity. The number of sentences which he shortened is impressive. In the manuscript the sentences are strung together by means of conjunctions or simply by commas and dashes. Slowly, from the proofs through the editions, the sentences have become briefer and terser, though a few overlong ones have not been eliminated. Clauses, as well as sentences, tend almost always in the first *jet* to be involved and cumbersome. These, too, have been simplified through successive changes. However, Balzac's endeavor to lighten his style sometimes finds itself in conflict with his inclination to tell the whole truth and consequently to accumulate details. In such cases his realism almost always triumphs over his desire for restraint, and his sentences become dilated with serried bits of information.

In his corrections Balzac had recourse, as we have seen, to a number of rhetorical devices. Amplifications and additions have increased the clarity and accuracy of the style. By means of omissions and compressions he has made his prose more concise and also, usually, clearer. A number of omissions were made to avoid redundancy. Transpositions within sentences were effected for the sake of clearness and for smoothness, and sometimes to produce a more pleasing combination of sounds. Figures of speech are not often affected in the variations. However, some of Balzac's most original and picturesque images were added in these corrections. The only important changes in dialogue were introduced in the Béchet text and have remained practically untouched since. These passages are interesting and move swiftly, proving Balzac's ability to invent dialogue. Speech-words were inserted for clearness and sometimes for dramatic effect. Rhetorical questions occurred infrequently in the variations, although Balzac was fond of inversions. An occasional new interjection or a repetition added intensity to his prose.

The changes involving the parts of speech were the most numerous in any revision. We have mentioned many times Balzac's search for the *mot propre*. Our study of the variations proves this trait to be the salient stylistic feature of his corrections for *Le Curé de Tours*. Verbs and conjunctions are more frequently affected than any other part of speech. As regards verbs, Balzac does not seem to have been always sure of himself, since his changes are at times restorations of earlier expressions. However, on the whole, the effort to find a forceful and exact verb is a strong objective in these revisions. The importance of conjunctions in the variants is due largely to Balzac's endeavor to shorten his sentences. Changes involving nouns are less numerous than those affecting verbs, probably because Balzac chose with greater ease concrete names to describe the men, women, and things he was depicting than he did the verbs with which he sought to show the interrelationship between "les personnes et la représentation matérielle qu'ils donnent de leur pensée." However, the variants in which nouns are concerned are sufficiently numerous to demonstrate Balzac's constant attention to this element of his prose and to prove that the effect of the exact, concrete noun in his style was not achieved without effort. The substitution of a noun for a pronoun is a very frequent change and again illustrates the author's bent for the concrete. This tendency is especially marked in the Furne edition, where the prose gains in exactness and concision from many small changes involving nouns and pronouns. This insistence on the exact word in the Furne indicates perhaps that definiteness and concreteness of style were increasingly important to Balzac. Of the other parts of speech which Balzac changed frequently in his various revisions, adverbs were most often affected. Adverbs were introduced principally for reasons of emphasis, color, and variety.

These minute changes involving the parts of speech contribute greatly to the vigor of the prose in *Le Curé de Tours*. The style of the story evolves slowly by means of literally thousands of corrections, but it gains through the years both in directness and in vividness. The general principle behind all the stylistic changes is Balzac's desire for clearness and exactness. His very faults derive from his desire to be clear and accurate, for he sometimes confuses these qualities with completeness of detail. On the whole, however, the style has been increasingly suited to the simple short narrative he is recounting.

The variations deriving from Balzac's realistic method are far from numerous, but they illustrate some of his salient traits. Changes involving his passion for truth are found in all the revisions. An effort to attain truth through greater accuracy of statement is seen from the first proof through the Furne edition. It is also for the sake of truth that some effort is made to correct inconsistencies of time, though Balzac has not concentrated on the time element when the psychological problem is more important. A number of variations involve money and things, but there is no tendency toward exaggeration of materialism. Sociological changes show Balzac continually striving to record society faithfully. *Dossiers* are inserted to build up social and biographical backgrounds. Additions to a legal contract illustrate Balzac's desire to expand the novel with technical documents. Two semitechnical digressions treat briefly of archeology and of semantics. Solidity, or the effort to link the novel with the *Comédie humaine*, accounts for a shift in the time of the action in the story and for the introduction of a reappearing character. These variations were naturally introduced after the 1832 edition and were made respectively in the Béchet and Furne texts.

When we turn to the changes involving the technical elements, we find that the plot and composition of the story are only slightly affected by the variations. A number of blocks of material which were transposed in the first proof show that Balzac had some trouble with organization. Passages of narration and dialogue inserted in the second edition add interest to the novel and contribute to the proportion and harmony of the composition. The sociophilosophic passage appended to the end of the story after the first edition is an example of the long-windedness of which Balzac is capable at times. The addition spoils the conclusion of the novel and so, from the point of view of technique, is unfortunate. As an example of his generalizing tendencies, the addition is, however, characteristic. A number of insertions are concerned with descriptions and characterization. Both the milieu and the characters are consistently built up from version to version by means of added details. This process exemplifies one of the cardinal principles of Balzac's literary method—his analytical technique.

As regards the realistic variations, the most important revisions were made for three texts: the first edition; the second edition, when the story was transferred from the *Scènes de la vie privée* to the *Scènes de la vie de province;* and the Furne, or first edition of the *Comédie humaine.* The most significant changes introduced for the *princeps* were the *dossiers* of Mme de Listomère, Mlle Salomon, and M. de Bourbonne. Salient in the Béchet edition are the variations which stress Balzac's sociological bent. A number of these serve to fit the story more completely into the *Scènes de la vie de province;* they frequently add a darkening touch to the picture and tend to bring out the somberness and mediocrity of provincial life. The second edition is also important because of additions which enrich the characterization in the novel and of other inserted fictional elements which perfect its composition. The Furne text is notable for the introduction of a reappearing character. It should be borne in mind, however, that *Le Curé de Tours* was well conceived in its main lines in the manuscript and that the realistic variations are, for the most part, small alterations. Nevertheless, these little changes in the aggregate contribute, in some measure, to the impression of reality which characterizes the novel.

If we examine Table 1 (p. 196) we note that the realistic variations increase after the first edition. This fact is largely accounted for by the details which Balzac added, particularly in Béchet, to round out characters and descriptions and by the small alterations which he made to set his story snugly in its proper niche. Contrary to the realistic variations, the stylistic variants are more frequent in the early versions of the novel through the *princeps.* The author would naturally make every effort to give his prose the most perfect finish possible before publication. The slowness with which the narrative portions of the text evolved, as compared to the swiftness with which the dialogue took form, is a salient feature of these variations, as it is, in fact, of Balzac's genius.

The realistic variations in their scope and variety are characteristic of Balzac's method, which aimed to portray with absolute fidelity the nineteenth-century comedy of manners and men which the author was watching. The stylistic changes bear mute witness to the price he paid in following his ideal.

BIBLIOGRAPHY

BALZAC, H. DE. *Avant-propos. Œuvres complètes*, Vol. I. Paris: Conard, 1912.

——. *Les Célibataires* (*Le Curé de Tours*) *1832*, Manuscrit et épreuves corrigées; *Supplement to Les Célibataires* (*Le Curé de Tours*) *1832*, Manuscrit et épreuves corrigées; in the University of Chicago Libraries. Bound photostatic copies (Paris, 1929) of the manuscript, *brouillons*, and author's proofs in the Lovenjoul Collection, listed in that collection as "A 11–A 12. *Les Célibataires* (*Le Curé de Tours*) *1832*, Manuscrit autographe et épreuves avec additions et corrections de l'auteur."

——. *Les Célibataires. Scènes de la vie privée*, Vol. III. Paris: Mame-Delaunay, 1832.

——. *Les Célibataires. Scènes de la vie de province*, Vol. II. Paris: Mme Charles-Béchet, 1834.

——. *Les Célibataires. Scènes de la vie de province*, Vol. II. Paris: Charpentier, 1839.

——. *Les Célibataires: Le Curé de Tours. La Comédie humaine*, Vol. VI. Paris: Furne, Dubochet et Hetzel, 1843.

——. *Les Célibataires: Le Curé de Tours. Œuvres complètes*, Vol. IX. Paris: Conard, 1913.

——. *Correspondance, 1819–1850. Œuvres complètes*, Vol. XXIV. Paris: Calmann-Lévy, 1876.

——. *Correspondance inédite avec Madame Zulma Carraud* (*1829–1850*). Paris: A. Colin, 1935.

——. *Le Député d'Arcis*, Vols. I and II. Paris: L. de Potter, 1854.

——. *Le Député d'Arcis. Œuvres complètes*, Vol. XXI. Paris: Conard, 1914.

——. *Lettres à l'Etrangère*. Paris: Calmann-Lévy, [1899], 1906, 1933. 3 vols.

——. *Letters to His Family, 1809–1850* (ed. Walter Scott Hastings). Princeton: Princeton University Press, 1934.

——. *Histoire intellectuelle de Louis Lambert*. Paris: Gosselin, 1833.

——. *Histoire intellectuelle de Louis Lambert. Le Livre mystique*, Vol. I. Paris: Werdet, 1835.

——. *Louis Lambert*. Paris: Charpentier, 1842.

——. *Notice biographique sur Louis Lambert. Nouveaux Contes philosophiques*. Paris: Gosselin, 1832.

——. *Le Prêtre catholique*, Manuscrit autographe inachevé, écrit en 1834. Lov. Coll., A 196.

ALAIN (pseud. of Émile Chartier). *Avec Balzac*. Paris: Gallimard, 1937.

ARRIGON, L.-J. *Les Débuts littéraires d'Honoré de Balzac*. Paris: Perrin, 1924.

BOUTERON, MARCEL (ed.). *Lettres de femmes adressées à Honoré de Balzac, première série* (*1832–1856*) ("Cahiers balzaciens," No. 3). Paris: Castellan, 1924.

CANFIELD, A. G. "Les Personnages reparaissants dans *la Comédie humaine*," *Revue d'histoire littéraire*, XLI (1934), 15–31; 198–214.

DARGAN, E. PRESTON; CRAIN, W. L.; and OTHERS. *Studies in Balzac's Realism*. Chicago: University of Chicago Press, 1932.

DUVIARD, FERDINAND. *Un Prédécesseur de Ferdinand Fabre, Balzac romancier clérical dans Le Curé de Tours*. Cahors: Bergon, [1927].

HANOTAUX, GABRIEL, et VICAIRE, GEORGES. *La Jeunesse de Balzac: Balzac imprimeur; Balzac et Madame de Berny*. New ed.; Paris: Ferroud, 1921.

SAINTE-BEUVE, CHARLES-AUGUSTIN. *Portraits contemporains*, Vol. II. Paris: Michel Lévy, 1869.

SPOELBERCH DE LOVENJOUL, CHARLES DE. *Histoire des œuvres de H. de Balzac*. 3d ed.; Paris: Calmann-Lévy, 1888.

WENGER, JARED. *The Province and the Provinces in the Work of Honoré de Balzac*. Princeton, 1937.

CHAPTER IV

AN INTRODUCTION TO A CRITICAL EDITION OF
LE SECRET DES RUGGIERI

By WILLIAM L. CRAIN

University of Kansas City

I

T HE fame of the *Comédie humaine* as a whole—magnificent in its scope, faithful in its recording of observed detail, penetrating in its analysis of contemporary French manners—has not prevented certain critics from perceiving that the man who fathered the realistic novel in France was at the same time an outstanding figure in an essentially romantic genre. Of the series of novels and *nouvelles* in which Balzac partly fulfilled his early intention of writing "a picturesque history of France," the most important is the trilogy *Sur Catherine de Médicis*, one of whose parts—originally called *Le Secret des Ruggieri*—is the subject of the present study.[1]

According to Wells, "the novel, as a whole, is sufficient to show that Balzac might have been as easily the first historical novelist of France as he is first in other fields of fiction."[2] Bellessort calls the work "une de nos plus fortes études de nos Guerres de Religion."[3] Both writers praise our author for his description of people and of places, remarking in this historical novel the same archeological preoccupation which anchors the rest of the *Comédie humaine* so firmly in time and space. For, as Bellessort points out,

[1] It should be explained that my dissertation, "A Critical Edition of Balzac's *Le Secret des Ruggieri*," complete in typewritten form, can be consulted at the University of Chicago Libraries under the call number "f PQ2163.C87 1937." In revising the Introduction for publication in the present volume I have eliminated, as far as possible, actual cross-references to the edition proper. Occasionally, however, it will be necessary to speak of readings that have nowhere been published or to refer to *Chronique de Paris* readings, the text of which is not available in America except in my unpublished critical edition.

[2] B. W. Wells, *A Century of French Fiction*, p. 146. See also p. 107.

[3] A. Bellessort, *Balzac et son œuvre*, p. 94.

Il ne pardonnait pas au progrès de la voirie la disparition d'un Paris dont son *Martyr calviniste* et *le Secret des Ruggieri* nous avaient donné de si pittoresques eaux-fortes; d'un Paris "qui n'existera plus que dans les ouvrages des romanciers assez courageux pour décrire fidèlement les derniers vestiges de l'architecture de nos pères."[4]

Wells finds *Sur Catherine de Médicis* "interesting for its minute archaeological reproduction both of buildings and of manners, and also for its analysis of the complex nature and policy of Catherine, *whom Balzac seems to have been one of the first to apprehend.*"[5]

It is this very point—as to whether Balzac really did apprehend the character of Catherine—which will determine for many readers the novel's truth, historically speaking. For Catherine's personality is the unifying force—the keynote—of the various parts. Several reviewers have recognized this fact, and one of them writes:

In Balzac's brilliant study she is the enigmatic "Mona Lisa," whose inward irony shines forth on subtle, sarcastic lips and in lustrous, sideward glancing eyes; an unintelligible woman, who combined serpent guile with dove-like wisdom, and who overshadowed her three kingly sons with the pure force of her virile and implacable nature. Florence never produced a more singular piece of mosaic than this woman.[6]

Some critics, notably Baldensperger and Saintsbury, feel that Balzac's *Etude philosophique* "on" Catherine[7] was not completely successful; Baldensperger, considering it "une des œuvres les plus prétentieuses de Balzac," goes so far as to call it "une des tentatives les moins réussies."[8] Before we can evaluate these unfavorable opinions of the novel, we ought to be more familiar with the history of its publication and with the subject matter of the different parts.

---

[4] *Ibid.*, p. 159. The Balzac quotation is taken from *Ce qui disparaît de Paris* (*OD.*, Vol. XXI), p. 437.

[5] *Op. cit.*, p. 145. Italics mine.

[6] Anonymous review of Katharine Prescott Wormeley's translation (Roberts Brothers' ed.), in *The Critic*, XXIII (January 12, 1895), 25–26. See also a review in *ibid.*, XXVIII (November 13, 1897), 281–82.

[7] It was George Saintsbury, in his Preface to the novel, who said that it was "important to remember the *Sur* if injustice is not to be done to the intentions of the author." The Saintsbury Preface has been reprinted several times (see Royce, *A Balzac Bibliography*, p. 186); in the Gebbie ed., from which we cite now and later, it occupies pp. ix–xiii.

[8] Fernand Baldensperger, *Orientations étrangères chez Honoré de Balzac*, p. ˙64 and p. 63.

II

In the history of the publication of *Sur Catherine de Médicis*[9] lies a partial explanation of the disparity in quality which we shall note in the four divisions that make up the complete novel.[10] For they were composed in exactly the reverse of their present order, and the dates of first publication extend over the period from 1830 to 1843. Only the "Préface" —or "Introduction," as it was later called—was *inédite* when, in January, 1843, the four divisions appeared under a collective title for the first time. Hippolyte Souverain was the publisher, and the title was *Catherine de Médicis expliquée* (three volumes in octavo, dated 1842). Since the order of the various parts was the one maintained ever since, it is convenient to continue with the history of the collective publications before going back to the previous history of the individual stories.

The Souverain arrangement (with the relative length of the divisions indicated by means of Conard paging) was as follows:

"Préface"[11] (occupying 46 pages in the definitive Conard edition)
"Première partie: *Le Martyr calviniste*" (210 pages in Conard)
"Deuxième partie: *Le Secret des Ruggieri*" (83 pages in Conard)
"Troisième partie: *Les Deux Rêves*" (18 pages in Conard)

The Souverain edition, with its original 1842 title-pages, is today extremely rare, for a large part of the edition appeared "En vente chez Chlendowski, rue du Jardinet, 8" with the *millésime* 1845.[12] The Chlendowski

[9] The starting-point for the history of publication of any novel by Balzac is, of course, Lovenjoul's *Histoire des œuvres de H. de Balzac* (3d ed.). *Sur Catherine de Médicis* is discussed on pp. 185–90 and 425–27. The present investigator has not limited himself to this work but has checked with the *Bibliographie de la France* and with the original editions themselves. An article by Lovenjoul, "Les *Études philosophiques* de Honoré de Balzac," *RHL*, 14th year (July–September, 1907), pp. 393–441, furnishes indispensable information concerning the history of *Le Secret des Ruggieri* and of *Le Martyr calviniste*. This article, still in process of publication at the time of Lovenjoul's death, was his last work; without it there would be a great gap in our knowledge of the *Études philosophiques*.

[10] Although the novel is properly called a trilogy, the "Introduction" is long and important enough to be designated one of the four divisions.

[11] Called "Introduction" in the subsequent editions and so referred to by Lovenjoul and in the Conard notes. Except for a long omission whose text is reproduced in Lov., *Hist.*, pp. 187–88, and which we shall discuss in connection with the interrelationship of the four divisions, the "Préface" remains substantially unchanged when it becomes the "Introduction." We shall, in general, refer to it by the latter title, and for the reader's convenience shall give both the Souverain and the Conard paging of any passages cited.

[12] The Conard notes (XXX, 397) are strangely misleading with reference to the dating and contents of the Souverain ed.: "La première et la deuxième partie, précédées

is not a genuine separate edition but merely a reissue with new title-pages. The text being that of Souverain, we shall use the latter name alone to designate the readings of either the original issue or the reissue.

In the Souverain edition (and consequently in the Chlendowski reissue) the work was dedicated thus:

DÉDICACE.[13]

À Monsieur le Marquis de Pastoret,

MEMBRE DE L'ACADÉMIE DES BEAUX-ARTS.

—INSTITUT.—

There followed, undated, the rather long dedicatory note which appears in subsequent editions with the date "Paris, janvier 1842." In this note Balzac laments the researches which have been wasted in an attempt to find, for example, the exact spot where Hannibal crossed the Alps, when modern history is so neglected and "les calomnies les plus odieuses pèsent encore sur des noms qui devraient être révérés." Especially does he regret that "l'histoire la plus importante au temps actuel, celle de la Réformation," is full of obscurities. But Balzac and the Marquis de Pastoret have made independently "les mêmes recherches sur la grande et belle figure de Catherine de Médicis," and in thus dedicating his novel our author desires to pay "au caractère et à la fidélité de l'homme monarchique, un public hommage, peut-être précieux par sa rareté."[14]

---

d'une introduction, furent imprimées, en volumes, en 1842 pour paraître chez Souverain, en 1845 (3 vols. in-8°), avec dédicace, datées de janvier 1843. L'ouvrage portait le titre général de: *Catherine de Médicis expliquée* et se divisait en: *Introduction;* I. *Le Martyr calviniste;* II. *Le Secret de Ruggieri.*" The annotator completely neglects the appearance of *Les Deux Rêves* in the Souverain, saying that this third part was *added* in 1846 for the Furne publication. Lovenjoul, cited as authority for the Conard note, avoids this error and also recognizes the true dating of the Souverain ed. as 1842; he does not mention the Chlendowski reissue. The present writer has seen one copy of the work bearing both the date 1845 and the name of Souverain as publisher, but ordinarily it is the Chlendowski sales announcement which appears. The *Bibliographie de la France* announced the Chlendowski contract as early as the August 31 and September 7, 1844, issues, and on September 21, 1844, stated that *Le Martyr calviniste* (actually the whole of *Catherine de Médicis expliquée*) was on sale.

[13] In subsequent editions the words "Dédicace" and "Institut" were dropped.

[14] The Marquis de Pastoret, whose historical researches and monarchical leanings Balzac praises, was the author of an anonymous work entitled *Le Duc de Guise à Naples,* or *Mémoires sur les révolutions de ce royaume en 1647 et 1648;* in 1828 Balzac, who was then in the printing business, printed the title-pages, if not the text proper, of the 2d ed. (see Conard notes, XXX, 398). The present writer has examined, in a Paris *librairie,* a copy of Pastoret's volume with the notation on the verso of the half-title: "IMPRIMERIE DE H. BALZAC/Rue des Marais S. G. n. 17."

The complete work next appeared in Volume XV (pp. 468–662) and Volume XVI (pp. 1–78) of the first edition of the *Comédie humaine*, published by Furne, Dubochet et Hetzel—familiarly called the "Furne edition." Both volumes appeared in 1846, although the former is dated 1845; they were the second and third volumes, respectively, of the fifth edition of the *Etudes philosophiques*. The novel bears its final title, *Sur Catherine de Médicis*. The word "expliquée" in the earlier edition perfectly expresses Balzac's intention as set forth in the "Préface," or "Introduction"; and, although one of the "explanatory" passages was deleted from the Furne text (see above, n. 11), the old title would still be appropriate. In the present title the "Sur" is pretty weak, and Saintsbury's gentle warning is needed.

In the Furne edition Parts I–III retained their earlier titles with the exception of *Le Secret des Ruggieri*, which was called *La Confidence des Ruggieri*. In the title of my unpublished critical edition (see above, n. 1), *Le Secret* has been preferred rather than *La Confidence*, because the former was the title under which the story had an independent existence. Incidentally, besides being somewhat ambiguous, *La Confidence* is the less intriguing title; *Le Secret* piques the reader's interest at once.

Changing none of the titles henceforth, Balzac still wrote textual corrections on the flyleaves and margins of his copy of the Furne edition, carrying on a process of revision which, for *Le Secret des Ruggieri* at least, had begun with the unfinished manuscript and had continued through several sets of proofs and the successive publications. Study of the proof sheets and editions of *Le Secret* discloses some oversights which, if detected in time, would have affected the final text; nevertheless, since Balzac personally revised the various forms, I believe the Conard editors had no choice but to use the corrected Furne text, embodying the author's final intentions, as the basis for their "definitive" edition.

Of the three stories that had an independent history prior to the Souverain edition, *Les Deux Rêves* was the earliest. If Balzac's dating ("Paris, janvier 1828") is correct, it ranks with *Les Chouans* and *La Physiologie du mariage* as one of the first works of the *Comédie humaine* to be composed. It was first published in *La Mode* of May 8, 1830; then in the December (1830) number of the *Revue des deux mondes* with a new title, *Le Petit Souper, conte fantastique*. Upon publication in volume form for the first time, in Volume III of the *Romans et contes philosophiques*,[15] it resumed its

---

[15] Published by Charles Gosselin, September, 1831; 3 vols., in octavo. *Les Deux Rêves* reappeared in Vol. II of the 1832 ed. of the *Contes philosophiques* (2 vols., in octavo), and in Vol. IV of the 1833 ed. of the *Romans et contes philosophiques* (4 vols., in octavo)—all published by Gosselin.

original title, which has since been maintained. It was published with three other *nouvelles* in Volume XII of the *Etudes philosophiques* in 1837, in the same *livraison* with *Le Secret des Ruggieri*, and under almost the same peculiar conditions as regards publishers' names and the dating of the volume (see below). This was its last independent publication.

Le Secret des Ruggieri first appeared in journal form in the *Chronique de Paris* of December 4, 11, and 18, 1836, and January 22, 1837. Its only publication in volume form before the Furne edition was as Volume XIII of the *Etudes philosophiques*, third *livraison*. Although bearing the name Werdet and the *millésime* 1836 on the title-page, it was not actually put on sale until August of 1837. For, as Lovenjoul explains,[16] the "quasi-faillite" of Werdet, occurring shortly after the appearance of the second *livraison* in August or September, 1836, required his successors to make important modifications in the subdivisions of the succeeding volumes of *Etudes philosophiques*. Most of them were delayed, the third *livraison* (5 vols.) appearing August 17, 1837, after having been "déposée et enregistrée dans la *Bibliographie de la France* du 8 juillet 1837." They were brought out by Delloye et Lecou, "acquéreurs des traités passés par Balzac avec Werdet."

Not only were publishers changed, but printers as well, even within the same volume; Lovenjoul warns us that when "les noms de Béthune et Plon, comme imprimeurs, sont inscrits à la seconde page de chacun des titres," this last indication, "malgré son apparence officielle," is far from being exact.[17] Later in the same article[18] we read:

Pour le tome treize: *Le Secret des Ruggieri*, cette déplorable combinaison d'impressions diverses se produit de nouveau. Les dix premières feuilles, dont la dernière page est chiffrée 117–118, furent imprimées et tirées chez Baudouin, 2, rue Mignon, et les feuilles onze à vingt, qui terminent le volume, sortent, ainsi que le titre et la couverture, des presses de Béthune et Plon. Néanmoins, l'exemplaire de Balzac porte un titre au nom de Werdet, avec le millésime de 1836. Ce titre, imprimé chez Baudouin, désigne donc ce dernier comme l'imprimeur de tout le volume!!

[16] Art. cit., *RHL*, 1907, pp. 394–95.

[17] *Ibid.*, p. 426. At this point Lovenjoul also states that "le nom de Werdet est remplacé, sur les titres et couvertures, par ceux de Delloye et Lecou, comme éditeurs." While true of other volumes of the third *livraison*, this is probably incorrect as regards the title-page of *Le Secret des Ruggieri*, which, in all the copies I have seen, keeps the name of Werdet. For Vol. XIII, the date 1837 and the names of Delloye et Lecou appear only on the covers.

[18] *Ibid.*, p. 430.

This information takes on special significance in connection with our study of proof sheets, for the first ten *feuilles*, printed by P. Baudouin, correspond exactly to Chapter I of the story; and the remaining ten, which Lovenjoul says were printed by Béthune et Plon, comprise Chapters II and III. Lovenjoul apparently thinks that the title-page of Balzac's copy was unique, but the present investigator owns one copy and has used two others, all of which agree with Balzac's in having the name of Werdet as publisher on the title-page. Since these copies are bound without the covers, the names of Delloye et Lecou do not appear at all. We shall therefore refer to this as the "Werdet edition" in spite of its being issued and sold by Delloye et Lecou.

The history of *Le Martyr calviniste* before the Furne edition likewise reflects an interesting phase of Balzac's life as "homme d'affaires," involving not only Werdet's pseudo-bankruptcy but also a struggle with Belgian pirating. In consequence of the Werdet affair, the story never appeared in the Werdet series of *Études philosophiques* at any time but was first published in *Le Siècle* under the title of *Les Lecamus*, from March 23 to April 4, 1841. However, it was written, at least in part, several years earlier—a fact we should keep in mind in view of the story's relationship with *Le Secret des Ruggieri*.[19] Exactly when it was written, and how completely at any one stage, we cannot determine; but Lovenjoul's article, already referred to, is very helpful. He says that it was first intended for publication as *Un Martyr* in Volume XII (1837) of the Werdet series and that it was then announced successively as *Le Pelletier de la Reine* and *Le Fils du pelletier* before it appeared as *Les Lecamus*.[20] Volume XII, like the volume which contains *Le Secret des Ruggieri*, was printed by two different firms: the first fourteen *feuilles*, in 1836, by Baudouin; and the remaining eight *feuilles*, together with the covers and title-page, by Béthune et Plon, in 1837. If Balzac had carried out his original plans, the last story in the volume would have been not *Les Martyrs ignorés* but the one which we now know as *Le Martyr calviniste*.[21]

---

[19] See pp. 345–59, below, for a discussion of variants in the published form of both stories as a result of their appearing together.

[20] *Ibid.*, p. 395. In Lov., *Hist.*, p. 186, the author gives still another announced title: *Les Lecamus ou Catherine de Médicis prise au piége.*

[21] A curiously ambiguous title-page, *Un Martyr*, intended for *Le Martyr calviniste* but kept for *Les Martyrs ignorés* because it was the last sheet of a *feuille* and could not be removed, serves to remind us of Balzac's change in publishing plans. From Lovenjoul's article we can piece together an almost complete history of *Le Martyr calviniste* while it was still called *Un Martyr*. He dates the conception of the story as 1835, or, at

So much for the delays in publication caused in part by Werdet's "bankruptcy." As for the effect of Belgian counterfeiting, a long note inserted by Balzac at the end of Volume I of the Souverain edition is significant. There he tries to explain away an error in the use of the term "Calvinistes"[22] in the early part of that edition by blaming it on the Belgians. "Talonnée par la contrefaçon," he says, "la littérature est obligée de ruser avec la Belgique"; and "les auteurs français, pour tromper l'avidité des pirates de Bruxelles, ne publient point en entier leurs romans dans les journaux." Alleging that the subscribers to *Le Siècle* found the appellation "Calvinistes" more intelligible than "Réformés," he pleads that in his preoccupation with enlarging *Les Lecamus* (9 chapters) into *Le Martyr calviniste* (18 chapters) he failed to correct the journal version with sufficient care.[23] The Belgian publication of *Les Lecamus* was by the firm of Meline, Cans et Compagnie, of Brussels, in 1841—two years before its first appearance in volume form in France—and, as Balzac points out, it follows the text of *Le Siècle*.

III

What was the nature of the three stories whose early history we have been tracing? What prompted Balzac to concern himself with Catherine for so many years, finally grouping the separate works under one title? Saintsbury's Preface contains some pertinent observations on these points:

And though it is, let it be repeated, a mistake, and a rather unfair mistake, to give such a title to the book as might induce readers to regard it as a single and definite novel, of which Catherine is the heroine, though it is made up of three parts written at very different times, it has a unity which the introduction shows to some extent, and which a rejected preface given by M. de Lovenjoul shows still better.

To understand this, we must remember that Balzac, though not exactly an

---

the very latest, 1836; my study of *Ruggieri* proof sheets makes me believe that, however early Balzac may have had the idea, he did not work on the actual Werdet manuscript of *Un Martyr* until late in 1836 or 1837 (for evidence see below, pp. 347–48). A few Werdet proof sheets of *Un Martyr* have been preserved which prove that printing was actually begun; and a note from Balzac to the printer Charles Plon (written on the last page of the manuscript of *Massimilla Doni* and reproduced on p. 437 of the Lovenjoul article) leads one to think that Balzac's interest in *César Birotteau* may have been an important reason for postponing the completion of *Un Martyr*.

[22] For Balzac's corrections of the word in *Le Secret des Ruggieri*, see pp. 346–47, below.

[23] *Catherine de Médicis expliquée*, I, 333–34. It is proposed to deal with the correction and expansion of *Les Lecamus* in a separate study.

historical scholar, was a considerable student of history; and that, although rather an amateur politician, he was a constant thinker and writer on political subjects. We must add to these remembrances the fact of his intense interest in all such matters as Alchemy, the Elixir of Life, and so forth, to which the sixteenth century in general, and Catherine de' Medici in particular, were known to be devoted. All these interests of his met in the present book.[24]

Les Deux Rêves (1830), as we have seen, was the first part to be published. There is not much to be said for the story as such: two strange men—a lawyer and a surgeon, who are finally identified as Robespierre and Marat, respectively—find themselves in unaccustomed society at the home of the wealthy Bodard de Saint-James, in the Place Vendôme, in the year 1786. At a late supper (supper and salon scenes abound in Balzac's work at this early period) they are plied with liquor by the other guests, among whom is Beaumarchais! Warmed with drink, the two men talk, each relating a strange dream: the lawyer reports a dream conversation with Catherine de Médicis in which she defends herself with respect to the St. Bartholomew Massacre; and the surgeon describes a fantastic operation upon a gangrened leg in such a way as to suggest, by analogy, the inevitability of a coming revolution in which blood would be shed to relieve the ills of the nation.

A detailed summary of *Le Secret des Ruggieri* (1836–37)—in preparation for our study of proof corrections—is given below (pp. 299 ff.). It is in this story that Balzac's interest in the occult sciences, as well as in Catherine's political credo, comes to the fore. In the final chapter Lorenzo Ruggieri's long exposition of the philosophy animating his researches is too diffuse for the taste of most readers; but in its characterization of Catherine, Charles IX, Marie Touchet, the Ruggieri, and a number of well-grouped minor personages the story is excellent. And the plot holds the reader's interest in spite of apparently excessive documentation; as for the documentation itself, it is essential to the general purpose of the *étude*. As to the historicity of *Le Secret des Ruggieri*, examination of source materials and comparison with modern authorities show that Balzac generally succeeds in infusing into his story the spirit of the "distracted and dishevelled times" in which Catherine lived.[25]

Most critics agree that *Le Martyr calviniste* is the best of the three parts, and at first I was decidedly of their opinion; now, upon further acquaintance, I am inclined to rate *Le Secret des Ruggieri* at least a very close

[24] *Op. cit.*, pp. ix–x.

[25] For further discussion of this point, see pp. 365–66, below.

second. The story of *Le Martyr calviniste* centers around the conspiracy of Amboise in 1560 and shows Catherine vacillating between Protestantism and Catholicism—sacrificing Christophe Lecamus, the young son of a furrier, to political expediency. The love story of Christophe and Babette Lallier is subordinated to the historical events, perhaps too much so for the general reader. For Balzac's own summary of the key situation, originally included in the text of *Le Secret des Ruggieri* but omitted from the Souverain and subsequent editions, see page 347, below. An anonymous reviewer, already quoted, says of *Sur Catherine de Médicis*, but with *Le Martyr calviniste* in mind:

No more harrowing or haunting picture has ever been painted of distracted and dishevelled times than the eloquent romancer, imitating the *Quentin Durward* of Scott, has painted in this book. . . . . The slender love story on which all this is hung is too frail to support the weight of the tragic events through which it meanders; but the reader cares nothing for this, so powerfully absorbing are the real events of the reign.[26]

Garnand and Dargan find in the story parallels with *Old Mortality* and *Woodstock*, and Dargan also points out resemblances to *The Abbot* and *The Fortunes of Nigel*.[27]

The "Introduction" (dated by Balzac, January, 1842, and first published in 1843) was written primarily to demonstrate the thesis underlying the three stories and to justify uniting them in a single *Etude philosophique*. This introductory essay is too long and ponderous for the ordinary reader of historical novels; the author seems to be too anxious to make a display of his erudition, bolstering up his thesis with a multitude of factual details and references to learned works. Although Baldensperger refers to Balzac's labor as "une documentation de fortune, que de doctes noms cités n'empêchent pas d'être précaire," Bourgeois, on the other hand, is sufficiently impressed to call it "presque digne d'un savant historien professionnel." For has he not utilized the *Mémoires* of Brantôme, the Protestant writers, Bayle's *Dictionnaire*, "et même, selon une bonne méthode scientifique, les registres du Parlement et de la Cour des Comptes"? In addition, there are those wordy and tiresome authors, Voûté and Du Tillet, whose completeness is their virtue. Bourgeois lets his enthusiasm overflow when he arrives at De Thou:

[26] *The Critic*, XXIII (January 12, 1895), 26.

[27] See E. P. Dargan, "Scott and the French Romantics," *PMLA*, XLIX (1934), 618–19.

Parmi les références, les plus importantes renvoient à l'histoire universelle de de Thou. Balzac ici encore a prouvé la solidité de son jugement par une confiance bien placée. Il cite sans cesse de Thou, il l'appelle le Tacite des Valois et salue à bon droit en lui un de nos historiens les meilleurs quoique les moins connus (il écrivit en latin), un de nos esprits les plus forts et les plus justes.[28]

We shall discover later that Balzac's erudition was not so profound as he wished it to appear, but at least the "Introduction" convinces most readers that he has a serious purpose.

IV

Both from the political side and from the occult side it is not hard to see why Balzac classified the novel (or novels) with the *Etudes philosophiques*. In his *Pensées, sujets, fragmens* we find this jotting:

19 Xbre 1836.—Résolu d'introduire dans les *Etudes philosophiques* autant de scènes historiques qu'il y a de siècles depuis l'invasion des Francs jusqu'en 1800, pour montrer le ravage des hautes idées dans la politique, ce qui a fait l'esprit des siècles, l'antagonisme, et cela dans les proportions du Secret des Ruggieri. Environ 15 scènes. —Les *Ruggieri* seront complétés par *Les deux Rêves*, dans l'édition future.[29]

When Saintsbury speaks of a "rejected preface" as showing the unity of Balzac's novel, he really means a part of the 1842 "Introduction" omitted in editions subsequent to Souverain.[30] From this rejected passage a few ideas concern us here. For, when the author of the *Etudes philosophiques* "eut résolu d'indiquer la pensée qui avait conduit chaque siècle antérieur au nôtre afin de démontrer l'activité des idées et leur puissance," he thought naturally of Catherine; and his opinion of this great queen had been formed as early as the publication of *Le Petit Souper* (i.e., *Les Deux Rêves*) in 1830. Perhaps, says Balzac, if this story had been entitled *Dialogue de Catherine de Médicis et de Robespierre*, then "l'analogie frappante entre les exigences politiques du principe de la domination démocratique et du principe de la domination monarchique" would have been better understood. As for the other two stories:

Le *Martyr calviniste* et le *Secret des Ruggieri* montrent Catherine de Médicis aux prises avec la première et la dernière grande difficulté de sa vie politique; mais en voyant combien de développemens exigent ces deux détails et combien de faits, d'hommes et d'intérêts s'y rattachent; en observant surtout avec quelle

---

[28] N. Bourgeois, *Balzac historien français et écrivain régionaliste*, p. 64.

[29] *Pensées, sujets, fragmens* (éd. J. Crépet), p. 138.   [30] See p. 282, n. 11.

sobriété l'auteur a procédé, l'on apercevra les énormes travaux auxquels doivent se condamner les historiens qui voudront entreprendre la peinture vraie de la France pendant la Réformation, ouvrage auquel travaille, dit-on, M. le marquis de Pastoret depuis quinze années.

Evidently, for this period two historians are necessary, a Protestant and a Catholic, since impartiality, "dans le sens que l'on donne à ce mot," is not permitted. And finally: "Quant à la conclusion à tirer de ces études sur Catherine, elle sera claire et visible: le pouvoir ne doit jamais être astreint aux règles qui constituent la morale privée. Cette maxime est directement contraire à celles [sic] avec laquelle la Bourgeoisie voudrait aujourd'hui diriger la politique des Etats."[31] This is Balzac's best statement of the unifying purpose of his *étude*. He feels that historians have misunderstood the character of Catherine, and he tries to support the thesis that her desire for domination was justified.

Even in *Les Deux Rêves*, as Balzac suggests in the passage just discussed, this vindication of Catherine was begun. In view of the general thesis the first of "the two dreams" is the more important. For example:

—Ma raison est confondue, dis-je à la reine. Vous vous applaudissez d'un acte que trois générations condamnent, flétrissent et ... —Ajoutez, reprit-elle, que toutes les plumes ont été plus injustes envers moi que ne l'ont été mes contemporains. Nul n'a pris ma défense. Je suis accusée d'ambition, moi riche et souveraine. Je suis taxée de cruauté, moi qui n'ai sur la conscience que deux têtes tranchées. Et pour les esprits les plus impartiaux je suis peut-être encore un grand problème. Croyez-vous donc que j'aie été dominée par des sentiments de haine, que je n'aie respiré que vengeance et fureur? Elle sourit de pitié.—J'étais calme et froide comme la raison même. J'ai condamné les Huguenots sans pitié, mais sans emportement, ils étaient l'orange pourrie de ma corbeille. Reine d'Angleterre, j'eusse jugé de même les Catholiques, s'ils y eussent été séditieux. Pour que notre pouvoir eût quelque vie à cette époque, il fallait dans l'Etat un seul Dieu, une seule Foi, un seul Maître. Heureusement pour moi, j'ai gravé ma justification dans un mot. Quand Birague m'annonça faussement la perte de la bataille de Dreux:—Eh! bien, nous irons au prêche, m'écriai-je. De la haine contre ceux de la Religion?

Her real hatred, she insists, was for the Cardinal de Lorraine and his soldier-brother. They spied upon her and wished to snatch the crown from her children. "Si nous n'avions pas fait la Saint-Barthélemi, les Guises l'eussent accomplie à l'aide de Rome et de ses moines." The Ligue, strong only in her old age, would have begun as early as 1573. Luther

[31] *Catherine de Médicis expliquée*, I, xlii–xlvii.

and Calvin, she continues, gave birth in Europe to a spirit of investigation which inevitably led the nations to examine everything. The aim of the reformers was nothing less than the annihilation of religion and royalty, and over their wreck the middle classes of all lands were to join in a common compact. "Ce fut un duel à outrance entre deux géants, la Saint-Barthélemi n'y fut malheureusement qu'une blessure." Catherine's misfortune consists in having no peers to judge her actions; fools are in the majority, and these two considerations explain everything. If she committed faults, she was, after all, only a woman. And why were there no men superior to their century? The Duc d'Albe, Philippe II, Henri IV, the Amiral de Coligny—all had their failings.

Louis XI vint trop tôt, Richelieu vint trop tard. Vertueuse ou criminelle, que l'on m'attribue ou non la Saint-Barthélemi, j'en accepte le fardeau: je resterai entre ces deux grands hommes comme l'anneau visible d'une chaîne inconnue. Quelque jour des écrivains à paradoxes se demanderont si les peuples n'ont pas quelquefois prodigué le nom de bourreaux à des victimes. Ce ne sera pas une fois seulement que l'humanité préférera d'immoler un dieu plutôt que de s'accuser elle-même.[32]

Thus, the slight framework of *Les Deux Rêves*, hardly justifying the name of *nouvelle*, serves as a vehicle for political ideas which really belonged in an essay.

An essay the 1842 "Introduction" frankly is—too pedantic to fit easily into a work of fiction, but growing out of convictions which Balzac, more than a decade before, had expressed in *Les Deux Rêves*. Concerning his defense of the maxim that public and private morality are different, that "the policy of a state cannot be, and ought not to be, governed by the same considerations of duty to its neighbors as those which ought to govern the conduct of an individual," Saintsbury reacts as follows:

But it was something of a mark of that amateurishness which spoilt Balzac's dealing with the subject to choose the sixteenth century for his text. For every cool-headed student of history and ethics will admit that it was precisely the abuse of this principle at this time, and by persons of whom Catherine de' Medici, if not the most blamable, has had the most blame put on her, that brought the principle itself into discredit.

The critic next poses the question: "Is the handling of this book the right and proper one for an historical novel? Can we in virtue of it rank Balzac (this is the test which he would himself, beyond all question, have ac-

[32] *Les Deux Rêves*, éd. Conard, XXX, 354–57. Save for minor variations, the text is the same as that of the original edition.

cepted) a long way above Dumas and near Scott?" Saintsbury's answer is:

> I must say that I can see no possibility of answer except, "Certainly not." For the historical novel depends almost more than any other division of the kind upon interest of story. Interest of story is not . . . . at any time Balzac's main appeal, and he has succeeded in it here less than in most other places. He has discussed too much; he has brought in too many personages without sufficient interest of plot; but, above all, he exhibits throughout an incapacity to handle his materials in the peculiar way required. . . . . In the best stories of Dumas (and the best number some fifteen or twenty at least) the interest of narrative, of adventure, of what will happen to the personages, takes you by the throat at once, and never lets you go till the end. There is little or nothing of the sort here. The three stories are excellently well-informed studies, very curious and interesting in divers ways. The "Ruggieri" is perhaps something more; but it is, as its author no doubt honestly entitled it, much more an "Etude Philosophique" (Philosophical Study) than an historical novelette. In short, this was not Balzac's way. We need not be sorry—it is very rarely necessary to be that— that he tried it; we may easily forgive him for not recognizing the ease and certainty with which Dumas trod the path. But we should be most of all thankful that he did not himself enter it frequently or ever pursue it far.[33]

Saintsbury is clearly at the opposite pole from Bellessort and Wells in his estimate of Balzac as a historical novelist. Many readers will agree, at least in part, with his criticisms; on the other hand, there are some confirmed Balzacians who would not expect or want Balzac to follow the path of Dumas. Accustomed to the fact that "interest of story is not . . . . at any time Balzac's main appeal," they find their compensation in the very qualities which make this novel a "philosophical study." As for plot interest itself, the present writer believes that *Le Martyr calviniste* and *Le Secret des Ruggieri* are considerably stronger than Saintsbury suggests. If we could ignore the pedantry of the "Introduction" and the slightness of *Les Deux Rêves*, would not the other two parts emerge as historical novels worthy of their author?

From the literary point of view Barrière has much good to say of the novel, comparing it favorably with *La Chronique du règne de Charles IX;* but he objects to Balzac's fanaticism and defense of Machiavellian principles, considering that "comme un traité philosophique de l'histoire de la Réformation" it is "pleine d'erreurs regrettables sur le devoir des monarques dont il excuse, dans un but politique, l'injustice et la violence ap-

33 *Op. cit.*, pp. x–xii.

portées au maintien de l'ordre."[34] Baldensperger, stressing the fact that Balzac offered *Sur Catherine de Médicis* as "une véritable page d'histoire," finds the interpretation of Catherine "un peu décevante":

> Avec ses tronçons peu cohérents et ses dates variées ... cette présentation soi-disant historique, avec ses citations d'autorités documentaires, ses exposés politiques et religieux, ne devient vraiment vivante qu'avec Cosme Ruggieri, l'astrologue favori, "à qui elle tient plus qu'à ses enfants." On regrette que Balzac, au lieu de chercher à comprendre, dans Catherine de Médicis, la femme et l'Italienne, s'applique à interpréter la reine contrainte, par la force des choses, de pratiquer une certaine diplomatie intérieure. "Un désir inné d'étendre la gloire et la puissance de la maison de Médicis": cette phrase de la première édition de la *Comédie humaine* aurait servi de point de départ à des considérations plus curieuses que celles qu'a développées le romancier, si Balzac avait eu la sagesse de ne pas jouer à l'augure. Une subtile Italienne, entre Napoléon, Italien francisé qui incarne l'action, et Dante, Italien tragique en qui il cherchera un guide et un garant, aurait complété la galerie que domine l'altière figure du poète de la *Divine Comédie*.[35]

Again one wonders if the "Introduction" has not prevented *Le Martyr calviniste* and *Le Secret des Ruggieri* from receiving their just due. Attempting a more serious task than the writing of novels *à la* Dumas, Balzac perhaps "protested too much" and defeated his own ends. Wells reminds us that he "seems to have been one of the first to apprehend" the character of Catherine. It is not surprising to one who has studied Balzac's source materials that he should have chosen to interpret her as "la reine contrainte, par la force des choses, de pratiquer une certaine diplomatie intérieure."

V

Let us now consider the circumstances which have prompted the preparation of a critical edition of *Le Secret des Ruggieri*. Judged in comparison with *Le Père Goriot* and *Eugénie Grandet*, it is not a really great novel—and perhaps, because of its shortness, it should not be called a "novel" at all—but it is distinctly Balzacian, and a study of its composition should throw considerable light on the author's general method. The availability of both manuscript and proof sheets is particularly fortunate, for most of Balzac's revising—as well as an appreciable proportion of fresh composing—was done in the proofs. The variations in the printed editions, while significant, are by no means so numerous or so interesting as those which precede the first publication. *Le Secret des Ruggieri* offers

[34] See Marcel Barrière, *L'Œuvre de H. de Balzac*, pp. 408-9.

[35] *Op. cit.*, pp. 164-65.

the student a second advantage: because it is a historical novel, he has more of an opportunity to investigate sources than is usually the case with other types of fiction. Having located a source, he can see how Balzac chose his materials and shaped them to his own ends.

My original choice of *Le Secret des Ruggieri* was due to the purchase by the University of Chicago, in 1927, of fifty-two sheets of proof extensively corrected and elaborated by Balzac in the margins and on the versos. Professor Dargan relates in "A Balzac Acquisition"[36] the means by which the University was enabled to possess what he rightly calls "a unique treasure." The fifty-two pages consist of *Chronique de Paris* proofs for the second and third chapters of our story—three sets of proofs for the second chapter and four for the third. After briefly describing the volume and characterizing the outstanding manuscript changes and additions, Professor Dargan expresses gratitude to Balzac for the lavishness of his corrections:

The result for posterity is that we are able, to a greater degree than with any other author, to determine the steps in his process. We pass with him into his fictional laboratory. We watch the slow heating of the furnace. We see the sorcerer, himself like one of the Ruggieri, surrounded by his crucibles. We follow his experiments, as he chooses and rejects his materials, tries this vial and that, incorporates fresh ingredients in the glowing mass, records the experiment, and finally blots the record for our admiration.

In the completeness with which it exploits such priceless materials and examines Balzac's method of documentation, the present writer's critical, or *variorum*, edition is believed to be practically unique among Balzacian studies.

As for the makeup of the Chicago volume, it is 444×345 mm. in size and consists of fifty-two sheets of various dimensions mounted in folio on hinges. It is half-bound in red *basane* and bears on the headband: "Le/Secret/de/Ruggieri/2ᵉ partie/Epreuves." The sides are of red quad-ruled paper, without corners.[37] The front flyleaf bears the following presentation inscription:

Mon vieux camarade Albert, ne valait-il pas mieux te réserver ceci où le travail de nain auquel m'a condamné une mauvaise fée se voit bien mieux.

Tout à toi,

Honoré de Bz.

[36] *The University Record*, new ser., XIII (1927), 124–26.

[37] Freely translated from a more complete technical description furnished by M. Marcel Bouteron at the time the proofs were purchased by Gabriel Wells. His notes, which will be referred to again, are laid in the Chicago volume.

The phraseology of the *envoi* shows that Balzac appreciated the importance of the proofs for a student of his method. The recipient of the volume was an old school-friend of Collège de Vendôme days, Albert Marchand (or Marchant) de la Ribellerie, to whom Balzac in 1846 dedicated *Le Réquisitionnaire*. Accompanying the proofs is a receipt (dated September 27, 1836) showing that Marchand de la Ribellerie had delivered a manuscript to the publisher. Probably, according to M. Bouteron, this was a fragment of Volume XII or Volume XVII of the *Etudes philosophiques*. Likewise preserved with the Chicago proofs is a letter to Marchand postmarked at Paris on February 10 and at Tours on February 11, 1837:

Mon vieux camarade,

Il y a pour toi Bureau restant, aux Messageries un livre d'épreuves, moins coquet que celui de Loiseau, mais plus curieux, va le quérir, et tu verras que je ne t'ai point oublié.

L'infâme Berrue avait mal envellopé [*sic*] le cadre, il y a d'horribles réparations; mais tu le verras à l'exposition dans toute sa gloire et moi dedans, je ne sais si je verrai l'exposition, je pars pour Milan dans trois jours.

t. à toi

honoré de Bz

Again M. Bouteron explains: "Le livre d'épreuves est le manuscrit acquis par Mr Wells; le cadre est un cadre acheté par Balzac, pendant un séjour en Touraine, en novembre 1836 et destiné à encadrer le portrait de Balzac par Louis Boulanger exposé en 1837."

The subsequent history of the proofs may be briefly sketched. They became the property of the Baron Auvray; on the latter's death they were sold at auction at Tours, June 29–30, 1920. They were acquired by the bookseller Conard, who resold them to the Parisian bookseller Davis; thence they passed into the hands of Gabriel Wells and William H. Royce, through whose agency they became the crowning jewel of Chicago's Balzac collection.

A treasure they are, indeed; but the fact remains that without the resources of Chantilly our knowledge concerning the composition of *Le Secret des Ruggieri* would still be very incomplete. For in the Lovenjoul Collection (under the *cote* A 210) there exist the original manuscript, forty-four pages long, and an additional one hundred and sixteen sheets of corrected proof,[38] besides four full pages, hand-written, which were

[38] These proofs were set up by Werdet (or rather, by Baudouin, his printer) for publication in Vol. XIII of the *Etudes philosophiques*. We shall call them "Werdet proofs."

really part of an insertion in the proofs but which, by mistake, were bound in with the manuscript proper. The volume bears on its flyleaf the inscription: "Offert à Madame la Comtesse de Sanseverino en témoignage de l'admiration de l'auteur De Balzac." Balzac had presented the volume, which in binding and general appearance resembles the one at Chicago, to the Comtesse Serafina Sanseverino, nee Porcia, in 1837.[39] After having been in the Sanseverino family for several decades, the proofs, like so many other precious Balzacian relics, became the property of the Vicomte Spoelberch de Lovenjoul.

The exact relationship of the Chicago proofs to those at Chantilly will be dealt with later. However, it may be said at once that we are entirely dependent upon the Chantilly volume for our knowledge of Chapter I, which comprises approximately half the story, and that the Chicago proofs of Chapters II and III represent an intermediate stage between the Chantilly proofs and the first publication. Lovenjoul, after studying the material he had acquired, suspected the existence of intermediary proofs. Believing that information from the family who had originally owned the first lot might aid him in his search for the others, he made inquiries of a certain C. Renman. The following reply, which is laid in the Chantilly volume and has not hitherto been published, put an end to his hopes:

Paris le 7 mars 95
9 rue Richepanse

Monsieur le Vicomte,

La Duchesse Litta ayant été malade, ce n'est qu'aujourd'hui que je reçois sa réponse à la question que je lui ai posée relativement à l'existence d'un tome II faisant suite au manuscrit de Balzac dont vous vous êtes rendu acquéreur. Voici ce qu'elle m'écrit à ce sujet:

"La Marquise Visconti-Sanseverino m'a de nouveau déclaré n'avoir jamais vu d'autre manuscrit de Balzac. Le volume acquis par M. de Spoelberck [sic] fut donné à sa mère par l'auteur lui-même, tel qu'il est, c'est-à-dire tout relié

---

[39] It was to this charming Milanese lady, living with her husband in Paris in the winter of 1837, that Balzac dedicated *Les Employés*. On the occasion of the author's first visit to Italy in February, 1837, she gave him letters of introduction to her brother, Prince Alfonso Serafino Porcia, and to her friend, Mme Claire Maffei. Professor Dargan (in an unpublished article, "Balzac and His *Gina*") says that Prince Porcia became "Gregorio" in Balzac's *Les Fantaisies de la Gina*, which he believes was probably written in May or June, 1838, but might even have been composed during the 1837 visit to Italy. On these various points, see also Conard notes, XIX, 369; Henry Prior, "Balzac à Milan. 1837," *Revue de Paris*, XXXII (1925), 283–302 and 602–20; and Bouteron's edition of *Les Fantaisies de la Gina* in the "Cahiers balzaciens," No. 2.

d'une reliure évidemment française. Il est probable qu'un second volume ait été offert en hommage à quelque autre personne: mais la Marquise croit pouvoir affirmer qu'il ne vint jamais dans la famille Sanseverino. Il aurait dû par contre exister des lettres adressées à ses parents par le célèbre auteur: mais il n'a pas été possible d'en retrouver une seule, malgré les recherches les plus diligentes."

Je regrette de ne pas pouvoir vous communiquer une information de nature à vous satisfaire davantage comme collectionneur et je m'empresse de vous renouveler, Monsieur le Vicomte, l'expression de mes sentiments les plus distingués.

C. Renman

We know now that the object of Lovenjoul's unsuccessful search was the volume presented by Balzac to Albert Marchand de la Ribellerie.

VI

So much for the history of the manuscript and proof sheets after they left the author's possession. But what were the conditions under which the story was written? *Le Secret des Ruggieri* has interested more than one Balzacian because of the novelist's claim that he wrote it in a single night.[40] In a letter[41] dated "Chaillot, 30 septembre—1ᵉʳ octobre 1836," to Mme Hanska, we read: "Pour savoir jusqu'où va mon courage, il faut vous dire que *le Secret des Ruggieri* a été écrit en une seule nuit. Pensez à cela quand vous le lirez." Balzac then boasts of the speed with which *La Vieille Fille* and other stories were written, "trois jours" or "trois nuits" being a favorite working unit. Many an author will envy him such fertility of invention, unless he reads on: "Ce qui me tue, c'est les corrections." By corrections, of course, Balzac means corrections on proof sheets. He goes on to say: "Enfin, au moment que je vous écris, j'ai devant moi les épreuves accumulées de quatre ouvrages différents qui doivent paraître en octobre ... . J'ai promis à Werdet de faire paraître sa troisième livraison d'*Études Philosophiques* ce mois-ci, et aussi ... ." In this third *livraison*, *Le Secret des Ruggieri* was to be included. When the letter was written, Balzac was living "dans l'ancienne mansarde de Jules Sandeau, à Chaillot," where he had "taken refuge" the thirtieth of September. He was profoundly discouraged: "N'être plus retenu dans la vie que par le sentiment du devoir! Je suis entré dans la mansarde où je suis avec la conviction d'y mourir épuisé de travail. J'ai cru que je

---

[40] Concerning the validity of this claim, see below, p. 304, n. 48, and p. 326.

[41] *Lettres à l'Etrangère*, I, 346–52. The various passages quoted below occur in this one long letter.

le supporterais mieux que je ne fais." For more than a month he had been rising at midnight and going to bed at six o'clock, and had imposed on himself a strict regimen in food as well as work. He was not well: "... non-seulement je sens des faiblesses que je ne puis décrire, mais tant de vie communiquée au cerveau amène de singuliers troubles .... Même dans mon lit, il me semble que ma tête tombe à gauche ou à droite, et je suis, quand je me lève, emporté par un poids énorme qui serait dans ma tête." With all his discouragements he could still work, and he had much to tell Mme Hanska of his performances, past and future. Finally, however, it was time to call a halt; his candles were paling, and he had proof sheets to correct:

Les épreuves attendent, il faut se plonger dans les écuries d'Augias de mon style et balayer les fautes. Ma vie n'offre plus que la monotonie du travail, que varie le travail lui-même. Je suis comme le vieux colonel autrichien qui parlait de son cheval gris et de son cheval noir à Marie-Antoinette; je suis tantôt sur l'un, tantôt sur l'autre, six heures sur *les Ruggieri*, six heures sur *l'Enfant maudit*, six heures sur *la Vieille Fille*. De temps en temps je me lève, je contemple cet océan de maisons que ma fenêtre domine, depuis l'École-Militaire jusqu'à la barrière du Trône, depuis le Panthéon jusqu'à l'Étoile, et après avoir humé l'air, je me remets au travail.

Such were the physical conditions under which *Le Secret des Ruggieri* was composed and its proofs corrected.

VII

The plot of *Le Secret des Ruggieri* is very simple, centering around the fears of Charles IX that Catherine intends to poison him. Perfectly evident to all the court is the fact that the twenty-four-year-old king—weakened in health, morbidly brooding over the horrors of St. Bartholomew's Day—has not long to live. For it is the latter part of October, 1573; if Catherine really wishes Charles out of the way, she has only to wait, but nonetheless his mind is obsessed with the dread of death by poisoning. The action of our story, the *drame* proper, may be said to begin with an after-supper court scene and to end the following afternoon with the interrogation of the Ruggieri brothers by Charles. The court scene gives an interesting picture of the strict etiquette enforced by Catherine. Everyone sits or stands, near or far away from royalty, according to his rank; and only the most intimate of the courtiers dare address the king. Charles is in somber mood, fatigued after a day of hunting; and the sad, pious Elizabeth of Austria is no doubt thinking of Charles's infatuation for his mistress, Marie Touchet, who has recently borne him a son. The atmosphere is so strained that most of the courtiers retire early, leaving only a few intimates in the presence of Charles and the queen-mother. Soon Catherine herself withdraws, making a secret sign that is understood by the Gondi brothers, Albert and Charles. The former has been appointed Maréchal de Retz, and the latter is master of the king's wardrobe; both are devoted to Catherine's interests. Charles IX meanwhile is exchanging glances with his own special followers, among whom is the Maréchal de Tavannes. It suits the secret plans of both Catherine and her son that a reconnoitering party should be formed which would include the Gondi brothers and Tavannes. "Vauriennerie" is the term used to describe their proposed activities: Charles IX and his party will explore the Saint-Honoré quarter, playing pranks upon innocent bourgeois, climbing roofs, and in general spying upon the inhabitants of the quarter. Charles says that he will pay a surprise visit to Marie; but near her home he is attracted by a single lighted window in the garret of a house belonging to René, the court perfumer. Now René has the reputation of being a master poisoner; Catherine may have employed him; Charles determines to investigate. While Albert and Charles de Gondi perch like cats upon the edge of a roof, Charles IX and Tavannes go ahead. They climb up to the lighted window; what they see is the laboratory of Catherine's astrologers, Cosimo and Lorenzo Ruggieri. After looking and listening for a while, Charles enters and has these men arrested and lodged in Marie Touchet's house in charge of a few soldiers of the king's own guard. Of his subsequent nocturnal activities, the most important is a secret interview with Catherine in his workshop shortly before dawn.

The next afternoon Charles visits Marie, who is expecting him. Their conversation shows in really charming fashion the genuineness of Marie's love for him and the young king's delight in having one refuge from his cares, where he may enjoy the companionship of his mistress and their little son. But Marie is curious about the strange prisoners in her house, and she must hear Charles's own story of the events of the night before. Then the Ruggieri are brought in and questioned. Charles had talked with them a little while on the previous evening and later had had their laboratory carefully searched. He had found no proofs of guilt; instead he is fascinated by the *grand œuvre* in which the brothers are engaged, and seeks to know more of its mysteries. The imposing old Lorenzo answers the king's questions with perfect self-possession; and when Charles finally leaves, the "secret des Ruggieri" is still undivulged.

This is the chronological order of events. But in what order does Balzac tell his story? He begins Chapter I *in medias res* with Albert and Charles de Gondi perched on the edge of a roof. Then, in order to explain why they are there, he loops back to the court scene at the Louvre; and then, in order to explain that scene, he loops back and presents the political situation of the previous six months. The first chapter is as long as Chapters II and III put together, for it contains nearly all the exposition of the story. Chapter II opens with a description of Marie Touchet's house and some characterization of the quarter in which she lived, partly repeating and reinforcing material of Chapter I. It is the day after the court scene; Marie is waiting for Charles to appear and tell her what has happened. From then on the story follows the order so briefly sketched in the preceding paragraph.

One of the most interesting facts I have discovered about the composition of *Le Secret des Ruggieri* is that Balzac wrote the manuscript version of Chapters II and III[42] first of all; had them set up in galley proof; then wrote the manuscript of Chapter I in shorter form than we now have it; had it set up in galley proof; and then (in the galleys) expanded Chapter I to about its present length and had it set up in the Werdet page proof before going on to correct the first galley proofs of Chapters II and III.[43] At many points in the present study we shall see the effects which this order of composition had upon the construction of the story. As evidence that Chapter I was the last of the three chapters to be composed and that it could not have been written in the same night as the others, two facts stand out as most important: First, in the manuscript and first galley proofs of Chapters II and III, the younger Ruggieri brother was called not Cosimo but Claude, and in the next set of proofs the name had to be changed many times. In the manuscript of Chapter I, however, the name was Cosimo from the first. Second, Balzac in the first galley proofs of Chapter II had not decided who were to be Charles's companions on the nocturnal excursion. He wrote in the name Cypierre and left a row of dots to show that he would fill in more later. But in the manuscript of Chapter I he has made up his mind; the Gondi brothers and Tavannes are already playing their roles, and the proofs of Chapter II must be corrected to correspond.

---

[42] Except for a little more than four pages of manuscript, at the very end of the story, added in the revision of the first set of Chicago proofs and then elaborated in succeeding sets.

[43] A study of the proof sheets shows also that Chapter II was corrected and expanded, probably to its final length, before the first proofs of Chapter III were corrected. For evidence of the order of proof corrections, see p. 312, n. 51, and p. 326, below.

VIII

Before discussing further the manifold corrections, elaborations, and rearrangements by means of which Balzac built up his original manuscript material to approximately double its length for the *Chronique de Paris* publication, it may be well to describe briefly the appearance of the manuscript and corrected proof sheets and to indicate a few of the technical problems which required solution before a critical edition could be made.

Both in the manuscript itself and in the marginal corrections on proof sheets the *ratures* afford an intimate glimpse into Balzac's thought-processes while composing. With strokes of the pen that frequently resemble brush strokes and almost blot out the original writing, or by means of horizontal spirals or crosshatching or other devices of the sort, our author has crossed out letters, words, and occasionally whole clauses or sentences. In these *ratures* we may see him struggling for a word and rejecting it half-written, only to employ it again later in the sentence; a short phrase may suggest an idea too extended for its original placing but capable of elaboration in a separate sentence. Sometimes substitutions or additions are made after a whole line or several lines are written, in which case we find interlinear or marginal corrections. More frequently the author becomes dissatisfied as soon as the word or phrase is written—perhaps even before it is completed—and changes it at once, either interlinearly or in the regular line of writing. Some notion of all this may be gained by examining the page of proof reproduced as the frontispiece of the present volume.[44]

In the critical edition of which the "Introduction," revised, constitutes the present study, an analysis of all the *ratures* in manuscript and proofs would have been a well-nigh endless task; and, more important, the mass of material might easily have obscured the main drive of the successive stages of correction. Consequently, it was decided that *ratures* in the proofs would not, in general, be recorded or discussed but that by a special space-economizing method[45] the manuscript *ratures* would be incorporated, without discussion, into the text.

[44] The new passages inserted in this page of proof are more straightforward in composition than is usually the case. The page was selected not for the frequency of *ratures* but for reasons explained on pp. 331–32, below.

[45] In part suggested by Pierre Masson's critical edition of *La Profession de foi du vicaire savoyard*. It is hoped that by means of this method a student examining the edition proper will be able to trace and characterize for himself the various stages by which Balzac arrived at the text which he was willing to have set up in the first proofs.

In the present study, as well as in the critical edition proper, it will often be necessary for us to identify accurately the particular set or sets of proofs from which a given reading is taken. Roman numerals will be used to designate which of the three chapters is concerned, and capital letters in alphabetical order will distinguish the successive sets of proofs. "Pr II A" means the first set of proofs of Chapter II; "Pr II B" the second; etc. When a set of proofs just preceding the journal form has not been preserved, but the readings can be reconstituted by means of the journal text, the capital letter is inclosed in brackets. Where it is quite clear that more than one set has been lost (this is true of Chapter I), a plus sign is used to indicate the fact; e.g., "Pr I [C+]." Balzac's handwritten corrections on a set of proofs are indicated by the notation "ms" after the capital letter identifying the set thus corrected. If the compositor follows Balzac's directions, the text of "Pr II A ms" will be identical with that of "Pr II B"; or, if "Pr II B" does not include that particular part of the chapter, "Pr II A ms" agrees with "Pr II C" or "Pr II D," etc., as the case may be. The number of proofs for a given text varies in different parts of the chapter.

The principal problem to be settled for the critical edition was that of enabling the reader to trace the evolution of the text from its manuscript form down to the definitive Conard edition. Wherever all the versions followed the same general order, the solution was simple, namely, to reproduce the manuscript text on the left-hand pages and the corresponding *Chronique de Paris* text on the right-hand pages immediately opposite. Two sets of notes were likewise required: the first set, immediately under the manuscript text, to describe Balzac's adaptation of source materials as well as to record and discuss the proof variations; and the second, on the opposite page, to record the variants in the volume publications (Werdet, Souverain, Furne, and Conard) as compared with the journal form. For convenient reference the lines of the *Chronique de Paris* text were numbered consecutively from the beginning to the end of the story: lines 1–1019 represent Chapter I; lines 1020–1621, Chapter II; and lines 1622–2113, Chapter III.[46]

[46] The story is divided into only two chapters in the Werdet ed.; in the Souverain there are five; and in the Furne and Conard there is no division into chapters at all. Since the line numbers of the *Chronique de Paris* text run consecutively from beginning to end, we can neglect these variations in chapter divisions in referring to the printed editions. By Chapters I, II, and III, we shall consistently mean the chapters as they appeared in the journal publication.

In four special cases the method discussed above was rendered impracticable by reason of the length of insertions in one of the proofs. Accordingly, a series of appendixes was prepared with the text of the proof insertion on the left-hand pages and the *Chronique de Paris* text on the opposite pages, with notes carrying the texts forward, as in the body of the edition. In order to keep each chapter a unit, the appendixes were inserted at the end of the chapter concerned rather than at the end of the volume: Appendixes I A, I B, and I C after Chapter I, and Appendixes II A and II B after Chapter II. For the edition proper the appendixes were indispensable, and even in the present "Introduction" we shall continue to identify these long passages as the "Appendix II A insertion" or the "Appendix I B transposition," as the case may be.[47]

In the following sections an attempt is made to furnish a guide to the larger problems of construction which arose as Balzac expanded and revised the successive chapters. Each chapter has its own particular interest. Chapter II, the first to be composed, contains a good deal of description; hence the notes of this chapter will pay special attention to stylistic variations. In Chapter III we shall be concerned with Lorenzo Ruggieri's philosophy and with the problem of bringing the story to a close. Chapter I includes most of the documentation and requires radical rearrangements before publication in the *Chronique de Paris*. These involved transpositions and Balzac's use of source materials will be discussed last of all.

IX

The earliest preserved manuscript version of *Le Secret des Ruggieri*[48] begins with a description of Marie Touchet's house. Knowing that description was Balzac's *bête noire*, and possessing false starts for Chapters I and III which show that he found any new division of the story hard to write, we are not surprised to discover that frequent changes, many of them stylistic, were made in the successive proofs of this opening description.

The first manuscript sentence of Chapter II is a typical Balzacian beginning, for it locates a street—and expresses an etymologist's interest in the name—in preparation for placing and describing a particular house

[47] Appen. I B, the second of the series, represents a very long transposition, which will be discussed below, pp. 337–42.

[48] The rough draft of Chapter II and a part of Chapter III are all of the finished story that Balzac could rightfully claim to have written in a single night, since they were set up in proofs before Chapter I was composed.

on that street. The sentence follows, exactly as Balzac wrote it: "La rue de l'autriche ou d'autruche, car les plus savans auteurs ne sont pas d'accord sur cette etymologie, était une rue du vieux Paris qui longeait l'ancien Louvre." Although this sentence was set up in Pr II A, it was not preserved with the rest of Pr II A ms in the Chantilly volume, for the reason that Chapter I (composed in the meantime) had treated the same material in greater detail. Because it was the opening sentence, Balzac easily snipped it off with his scissors as he pasted columns of proof in the middle of large pages, ready for marginal corrections. Elsewhere in the description he blots out unwanted Pr II A text with brushlike strokes of his pen.

Most of the significant revisions were effected in the manuscript corrections to the first set of proofs (i.e., Pr II A ms) and were embodied in the next set (Pr II B) only to be further corrected later. For the present let us content ourselves with examining only the first and second stages of the text arranged in parallel columns, with italics to indicate substitutions, insertions, or omissions, and with broken brackets in both texts to indicate the passages transposed. The latter are numbered in the margins according to their order in the first column. Boldface type indicates transpositions within a given passage. (In the MS, Pr II A text below, as in all later examples of readings from the manuscript plus the first set of proofs, we shall neglect minor peculiarities of spelling, capitalization, and punctuation in the manuscript and use the proof-sheet version as accepted by Balzac and maintained in later proofs. For certain words, like *âme*, the printer himself determined what form was to be used; where the first Werdet proofs print *âme*, the *Chronique de Paris* proofs print *ame*, with no special directions from the author.)

MS, Pr II A

Vers le milieu de cette rue étroite et sombre se trouvait un petit hôtel bâti entre cour et jardin. La cour n'avait pas cinquante pieds carrés, ⟨*le jardin était* **un jardin de Paris, vingt-cinq** *perches au plus; mais* les fleurs rares *y* abondaient, une vigne *y* tapissait les murailles; au milieu s'élevait un pin argenté; *au fond étaient* des tilleuls. La maison

Pr II A ms, B

La petite *maison où demeurait la dame de Belleville et où Charles IX avait déposé ses prisonniers, était l'avant-dernière dans la rue de l'Autruche, du côté de la rue Saint-Honoré.* ⟨La porte de la rue, flanquée de deux petits pavillons en brique, *semblait fort simple* dans un temps où les portes et leurs dessus étaient si curieusement façonnés; *elle se composait de deux pilastres en pierre taillée en pointe de diamant,* le cintre représentait une femme cou- (3)

avait un *seul* étage au-dessus *d'un* rez-de-chaussée, *et cet étage couronné* par une frise sculptée *supportait* un toit *très élevé* percé de trois croisées en saillie, ornées de tympans et de chambranles que le ciseau avait **couvert** *de dentelles.* Chacune des trois croisées du premier étage se recommandait également par ses broderies *en* pierre *de taille* que la brique des murs

(1) faisait *parfaitement* ressortir. Au rez-de-chaussée *la* **porte d'entrée** *qui s'élevait sur* un perron **délicatement** *construit* et dont la tribune *offrait* un M et un C mariés dans un lacqs d'amour, *était* en bossages vermiculés, *ainsi que* la croisée *qui se trouvait à* droite et *à* gauche. La façade du jardin offrait *les mêmes décorations.* **Des deux côtés la croisée du milieu** *avait* **un joli balcon travaillé.**⟩ ⟨*La* **cour**

(2) *était* pavée à la vénitienne.⟩ ⟨La porte de la rue flanquée de deux petits pavillons en brique *n'avait rien de remarquable* dans un temps où les portes et leurs dessus étaient si curieusement façonnées. *C'était des bossages simples.* Le cintre *de la porte* représentait une femme couchée

(3) *sur* une corne d'abondance. La porte *était en bois garni* de ferrures énormes, *il y avait* un guichet pour examiner ceux qui *frappaient, et* chacun des pavillons logeait un concierge. *Il y avait le* concierge *de* jour *et le* concierge *de* nuit.⟩ Malgré le goût exquis qui respirait dans

chée *qui tenait* une corne d'abondance. La porte *garnie* de ferrures énormes *avait, à la hauteur de l'œil,* un guichet pour examiner ceux qui *demandaient à entrer.* Chacun des (pavillons logeait un concierge, *car le plaisir extrêmement capricieux du roi Charles exigeait* un concierge le jour, *un la* nuit.⟩ ⟨*La maison avait une petite* **cour** pavée à la véni- (tienne,⟩ ⟨*et* **un jardin** *d'environ trente* perches *où* les fleurs *les plus* rares abondaient, une vigne tapissait les murailles, au milieu s'élevait un pin argenté, *dans le* fond se trouvait un couvert de tilleuls. La maison *élevée d'*un étage au-dessus *du* rez-de-chaussée, *était couronnée* par une frise sculptée *sur laquelle s'appuyait* un toit *à quatre pans dont le sommet formait une plate forme. Ce toit était* percé de trois croisées en saillie, ornées de tympans et de chambranles que le ciseau avait *dentelés et* **couvert** *d'arabesques.* Chacune des trois croisées du premier étage se recommandait également par ses broderies *de* pierre, que la brique des murs faisait ressortir. Au rez-de-chaussée, un *double* perron *décoré fort* **délicatement** et dont la tribune *se distinguait par* un M et un C mariés dans un lacqs d'amour, *menait à une* **porte d'entrée** en bossages vermiculés, *système de décor qui se retrouvait dans* la croisée *de* droite et *dans* celle de gauche. La façade du jardin, *semblable à celle de la cour,* offrait *comme elle* **un joli balcon travaillé** *qui surmontait la* porte et embellissait **la croisée du milieu.** **Des deux côtés,** *les ornemens de cette croisée montaient jusqu'à la frise, ce qui simulait un petit pavillon en pierre, nommé, je crois, une lanterne.*⟩ ⟨Les appuis *des autres croisées* étaient incrustés de marbres rares encadrés dans la pierre.⟩ Malgré le goût exquis qui

4) cette maison ⟨*où* les appuis *de chaque croisée* étaient incrustés de marbres rares encadrés dans la pierre,⟩ elle avait une physionomie triste. Le jour y était obscurci par la hauteur des maisons voisines, il y régnait un profond silence; mais ce silence, cette ombre, cette *mélancolie de* solitude faisaient du bien à l'âme. *C'était* un cloître où l'on se recueille, ou *bien* la jolie maison *seulette* où l'on aime. *Ce logis appartenait à une femme d'une rare beauté qui se nommait Marie et qui n'aima qu'un homme; cet homme était le roi Charles IX.* Qui ne devinerait pas maintenant les recherches intérieures de cette retraite, seul lieu de son royaume où l'avant-dernier Valois pouvait épancher son âme, dire ses douleurs, déployer son goût pour les arts, se livrer à la poésie qu'il aimait, affections contrariées. Là seulement, sa grande âme et sa haute valeur étaient appréciées; là seulement il *était heureux père.*

respirait dans cette maison, elle avait une physionomie triste; le jour y était obscurci par la hauteur des maisons voisines *et par les toits de l'hôtel d'Alençon qui projetaient leur ombre sur la cour et sur le jardin;* il y régnait un profond silence. Mais ce silence, cette ombre, cette solitude faisaient du bien à l'âme *qui pouvait s'y livrer à une seule pensée, comme dans un* cloître où l'on se recueille, ou *comme on doit être dans* la *coite* maison où l'on aime. Qui ne devinerait pas maintenant les recherches intérieures de cette retraite, seul lieu de son royaume où l'avant-dernier Valois pouvait épancher son ame, dire ses douleurs, déployer son goût pour les arts *et* se livrer à la poésie qu'il aimait, *toutes* affections contrariées *par les soucis de la plus pesante des royautés.* Là seulement sa grande ame et sa haute valeur étaient appréciées; là seulement il *put se livrer durant quelques mois fugitifs, les derniers de sa vie, aux jouissances de la paternité, plaisirs dans lesquels il se jetait avec la frénésie que le pressentiment d'une horrible et prochaine mort imprimait à toutes ses actions.*

Fundamentally the description consists of two parts, both suggested by the first sentence in the left-hand column; one is the physical makeup of the house with its accompanying garden and courtyard (cf. the manuscript form, "un petit hôtel bâti entre cour et jardin"), and the other is the atmosphere of the place (cf. "cette rue étroite et sombre"). It is the physical aspect which taxes Balzac's descriptive powers; in his anxiety to put on paper the many specific details that occur to his imagination, he loses sight of coherent order in the manuscript form. First he gives the dimensions of the court and the garden and briefly describes the flowers and trees in the latter; then he describes the house, subordinating details of its elaborate decoration to an exposition of how it was constructed; next he mentions that the courtyard was paved in the Venetian manner, and passes on to a description of the street gate with its decorations, its peephole, and its lodges for two gatekeepers. This would seem to conclude the physical description, but in the opening sentence of the second part he interrupts himself to loop back and mention the rare marbles incrusted in the sills of the windows.

In the first proof corrections (shown in the right-hand column, above) Balzac sets about improving the organization of the foregoing description. Neglecting the court and garden for the moment, he moves the part concerning the street gate (passage 3) to its logical position near the beginning, immediately after the street location of the house. Then he transfers the short sentence concerning Venetian paving (passage 2) so that it constitutes his first mention of the courtyard; except for the adjective *petite* he neglects the dimensions. Without a sentence break he goes back to the original description of the garden and house (passage 1), but this time his main concern is elaborateness of decoration rather than construction. The sentence structure is completely changed, and particular attention to verbs is required in order to emphasize the new keynote and harmonize with it the mass of accumulated detail. Finally, Balzac painlessly amputates the clause concerning rare marbles (passage 4) from the second part and makes of it a separate sentence to conclude logically the physical description of the house.

Comparison of the two parallel columns will impress us with the minute attention to detail which accompanied Balzac's rearrangement. Verbs, nouns, pronouns, adverbs, adjectives, prepositions, conjunctions—all are changed many times in the course of the re-writing. But it is not so much dissatisfaction with single words that motivates the correction as it is the larger purpose of keynoting properly the description and harmonizing the details so as to produce a unified, coherent, vivid effect.

The changes thus far discussed were all made in a single stage of proof correction; for our material we have depended upon the two sets of Werdet proofs preserved at Chantilly. But if we imagine that the process was complete and the description was ready for the journal publication, we do not yet know Balzac. For we have the three additional sets owned by the University of Chicago, and in each of them further modifications take place. They are not so numerous in this part of the chapter as later on; but they are, nevertheless, significant.

Now that the rearrangement is nearly complete, the new combination of ideas stimulates Balzac to add further elaboration for the third set of proofs (first set of the Chicago volume). An example is the Venetian paving of the courtyard. Balzac has had to sacrifice temporarily the manuscript idea of "le jardin était un jardin de Paris"; instead, he turns to the paving and in a few lines, inserted, transports us to a former age. The elaborated passage reads as follows in Pr II B ms, C:

La maison avait une petite cour pavée à la vénitienne; car à cette époque les voitures n'étaient pas inventées, les dames allaient à cheval ou en litière et les cours pouvaient être intérieurement magnifiques sans que les chevaux ou les voitures les gâtassent, et il faut sans cesse penser à cette circonstance pour s'expliquer l'étroitesse des rues et des cours, et beaucoup de détail des habitations de cette époque en tout pays.

The characteristic *apologie* which closes the insertion serves a double purpose: at the same time that it expresses Balzac's sociohistorical interest in the evolution of manners as reflected in architectural styles, it also provides a satisfactory transition to the description of the house proper and its ornamentation. Five minor changes are made in this insertion in the succeeding proofs.

So convenient is the transition just discussed that Balzac, continuing his revision of Pr II B, postpones the description of the garden so that in Pr II C it immediately precedes the sentence beginning "La façade du jardin, semblable à celle de la cour" (near end of passage 1 as located in the second column above). This short description assumes so many forms in its progress from the manuscript to the *Chronique de Paris*, that it may be interesting to compare them all. After the first form, italics and boldface type are used to indicate variations from the preceding form only. Since no changes were made in Pr II D ms, E, there are five versions in all:

MS, Pr II A
Le jardin était **un jardin** *de Paris, vingt-cinq* perches *au plus; mais* les fleurs rares *y* abondaient, une vigne *y* tapissait les murailles; au milieu s'élevait un pin argenté; *au* fond *étaient des* tilleuls.

Pr II A ms, B [transposed with rest of passage 1]
... *et* **un jardin** *d'environ trente* perches *où* les fleurs *les plus* rares abondaient, une vigne tapissait les murailles, au milieu s'élevait un pin argenté, *dans le* fond *se trouvait un couvert de* tilleuls.

Pr II B ms, C [transposed again, separately]
Un jardin où les fleurs les plus rares abondaient *occu-*

> pait, derrière la maison, un espace égal en étendue à celui
> de la cour. C'était le jardin de ce temps. Une vigne ta-
> pissait les murailles, au milieu de quelques carrés de
> fleurs s'élevait un pin argenté, dans le fond se trouvait
> un *petit bouquet d'ifs taillés.*

Pr II C ms, D; D ms, E

Un jardin où **abondaient** les fleurs rares, occupait derrière la maison un espace égal en étendue à celui de la
cour. *Ce* jardin *était distribué et planté à la mode* **de ce
temps:** une vigne tapissait les murailles, au milieu de
quelques carrés de fleurs s'élevait un pin argenté, dans
le fond se trouvait un petit *bosquet* d'ifs taillés.

Pr II E ms, *C. de P.* [identical with Pr
II C ms, etc., except for following insertion at the end]

*... ; les murs étaient revêtus de mosaïques composées de
différents cailloux assortis, et dont les dessins quoique
grossiers plaisaient à l'œil par la richesse des couleurs,
en harmonie avec celles des fleurs.*

The Pr II B ms, C form takes a final step away from definiteness in dimensions by omitting "d'environ trente perches" and inserting "occupait, derrière la maison, un espace égal en étendue à celui de la cour."
The phrase "derrière la maison" fits the transposed material into its new
location just following the description of the house proper. The insertion
of "C'était le jardin de ce temps" takes up again the manuscript thread of
"le jardin était un jardin de Paris," temporarily neglected in Pr II A ms,
B; seldom does Balzac abandon an idea permanently. In Pr II C ms,
etc., the insertion is elaborated into "Ce jardin était distribué et planté à
la mode de ce temps," with a colon to emphasize its function as a topic
sentence for the details which follow. Finally, Pr II E ms and *C. de P.*
insert, at the end, several lines which add one more touch to the accumulated richness and harmony of the description.

Despite the re-working the passage has undergone in the proofs, Balzac
is still dissatisfied. On examining the variations in the volume publications, we discover that it was broken up into shorter, crisper sentences
for the Souverain edition and completely re-written for the Furne. The
two versions, with italics and boldface type to facilitate comparison,
follow:

SOUVERAIN

Un jardin où abondaient les fleurs rares, occupait derrière la maison un espace égal en étendue à celui de la cour. *Ce jardin était* distribué *et* planté à la mode de ce temps. Une vigne tapissait les murailles. Au milieu *de quelques carrés de fleurs* s'élevait un pin argenté. *Dans le* fond se trouvait un petit bosquet d'ifs taillés. Les murs *étaient* revêtus de mosaïques composées de différents cailloux assortis, *et dont les* dessins *quoique* grossiers plaisaient à l'œil par la richesse des couleurs en harmonie avec celles des fleurs.

FURNE

Un jardin distribué planté à la mode de ce temps, *et* où abondaient les fleurs rares, occupait derrière la maison un espace égal en étendue à celui de la cour. Une vigne tapissait les murailles. Au milieu *d'un gazon* s'élevait un pin argenté. *Les plate-bandes étaient séparées de ce gazon par des allées sinueuses menant à* un petit bosquet d'ifs taillés *qui* se trouvait *au* fond. Les murs revêtus de mosaïques composées de différents cailloux assortis, *offraient* à l'œil *des* dessins grossiers, *il est vrai, mais qui* plaisaient par la richesse des couleurs en harmonie avec celles des fleurs.

By transposition and omission Balzac reduces in importance the former topic sentence, with its implied restrictions, and leaves himself free to elaborate. In the Furne text (unchanged for the Conard) we have the added detail of the lawn and the winding paths, with changes in sentence structure to show their exact placing and also to throw into greater relief the qualities of the pebbled mosaics.

After all the labor which Balzac expended upon the physical description of the house with its courtyard and garden, it is a relief to note the comparative ease with which he suggests the atmosphere and spirit of the place. Referring back to the parallel columns on pages 305–7, we find that, aside from the omission of a manuscript sentence rendered unnecessary by the composition of Chapter I, the Pr II A ms, B changes consist mainly of happy elaborations of ideas already in the text. The first of these provides a link with Chapter I, and the last reinforces very effectively the theme of the story: Haunted by his fear of a horrible death near at hand, Charles IX finds in Marie's house the one refuge where he can enjoy the privileges of a father. After the Pr II A ms, B form, shown in the second column, only a few changes (five in all) are made in succeeding proofs, and even these are of minor importance; mainly they are substitutions to avoid repetition. After the *Chronique de Paris* we find only one verbal change; the five other variations concern typographical points.

If critics are justified in deploring the heaviness of Balzac's style in descriptive passages—particularly those which list material objects in catalogue-like profusion—at least we have in the foregoing analysis ample evidence that he realized his own deficiencies and strove to overcome them. Why else would he have composed seven distinct versions to describe a small garden which plays no part in the story except that it belongs to the house where Marie Touchet lived? In suggesting atmosphere Balzac's pen is relatively facile and sure, he works with economy of effort; where *things* are involved, he arranges and rearranges, cutting down where absolutely necessary, but more often adding details to complete the picture. Scholars differ in their classification of Balzac with the romanticists or the realists. Perhaps, on the evidence of the characteristic proof corrections analyzed above, we may say that he was a romanticist by nature,[49] a realist by conscious design and self-imposed discipline. To take a hint from the recapitulation theory of the biologists, perhaps we may discern in the development of the fictional embryo some reminders of Balzac's evolution between 1829—the year of *Les Chouans*—and 1836, when *Le Père Goriot* and *Eugénie Grandet* were already in print and the writing of *César Birotteau* was shortly to be completed.

Now that the description of the house and its surroundings is complete, Balzac allows himself three short paragraphs to prepare for the conversation between Marie and Charles which takes up nearly all the remainder of Chapter II. These transitional paragraphs assume as many as six different forms[50] in their progress from manuscript to the *Chronique de Paris*. When the process of correcting them is complete, the main difficulties of the first part of the chapter have been cleared away; at the point where Charles slips in unobserved while Marie is arranging her hair and smoothing her gown, the short second set of proofs[51] comes to an end. Henceforth we pass directly from Pr II A ms to Pr II C.

Upon reaching the dialogue we are immediately struck by the greater

[49] And, of course, by literary inheritance—influence of Scott, etc.

[50] We may pass over the actual revisions, which interest us mainly because of variation in the exact dating of the story (year, day, and hour) and also because of one or two significant changes in the description of Marie herself: it seems she has black hair instead of a *chevelure d'or* (in fictional characters Balzac almost never changes the color of hair or eyes) and that she wears an *escoffion*—this is a specific sixteenth-century term —rather than a mere *chaperon*.

[51] Besides proving useful to Balzac in clarifying the description of Marie Touchet's house, this special set of Werdet page proof, only 7 pages long, provides us additional evidence of the order which Balzac followed in composition and proof correction. For its pages were numbered in the 120's, and Chapter I as finally printed by Baudouin for the Werdet ed. ends with p. 118. This shows that Chapter I was expanded to its full length and set up in Werdet page proof before Pr II B was run off at all. As has already been stated, the final proofs of Chapter I have unfortunately been lost.

ease with which Balzac composed this kind of material. The comparative infrequency of manuscript *ratures* would indicate that the wording of speeches was clean cut in his imagination from the first. While in general Balzac did not succeed remarkably well as a dramatist proper, the dramatic form had a certain appeal for him, an appeal no doubt enhanced by his ability to think rapidly in terms of dialogue. As we examine proof corrections, we shall find that, in the main, they involve changes in stage directions or expansion of the dialogue by means of long or short insertions, rather than numerous stylistic variations. Occasionally the expansion of Chapter II—which twice in our edition requires a special appendix to handle the longest insertions—necessitates omitting or rearranging manuscript dialogue which only sketches or suggests the more elaborate treatment. Occasionally, too, a passage requires re-working because of the intervention of Chapter I. It is significant that stylistic difficulties account for so few variants within the speeches.

Changes in stage directions are particularly numerous in the early part of the conversation, where Marie is trying, by the force of her love and sympathy, to arouse Charles from his profound melancholy. The re-working and elaboration take place mainly in the Pr II A ms, C form, as Balzac prepares for a long insertion.

MS, Pr II A	Pr II A ms, C
Elle lui ôta son chapeau, son manteau, lui passa les mains dans les cheveux, comme si elle eût voulu les lui peigner avec ses doigts; *il* se laissa faire sans répondre, *elle* vit alors les traces *de la profonde* mélancolie *qui le dévorait;* elle baisa *son* front sillonné de rides précoces, *ses* joues décomposées, *elle essaya quelques* caresses qui n'eurent pas de succès; elle se mit à genoux *devant lui,* leva la tête à la hauteur de *la sienne en l'étreignant* doucement de ses bras mignons, et *lui dit:*	Elle lui ôta son chapeau, son manteau, lui passa les mains dans les cheveux, comme si elle eût voulu les lui peigner avec ses doigts. *Charles se laissa faire sans rien répondre. Étonnée, Marie se mit à genoux pour bien étudier le pâle visage de son royal maître, et vit alors les traces d'une fatigue horrible et d'une* mélancolie *plus dévorante que toutes les mélancolies qu'elle avait déjà dissipées. Elle retint une larme, elle garda le silence pour ne pas irriter des douleurs qu'elle ne connaissait point par d'imprudentes paroles; elle fit ce que font les femmes tendres,* elle baisa *ce* front sillonné de rides précoces, *ces* joues décomposées, *en essayant d'imprimer la fraîcheur de son âme à cette âme soucieuse en la faisant passer dans de suaves* caresses qui n'eurent pas de succès; elle leva la tête à la hauteur de *celle du roi, qu'elle étreignit* doucement de ses bras mignons, *et se tint coi, le visage appuyé sur ce sein douloureux, en épiant le moment pour questionner ce malade abattu.*

In the long insertion (composing Appen. II A in our edition) for which this expanded paragraph prepares, Charles compares his own lot with that of the various kings who have borne his name. Marie's role in that scene is the rather unimportant one of interlocutor; but because of the present elaboration of detail, we are early impressed with the sincere and selfless quality of her love for Charles. The expanded stage directions shown in italics in the right-hand column above do not represent pure insertions in the sense of fresh composition; nor, on the other hand, are they directly transposed from some other point in the proofs. Rather, they are a somewhat free adaptation from an MS, Pr II A passage which originally came later in the chapter; in the scissoring process involved in arranging Pr II A ms to be set up as Pr II C, the proof of the latter passage was destroyed.

The passage thus omitted illustrates very well not only the re-use, by adaptation, of stage directions no longer needed in their original placing but also other redistributions of manuscript material resulting from the composition of Chapter I. It is therefore quoted in its entirety as it appeared in its manuscript form:

Après ces paroles, le Roi tomba dans une de ces rêveries sombres qui furent les préludes et les causes de sa mort. *Marie resta silencieuse comme le Roi, tout en s'agenouillant de nouveau devant lui et lui mettant sa blonde tête dans les mains comme pour l'inviter à jouer. Elle savait les ménagemens infinis qu'elle devait employer pour dissiper cette humeur noire qui saisissait Charles IX; à quel moment sa voix douce pouvait s'elever, quand il fallait lui offrir entre deux baisers souvent mal reçus, le rebec espèce de mandoline sur laquelle le Roi s'accompagnait en chantant quelque romance faite par lui.* Moins celebre que ne le furent la duchesse d'Etampes, et Diane de Poitiers, Marie fille d'un apothicaire d'orléans ne voulut ni titres, ni richesses ni honneurs. *Son sincère amour se déploya dans l'ombre, comme une de ces fleurs qui ne s'ouvrent qu'au coucher du soleil,* touchante harmonie avec la destinée des Valois qui s'éteignaient. Charles IX avait le pressentiment de l'extinction de la race artiste et voluptueuse des Valois, à laquelle le royaume devait tant, mais qui ne sauva point la royauté. Marie Touchet dont la beauté parfaite est celebrée par l'histoire fut la dernière des illustres femmes que l'amour plaça aux pieds du trône pour en chasser les ennuis, mais la plus heureuse en ce qu'elle ne connut point les horreurs de l'abandon. Sa modestie la protégea. [Italics distinguish the portions adapted in the elaborated stage directions of Pr II A ms, C, quoted on p. 313.]

To take up the stage directions first, we may note that Balzac in Chapter I has already described Marie as a loving, self-effacing mistress. Placing the modified stage directions at a point so early in Chapter II reinforces the effect of the previous exposition: we are convinced of its truth, without delay, by the naturalness of Marie's actions and words. It is regrettable, however, that the characteristic detail of the *rebec* should have been lost in the transfer.

However effective we may find the new placing and the adaptation of these stage directions, they were probably not the primary reason for omitting the MS, Pr II A passage quoted above. A more important consideration is Balzac's use of the factual material of the passage. Let us center our attention for a moment on the first sentence. Conjectures as to the reasons for Charles's death appear in more specific and more elaborate form elsewhere: first, in a passage of Chapter I referring to Elizabeth of Austria, and, more especially, in part of a second long insertion in Chapter II (the one composing Appen. II B in our edition). In Chapter I we read: "Pendant l'absence de sa maîtresse, le roi s'était rapproché de sa femme avec un emportement que l'histoire a mentionné parmi les causes de sa mort."[52] In the Pr II A ms, D insertion that constitutes our Appendix II B, Marie, rather than Elizabeth, is held responsible for Charles's excesses. Note how "une de ces rêveries sombres, etc." is elaborated:

Charles était, en effet, en proie à l'une de ces prostrations complètes de l'esprit et du corps, produites par la double fatigue de toutes les facultés, et augmentées par le découragement que cause l'étendue du malheur, l'impossibilité reconnue du triomphe, ou l'aspect de difficultés si multipliées, que le génie lui-même s'en effraye. L'abattement du roi était en raison de la hauteur à laquelle s'était monté son courage et ses idées. Puis un accès de mélancolie nerveuse engendré par la maladie elle-même, l'avait saisi au sortir du long conseil qui s'était tenu dans son cabinet. Marie devina qu'il se trouvait en proie à l'une de ces crises où tout est douloureux et importun, même l'amour; elle demeura donc agenouillée ... .[53]

Les deux amants restèrent ainsi dans le plus profond silence pendant un long moment, une de ces heures où toute réflexion fait plaie, où les nuages d'une tempête intérieure et continue voilent jusqu'aux souvenirs du bonheur. Marie se crut pour quelque chose dans cet effrayant accablement; elle se demanda, non

[52] Quoted from *C. de P.*, ll. 85-87. In the revision of Chapter I these lines were moved from place to place and their original manuscript form was modified several times in proofs. Balzac agrees with his source (i.e., Dreux du Radier; for the general question of the documentation for Chapter I, see below, pp. 349-65) in suggesting now Marie, now Elizabeth, as contributing to Charles's malady.

[53] The ensuing stage directions (not quoted here) are similar in tone to those already examined.

sans terreur, si les joies excessives qui marquaient son retour, si le violent amour du roi qu'elle n'avait pas la force de combattre, n'avaient pas affaibli l'esprit et le corps de Charles IX. Au moment où elle leva ses yeux, baignés de larmes comme son visage, vers son amant, elle vit des larmes dans les yeux et sur les joues décolorées du roi. Cette entente qui les unissait jusques dans la douleur, émut si fort Charles IX, qu'il sortit de sa torpeur comme un cheval éperonné. Il prit Marie par la taille, et, avant qu'elle pût deviner la pensée de Charles, il l'avait posée sur le lit de repos.

—Je ne veux plus être roi, dit-il, je ne veux plus être que ton amant, et tout oublier dans le plaisir! Je veux mourir heureux, et non dans les soucis du trône.

L'accent de ses paroles, et le feu qui brilla dans les yeux naguère éteints de Charles IX, au lieu de plaire à Marie, lui fit une peine horrible; car en ce moment elle accusait son amour de complicité avec les causes inconnues qui tuaient le roi.

Of the one hundred and four *Chronique de Paris* lines taken up by the Appendix II B insertion, nearly a third (ll. 1259–91) are thus expanded from the original short manuscript sentence. It is characteristic that Balzac should lighten the exposition by interpolating Charles's speech near the end. Marie breaks into her royal lover's melancholy mood by rising energetically with the words: "Vous oubliez vos prisonniers."

The omission of the Chapter II details concerning Marie Touchet's origin and position at court follows naturally because her *dossier* has been given at length in Chapter I. In the *Chronique de Paris*, lines 92–132 explain why Catherine favored her son's affair with Marie, the principal reason being the young woman's modesty and that of her family—in marked contrast with the ambition of Diane de Poitiers and the Duchesse d'Etampes, "qui combattaient pour leurs maisons avec les armes secrètes de l'amour."

Thus the MS, Pr II A passage quoted on page 314 is omitted in Pr II A ms, C, only to be exploited elsewhere in a variety of ways. Let us now return to the early part of the conversation between Charles and Marie. It was stated on page 314 that the introductory paragraph as expanded in Pr II A ms, C prepared the way for the long Appendix II A insertion (corresponding to ll. 1104–57 of the *Chronique de Paris*). What prompted this insertion? The germ of it we find in an MS, Pr II A passage occurring later in the chapter and maintained with almost no changes through the *Chronique de Paris:*

—Ma sorcellerie est l'amour, reprit-elle en souriant. Depuis le jour heureux où vous m'avez aimée, n'ai-je pas deviné vos pensées? Et les pensées qui vous tourmentent aujourd'hui ne sont pas dignes d'un roi.

—Suis-je roi? dit-il avec amertume.

—Ne pouvez-vous l'être? Comment fit Charles Sept, *de qui vous portez le nom?* Il écouta sa maîtresse, monseigneur, et il reconquit son royaume envahi par les Anglais, comme le vôtre l'est par ceux de la Religion. Votre dernier coup d'état vous a tracé une route qu'il faut suivre. Exterminez l'hérésie.

—Tu blâmais le stratagème, dit Charles et aujourd'hui ...

—Il est accompli, répondit-elle.

—Charles VII n'avait que des hommes à combattre, et je trouve en face de moi des idées, reprit le roi. On tue les hommes, on ne tue pas des mots! [Italicized clause is discussed below.]

The manuscript comparison of Charles IX with Charles VII, and especially Marie's observation, "de qui vous portez le nom," contains a suggestion which Balzac could not neglect. Why not extend the process in Pr II A ms, C, and see what became of the other French kings who had borne that fateful name? Material for such an expansion was not hard to find[54]—if, indeed, Balzac needed to refresh his history-laden memory with regard to facts (or supposed facts) so commonly known. The insertion consists almost entirely of dialogue and requires little modification between Pr II C and the *Chronique de Paris*.

With every long insertion the problem arises of fitting it smoothly into the original text, and usually it is easier to lead up to the insertion than it is to taper away from it. Both the long insertions of Chapter II postpone Charles's report of the previous evening's activities. Accordingly, some of Marie's original manuscript questions are either crowded out or are worked in toward the end of the second insertion so as to prepare for the narrative proper. The printed proof of three manuscript speeches was destroyed in the scissoring process with which we have become acquainted. One short passage was cut out with scissors and pasted very close to the end of the Appendix II B insertion, where it resembles a small island emerging from a sea of manuscript. The ending of the Appendix II A insertion interests us because therein Balzac again adapted stage directions from manuscript material no longer needed in its original form or location. In the later proofs the passage underwent successive modifications which indicate once more that Balzac was more sure of his dialogue than of the accompanying gestures.

As for the subject matter and motivation of the Appendix II B insertion,[55] we have already analyzed (on pp. 315–16) approximately the

[54] For two sources upon which Balzac may well have drawn, see pp. 350–51, below.

[55] This insertion fills four handwritten pages in the corrections to Pr II A ms; it was first set up in type for Pr II D, the second and third sets of proof having been too short

middle third. The keynote to the first part (a little less than a third of the whole insertion in its *Chronique de Paris* form) is given in Charles's opening remark: "Nous sommes deux enfants en politique." In the manuscript version, just before the point where the long proof insertion is made, Marie, to distract Charles from his fears of poison, has given him vigorous advice: "Eh, soyez un tyran à la façon de Louis XI, inspirez une profonde terreur; imitez Don Philippe, bannissez les Italiens, donnez la chasse aux Guises et confisquez les terres des calvinistes, vous vous éleverez dans cette solitude, et vous sauverez le trône. Le moment est propice, votre frère est en Pologne." In the ensuing manuscript text we do not get Charles's reaction to this advice; instead, rather abruptly and artificially, we are pulled back to the happenings of the night before. In Pr II A ms, D, Balzac remedies this defect by omitting the abrupt transitional material and beginning the long insertion as follows:

—Nous sommes deux enfants en politique, dit Charles avec amertume; hier, je songeais à tout ceci, je voulais accomplir de grandes choses; ma mère a soufflé sur mes châteaux de cartes. *Tu ne connais pas, Marie, les difficultés de détail, les impossibilités que créent les intérêts de chacun.* Ma mère m'a démontré l'inanité de mes plans; nous sommes environnés de sujets qui narguent la justice; et faute de la hache de Louis XI, de qui tu parles, il faudrait avoir le courage que veut l'assassinat; le parlement ne condamnerait pas les Guises; je suis dégoûté de tout.

Et il retomba dans une morne somnolence. [Italicized sentence discussed below.]

Even in this version the subject has obviously not received the treatment it deserves. Consequently, we find that Pr II D ms, E, substitute for the italicized sentence a passage (corresponding to ll. 1234–46 of the *Chronique de Paris*) in which Balzac makes a serious attempt to analyze the political capital made of religious dissension by those who would gain power. The passage fits in nicely as a reaction to Marie's advice. The other proof variations in the first third of the insertion need not be discussed here.

The last third is less unified than the other two sections, partly because of the necessity of bringing the conversation back to Charles's nocturnal adventure. It is worth noting that into this section is introduced a scene

---

to include it. We may observe that the number of corrections in any given set of proofs (after the first) increases as the end of the set is approached. The effect has been compared, by Professor Dargan, to the action of a snowplow clearing away snowdrifts by a series of starts; Balzac's progress through the early pages of comparatively clean proof gives him the momentum necessary for attacking the heavier drifts which remain.

wherein appears the little son of Marie and Charles. Here we are reminded of Balzac's earlier remark that this house was the only place where Charles could give himself over to the delights of paternity. One of Marie's manuscript questions, deleted in Pr II A ms, was: "Veux-tu que j'aille te chercher notre cher enfant, le petit duc d'Angoulême ... . Non." This is but one more example of Balzac's tenacity; an idea may be crowded out at one point, but if there is any opportunity it is put back at another—and usually in elaborated form.

The insertions thus far discussed have been complicated by redistributions of material. Through the rest of Chapter II much of the expansion is accomplished by a simpler process of interpolating additional dialogue and stage directions. When original manuscript speeches are changed, it is frequently because Balzac, having written Chapter I, has a clearer conception of what transpired on the night before. As long as the actual events are clear in his mind, there are relatively few changes as a result of fumbling for words. In the following example, occurring just after Charles has resumed the main course of his narrative, the dialogue is augmented in three consecutive proofs with little disturbance of original speeches. Italics indicate the variants:

MS, Pr II A

—Rue Saint-Honoré, *ma chère, et* mes yeux furent attirés par une vive clarté des combles de la maison où demeure Réné le parfumeur et le gantier de ma mère, le tien, *le mien,* celui de la cour.

Pr II A ms, D

—Rue Saint-Honoré, *mon minon, dit le roi qui parut s'être remis, et qui, en reprenant ses idées, voulut mettre sa maîtresse au fait de la scène qui allait se passer chez elle. En y passant hier,* mes yeux furent attirés par une vive clarté des combles de la maison où demeure Réné le parfumeur et le gantier de ma mère, le tien, celui de la cour. *J'ai des doutes violents sur ce qui se fait chez cet homme, et si je suis empoisonné, là s'est préparé le poison.*

Pr II D ms, E [similar to the preceding version except for addition of two speeches, as follows:]

—*Dès demain je le quitte, dit Marie.*
—*Ah! tu l'avais conservé quand je l'avais quitté, s'écria le roi. Ici était ma vie, on y a mis la mort.*

Pr II E ms, *C. de P.* [First part identical with
Pr II A ms, D; ending augmented as follows:]
—Dès demain je le quitte, dit Marie.
—Ah! tu l'avais conservé quand je l'avais quitté, s'écria
le roi. Ici était ma vie, *reprit-il d'un air sombre,* on y a mis
la mort....
  —*Mais, cher enfant, je reviens de Dauphiné, avec notre
dauphin, dit-elle en souriant, et Réné ne m'a rien fourni depuis
la mort de la reine de Navarre.... Continues, tu as grimpé sur
la maison de Réné?*
—*Oui, reprit le roi.*

The mere omission of "le mien" from the manuscript version makes the
interpolations possible. The added speeches link up with information furnished in Chapter I but do not involve transposition.

The examples thus far analyzed illustrate the chief problems of construction—or reconstruction—encountered in Chapter II. Detailed treatment of many proof corrections occurring in the remainder of the chapter
we may leave for the edition proper. It may be well, however, to indicate
a few of the more important passages. For example, at a point corresponding to line 1355 of the *Chronique de Paris,* Pr A ms introduces Tavannes as co-investigator (along with Charles and the Gondi brothers)
into the mysteries of the Ruggieri laboratory; this harmonizes with Chapter I, where the king's companions have been named. Several times, as
Charles's narrative continues, successive modifications in the proofs aug-
ment the importance of Tavannes's role and heighten the dramatic qualities of the recital. A favorite device is to interrupt a description with a bit
of dialogue, accompanied by stage directions that indicate the effect of
the scene upon one or the other of the two observers. In other words,
Charles as narrator uses Balzac's own technique for breaking up and
lightening long descriptions. The workroom, as pictured by Charles, reminds us somewhat of Gautier's *La Maison de la sorcière;*[56] as we might
expect, details descriptive of the room, the Ruggieri, and the strangely
beautiful woman whom Charles judged to be the subject of an experiment
—she was "fine et longue comme une couleuvre, blanche comme une
souris, livide comme une morte, immobile comme une statue"—are
changed in the different proofs. The variants are, however, not nearly so

---

[56] This poem, published in 1832, may possibly have influenced Balzac; in its concrete
details it is more suggestive than Dumas's *Henri III et sa cour,* where Cosimo Ruggieri
plays a part (see n. 61 below).

frequent as in the description of Marie's house at the beginning of the chapter.

Charles is particularly fascinated by the imposing figure of old Lorenzo Ruggieri. "Je le regardais," he says, "si curieusement que son esprit a, je crois, passé en moi." This recalls to our minds the opening of *Facino Cane*, wherein Balzac analyzes his own faculty of observation. At a point corresponding to line 1361 of the *Chronique de Paris*, the name of the younger Ruggieri is mentioned for the first time in Chapter II, and the process of changing "Claude" to "Cosme" begins.[57] It is curious that Balzac should have confused the name of Claude Ruggieri, who in real life was *artificier du roi* under Charles X, with that of Catherine's astrologer, especially in view of the fact that Cosimo was so well known and is mentioned in so many histories of France. On the other hand, historical information concerning the other members of the family is almost nonexistent. Balzac himself, in a manuscript *rature* in Chapter I, admits that the life of Lorenzo "a échappé à l'histoire," or, at any rate, "a échappé aux investigations purement historiques." The manuscript text of Chapter I also hints that Balzac obtained his information concerning Lorenzo and Ruggieri-le-vieux from certain "auteurs cabalistiques," which the present investigator, much to his regret, has been unable to identify. It may be that Cosimo's brother Lorenzo actually existed; but in that case it seems strange that, as Balzac says, there should be no mention of him in "purely historical" works. In our examination of Chapter I (both variations and sources) we shall see what liberties Balzac had to take with his principal historical source, identified in this study for the first time, in order to eke out such information as he possessed with regard to Lorenzo. It is quite possible that Lorenzo was an invention of Balzac's own and that the vague reference to "auteurs cabalistiques" was thrown in to lend an air of authenticity to spurious documentation.[58]

If only Balzac had given Cosimo his right name from the beginning, the choice of the name "Lorenzo" would be easy to account for. In the manuscript version (Chap. I) we read that "Paul Ruggieri-le-vieux était si con-

[57] These changes have been brought forward on p. 301 as evidence that Pr II A and Pr III A were set up before Chapter I was written.

[58] Since this conjecture was first arrived at, my belief that Lorenzo was a fictional character has been further strengthened by the fact that Mr. Furman Bridgers, of Duke University, working upon *An Index of Proper Names in the "Comédie Humaine,"* has unearthed no evidence that Lorenzo was an actual person.

sidéré par les Médicis, qu'ils furent les parrains de ses deux enfants."[59] With the historical Cosimo as a point of departure and with the Medici put forward as godfathers, Lorenzo would be the logical name for a fictional brother. Unfortunately for such reasoning, Balzac used the name "Laurent" for many pages in the manuscript and first proof of Chapters II and III before discovering that the younger brother should have been called "Cosme" instead of "Claude."

Let us continue in our belief that Lorenzo was a fictional character and see how Balzac makes his association with historical characters plausible. How does it happen, for example, that Cosimo was the only one to suffer for his implication in the La Mole–Coconnas conspiracy?[60] Balzac gets around this difficulty by explaining in the manuscript of Chapter III that Lorenzo had left the kingdom immediately. Pr III D ms and subsequent forms, omitting "aussitôt," merely state that he had left. Balzac cleverly uses the fictional events of Le Secret des Ruggieri to account for Charles's historically recorded animosity against Cosimo:

> Ce soupçon explique la haine que manifesta le roi contre Cosme lors de la découverte de la conspiration de La Mole et Coconnas; en le trouvant un des artisans de cette entreprise, *il crut avoir été joué par les deux Italiens*, il lui fut

---

[59] A curious footnote in Eugène Defrance, *Catherine de Médicis, ses astrologues et ses magiciens-envoûteurs*, pp. 188–89, takes with complete seriousness Balzac's information concerning the two sons of Ruggieri-le-vieux, paraphrasing this portion of *Le Secret des Ruggieri*, though with no mention of Balzac as the source. (In another connection, p. 30, where ultimate sources are lacking, he does cite Balzac as authority.) In Collin de Plancy's *Dictionnaire infernal*, a whole article, "Universités occultes," consists of an acknowledged quotation from *Le Secret des Ruggieri* (corresponding to ll. 180–286 of the *Chronique de Paris*). Apparently Balzac's desire to be considered a serious historian was granted!

[60] In Chapter I, at some length, Balzac writes up the La Mole–Coconnas conspiracy as an attempt to place Henri de Navarre and Charles IX's younger brother, the Duc d'Alençon, at the head of the Protestants. Charles himself was to be made prisoner. Involved in the plot were the Comte de La Mole, who was a lover of Marguerite de Navarre, and the Comte de Coconnas. Cosimo Ruggieri was implicated because a wax figure which he had made was found, pierced through the heart with two needles, in La Mole's possession. The accusation was made that by this form of magic, called *envoûtement*, the conspirators were attempting to do Charles bodily harm. Any defense claim that the wax effigy was only a love charm and did not represent the king proved futile. La Mole and Coconnas were beheaded in April, 1574, and Cosimo was condemned to the galleys. According to Balzac, Catherine had secretly encouraged the plot but, for reasons of her own, exposed it a few months after the main action of our story. She made possible a light sentence for Cosimo and arranged for his release after Charles's death.

prouvé que l'astrologue de sa mère ne s'occupait pas exclusivement des astres, de la poudre de projection et de l'atome pur. *Laurent avait quitté le royaume* [*C. de P.*, ll. 2078-83; italics mine].

To return to Chapter II, Charles displays special curiosity concerning Lorenzo, the more mysterious of the two brothers. A sentence inserted in Pr II A ms, and maintained thereafter, is significant; Charles says to Marie: "Tête-Dieu pleine de reliques, je trouvais qu'il y avait bien assez d'un Ruggieri dans le royaume, et voilà qu'il s'en trouve deux." Thus a reader already acquainted with the historical Cosimo is led to accept his brother as well. If, as appears likely, Lorenzo is indeed a product of the author's imagination, then Balzac has solved satisfactorily a problem which confronts every writer of historical novels.

Whether Lorenzo was a fictional character or merely a real person about whom Balzac had little information, the following passage will be of interest. In its concentrated mass of corrections it represents several types of variants which are characteristic of the latter part of the chapter but which, in general, are distributed over a wider area. In the MS, Pr II A version presented below, all expressions changed before journal publication are put in italics or boldface; after the first form, only the variations from the preceding version are so designated:

MS, Pr II A

Quoique je fusse placé de manière à ne pas être vu, *Claude s'écria:* —Il y a quelqu'un près de nous! Qui est-ce? demanda-t-il *à la morte* [i.e., the beautiful woman "livide comme une morte" mentioned above, p. 320].—Le roi! dit-elle. *Nous sommes perdus! entendis-je.* Je me suis montré, Ruggieri m'a ouvert la croisée, et j'ai sauté dans *le laboratoire en laissant mes compagnons à leurs affaires.*—Oui, le roi, dis-je aux deux Florentins qui *se tenaient debout et découverts en grande peur. Je veux savoir ce que vous faites ici et à l'hôtel de Soissons; vous pouvez avoir des secrets dans lesquels vous ne vouliez mettre personne autre que moi du royaume, voilà pourquoi je suis venu par ce chemin, et je leur montrai la croisée. Il doit se trouver quelque chose au fonds de ceci, leur dis-je en montrant les* four- neaux et *les* livres. *Maître Claude et vous, maître Laurent, vous êtes deux savans, vous avez hérité des connaissances de votre père qui, s'il faut en croire madame Catherine* ma mère, *était un homme adonné à l'astrologie judiciaire et qui a formé le sieur Galilée; vous n'êtes pas des gens ordinaires,* vous puisez dans *beaucoup* de bourses *et* vous ne devez pas vous jeter en étour- neaux dans cette cuisine. Vous avez *une idée,* je suis homme à l'entendre, ...

Pr II A ms, D

Quoique je fusse placé de manière à ne pas être vu, *Cosme* s'écria: —Il y a quelqu'un près de nous! Qui est-ce? demanda-t-il à la morte.—Le roi! dit-elle. Je me suis montré, Ruggieri m'a ouvert la croisée, et j'ai sauté dans le laboratoire, en laissant mes compagnons à leurs affaires.—Oui, le roi, dis-je aux deux Florentins qui se tenaient debout et découverts en grande peur. *Malgré vos* fourneaux et *vos* livres, *vos sorcières et votre science, vous n'avez pas deviné cette visite. Vous êtes le fameux Laurent Ruggieri, dis-je au vieillard de qui parle si mystérieusement la reine* ma mère, *pour qui vous travaillez peut-être ici. Je veux savoir la vérité tout entière. Or,* vous puisez dans *tant* de bourses *que depuis long-temps des gens cupides eussent été rassasiés d'or; vous êtes des gens trop rusés pour vous jeter imprudemment dans des voies criminelles, enfin* vous ne devez pas *non plus* vous jeter en étourneaux dans cette cuisine, vous avez *donc* une idée, je suis homme à l'entendre ...

Pr II D ms [Pr II E does not include this portion of chapter]

Quoique je fusse placé de manière à ne pas être vu, Cosme s'écria: —Il y a quelqu'un près de nous! Qui est-ce? demanda-t-il à la *jeune* morte.—Le roi! dit-elle. Je me suis montré, Ruggieri m'a ouvert la croisée, et j'ai sauté dans *cette cuisine de l'enfer, suivi de Tavannes.*—Oui, le roi, dis-je aux deux Florentins qui *nous parurent saisis de terreur.* Malgré vos fourneaux et vos livres, vos sorcières et votre science, vous n'avez pas deviné *ma* visite. *J'étais bien aise de voir ce* fameux Laurent Ruggieri, de qui parle si mystérieusement la reine ma mère, *dis-je au vieillard qui se leva et s'inclina. Vous êtes dans le royaume sans mon agrément, bon homme? Pour qui travaillez-vous ici, vous qui, de père en fils, êtes au cœur de la maison de Médicis? Écoutez-moi bien!* Vous puisez dans tant de bourses, que depuis long-temps des gens cupides eussent été rassasiés d'or; vous êtes des gens trop rusés pour vous jeter imprudemment dans des voies criminelles, *mais* vous ne devez pas non plus vous jeter en étourneaux dans cette cuisine, vous avez donc *de secrets desseins, vous qui n'êtes satisfaits ni par l'or, ni par le pouvoir? Qui servez-vous? Dieu ou le Diable. Que fabriquez-vous ici?* Je veux la vérité tout entière, je suis homme à l'entendre ...

Pr II [F], *C. de P.*

Quoique je fusse placé de manière à ne pas être vu, Cosme *dit en prenant la main de* la jeune morte:—Il y a quelqu'un près de nous! Qui est-ce? demanda-t-il.—Le roi! dit-elle. Je me suis montré *en frappant au vitrail,* Ruggieri m'a ouvert ... visite. *Je suis* bien aise .... Écoutez-moi! Vous puisez .... Je veux la vérité *toute* entière, je suis homme à l'entendre ... [The omitted lines are identical with Pr II D ms.]

Let us limit ourselves here to a general comparison of the manuscript passage with the versions which replace it. The manuscript sentence "Nous sommes perdus! entendis-je" was rather too obvious an admission of guilt on the part of the Ruggieri; since in the *Chronique de Paris* we are to be kept in suspense on this point through the entire story, omission of the sentence is desirable. Self-possession and dignity in the face of royal wrath are later shown to be Lorenzo's outstanding characteristics. Charles's manuscript explanation of why he entered by the window was wordy and lacking in dramatic sense, and his wheedling curiosity concerning the Ruggieri's researches did not accord with kingly character. In the revised versions, on the other hand, the sentence beginning "Malgré vos fourneaux et vos livres, vos sorcières et votre science," is a striking expression of his disbelief in the Ruggieri. The threat implied in "Vous êtes dans le royaume sans mon agrément, bon homme?" is calculated to inspire fear in the alchemists; and when, later on, Charles demands "la vérité toute entière," he does so with an air of authority. Lastly, we may note the diminished importance of Ruggieri *père* in the revised versions, as compared with his manuscript role. Chronology would account, in part, for Balzac's modifications. At the time of our story Catherine de Médicis could not have talked of Ruggieri *père*, or of Lorenzo himself, as having "formé le sieur Galilée," for Galileo was not born until 1564. That Balzac originally had the wrong dates in mind is clear from a *rature* in the manuscript: "Galilée est en prison"; the scientist's imprisonment by the Inquisition took place from 1633 on. Hence the omission, in Pr II A ms, etc., of the reference to Galileo. Balzac also fixes his attention not on the father but on Lorenzo, who becomes an increasingly impressive figure in the revisions of Chapters II and III. It is likely that in building up Lorenzo he made use of a number of details originally associated in his mind with Ruggieri *père*.

Several times in the proof revision of this portion of Chapter II other proper names—"Agrippa," "le vieux Bodin," and "Bernard de Palissy"—

are omitted or juggled under circumstances which lead one to suspect that Balzac did not always have definite authority for attributing particular ideas to particular thinkers but that, instead, he indulged in a general pseudo-philosophical "patter," to which he gave apparent authenticity by introducing well-known names.

At the point where the Ruggieri are brought before Charles and Marie for questioning, marginal directions in Pr II A ms show Balzac's momentary intention of beginning Chapter III, "Fin contre Fin," at once; but he crosses them out and expands his manuscript version of the preparations for the interrogation scene. The few remaining pages of Chapter II include some preliminary verbal skirmishing between Charles and Lorenzo; some description of the room where the inquiry is to be held; and the impression produced on Marie by the sight of the Ruggieri—Lorenzo in particular. The proof corrections are fairly numerous. The most interesting one as a preparation for Chapter III is a remark by Lorenzo inserted in Pr II D ms: "Celui que vous voyez devant vous, Madame, dit alors le grand vieillard, est autant au-dessus des rois que les rois sont au-dessus de leurs sujets, et vous me trouverez courtois, alors que vous connaîtrez ma puissance." The special significance of this insertion for our study of proof corrections is that it motivates the long Pr III A ms insertions at the very beginning of Chapter III (discussed below, p. 327). The fact that it was not inserted until Pr II D ms indicates that Balzac made all, or very nearly all, his corrections for Chapter II before beginning his revisions of Pr III A. It is the last link in the chain of evidence; from the manuscript to the *Chronique de Paris* we know in what order the three chapters were composed and revised. With this final confirmation of the order presented on page 301 we bring to a close our analysis of proof variations in Chapter II.

X

Even leaving out of consideration Chapter I, not composed until after the proofs of Chapter II and III were set up, we begin to perceive how exaggerated was Balzac's boast that he had written *Le Secret des Ruggieri* in a single night. If Chapter II, relatively complete, required so much elaboration in the proofs, the situation is still worse with regard to Chapter III. For the manuscript version of this part of the story is left dangling in the middle of a sentence; and several pages of close handwriting—included in the Chicago proofs—are required to finish it. The original first draft of the story contained no chapter divisions at all; indeed, the manuscript form of the third chapter would have made a sorry showing if lopped off from its parent-stem, Chapter II. We have already seen how Balzac made one attempt, in Pr II A ms, to begin the new chapter a few pages earlier; we have also studied the important subsequent insertions which laid the groundwork for Chapter III as printed in the *Chronique de Paris*. Using the one set of proofs at Chantilly and the four at Chicago and reconstructing the missing set or sets, Pr III [F], we are now ready to examine the revisions and fresh composition which expanded the manuscript material of Chapter III at least threefold before it was published.

The most fascinating pages of the Chicago proofs, aside from the handwritten ending of the story, are those which begin Chapter III. The heading of the chapter, "III. Fin contre Fin," was inserted in Pr III A ms, together with an opening paragraph, which, revised and augmented in each and every set of proofs, finally occupies lines 1622–50 of the *Chronique de Paris*. The keynote of the paragraph was furnished by the Chapter II insertion (see p. 326, above) in which Lorenzo, with dignity and self-possession, declares that he is "autant au-dessus des rois que les rois sont au-dessus de leurs sujets." The new introduction, then, sets off the astrologer against the king, pointing out that only Cosimo could appreciate the finesse of his brother's challenge. If Lorenzo is clearly supreme in the realm of pure thought, at least Charles IX, as head of his temporal kingdom, has the power of life and death over these two old men suspected of plotting against the sovereign. What will be his verdict? In the clash of wills we have, to repeat a favorite phrase of Balzac's, "toute une scène."

Most of Chapter III is taken up by Lorenzo's demonstration of the *grand œuvre* to which he and Cosimo, as well as generations of researchers before them, have devoted their lives. Fascinated by these glimpses into the mystery of creation, Charles is diverted from his earlier suspicions; if momentarily he returns to them, Lorenzo suavely avoids the issue. But much of the time Balzac seems to be writing only incidentally in the interests of plot; in this portion of the story he is less the historical novelist than the author of *Louis Lambert*, giving rein to his fondness for philosophical speculation.

For the stages in the expansion from the manuscript to the *Chronique de Paris* the reader is, in general, referred to the edition proper; but we may note here that the principal philosophical or pseudo-philosophical ideas are sketched in the manuscript. The first of these is Lorenzo's belief that God does not intervene in the daily affairs of the world. In a

Pr III B ms insertion—which also points out the error of the popular notion that the purpose of alchemy is to discover the composition of gold —he says: "Si j'admettais la présence de Dieu dans la matière à ma voix, la flamme des fourneaux allumés depuis des siècles s'éteindrait demain. Mais nier l'action directe de Dieu, n'est pas nier Dieu; n'accusez pas d'athéisme ceux qui veulent l'immortalité!" This represents a partial shift from the manuscript idea that "Cette croyance [in the nonintervention of God] n'est pas essentielle à nos recherches." In the manuscript Lorenzo cites as evidence the fact that his brother—named "Cosimo" only in the proofs—believes in the practices of the church[61] while still pursuing the *grand œuvre*. In a Pr III A ms insertion Lorenzo says that Cosimo will die "presque centenaire"—a sign that the Ruggieri expect to escape from their present predicament—and will, at the end of his life, agree with his brother's opinions. A Pr B ms elaboration gives the reason: "... car il est impossible d'être alchimiste et catholique, d'avoir foi au despotisme de l'homme sur la matière et au règne de l'esprit sur la matière." The insertion, as a whole, seems to be partly a concession to the plot; the reader is reminded that Lorenzo's disquisition is intended to save the lives of the astrologers.

Next, in the manuscript version, Lorenzo says that the earth belongs to man; he does not recognize the world of the soul, for after death the substances of man's body return to their "primitive expressions"—water to water, fire to fire, metal to metal. Successive insertions enlarge upon the idea. According to Pr III B ms, man is a terrestrial creation: "... s'il portait en lui-même une portion de Dieu, il ne périrait pas, et il périt." Socrates and his school invented the soul, but Lorenzo stands "pour les transformations de la matière que je vois, contre l'impossible éternité d'une âme que je ne vois pas." The extreme materialism of this conception of creation is modified in a Pr III D ms elaboration:

L'homme n'est pas une création immédiatement sortie des mains de Dieu, mais une conséquence des principes semés [changed to "du principe semé" in the lost set of proofs] dans l'infini de l'éther où se produisent des milliers de

---

[61] And, consequently, in the importance of God in the life of the individual. Cf. Act I, scene 3, of Dumas's *Henri III et sa cour*, where Cosimo says to the young aristocrats who seek the aid of his magical powers: "Rassurez-vous, messieurs, je suis aussi bon chrétien que vous." However, in view of the frequency with which the name "Côme Ruggieri" appears in the play, Balzac was probably not using Dumas directly; otherwise he would hardly have referred to Catherine's astrologer as "Claude." There is, of course, no mention of Lorenzo by Dumas.

créatures dont aucune ne se ressemble d'astre à astre, parce que les conditions de la vie y sont différentes. Oui, sire, le mouvement subtil que nous nommons la vie a sa source au-delà des mondes visibles; les créations se le partagent au gré des milieux dans lesquelles elles se trouvent, et les plus infîmes d'entre elles y participent en en prenant tant qu'elles en peuvent prendre, à leurs risques et périls. L'alchimie est là tout entière.

Even supposing that something of man survives death, says Lorenzo in a Pr III A ms insertion, it is not the *"moi* actuel." The old alchemist's devotion to the *grand œuvre* is the result of his desire to prolong the "transformation présente," to extend man's life on earth. And he has faith: "Déjà nous avons étendu nos sens, nous voyons dans les astres! ... La vie sera quelque jour à nous!"

Chapter III offers some striking examples of a type of variation that occurs occasionally in other portions of the story—namely, cases in which a compositor's misreading or his confusion regarding marginal directions influences the final form or placing of a passage. The following example, occurring in one of the insertions just discussed, is especially interesting because of Balzac's elaboration of a misreading. In a Pr III B ms insertion the author wrote: "Quoi! les arbres vivent des *centaines d'années*, et les hommes ne vivraient que des années, tandis que *l'homme est actif, là ou l'arbre est passif*" (italics in this and following version indicate variants). In both Pr III C and D the passage remains unchanged, except that the compositor set up "l'autre" for "l'arbre." The misreading was so plausible that Balzac probably did not recognize it as such, but it suggested an antithesis which he elaborates in Pr III D ms to the form maintained through the *Chronique de Paris:* "Quoi! les arbres vivent des *siècles*, et les hommes ne vivraient que des années, tandis que *les uns sont passifs et que les autres sont actifs; que les uns sont immobiles et sans parole, et que les autres se parlent et marchent!*" In view of such elaboration it would be impossible, in a definitive or critical edition, to correct the compositor's error; one can only note the changes and explain the circumstances which caused them to be made.

Soon after this misreading we come upon an instance where the compositor setting up Pr III B misunderstood Balzac's marginal directions concerning a series of transpositions. The original directions were given in Pr III A ms; if they had been carried out to the letter, four passages which together occupy lines 1751–1848 of the *Chronique de Paris* would have occupied the same location, it is true, but in a different order with respect to each other. Their history is too involved to trace here; we merely note that Balzac accepted the order laid down by the compositor of Pr III B and went on elaborating in the succeeding proofs.

One of the four passages—first in manuscript order, though last in the *Chronique de Paris*—expresses vividly Lorenzo's faith in the continuity of his work, implying that Charles's inquiry is but an unimportant and momentary interruption. It begins with Lorenzo's statement: "Je me suis donc pris corps à corps avec la matière à laquelle je crois, et je la veux pénétrer." As a "patient observateur des atomes," he knocks ceaselessly at the door of creation; and when he dies, his hammer will pass into other hands. The hope of discovering the secret of life was born with the human race; and succeeding generations of researchers have passed on their discoveries. The order of the Templiers was formed for this purpose. Though one of Charles's predecessors, Philippe-le-Bel, burned the men who belonged to that order, their secrets were not destroyed. Lorenzo is the elected sovereign of the new Templiers, a race of intrepid and inseparable seekers after ultimate truth. "Je les dirige tous," says he, "vers l'essence, nous suivons tous la molécule imperceptible qui fuit nos fourneaux, échappe à nos yeux; mais nous nous ferons des yeux plus puissants que les nôtres, nous atteindrons l'atome primitif, l'élément corpusculaire intrépidement cherché par tous les sages qui nous ont précédés dans cette chasse sublime."

The other three passages likewise expound Lorenzo's philosophy, but they are so general in their nature and so loosely constructed that the transitional sentences would have required considerable re-working in whatever order they might be arranged. The prolixity of this part of the chapter is perhaps the chief defect of *Le Secret des Ruggieri* as a historical novel.

Nevertheless, Lorenzo—reflecting Balzac's own enthusiasm for philosophical speculation—does, in some of these very passages, give us a vivid impression of his sincerity; and this impression is reinforced in each successive set of proofs. Our sympathy for him is so strong at this stage that we are regretful, later on, when exigencies of plot cause Balzac to characterize the Ruggieri as conscious charlatans. The following Pr III B ms, D insertion is a case in point:

> Malgré son désir de ne pas se laisser surprendre par les ruses florentines, le roi, de même que sa naïve maîtresse, étaient déjà saisis, enveloppés dans les ambages et les replis de cette pompeuse loquacité de charlatan; leurs yeux attestaient l'éblouissement que leur causait la vue de ces richesses mystérieuses étalées, ils apercevaient comme une enfilade de souterrains pleins de gnomes en travail. Les impatiences de la curiosité dissipaient les défiances du soupçon.

—Mais alors, s'écria le roi, vous êtes de grands politiques qui pouvez nous éclairer.

—Non sire, dit naïvement Laurent.

As we approach the end of the original manuscript version,[62] the connection of the Ruggieri with political affairs—and the question of their guilt or innocence—comes more sharply into focus. In the manuscript Charles asks a direct question involving René the perfumer and Catherine, and receives in answer a direct defense of the Ruggieri themselves, of René, and of Catherine, which by its very emphasis arouses suspicion. In the final form Charles's questions are more general, and Lorenzo answers with suave generalities of a sort to exonerate Catherine. René is left out of consideration. As for their own guilt, the Ruggieri pretend not to be aware of the king's suspicions. In characterization, then, the revised version is consistent with the picture of Lorenzo which has already been presented—an imposing old man before whose calm dignity even a king felt humble. Three versions[63] will be sufficient to show the trend of the revisions:

MS, Pr III B

Avez-vous vendu des poisons *à Réné le parfumeur?* ma mère en a-t-elle demandé?

Le roi *était haletant.*

—Sire, *dit Laurent, jamais ni moi, ni mon frère nous n'avons fait usage ou donné connaissance à autrui de nos découvertes. Réné le parfumeur ne nous a jamais demandé de poison.* La reine Catherine *a des bras assez dévoués à son service pour se passer de ces moyens.* Mon frère ne l'a pas quittée depuis sa venue en France, *et* sait combien madame Diane lui a donné de chagrin, elle n'a jamais pensé à la faire empoisonner, *cependant Cosme aussi bien que moi connaît de terribles poisons, particuliers aux Ruggieri. Nous ne livrerons jamais à personne ces secrets.*

—*Mais à moi! dit Charles IX avec un accent de fureur concentrée.*

Les deux frères se regardèrent.

—*Vous êtes le maître, dit Cosme Ruggieri.*

[62] Pr III A ends with the words: "—Sire, dit Marie Touchet, les Ruggieri ont votre parole de gentilhomme." The final page of the incomplete manuscript was not set up before Pr III B; for the text of the ending, see the frontispiece of the present volume, where p. 8 of Pr III B is reproduced, together with Balzac's marginal corrections, which we call "Pr III B ms." In the final manuscript page Balzac substitutes "Cosme" for "Claude" wherever it occurs, by writing one name directly on top of the other. Otherwise the corrections are made in Pr III B ms and subsequent proofs.

[63] The first two of these versions transcribe a part of the proof sheet reproduced as our frontispiece.

Pr III B ms, C

Vous occupez-vous à chercher, à combiner des poisons?
—*Pour connaître ce qui fait vivre, il faut bien savoir ce qui tue.*
—*Vous possédez le secret de plusieurs poisons.*
—*Oui, sire.*
—Ma mère en a-t-elle demandé?
Le roi était haletant.
—Sire, dit Laurent, la reine Catherine *est trop habile pour employer de semblables moyens. Elle ne partage aucune de mes idées, et sait que le souverain qui se sert de poison périt par le poison, les Borgia offrent un célèbre exemple des dangers que présentent ces ressources. Tout se sait à la cour. Vous pouvez tuer un pauvre diable, et alors à quoi bon? Mais s'attaquer aux gens en vue, y a-t-il une seule chance de secret? Qui tira sur Coligny? ce ne pouvait être que vous, ou la reine, ou les Guise. Personne ne s'y est trompé. Croyez-moi, l'on ne se sert pas deux fois impunément du poison en politique. La reine le sait, elle est de Florence.* Mon frère qui ne l'a pas quittée depuis sa venue en France, sait combien madame Diane lui a donné de chagrin, elle n'a jamais pensé à la faire empoisonner. *Elle le pouvait. Qu'eut dit le roi votre père? Jamais femme n'a été plus dans son droit, ni plus sûre de l'impunité. Madame de Valentinois vit encore.*

Pr III C ms, D

Vous occupez-vous des poisons?
—Pour connaître ce qui fait vivre, il faut bien savoir ce qui *fait mourir.*
—Vous possédez le secret de plusieurs poisons.
—Oui, sire*; mais par la théorie et non par la pratique, nous les connaissons sans en user.*
—Ma mère en a-t-elle demandé? *dit* le roi *qui haletait.*
—Sire, *répondit* Laurent, la reine Catherine est trop habile pour employer de semblables moyens. Elle sait que le souverain ... présentent *d'aussi misérables* ressources ... . Croyez-moi, l'on ne se sert pas deux fois impunément du poison en politique. *Les princes ont toujours des successeurs. Quant aux petits, si, comme Luther, ils deviennent des souverains par la puissance des idées, on ne tue pas leurs doctrines en se débarrassant d'eux. La reine est de Florence et sait que le poison est l'arme des vengeances personnelles.* Mon frère ... vit encore.

The defense of St. Barthélemy inserted in the second version reminds us of *Les Deux Rêves*. Catherine, thus capable of open and direct attack when she feels it necessary for the public good, might, as a Florentine, recognize in poison a legitimate means of obtaining personal vengeance; but even here, under great provocation, she scorns "d'aussi misérables ressources."

What of *envoûtements?* Charles is still apprehensive on this point. The defense—proffered by Cosimo, which is significant in view of the part he is later accused of playing in the La Mole–Coconnas conspiracy—is a similar one: Catherine, with every resource at her command, has no need of a practice so innocuous that it resembles the administering of bread pills to a hypochondriac. Except for an unfinished sentence, deleted in the proofs, the manuscript version ends as follows: "La reine Catherine pourrait-elle vous sauver en ce moment? dit le roi d'un air sombre. —Mais nous ne sommes pas en danger, sire, répondit tranquillement Laurent Ruggieri." The ending of the story is neglected until Pr III B ms, when an insertion of a little more than four handwritten pages—expanded and added to in later proofs—brings it to a close. In this insertion Lorenzo claims to see into the future. Not only will he leave Marie's house unharmed, but Cosimo will finally triumph over the king's anger (when the La Mole–Coconnas conspiracy is discovered, a few days later). The king is curious to learn of coming events; he is told of the fate of the Valois house, of Henri de Bourbon, and of Marie Touchet. Charles goes to get his son, the little Comte d'Auvergne; during his absence Marie asks why Lorenzo had said that she would be married to Balzac d'Entragues,[64] have children, and live to be more than eighty years old. Lorenzo replies with dignity that he was required to tell the truth. Pr III C ms elaborates their conversation in such a way that our faith in the Ruggieri is once more undermined. But Charles has forgotten his suspicions; in the same Pr III C ms insertion he receives a note from the physician Chapelain which, as he expects, exonerates the alchemists. While Cosimo looks at the child's hand, the king listens to Lorenzo discoursing on alchemy as "le matérialisme expliqué" (in Pr III B ms, C) or "la mathématique du matérialisme, la loi vivante de ses phases" (in Pr III C ms, etc.). With good humor restored, Charles even comes to feel that Catherine's interest in the Ruggieri is the same as his own:

[64] Or "Charles de Balzac, marquis d'Entragues, gouverneur d'Orléans," as he is called nearer the end of the chapter. Honoré *de* Balzac has been taxed with claiming to be descended from the same family as Balzac d'Entragues. Does this partly explain his desire to write up the story of Marie Touchet? For a jibe at these pretensions to aristocracy, see Lovenjoul, *Un Dernier Chapitre de l'histoire des œuvres de H. de Balzac* (Paris: Dentu, 1880), p. 24, where a document relating to Balzac's lawsuit with the *Revue de Paris* is reproduced.

—L'alchimie est donc alors la science des sciences! s'écria Charles IX en-
thousiasmé. Je veux vous voir à l'œuvre....

—Toutes les fois que vous le voudrez, sire; vous ne serez pas plus impatient
que la reine votre mère...

—Ah! voilà donc pourquoi elle vous aime tant, s'écria le roi.

—La maison de Médicis protége secrètement nos recherches depuis près d'un
siècle.

Cosimo then predicts a long and happy life for the little Comte d'Auvergne, and the Ruggieri are released. They go down the Rue d'Autruche
toward the Louvre without saying a word; but when they are alone, they
congratulate each other, in their Florentine speech, on having served their
queen so well. They have kept their secret.

The story proper is finished, but Balzac gives us a rapid sketch of subsequent historical events to show how faithfully the predictions of the
astrologers were fulfilled. The final paragraph in Pr III B ms, C whets
our curiosity with a reference to the Comte de Saint-Germain. In its
Chronique de Paris form the passage reads:

Laurent et Cosme ont eu pour élève le fameux comte de Saint-Germain, qui
fit tant de bruit sous Louis XV. Ce célèbre alchimiste n'avait pas moins de cent
trente ans, l'âge que les biographes donnent à Marion Delorme. Le comte pouvait savoir par les Ruggieri les anecdotes sur la Saint-Barthélemy et sur le règne
des Valois, dans lesquelles il se plaisait à jouer un rôle en les racontant à la
première personne du verbe. Le comte de Saint-Germain est le dernier des al-
chimistes qui ont le mieux expliqué cette science; mais il n'a rien écrit. La doctrine cabalistique exposée dans cette étude procède de ce mystérieux personnage.

The paragraph is further elaborated in Pr III C ms, D by the following
addition, quoted in its *Chronique de Paris* form:

N'est-il pas singulier que trois existences d'hommes, celle du vieillard de qui
viennent ces renseignements, celle du comte de Saint-Germain et celle de Cosme
Ruggieri suffisent pour embrasser l'histoire européenne depuis François Ier jusqu'à Napoléon? Il n'en faut que cinquante semblables pour remonter à la première période connue du monde.—"Que sont cinquante générations, pour étudier les mystères de la vie?" disait le comte de Saint-Germain.

What was the immediate source of the "doctrine cabalistique"? We have
been told that the Comte de Saint-Germain wrote nothing. Was the
"vieillard" one of the "auteurs cabalistiques" referred to on page 321?
Perhaps he was even a compiler (cf. Dreux du Radier) who cited various
authors of this type. An oral source is hardly likely here. The clues offered
by the life of the Comte de Saint-Germain have proved unfruitful; and I

have reluctantly limited myself to presenting certain historical, rather than cabalistic, sources for *Le Secret des Ruggieri*.

The insertion, as a whole, reminds us that Balzac, nineteenth-century realist, is also the author of *Le Livre mystique* and *La Recherche de l'absolu*. Impelled by curiosity concerning the "mysteries of life," he is willing to study a former century in order to add *Le Secret des Ruggieri* to his series of *Etudes philosophiques*.

XI

The proof corrections of Chapters II and III have familiarized us with important features of Balzacian method. Here, as in other variation studies, we have been conscious of Balzac's eternal struggle with the "écuries d'Augias" of his style, particularly in physical descriptions. We have also remarked his comparative ease in the actual wording of dialogue, the main preoccupation being expansion in successive proofs. We have watched him elaborate stage directions as well, tenaciously refusing to sacrifice material once written if it could be re-used or adapted elsewhere. Even a chance reading due to a compositor's error was occasionally grist to his mill. We have followed the stages in the development of his plot and characters from what might almost be called the "scenario form," the unfinished manuscript of Chapters II and III. We have learned how he mingled historical and fictional (or semifictional) personages, taking advantage of the greater freedom of invention offered the historical novelist when a character is unknown to his readers or is only vaguely familiar. In company with Charles IX we have sought to explore the realm of the occult sciences and have fallen under the spell of the mysterious Lorenzo, who grows in stature as proof follows proof. Through the sometimes incoherent and nebulous demonstration of the astrologer's philosophy we have come a little closer to understanding the importance which Balzac attached to his *Etudes philosophiques* as a division of the *Comédie humaine*.

Even so, we have studied only the last half of *Le Secret des Ruggieri* as it was arranged in the published versions. We have yet to take into account the revisions of the lengthy Chapter I, composed after the manuscript of the other two chapters was set up in proofs, but corrected and expanded before those chapters were revised. It is here that we can begin to evaluate Balzac as a serious student of history. For this was the chapter in which he developed the historical background for his novel, supplementing his general knowledge of the sixteenth century by documentary research. The nature of this documentation we shall inquire into later (see pp. 349–64, below). For the present, saving for the critical edition most of the individual variants, let us confine our attention to the larger problems of construction and reconstruction. These completely overshadow the redistributions made in Chapters II and III; in the manuscript corrections to the first set of proofs Balzac composes the longest insertion of the whole story and transposes twenty-two pages of proof at one fell swoop, only to break up the transposition later and redistribute it in an effort to see that the documentation is properly assimilated.

In view of the radical rearrangements of manuscript and proof materials it was necessary to devise a special technique for the critical edition in order that the reader might be able to trace the entire progression from the manuscript to the *Chronique de Paris* form. For our present purpose we need not concern ourselves with this apparatus in detail, but it will help keep the general process of revision clear if the reader will allow the longest insertion to be identified as the "Appendix I A" insertion.[65] Similarly, the twenty-two-page proof transposition which immediately follows this insertion in the Pr I A ms, B form will be called the "Appendix I B" transposition; and the shorter insertion which follows immediately upon these two sections in the Pr I A ms, B form will be referred to as the "Appendix I C" insertion. The comparative length of the three sections will be approximately indicated by giving the number of *Chronique de Paris* lines which each eventually occupies. Only three actual stages of the text have been preserved:

1. The MS, Pr I A form
2. The Pr I A ms, B form (here the second set of proofs has been lost, but except for compositor's errors the readings can be reconstituted from the manuscript corrections to Pr I A)
3. The Pr I [C+], *C. de P.* form (from the number and intricacy of the corrections it is clear that there must have been more than one set of proofs lost between Pr I B and *C. de P.*)

As we have already seen (pp. 299–300, above), the action of our story really commences with an after-supper court scene at the Louvre, but Balzac begins Chapter I *in medias res* with Albert and Charles de Gondi exercising "le métier des chats" on the roof of a house in the Rue Saint-Honoré and then, in explanation of their strange conduct, loops back to the court scene. Lines 1–21 of the *Chronique de Paris* correspond to the original manuscript order.

[65] See above, p. 304.

In the MS, Pr I A form there was at this point the following very brief summary of the court scene:

Pendant la soirée, le roi Charles avait effrayé sa mère par son attitude sombre et pensive. Elle devinait les pensées qui agitaient ce prince, et quand il ne resta plus que quelques courtisans admis dans l'intimité de la mère et du fils, Catherine quitta le salon, sans que le roi s'en aperçut. Elle le laissa entre les maréchaux de Tavannes et de Retz, M. de Gondi-La Tour et le comte de Solern. Ce dernier était un seigneur allemand que la reine de France, Elisabeth d'Autriche, avait amené en France, et qui y resta par attachement pour elle et pour Charles IX auquel il se dévoua malheureusement trop tard. La dissimulation de ce malheureux prince obligé de cacher ses pensées intimes à tous ses serviteurs, fit qu'il ne se confia que dans les derniers jours de sa vie à cet allemand auquel il avait inspiré la plus profonde compassion.

This passage was omitted in Pr I A ms, B to make way for the very long Appendix I A insertion, followed in turn by the Appendix I B transposition (pp. 14–35 in Balzac's original numbering of Pr I A) and the shorter Appendix I C insertion. The ideas of the omitted MS, Pr I A passage were not thrown out of the story entirely; instead, according to a practice familiar to us from our study of Chapter II, they were reserved for more elaborate treatment—either within the long insertion itself or in proof corrections of ensuing manuscript material.

What was the nature of the Appendix I A insertion? It starts out with a typical Balzacian apology, "Mais pour expliquer comment et pourquoi les deux courtisans étaient là, etc.," and then describes the court scene in great detail. We are made sensible of the strict etiquette which prevailed under Catherine. Employing all the care of a Saint-Simon, Balzac tells us where each of the eminent personages sat or stood and, with a word concerning ancestry or high office, explains the greater or lesser degree of intimacy which each enjoyed in association with royalty. For example, the Comte de Solern, "seigneur allemand," stood in the corner of the fireplace "auprès de la petite-fille de Charles-Quint qu'il avait accompagnée en France." The Comtesse de Fiesque, "une Strozzi, parente de Catherine et dame d'honneur," sat on a stool near Catherine, while "la belle madame de Sauves, une descendante de Jacques Cœur, maîtresse du roi de Navarre, du roi de Pologne et du duc d'Alençon," remained standing ("quoique son mari fût secrétaire-d'état," adds Balzac in Pr I [C+]). The description of the men grouped around Charles hints of factions at court, for besides Tavannes and Villeroy there were:

MM. de Biragues et de Chiverny, l'un l'homme de la reine-mère, l'autre le chancelier d'Anjou et de Pologne, l'homme du frère que Charles IX regardait comme son ennemi; Strozzi, le cousin de la reine-mère, puis quelques seigneurs parmi lesquels tranchaient le vieux cardinal de Lorraine, et le jeune duc de Guise tous deux également tenus à distance par Catherine et par le roi.

Two sentences added to this passage in Pr I [C+], *C. de P.* are typical of Balzac's re-working of all parts of the Appendix I A insertion. The continuation reads:

Ces deux chefs de la Sainte-Union, plus tard la Ligue, qu'ils avaient fondée depuis quelques années d'accord avec l'Espagne, affichaient la soumission de ces serviteurs qui se savent les maîtres; contenance que Catherine et Charles observaient avec une égale attention. Dans cette cour aussi sombre que la salle où elle se tenait, chacun avait ses raisons pour être ou triste ou songeur.

Notwithstanding the large number of secondary characters thus introduced in Pr I A ms, B to give a more complete picture of the intimate assemblage, Balzac remembers that the reader's main interest must be centered upon Charles IX and Catherine, upon Elizabeth of Austria and Marie Touchet (the latter, of course, was not present except in the thoughts of the others). But he has dealt with these important personages also in the manuscript version of the Appendix I B transposition. His principal task in the Pr I [C+], *C. de P.* stage of revision will be to organize properly these two large sections so that they become fully amalgamated.

It is most essential to acquaint ourselves with the makeup of the Appendix I B material in order to understand how it could be broken up and redistributed for the *Chronique de Paris* form. It will be necessary to distinguish between transpositions of large blocks of material and transpositions of individual sentences or parts of sentences. The latter are so numerous and are so thoroughly re-worked in the moving process that only in the critical edition proper, with its carefully planned system of cross-references, could their history be adequately treated. But if we gain sufficient perspective, we can see that the long transposition is logically divided into seven blocks, whose history, in the large, we can trace here. Although transposed, as a whole, from their manuscript location, the seven blocks still keep in Pr I A ms, B the same order with respect to each other. The unifying principle is that they analyze Catherine's character, of which the "thème prédominant" is her passion for power; this analysis involves a discussion of the means by which she maintained her supremacy, which, in turn, necessitates an explanation of her relationships with people like Charles IX, Marie Touchet, and Cosimo Ruggieri. The following table showing the subject matter of the different blocks will be found convenient for reference:

Block I   Catherine's passion for power
Block II   Her belief in policy "diviser pour régner"
Block III   Degeneration of Charles IX as result of latter policy
Block IV   Catherine's attitude toward Marie Touchet
Block V   Her participation in La Mole–Coconnas conspiracy through Cosi-
             mo Ruggieri, her astrologer
Block VI   Her belief in astrology
Block VII   "Combat sourd" between Catherine and Charles, caused by lat-
             ter's suspicions of mother

Some of these blocks are longer than others; their relative lengths will be indicated below.

Having made this preliminary survey of the Appendix I B transposition, let us return to the Appendix I A insertion and discover what Balzac did with it in the lost proofs, Pr I [C+], so that it might be set up in the *Chronique de Paris* form. For some time (ll. 22–89 of the *Chronique de Paris*) the journal version follows the same order as the first part of the long insertion. This ends with a brief portrait of the young queen, Elizabeth of Austria, seated with Catherine at the left of the fireplace, trying vainly to hide her sorrow at having been abandoned by Charles IX upon Marie's return from the Château de Fayet. What could be more natural than for the *Chronique de Paris* to transfer here (ll. 89–153) Block IV of Appendix I B, in which is explained Catherine's attitude toward Marie and her infant son? Only a few lines of introduction need be inserted in the *Chronique de Paris* to shift the spotlight: "Ce n'était pas la seule déception que la reine éprouvait en cette affaire. Jusqu'alors Catherine de Médicis lui avait paru son amie; et c'était sa belle-mère qui, par politique, avait favorisé cette trahison, en aimant mieux servir la maîtresse que la femme du roi. Voici pourquoi." From sympathizing with Elizabeth's disappointment we turn to appraising Catherine's self-interested policy. Marie's *dossier* follows as a matter of course. She really loves Charles IX, we are told in Block IV; she comes from a modest family, and she has no desire to follow in the footsteps of royal mistresses like the Duchesse d'Étampes and Diane de Poitiers. In short, she will never be a rival for political power, and Catherine can safely encourage Charles IX in his infatuation for her. This brings us back to the subject of Catherine's relations with Charles, whose mood of forced gaiety during supper has attracted the queen-mother's attention and aroused her fears that he might be planning some act of violence against her. Thus, for a short space (ll. 154–65) the *Chronique de Paris* returns to Appendix I A material, down through the following sentence, maintained in the *Chronique de*

Paris without change from its Pr I A ms, B form: "Par la force de ses combinaisons, Catherine était au-dessus de toutes les circonstances; mais elle ne pouvait rien contre une violence."

The sentence suggests to Balzac that this is the proper location for five of the seven blocks listed above. He rearranges them in the *Chronique de Paris* so that Block I occupies lines 166–79; Block VI, lines 180–286; Block II, lines 287–333; Block V, lines 333–59; and Block VII, lines 359–414. A point especially to be noted in this rearrangement is the fact that Block VI, dealing with Catherine's belief in astrology, no longer follows the account of her participation in the La Mole–Coconnas conspiracy through Cosimo Ruggieri; instead, it succeeds Block I, treating of Catherine's passion for power. To make the shift in order and to fuse together two blocks originally several hundred lines apart, the end of Block I is ingeniously re-worded and expanded in the *Chronique de Paris* so that the new order seems as natural as the old. So illuminating is this particular example that both versions are reproduced here:

Pr I A ms, B

Exclusivement ambitieuse, Catherine de Médicis n'eut d'autre passion que celle du pouvoir. Sans ce thème *prédominant de sa vie*, elle restera toujours incomprise.

Pr I [C+], *C. de P.*

Deux mots expliquent cette femme si curieuse à étudier, et dont l'influence laissa de si fortes impressions en France. Ces deux mots sont Domination et Astrologie. Exclusivement ambitieuse, Catherine de Médicis n'eut d'autre passion que celle du pouvoir. *Superstitieuse et fataliste comme le furent tant d'hommes supérieurs, elle n'eut de croyances sincères que dans les sciences occultes.* Sans ce *double* thème, elle restera toujours incomprise. *En donnant le pas à sa foi dans l'astrologie judiciaire, la lueur va tomber sur les deux personnages philosophiques de cette Etude.*

Other transitions, simpler to write or re-write, likewise succeed in fitting the various blocks into their *Chronique de Paris* order.

Faulty organization of the manuscript and Pr I A ms, B forms is the principal reason why such rearrangement and re-working of the blocks was desirable. The subject of Block VII is the struggle between Catherine and Charles now that the latter has taken a new resolution to act for himself. Upon examining the details of the preceding blocks (Pr I A ms, B form) we find the logical progression of ideas marred by scattered sentences which anticipate Block VII instead of sticking to the immediate subject. In the process of reorganization which takes place for the *Chro-*

nique de Paris, Balzac takes out these unity-destroying sentences and moves them in modified form to Block VII. Occasionally a sentence occurring in an earlier block almost duplicates a sentence already part of Block VII, so that one of them must give way to the other. It is amazing (or would be if we did not know Chapter II) that in the welter of transpositions Balzac should have had to sacrifice so little of what he had already written and that the final result should hang together as well as it does.

After having absorbed five blocks, the *Chronique de Paris* version (ll. 414–67) again returns to Appendix I A material. The transition causes little trouble. A two-line insertion (and one of these lines an adaptation, transposed) is sufficient: "En de pareilles circonstances, et dans un moment où le fils et la mère faisaient assaut de fourberie, le roi surtout devait occuper les regards." The technique is already familiar. The spotlight is now on Charles; in its merciless glare we perceive the many evidences of his physical and moral degeneration.[66] But was not that also the subject of Block III of the Appendix I B transposition? As if by foreordination, this one remaining block is moved to occupy lines 468–83 of the *Chronique de Paris.* The block is short, but it has had a most interesting history, beginning with its source in an eighteenth-century historical compilation (see pp. 359–60, below). The stylistic changes between the manuscript and Pr I A ms, B were rather numerous; they are even more so between the second form and the *Chronique de Paris.* In the journal form an inserted introduction shows that the author himself is appalled by what the spotlight reveals. Let us examine more closely than usually the last two versions:

Pr I A ms, B

Ce roi si vigoureux *devint* débile, cet esprit si fortement trempé se *trouva* plein de doutes *et* sans appui, *sans* **confiance en** *lui;* ce caractère ferme *était sans force,* la valeur guerrière *devint* férocité, la discrétion *devenait* dissimulation, l'amour fin et délicat des Valois *devenait* une inextinguible rage de *plaisirs.* Ce grand *roi* méconnu, perverti, *s'usait par* les mille faces de sa belle ame; roi sans pouvoir, ayant un noble cœur et n'ayant pas un ami; tiraillé par mille desseins contraires, il avait *fini par apercevoir la haine* que *lui portait* sa mère, *et la lui rendit avec usure;* mais la lumière *venait quand la* lanterne *était* brisée.

---

[66] See below, pp. 357–61, for a comparison of part of this text with Balzac's principal historical source.

Pr I [C+], *C. de P.*

La reine-mère en voyant son ouvrage devait avoir des remords, si toutefois la politique ne les étouffe pas tous au moment où les gens couverts de pourpre atteignent à leur but. Si Catherine avait su l'effet de ses intrigues sur son fils, peut-être aurait-elle reculé! Quel affreux spectacle! Ce roi si vigoureux *était devenu* débile, cet esprit si fortement trempé se *trouvait* plein de doutes, *cet homme, en qui résidait l'autorité, se sentait* sans appui; ce caractère ferme *avait peu de* **confiance** en *lui-même;* la valeur guerrière *s'était changée par degrés en* férocité, la discrétion en dissimulation, l'amour fin et délicat des Valois *en* une inextinguible rage de *plaisir.* Ce grand *homme* méconnu, perverti, *usé sur* les mille faces de sa belle ame, roi sans pouvoir, ayant un noble cœur et n'ayant pas un ami, tiraillé par mille desseins contraires, *offrait la triste image d'un homme de vingt-quatre ans désabusé de tout, se défiant de tout, décidé à tout jouer, même sa vie. Depuis peu de temps,* il avait *compris sa mission, son pouvoir, ses ressources, et les obstacles* que sa mère *apportait à la pacification du royaume;* mais la lumière *arrivait dans une* lanterne brisée.

Prominent among the stylistic variations are the verb changes. Where Pr I A ms, B had replaced the imperfects of the manuscript by past definites, the Pr I [C+], *C. de P.* form makes frequent use of the pluperfect; Catherine's influence had already had its effect. Where Pr I B purposely employed *devenir* several times, the *Chronique de Paris* seeks variety in verbs. A noun change is significant; twice *homme* is used in the *Chronique de Paris*, putting the emphasis on Charles as a man rather than as a king. And, indeed, the elaborations in the later version do give us more respect for the man Charles had been. The reasons given, toward the end of the passage, for Charles's change of heart toward his mother rise above the merely personal feeling expressed in Pr I A ms, B; he hates Catherine now because she is an obstacle to peace within the kingdom. We begin to think that Charles, had the lantern not already been broken, might actually have been a ruler, not a puppet king. The whole tragedy of his reign is there.

We are nearing the end of the Appendix I A insertion. With the interpolation of Block III accomplished, we realize that none of the Appendix I B transposition remains to be absorbed. Our long insertion, in developing a scene only briefly sketched in the manuscript passage which it displaced, has diverted the course of Chapter I into another channel. The current is full and strong, so that Balzac in Pr I [C+] has been able to drop into it seven blocks of transposed material without appreciably retarding the flow.

Only the final section of the long insertion must now be adapted to occupy lines 484–511 of the *Chronique de Paris*. It begins with a mention of the king's physicians, Paré and Chapelain, who were anxiously observing their master. As usual with Balzac, a bit of conversation with Chiverny and Tavannes lightens the end of the very long exposition whose complex history we have been studying.

Because the long transposition has been completely disposed of, Balzac must now pass directly from the material of Appendix I A to that of Appendix I C. The fusion of the two insertions is accomplished with less difficulty than one might expect:

LAST SENTENCE OF APPENDIX I A	Pr I [C+], *C. de P.*
Charles IX *revint à son fauteuil accompagné* de son ancien favori, avec lequel il parut s'entretenir *du siège de la Rochelle.*	Charles IX *se promena, le bras appuyé sur l'épaule* de son ancien favori, avec lequel il parut s'entrenir *de ses souffrances pour tromper les curieux;*
FIRST SENTENCE OF APPENDIX I C	*puis craignant* de rendre sa froideur
Le roi craignit de rendre sa froideur trop visible, il *se leva,* vint causer avec les deux reines en appelant auprès d'elles *son médecin.*	trop visible, il vint causer avec les deux reines en appelant *Birague* auprès d'elles.

Thus, within a single transitional sentence—requiring not elaboration but merely modification of details already present—the *Chronique de Paris* joins two sentences, and two sections of material, which in Pr I A ms, B were widely separated in space though not in time of composition. Appendix I C is short, and the *Chronique de Paris* (in ll. 512–35) quickly brings the court scene to an end. We have learned in the course of the first insertion that the reconnoitering of the Saint-Honoré quarter is planned; and, at the very end of the second insertion, Catherine, about to leave the room, whispers to Charles words which are prophetic of the closing scene of Chapter I: "Monsieur, j'ai des choses importantes à vous confier."

For the rest of the chapter the three versions follow the same order, due allowance being made for leaving out pages 14–35 of Pr I A, whose history as a transposition we know. We shall therefore dispense with further analysis of subject matter, except for a significant Pr I [C+], *C. de P.* insertion which occurs toward the end of the final interview between Catherine and Charles. It extends from "Vous vous reprochez" in line 956 of the *Chronique de Paris* through "domine les empires?" in line 1005; for the text, very little changed in intervening publications, see the

Conard edition, XXX, 299–300. If Balzac wrote *Sur Catherine de Médicis* to defend Catherine for seeking absolute power, no passage of his long study succeeds better than the present insertion. With true political genius she outlines a gigantic scheme for uniting France and Spain and Italy under one house, the Valois, and with one religion, Catholicism. If Austria aids the Protestants, she must be put down, notwithstanding the feeling of Elizabeth for her native land. Friends of the Protestant cause, says Catherine, take pleasure in promoting discord between Charles and his mother. But is it her fault that his only son is illegitimate? If Elizabeth had borne him three sons, instead of a daughter, would there have been a La Mole–Coconnas conspiracy? Catherine's face becomes beautiful in its animation; she fixes upon Charles "le coup d'œil fascinateur de l'oiseau de proie sur sa victime." The king, we are told, "ne vit plus la mère d'un seul homme, mais bien ... la mère des armées et des empires (*mater castrorum*)." But Charles has observed the special precautions taken by his mother to arrange their meeting; "sa défiance ne pouvait tomber devant des phrases." Catherine is astonished to find how deepseated are the suspicions in the heart of her son.

Once the insertion is finished, we recall that Charles is not the instrument by means of which Catherine's dreams will be realized. They both agree that the moment has come to act, but for the young king it is too late. No longer the purposeful leader, persuasive and statesmanlike, he becomes once more the melancholy weakling of the earlier court scene; and though he prays heaven for guidance in questioning the Ruggieri, his real desire is for death to release him from the contradictions of life.

The insertion, as a whole, is a magnificent illustration of Balzac's ability to tell a story. Just when we are deciding that the chapter contains too much documentation, and recalling Henry James's phrase about "huge feet fairly ploughing the sand of our desert," we are lifted up in spite of ourselves to a lookout from which the pattern of the story may be clearly perceived. We have sympathized with Charles and Marie and Elizabeth; we have followed the intrigues which menace their happiness; but perhaps, after all, Catherine is the really tragic figure. At any rate, the scene is one that will remain long in the memory.

It may seem surprising, in view of the importance of the insertion with respect to Balzac's general scheme, that the whole scene between Catherine and Charles was, in a sense, an afterthought in *Le Secret des Ruggieri*. But such is the case. The evidence appears in a manuscript *rature* (at a point corresponding to line 897 of the *Chronique de Paris*), where, in the body of the page, we find the chapter heading "Marie Touchet" and the notations "fx titre" and "II" to prove that Balzac intended to begin at once our present Chapter II. However, he does not hesitate for long; blotting out the headings, he writes the words "Aux premières lueurs de l'aube" and launches forth into the last part of the chapter. After some preliminaries that have nothing to do with Marie Touchet, comes the scene in Charles's atelier.

The close of the chapter, therefore, amounts to an insertion in the manuscript. To the reader familiar with *Sur Catherine de Médicis* as a whole, it is almost inconceivable that the final scene should so narrowly have escaped exclusion from *Le Secret des Ruggieri*. It seems, and is, central in the author's general intention. Its presence in the *Chronique de Paris* version indicates that Balzac already had his fundamental thesis in mind in 1836; the inserted passage harmonizes with the "Introduction" composed some six years later. Nor does it merely harmonize; the thought which is expounded so lumberingly and pedantically in the "Introduction" is here made incandescent in a flame brighter and hotter than that of Charles's forge.

XII

As compared with the extensive re-workings in proof sheets, the variants in printed editions are infrequent and relatively unimportant. The example quoted on page 311 is exceptional. Many of the variations in the volume publications (recorded in right-hand-page notes in our critical edition) concern typographical inconsistencies in paragraphing, sentence division, spelling, capitalization, punctuation, and the like. Occasionally one of these may be interesting—for instance, the progression from "lacqs" to "lacs" to "lac" in line 1042 of the *Chronique de Paris*—but usually they are recorded because without them a critical edition would be incomplete. Most of the true variants are stylistic and involve single words or short expressions. If we possessed only the printed editions, we might learn something of Balzac's method from analyzing these stylistic variants; but the proof corrections are much more revealing and consequently have been written up more fully. The stylistic variants interest us most when they continue a process of correction already begun in the proofs; accordingly, cross-references to the earlier stages are included in the notes. The most frequent variations are found in the Souverain edition; very few are initiated in the Werdet, which was published very shortly after the *Chronique de Paris*.

A few of the variations in published editions do, however, deserve special attention here. These are changes in *Le Secret des Ruggieri* that could not have occurred in the proofs, since they grow out of the writing of *Les Lecamus* (1841) and its expansion, under the title of *Le Martyr calviniste*, to form Part I of *Catherine de Médicis expliquée* (Souverain, 1842). Take, for example, one which occurs in the passage whose earlier history as a proof insertion we have indicated on pages 313 and 316. In the *Chronique de Paris* and the Werdet form we read:

—A l'exception de Charlemagne, dit-il d'une voix sourde et creuse, tous les rois de France du nom de Charles ont fini misérablement.
—Bah! dit-elle, et Charles VIII?
—A la fleur de l'âge, reprit le roi, ce pauvre prince s'est cogné la tête à une porte basse, au château d'Amboise qu'il embellissait, et il mourut en d'horribles souffrances; *on lui a percé le crâne avec un effroyable instrument que Paré s'occupe à perfectionner, et que je croyais sentir dans ma tête, à mesure qu'il me décrivait l'opération. Cette horrible torture* a donné la couronne à notre maison. [Italics indicate variants discussed below.]

Replacing "Cette horrible torture" by "Sa mort," Souverain, Furne, and Conard omit all the preceding reference to the operation of trepanning because it has been expanded most dramatically, in a different setting, in *Les Lecamus* and *Le Martyr calviniste*. The occasion is the deathbed scene of François II, and only incidentally is reference made to a similar operation on Charles VIII. For nearly forty pages in the Souverain edition of *Le Martyr calviniste* Ambroise Paré and his instrument are a matter of almost breathless interest to the reader. Skilfully developing the idea of the three simple lines dropped from *Le Secret des Ruggieri*, Balzac even manages, at one point or another, to adapt their wording.

Another special type of variation occurs in the passage whose history as an Appendix II B proof insertion we have discussed on pages 315–16 and 317–20. Here the Souverain, Furne, and Conard editions several times replace the words "protestantisme" and "protestant" by "Calvinisme" and "Calviniste," respectively. The latter appellations were prevalent at the time of our story, as we see in the note which Balzac wrote for the end of Volume I of *Catherine de Médicis expliquée*. There he apologizes for having used the terms incorrectly in *Le Martyr calviniste* in connection with events which preceded the "Tumulte d'Amboise":

Comme on le verra dans le volume suivant, ce ne fut que postérieurement au tumulte d'Amboise que la Réformation s'appela le Calvinisme, et l'auteur, faisant ce récit dans l'époque actuelle, s'est servi des mots Calvinisme et Calviniste plusieurs fois dans ce volume. En s'apercevant de sa faute, il a cru pouvoir arriver à tems pour la réparer; mais son ouvrage s'imprimait en province, et il a trouvé les feuilles tirées.

A l'époque où se passe le drame du MARTYR CALVINISTE, le parti de Calvin n'avait pas de nom fixe, on le nommait *la nouvelle doctrine*, la *Religion*, la *Réformation*, le *Prêche*, et ses adhérens étaient des Huguenots, nom dont l'origine a donné lieu à des controverses et qui, dit-on, vient de la porte Hugon à Tours, où s'assemblèrent les premiers Réformés, car ce nom est d'abord écrit Hugonneaux et prononcé Huguenaux, puis Huguenots. On les appelait encore Religionnaires, Réformés ou Ceux de la Religion. Enfin, en 1562, les mots Calvinisme et Calviniste prévalurent [*Sou.*, I, 340–41; italics Balzac's].

When writing this note, Balzac may well have been acquainted with a chapter from Estienne Pasquier's *Les Recherches de la France* entitled "Du Mot Huguenot" (livre VIII, chap. lv, cols. 857 ff.), where the essential facts are given.

A Chapter I omission in Souverain and subsequent editions is of special interest because it summarizes the plot of *Les Lecamus* or *Le Martyr calviniste* in such a way as to throw some light upon Balzac's original conception of that story. The passage later omitted reads as follows in *Chronique de Paris* and Werdet:

Mais les Guise se défièrent tellement de leur alliée [Catherine], qu'ils la firent espionner par la jeune reine Marie Stuart, leur nièce, femme de François II. Comment le roman et le drame ne se sont-ils pas encore emparés de l'aventure de ce marchand pelletier, nommé Lecamus, qui, sous prétexte de faire voir des fourrures à la reine-mère, lui apportait à examiner un traité avec les calvinistes. Surprise par sa belle-fille, qui s'était défiée du pelletier, Catherine livra les papiers aux Guise, qui mirent le marchand à la question. L'émissaire sacrifié garda le silence le plus profond à la reine-mère. Quels hommes étaient les bourgeois de ce temps!

We may note that in the earlier proofs Catherine was to sign, not merely examine, the treaty; also, at no stage of the *Secret des Ruggieri* passage was it evident that Christophe, "le fils du pelletier," was involved rather than his father. Thus it would appear that in 1836 Balzac did not yet have the outlines of his story clearly in mind. We have remarked (p. 286, n. 21) upon Lovenjoul's evidence that a considerable part of *Les Lecamus*—first planned for publication by Werdet as *Un Martyr*—was written by the summer of 1837, and upon his conjecture that Balzac may have worked on the story as early as 1835 or 1836. The passage we have been considering would seem to indicate that Balzac did not prepare the Werdet manuscript of *Un Martyr* until after he had published the *Chro-*

nique de Paris form of *Le Secret.* Why did he not omit the summary from the Werdet edition of *Le Secret*, or at least change it so as to make the furrier's son the hero? This may be accounted for by the fact that, though our story did not appear until August of 1837, Chapter I was printed in 1836 by Baudouin—months before the other chapters were printed by Béthune et Plon.

Bourgeois[67] cites a passage from De Thou's *Histoire universelle*, livre XXV, as a possible source for the theme of *Le Martyr calviniste.* We may consider as another possibility a passage from Garnier's continuation of Velly, *Histoire de France depuis l'établissement de la monarchie jusqu'au règne de Louis XIV.*[68] Garnier's account is based upon La Planche and La Place as well as upon De Thou. Like the passage quoted above from the earlier versions of *Le Secret des Ruggieri*, De Thou and Garnier furnish in condensed form the central situation of *Le Martyr calviniste.* Both sources are definite in their references to the furrier's *son* as the agent who carried the treaty to Catherine. In certain details—e.g., the names "le Camus" and "Chandieu" rather than "Camus" and "Chandey"—Garnier's version seems slightly closer to Balzac than does De Thou's, but neither can be considered an exclusive source. Many actual personages not mentioned by them play a part in the novel, and the author must draw upon various other historical and semihistorical works for additional material. It is interesting that Balzac should have transformed, or deformed, the name "Chandieu" into "Chaudieu." The fictional element bulks much larger in this novel than in *Le Secret des Ruggieri.* In inventing the romance of Christophe and Babette Lallier, Balzac copies, to a certain extent, Scott's technique of focusing the plot interest upon fictional characters; but, as suggested by the reviewer quoted on page 289, the love story in *Le Martyr calviniste* is so slight that it is overshadowed by the real events of Catherine's reign. The offense, if such it be, is mitigated by the novel's inclusion in the larger study of which Catherine is, by design, the central figure.

We pass over several other examples of variations due to the grouping.

[67] *Op. cit.*, pp. 65–67.

[68] 15 vols.; Paris: Desaint et Saillant, 1770–86. The passage occurs on pp. 464–65 of Vol. IV (1781), which was part of Garnier's continuation and was published by Desaint and Nyon l'aîné. Both De Thou (in French translation) and Velly appear in Balzac's lists of readings for *Sur Catherine de Médicis;* see below, pp. 349–51. Working independently of these lists, Mr. Furman Bridgers, of Duke University, came across the passage from Velly referred to here and was kind enough to permit its use in this study without previous announcement of the discovery.

In one case Balzac makes an insertion for the Souverain edition of *Le Martyr calviniste* in which the facts should harmonize with *Le Secret des Ruggieri* but do not completely succeed in doing so. This is exceptional; usually, by means of insertions, omissions, or substitutions in the one story or the other, or in both, Balzac brings them closer together and places his material where it most logically belongs in the novel as a whole. Thus, he injects into the revision of printed editions the same zeal for redistributing and harmonizing his materials which was so notable a feature of the corrections in proofs.

XIII

We come, last of all, to the most engrossing problem of the present study, one that hitherto has only been broached—namely, an investigation of Balzac's documentation, the probable reading which he did in order to get the historical background for *Le Secret des Ruggieri*.

At the Musée Lovenjoul in Chantilly there is a collection of Balzac jottings which Lovenjoul has bound together under the title "Recueil de fragments manuscrits" (*cote* A 158). A section of this volume concerns possible readings for *Catherine de Médicis;* there we find, in six or more pages, a long list of titles: sets of memoirs, general histories of France, biographies, controversial pamphlets, etc. Or rather we find, in addition to miscellaneous bibliographical notes, three lists, drawn up at different times, in which a number of titles are repeated. Usually the titles are abridged, and frequently they are inexact. Sometimes the place and date of publication are given, sometimes not; and sometimes they vary from one list to another. The lists are truly formidable. For example, a line in the first one reads: "... tomes 11. 12. 13. 14. 15. 16. 17. des Vies des hommes illustres de France—1747 in 12." For a while this work eluded identification, but finally a clue was furnished by information in Quérard, *La France littéraire*, with regard to an item on the second list, "Vie de Gaspard M. Coligny par l'abbé Pérau 1747 in-12." The latter work proved to be Volume XIV of a twenty-six-volume series, dated 1739-68, entitled *Les Vies des hommes illustres de la France, depuis le commencement de la monarchie jusqu'à présent, par M. d'Auvigny.* Volume XIV itself is anonymous, but it bears the desired date, 1747; and Quérard tells us that Pérau wrote it. Balzac thus gave to his whole series the date 1747, which properly belongs only to Volumes XIV and XV. Had it not been that Pérau's biography of Coligny was one of the volumes in the series, the latter might have failed of identification. This is but one illustration of the difficulties encountered in checking Balzac's informal bibliography

—eliminating inaccuracies and filling in where the information was incomplete.

Although time was lacking in which to examine in detail all the volumes on Balzac's lists, even when they could be definitely identified, thousands of pages have been read, and many more have been skimmed, in a search for sources. To give full bibliographical data concerning the works consulted would occupy too much space with problems of identification comparable to the one just discussed. However, we may note that on Balzac's lists appeared the histories of France by Velly, Mézeray, and De Thou; the memoirs of Condé, Castelnau (including the "additions" of Le Laboureur), La Noue, the Duc de Nevers, Brantôme, Marguerite de Navarre, and others; and works dealing with the French civil wars, such as Davila's *Historia delle guerre civili di Francia* (in French translation) and various anonymous "remonstrances" or "commentaries" on the conditions obtaining under Henry II, Francis II, or Charles IX.

With works so numerous, so broad in scope, and in many cases covering the same field, mere correspondence of certain facts with those given by Balzac was, of course, not considered sufficient to establish one of them as a definite source. The objective was unmistakable evidence that our author knew, read, and *used* a particular work—evidence that he must have got his facts directly from that work and not from some other book containing similar information.

We have already mentioned the possible influence on *Le Secret des Ruggieri* of several authors whose names appear on these lists: Estienne Pasquier, De Thou, and Velly (in Garnier's continuation). Another such work, Belleforest's *Histoire des neuf Charles*,[69] together with a chapter from Pasquier entitled "De la Fatalité qui se trouve quelquefois és noms,"[70] may well have influenced the insertion in which Balzac compared Charles's lot with that of other kings who had borne his name (see above, pp. 314 and 317). Pasquier begins his chapter with the remark that, although the subject may seem "plus digne de risée que d'observation," he does not wish to pass over it in silence "parce que l'on trouve quelques exemples en nostre France qui concernent telle matiere." After citing

---

[69] The full title is *L'Histoire des neuf roys Charles de France: contenant la fortune, vertu, & heur fatal des roys, qui sous ce nom de Charles ont mis à fin des choses merueilleuses.* (Le tout comprins en dix-neuf liures, auec la table sur chacune histoire de roy. Par François de Belle-Forest Comingeois. A Paris. A l'Oliuier de P. L'Huillier, rue S. Iacques. 1568.)

[70] *Op. cit.*, livre IV, chap. xxv; tome I, cols. 419 ff.

the names of Brutus, Augustus, and Constantine from ancient history, he arrives at the example which concerns us:

Tout de la mesme façon en est-il souvent advenu aux nostres. Car tout ainsi que sous Charles Martel sa lignée prit premier accroissement de grandeur, & que sous un Charles le Grand son petit fils, elle vint en toute extremité, aussi sous Charles le Simple commença-elle à perdre sa force, & sous un Charles que Hugues Capet frustra du Royaume qui luy appartenoit, elle perdit toute authorité.

This accords very well with the spirit of Balzac's insertion, in which Charles IX says, "A l'exception de Charlemagne tous les rois de France du nom de Charles ont fini misérablement," and gives facts to support his statement.

The very title of Belleforest's book, with its emphasis on the nine Charleses and their "heur fatal," suggests that it would be a natural source for Balzac to use for these supporting details. Except for Charles VIII, who died, says Belleforest, of a stroke of apoplexy while "aduisant ioüer les gentils-hommes de sa maison à la paume," the facts as given in *L'Histoire des neuf Charles* agree pretty closely with those in Balzac's insertion.[71] It seems very probable that both Pasquier and Belleforest influenced our author when he composed it.

Such influences, however, were rather general in nature, and at best the various works already discussed are but secondary sources; they account for a very small proportion of the historical information utilized in *Le Secret des Ruggieri*.

In contrast with these, one title included in two of Balzac's lists does meet all the tests necessary to prove that the novelist used it directly; and it accounts so largely for the documentation of *Le Secret des Ruggieri*, both in spirit and in matter, that I feel justified in considering it the principal historical source of the story.[72] That work, as has already been indicated, was written by an eighteenth-century historian or compiler by the name of Dreux du Radier. Its full title is *Mémoires historiques, critiques, et anecdotes des reines et régentes de France*. It was first published, anonymously, in four duodecimo volumes in Amsterdam in 1764. Expanded to six octavo volumes, it was published in Amsterdam in 1776. The larger edition was reprinted in Paris in 1808 by the Frères Mame; this time the

---

[71] A more complete comparison is made in the critical edition proper, p. 236.

[72] It also accounts for a significant proportion of the documentation in the "Introduction" but for very little of *Le Martyr calviniste*. For reasons inherent in the fantastic nature of the story, *Les Deux Rêves* is considered to be outside the field of serious historical documentation.

author's name appeared on the title-page. In all probability the Paris edition of 1808 was the one used by Balzac,[73] and we cite from it.

The volumes are not divided into numbered chapters but consist of many sections or "articles"—in the French sense—each with its own heading. The sections which Balzac used most frequently were: (1) "Catherine de Médicis, femme de Henri II," (2) "Marie Touchet, maîtresse de Charles IX," and (3) "Marguerite de Valois, femme de Henri IV." Of these, the most important article, as might be anticipated, is the one on Catherine herself; pages and pages of *Le Secret des Ruggieri*, as well as of the long "Introduction," owe their inspiration directly to this. While Balzac unquestionably absorbed the entire article, as well as the two others mentioned, he did not stop there. When occasion demanded, he took facts from articles on Diane de Poitiers, on Anne de Pisseleu, on Elisabeth d'Autriche, on one of Henri III's mistresses called "N... Flamin" (a French version of the Scotch name Fleming), and even on Marie de Médicis. We suspect Dreux du Radier of having been a *livre de chevet*, so familiar was Balzac with widely separated portions of the work.

Let us examine our author's borrowings. The first example, below, concerns an event of Catherine's girlhood. It is quoted from Balzac's "Introduction" for three reasons: (1) because it follows Dreux du Radier very closely, establishing him as an unmistakable source; (2) because it shows that for his adaptation Balzac did not need more information than Dreux du Radier provided; and (3) because a proof correction in Chapter I of *Le Secret* refers again to the anecdote. The material from both authors is arranged in parallel columns in order that the resemblances in wording, as shown by italics, may be more evident:

DREUX DU RADIER	BALZAC
Le Milanais avoit été rendu à François Sforce, et la maison papale *rétablie dans Florence* après un violent orage élevé contre cette maison. La révolte contre *les Médicis* avoit été poussée si loin, que les Florentins ne s'étoient pas *contentés d'enfermer Catherine* de Médicis, qui n'avoit que *neuf ans, dans un monastère, après l'avoir dépouillée de tous les biens de sa*	Ce fut *pendant le siège de Florence,* entrepris par *les Médicis,* pour *y rentrer,* que le parti républicain, non *content d'avoir enfermé Catherine,* âgée de *neuf ans,* dans un *couvent, après l'avoir dépouillée de tous ses biens,* voulut *l'exposer entre deux créneaux au feu de l'artillerie,* sur la *proposition* d'*un nommé Baptiste*

[73] Since he almost certainly used the expanded version, which was printed only once in France; and we know that Mame-Delaunay were among the early publishers of his novels.

maison; pendant le siège de Florence, un des séditieux, nommé Baptiste Cei, alla jusqu'à proposer de mettre la jeune princesse sur les murs de la ville entre deux créneaux, pour *l'y exposer au feu de l'artillerie. Bernard Castiglone* avoit opiné d'une manière encore plus cruelle contre Catherine; et, *dans le conseil, son avis avoit été, "que, bien loin de la remettre au pape, qui la redemandoit, il falloit la* rendre la victime de la débauche et de la brutalité *du soldat."* Il n'y eut que l'horreur qu'inspirent naturellement de pareilles *propositions,* même aux plus emportés, qui sauva la princesse [*op. cit.,* IV, 212–13].

Cei. Bernard Castiglone alla plus loin *dans un conseil* tenu pour aviser à terminer les affaires, *il fut d'avis que, loin de remettre Catherine au pape qui la redemandait, il fallait la* livrer *aux soldats* pour la déshonorer. On voit que toutes les révolutions populaires se ressemblent. La politique de Catherine qui favorisait tant le pouvoir royal, pouvait avoir été conseillée par de telles scènes, qu'une Italienne de neuf ans ne pouvait pas ignorer [*Sur Catherine de Médicis,* éd. Conard, XXX, 19–20; wording identical with Souverain, 1842].

How familiar all this seems to one who has been working with Balzac's variations! Almost with a start of surprise we remind ourselves that the name at the top of the first column is Dreux du Radier; it might so easily be Balzac, with the second column representing merely the author's later version of his own material. For here is the same technique of revision which we know so well: changes in word order; transposition of ideas; substitution of nouns, verbs, etc. But, nevertheless, whole phrases remain absolutely unchanged. The only important respect in which the "revised" version does not follow Balzac's usual practice is its condensation of the "original" form. This is compensated for by an ensuing characteristic elaboration: whereas Dreux du Radier was merely relating an anecdote, drawing no conclusions from it, Balzac sees in this childhood experience an influence that helped shape Catherine's later political credo, molding her into so fanatical an exponent of royal absolutism.

The example cited illustrates very well the dangers attending a search for sources. Before discovering Dreux du Radier, the present investigator copied from the *Discours merveilleux*[74] a passage concerning Catherine which might easily have been considered one of Balzac's sources:

Les vns proposerent de la mettre dedans vn panier, & le pendre dessus le rempart entre deux creneaux: à fin que quelque cannonade l'emportast: mesmes

---

[74] Full title of edition cited: *Discours merveilleux de la vie, actions et déportements de la reine Catherine de Médicis* (attributed to Henri Estienne; Cologne: P. du Marteau, 1663). The work was first published as early as 1575. The excerpt quoted occurs on pp. 11–12.

y eut quelque prescheur, qui exhorta les Seigneurs publiquement, à ce qu'il s'en deffissent de telle sorte. Autres de la mettre en vn bordeau, quand elle seroit en aage, aucuns de l'oster aux religieuses qui l'auoyent en garde, & la mettre au conuent des Emmurees, dont elles ne sortent iamais: tous d'un accord, de ne la rendre iamais à son oncle.

Certain phrases in this passage show some kinship with Balzac's wording, but the resemblances are slight, as compared with the almost word-for-word correspondence between Balzac's text and that of Dreux du Radier; and the phrases concerned appear in all three authors. The facts in the *Discours merveilleux* are insufficient to account for either of the other two versions, whereas in the latter the facts are duplicated. Dreux du Radier cites the *Discours merveilleux* as authority for other portions of his article on Catherine but not for this one. The probability is that, although he was acquainted with the passage, he depended upon other, more definite sources for the details of his anecdote. For us the significant point is that Balzac did not need to go back of Dreux du Radier for the factual details but found all the material ready to his hand in the *Mémoires et anecdotes des reines et régentes de France*.

As stated above, the anecdote so fully narrated in the 1842 "Introduction" was briefly referred to in a proof correction of *Le Secret*, Chapter I, written six years before—one of the many evidences that Balzac knew and used Dreux du Radier while writing the earlier work. The circumstances leading up to this revision are enlightening as regards both the frequency of borrowings and our author's method of adapting them to his own purposes. Together with other closely related manuscript passages and proof corrections, this particular example has some bearing on the question of whether Lorenzo Ruggieri was or was not a fictional character. Both Dreux du Radier and Balzac treat in some detail predictions by various astrologers like Bazile, Nostradamus, etc.; the importance of these in *Le Secret* is that they make our story of the Ruggieri family more plausible. Except for Cosimo's connection with the La Mole–Coconnas conspiracy, Balzac has little information about the Ruggieri—and probably none about Lorenzo—but, as a story-teller, he must keep them as much as possible in the center of the picture. How does he do so? He builds up the Ruggieri by attributing to them accomplishments which history, as represented by Dreux du Radier, etc., credits to other astrologers. In the manuscript, for example, he says that Ruggieri-le-vieux alone "fit le thème de nativité de Catherine, en sa qualité de mathématicien, d'astrologue et de médecin de la maison de Médicis." But from a Dreux du

Radier passage (IV, 261) we learn that it was "le fameux mathématicien Bazile" who drew up a "thème natal" for Catherine. In Pr I A ms, B, Balzac compromises with Dreux du Radier by saying that Ruggieri-le-vieux "dressa, de concert avec le fameux mathématicien Bazile, le thème de nativité de Catherine." Dreux du Radier also tells of a famous consultation at Chaumont in which a magician allowed Catherine to see in a magic mirror a spinning-wheel at which François II, Charles IX, and Henri III—still children—were placed one after the other; by the number of turns each made she could tell how many years each child would reign. Henri IV, placed next at the wheel, made twenty-two turns, thus arousing, says Du Radier (and Balzac as well), the undying hatred of Catherine. Balzac, reporting the consultation, says that it confirmed the *thème* which Bazile and Ruggieri-le-vieux had drawn up. What is the significance of using the scene as a confirmation of the earlier prophecy? Simply, that by this ingenious device Balzac justifies himself for reading into the Bazile-Ruggieri *thème* a good many details which Dreux du Radier's report on Bazile had not mentioned. Among the elaborations is the following: "Les malheurs par lesquels elle [Catherine] commence sa vie" (manuscript form) is changed in Pr I A ms, B to "Les malheurs qui pendant le siège de Florence signalèrent le commencement de sa vie." The insertion of the phrase "pendant le siège de Florence" shows clearly that Balzac is referring to the anecdote with which we began our study of Dreux du Radier. In thus elaborating upon the originally meager prophecy of Bazile, Balzac also compensates for his even more meager knowledge of Ruggieri *père*. If, as the adaptation indicates, he knew so little about Ruggieri-le-vieux, it is probable, as already suggested, that he knew still less about Lorenzo and even invented him out of whole cloth.

Balzac made extensive use of Dreux du Radier, not merely in the 1842 "Introduction," but also at every stage of the first chapter of *Le Secret des Ruggieri*. The examples which we shall examine here are cited now from the manuscript, now from Pr I A ms, B, and now from Pr I [C+], *C. de P.* Occasionally the complete story of a particular borrowing requires us to take into account all three forms, with their progressive elaborations. The most numerous borrowings occur in the first long insertion of Chapter I or in the proof elaborations of the long passage first transposed *en bloc* and then broken up and redistributed. It was, in fact, the accumulation of documentary material in these portions of the story which necessitated the complete rearrangement of Chapter I. Balzac may have been acquainted with Dreux du Radier before writing his first draft of Chapters

II and III, but he probably did not study the work intensively until he began the composition of Chapter I itself. Otherwise he would hardly have applied the name "Claude" to Catherine's astrologer; the change to "Cosme" appears for the first time, as we have seen, in the manuscript of Chapter I. The influence of Dreux du Radier upon Chapters II and III shows up mainly in proof corrections or insertions which harmonize with material already used in the first chapter.

How faithfully does Balzac, in *Le Secret des Ruggieri*, follow the wording of his source? Sometimes, as in the example concerning Elizabeth of Austria (pp. 362–63, below), a fairly long passage is close enough to the original source to justify quoting both forms in parallel columns. More frequently, however, Balzac borrows specific facts or ideas and uses them wherever it best suits his needs. Consequently, a single page of Dreux du Radier may contain several bits of information which are exploited at widely separated points in *Le Secret;* or the reverse may be true, Balzac collecting facts from various pages of the *Mémoires et anecdotes* and using them in illustration of a single idea.

Again, we find in Dreux du Radier certain general ideas which Balzac develops in his own fashion; though the parallels in expression are less striking, such borrowings are among the most important in the novel. In the anecdote of Catherine's childhood we have noted that Balzac draws conclusions bearing upon the thesis which he defends in his "Introduction." The next example is chosen partly because the idea of it is central for the plausibility of *Le Secret des Ruggieri* and partly because of the social generalizations it suggests to the author. Without a wide belief in astrology in sixteenth-century France we should have no story. Du Radier says of Catherine:

> Sa faiblesse pour l'astrologie judiciaire, les devins et son caractère superstitieux, sont bien mieux prouvés que sa religion. Jamais on ne vit tant de *nécromans*, de *sorciers* et de *magiciens*, qu'il en eut sous son règne, où la France en fut inondée [*ibid.*, IV, 261; italics Du Radier's].

In a footnote of the article "Agnès Sorel, maîtresse de Charles VII" we read:

> La manie des *astrologues* a été long-temps celle de la cour de France. Cette science y étoit en honneur dès le temps de Louis le Débonnaire, qui y avoit beaucoup de foi. Celui des auteurs qui a le mieux réussi à écrire l'histoire des règnes de Pepin, de Charlemagne et de Louis son fils, prend le titre d'*astronome*. Tout sage que fut Charles V, on voit un astrologue à ses gages; ils y brillèrent sous Charles VII, et Louis XI eut un maître d'*astrologie* dans sa jeunesse. Il est même

à croire qu'il y avoit sous ces règnes un *astrologue en titre*. Catherine de Médicis en réveilla le goût, et les règnes de Henri II, et de ses trois fils, François II, Charles IX, et Henri III furent infectés d'astrologues et de magiciens [*ibid.*, III, 185; italics Du Radier's].

Balzac, after presenting several instances of Catherine's superstitious belief in "l'astrologie judiciaire," generalizes concerning the period: "A cette époque, les sciences occultes se cultivaient ouvertement avec une ardeur qui peut surprendre les esprits incrédules de notre siècle si souverainement analyseur" (manuscript and Pr I A ms, B forms). And then he goes on with a characteristic comparison of the sixteenth and nineteenth centuries, saying that perhaps in the sixteenth-century occult sciences one finds the germ of nineteenth-century positive science, with one advantage in favor of the earlier period: "... les audacieux chercheurs du seizième siècle, au lieu de faire de l'industrie, faisaient de l'art, de la pensée, de la poésie" (manuscript form). Thus, for all he has steeped himself in the atmosphere of the sixteenth century, he remains himself—a nineteenth-century realist, observing contemporary society and preserving the record for later generations who might also wish to compare the present with the past. Noteworthy in our study of proof corrections is the fact that here, in these generalizations, a sudden crop of stylistic variations should spring up. For pages Balzac has been preoccupied with adding facts, many of them borrowed, and the stylistic variations have been less numerous; but the conclusions are peculiarly his own, and he becomes more self-conscious with regard to style.

Space forbids discussing here more than a few further examples of Balzac's adaptation of his source. The following passage, taken from the first long insertion of Chapter I, is selected for four reasons: (1) the ideas contained therein are significant as regards the theme of our story; (2) it concentrates into brief space rather extensive borrowings from Dreux du Radier; (3) occasionally the wording is close enough to the source to indicate that Balzac must have had the *Mémoires et anecdotes des reines et régentes de France* open before him as he composed and corrected; and (4) the passage illustrates Balzac's fondness for extracting factual details from footnotes and running them smoothly into his text. In its Pr I A ms, B form the passage reads:

En ce moment Charles IX âgé d'environ vingt-quatre ans, paraissait en avoir quarante, il était déjà la proie de la maladie dont il mourut et qui fit croire à des personnes d'une haute autorité qu'il fut empoisonné. *Selon de Thou*, le

Tacite des Valois,[75] *les chirurgiens trouvèrent dans le corps de Charles IX des tâches suspectes (**ex causâ incognitâ reperti livores**)*. Néanmoins il peut être permis aujourd'hui de croire que Charles IX mourut d'une maladie de poitrine. Mais les excès de Charles IX, son genre de vie, le développement subit de ses facultés, ses derniers efforts pour ressaisir les rênes du pouvoir, son désir de vivre, l'abus de ses forces, ses dernières souffrances et ses derniers plaisirs, tout démontre aux esprits impartiaux qu'il mourut d'une maladie de poitrine, affection peu connue alors, mal observée et dont les symptômes purent autoriser Charles IX lui-même à se croire empoisonné. Ce prince qui par les funestes conseils des Gondi, et des courtisans placés à dessein par Catherine autour de lui, gaspilla ses forces intellectuelles autant que ses forces physiques, et dont la maladie dut être tout occasionnelle et non constitutive, fit preuve de si belles qualités, il dut être un si grand roi que sa mère le prit en haine, tant elle craignit de perdre le pouvoir qu'elle avait conquis. Les sentiments de Catherine éclatèrent surtout *aux funérailles de ce fils qui furent encore plus négligées que celles de François II, au drap mortuaire duquel on attacha un écriteau où se lisaient:* **Tanneguy du Chastel, où es-tu? Mais il était Français.** *De Saint-Lazare à Saint-Denis*, Charles IX fut conduit *par quelques archers de la garde et par Brantôme.* *Tanneguy du Chastel avait dépensé trente mille écus du temps*, somme énorme, *pour la pompe funèbre de Charles VII, le bienfaiteur de sa maison.* [Ordinary italics indicate passages where the wording follows Dreux du Radier closely; boldface italics indicate expressions italicized by Balzac as they were in the source.]

Let us now see how Dreux du Radier regarded the possibility that Catherine de Médicis may have had her son poisoned. The footnotes (indicated by asterisks) are Du Radier's:

Si le roi ne fût pas mort, Catherine eût survécu au pouvoir souverain qu'elle avoit usurpé. On renouvela contre elle l'accusation de poison, et elle n'est pas mieux fondée. Sans lui prêter un crime, dit très judicieusement un moderne, on peut croire que le chagrin et les remords furent le seul poison qui abrégea sa vie ... . Enfin, Henri Estienne n'accuse point encore Catherine de la mort de Charles IX.* Ce prince, à sa mort, l'avoit déclarée régente jusqu'au retour de son successeur. Elle donna tous ses soins à s'assurer de sa nouvelle régence; et *les funérailles de Charles IX furent aussi négligées que celles de François II.* Catherine, qui avoit fait une dépense toute royale aux obsèques du père, ne pensa presque pas à celles des enfants.** Elle fit confirmer sa régence au parle-

---

[75] We have observed on p. 290 how Bourgeois praises Balzac for drawing upon De Thou and saluting in him the "Tacitus of the Valois." But we shall shortly realize that in the very passage under consideration Balzac was actually using Dreux du Radier without acknowledgment. As for our author's tribute to De Thou, we find a somewhat similar one in the "Avertissement" of the *Mémoires et anecdotes* (I, 18), where the historian is referred to as "l'inestimable de Thou, notre Tite-Live."

ment le 3 juin [*op. cit.*, IV, 244–46; ordinary italics designate the passages which correspond closely with Balzac; boldface italics indicate expressions italicized by Du Radier].

    * Il faut pourtant convenir que M. de Thou penche pour le poison, qu'il en accuse même indirectement la reine, et qu'il dit qu'*à l'ouverture de son corps on trouva des taches **ex causâ incognitâ reperti livores.*** Thuan. lib. 57, vers la fin. Mais voy. le procès-verbal d'ouverture de son corps, du dernier mai 1574, dans Papire-Masson, Éloge, tome 2, p. 553.

    ** Il n'y eut dans toute la cour que La Brosse et Sausac, et des prélats, que Guillard, évêque de Senlis, aveugle pour lors, qui suivirent le corps de François II à *Saint-Denis. On attacha au drap mortuaire* qui couvroit le corps *un écriteau où étoient ces mots:* **Tannegui du Chastel, où es-tu? Mais il étoit Français.** En semblable occasion *Tannegui du Chastel* (vicomte de la Bellière, grand-écuyer de France, mort au siège de Bouchain le 29 mai 1477, et neveu de Tannegui, favori de Charles VII, mort avant son maître, en 1449) *avoit employé trente mille écus de ses deniers pour faire la pompe funèbre de Charles VII, bienfaiteur de sa maison.* Voyez de Thou, sous l'an 1560, liv. 18. Ce grand homme paroît confondre Tannegui du Chastel, dont il s'agit ici, avec Tannegui du Chastel son oncle, prévôt de Paris, mort douze ans avant Charles VII. Tous les princes et les seigneurs quittèrent le convoi de Charles IX à *l'église de Saint-Lazarre,* et *il n'y resta que Brantôme,* quatre gentilshommes de la chambre, *et quelques archers de la garde.* La Popélinière parle autrement.

Comparison of Balzac and Du Radier discloses a more scientific analysis of Charles's malady on the part of the former, but both agree that poison was not the agent which caused the young king's death. As a definite proof that Balzac used the text just quoted, the footnotes are significant. His attention was attracted to the Latin phrase from De Thou, with which he might "épater le bourgeois," and to the phrasing of the sign fastened on the bier of François II. The two footnotes treat different subjects; choosing and rejecting according to his needs, Balzac adapts them both within a single paragraph. He modifies the wording and shifts the order of facts slightly, but not enough to disguise their origin. So closely does he follow the text of his source that he inadvertently employs a plural verb *se lisaient* (cf. Du Radier, *ou étoient ces mots*) when a singular was required; in a subsequent set of proofs he corrects the error. We can hardly doubt that he was reading the page from Du Radier as he wrote.

In the same Balzac passage it is suggested that, while Catherine did not actually poison Charles, she used more subtle means of accomplishing his ruin; namely, the choice of counselors devoted to her interests rather than his. Such is the belief of Dreux du Radier also:

Un reproche ineffaçable qu'on fera toujours à Catherine, c'est l'éducation qu'elle donna à ses enfants, à l'infortuné Charles IX, ce génie si beau, si élevé; ce prince né pour être l'un de nos plus grands rois, s'il eût été conduit par une autre mère. Elle sut faire des vices de toutes les semences de vertu qui étoient en lui, et de toutes ses grandes qualités autant de grands défauts. Elle changea sa prudence et sa discrétion en une noire politique, sa vivacité en fureur, son courage en férocité: il n'y eut que sa tempérance pour le sexe qu'elle ne put changer entièrement. Brantôme, qui ne doit pas être suspect, après les éloges dont il comble Catherine de Médicis, dit que "ce fut le maréchal de Retz qui le pervertit du tout, et lui fit oublier et laisser toute la belle nourriture que lui avoit donnée le brave Cipière." Le maréchal de Retz, Florentin, étoit une créature de Catherine: ce fut elle qui le mit auprès du roi, qui éleva sa fortune [*op. cit.*, IV, 242–43].

The *Chronique de Paris* text of one Balzac sentence already quoted (toward the end of the Pr I A ms, B passage on p. 358, above) is re-worked in such a way that the Dreux du Radier influence is more evident. The sentence reads as follows in the *Chronique de Paris:* "MM. de Ci-pierre [later changed to "Cypierre"] le gouverneur, et Amyot le précep-teur de Charles IX avaient fait de leur élève un si grand homme, ils avaient préparé un si beau règne, que la mère prit son fils en haine, tant elle craignit de perdre le pouvoir qu'elle avait conquis." Besides being re-worked, this sentence was moved to another location for the *Chronique de Paris.* One result of the general rearrangement of Chapter I is that borrowings from Dreux du Radier, formerly consecutive, became scat-tered by the time they were published in the journal form.

In still other passages Balzac follows Dreux du Radier in placing the responsibility for Charles's degeneration squarely on Catherine. Two sen-tences[76] of the source concern us particularly: "Elle sut ... changer en-tièrement." Balzac utilizes the idea of the first sentence in elaborating the Chapter II dialogue between Marie Touchet and Charles IX. There, in a Pr II A ms, D insertion, Marie is made to say:

—Les femmes dont l'âme est grande et dont les intentions sont pures se servent des vertus pour dominer les hommes qu'elles aiment, et les femmes qui ne leur veulent pas de bien, les gouvernent en prenant des points d'appui dans leurs mauvais penchants. Or, la reine a fait des vices de plusieurs belles qualités, et vous a fait croire que vos mauvais côtés étaient des vertus. Etait-ce là le rôle d'une mère?

The novelist's adaptation of the second sentence undergoes considerable stylistic revision in later versions, but the manuscript form will be enough to show its general nature:

[76] The second and third sentences in the Du Radier passage last quoted.

Après avoir donné au roi une sombre et secrète jalousie contre son frère, elle se servit de cette passion pour miner sa forte constitution par les entraves qu'elle lui suscitait; ses efforts rencontraient des barrières impénétrables. Ce roi si vigoureux était débile, cet esprit si fortement trempé était plein de doutes, ce caractère ferme était sans trône, la valeur inactive devenait férocité, la discrétion devenait dissimulation, l'amour fin et délicat des Valois devenait une rage inextinguible.

The influence of Du Radier's second sentence upon this passage is unmistakable; specific resemblances in wording show, beyond doubt, the connection between the two. But Balzac is here no slavish imitator. Using Dreux du Radier as a starting-point, he develops some of the possibilities suggested by that writer's spirited contrasting of the old Charles with the new. Quality by quality, Du Radier has compared the Charles of good natural endowments—fostered by his preceptor Cypierre—with the Charles preyed upon by the intrigues of the ambitious queen-mother. Balzac does likewise, now taking up the same qualities as his predecessor, now adding others to the list. With one exception the spirit of the two passages is the same; the exception concerns the young king's moderation in love. Whereas Dreux du Radier says that Catherine could not change entirely Charles's "tempérance pour le sexe," Balzac believes that she was successful, so that (to use the Pr I A ms, B expression) "l'amour fin et délicat des Valois devenait une inextinguible rage de plaisirs." This is consistent with the other passages in Balzac where the author is inclined to agree with those who think Charles's death was hastened by his excessive love for Marie Touchet.

In the next example Balzac makes a specific reference to Brantôme as if he had used the sixteenth-century source directly. Notwithstanding the impression of erudition thus produced, he still is depending upon the eighteenth-century compiler—and drawing upon Brantôme *through him*. The passage in question has the further interest of being an insertion in Pr I [C+], *C. de P.* It is one of several evidences that our author not only knew Dreux du Radier before he began the manuscript of Chapter I but also had the work open before him while correcting each new set of proofs. The inserted passage concerns Elizabeth of Austria at the time when Catherine was openly encouraging Charles's affair with Marie Touchet. Italics indicate exact, or nearly exact, duplications in the two forms; boldface italics indicate expressions italicized by Balzac in passages adapted from Du Radier; and boldface roman indicates an expression italicized by Du Radier but not occurring in Balzac's adaptation.

DREUX DU RADIER (V, 26 ff.)

Pr I [C+], *C. de P.*

J'entends parler de *Brantôme:* c'est ainsi qu'il s'exprime (**Dames Galantes**, t. 2, p. 62.) "Nous avons eu notre reine de France, donna Isabel d'Autriche, laquelle nous pouvons dire par-tout *avoir été une* des meilleures, *des plus douces*, des plus sages et des plus vertueuses *reines* qui régna depuis le règne de tous les rois et reines *qui ayent jamais régné.* Je le peux dire et un chacun avec moi, qui la [*sic*] vue ou ouï parler, sans faire tort aux autres, et avec une très grande vérité." Après cet éloge, il parle de la beauté d'Élisabeth, pour rendre ce qu'il avoit à dire de sa piété d'autant plus admirable; et tel est *le portrait qu'il fait de cette princesse.* "Elle étoit une très belle princesse, *ayant le teint de son visage aussi beau et délicat que dame de sa cour, et fort agréable. Elle avoit la taille fort belle, encore qu'elle l'eût moyenne assez.*" Passant ensuite aux qualités de l'esprit et du cœur: "Elle étoit très sage, dit-il, et aussi très vertueuse, très bonne; *et qui ne fit* jamais *mal ni déplaisir à personne* quelleconque; non pas offenser la moindre du monde ..."

[Then follows more than a page concerning Elizabeth's piety and modesty, ending:]

"... pour lire et prier Dieu dans *ses heures.....* Telles formes de prières ne tenoient rien de celles des hypocrites, qui, voulant paroître entièrement devant tout le monde, font leurs prières et dévotions publiquement et en marmottant, afin qu'on les trouve plus dévotes et saintes."

(V, 19 ff.)

Après *la mort du roi*, pénétrée d'une tristesse profonde, elle n'éclata point en regrets; on ne l'entendit point se plaindre du ciel ni de son sort ... . *Quelques unes de ses dames lui disant:* "Au moins, madame, *si Dieu*, au lieu d'une fille, *vous eût laissé un fils, vous seriez reine mère;* votre sort seroit moins à plaindre." "*Ah! louons Dieu, répondit-elle, de ne m'avoir pas donné de fils.* La France est déjà assez à plaindre, sans avoir encore un enfant pour roi, et retomber dans les

Les raisons qui faisaient agir en cette affaire Catherine de Médicis échappaient donc aux yeux de *dona Isabelle qui,* selon *Brantôme, étoit une des plus douces reines qui aient jamais régné, et qui ne fit mal ni déplaisir à personne, lisant même ses Heures en secret.* Mais cette candide princesse commençait à entrevoir les précipices ouverts autour du trône, horrible science qui pouvait bien lui causer quelque vertige; elle dut en éprouver un grand pour avoir pu *répondre* à *une de ses dames* qui *lui disait, à la mort du roi,* que *si elle avait eu un fils, elle serait reine-mère* et régente: —"*Ah! louons Dieu de ne m'avoir pas donné de fils. Que fût-il arrivé? Le pauvre enfant eût été dépouillé comme on a voulu faire au roi mon mari, et j'en aurais été la cause. Dieu a eu pitié de l'état, et il a tout fait pour le mieux.*"

Cette princesse, dont Brantôme croit *avoir fait le portrait* en disant qu'elle **avait le teint de son visage aussi beau et délicat que les dames de sa cour, et fort agréable; qu'elle avait la taille fort belle, encore qu'elle l'eût moyenne assez,** *comptait pour fort peu de chose à la cour;* mais l'état du roi lui permettant de se livrer à sa

malheurs d'une nouvelle minorité. *Que fût-il arrivé?* Victime des passions des grands, *le pauvre enfant eût été dépouillé comme on a voulu faire au roi mon mari, et j'en aurois été la cause.* Dieu a eu pitié de l'État; il a tout fait pour le mieux; remercions-le de ses bontés." Élisabeth ne pouvoit donner de marques plus certaines de sa sagesse et de son attachement pour la France. Elle résolut pourtant de la quitter.

(V, 18)

Entièrement occupée des exercices de *piété,* et du soin de plaire au roi, Élisabeth *n'eut que très peu de part à tout ce qui se passa* en France sous le règne tumultueux de Charles IX.

double douleur, son attitude ajoutait à la couleur sombre du tableau, qu'une jeune reine, moins cruellement atteinte, aurait pu égayer. La *pieuse* Élisabeth prouvait en ce moment que les qualités qui sont le lustre des femmes d'une condition ordinaire, peuvent être fatales à une souveraine; car une princesse, occupée à tout autre chose qu'à *lire ses Heures pendant la nuit,* aurait été d'un utile secours à Charles IX, qui ne trouva d'appui ni chez sa femme, ni chez sa maîtresse.

Comparison with Brantôme[77] shows that Dreux du Radier quotes his text pretty faithfully, orthographical changes and certain slight condensations aside. The explanatory transitions for the first three quotations divide up what was continuous text in Brantôme. These transitions are Dreux du Radier's own; it is therefore especially significant that Balzac should have adapted one of them: "... tel est le portrait qu'il fait de cette princesse." Although referring to Brantôme by name, he has taken *all* of his material from the text quoted in the left-hand column above. Condensing the direct quotations to a much greater extent than did Dreux du Radier, he uses nothing from Brantôme that is not also in the intermediary source. The un-italicized portions of the text in the right-hand column integrate the quotations with the court scene which forms so important a part of Chapter I.

All this does not mean that Balzac was unacquainted with writers like Brantôme and Le Laboureur.[78] He doubtless knew them in a general way, and the names are on his lists to show that he had them in mind as storehouses of sixteenth-century information. But as a working tool he found

---

[77] *Œuvres complètes de Brantôme,* éd. Lalanne, IX, 594–95. The section in which Lalanne gives a fuller text than Du Radier does is the part concerning the evils which would befall the kingdom if Elizabeth had a son. For our present purpose we need not go back to the edition which Du Radier used, since Balzac condenses even more.

[78] Le Laboureur is cited by name in connection with the La Mole–Coconnas conspiracy.

Dreux du Radier, compact with citations from early writers, more convenient to use. And, like a college Freshman who has not been trained to scrupulous bibliographical honesty, he drew a herring across the trail by referring to the original, rather than the intermediate, source.

Specific references of the sort are less numerous in *Le Secret* than in the "Introduction." More frequently, in passages of our story where Balzac is borrowing from his familiar source, he takes refuge in vague, general references like "Les mémoires du temps rapportent un autre fait non moins étrange" or "L'histoire a enregistré les instances que fit Catherine pour engager Henri II à ne pas descendre en lice." Such expressions soon become recognizable as so many signboards pointing to Dreux du Radier, or possibly, on rare occasions, to some other historian of his type.

Does Balzac ever publicly acknowledge his indebtedness to the eighteenth-century compiler? Only once—in the "Introduction"—and without giving his name. On a page strewn with borrowings from the *Mémoires et anecdotes* we read:

> Diane, qui avait pour gendres les ducs d'Aumale et de Bouillon, alors prince souverain, conserva toute sa fortune et mourut en paix en 1566, âgée de soixante-six ans. Elle avait donc dix-neuf ans de plus que Henri II. Ces dates, tirées de son épitaphe copiée sur son tombeau *par l'historien qui s'est occupé d'elle vers la fin du dernier siècle*, éclaircissent bien des difficultés historiques; car beaucoup d'historiens, etc. [*Con.*, XXX, 44; italics indicate the veiled reference to Dreux du Radier].

But how grudging is the acknowledgment! For we know that Dreux du Radier furnished not only the information about Diane[79] but much besides. With "beaucoup d'historiens" Balzac hastily retreats from even so slight an admission of his pillaging; he pretends, as usual, that he himself is an "abyss of knowledge."

In judging the relative importance of the historical sources for *Le Secret*, Dreux du Radier must be accorded first rank. The very number and bulk of the borrowings, and their intimate bearing on the central theme of our story, lead inevitably to this conclusion. In parallel passages we find repeated testimony to Catherine's overweening ambition: her share in the La Mole–Coconnas conspiracy; her corruption and weakening of Charles; and her setting of one party against another, one religion

---

[79] "Elle y mourut, suivant son épitaphe dont j'ai fait tirer la copie sur son tombeau, le 22 avril 1566, âgée de soixante six ans, trois mois et vingt-sept jours. Comme cette pièce rectifie une infinité d'erreurs dans nos historiens, que Bayle même n'en a pas eu une note régulière, je crois qu'on trouvera ici cette copie exacte avec plaisir; elle m'a servi de guide pour les faits chronologiques de ce mémoire" (*op. cit.*, IV, 335–36).

against another, so that in the conflict of interests she might retain the balance of power. For biographical details Du Radier is a constant mine of information; and here, in particular, Balzac is clever in extracting details from footnotes and running them smoothly into his text. If the source tries to present all sides of a disputed point, he chooses the side which best suits his theme and avoids controversy by means of vague, general references similar to those already discussed.

XIV

All this accumulation of historical detail—fused by Balzac's penetrating generalizations and lending plausibility to the thoughts and words and actions of characters quite foreign to the modern world of the *Comédie humaine*—all this massing produces upon the reader an impression of historicity not to be denied. Modern authorities[80] may doubt that the Hôtel de Soissons was built for astrological purposes; the fact remains that many people, including some historians, believe that Catherine's interest in occult sciences was responsible for its construction. At the time of the La Mole–Coconnas conspiracy she may not have protected Cosimo Ruggieri to the extent that Balzac, relying on his principal source, suggests; but she was fascinated by his "magic" and is generally thought to have been a sponsor for him. Astrology as a science is discredited now; but Balzac would be untrue to the sixteenth century if he did not play up its widespread belief in that and other occult sciences. Historians today do not hold that Catherine was guilty of the numerous poisonings with which tradition has credited her; neither does Balzac. There is no doubt that the end of Charles's life was filled with morbid fears, that lethargy alternated with sudden bursts of activity; Balzac seems to have diagnosed his malady in quite modern fashion. Some of our more recent historians suspect that Catherine was less a virile, masterful woman than she was a vacillating opportunist; but Balzac really believes—with Dreux du Radier, who is representative of the eighteenth (and nineteenth) century attitudes on the subject—that power was her single aim and that she employed Machiavellian tactics to achieve it. Her policy of maintaining the balance of power by playing off one party against another marks her as truly one of the Medici, whose ability to compromise is recognized[81]

[80] Of the sort represented in our critical edition by Mariéjol, Thompson, Grant, and Colonel Young. Our references to these authorities in the edition will show that substantially Balzac is still considered to be in the right, historically speaking.

[81] By Ralph Roeder, among others. His *Catherine de' Medici and the Lost Revolution* (New York: Viking Press, 1937) is of particular interest in view of Catherine's defense of St. Bartholomew's Day in *Les Deux Rêves*.

as an important factor in their rise to wealth and political influence. She was a Medici, too, in her wish to extend the prestige of her family by shrewdly arranged marriages; Balzac does not overlook the fact. Our author believes that Catherine was justified in her efforts to keep the power she had so painfully acquired; this is a matter of opinion, but he defends his thesis. If he does so a bit pedantically and unconvincingly in the 1842 "Introduction," he makes amends in advance with the eloquent insertion near the end of Chapter I. And finally, if, after having in the main followed his authorities pretty closely, he consciously juggles information irt order to make some of his characters more plausible, he is only taking advantage of a license invoked by nearly all historical novelists, including Scott the master. In short, there lives and breathes in *Le Secret des Ruggieri* the spirit of the sixteenth century. This will become increasingly evident to those who will ponder over the text and annotations of our edition.

BIBLIOGRAPHY

ANONYMOUS. *"About Catherine de' Medici,* Translated by Clara Bell" (review of the Macmillan edition), *Critic,* XXVIII (November 13, 1897), 281–82.

———. "Catherine de' Medici" (review of Katharine Prescott Wormeley's translation, Roberts Brothers' edition), *ibid.,* XXIII (January 12, 1895), 25–26.

BALDENSPERGER, FERNAND. *Orientations étrangères chez Honoré de Balzac.* Paris: Champion, 1927.

BALZAC, HONORÉ DE. *La Comédie humaine,* texte revisé et annoté par Marcel Bouteron et Henri Longnon. (*Œuvres complètes de Honoré de Balzac.*) Paris: Louis Conard, 1912–28. 33 vols.

———. *Lettres à l'Etrangère.* Vol. I, *1833–1842.* Paris: Calmann-Lévy, [1899].

———. *Pensées, sujets, fragmens,* avec une préface, et des notes de Jacques Crépet. Paris: Blaizot, 1910.

BARRIÈRE, MARCEL. *L'Œuvre de H. de Balzac.* Paris: Calmann-Lévy, 1890.

BELLEFOREST, FRANÇOIS DE. *Histoire des neuf roys Charles de France: contenant la fortune, vertu & heur fatal des roys, qui sous ce nom de Charles ont mis à fin des choses merueilleuses.* Le tout comprins en dix-neuf liures, auec la table sur chacune histoire de roy. Par François de Belle-Forest ... . Paris: Imprimé par F. Le Blanc pour P. L'Huillier, 1568.

BELLESSORT, ANDRÉ. *Balzac et son œuvre.* Paris: Perrin et Cie, 1924.

BOURGEOIS, NICOLAS. *Balzac historien français et écrivain régionaliste.* Paris: Bloud et Gay, 1925.

BRANTÔME, PIERRE DE BOURDEILLE, SEIGNEUR DE. *Œuvres complètes de Pierre de Bourdeille, seigneur de Brantôme,* publiées d'après les manuscrits avec variantes et fragments inédits pour la Société de l'histoire de France, par Ludovic Lalanne ... . Paris: Mᵐᵉ Vᵛᵉ Jules Renouard, 1866. 11 vols.

COLLIN DE PLANCY, J. *Dictionnaire infernal ...* . 6th ed. Paris: Henri Plon, 1863.

DARGAN, E. PRESTON. "A Balzac Acquisition," *University Record*, new ser., XII (1927), 124–26.

———. "Balzac and His *Gina*." Unpublished article.

———. "Scott and the French Romantics," *Publications of the Modern Language Association*, XLIX (1934), 599–629.

DARGAN, E. PRESTON; CRAIN, W. L.; and OTHERS. *Studies in Balzac's Realism*. Chicago: University of Chicago Press, 1932.

DEFRANCE, EUGÈNE. *Catherine de Médicis, ses astrologues et ses magiciens-envoûteurs ...* . Paris: Mercure de France, 1911.

DU RADIER, DREUX. *Mémoires historiques, critiques, et anecdotes des reines et régentes de France*. Paris: De l'imprimerie des Frères Mame, 1808. 3 vols.

[ESTIENNE, HENRI.] *Discours merveilleux de la vie, actions et déportements de la reine Catherine de Médicis*. Cologne: P. du Marteau, 1663.

GARNAND, H. J. *The Influence of Walter Scott on the Works of Balzac*. New York: [Columbia University Press], 1926.

MASSON, PIERRE MAURICE (ed.). *La "Profession de foi du vicaire savoyard" de Jean-Jacques Rousseau;* édition critique ... . Paris: Hachette, 1914.

PASQUIER, ÉTIENNE. *Les Œuvres d'Estienne Pasquier*, contenant ses Recherches de la France; son Plaidoyé pour M. le duc de Lorraine; celuy de Mᵉ Versoris, pour les jesuites ... . Ses lettres; ses œuvres meslées; et les Lettres de Nicolas Pasquier, fils d'Estienne ... . Amsterdam: Aux depens de la Compagnie des libraires associez, 1723. 2 vols.

PRIOR, HENRY. "Balzac à Milan. 1837," *Revue de Paris*, XXXII (1925), 283–302, 602–20.

ROYCE, WILLIAM H. *A Balzac Bibliography*. Chicago: University of Chicago Press, 1929.

SAINTSBURY, GEORGE. Preface to *About Catherine de' Medici* (trans. by Clara Bell). Philadelphia: Gebbie Publishing Co., Ltd., 1899.

SPOELBERCH DE LOVENJOUL, CHARLES DE. *Histoire des œuvres de H. de Balzac*. 3d ed. Paris: Calmann-Lévy, 1888.

———. "Les *Etudes philosophiques* de Honoré de Balzac," *Revue d'histoire littéraire de la France*, 14th year (July–September, 1907), pp. 393–441.

VELLY, [PAUL FRANÇOIS]. *Histoire de France depuis l'établissement de la monarchie jusqu'au règne de Louis XIV*. Par M. l'abbé Velly ... . Paris: Desaint et Saillant, 1770–86. 15 vols.

WELLS, B. W. *A Century of French Fiction*. New York: Dodd, Mead & Co., 1898.

For editions of *Le Secret des Ruggieri*, see the section on the history of publication, pp. 282 ff., above; for information concerning Balzac's proposed readings, see pp. 349 ff.; and for symbols distinguishing the various sets of proofs, etc., see pp. 303–4.

CHAPTER V

SUMMARIES OF VARIANTS IN TWENTY-SIX STORIES

Prepared by BERNARD WEINBERG

Washington University

THE following summaries of variation studies fall into two groups. In the first (Secs. I–X) are included fairly complete résumés, arranged chronologically according to the dates of first editions and rather fully illustrated with examples. In the second (Sec. XI) are contained very brief indications, in the same arrangement, of the principal findings of additional investigations, usually without examples.

I. *UN EPISODE SOUS LA TERREUR*

By HENRY L. ROBINSON

Editions collated.—

1. 1830, as the Introduction (without title) to *Mémoires pour servir à l'histoire de la Révolution française*, by Louis François L'Héritier de l'Ain, I, v–lxvii (*Mém.*).

2. Conard, XXI (*Scènes de la vie politique*), 1–25. This edition is practically identical with the Furne edition of 1846, XII, 209–25 (*Con.*).

The brief story consists of "une messe en 1793" (title of the 1842 edition) and the circumstances, both political and private, which surround this expiatory Mass for Louis XVI. Revolutionary Paris is depicted under several aspects, and the political considerations involved justify the inclusion of the work in the *Scènes de la vie politique*.

Preliminary changes.[1]—In the first two editions the work has no specific title. In the *Journal de Paris* edition of 1839 the story is called *Un Inconnu, Épisode de la Terreur*. The second part of this title remains with the story (in slightly modified form) in all editions except that of Janet's *Royal Keepsake* (1842); here it is called *Une Messe en 1793*. The Dedication to M. Guyonnet-Merville and the date, "Paris, janvier 1831," appear first in the Furne edition. The variations between the editions collated are most frequent at the beginning and become less and less frequent

---

[1] This term will be applied throughout to alterations in the "preliminaries," i.e., in material preceding the text of the story, including the title.

as the story proceeds. Changes in the dialogue are few. The paragraphing is reduced, with the loss of certain special effects, such as that of making a single sentence stand out.

Solidity.—Balzac's constant effort to link individual works to the body of the *Comédie humaine* is again exemplified here, with a twofold effect on the nature of the revisions. First, changes in name occur as follows:

1830	CONARD
le duc de Lorge [p. xxiv]	le duc de Langeais [p. 11]
le marquis de Béthune [p. xxiv]	le marquis de Beauséant [p. 11]
la sœur Agathe, celle des deux religieuses qui appartenait à la maison de Béthune [p. xxx]	la sœur Agathe, celle des deux religieuses qui appartenait à la maison de Langeais [p. 13]
mademoiselle de Charost [p. xxxiv]	mademoiselle de Beauséant [p. 16]
mademoiselle de Charost [p. xlvi]	mademoiselle de Langeais [p. 20]
mademoiselle de Charost [p. l]	mademoiselle de Langeais [p. 23]
mademoiselle de Charost [p. li]	mademoiselle de Langeais [p. 23]
. . . .	Ragon [p. 24]
. . . .	madame Ragon [p. 24]

There is some confusion in this scheme. Lorge = Langeais once, Béthune = Beauséant and Langeais once each, Charost = Beauséant once and Langeais three times. Note the predominance, in the Conard version, of the house of Langeais, previously presented in *La Duchesse de Langeais* (1833). With the addition of the Ragons in the new ending of 1842, the total of reappearing characters is brought up to four. Moreover, the nuns, although they do not themselves reappear, are related to families of importance in the *Comédie humaine*.

Second, the ending of the story is completely re-written. In 1830, when the story served as the Introduction to the *Mémoires*, its ending was adapted to that purpose. It included historical details and an account of how the executioner Sanson's papers, now published in the *Mémoires*, came to be preserved. For this epilogue of some two thousand words Balzac substituted a shorter one of slightly over three hundred words, which introduced the Ragons and their perfumery, so frequently a meeting place for the royalists in the *Comédie humaine*.[2]

Sociological features.—Two insertions are of sociological interest. One refers to the relative value of a nun's life as against that of a priest. The priest is speaking:

[2] The original ending may be read in Lov., *Hist.*, pp. 147–51.

C'est de vous et non de moi qu'il faut s'occuper.
—Non, dirent les deux vieilles femmes. [*Mém.* xxiii]

C'est de vous et non de moi qu'il faut s'occuper.
—Non, dit l'une des deux vieilles femmes, *qu'est-ce que notre vie en comparaison de celle d'un prêtre.* [*Con.* 10]

The other refers to the confusion following the king's death and is added to a speech of the "inconnu":

... sachez ... que s'il est quelque bon office que je puisse vous rendre, vous pouvez m'employer sans crainte ... [*Mém.* xxx]

... sachez ... que, s'il est quelque bon office que je puisse vous rendre, vous pouvez m'employer sans crainte, *et que moi seul, peut-être, suis au-dessus de la loi, puisqu'il n'y a plus de roi* ... [*Con.* 13]

Thus Sanson hints at his mysterious power.

Detail.—A number of changes in detail are effected to add to the realistic exactness of the narrative. In the opening sentence an approximate date is changed to an exact date:

Vers la fin du mois de janvier 1793 ... . *Il était environ* huit heures du soir. [*Mém.* v]

Le 22 janvier 1793, *vers* huit heures du soir ... [*Con.* 3]

This specific night is referred to later as

la nuit du 27 janvier 1793. [*Mém.* xlviii]

la nuit du 22 janvier 1793. [*Con.* 22]

In 1830 the date given is wrong, whereas in the Conard text it is consistently correct.

In one instance an indefinite time indication is made definite by changing "depuis quelques jours" to "depuis hier" (*Mém.* xxii, *Con.* 10). In three other cases a definite interval which would have required a stop watch, so to speak, is changed to an indefinite interval or suppressed in the interests of verisimilitude; for example, "fut fait en deux secondes" becomes "fut bientôt fait" (*Mém.* xxix, *Con.* 13).

Several times, Balzac heightens the keynote of wretchedness, applied to the dwelling of the *proscrits*, by the insertion of an additional detail:

La bise ... sifflait à travers les maisons, ou plutôt les chaumières, semées dans ce vallon presque inhabité. *Rien ne peignait mieux la désolation, et cet endroit* semblait être l'asile naturel de la misère et du désespoir. [*Mém.* xviii–xix]

La bise ... sifflait à travers les maisons, ou plutôt les chaumières, semées dans ce vallon presque inhabité *où les clôtures sont en murailles faites avec de la terre et des os. Cet endroit désolé* semblait être l'asile naturel de la misère et du désespoir. [*Con.* 9]

... le prêtre ... regarda les trois assistans qui figuraient la France chrétienne, et leur dit: —Nous allons entrer dans le sanctuaire de Dieu! ...
[*Mém.* xxxix]

... le prêtre ... regarda les trois assistants qui figuraient la France chrétienne, et leur dit, *pour effacer les misères de ce taudis:* "Nous allons entrer dans le sanctuaire de Dieu!"
[*Con.* 17–18]

Additional details are also introduced to correct the obscurity of certain passages. Where they are not essential to the comprehension of a passage, Balzac is just as likely to suppress as to insert them.

Style.—Ten variations illustrate Balzac's endeavor to tone down, simplify, or render his expression more compact. We present an example of each of these:

Toning down, by removal of unsuitable expression:

—Veux-tu nous faire couper le cou ... aristocrate? ... s'écria-t-il *avec une fureur qui lui glaçait la langue.*
[*Mém.* xvi]

—Veux-tu nous faire couper le cou, misérable aristocrate? ... s'écria-t-il *avec fureur.* [*Con.* 8]

This change also eliminates the absurdity contained in the paradox of the original form.

Simplification and compactness:

Le passant *resta immobile occupé à contempler* cette maison. *Elle offrait* en quelque sorte le type des *habitations qui rendent si misérable l'aspect des faubourgs de Paris.* [*Mém.* xx]

Le passant, *immobile, contemplait* cette maison, *qui présentait* en quelque sorte le type des *misérables habitations de ce faubourg.* [*Con.* 9]

Toning down and compactness, together with an uncharacteristic diminution of the realistic coloring:

Mademoiselle de Charost y trouva un *long* mouchoir de batiste très-fine. Il était souillé *par quelques taches* de sueur. *Après l'avoir examiné tous trois à la lumière avec une attention scrupuleuse,* ils y reconnurent *de petits points presque noirs et clair-semés, comme si le linge avait reçu des éclaboussures.*
[*Mém.* xlvi]

Mademoiselle de Langeais *ouvrit la boîte,* y trouva un mouchoir de batiste très-fine, souillé de sueur; *et en le dépliant,* ils y reconnurent *des taches.*
[*Con.* 20]

Problems of style were responsible for the greatest number of revisions. Of the total of one hundred and seventy-three variations (not including mechanical variations or those pertaining to sentence structure), as many as thirty-five arose from the search for the right word or expression, while fourteen involved addition or deletion of descriptive adjectives and adverbs. Changes in sentence structure were made for all but one of the sixty-two pages of the 1830 edition. The stylistic changes are, with rare exceptions, fortunate and show a determined effort to improve expression.

II. *LA VENDETTA*

By FRANCES BRIXEY

Editions collated.—

1. 1830, in *Scènes de la vie privée*, éd. Mame et Delaunay-Vallée, I, 9–165 (*Mame*). All *"Mame"* references are to this edition.
2. 1832, in *Scènes de la vie privée*, éd. Mame-Delaunay, I, 5–161. This is the second edition of the *Scènes*, and *La Vendetta* is reprinted without alterations.
3. 1835, in *Scènes de la vie privée* (*Etudes de mœurs au XIXe siècle*, Vol. I), éd. Mme Charles-Béchet, I, 267–401 (*Béch.*).
4. 1839, in *Scènes de la vie privée*, éd. Charpentier, II, 1–105 (*Char.*). Aside from a small number of corrections in punctuation and spelling, there is only one variation between the texts of 1835 and 1839.
5. 1842, in the *Comédie humaine*, éd. Furne, Dubochet et Hetzel, I (Vol. I of the *Scènes de la vie privée*), 168–230 (*Fur.*).
6. Conard, III (Vol. III of the *Scènes de la vie privée*), 137–220 (*Con.*).

La Vendetta is a melodramatic, though rather poignant, story of the conflict of two passions—love and hate—and of two wills.

*Changes in preliminaries and makeup.—*Since the 1830 and 1832 editions are identical and the 1835 and 1839 editions practically so, there were only three significant stages in the work of revision. The story was originally divided into five parts: an introduction and four chapters; but all chapter titles and divisions were removed in 1835. The Dedication (to Puttinati, Milanese sculptor) and date line were added in 1842. The material was progressively condensed: one hundred and fifty-two paragraph indentations were removed for the 1835 edition, thirty-six more for the Furne, five more for the Conard.

*Stylistic and linguistic changes.—*As is generally the case, these types of variations predominate and include changes in sentence structure, transpositions, omissions and compressions, amplifications and additions, and other rhetorical devices.

If we consider the various versions collectively, we find altogether three hundred and thirty-seven changes involving sentence structure. Of this number, two-thirds concern changes from dependent to independent clauses, or the reverse. A large percentage of these involve treatment of the conjunction. In twenty-two cases Balzac links an independent clause to another clause or sentence by subordinating the clause with an adjectival, pronominal, or participial form. The following citation is taken from the description of Ginevra's entrance into the atelier:

... elle se dirigea lentement vers sa place ... *Mais elle ne s'aperçut pas* de la curiosité particulière et toute nouvelle qu'excitait sa présence. [*Mame* 39–40]	... elle se dirigea lentement vers sa place ... *sans s'apercevoir* de la curiosité particulière qu'excitait sa présence. [*Béch.* 294]

The sentence is thus made more compact and more vivid.

The substitution of finite for participial forms often clarifies or emphasizes the expression. In the following example Ginevra has heard noises behind the closed door of a cabinet in the atelier:

Alors elle approcha de la cloison une table ... *puis, grimpant* lestement sur cet échafaudage, elle atteignit à la crevasse. [*Mame* 42]	Elle approcha de la cloison une table ... *elle grimpa* lestement sur cet échafaudage, et atteignit à la crevasse. [*Béch.* 295–96]

Balzac's striving for clarity and emphasis led him to make almost five hundred changes in rhetorical devices alone. These may involve additions, omissions, or transpositions. The following citation is a good example of Balzac's condensation of a florid description into a terse, compact phrase:

... Ginevra tressaillit, tourna la tête, vit son ennemie, devint aussi rouge que le plus éclatant coquelicot des champs ... [*Mame* 50]	Ginevra tressaillit, tourna la tête, vit son ennemie, rougit ... [*Béch.* 303]

Numerous examples of transpositions are found in the revisions of pronominal clauses. In every case where possible (and in many where it is neither advisable nor excusable) Balzac preserves the *dont* clause by revising and transposing. But sometimes, as in the example below, he is forced to substitute a relative clause, and the resultant sentence is improved. Ginevra and Luigi look over their house for the first time:

Ils parcoururent ensemble les trois chambres *dont leur logement était composé*. [*Char.* 87]	Ils parcoururent ensemble les trois chambres *qui composaient leur logement*. [*Fur.* 220]

Changes in parts of speech total nine hundred and forty-two. Balzac sorted, discarded, and added material with painstaking care. A great number of changes involve substitution of more forceful or more appropriate terms for words used earlier; so Luigi's statement after the discovery of his identity:

Nous serions *ennemis!* demanda Luigi en tremblant. [*Char.* 66]	Nous serions *en vendetta,*[3] demanda Luigi en tremblant. [*Fur.* 207]

In the next citation Balzac has substituted the proper technical term for one which was much more general:

... [Ginevra] se mit à *exécuter* à la seppia la tête du pauvre reclus. [*Mame* 52]	... [Ginevra] se mit à *croquer*[4] à la seppia la tête du pauvre reclus. [*Béch.* 304]

Variations concerning realistic elements.—There are only eighty-nine variations which may be classed under this category. Of that number, over a third deals with figures, dates, and money; a second third concerns changes which made the story historically accurate; and the last group contains sociological, scientific (or pseudo-scientific), and consolidating revisions.

In several instances Balzac has added psychological material which would enrich the character of his personage. For example, Piombo has warned Ginevra that he would kill Luigi rather than allow him to marry her: "... je ne crains pas *la justice des* hommes. *Nous autres Corses, nous allons nous expliquer avec Dieu*" (*Char.* 71, *Fur.* 210).

Figures, dates, sums of money—here as elsewhere—change often and sometimes without evident reason. In the 1835 edition Balzac alters the number of students in Servin's atelier from "dix" (*Mame* 28) to "plusieurs" (*Béch.* 283). In the same edition an added text reads: "... *seize ans* s'écoulèrent entre l'arrivée de la famille Piombo à Paris et l'aventure suivante" (*Béch.* 279). Since the date of arrival is given as 1800, the above statement is changed to "quinze ans" (*Fur.* 173) to make the account of Labédoyère's trial and execution historically accurate. In another variation Piombo's wealth is increased, in accordance with Balzac's usual practice, from "*une douzaine* de mille livres de rente" to "*une vingtaine* de mille livres ..." (*Mame* 83, *Béch.* 331).

As for historical truth, it is to be noted that this is one of the few stories in which Napoleon actually appears on the scene for a brief period. (The other two are *La Femme de trente ans* and *Une Ténébreuse Affaire.*) Revisions are made to include references to "Waterloo, les Cent Jours, le

---

[3] The Italian word is italicized by Balzac.

[4] Italics by Balzac.

maréchal Feltre, Napoléon, le sauveur de la France, les Ultra, le maréchal Ney, le Côté Droit, le Côté Gauche."

Solidity.—Eight reappearing characters are added in the Furne text and serve to link this story with the others in the *Comédie humaine.* Four of these (Élie Magus, Thirion, Bidault, and Gigonnet) are only mentioned, while four others (Vergniaud, Roguin, Mathilde Roguin, Amélie Thirion) now appear in the action under their own names. In two instances Balzac introduces descriptive material about Ginevra which foreshadows the climax of the plot. In a third instance such a passage is removed as being obviously repetitious. The *dossiers* given in 1830 remain fundamentally unchanged; descriptive details are added, deleted, or rearranged; but the essential character of each person remains constant.

Although *La Vendetta* is a comparatively short story, Balzac subjected it to more than nineteen hundred variations. Over nine hundred of these were made for the edition of 1835; about a thousand, in 1842. Balzac's main effort bore on style: he attempted to balance his sentences, give them grace, smoothness, harmony, polish, precision, and accuracy.

III. *ETUDE DE FEMME*
By ROSE GOLDSMITH

Editions collated.—

1. 1831, in *Romans et contes philosophiques*, éd. Gosselin, III, 301–20 (*Gos.*).

2. 1835, in *Scènes de la vie parisienne* (*Etudes de mœurs au XIXᵉ siècle*, Vol. XII), éd. Mme Charles-Béchet, IV, 111–31, under the title of *Profil de marquise* (*Béch.*).

3. Conard, III (Vol. III of the *Scènes de la vie privée*), 381–94, with the original title (*Con.*).

This brief sketch presents a side light on the character of the Marquise de Listomère at a time when she imagines herself courted by Rastignac.

Preliminary changes.—The title of the story remained the same throughout, except in the 1835 edition, where it was temporarily changed to *Profil de marquise*. In 1842 Balzac dedicated the work to Jean-Charles di Negro.

Characters.—The most significant variations are those which affect the names and the histories of the personages. Following is a table of the names given in the various editions:

GOSSELIN	BÉCHET	CONARD
[Anonymous]	Raphaël	Horace [Bianchon][5] [the narrator]
Comtesse de ***	Marquise de Listomère	. . . . . .
Thérèse	Clémentine	Caroline [her maid]
Comte de ***	Marquis de Listomère	. . . . . .
Ernest de M ...	Eugène de Rastignac	. . . . . .
Jean	Joseph	. . . . . [his servant]
Marquis de L ...	Marquis de Beauséant	. . . . . .
Vicomtesse de B ...	Baronne de Nucingen	. . . . . .
		Mme de Mortsauf
		[Félix de Vandenesse][5]

The Béchet edition thus replaces the incomplete indications of the Gosselin text by full names, most of which are already familiar in the author's works. There is a possibility that the Raphaël of Béchet was meant to be Raphaël de Valentin, who, like the narrator, was a writer and an intimate friend of Rastignac (cf. *La Peau de chagrin*). The two people added in Conard do not enter into the action; the first is mentioned, the second merely alluded to, though not by name. All the names are changed at least once in the course of the revisions, and in the final form nine[6] out of ten of the characters are reappearing (Caroline constituting the only exception).

These changes lead to certain modifications in the details concerning people; for example, when Raphaël becomes Horace, the following variation is introduced in connection with

l'expédition d'Alger, dans laquelle je désirais être employé en qualité d'*historiographe et rédacteur de bulletins militaires*. [*Béch.* 121]	l'expédition de Morée, dans laquelle je désirais être employé en qualité de *médecin*. [*Con.* 387]

The same change motivates the addition, in 1842, of a conclusion to the story. Dr. Bianchon is speaking of the Marquise de Listomère: "Moi qui la soigne et qui connais son secret, je sais qu'elle a seulement une petite crise nerveuse de laquelle elle profite pour rester chez elle" (*Con.* 394). Similarly, the shift in names necessitates changes like the following:

Le marquis de L ... étant son *oncle* ... [*Gos.* 312]	Le marquis de Beauséant étant *un peu parent* à monsieur de Rastignac ... [*Con.* 389]

[5] The names bracketed do not actually appear in the story.

[6] Miss Preston counts only eight.

The addresses of the Comtesse de *** and the Vicomtesse de B... become the traditional abodes of the Marquise de Listomère and the Baronne de Nucingen (Rue Saint-Dominique and Rue Saint-Lazare, respectively) with the substitution of names.

Somewhat comparable, but in the nature of an elaboration, is the addition to the discussion of the Marquise de Listomère. The new material seems to serve the purpose of claifying the motivation in this "étude de femme."

Elle est mariée depuis sept ans au comte de *** . [*Gos.* 304]	Mariée depuis sept ans au marquis de Listomère, *un de ces députés qui attendent la pairie, elle croit peut-être aussi servir par sa conduite l'ambition de la famille. Quelques femmes attendent pour la juger le moment où M. de Listomère sera pair de France, et où elle aura trente-six ans, moment de la vie où la plupart des femmes s'aperçoivent qu'elles sont dupes des lois sociales.* [*Béch.* 114]

Generalizations.—The last part of the preceding quotation is one of a group of generalizations added to the tale. Usually these contribute additional insights into character.

Il faut être bien vieux pour ne pas rougir en entendant prononcer le nom d'une *bien-aimée*.[7] Néanmoins il [Rastignac] dit avec assez de sangfroid: —Oh! non, madame! [*Béch.* 130]	Il faut avoir plus de vingt-cinq ans pour ne pas rougir *en se voyant reprocher la bêtise d'une fidélité que les femmes raillent pour ne pas montrer combien elles en sont envieuses.* Néanmoins il dit avec assez de sang-froid: "Pourquoi pas, madame?" [*Con.* 393]

The change of the answer itself is here in keeping with the conception of Rastignac's character.

Dossiers (*partial*).—In the Gosselin edition, page 309, Balzac uses the word "bourguignon," which he stars and defines in a footnote. In the Béchet edition, page 120, he incorporates this definition into the text and prefaces it with the remark: "A ce mot arrêtons-nous et plaçons ici pour les ignorans une explication due à un étymologiste très distingué qui a désiré garder l'anonyme." This transitional explanation might be considered as part of a *dossier.*

The reader will understand that in this story, as elsewhere, the most

---

[7] Italicized by the author.

frequent variations are those which concern style and language. The familiar substitution of finite constructions for participial phrases, of rhetorical questions for statements, the changes in words and sentence structure, and so forth, are again in evidence. But the most important variations, here, are those which tend to link the story with the mass of the *Comédie humaine* and thus to solidify the entire work.

IV. *L'AUBERGE ROUGE*
By RUTH B. DUNN

Editions collated.—

1. 1832, in the *Nouveaux Contes philosophiques*, éd. Gosselin, pp. 179–269 (*Gos.*).
2. 1837, in the *Etudes philosophiques*, éd. Werdet (by Delloye et Lecou), XVII, 5–144 (*Wer.*).
3. Conard, XXIX (Vol. III of the *Etudes philosophiques*), 273–317 (*Con.*).

L'Auberge rouge presents the familiar narrative device of a story within a story; the two parts are joined by the person of Frédéric Taillefer, who is at the same time one of the actors in the inset story and one of those who hear it told. The narrator of the external story is considering marriage with Victorine Taillefer, and the problem arises for him as to whether it is ethical to marry a woman whose father has acquired wealth through murder.

Changes in preliminaries and makeup.—Both Gosselin and Werdet are divided into a number of chapters, and those which give the inset story are themselves divided into the narrative, "interruptions," and "continuations." These divisions are eliminated in the Furne edition of 1846 (XV, 359–90), which substitutes for them two general headings: "L'Idée et le fait" and "Les Deux Justices." In the same edition appears the Dedication to "Monsieur le Marquis de Custine." Werdet alone has a prefatory quotation from *Louis Lambert:* "Une idée causer des souffrances physiques, hein! qu'en dis-tu?"

Characters.—Before the 1837 edition the story was not connected with the body of the *Comédie humaine*. But in that edition Balzac made reappearing characters of the principal personages, and thus related the work to several others. The changes brought about constitute the most interesting aspect of the variations, and we shall treat only them in the present study.

Frédéric Taillefer, the banker, was at first called "Frédéric Mauricey"

(*Gos.* 196). Before the new name was introduced into *L'Auberge rouge* (*Wer.* 34), however, it had already been used in *Le Père Goriot*, as early as 1834. There, Taillefer is described thus: "Le père Taillefer est un vieux coquin qui passe pour avoir assassiné l'un de ses amis pendant la Révolution .... Il est banquier, principal associé de la maison Frédéric Taillefer et Compagnie" (preoriginal edition, *Revue de Paris*, XII [1834], 256). *Le Père Goriot*, further, discusses at length the Taillefer family, the disowned daughter Victorine, and the son, after whose death in a duel Victorine returns to her home from a long sojourn at the Maison Vauquer. It is likely that at the time of writing *Le Père Goriot* Balzac had in mind the events of *L'Auberge rouge;* the existence of a banker-murderer whose given name is Frédéric and the fact that he has a daughter are common to the two. But differences are found in the circumstances that Mauricey-Taillefer had not, in *L'Auberge rouge*, literally "assassiné l'un de ses amis," since he had attributed to a friend a murder which he himself had committed, and that his daughter, in *L'Auberge rouge*, had been in a convent, not in a boarding-house. The likelihood of a cross-reference seems greater when one remembers that in 1833, shortly before the composition of *Goriot*, Balzac had evolved the plan of the *Comédie humaine* and the notion of reappearing characters.

There can be no doubt, however, that Balzac was referring specifically to events in *Le Père Goriot* in an insertion in the Werdet edition of *L'Auberge rouge:*

Il [Taillefer] a une jolie fille que, pendant fort long-temps, il n'a pas voulu reconnaître; mais la mort de son fils, tué en duel, l'a contraint à la prendre avec lui, car il ne pouvait plus avoir d'enfans. La pauvre fille est ainsi devenue tout-à-coup une des plus riches héritières de Paris. La perte de son fils unique a plongé ce cher homme dans un chagrin qui reparaît quelquefois [pp. 17–18].

Thus the two families are definitely amalgamated by 1837.

By way of linking, this same amalgamation is made again a year later, in the 1838 edition of *La Peau de chagrin;* Balzac links up a hitherto anonymous character with the banker of *L'Auberge rouge* and gives him the name of Taillefer. Earlier editions of *La Peau* had spoken merely of a "banquier," a "capitaliste," to whom several murders were attributed. He is now associated by name with the banker of *Le Père Goriot* and by deed with the banker-murderer of *L'Auberge rouge*. The variations of the most important passage in question are given below:

La Peau de Chagrin (Second edition, 1831)	La Peau de Chagrin (Conard edition)
S'il faut croire les envieux et ceux qui tiennent à voir les ressorts de la vie, cet homme aurait tué, pendant la révolution, *je ne sais quelle vieille dame asthmatique, un petit orphelin scrofuleux et quelque autre personne.* Peux-tu donner place à des crimes sous les cheveux grisonnans de notre vénérable *amphitryon?* Il a l'air d'un bien bon homme. [Gosselin, I, 151]	S'il faut croire les envieux et ceux qui tiennent à voir les ressorts de la vie, cet homme aurait tué, pendant la.révolution, *un Allemand et quelques autres personnes qui seraient, dit-on, son meilleur ami et la mère de cet ami.* Peux-tu donner place à des crimes sous les cheveux grisonnants de ce vénérable *Taillefer?* Il a l'air d'un bien bon homme. [P. 51][8]

Therefore, the situation with regard to Taillefer is, in summary, as follows: (1) In 1831 Balzac creates two banker-murderers, the first of whom (in *L'Auberge rouge*) is called "Mauricey," the second of whom (in *La Peau de chagrin*) is anonymous; there is no apparent relationship between them. (2) In 1834 he sets up a character of this type (in *Le Père Goriot*), whom he calls "Taillefer" and in whom there may be a reminiscence of Mauricey. (3) In 1837 Balzac actually introduces into *L'Auberge rouge* the name and the passage (quoted above) relating this story to *Le Père Goriot*. (4) In 1838 the identification is extended to *La Peau de chagrin*. The three works now distinctly concern the same man.

Similar, although less complicated, changes affect the other members of the Taillefer family. The daughter, Victorine, is called Joséphine in the Gosselin text, page 258. In this edition the first mention of her omits her given name: "C'est mademoiselle Mauricey" (p. 251). By 1837, however, she has become known to readers of *Père Goriot;* and in order that she may be recognized immediately in the present story, she is introduced as "Mlle Victorine Taillefer" (*Wer.* 115). Several modifications to her portrait change her personality to make it agree with other appearances:

Elle cause avec réserve, *elle est accorte, gaie.* Son caractère a des *attraits* auxquels personne ne sait résister. [*Gos.* 258]	Elle cause avec réserve; et son caractère a des *grâces mélancoliques* auxquelles personne ne sait résister ... [*Con.* 311–12]

Thus her description is brought into harmony with her character in *Goriot*, where "tristesse habituelle," "grâce," and "douceur" had been applied to her (*Con.*, VI, 232–33).

---

[8] This is the text of the 1838 edition, by Delloye et Lecou, pp. 65–66.

Mme Taillefer also appears in *L'Auberge rouge;* but here we have the curious phenomenon of a character who, by successive steps, is eliminated from active participation in the story. In the Gosselin edition, she is the banker's first wife and Joséphine's mother. However, since *Le Père Goriot* reports her as dead and Victorine as "orpheline de mère," Werdet gives her the role of second wife in our story. An addition to Taillefer's history states: "Il s'est remarié par spéculation" (*Wer.* 17), and in two cases references to Victorine's "mère" are changed to "belle-mère." In *Goriot*, too, Victorine's extreme devotion to her father had been emphasized; this accounts for her assuming, to a certain extent, the role of her stepmother in Werdet. Here are some of the significant passages, taken from the conclusion of the banquet scene:

Si *madame Mauricey* entendait son *mari*, elle pourrait bien avoir une attaque de nerfs! ...	Si *mademoiselle Taillefer* entendait son *père*, elle pourrait bien avoir une attaque de nerfs!
Le banquier rentra dans le salon, y chercha *madame Mauricey*, lui dit un mot à voix basse; et aussitôt jetant un cri, elle s'élança vers la porte et disparut. [*Gos.* 252]	Le banquier rentra dans le salon, y chercha *Victorine*, et lui dit un mot à voix basse. Aussitôt *la jeune personne* jeta un cri, s'élança vers la porte et disparut. [*Wer.* 117]
Madame Mauricey essayait d'étouffer les gémissemens de son *mari*, en lui couvrant la bouche d'un mouchoir. [*Gos.* 256]	*Mademoiselle Taillefer* essayait d'étouffer les gémissemens de son *père* en lui couvrant la bouche d'un mouchoir. [*Wer.* 122]

This process is continued in the variations between the Werdet and the Conard editions, with the result that in the final version Mme Taillefer's part is reduced to a few simple allusions. The first of these changes concerns Taillefer's violent attacks of illness:

... sa *femme* est forcée de le faire attacher sur son lit ... [*Wer.* 119]	... sa *fille* fut alors forcée de le faire attacher sur son lit ... [*Con.* 309–10]

The second refers to Victorine's fortune:

... si donc je [the narrator] lui propose de se priver de quinze cent mille francs ... sa *belle-mère* me prendra pour un mauvais plaisant. [*Wer.* 142]	... si donc je lui propose de se priver de quinze cent mille francs ... sa *femme de confiance* me prendra pour un mauvais plaisant. [*Con.* 316]

"Femme de confiance" doubtless refers to Mme Couture, who in *Le Père Goriot* had cared for Victorine, and whom she had kept "comme demoiselle de compagnie."

Taillefer's son figures in *L'Auberge rouge*, beginning with the second edition, where, as we have seen, he is mentioned in an expository passage (*Wer.* 17; quoted above).

In *L'Auberge rouge*, then, we have an excellent example of a work which, originally independent, is linked to the *Comédie humaine* through changes in successive editions. Balzac's growing conception of the story leads to similar alterations in other works—alterations which serve to bind at least three stories more closely together.

V. *HISTOIRE DES TREIZE*

PART II: *LA DUCHESSE DE LANGEAIS*

By MARGUERITE RICE CRAIN

Editions collated.—

1. 1834, in *Scènes de la vie parisienne* (*Etudes de mœurs au XIXᵉ siècle*, Vol. XI), éd. Mme Charles-Béchet, III, 1–289, under the title of *Ne Touchez Pas la Hache* (*Béch.*).
2. Conard, XIII (Vol. I of the *Scènes de la vie parisienne*), 151–317 (*Con.*).

The second episode of the *Histoire des Treize* combines a *roman-complot* with a *roman de mœurs;* but the melodramatic machinery is only a slight framework surrounding a detailed study of the Faubourg Saint-Germain in 1818–19. *La Duchesse de Langeais* falls into three parts, sharply divided: the beginning *in medias res;* a long Balzacian "loop" of explanation; a return to the action of the first part and the denouement.

*Preliminary variations.—*The change in title from *Ne Touchez Pas la Hache* to *La Duchesse de Langeais* is not explicable entirely as resulting from a shift in emphasis with the passing of years. For Balzac had used both titles before the appearance of the Béchet edition, in a letter to Mme Hanska.[9] It was not until 1839, however, that the present title was adopted. The final title stresses sociological groupings, as against the strictly fictional implications of its predecessor. The Furne edition (IX, 111–235), which first bore the dedication to Franz Liszt, suppressed the chapter divisions, the titles, and the mottoes which had originally preceded each chapter.

*Linguistic and stylistic variations.—*The large number of changes in sentence structure, word order, and parts of speech show that Balzac was constantly trying to make this novel more forceful by adding to the clarity and the conciseness of its style. The same effort is disclosed in the substi-

[9] Sunday, March 9, 1834, in *LEt.*, I, 138. The Béchet volume appeared during the week ending April 19, 1834.

tution of more vivid words for colorless ones; the quest of the *mot juste* is a part of his realistic method. This is particularly striking in the case of verbs; note, for example, the relief added to the following sentence by the two changes:

Armand *attendit* dans le salon *en examinant* le goût répandu dans les moindres détails. [*Béch.* 113]	Armand *se promena* dans le salon *en étudiant* le goût répandu dans les moindres détails. [*Con.* 215]

Frequently, *être* is supplanted by words which add to the significance or the force of the idea expressed.

Among the numerous additions to the text those in the dialogue are especially prominent. Some of these additions take the form of descriptive phrases; for example, "dit-elle *aussi* indifférement *qu'elle le put* à Julien ..." (*Béch.* 223, *Con.* 280). Such speech-words as "*dit-elle après avoir embrassé sa nièce*" (*Béch.* 252, *Con.* 299) and "*reprit-elle après une pause*" (*Béch.* 131, *Con.* 226) are added to accompany the speaker's words with action. Other changes in dialogue consist of additions or intensifications of the speeches proper, as in the following example:

Ce sont des douleurs de riche! [*Béch.* 223]	Une des mille douleurs du riche! [*Con.* 280]

Variations in realistic elements.—What may be styled a change in a social generalization is presented in a passage which relates to the *mariage de convenance:* "Que prouve un mari? Que, jeune fille, une femme était ou richement dotée, ou bien élevée, avait une mère adroite, *ou satisfaisait aux ambitions de l'homme*" (*Béch.* 81, *Con.* 196); here the italicized phrase is added. Another such generalization is made to bear more directly upon Balzac's conception of society; the use of the expression "comédie historique" is noteworthy in the light of the ultimate title for his work:

Ce qui est vrai dans la comédie historique des siècles, est également vrai dans la sphère plus étroite des scènes partielles *de ce drame.* [*Béch.* 71]	Ce qui est vrai dans la comédie historique des siècles est également vrai dans la sphère plus étroite des scènes partielles *du drame national appelées les Mœurs.* [*Con.* 190]

Thus Balzac calls attention to the general division of the *Comédie humaine* under which this story falls, the "Etudes de mœurs." The passage also shows Balzac's tendency to compare the past with the present, a tendency manifested again by the introduction of the contemporary allusion into the following: "Un beau théorème vaut un grand nom. *Les Rotschild*, ces Fugger modernes, sont princes de fait" (*Béch.* 58, *Con.* 182).

Other realistic variations are miscellaneous in nature. One involves the correction of a contradiction in the story. The Duchesse de Langeais was abducted in her own carriage; this could not, therefore, have been seen just at that time in Mme de Sérisy's court, as the latter had originally stated:

... mon frère Ronquerolles m'a dit avoir vu *votre voiture dans la cour.* [*Béch.* 210]	... mon frère Ronquerolles m'a dit avoir vu *vos gens qui vous attendent.* [*Con.* 273]

Two changes substitute appropriate military terms for incorrect terms used in the earlier edition (*Béch.* 20, *Con.* 161; *Béch.* 106, *Con.* 211). By supplying "A Paris" in place of "En France," Balzac reminds the reader that the true subject of the novel is Paris (*Béch.* 103, *Con.* 209). The tendency away from the fictional approach is evident in changes of another order. In the variation affecting the Duchesse de Langeais's definition of coquetry, the meaning of the original passage is completely transformed, resulting in a modification in the portrayal of the heroine's character:

Etre coquette, Armand; mais *c'est être constamment fausse.* Se faire mélancolique avec les humoristes, gaie avec les insoucians, politique avec les ambitieux, écouter avec admiration les bavards, s'occuper de guerre avec les militaires, être passionée pour le bien du pays avec les philantropes, *prendre enfin pour plaire à chaque homme le vêtement d'esprit, l'allure de caractère qui peut le séduire sans donner une miette de son âme, les amuser tous, les captiver, s'en moquer, voilà ce que c'est d'être coquette!* [*Béch.* 125]	Etre coquette, Armand, mais *c'est se promettre à plusieurs hommes et ne pas se donner. Se donner à tous est du libertinage. Voilà ce que j'ai cru comprendre de nos mœurs. Mais* se faire mélancolique avec les humoristes, gaie avec les insouciants, politique avec les ambitieux, écouter avec *une apparente* admiration les bavards, s'occuper de guerre avec les militaires, être passionnée pour le bien du pays avec les philanthropes, *accorder à chacun sa petite dose de flatterie, cela me paraît aussi nécessaire que de mettre des fleurs dans nos cheveux, des diamants, des gants et des vêtements. Le discours est la partie morale de la toilette, il se prend et se quitte avec la toque à plumes. Nommez-vous ceci coquetterie?* [*Con.* 222–23]

This closer notation of the methods ascribed to the Duchesse de Langeais is doubtless connected with Balzac's memories of those actually practiced by the Duchesse de Castries.

In both abductions of the duchess, dramatic exclamations and theatrical and technical details were at first heaped up to the point of tire-
someness. By making the changes in question Balzac tries to give a more
sober tone to these scenes.

A moi les Treize! Il faut l'enlever d'ici.   ... il faut l'enlever d'ici.   [*Con.* 177]
     [*Béch.* 44]

Elle se croyait aimée. *Erreur!*   ... elle se croyait aimée.   [*Con.* 270]
     [*Béch.* 205]

The red dominoes of the Treize are deleted for the same reason: "Tout-à-
coup les reflets devenus plus vifs avaient illuminé trois personnes masquées
enveloppées de dominos rouges" (*Béch.* 194, *Con.* 262); "et revit distincte-
ment les trois hommes masqués *vêtus de leurs longues robes rouges*" (*Béch.*
203, *Con.* 268).

Reappearing characters.—Twenty-one characters figured in the Béchet
edition of *Ne Touchez Pas la Hache.* Of these, five had already appeared
in novels written in 1832–33. Eight of the original personages disappear
in the Furne and Conard editions, four of them being replaced by well-
known characters of the *Comédie humaine.* Nine other reappearing characters are brought into these editions, largely in the background. Examining the persons who replace the eight "disappearing" characters, we find
that two of them are historical—Talleyrand and the Chevalier de Jau-
court—and two nonreappearing—Mme de Marigny and her son. The other
four are reappearing: M. de Genouilhac, who is to escort the Duchesse
de Langeais to Mme de Sérisy's ball, is replaced by Henri de Marsay
(*Béch.* 175, *Con.* 253); the place of the Marquis de Cassan, one of a group
of Parisian aristocrats, is taken by the Duc de Grandlieu (*Béch.* 224, *Con.*
280); a Mme Bouvry becomes Mme Keller, the wife of the banker (*Béch.*
235, *Con.* 288); and Mme de Montignon is supplanted by the Comtesse de
Granville (*Béch.* 227, *Con.* 283).

The aristocratic, the financial, and the judicial worlds are represented
by these four people. The distribution among social groups is carried further through the addition of still other reappearing figures. The Duc and
the Duchesse de Maufrigneuse (*Con.* 197, 299), the Vicomtesse de Fontaine (*Con.* 196), the Comtesse de Soulanges (*Con.* 287), M. d'Aju-
da-Pinto, and Mlle de Rochefide (*Con.* 223) add to the splendor of the
aristocratic background of the novel. The variation concerning the last
two is of particular interest, since it links up more fully with a situation of
Le Père Goriot and is made to accord with the chronology of the two novels:

Bien mieux, *la récente aventure de ma-dame de Beauséant* m'a prouvé que ces mêmes sacrifices sont presque toujours les causes de notre abandon.

[*Béch.* 126]

Bien mieux, *la rupture que chacun prévoit entre madame de Beauséant et monsieur d'Ajuda, qui, dit-on, épouse mademoiselle de Rochefide,* m'a prouvé que ces mêmes sacrifices sont presque toujours les causes de notre abandon.

[*Con.* 223]

This speech, spoken in 1819, must of necessity look forward to the rupture mentioned, which does not take place until 1820. With the insertion of Gondreville (*Con.* 288) the political circles are given another representative in the novel. The Marquis d'Aiglemont (*Con.* 277), because of his wide experience and interests, might be classed with the aristocratic, the military, or the financial groups.

In its final form *La Duchesse de Langeais* has twenty-five characters, and all but three are reappearing. They link this novel with forty-eight other works, as compared with the thirty-eight novels represented by the personages in the original edition.

VI. *LE COLONEL CHABERT*
By Juanita Kramer Bromberg

Editions collated.—

1. 1835, in *Scènes de la vie parisienne* (*Etudes de mœurs au XIXe siècle*, Vol. XII), éd. Mme Charles-Béchet, IV, 253–390, under the title of *La Comtesse à deux maris* (*Béch.*).[10]

2. 1844, in the *Comédie humaine*, éd. Furne, Dubochet et Hetzel, X (Vol. II of the *Scènes de la vie parisienne*), 1–60 (*Fur.*).

3. Conard, VII (Vol. VII of the *Scènes de la vie privée*), 1–80 (*Con.*).

The situation in *Le Colonel Chabert*, that of the return of a husband, supposed dead, to his wife, who has remarried, is essentially unreal in conception. But by approaching the plot from the standpoint of the legal considerations involved and of the psychology of the actors and by dwelling upon the physical and social background of the incidents Balzac has made of this situation a convincingly realistic study. In the present analysis these realistic elements will be discussed to the exclusion of stylistic matters.

Preliminary variations.—As Balzac's emphasis shifted from one aspect of the story to another, the title underwent significant changes. In the

---

[10] Contrary to general practice in these studies, the first edition has not been collated for this particular tale, since Volume I of *Salmigondis*, where it first appeared in volume form, was unfortunately not available to the writer.

preoriginal edition it was called *La Transaction* ("The Compromise"), and the stress was on the legal implications. The civil, rather than the military, status of the leading personage was brought into relief by the first edition, when the title was changed to *Le Comte Chabert*. In Béchet and Charpentier (*Scènes de la vie parisienne*, Vol. I [1839]), the purely fictional interest was suggested by *La Comtesse à deux maris*. Finally, the present title was adopted in Furne, thus focusing the attention on the central figure, now in his capacity as an officer under Napoleon. In Furne, also, the chapter headings are omitted, and the Dedication added. It is not until Conard, however, that the classification was changed from the *Scènes de la vie parisienne* to the *Vie privée*.

Variations concerning realistic elements.—The opening scene of the story depicts a typical *étude d'avoué*. Balzac made numerous additions to this scene for the purpose of increasing the impression of reality. For example, one supplementary detail describes the actions of the clerks:

... dit le troisième clerc, qui cessa son argumentation. [*Béch.* 272]	... dit-il en cessant son argumentation *étouffée par le rire des autres clercs.*
	[*Con.* 12]

Another addition treats the noises of the office: "les plumes recommencèrent à crier sur le papier timbré *en faisant dans l'Etude le bruit de cent hannetons enfermés par des écoliers dans des cornets de papier*" (*Béch.* 273, *Con.* 13). A third expands the conversation to include more bantering of Godeschal by the other clerks. Godeschal defines his terms with reference to a waxworks museum:

Je parie cent francs contre un sou ... que le cabinet de Curtius constitue *un spectacle.*	Je parie cent francs contre un sou ... que le cabinet de Curtius constitue *l'ensemble de choses auquel est dévolu le nom de spectacle. Il comporte une chose à voir à différents prix, suivant les différentes places où l'on veut se mettre.*
Les clercs haussèrent les épaules. [*Béch.* 272]	*—Et berlik berlok,*[11] *dit Simonnin.*
	—Prends garde que je ne te gifle, toi! dit Godeschal.
	Les clercs haussèrent les épaules.
	[*Con.* 12]

The dictation of a long legal document extends through a large part of this scene. Several remarks and interjections are inserted in it for the pur-

---

[11] Italicized by the author.

pose of breaking the monotony. In the following addition Boucard, who has been calculating accounts, interrupts Godeschal:

... il faut que je relise ma phrase; je ne me comprends plus moi-même). *Nous espérons que Messieurs* ...[11]

[*Béch*. 273–74]

... il faut que je relise ma phrase, je ne me comprends plus moi-même.

—*Quarante-six ... Ça doit arriver souvent! ... et trois quarante-neuf, dit Boucard.*

Nous espérons, reprit Godeschal après avoir tout relu, que Messieurs ...[11]

[*Con*. 13]

The time references in *Le Colonel Chabert* are carefully worked out and are subjected to numerous revisions. The period spent by Chabert in the Heilsberg hospital before recovering his memory is reduced from fifteen months to six months (*Béch*. 287–88, *Con*. 23), probably for the sake of verisimilitude. Derville's visit to the countess is advanced one year, from 1817 to 1818 (*Béch*. 337, *Con*. 50); and consequently the date of Chabert's entrance to Bicêtre must be similarly advanced (*Béch*. 389, *Con*. 78). Finally, the year of the last visit of Derville to Chabert (and, besides, the year in which the former sold his *étude* to Godeschal) is changed from 1832 to 1840, probably to extend Derville's brilliant career over a longer period of time (*Fur*. 57, *Con*. 76).

Balzac's efforts toward careful distinctions, toward precision of analysis, and toward appropriate expression are visible in another group of variations. When he changes "le silence nécessaire *aux grandes conceptions*" to "le silence et la tranquillité nécessaires *à la conception des bonnes idées*" (*Béch*. 275, *Con*. 15), he is describing more adequately the type of mental activity of the lawyer Derville. He comes nearer to scientific truth by altering "là où j'étais, *il n'y avait pas d'air*" to "là où j'étais, *l'air ne se renouvelait point*" (*Béch*. 284, *Con*. 21). Again, the addition of "sociale," that favorite adjective, to "cet homme rebuté ... par la création *sociale* entière" (*Béch*. 293, *Con*. 26) makes an essential distinction and illustrates, at the same time, Balzac's constant tendency to divide the world into physical and social. Finally, a more distinct causal relationship is achieved when the phrase "Combien de choses n'ai-je pas apprises *pendant le temps que j'ai été avoué?*" becomes "Combien de choses n'ai-je pas apprises *en exerçant ma charge!*" (*Béch*. 389, *Con*. 79).

Variations affecting the personages of the story are of two types: (1) those which add to the characterization of the individual and (2) those which serve to link this story with others from Balzac's pen. The second type will be treated later in connection with linking. Of the first type, only one refers to Chabert himself: by suppressing "doucement" in the sentence "En ce moment, le colonel entra et demanda *doucement* Derville" (*Béch.* 350, *Con.* 58), Balzac conforms more closely to the personality of Chabert after he has once again assumed a military bearing and appearance. Three changes fill out the characterization of Simonnin, the *petit clerc:* The first relates to his activities:

Le saute-ruisseau ... se trouve sous la domination spéciale du principal clerc *dont il fait les commissions, dont il porte les billets doux.* [*Béch.* 258]	Le saute-ruisseau ... se trouve sous la domination spéciale du Principal clerc *dont les commissions et les billets doux l'occupent tout en allant porter des exploits chez les huissiers et des placets au Palais.* [*Con.* 4]

The second, to his calling:

Il tient au gamin de Paris par ses mœurs, et à la Chicane par sa *ruse.* [*Béch.* 258]	Il tient au gamin de Paris par ses mœurs, et à la Chicane par sa *destinée.* [*Con.* 4]

And the third, a long addition, to his background and personal traits:

> Cet enfant est presque toujours sans pitié, sans frein, indisciplinable, *faiseur de couplets, goguenard, avide et paresseux. Néanmoins presque tous les petits clercs ont une vieille mère logée à un cinquième étage avec laquelle ils partagent les trente ou quarante francs qui leur sont alloués par mois.* [*Béch.* 258, *Con.* 4]

These statements about Simonnin concern the general type of *petit clerc* as much as they concern Simonnin himself. They thus lead to an analysis of the sociological generalizations found in the story. Among such variations, there is one of considerable length and equal importance. Prefatory to his summary of *choses vues,* Derville remarks that three categories of men—the priest, the doctor, and the lawyer—can have no esteem for the world. By way of elucidation he adds:

> Le plus malheureux des trois est l'avoué. Quand l'homme vient trouver le prêtre, il arrive poussé par le repentir, par le remords, par des croyances qui le rendent intéressant, qui le grandissent, et consolent l'âme du médiateur, dont la tâche ne va pas sans une sorte de jouissance: il purifie, il répare, et réconcilie. Mais, nous autres avoués, nous voyons se répéter les mêmes sentiments mauvais, rien ne les corrige, nos Etudes sont des égouts qu'on ne peut pas curer.
>
> [*Con.* 79]

These sentences appeared first in the Furne edition; they represent the philosophy of the lawyer at the close of his career.

Variations concerning linking.—The present story, through successive changes, is related more and more intimately to the *Comédie humaine*. Two methods are employed—that of introducing allusions and that of developing reappearing characters. In editions before the Furne the nature of the legal document (discussed above) is not specified; but the following passage, added in the Furne after "valse jusqu'aux Invalides" (*Fur.* 10), clears up its relationships:

... *Que nous établissons ici,* reprit Godeschal. Ajoutez: *dans l'intérêt de madame* ... (en toutes lettres) *la vicomtesse de Grandlieu* ...
—Comment! s'écria le Maître-clerc, vous vous avisez de faire des requêtes dans l'affaire Vicomtesse de Grandlieu contre Légion-d'Honneur, une affaire pour compte d'Etude, entreprise à forfait? Ah! vous êtes un fier nigaud! Voulez-vous bien me mettre de côté vos copies et votre minute, gardez-moi cela pour l'affaire Navarreins contre les Hospices. Il est tard, je vais faire un bout de placet, avec des *attendu,* et j'irai moi-même au Palais ...   [*Con.* 14][12]

Thus the documentary method, as here amplified, includes allusions to reappearing characters. Earlier in the dictation, reference had been made to the claims of "l'administration *des hospices*"; since the document now relates to the "affaire Vicomtesse de Grandlieu contre Légion-d'Honneur," the phrase must be changed to "l'administration *de la grande chancellerie de la Légion-d'Honneur*" (*Béch.* 274, *Con.* 13). However, Balzac had in mind from the first some suit against the hospitals, which is now subordinated to the Grandlieu case in the form of the Navarreins case.

The most sweeping of the passages which allude to other stories and figures of the *Comédie humaine* is the famous *tirade* of Derville. This did not appear either in *L'Artiste* or in *Salmigondis* but was printed first in the Béchet edition, page 390.[13] Here situations similar to those in several other stories, as well as the story of *Chabert* itself, are summarized. In the Furne text Balzac was obliged to correct one part of this passage, as follows:

... un père ... abandonné par ses deux filles *à chacune desquelles* il avait donné quarante mille livres de rente! [*Béch.* 390]	... un père ... abandonné par deux filles *auxquelles* il avait donné quarante mille livres de rente. [*Con.* 79]

[12] Italics are the author's.

[13] Mario Roques, "Manuscrit et éditions du *Père Goriot,*" *Revue universitaire*, II (1905), 34, n. 3.

The situation is that of *Le Père Goriot*. In that novel (*Con.* VI, 314–15) it is stated that Goriot had 60,000 *livres de rente* and that, after having given to each of his daughters 500,000 or 600,000 francs (p. 298), he retained only 8,000–10,000 *livres de rente* for himself.[14] Therefore, he could not possibly have had much more than 50,000 *livres de rente* to divide between his daughters, and the assertion of the Béchet edition of *Le Colonel Chabert* becomes erroneous.

Finally, subsequent to the publication of Furne, Balzac added a closing line, with reference to legal experiences, to the story: "J'en ai déjà bien vu chez Desroches, répondit Godeschal" (*Con.* 80). This line alludes to *Un Début dans la vie* (1842), where Godeschal is first clerk of Desroches, who, after leaving Derville, had begun an independent practice.

Thus Desroches and Godeschal, both of whom had their "start in life" under Derville, later became important figures in the ensemble of Balzac's work. Successive editions of *Le Colonel Chabert* tend to bring them into increasing prominence. Desroches, for example, does not appear at all in Béchet; his name occurs only once in Furne (where he is the neophyte of the *étude*); but he is named frequently in Conard, as the fourth clerk. One passage shows this development:

M. *Godeschal*, vous irez au spectacle
sans payer, dit le quatrième clerc au
nouveau-venu ...   [*Béch.* 271]

> Monsieur *Desroches*, vous irez au spec-
> tacle sans payer, dit Huré, *le* quatri-
> ème clerc, à *un nouveau venu* ...
>   [*Fur.* 8]

> > Monsieur Desroches, vous irez au
> > spectacle sans payer, dit Huré *au* qua-
> > trième clerc ...   [*Con.* 11]

As a result of these changes Desroches, absent at first, replaces Godeschal as the newcomer and is finally advanced to the position of fourth clerk. Other insertions of his name are introduced between the Furne (pp. 2, 3, 9) and the Conard (pp. 4, 5, 13) editions.

The first of the above passages indicated that Godeschal was then considered as the new clerk. When that position was given to Desroches in the Furne text, Godeschal was made third clerk (*Béch.* 259, *Fur.* 2). He

---

[14] The figures already appear thus in the periodical form, *Revue de Paris*, December 14, 1834.

remains third clerk throughout, and his name is written into the text several times (*Béch.* 261, 266, 269; *Con.* 5, 6, 10). Still more important, however, is the role which he assumes at the end of the story. In all the editions up to and including the Furne, the successor of Derville, who accompanies that lawyer on his last visit to Chabert, is anonymous. In the Conard version, however, the part is given to Godeschal:

En 1832, vers la fin du mois de juin, *un jeune avoué* allait à Ris, en compagnie de son prédécesseur. [*Fur.* 57]	En 1840, vers la fin du mois de juin, *Godeschal, alors avoué,* allait à Ris, en compagnie de *Derville* son prédécesseur. [*Con.* 76–77]

The name is added to the text four more times in the final pages of the story. In this manner Godeschal, whose original role was very small, is, step by step, raised in dignity until he finally becomes the successor of Derville himself. The change in the date of the final episode and the closing line of the story also have bearing upon Godeschal's career.

The case is somewhat different with the treatment of another reappearing character, Vergniaud. Here changes are introduced either to solidify Vergniaud's relationship with Chabert, under whom he had served in the Egyptian campaign, or to connect up with details of *La Vendetta*. The two examples which follow belong to the first category. In one, Chabert explains his attachment to Vergniaud:

—Nous appelons ainsi [i.e., "égyptien"] les troupiers qui sont revenus de l'expédition d'Egypte, dont j'ai fait partie; *mais* tous ceux qui en sont revenus sont un peu frères. [*Béch.* 318]	Nous appelons ainsi les troupiers qui sont revenus de l'expédition d'Egypte de laquelle j'ai fait partie. *Non seulement* tous ceux qui en sont revenus sont un peu frères, *mais Vergniaud était alors dans mon régiment, nous avions partagé de l'eau dans le désert.* [*Con.* 39]

In the other, Vergniaud, in turn, refers to Chabert as "un égyptien" (*Béch.* 329); in later editions he adds "le premier lieutenant sous lequel j'ai servi" (*Con.* 45–46). The second type of change is motivated by the desire to connect Vergniaud with a character in *La Vendetta*. In that story one of the witnesses to Luigi's marriage was described as an "ancien maréchal-des-logis de hussards ... il s'était mis loueur de voitures et possédait quelques fiacres" (*Con.* III, 200–201). In all editions previous to the Furne this man was called Hardi. In Furne, however, we find the following change in a speech of Luigi:

La Vendetta (Charpentier edition, II, 98)	La Vendetta (Furne edition, I, 226)
Hardi, mon pauvre Hardi, le brave maréchal-des-logis, est impliqué dans une conspiration ...	*Vergniaud, le nourrisseur, mon vieil Egyptien*, est impliqué dans une conspiration ...

That Balzac here had the personage of *Chabert* in mind is shown by his name, his history, and his profession. But in order to complete the identification and to link *Chabert* with the first "maréchal-des-logis" passage of *La Vendetta* (quoted above), Balzac makes this corresponding change in *Chabert:*

Le comte Chabert ... demeurait ... chez un nourrisseur nommé Vergniaud.　　　　　[*Béch.* 311]	Le comte Chabert ... demeurait ... chez *un vieux maréchal-des-logis de la garde impériale, devenu* nourrisseur, et nommé Vergniaud.　　[*Con.* 35]

In their totality, then, the variations show two trends—the one toward consistency and clarity within the story, the other toward a firmer concatenation with the whole structure of Balzac's work. Through the devices for linking described above, a connection is made with at least six specific novels and with many people who are recurrent in numerous parts of the *Comédie humaine.*

VII. *LE CABINET DES ANTIQUES*

By Mary Harmon Maxam and Frank R. Bartlett

Editions collated.—

1. 1839, éd. Souverain, I and II, 1–83, with subtitle *Scène de la vie de province* (*Sou.* I and *Sou.* II).
2. 1844, in the *Comédie humaine*, éd. Furne, Dubochet et Hetzel, VII (Vol. III of the *Scènes de la vie de province*), 120–244 (*Fur.*). The Furne text is reproduced in the *Bibliotheca romanica*, Nos. 96–98, which also gives variants from the Souverain edition.
3. Conard, XI (Vol. IV of the *Scènes de la vie de province*), 1–168 (*Con.*).

Balzac develops the present novel on the basis of several social problems which were of broad significance in contemporary France: the struggle of the impoverished nobility against the wealthy bourgeoisie, the clash of conservatism and liberalism, the growth of political ambition, and the attraction of provincials toward Paris. These problems are represented by personages or incidents in the story, and in some respects a typical solution is offered.

Preliminary variations.—The Souverain edition was accompanied by a preface which set forth Balzac's aims in the *Vie de province* series and explained his method of converting life about him into fictional material, of deriving the *vraisemblable* from the *vrai*. It stated, also, that such prefaces would be useless when the entire *Comédie humaine* was completed. Consequently, this preface was removed from later editions. The Dedication to "Monsieur le Baron de Hammer-Purgstall" bore the date "Aux Jardies, février 1839" in the Souverain edition only, and no date thereafter. The story itself was dated "Aux Jardies, septembre 1838" in that edition; the Furne and the Conard texts, however, have as date line "Aux Jardies, juillet 1837." The former date is apparently correct for the second part of the tale, since on September 17, 1838, Balzac announces to Mme Hanska: "Je viens d'écrire pour *le Constitutionnel*, la fin du *Cabinet des Antiques*, sous le titre de: *les Rivalités en Province*."[15] The original chapter headings, most of which indicated the principal "taps" of the story, were suppressed in the Furne edition.

Variations in style and language.—Of the six hundred and two variations of all types between Souverain and Conard, about three hundred and eighty-six belong to this category; this proportion of slightly less than two-thirds is smaller than in most novels studied. They are as diversified as they are numerous, and we can attempt to give here only a sample of the different kinds. There are some forty cases of change in order of words or phrases with a view to producing smoothness or a relative compactness; for example,

c'eût été pour lui comme un coup de foudre que la révélation des excessives précautions employées afin de *joindre les deux bouts de l'année*,[16] suivant l'expression des ménagères.	La révélation des excessives précautions employées pour *joindre les deux bouts de l'année*,[16] suivant l'expression des ménagères, eût été pour lui comme un coup de foudre.　[*Con.* 23–24]
[*Sou.* I, 66–67]	

In six passages Balzac converts a declarative sentence into a rhetorical question, with a decided gain in effectiveness:

Le rôle de Camusot était de se faire un marchepied de ce procès criminel ...	Le rôle de Camusot n'était-il pas de se faire un marchepied de ce procès criminel ...
[*Sou.* II, 19]	[*Con.* 142]

---

[15] *LEt.*, I, 488. For dating the two parts, see Lov., *Hist.*, pp. 93–94.

[16] Italicized by the author. Unfortunately, in this particular example, the subject is now too far from the verb. But the gain in periodic structure is evident.

Passing on, now, to the parts of speech, we find that in about ten sentences a pronoun subject is introduced to avoid ambiguity and that some twelve times it is suppressed where unnecessary. Verbs are altered frequently in form and in tense; as late as the Conard edition, a passage describing Mme Camusot is changed from the imperfect to the present (*Sou.* II, 17–18; *Con.* 141). The usual replacing of weak by strong verbs is again to be noted; in each of the following cases we observe a marked increase in vividness or precision:

... l'impudeur de saisir un ange comme ils *saisiraient* l'un de nous. [*Sou.* I, 187]	... l'impudeur de saisir un ange comme ils *empoigneraient* l'un de nous. [*Con.* 76]
Du côté de la rue ... *il y avait* une vieille grille ... [*Sou.* I, 294]	Du côté de la rue ... *s'étendait* une vieille grille ... [*Con.* 124]

In the first of these examples a repetition of words is avoided by the variation.

We shall note later that additions in the text largely concern realistic elements; omissions, however, aim especially at concision in the style. One example chosen from twenty-three is given below; in this passage Balzac is comparing the standards of the nobility to those of an antiquary:

... pour un antiquaire, le poids de la médaille *ne signifie rien; la beauté de la pièce consiste dans* la pureté des lettres et de la tête, *dans sa rareté, dans* l'ancienneté *de son* coin. [*Sou.* I, 44]	... pour un antiquaire, le poids de la médaille *est peu de chose en comparaison et de* la pureté des lettres et de la tête et de l'ancienneté *du* coin. [*Con.* 13]

Substitutions involving a search for the *mot juste* are found in abundance; thus, it is more appropriate to say "l'amour divin émanait de ce cœur" than to say "était dans ce cœur" (*Con.* 94; *Sou.* 223). Somewhat similar in tendency are those alterations in readings where there might be a doubt as to the precise reference: "ce sobriquet" becomes "le mot Cabinet des Antiques" (*Sou.* I, 47; *Con.* 14) and "la personne" is superseded by the proper name "Blondet" (*Sou.* I, 38; *Con.* 10). Finally, attention may be called to a group of additions which heighten the effect of the passage concerned, frequently by introducing adjectives or adverbs; for example, "Monsieur du Croisier, répéta le vieillard *si cruellement* atteint jusqu'au cœur" (*Sou.* I, 198; *Con.* 104) and "l'aspect de *son cher* Victurnien" (*Sou.* I, 222; *Con.* 116).

Variations concerning the nobility.—In working out the social problem of his novel Balzac shows a marked tendency to dwell increasingly on the role of the nobility. This is in line with his firm belief in the hereditary aristocracy, in the principle of *noblesse oblige*, and in family traditions. A whole group of variations is important as bearing upon this class. Some of these deal with minor matters, such as the device or the name of a family; for example, the following additions: "marquis d'Esgrignon *ou des Grignons, suivant d'anciens titres*" (*Sou.* I, 24; *Con.* 4) and "les Troisville (*prononcez Tréville*), les la Roche Guyon" (*Sou.* I, 68; *Con.* 24). Along this line the father's advice to young D'Esgrignon is typical:

—Souvenez-vous ... que votre écusson *est sans tache*, qu'il vous permet d'aller partout ... [*Sou.* I, 122]	—Souvenez-vous ... que votre écusson *a pour devise: Cil est nostre!*[17] qu'il vous permet d'aller partout ... [*Con.* 49]

Such changes exemplify Balzac's well-known concern with titles and etymologies. Closely connected with the pride in the family name is the pride in the family history; this is intensified in a number of variations. Sometimes the change may involve merely a small addition: "Le vieillard, *posé sur son arbre généalogique*, se balançait d'un air fat" (*Sou.* I, 205; *Con.* 85) and "le prince de Chinon, *le dernier des Richelieu*" (*Sou.* I, 97; *Con.* 37). Sometimes, however, it may constitute elaborate developments in successive editions. In the Souverain edition (I, 38), for example, the old marquis states: "Une d'Esgrignon peut épouser un Montmorency, notre sang n'est pas aussi mêlé que l'a été le leur." Another sentence is added to this in the Furne (p. 126): "Les d'Esgrignon *portent d'or à deux bandes de gueules*, et rien, depuis neuf cents ans, n'a changé dans leur écusson; il est tel que le premier jour." As late as the Conard (p. 10), still another sentence is added to the preceding: "De là notre devise *Cil est nostre* qui fut prise au tournoi de Philippe-Auguste, ainsi que le chevalier armé d'or tenant de droite et le lion de *gueules* à gauche."[18] Thus, piece by piece, Balzac constructs a scutcheon for the family and builds up an extended statement of the nobleman's vanity. As the historian, too, he modifies the account of the Carol family in the same direction:

... leur titre de marquis était *réel* ... [*Sou.* I, 25]	... leur titre de marquis était à *la fois un devoir, un honneur, et non le simulacre d'une charge superposée* ... [*Con.* 4]

Finally, Balzac produces a specific example in support of one of his generalizations on the nobility:

[17] The motto is italicized by the author.

[18] The heraldic terms are all italicized in the text.

Une famille noble, inactive, oubliée est une fille sotte, laide, pauvre et sage, les quatre points cardinaux du malheur. *Le mariage d'une demoiselle de Trois-ville avec le général Montcornet, loin d'éclairer le Cabinet des Antiques, faillit causer une rupture entre les Troisville et le salon d'Esgrignon qui déclara que les Trois-ville* se galvaudaient. [*Sou.* I, 69; *Con.* 26]

Other variations which we may consider in this category concern Michu's devotion to the nobility (*Sou.* II, 39; *Con.* 150); the description of Victurnien as "ce charmant débris d'une vieille famille" (*Sou.* I, 145; *Con.* 58); the author's comment on D'Esgrignon's last tribute to the re-treating Charles X: "Acte de courage qui semblera tout simple aujourd'-hui, mais que l'enthousiasme de la Révolte rendit alors sublime!" (*Sou.* II, 80; *Con.* 167); and the change from "Les guerres" to "Le Code civil" in the passage: "... il n'y a plus de noblesse, il n'y a plus que de l'aristo-cratie. *Le Code civil* de Napoléon a [*Sou.: ont*] tué les parchemins comme le canon avait déjà tué la féodalité" (*Sou.* II, 72; *Con.* 163).

A small group of changes, comparable to the preceding since it affects another class of society, consists of variations concerning judicial matters. Such, for example, is the augmented description of the elder Blondet: "Ça m'a *pourtant* l'air d'être un faux, dit le vieux Blondet, *chez qui nulle passion ne pouvait obscurcir la clarté de la conscience judiciaire*" (*Sou.* II, 52; *Con.* 155). Such, again, is the change in a generalization on provincial judges:

La province est le séminaire des ambitions judiciaires. Les juges et les gens du Roi forcés de commencer *là* leur carrière voient tous Paris ... [*Sou.* I, 287]

Les juges et les gens du Roi forcés de commencer leur carrière *en province où s'agitent les ambitions judiciaires,* voient tous Paris ... [*Con.* 121]

A definition of a legal term constitutes a display of technical erudition: "Eh! bien, où voyez-vous *donc* un faux? dit le vieux juge. *L'essence du faux, en matière civile, est de constituer un dommage à autrui*" (*Sou.* II, 52; *Con.* 156). These changes are unimportant, however, compared to the great increase in attention to judicial circles between the preoriginal edi-tion in *Le Constitutionnel* (September 22–October 8, 1838) and the Sou-verain. Lovenjoul reprints[19] the original version of a passage which, as re-written, contains an extended generalization on lawyers and the law, *dossiers* on Du Ronceret, Blondet *père*, Michu, Sauvager, Camusot de Marville, and his wife, and considerable plot elaboration (*Con.* 120, l. 15,

[19] *Hist.*, pp. 94–95.

to 160, l. 8). This notable addition to the story gives striking evidence of Balzac's growing interest in political life.

Other realistic variations.—Aside from those changes pertaining to the social groups studied above, we find others of less limited application. Several generalizations are altered in the course of the re-workings; one emphasizes the function of the author:

... les noms de cette rue et de cette ville doivent être *un secret. L'aventure dite,* chacun appréciera les motifs de *la* sage retenue *que s'impose le narrateur.* [*Sou.* I, 23]	... les noms de cette rue et de cette ville doivent être *cachés ici.* Chacun appréciera les motifs de *cette* sage retenue *exigée par les convenances. Un écrivain touche à bien des plaies en se faisant l'annaliste de son temps!* [*Con.* 3]

Another derives an antithetical statement from an exemplary case: "[En effet] Une mère prévoit le mal long-temps avant qu'une fille comme mademoiselle Armande ne l'admette, même quand il est fait. *L'une prévoit le désastre, l'autre y remédie*" (*Sou.* I, 74; *Con.* 28). Among the changes in characterization, one omission of an exaggerated, melodramatic speech improves the tone of the passage; Diane de Maufrigneuse is speaking:

Ne sais-je pas bien jouer mon rôle d'homme? reprit-elle en rehaussant les faces de sa perruque à la Titus et agitant sa cravache. *Postillon, en avant, dit-elle en grossissant sa voix. Faut-il que je jure, que je sacre, que je fume? Je fumerais, jurerais, sacrerais pour sauver ce malheureux enfant.* [*Sou.* II, 27; *Con.* 144]

Variations involving money are comparatively numerous. The longest of these affects the financial statement of Camusot de Marville:

Il n'avait pas eu plus de mille écus de rente constitués par ses père et mère à son contrat, mademoiselle Thirion ne lui avait pas apporté plus de vingt mille francs de dot, *c'était donc un pauvre ménage que le sien ...* [*Sou.* II, 10]	*Son père ne lui avait donné en le mariant que six mille francs de rente, la fortune de feu sa mère, toutes déductions faites de ses avantages d'époux; et comme* mademoiselle Thirion ne lui avait pas apporté plus de vingt mille francs de dot, *ce ménage connaissait les malheurs de la pauvreté caché ...* [*Con.* 138]

Thus the desperately poor state of the couple's finances is bettered in the second version. We shall note below the bearing of this version upon the problem of linking. In order to conform to the depleted resources of the D'Esgrignons, Victurnien's monthly allowance is reduced from 3,000 to 2,000 francs (*Sou.* I, 127; *Con.* 51) and the total sum to be spent on his Parisian sojourn from 100,000 to 60,000 francs (*Sou.* I, 129; *Con.* 52). On the other hand, the dowry of Mlle Duval is raised from two to three million francs (*Sou.* II, 81; *Con.* 167); Balzac, as usual, is lavish in bestowing large sums of money upon those who are already wealthy.

Reappearing characters.—In its first form the novel included a large number of reappearing characters, most of whom were members of the aristocracy. Still others are added to these in the course of the revisions, sometimes by means of long enumerations. Thus, for "une Montmorency, une Rohan, une de Lorges, une Fesenzac, une Bouillon," Balzac substitutes "une Navarreins, une Cadignan, une d'Uxelles, une Beauséant, une Blamont-Chauvry" (*Sou.* I, 67; *Con.* 24); "les ducs d'Avaray, de Blacas, les Rivière" is changed to "les ducs de Navarreins, de Lenoncourt, de Maufrigneuse, de Chaulieu" (*Sou.* I, 106; *Con.* 41). In both passages *Comédie humaine* people take the place originally occupied by historical personages. In other enumerations, which already contain reappearing characters, additions are made; "les d'Hérouville" (*Sou.* I, 142; *Con.* 56), "les Manerville" (*Sou.* I, 143; *Con.* 57), the Duchesse de Chaulieu, and Mme Firmiani (*Sou.* I, 144; *Con.* 57) gain admission to the novel in this fashion. "Qu'a-t-on fait pour les Montauran, pour les Ferdinand ... ?" becomes, with additions, "Qu'a-t-on fait pour les du Guénic, pour les Ferdinand, pour les Fontaine et pour le frère de Montauran ... ?" (*Sou.* I, 111; *Con.* 44). This last variation assembles a number of *Chouan* characters, who tend to form a group apart in Balzac's work. In still other lists of names, unknown individuals are replaced by familiar figures; such are "les Gordon," who are superseded by "les Verneuil" (*Sou.* I, 44; *Con.* 13), and the Marquis de Berines, who is omitted in favor of Canalis (*Sou.* I, 170; *Con.* 70). Mlle des Touches, absent from the first edition, figures later in her important salon (*Sou.* I, 157; *Con.* 64); but Mme de Grandlieu, whom she succeeds in this particular passage, is retained elsewhere in the story. François Michu assumes, throughout the novel, the role originally given to the Baron de Granville (e.g., *Sou.* II, 39; *Con.* 150); as a consequence, Michu's biography is filled in and his *dossier* enlarged. There are, in addition, several interesting changes in given names; Émile Blondet is at first called "Alfred" (*Sou.* I, 302; *Con.* 150), and Fabien du Ronceret is named "Félicien" (*Sou.* I, 90; *Con.* 33). The novels in which these persons appear are all posterior to *Le Cabinet des antiques*, which thus introduces them into the fictional world of Balzac.

A number of the inserted personages had appeared in *La Vieille Fille*, which, in so far as elements of plot are concerned, gives the antecedents of *Le Cabinet des antiques*. Another link between the two novels is accomplished through the introduction of an allusion into the latter: "Brigitte réveilla le premier clerc, et l'envoya surveiller les bords de la rivière, *devenus fatalement célèbres depuis le suicide d'un jeune homme plein d'avenir, et la mort récente d'une jeune fille séduite"* (*Sou.* I, 253; *Con.* 106). The young man in question is Athanase Granson, who, in *La Vieille Fille* (*Con.* X, 387), had committed suicide when Mlle Cormon's marriage was announced. An addition link is constituted by the pointing-out that a person elsewhere called the "Chevalier" is really the Chevalier de Valois (*Sou.* I, 150; *Con.* 60), an important actor in *La Vieille Fille.* The inserted passages on the coat-of-arms and motto of the D'Esgrignons (cf. above) parallel a similar development for the Troisvilles in the last-mentioned novel (*Con.* X, 265). The passage on Camusot de Marville's finances cited above, while it does not bear upon *La Vieille Fille,* does, however, involve other novels; since the revised form speaks of Camusot de Marville's mother as dead, it echoes the situation of stories written after the Furne edition (where the passage is unchanged)—stories in which the elder Camusot has a second wife.[20]

On the whole, the variations in *Le Cabinet des antiques* are considerable in number. Balzac expended a notable effort on improving the style. The changes involving realistic elements tend to emphasize the original social preoccupations of the novel; and the addition of characters, most of whom are members of the nobility, carries this trend still further. Alterations in fictional elements make the story more distinctly a sequel to *La Vieille Fille;* variations in the latter novel show that a similar effort was there made to combine and harmonize the two works.

VIII. *GAMBARA*
By HENRIETTA GRAYBILL
Editions collated.—

1. 1839, in *Le Cabinet des antiques, Scène de la vie de province, suivie de Gambara,* éd. Souverain, II, 85–267 (*Sou.*).
2. 1846, in the *Comédie humaine,* éd. Furne, Dubochet et Hetzel, XV (Vol. II of the *Etudes philosophiques*), 74–128 (*Fur.*).
3. Conard, XXVIII (Vol. II of the *Etudes philosophiques*), 35–107 (*Con.*).

Gambara, because of its preoccupations with music and its depiction of Italians, is a companion piece to *Massimilla Doni* (*Les Fantaisies de la Gina* would also belong in this class). The first two novels were written in

[20] Cf. Cerfberr et Christophe, *Répertoire de la "Comédie humaine"* (Paris, 1893), p. 77.

1837, shortly after Balzac's return from Italy; both figure together in his correspondence.[21] With *Le Chef-d'œuvre inconnu*, they illustrate how a superabundance of creative power may frustrate creation itself. As studies of master-passions, they are well classified in the *Etudes philosophiques.*

Preliminary and similar variations.—In its first edition *Gambara* was dedicated, in cordial terms, to the Marquis de Belloy, one of Balzac's secretaries at the time of his political aspirations. The Dedication persists in later editions but is reduced to a mere mention of the name: "A Monsieur le Marquis de Belloy." The chapter headings found in the *feuilleton* edition (*Revue et gazette musicale de Paris*, July–August, 1837) and the Souverain are subsequently removed.

Stylistic variations.—The small total number of variations (one hundred and thirty-four) between the Souverain and the Furne editions, and the much smaller number (six) between the Furne and the Conard, seem to indicate that Balzac did not consider *Gambara* as in great need of revision, either because of its relative unimportance in the scheme of the *Comédie humaine* or because he had worked it out more carefully in the first writing than was usually his custom. Of the purely stylistic variations, those affecting sentence structure are, as usual, prominent; changes to longer and to shorter sentences occur in almost equal numbers, although the tendency to longer and more solid sentences is somewhat stronger (cf. *Sou.* 106–7, *Con.* 42). Most of the changes in word order occur in clauses introduced by *dont*, the handling of which troubled Balzac constantly.

But the great bulk of stylistic and linguistic changes are those made by substituting one part of speech for another, for purposes of clearness and accuracy. The few noun changes are motivated by a search for the *mot propre;* such is the case in the description of Andrea's first meeting with Marianna:

Trop sérieusement épris pour ne pas épier le moindre indice de *retour*, le comte se crut aimé en se voyant si bien compris. [*Sou.* 124]

Trop sérieusement épris pour ne pas épier le moindre indice de *complaisance*, le comte se crut aimé en se voyant si bien compris. [*Con.* 50]

The revised form of the following passage makes the allusion more specific:

Sa pauvre femme est réduite à travailler pour toute sorte de monde, *le monde de la rue!* [*Sou.* 113]

Sa pauvre femme est réduite à travailler pour toute sorte de monde, *le monde de la borne!* [*Con.* 45]

---

[21] *LEt.*, I, 398, 407, 412.

Whereas the first class of people is indeterminate, the second can refer only to prostitutes. Again, Andrea speaks of Meyerbeer's opera, *Robert-le-Diable*, as "un tableau musical" (*Sou.* 218), but this phrase later becomes the more appropriate "une composition si vaste" (*Con.* 87). Sometimes the meaning may be completely altered by a verbal change, as in this passage on Gambara's ruling passion, music, where it is difficult to divine the meaning of an "entière maîtresse":

Gambara s'était donné ... à l'orgueilleuse et *entière* maîtresse ... [*Sou.* 164]	Gambara s'était donné ... à l'orgueilleuse et *vindicative* maîtresse ... [*Con.* 66]

Again, the change of "cette musique *nouvelle*" to "cette musique *impossible*" (*Sou.* 194, *Con.* 78), as applied to Gambara's art, represents a shift in Balzac's point of view with regard to his character's achievements. Of the eighteen noun-for-pronoun substitutions, at least twelve serve to elucidate obscure references; they indicate a distinct interest in clarity of presentation. Verbs are changed in tense or are replaced one by another, but without the striking improvement usually resulting from such changes.

Realistic variations.—Whether in the number or in the significance of such variations, *Gambara* is by no means comparable to works in the *Etudes de mœurs*. Yet these changes are more variegated and more representative than their counterparts in *Massimilla Doni*. A few of them affect numbers; the length of Andrea's political exile in Paris is made much less definite in the later editions by changing "depuis *trois ans*" to "depuis *quelques années*" (*Sou.*109, *Con.* 43); perhaps Balzac feared, with the story dated as taking place in 1831, to make other dates too exact. Twice numbers are increased in size, a variation typical of Balzac's tendency to exaggeration of his statements; a guess at the number of opera houses in Europe is raised from forty to one hundred (*Sou.* 135, *Con.* 55), and a prediction of the "run" of Meyerbeer's opera, from two hundred to five hundred performances (*Sou.* 243, *Con.* 99). The local color of the story is made more convincing through the adoption of several additional Italian terms; "*le* signor" is changed to the more correct "*il* signor" (*Sou.* 112, *Con.* 44; cf. *Sou.* 111), and "la patrie" to "la cara patria" (*Sou.* 210, *Con.* 86). In the same way, an effort is made to correct and enlarge portions of the musical theory found in the story. The following are examples of technical erudition: the addition in "L'harmonie règne souverainement, *au lieu d'être le fonds sur lequel doivent se détacher les groupes du tableau musical*" (*Sou.* 218, *Con.* 87) and the change of "ton relatif" to "temps relatif" (*Sou.* 178, *Con.* 71) in a study of the opera.

A second group of realistic variations may be classified under the head of fictional technique. There are, however, but few examples of each type. By the use of additional detail Balzac completes a description or a characterization; the addition of "l'air écossais" in the following sentence not only clears up a vague reference but also shows Gambara's concern with the various ramifications of the musical field: "Le morceau de: *Gloire à la Providence!* ressemble un peu trop à un morceau de Haendel, le chœur des chevaliers allant au combat est parent de *l'air écossais dans la Dame blanche*"[22] (*Sou.* 252, *Con.* 103). Again, the added phrase here intensifies the scorn of Gambara's attitude toward the Italian masters: "Grâce à Dieu, je suis en dehors de ces pauvretés *plus ou moins* mélodiques!" (*Sou.* 138, *Con.* 56). In another direction intercalated speech-words (*Sou.* 223 and 239, *Con.* 90 and 97) separate more distinctly the dialogue from preceding descriptive passages. In still another direction there is one example making for consistency within the story:

Je conviens avec vous que la science *règne en souveraine* dans l'opéra de Meyerbeer ...   [*Sou.* 220]

Je conviens avec vous que la science *est grande* dans l'opéra de Meyerbeer ...   [*Con.* 88]

The original statement was in contradiction with a remark made several pages earlier that "*L'harmonie* règne souverainement" (*Con.* 87); hence it was changed. The desire to avoid repetitious phraseology may also have motivated the change. Finally, we may point to one insertion which forms a more solid link with the companion novel, *Massimilla Doni*. In their first forms these two works had been connected (cf. *Con.* XXVII, 428, and XXVIII, 106). But the added sentence, epitomizing, as it does, the story of Massimilla and her husband, makes this linking considerably stronger:

—Ne lui écrivez pas, madame, dit Marianna, et que Dieu vous conserve toujours belle.

—*Chargeons-nous d'eux?* demanda la princesse à son mari, car cet homme est resté fidèle à *l'IDEAL que nous avons tué.*

En voyant la pièce d'or, le vieux Gambara pleura ...   [*Sou.* 266, *Con.* 107]

To summarize, then, the total number of variations in *Gambara* is not large, even for a novelette of seventy pages. In neither the Furne nor the Conard editions are there variations which change the identity of a character, and only once is a passage inserted for a closer co-ordination of *Gambara* with the *Comédie humaine*. Nor are there changes which affect

---

[22] The names of the compositions are italicized by Balzac.

the characterizations or the action of the story. Perhaps by 1837 the structure of the *Comédie humaine* and the place of this novel in it were sufficiently clear in the author's mind to obviate thoroughgoing alterations.

IX. *MASSIMILLA DONI*

By SISTER MARIE PHILIP HALEY

Editions collated.—

1. 1839, in *Une Fille d'Ève suivie de Massimilla Doni*, éd. Souverain, II, 71–303 (*Ève*).[23]

2. 1840, in *Le Livre des douleurs*, éd. Souverain, Vols. II (pp. 119–210) and III (*Liv.* II and *Liv.* III).

3. 1846, in the *Comédie humaine*, éd. Furne, Dubochet et Hetzel, XV (Vol. II of the *Etudes philosophiques*), 1–73 (*Fur.*). Dated 1845, this volume did not appear until October, 1846.

4. Conard, XXVII (Vol. I of the *Etudes philosophiques*), 375–471 (*Con.*).

In *Massimilla Doni* Balzac writes a philosophical novel in which, he says, "La fantaisie ... dominera d'une manière sensible, et s'opposera vigoureusement à la constante réalité qui sera le cachet des Etudes de mœurs."[24] It is not surprising, then, that Balzac's changes are seldom toward realism and that his attention should have been directed toward improvement of style almost exclusively.

Before taking up the variations themselves, however, we must discuss a problem which arose from the study of them. This problem concerns the priority of the 1839 or the 1840 text. There can be no doubt that the edition of 1839 was the first to appear and that it constitutes the genuine *princeps;* yet it was apparent from the comparison of these two editions that the one of 1840 represented an earlier state of the text than that of 1839. Besides, Furne is based on 1839, thus indicating that the sequence is 1840–1839–Furne. A few words on the composition and publication of the novel are necessary to explain this paradoxical situation.

Balzac began the writing of the work either during his visit to Italy in the spring of 1837 or immediately after his return to Paris. For on May 24, twenty-one days after his arrival home, he announced the completion of the novel; and the next day he sent the copy to the printer, Charles

---

[23] The copy at the University of Chicago bears the date 1840 on the title-page; otherwise it agrees in all details with the 1839 edition as described by Carteret, in *Le Trésor du bibliophile romantique et moderne* (Paris, 1924), I, 74, and is apparently a reprint of the latter. We shall speak of this as "1839."

[24] Suppressed Preface to *Ève*, I, 38.

Plon of the firm of Béthune et Plon.[25] The work was at that time complete except for the chapter on *Mosè*, which was not written until much later. By July 19, 1837, Balzac had finished correcting the proofs; but publication was indefinitely held up by the decision to write an additional chapter.[26] This chapter was not terminated until two years later, when it appeared separately in *La France musicale* of August 25, 1839, under the title of "Une Représentation du *Mosè* de Rossini, à Venise." The work as a whole appeared first in the *Fille d'Ève* edition of 1839, over the Souverain imprint; but it is significant to note that the printer of this edition was E. Jacquin of Fontainebleau. On the other hand, the *Livre des douleurs* edition of our story, also published by Souverain, was printed by Béthune et Plon—the firm which had set the story (except for the interpolated chapter iii) as early as July, 1837.

Briefly, then, the situation is as follows: *Massimilla Doni*, with the exception of one chapter, was set by Béthune et Plon in May–July, 1837; but the edition made from their type was not put on sale until 1840. In the meantime, the *Fille d'Ève* edition, printed by E. Jacquin, had been offered for sale in 1839; the text of this edition consists of the Béthune et Plon text plus corrections by Balzac. In both cases Souverain was the publisher; he merely allowed the later form of *Massimilla Doni* to appear with *Une Fille d'Ève* while awaiting the completion of the five volumes of *Le Livre des douleurs*, Volumes II and III of which contained the earlier form of the story. The variations will bear out these conclusions.[27]

Changes in préliminaires and makeup.—The preliminary and mechanical variations, if read from 1840 to 1839, are in accord with Balzac's usual procedure, as revealed by the study of variations in other novels. The *Livre* text is the only version with chapter titles; there are four chapters: "Les Deux Amours," "Les Extrêmes Jouissances," "L'Opéra de Mosè," and "Les Deux Guérisons." *Ève* preserves the chapter divisions i–iv but without chapter headings; all divisions are suppressed in the Furne edition. The dedication to the Bavarian musician Jacques Strunz is absent

[25] *LEt.*, I, 398–99; cf. Lovenjoul, "Les *Etudes philosophiques* de Honoré de Balzac," *RHL*, 14th year (1907), p. 437.

[26] *LEt.*, I, 412, 434.

[27] Chapter iii of the novel presents a special problem. It is evident from a letter to Souverain (Hastings, *Balzac and Souverain* [New York, 1927], pp. 18–19) that the latter had proofs of this section before its appearance in *La France musicale*. But whether the journal form or the *Livre* edition constitutes the original text could be ascertained only by comparison with the periodical, which was not available to the writer.

from *Livre;* it appears first in *Ève* and then in all subsequent editions. In *Livre* the date given to the story by Balzac is "Paris, 25 mai 1837"; this is in accord with the dated manuscript. But *Ève* changes this date to "Paris, 25 mai 1839," altering only the year; month and day should also have been changed, since Balzac did not complete the story until August of 1839. A preface to *Une Fille d'Ève* and *Massimilla Doni*, dated "Aux Jardies, février 1839," opens Volume I of *Ève* and justifies the appearance of an *Etude de mœurs* and an *Etude philosophique* in the same edition. Finally, the changes between *Livre* and *Ève* include eighteen cases of the typical combination of paragraphs, and those between *Ève* and Furne an additional eighteen cases. The mechanical changes, then, point conclusively to the same order as derived from the study of the publications as a whole: to wit, *Livre–Ève*–Furne.

Stylistic and linguistic variations.—Of the one hundred changes in the *Livre-Ève* stage of the variations, thirty-one seem to show improvement in the *Ève* version. For example: Emilio, finding his palace lighted up, hurries through the peristyle

pour *reconnaître* la cause de cette singulière aventure.   [*Liv.* II, 160]

pour *connaître* la cause de cette singulière aventure.   [*Ève* 180, *Con.* 389][28]

A loose and incorrect construction is avoided in *Ève:*

Par momens, il lui [Emilio] suffisait de voir les beaux cheveux noirs de cette tête adorée serrés par un simple cercle d'or *et s'échapper* en tresses luisantes ...
    [*Liv.* II, 137]

Par momens, il lui suffisait de voir les beaux cheveux noirs de cette tête adorée serrés par un simple cercle d'or, *s'échappant* en tresses luisantes ...
    [*Ève* 90, *Con.* 381]

Not all the changes made are demonstrably for the better, but they can usually be justified. The reader will note, in most of the examples involving the first two editions, that it would be difficult to accept them as changes from *Ève* to *Livre* (i.e., from 1839 to 1840), whereas they are absolutely consistent with Balzac's habitual method when taken as changes from *Livre* to *Ève*. In our study of variations, examples will be selected from all stages of the revisions and grouped together.

Variations affecting sentence structure total seventeen; their result is usually a more intimate relationship between the components of the sentence:

[28] To show the continuation of the *Ève* readings even in the definitive text, Conard references will be given in all cases of *Livre-Ève* changes.

La Tinti *fut* rappelée *et* reparut seule, elle fut saluée par des acclamations ... [*Fur.* 60]

La Tinti rappelée reparut seule, elle fut saluée par des acclamations ... [*Con.* 452]

Cette illustre cantatrice était une simple servante d'auberge. *Sa* voix merveilleuse avait surpris un grand seigneur en voyage ... [*Liv.* II, 147]

Cette illustre cantatrice était une simple servante d'auberge, *dont la* voix merveilleuse avait surpris un grand seigneur en voyage. [*Ève* 98, *Con.* 385]

Transposition often produces a gain in clarity and smoothness, as shown below, where the first construction was manifestly incorrect:

Je rends *à notre mère son enfant*, l'Adriatique recevra mon dernier soupir, *après avoir tenté mon dernier effort.* [*Ève* 249]

Après avoir tenté mon dernier effort, je rendrai *son enfant à notre mère*, l'Adriatique recevra mon dernier soupir! [*Fur.* 56]

Among rhetorical changes we may include elaborations, exclamations, interrogations, and figures of speech. Elaboration frequently results in definiteness and clearness: "Jamais Rossini ne s'élèvera plus haut *que dans cette prière*, il fera tout aussi bien, jamais mieux ... " (*Ève* 264, *Fur.* 61). Interjections are added several times in the *Ève*-Furne stage; and, to avoid a pronominal ambiguity, there is one instance of a change from a declarative to a semi-interrogative sentence:

L'auteur n'ose pas dire le dénouement de cette aventure, il est trop horriblement bourgeois. [*Fur.* 73]

Comment dire le dénouement de cette aventure, car il est horriblement bourgeois. [*Con.* 470]

Figures of speech may be added or omitted; one drawn from the field of art is introduced into Furne: "Mes yeux, *comme ceux de sainte Cécile*, aperçoivent des anges ... " (*Ève* 294, *Fur.* 70). A confused and exuberant figure is deleted from a passage on Emilio's love for Clarina:

Son âme, son cœur, sa raison, toutes ses volontés se refusaient à l'infidélité; mais la brutale et capricieuse infidélité *se dressait flagrante, échevelée, furieuse, par la toute-puissance de la Nature.* [*Liv.* II, 165]

Son âme, son cœur, sa raison, toutes ses volontés se refusaient à l'Infidélité; mais la brutale et capricieuse Infidélité *dominait son âme.* [*Ève* 112, *Con.* 391]

The bulk of the variants found in the four successive texts are verbal changes that will be classified under the parts of speech. Adjective additions intensify or clarify the thought, while substitutions bring exactness or elegance—for example, the change from "un décret *impérial*" to "un décret *autrichien*" (*Ève* 100, *Fur.* 8). In one passage Balzac comes progressively closer to the color that he wishes to describe:

bassins clairs où nageaient des pois-
sons *dorés*.   [*Liv.* II, 132]

> bassins clairs où nagent des poissons
> *d'azur et d'or*.   [*Ève* 87]

> > bassins clairs où nagent des poissons
> > d'azur et *de cinabre*.   [*Fur.* 3]

Changes in possessives, articles, adverbs, and conjunctions are, in this story, of little interest to style as such; they merely bring the text into conformity with the rules of usage. But modifications in nouns are significant since they generally work toward euphony and definiteness; the latter is well illustrated by this example:

Massimilla regarda *tout* autour d'elle, fut conduite par sa mère à la Pergola, dans *le monde*, aux Cascine, partout ... [*Liv.* II, 139]	Massimilla regarda *le monde qui se pressait* autour d'elle, fut conduite par sa mère à la Pergola, dans *quelques maisons diplomatiques*, aux Cascine, partout ... [*Ève* 92, *Con.* 382]

Pronoun alterations result in greater clarity, as a rule, while those affecting prepositions make for smoothness. As usual, vigorous verbs supplant commonplace ones—"accoururent" for "vinrent" (*Ève* 303, *Fur.* 73)—and tenses are frequently modified.

Summing up our results thus far, we find that Balzac modified the original version of the novel by some four hundred stylistic variations—a comparatively small total—with obvious gains in clarity, smoothness, and emphasis. The majority of the changes occur between the *Ève* and the Furne editions. The one hundred variants between *Livre* and *Ève* are found almost entirely in the first chapter, and they bear out our conclusions as to the chronology of these two texts.[29]

Realistic and fictional variations.—The "materialistic" changes which are usually so prominent in the revisions are here represented by only one variation, which makes the heroine a year younger (*Ève* 94, *Fur.* 6). There are, however, a number of alterations involving detail of one kind or another. Some of these introduce additional facts which contribute to the concreteness of the description: "... jamais la fée n'a montré de plus

[29] A study of chapter iii for *Livre-Ève* changes shows that the only variations between them are mechanical—having to do with spelling, punctuation, accents, etc. They are thus of no help in solving the question of priority referred to above, p. 405 n.

beaux bras, n'a souri plus amoureusement, n'a mieux relevé sa tunique *jusqu'à mi-jambe*" (*Ève* 195, *Fur.* 39). Others are causal in nature: " ... le médecin cherchait à comprendre et comprit; *car il appartenait à cette pléiade de beaux génies de l'Ecole de Paris, d'où le vrai médecin sort aussi profond métaphysicien que puissant analyste*" (*Ève* 196, *Fur.* 39–40). Occasionally, a superfluous detail may be deleted from the text: "Sur le devant, toutes les loges *de la salle* sont drapées en soie ... " (*Liv.* III, 11; *Ève* 155; *Con.* 408); "Mais comme celui qui dépasse le but *avec sa flèche* en est aussi loin que celui dont le trait n'y arrive pas ... " (*Liv.* II, 143; *Ève* 95; *Con.* 383).

Along the line of fictional technique there are two developments worthy of attention. The first has to do with the problem of dialogue. Balzac's ordinary procedure is to develop a conversation or to transform exposition into direct speech; an example of the latter follows:

Il me semble avoir assisté à la libération de l'Italie, pensait un Milanais. Cette musique relève les têtes courbées, et donne de l'espérance aux cœurs les plus endormis. [*Ève* 264]	Il me semble avoir assisté à la libération de l'Italie, pensait un Milanais. —Cette musique relève les têtes courbées, et donne de l'espérance aux cœurs endormis, *s'écriait un Romagnol.* [*Fur.* 61]

Speech-words, when inserted, remove the danger of ambiguity (*Ève* 285, *Fur.* 67). In two instances the vulgarity of Clarina's speech is attenuated by omission, and a third change in this direction attests Balzac's concern with the charges of immorality which were then being leveled at him:[30] "Au milieu des torrens d'amour *de cette coucherie*, il s'élevait un rocher contre lequel se brisait l'onde" (*Liv.* II, 186; *Ève* 130; *Con.* 399). Two other changes in dialogue will best be treated under the second group of fictional changes.

This group affects principally the character of Massimilla Doni, as contrasted with that of a French doctor. At two successive performances of the Venice opera she has the opportunity of carrying on extended conversations with him and of comparing French and Italian points of view. The first of these conversations is broken up by added interruptions and interjections (*Ève* 168, *Fur.* 30). The second is amplified by the insertion

---

[30] On January 22, 1838, he wrote to Mme Hanska: "Vous ne sauriez croire avec quelle résignation j'envisage les mauvaises et méchantes sottises que cette œuvre de *Massimilla Doni* m'attirera. Vu d'un côté, le sujet donne prise à la critique: on dira que je suis un homme obscène. Mais, voyez le sujet psychique: c'est une merveille, selon moi ..." (*LEt.*, I, 457).

of several speeches: "Si vous vouliez me dire d'où vient leur folie, je les guérirais, s'écria le médecin.—Depuis quand un grand médecin n'est-il plus un devin? demanda railleusement la duchesse" (*Ève* 252, *Fur.* 57). After the first meeting, Massimilla's intelligence and wit are made the subject of remarks by outsiders both at the opera and at the Café Florian:

> Après quelques instans, pendant lesquels la conversation s'anima entre le Français et la duchesse, qui se montra finement éloquente, les Italiens se retirèrent un à un *pour aller dire dans toutes les loges que la Cataneo qui passait pour être una donna di gran spirito avait battu sur la question d'Italie, un habile médecin français. Ce fut la nouvelle de la soirée.* Quand le Français se vit seul entre le prince et la duchesse, il comprit qu'il fallait les laisser seuls et sortit.
>
> [*Ève.* 181, *Fur.* 34]

The matter is mentioned again among the subjects of discussion at the café: "*puis la lutte entre la duchesse et le médecin français*" (*Ève* 186, *Fur.* 36). These additions are evidence of Balzac's interest in developing the depiction of his heroine both through her own speech and through the opinions of others about her.

The realistic and fictional variations are thus rather limited and one-sided in character. Many of the types ordinarily found are here omitted; there are no changes affecting reappearing personages or linking, although at this period Balzac was much concerned with multiplying devices of solidification. The reason, as has been suggested, is probably the nature and the setting of the story itself, which remains apart from the tendencies of most of his other works.

X. *LES SECRETS DE LA PRINCESSE DE CADIGNAN*
By OLIVER E. JACKSON

Editions collated.—

1. 1840, as *La Princesse parisienne*, in *Le Foyer de l'Opéra*, éd. Souverain, Vol. I (*Sou.*).

2. 1844, in the *Comédie humaine*, éd. Furne, Dubochet et Hetzel, XI (Vol. III of the *Scènes de la vie parisienne*), 81–132 (*Fur.*).

3. Conard, XVI (Vol. IV of the *Scènes de la vie parisienne*), 299–368 (*Con.*).

This *nouvelle* is of importance since it supplies the conclusion to two brilliant careers in the *Comédie humaine*, that of the famous Diane de Maufrigneuse and that of the illustrious Daniel d'Arthez. The emphasis, however, is not so much on the plot elements as on the characterization of the heroine; the story is really another *étude de femme*, comparable in this respect to two other novelettes by Balzac.

Preliminary variations.—The story is called *La Princesse parisienne* on the title-page and *Une Princesse parisienne* on the half-title of the Souverain edition. Here, the Dedication reads: "A Théophile Gautier, Son ami, H. de Balzac." In Furne the definitive title is adopted, and the Dedication simplified to "A Théophile Gautier." Chapter headings are suppressed as usual, and there are thirteen changes in the paragraphing, making the story more compact.

Changes in style and language.—Virtually all of these variations are made between the Souverain and the Furne editions, since only six out of two hundred and seventeen such changes are found between the Furne and the Conard. A number of the alterations are minor revisions, involving addition or deletion of conjunctions, pronouns, prepositions, etc. Others really make a contribution to the style, as does this insertion of an adverb: " ... ces deux corrupteurs plaignaient d'Arthez ... et stimulaient *vivement* sa curiosité" (*Sou.* 81, *Con.* 320). Often, for reasons of definiteness, clarity, or emphasis, a pronoun or a common noun will be replaced by a proper noun; here, the italicized phrase supplants "cette rencontre": "Jamais le hasard ne s'était permis de préparations plus savantes que pour *la rencontre de d'Arthez et de madame de Cadignan*" (*Sou.* 95, *Con.* 323). Similarly, "le duc de Maufrigneuse" becomes "Georges de Maufrigneuse" (*Sou.* 29, *Con.* 306). Among noun changes introducing the *mot propre* the following is worthy of notice:

Le marquis d'Esgrignon ... a fini par faire un très beau mariage ... [*Sou.* 206]	Le marquis d'Esgrignon ... a fini par faire un très-*riche* mariage ... [*Con.* 354]

Other substitutions involve a whole phrase; in them the improvement is usually patent:

—*Voilà de Marsay bientôt mort,* ... et avec lui votre dernier espoir de fortune pour le duc de Maufrigneuse ... [*Sou.* 44]	—*Nous perdrons bientôt de Marsay* ... et avec lui *s'en ira* votre dernier espoir de fortune pour le duc de Maufrigneuse ... [*Con.* 309]
Ces paroles ... *étaient celles d'un ange de sensibilité.* [*Sou.* 174]	Ces paroles ... *révélaient une sensibilité angélique.* [*Con.* 345]

Variations in the verb play their part in improving the style; they may concern tense, agreement, or usage. In a few cases Balzac's predilection for the *mot propre* is again evident:

D'après la connaissance qu'elle avait prise ... elle *avait deviné* que ce désir ne serait pas assez tôt exprimé ... [*Sou.* 142–43]	D'après la connaissance qu'elle avait prise ... elle *avait soupçonné* que ce désir ne serait pas assez tôt exprimé ... [*Con.* 337]

Transpositions are usually motivated by the desire to bring related parts of the sentence more closely together; in some cases, as here, the gain in clarity is offset by a loss in the unity of the sentence:

Quand la duchesse d'Uxelles maria sa fille au duc de Maufrigneuse, elle *avait quarante-cinq ans, et depuis long-temps* assistait ... aux succès de son ancien ami. [*Sou.* 162]	La duchesse d'Uxelles *avait quarante-cinq* ans quand elle maria sa fille au duc de Maufrigneuse, elle assistait donc *depuis long-temps* ... aux succès de son ancien ami. [*Con.* 343]

Frequently a revision, while correcting usage or style, detracts from the original vigor of the expression.

Realistic and fictional variations.—In the present novel, only a relatively small number of the realistic qualities usually found is in evidence; the principal function of the work is character portrayal rather than the depiction of *mœurs;* and hence the subject matter limits, in a sense, the application of the realistic method. However, the comparatively few categories of this kind appearing in the revisions are represented by a large number of cases. Such is the situation with regard to time. Most of these alterations result from the important change of date for the beginning of the action from "un des derniers beaux jours du mois d'octobre 1835" to "un des premiers beaux jours du mois de mai 1833" (*Sou.* 43, *Con.* 309); the new date brings the story closer to the Revolution of July, when Diane's adventures, along with her fortune, came to an end. Consequently, a statement about those adventures must also be modified:

En 1835, cinq années avaient jeté leurs tas de neige sur les aventures de la duchesse de Maufrigneuse ... [*Sou.* 24]	*En 1832, trois années* avaient jeté leurs tas de neige sur les aventures de la duchesse de Maufrigneuse ... [*Con.* 304][31]

The period elapsed between the revolution and the action of the story, a period which Diane spent in retirement, is also reduced from four to three years (*Sou.* 46, *Con.* 310). Finally, Diane's age is reduced from thirty-seven to thirty-six years (*Sou.* 25, *Con.* 304), and the date of her marriage becomes 1814 instead of 1815 (*Sou.* 193, *Con.* 349; also *Sou.* 157,

---

[31] The change here is not absolutely consistent, since the difference in date is three years and that in time only two years. Similar inconsistencies will be noted in other time-changes; they most probably resulted from Balzac's haste in revising.

Con. 342). This foreshortening in the events of Diane's life affects also that of her son, whose marriage is placed five, instead of seven, years in the future (*Sou.* 25, *Con.* 304). In another direction a plausible change is made in the length of D'Arthez' courtship before he casts formality aside; "après quinze jours" is replaced by "après soixante jours" (*Sou.* 185, *Con.* 348).

Against these numerous alterations in time elements we find only one affecting money matters; D'Arthez' fortune, originally 20,000 *livres de rente,* is increased to 30,000 (*Sou.* 82, *Con.* 320), to correspond with the general rise in his fortunes. Sociological changes are also rather sparse; we find two of them offering characteristic comment on the bourgeoisie: "A l'abri de ces occupations, elle put tromper l'un de ses premiers amants, de Marsay, le plus influent personnage de la politique *bourgeoise intronisée en juillet 1830*" (*Sou.* 36–37, *Con.* 308); "elles [les grandes dames] arrivent à être, dans cette situation, comme des statues antiques; si elles gardaient un chiffon, elles seraient impudiques. *La bourgeoisie essaie toujours de s'envelopper*" (*Sou.* 241, *Con.* 363). A third shift in social viewpoint affects a speech of Diane's, who characterizes her opinions first as "aristo-cratiques," later as "monarchiques" (*Sou.* 104, *Con.* 326). Only one animalism is modified in the course of the revisions, by means of a rather grotesque addition: "Ce fut leste et net comme un geste de chatte *prenant une souris*" (*Sou.* 184, *Con.* 348).

Alterations in dialogue, making for closer conformity to reality, are somewhat more numerous; one of Nucingen's speeches is translated from French into his own particular Alsacian, familiar to readers through such works as *La Maison Nucingen:*

—C'est sans doute pour elle que vous négligez la chambre ... [*Sou.* 244]	—C'esde sans titte bir elle que fus néclichez la Jampre ... [*Con.* 364]

Weird as the product is, Balzac's phonetics were thoroughgoing. An impassioned declaration of D'Arthez to Diane gains in dramatic effect through an elaboration: "Combien de fois n'ai-je pas reçu la pluie en accompagnant votre voiture jusque chez vous ... pour nous maintenir au même point sur une ligne parallèle, *afin de vous voir ... de vous admirer!*" (*Sou.* 107, *Con.* 327). In Diane's long description of her past life, the phrase "une jeune fille aime toujours à *jouer à la maternité*" is altered to the more colloquial "une jeune fille aime toujours à *jouer à la maman*"[32] (*Sou.* 202, *Con.* 352). One important *dossier* change occurs; in the first

---

[32] Italics here, as in the speech of Nucingen quoted above, are Balzac's.

edition D'Arthez is presented first at a soiree, and then a four-page discussion of him follows. In the later forms the paragraph introducing the *dossier* is split up; the second part, looking forward to the soiree, is put first, then the *dossier* itself is intercalated, then the rest of the paragraph is made to lead directly into the soiree (*Sou.* 69–70, *Con.* 317–23); the necessary changes in wording are made to correspond.

So much for realistic variations, broadly speaking. Those concerning fictional technique are almost as numerous and diversified. We might point first to the new conclusion appended to the novel; it is significant as epitomizing Balzac's attitude toward the indeterminate ending: "D'Arthez ne se montre qu'à la Chambre. Enfin, ses publications sont devenues excessivement rares. *Est-ce un dénouement? Oui, pour les gens d'esprit; non, pour ceux qui veulent tout savoir*" (*Sou.* 258, *Con.* 368). Again, the note of impersonality is enhanced by the ascription of an idea, originally given as the author's, to one of his characters, Michel Chrestien: " ... plus une femme était accomplie, plus elle perdait à leurs yeux; *car selon lui*, leur imagination n'avait rien à y faire" (*Sou.* 77, *Con.* 319). Most of the fictional changes, however, belong to the general practice of linking; one aspect of this is the introduction of narrative elements harking back to other stories. In the following example the revised version agrees with events related in *La Muse du département* (1843), where Diane, in financial difficulties, is obliged to sell her château of Anzy to the La Baudraye family. Here Diane says:

J'avais une belle fortune ... en forêts, que la révolution avait oublié de vendre *en Alsace* ... , le théâtre de la guerre était là. [*Sou.* 197]	J'avais une belle fortune ... en forêts, que la Révolution avait oublié de vendre *en Nivernais ... et qui dépendaient du château d'Anzy ...* [*Con.* 351]

New data on Lucien de Rubempré, added in the Furne marginalia, correspond to his love affairs as developed in *Splendeurs et misères des courtisanes;* Diane is just finishing a remark with regard to Henri de Marsay:

Nous n'aimons jamais les hommes qui se font nos instituteurs, ils froissent trop nos petites vanités.

—*Et ce petit misérable qui s'est pendu?*

—*Lucien? c'était un Antinoüs et un grand poëte, je l'ai bien consciencieusement adoré, j'aurais pu devenir heureuse, mais il aimait une fille et je l'ai cédé à madame de Sérisy; s'il avait voulu m'aimer, l'aurais-je cédé?*

—*Quelle bizarrerie! vous heurter contre une Esther!*

—*Elle était plus belle que moi, dit la princesse.* Voici bientôt trois années que je passe dans une solitude entière ... [*Fur.* 88, *Con.* 310]

But already in the Furne edition Rubempré had been inserted into a list of Diane's lovers (*Sou.* 220, *Con.* 358), as had also Ronquerolles (*Sou.* 27–28, *Con.* 305). Another elaboration in Conard brings in two other reappearing persons by way of comparison: "Le génie seul a la foi de l'enfance, la religion de l'amour, et se laisse volontiers bander les yeux. *Voyez Canalis et la duchesse de Chaulieu*" (*Fur.* 90, *Con.* 313). The Marquise de Cinq-Cygne and her daughter Berthe are also mentioned (*Sou.* 45, *Con.* 309).

Les Secrets de la princesse de Cadignan, although rather short and limited in content, nevertheless presents a very representative group of changes, both stylistic and realistic. The former are the standard variations that we have encountered in so many studies; the latter, however, seem to show an increased preoccupation with the problem of harmonizing the story, both within itself and with other works of the *Human Comedy*. Most of the realistic, as well as the fictional, changes could be explained on this basis.

XI. ADDITIONAL MATERIALS FROM OTHER TALES

The following brief remarks present, in a greatly condensed form, the conclusions resulting from studies of sixteen additional stories. They are arranged chronologically according to the dates of the first editions.

"*L'Enfant maudit*" (*1831*).[33] —This story was expanded, in 1836, from a short descriptive sketch into a complete tale. Hence, the variations between the Gosselin and Werdet editions effected not a revision but a thorough re-writing of the original Part I. This re-writing involved extensive changes in style—in the direction of greater smoothness, compactness, clearness, and precision—and in fictional elements. The latter included anticipatory statements, additions to plot and to character portrayal, and changes in tone and in psychology. These trends were further developed in the preparations for Furne, with respect to both parts. It is noteworthy that, in spite of the fact that this story is set in the sixteenth century, Balzac linked it to the world of the nineteenth-century *Comédie humaine*, introducing ancestors for later heroes. One such revision, giving the name of Rubempré to the hero, had later to be withdrawn; Balzac discovered that, since the persons bearing the name died without leaving offspring, it would be impossible to connect them up with the nineteenth-century Rubempré lineage.

[33] Editions collated (by J. D. Brennard): 1831, *Revue des deux mondes;* 1831, Gosselin; 1837, Werdet; 1846, Furne, Dubochet et Hetzel; Conard.

"*Jésus-Christ en Flandre*" and "*L'Eglise*" (*1831*).[34]—Besides the customary stylistic and linguistic variations, the majority of which occur between the Gosselin and Werdet editions, this tale offers interesting examples of changes in both realistic and technical elements. With respect to the latter, the story presented a special problem, since in its final form it combined two originally distinct narratives. These two were not amalgamated until the Furne edition, and at that time Balzac made a number of changes in order to harmonize them in time, in place, in ideology. In the last connection Balzac so modified the work as to make it represent his current ideas on religion and on monarchy—ideas which he had but recently expressed in the *Avant-propos*. Other variations indicate Balzac's constant striving for accurate and apt characterization, especially the eight changes in the description of Jesus. As for realism, the variants demonstrate again the author's efforts toward impersonality, authenticity, and accuracy and his interest in sociological generalizations.

"*Madame Firmiani*" (*1832*).[35]—We here find a resemblance to other stories already studied, in the fact that reappearing characters, absent from the primitive form, are introduced into later editions; much of the aristocracy of the *Comédie humaine* is ultimately incorporated. But, with one exception, the change was not effected until the Furne edition of 1842; only the "princesse de Blamont-Chauvry" was written into Béchet. The same holds true for realistic variations in general: they were much more numerous, proportionately, in the Béchet-Furne stage than in the Gosselin-Béchet. This may be explained by the fact that in 1835, at the time he was revising his first edition, Balzac's scheme for the *Human Comedy* was not so fully developed as it was to be later. These realistic variations deal with matters of chronology, of money, of place, and with generalizations on social types. An interesting group of changes affects the development of characterization, especially with respect to the heroine.

"*La Femme abandonnée*" and "*La Grenadière*" (*1833*).[36]—The majority of the variations in these two stories are, as usual, linguistic and stylistic. There are surprisingly few changes affecting realistic elements, and practically none which serve to form links with the rest of Balzac's work. The

[34] Editions collated (by Carl O. Hedeen): 1831, Gosselin; 1836, Werdet; Conard.

[35] Editions collated (by Miss Stella M. Coesfeld and Miss Helen Williams): 1832, Gosselin; 1835, Béchet; Conard.

[36] Editions collated (by N. E. Saxe): 1833, Béchet; Conard.

plot of *La Femme abandonnée* forms a partial sequel to *Le Père Goriot;* that of *La Grenadière*, a sequel to *Le Lys dans la vallée*. The actual task of linking was done at the time of composition of the longer works, both of which presented the main events in the lives of characters earlier treated in the short stories. Hence, there is here only one variant affecting reappearing characters; its effect is to replace historical families by Balzacian families.

"*Le Médecin de campagne*" (*1833*).[37]—Of the nine chapters for which variations were studied, the first three showed the most extensive revisions of stylistic elements—revisions bearing on sentence structure, on rhetorical devices, such as amplification, condensation, and repetition, and on parts of speech. The proportion of realistic and technical changes was larger in the succeeding chapters. The longest additions were to passages of a sociological import, to the disquisitions on religion, universal suffrage, the professions, and so on; this was to be expected, granted the considerable place of theoretical considerations in the whole concept of the work. On the fictional side there are important contributions to characterization through the addition of detail and of facts about milieu. It is again surprising to note that there are no changes affecting reappearing characters and that in its final version the novel still remains independent of the *Comédie humaine*.[38]

"*Ferragus, Chef des dévorants*" (*1834*).[39]—The first episode of the *Histoire des Treize* contains a general introduction to the trilogy.[40] Among its significant variations we may single out those affecting dialogue and producing greater realism in conversation; those concerning reappearing characters, which add seven to the original eleven; and those involving developments in characterization. Several notable changes improve the story artistically. In one case an episode similar to another in *Gobseck* was deleted in order to avoid repetition. In a second case an episode (the finding of a suicide's body) was shortened considerably, since the incident was not directly connected with the central action of the story. This striving for artistic excellence was, as usual, manifested by a number of revisions of style and language.

[37] Editions collated (by Miss Alice Whitcomb): 1833, Mame; 1836, Werdet. The nine chapters referred to are the first nine of the original edition.

[38] Marcel Bouteron (*Con.* XXIV, 282) remarks that there are no reappearing characters in the novel, although Miss Preston (*op. cit.*, p. 280) counts two.

[39] Editions collated (by Albert D. Lippman): 1834, Béchet; Conard.

[40] Cf. above, pp. 382–86, for a study of the second episode, *La Duchesse de Langeais*.

"*La Fille aux yeux d'or*" (*1834–35*).[41]—The third episode of the *Histoire des Treize* was, from the outset, written as a part of this trilogy. Therefore, practically all of the desired connections with the other episodes were made at the time of original composition, and very few variants had to be introduced for purposes of harmonization. Similarly, the story was composed in the context of the *Comédie humaine;* and only one reappearing character, the Baron de Nucingen, was added in later versions. The total number of variations is small, and some two-thirds appear in the first part of the story, called "Physionomies parisiennes"; it would seem that Balzac was more concerned with improving this chapter of sociological generalizations and observations on Parisian life than with the remaining sections of romantic intrigue. This holds true for all three parts of the trilogy. Among stylistic changes there is an unusually large group which aims to improve the harmony of the style and to correct dissonance.

"*Un Drame au bord de la mer*" (*1835*).[42]—Balzac left this story practically unchanged; only eight changes were made at the Werdet-Souverain stage, and these were not carried on into the Furne; the Furne, based upon the Werdet again, differed from it only in thirty passages; the Conard is identical with the Furne text. The fact that Balzac should have skipped over the Souverain text and prepared the Furne from the Werdet is of interest; we shall find another example of the same procedure in *Facino Cane*. In both cases the low quality of the Souverain edition, typographically, may have been the reason. Of further importance is the remark that all the changes in the present story affect stylistic and linguistic elements; none are of realistic or technical character. These conclusions indicate that Balzac did not subject this story to the rigorous revisions undergone by most of the other stories: the number of variations is small, and there is little obvious improvement resulting from them.

"*Melmoth réconcilié*" (*1836*).[43]—Two types of variations important in Balzac's allusive technique make an early appearance in this story. The first involves the replacing of reappearing characters—rather than non-recurrent names—by other reappearing characters, with the change

---

[41] Editions collated (by Bredelle Jesse): 1834–35, Béchet; Conard.

[42] Editions collated (by Stratton Buck): 1835, Werdet; 1843, Souverain; 1846, Furne, Dubochet et Hetzel; Conard. Cf. below, p. 419, the situation with respect to *Facino Cane*.

[43] Editions collated (by Miss Eula May): 1836, Werdet; Conard.

motivated by the desire to find personages more appropriate to the milieu and the situation. The second concerns the reference by name to another novel; "Voyez *les Employés*," says Balzac after a generalization on the system of bureaucracy (*Con.* XXVII, 323). This addition is all the more noteworthy since, about the same date, 1836, Balzac began introducing the general system of cross-reference into new novels. Also of interest is the removal of the historical Marchangy both from this story and from *César Birotteau*.

"*La Vieille Fille*" (*1837*).[44]—Over 98 per cent of the total number of variations are here of a stylistic character and fall into four categories representing Balzac's efforts toward concision, clearness, vividness, and grammatical correctness. The small group of realistic variations is significant for its examples of truthfulness, materialism (changes affecting money, dates, animalisms, external objects), and social distinctions. There are three kinds of changes concerning fictional technique: those which harmonize the story within itself; those which connect it more intimately with its sequel, *Le Cabinet des antiques;* and those which integrate it with the larger structure of Balzac's works. The second group is especially interesting. Apparently, Balzac did not originally intend to bind these two studies closely together, and it was not until he corrected his copy of Furne with a view to later publication that he effected the combination. This was done through the changing of names ("Gordes" becomes "D'Esgrignon," "Choisnel" becomes "Chesnel"), the uniformization of the social background, and the introduction of parallel passages. Integration with the *Comédie humaine* was in part achieved by the introduction of direct cross-references to other novels, a technique which Balzac was just developing at this time.

"*Facino Cane*" (*1837*).[45]—The extremely small total of variations is interesting chiefly for a bibliographical indication. As in the case of *Un Drame au bord de la mer*, the Furne edition was based not on the Souverain edition of the preceding year but on the original Werdet form. Changes in the Souverain appear in no later editions, and in each case the adequate Werdet text is found restored in the Furne. Here is an example:

---

[44] Editions collated (by Miss Rachel Wilson): 1837, Werdet; 1844, Furne, Dubochet et Hetzel; Conard.

[45] Editions collated (by Miss Helen Williams): 1837, Werdet; 1843, Souverain; 1844, Furne, Dubochet et Hetzel; Conard.

... les danseurs ne s'en apercevaient
pas plus que les deux acolytes de mon
italien; *car je voulais que ce fût un ita-*
lien, et c'était un italien.
   [Ed. Werdet, *Etudes phil.*, XII, 134]

> ... les danseurs ne s'en apercevaient
> pas plus que les deux acolytes de mon
> italien, et c'était un italien.
>   [Ed. Souverain, *Muse du département,*
>   IV, 279–80]

> > ... les danseurs ne s'en apercevaient
> > pas plus que les deux acolytes de mon
> > Italien; *car je voulais que ce fût un Ita-*
> > *lien,* et c'était un Italien.
> >   [Ed. *Fur.* X, 64]

"Splendeurs et misères des courtisanes" *(1838–47)*.[46]—Since this work,
one of the most important of the *Comédie humaine,* grew from a short
story to a large four-part novel, it furnishes excellent materials for a study
of Balzac's methods and intentions. A preliminary examination of the
various stages of Parts I and II has shown the general trend of the variations. Between the Werdet and the De Potter editions (the *La Torpille*
section) the revisions were predominantly stylistic. But between the De
Potter and the Furne (for both parts) there was a much larger proportion
of realistic and fictional changes; these included a number of important
expansions of *dossiers,* many sociological details, and new reappearing
characters. At the Furne-Conard stage the variants were again mainly
of a linguistic character.

"Une Fille d'Ève" *(1839)*.[47]—The statistics of variations are in this case
somewhat unusual. Although the novel was written late, it was revised
extensively for the Furne edition. Excluding mechanical variations, we
find that the realistic changes represent 17 per cent of the total; this is
very high. Almost half of these are accounted for by Balzac's sociological
approach, which leads him to capitalize certain abstract words and to
stress the professions of his characters. Development of characterization

---

[46] Editions collated (by Robert Strozier): 1838, Werdet (*La Torpille*); 1844, De
Potter (dated 1845); 1844, Furne, Dubochet et Hetzel; Conard.

[47] Editions collated (by Mrs. Dorothea Davis): 1839, Werdet; 1842, Furne, Dubochet et Hetzel.

and addition of materialistic detail are responsible for most of the others. Six reappearing characters are inserted in the Furne text.

"*Béatrix,*" *Parts II and III (1840–45)*.[48]—In comparison with novels of an earlier period, this work has a very small number of variations. It would seem that in composing these later novels Balzac was applying a literary and realistic method developed over a long period of years and now fairly completely elaborated. Consequently, his task of revision was progressively lightened. However, we still find numerous changes in style, aimed especially at rhetorical effectiveness and at clarity. Realistic variations are hardly more abundant than in other late novels, and they affect essentially the same categories. The fact that we are here again dealing with a trilogy explains the existence of so many alterations relative to narrative technique. Some of these are necessary for the concatenation of the three parts: insertion and deletion of summarizing paragraphs, additions to characterization, and changes in time. Moreover, we find the customary introduction of reappearing characters and cross-references to the rest of the *Comédie humaine;* but this, again, is much less extensive than in the case of novels written before the evolution of the whole scheme of interrelated stories.

"*Honorine*" *(1844)*.[49]—The latest of the works here analyzed again has very few variations; the total is only sixty-seven (excluding mechanical changes). There are no changes involving reappearing characters. Realistic variations concern sociological aspects, characterization, and especially matters of date and chronology. Stylistic variations affect largely matters of euphony and clarity, rhetorical devices, and the use of the *mot propre.*

[48] Editions collated (by Miss Brucia L. Dedinsky): for Part II, 1840, Souverain; 1842, Furne, Dubochet et Hetzel; Conard; for Part III, 1845, Chlendowski; 1845, Furne, Dubochet et Hetzel; Conard. Part I of this novel was studied by Joachim Merlant in the *RHL*, XX (1913), 602–36.

[49] Editions collated (by Archie G. Ryland): 1844, De Potter; Conard.

CHAPTER VI
GENERAL CONCLUSION
By the EDITORS

I
T IS apparent from the preceding studies on textual variations that, whereas the kinds of variations are fairly constant throughout the stories, the thoroughness of revision depends upon a number of more or less predictable factors. Balzac's liking or dislike for a given story may account for his repeated effort to improve it or his complete failure to do so. Again, his conception of its importance in the structure of the *Comédie humaine* may be a determining consideration. Still again, his decision to unite it with some other work may lead to extensive alterations. Or the accidents of publication—the haste of a printer, his desire to save space— may preclude desired changes.

Nevertheless, it is possible to derive from these studies certain clear conclusions with respect to the history of Balzac's revisions of his novels. These conclusions will throw light on the periods of revision rather than on the nature of the variations, already described in the Introduction.

Balzac revised constantly, from the beginning of his career as a realistic novelist to the end; for each story, from the time of drafting the original manuscript to that of jotting down the marginalia on his own copy of the Furne edition. But in this constant process two periods stand out as those in which he did the major work of revision: the years around 1834– 37, when Balzac was preparing his early works for reprinting in the Béchet and the Werdet editions, and the years following 1841, when he was preparing his complete works for inclusion in the first edition of the *Comédie humaine*, that is, the Furne edition. Already in the first of these periods part of the task consisted in the integration of the separate stories into a complete whole, then known as the *Etudes de mœurs au XIXᵉ siècle* and the *Etudes philosophiques;* adjustments must be made in dates and places, reappearing characters and cross-references must be added, the tendency of the whole must be made more definitely realistic. In the second period these same efforts were continued and in some cases even intensified. Throughout, of course, Balzac was preoccupied with the improvement of his language and of his style.

The degree of revision of any given story depended usually upon the date of its original composition. If it came early in Balzac's career, it had to be revised extensively in order that it might grow with the growing conception of the *Comedy*. Stories written around 1830 in some cases underwent as many as six revisions. If, however, it came somewhat later, the amount of change would be smaller, since from the start the tale would have been written into the context of the whole series. If it came very late—during or after the publication of the Furne edition—the chances are that it would undergo very slight alteration indeed (with the exception, of course, of stylistic changes, which might occur in any quantity at any time).

What was achieved by this work of revision is hence apparent. That it led to a notable superiority of the final over the original product is unquestionable; and this superiority is not only one of language and expression, but it is also the peculiarly Balzacian superiority of a vast group of novels existing as a world apart, organized and interrelated like the world of reality.

A few further points may be made if we run over, in reverse order this time, the three central studies in this volume. Each of these offers special problems and results. Mr. Crain's task (somewhat like that of Mr. Chamberlin, in the Appendix) was to dig out the original core and to show how the manuscript was developed, through phases, into something quite different. His Introduction had to synthesize what appears concretely on every page of his edition: how Balzac's primary aim here was historical truth, and how he made it alive. Mr. Crain could also give us a shortened view of how, at a nod of the master-builder, sizable blocks of material were swung into new and effective positions.

We must next mention the paradoxical findings of Miss Wilson and of Miss Margaret Anderson in her unpublished University of Chicago dissertation on *Illusions perdues*. The former, in a story of some eighty pages, finds no less than five thousand variations, while the latter, in one of Balzac's largest frescoes (*ca.* 745 pages in Conard), brings to light only about thirty-five hundred changes. One answer to this puzzle is that the first writer deals with nine versions (complete or incomplete) of the *Curé de Tours*, while the second leaps directly from *princeps* to final edition of *Illusions perdues*. Another reason will appear in a moment.

First, let us emphasize some of Miss Wilson's particular discoveries. Balzac's great quantity of re-writing (as often) has made the style from the manuscript to the Conard edition both more correct and more telling.

Also, the changes effected in the direction of a realistic approach are usual-ly characteristic of the author. They are, too, the more interesting kind, in spite of the fact that here—as in the great majority of novels revised—they are numerically far below the stylistic alterations. The latter aim primarily at precision (the *mot propre*), simplicity, and clarity. Both of the last statements are typical and true of the *Comédie humaine* as a whole. Nor, among realistic procedures, are we surprised to find the usual emphasis placed on truth or *vraisemblance* as an abiding aim or upon the building of *dossiers* and characterization.

Now let us turn to a large-scale affair, such as the direct comparison of the earliest available texts to the latest, in the printing of *Illusions perdues*. We cover 746 pages; yet we find the comparatively moderate total of some thirty-five hundred variations. The great majority of these are of the routine kind. The difference in the total of variations between the versions studied of the last two novels discussed will help to demonstrate this further fact: it is when you start with the manuscript that the fre-quency of variations seems overwhelming. Mr. Crain, who took the trouble to decipher many of Balzac's original erasures, can also testify to this effect. Several of the smaller stories (particularly in the early *Scènes de la vie privée*), which have not been given full discussion here, would again indicate that Balzac's manuscripts were meant to be preliminary sketches and little more.

The third of our major studies in this recessional movement has already spoken so well for itself that we need add but little more. Miss Dedinsky believes that, just as the changes in each novel show a forward march in style and structure, so in all its changes and shiftings of titles the *Comédie humaine* evinces an effort, largely successful, toward a better classification and nomenclature of the novels.

It will be understood that all titles discussed represent only a portion —though a fairly representative portion—of the material available and the work done at the University of Chicago. Hints will be found through-out the volume that other such undertakings (see especially the Appendix) are in progress. The earliest printed study of this kind was the mono-graph on *Les Chouans* by Mrs. Helen Barnes Wodrada (1923). Latterly, the system which is the basis of our Volume III, as well as of this volume, namely, the arrays of "realistic qualities" and the like, has been adapted and applied successfully on this campus to two such different novelists as George Sand and Galdós. Still other "variation studies" have been completed as Princeton dissertations: by R. W. Elliott, on *Ursule Mirouët,* and by A. J. Williamson, on *La Recherche de l'absolu.* These gentlemen— and others too—have naturally not felt themselves tethered by any scheme exhibited here. If there is any outstanding thing about Balzac, it is his great and ever fertile variety. So let us add our small pile of "variations" to a pile which already seems as various and manifold as the man himself.

APPENDIX

THE ZWEIG MANUSCRIPT PROOF OF
UNE TENEBREUSE AFFAIRE

By WELLS CHAMBERLIN
University of Illinois

THE study now in progress of the text of *Une Ténébreuse Affaire* is based on a comparison of the manuscript proof with the available editions of the novel; the conclusions here presented are tentative, since the investigation is still in the preliminary stages. The volumes of manuscript proof, owned by Mr. Stefan Zweig, were photographed in London in 1937 at the instance of Professor Dargan. These copies, totaling about seven hundred pages, are now an important part of the University of Chicago's Balzac Collection. The photographing was done in such a manner that all sheets of proof and all manuscript, including long additions, minute notes, "bouteilles," and directions to the compositor, are available for examination.

The material consists of both proof sheets and manuscript additions, covering practically all of the first edition of the novel. Examination has revealed the presence of some hundred-odd sheets of continuous proof, which form a complete story, roughly similar in outline to the published novel. We shall refer to this continuous proof as the "earliest" version of *Une Ténébreuse Affaire;* however, it must be assumed that this proof was set up from an original continuous manuscript, which we do not have. In revising, Balzac broke the continuity of the earliest version by inserting wedges of lengthy new material in manuscript between sections of the proof, by deleting some of the original text, and by revising minutely that part of the proof which was to be retained. The sum of this material forms a new version of the story, which we call the "first stage" of revision. Another proof repeats nearly all of the new version and forms a second stage; the author then revises this proof by means of marginal notes. Samplings show that for some chapters we have a subsequent proof (third stage) repeating the revised second stage. However, no set of proof other than that forming the earliest version is continuous throughout the story; the later proofs appear to have been set up chapter by chapter, as revision progressed. We find gaps and differences in type face in these proofs.

The problem of the textual relationships between the various revision stages cannot be solved at this time. An examination of the first two stages of two early chapters shows that in one case the second stage (proof) was set up directly from the first; in the other case, however, the second stage introduces variations which indicate that a set of proof is missing between the stages which are available for examination.

Were the cumulative revisions of the story intended for the preoriginal edition, which appeared in *Le Commerce* from January 14 to February 20, 1841,[1] or were they intended for the first edition, published in 1842 (dated 1843) by Souverain? Since the preoriginal text is not available at the moment, we have made a comparison of the last stage of revision and the first edition. This comparison, a sampling covering the first third of the novel, shows that in some six hundred and eighty cases the text of the first edition does not follow exactly the last revised stage. This means that there is at least one stage between the last version available to us and the first edition; the 1841 preoriginal may be that missing stage. Other facts appear to support this hypothesis. The numbers and titles of the twenty chapters in their last revised form in the manuscript proofs correspond almost exactly to the numbers and titles which, according to Spoelberch de Lovenjoul, are found in the preoriginal edition. When compared with the last revised form, however, the Souverain edition shows several changed titles and two additional divisions. Moreover, the type face of the Souverain edition is quite different from that of the last available proofs. However, it is apparent from the nature of the variations so far discovered between the last available stage and the first edition that the missing stage (or stages) closely resembled the Souverain text except for minor stylistic differences.

A comparison of the broad outlines of the earliest version (contained in the hundred continuous proof sheets) with the Souverain edition illustrates, even at this preliminary phase of the investigation, the author's narrative technique and his interest in history. In order to make this comparison, we have reassembled the earliest proof sheets in their original sequence, determined by a partly obliterated numbering system and by subject matter.

The first available version of *Une Ténébreuse Affaire* lacks development of dramatic scenes, especially in the early chapters. This version began with expository material on Gondreville and on the Simeuse family; later, Balzac makes a new start with the episode of Michu and the rifle. The reader thus senses from this beginning *in medias res* the element of mystery which surrounds Michu. After working in the exposition, the author now returns to Michu and adds, in manuscript, his long conversation with the police agents. In the later versions Michu does not merely refer to the cavern as a possible hiding place for the nobles; he takes the heroine there and proves to her that the fugitives will be safe. A decided improvement on the original proof is the addition of the struggle between Laurence and Corentin over the box of keepsakes. This inci-

[1] Lov., *Hist.*, pp. 151–52.

dent symbolizes the undying enmity between the two: the blow which Corentin receives across the knuckles motivates his thirst for vengeance.

Another group of additions complicates the detective story and emphasizes the cleverness of policemen and lawyers. For example, in the earliest version the police simply follow Marthe Michu to the cavern. In the revised version they employ a more subtle means of discovering the hiding place: a shoemaker-spy marks the shoes of the Simeuse horses, and the police follow the trail. The amusing episode of the plaster, on which so much of the courtroom debate turns, is an added complication. In the early version Michu must free himself from the spy Violette, who has made an inopportune visit. Michu simply tells him that the nobles are planning to burn his farm, and the spy rushes home. In the new version Michu has to spend several hours offering a mixture of wine and brandy to Violette. When the spy is sufficiently intoxicated, Michu escapes to warn the nobles that their plot against Napoleon has been discovered.

It is important to note that several of the reappearing characters in *Une Ténébreuse Affaire* did not appear at all in the earliest proof. The two police agents, Corentin and Peyrade, were unnamed in that version. In the Souverain edition we find a second defense attorney, M. de Granville. This case becomes his steppingstone to fame. In the earliest version Bordin defended the nobles and Michu together. However, the final scene, which presents the Princesse de Cadignan and De Marsay, appears in the earliest proof in a form closely resembling that of the first edition.

A second main objective in the expansion of the early sketch to the proportions of a novel was that of presenting a work of greater historical content. For example, in the earliest version the author writes a hasty and poorly organized description of the principal characters as they sit one fateful evening in the salon at Cinq-Cygne. He has the mayor arrive unexpectedly, to warn them of impending danger, but abandons the mayor in order to describe the faces in the room. In revising for publication Balzac gives to this episode the flavor of the historical novel. He declares that, even if these individuals were not involved in a drama, they should, nevertheless, be presented here as typical royalists of the day. Hence, in the new treatment the figures in the room first receive a leisurely study. *Dossier* material is expanded. Balzac dwells on harmony of dress and character, as well as on the general harmony of the scene. Then, and only then, does the mayor arrive to disturb the tranquillity of these historical types who have been sitting for a tableau. Changes in the chapter title illustrate the change in Balzac's attitude toward the function of the episode: rejecting "Les Habitans de Cinq-Cygne," he considers "Le Moment avant l'orage," but finally decides upon "Intérieur et physionomies royalistes sous le consulat." In other words, the author seems to have considered the chapter first in relationship to characterization, then in relationship to plot, and finally in relationship to his own position as secretary of society.

The addition of Napoleon as an active character in two scenes heightens the historical interest of the novel. In the original proof Laurence refuses to ask a pardon from Napoleon, and the mission is undertaken for her by Bordin and M. de Charsebœuf (*sic*). However, in the revised version the heroine submits and goes with her elderly relative to Napoleon, who receives her graciously.

Thus, even at this point in the investigation we can discern the major changes effected in the general plan of *Une Ténébreuse Affaire* between the earliest proof and the first edition. Moreover, we can already distinguish the existence of thousands of variations of a realistic or stylistic character. Any estimate of the number and significance of these changes must, of course, await completion of the study, which will ultimately include an examination of all the available editions.

INDEX

This Index lists Balzacian characters and works, the latter under their definitive titles; selected subject matters, especially those which figure prominently in the variations; modern scholars and critics only when their findings are upheld or contradicted by additional evidence; and persons connected with Balzac and his writings.